GERHARD ULLRICH

# The Law of the International Civil Service
## Institutional Law and Practice in International Organisations

# The Law of the International Civil Service

## Institutional Law and Practice in International Organisations

By

Gerhard Ullrich

Duncker & Humblot · Berlin

Bibliographic information published by the Deutsche Nationalbibliothek

The Deutsche Nationalbibliothek lists this publication in
the Deutsche Nationalbibliografie; detailed bibliographic data
are available in the Internet at http://dnb.d-nb.de.

Enlarged, updated, and translated edition published
in the year 2009 by Duncker & Humblot
Gerhard Ullrich: Das Dienstrecht der Internationalen Organisationen.
Institutionelles Völkerrecht, Recht und Praxis. ISBN 978-3-428-12947-8.


Printing: CPI buchbücher.de gmbh, Birkach
Printed in Germany

ISBN 978-3-428-14914-8 (Print)
ISBN 978-3-428-54914-6 (E-Book)
ISBN 978-3-428-84914-7 (Print & E-Book)

Printed on no aging resistant (non-acid) paper
according to ISO 9706 ♾

Internet: http://www.duncker-humblot.de

# Preface

In a world of increasing globalisation, sovereign states, as the classic actors in international relations, find themselves in growing need of transnational cooperation. More than ever, international organisations are important players in global governance and the interdependency of states. In coping with world issues such as climate change, financial stability, poverty, ageing populations and terrorism, the tasks of international organisations have taken on a new dimension. While the material tasks and fields of competence of international organisations range across all aspects of human life, the structures of the institutional law of international organisations have much in common. Indeed, international organisations face similar problems in the context of their institutional law and one international organisation will frequently rely extensively on the proven experience of others. This is especially true for the employment law of international organisations. When setting up their rules of employment, they do not re-invent the wheel but take inspiration from the civil service law of comparable existing organisations. This book categorises the various civil service rules of organisations into four schemes, it aims at contributing to a better understanding of the similarities and differences of the employment law of international organisations.

Since the first edition of this book in 2009, the law of the international civil service has undergone substantial changes.

The global financial crisis was not without repercussion for the financing of international organisations. As a result, most organisations have introduced moderation and exception clauses into their regular salary adjustment systems.

The increase in life expectancy is leading to a lengthening of the time during which pension benefits are being paid out. In parallel to national legislation, ever more organisations have shifted the right to an unreduced pension payment to a higher retirement age and reduced the yearly rates of acquired pension claims, or even replaced the defined benefit scheme by a defined contribution scheme.

In other fields of institutional law, like data protection, measures against corruption, whistle-blowing and harassment, there has been a flood of new rulings with an impact on the employment law of international organisations.

The first addition of this book was published in German in 2009. Many people have assisted me in the accomplishment of this book. I would like to repeat the acknowledgment of the previous edition of this book to my former colleagues. In order to achieve a wider circulation of this book it has been decided to publish this edition in English, the *lingua franca* of international organisations today.

Munich, April 2018 *Gerhard Ullrich*

# Summary of Contents

# Table of Contents

*Chapter 3*

**The typical structures and elements of employment rules** 258

# Abbreviations

| | |
|---|---|
| AAFI/AFICS | Association of Former International Civil Servants – Geneva |
| ADR | Alternative dispute resolution |
| AöR | Archiv des öffentlichen Rechts (German Law Journal) |
| Art. | Article |
| ASG | Assistant Secretary-General of the UN |
| AT/EPO agreement | Agreement between the EPO and the Republic of Austria concerning the headquarters of the Vienna sub-office of the EPO of 2 July 1990, AT/BGBl. No. 263 of 6 November 1990, pp. 4071 et seq. |
| BGBl. | Bundesgesetzblatt (German Federal Law Gazette) |
| CCFSR | Community Charter of Fundamental Social Rights of Workers of 9 December 1989 |
| CCISUA | Co-ordinating Committee for International Staff Unions and Associations of the UN System |
| CCR | Co-ordinating Committee on Remuneration |
| CERN | European Organisation for Nuclear Research |
| CERN/ESO-PF | Pension Fund of CERN and ESO |
| CFREU | Charter of Fundamental Rights of the European Union |
| CJEU | Court of Justice of the EU (before 1 December 2009 European Court of Justice) |
| CJEU (CST) | The European Civil Service Tribunal of the CJEU (until 1 September 2016) |
| CJEU (GC) | The General Court of the CJEU (before 1 December 2009 Court of First Instance) |
| CO | co-ordinated organisations |
| CoE | Council of Europe |
| CoE-GAPI | General Agreement on Privileges and Immunities of the CoE |
| CoE-NPS | New Pension Scheme of the CoE (Appendix Vbis CoE-SR) |
| CoE-SR | Staff Regulations of the CoE |
| CoE-TPS | Third Pension Scheme of the CoE (Appendix Vter CoE-SR) |
| CVPO | Community Plant Variety Office |
| DBPS | Defined benefit pension scheme |
| DCPS | Defined contribution pension scheme |
| DE/EPO agreement | Headquarters Agreement between the EPO and the Government of the Federal Republic of Germany of 19 October 1977, DE/BGBl. II No. 17 of 4 April 1978, pp. 337 et seq. |
| doc. | Document |
| EC | European Communities |
| ECB | European Central Bank |

| | |
|---|---|
| ECB-SR | Conditions of employment for staff of the ECB |
| ECGAB | European Code of Good Administrative Behaviour |
| ECHR | European Court of Human Rights |
| ECMWF | European Centre for Medium Range Weather Forecast |
| EConHR | European Convention for the Protection of Human Rights and Fundamental Freedom |
| EFTA | European Free Trade Association |
| EGV | Vertrag zur Gründung der Europäischen Gemeinschaft (TEC, Treaty establishing the European Community) |
| EIB | European Investment Bank |
| EIF | European Investment Fund |
| EJIL | European Journal of International Law |
| EMBL | European Molecular Biology Laboratory |
| EP | European Parliament |
| EPO | European Patent Organisation |
| EPO (Office) | European Patent Office |
| EPO-Codex | EPO documents on personnel/policy and personnel/operational matters published on the website of the EPO Administrative Council since 30 September 2015 |
| EPO-EPC | European Patent Convention |
| EPO-PPI | Protocol of Privileges and Immunities of the EPO |
| EPO-PRF | Pension Reserve Fund of the EPO |
| EPO-PS | Pension Scheme regulations and rules of the EPO |
| EPO-RFPSS | Reserve Funds for Pensions and Social Security of the EPO |
| EPO-SR | Service Regulations for permanent employees and the conditions of employment of other employees of the EPO |
| EPPO | European and Mediterranean Plant Protection Office |
| EPSO | European Personnel Selection Office |
| ES | European School |
| ESA | European Space Agency |
| ESC | European Social Charter |
| ESM | European Stability Mechanism |
| ESMAT | Administrative Tribunal of the ESM |
| ESO | European Southern Observatory |
| et seq. | and following pages |
| EU | European Union |
| EU-CEOS | Conditions of employment of other servants of the EU |
| EUIPO | EU Intellectual Property Office |
| EU-PPI | TEU Protocol No. 7 on the privileges and immunities of the EU |
| EU-PS | Pension Scheme of the EU (Annex VIII of the EU-SR) |
| EUR-LEX | Database of EU law |
| Eurocontrol | European Organisation for the Safety of Air Navigation |
| FAO | Food and Agriculture Organization of the UN |
| footn. | footnote |

| | |
|---|---|
| GRUR Int | German Journal of Intellectual Property Law and Practice, international part |
| IAEA | International Atomic Energy Agency |
| IBRD | International Bank for Reconstruction and Development |
| ICAO | International Civil Aviation Organization |
| ICC | International Criminal Court |
| ICJ | International Court of Justice |
| ICSC | International Civil Service Commission |
| ICSID | International Centre for Settlement of Investment Disputes |
| IDA | International Development Association |
| IFAD | International Fund for Agricultural Development |
| IFC | International Finance Corporation |
| IGO | Intergovernmental IO |
| IIB | International Patent Institute |
| ILC | International Law Commission |
| ILO | Internation Labour Organization |
| ILOAT | Administrative tribunal of the ILO |
| IMF | International Monetary Fund |
| IMFAT | Administrative Tribunal of the IMF |
| INPADOC | International Patent Documentation Centre |
| IO | International Organisation(s) |
| IOLR | International Organizations Law Review |
| IOM | International Organization for Migration |
| IPSAS | International Public Service Accounting Standards |
| IPU | Inter-Parliamentary Union |
| ISA | International Seabed Authority |
| ISR | Internationale Steuer Rundschau (German international tax review) |
| ISRP/SIRP | International Service for Remuneration and Pensions |
| ITLOS | International Tribunal for the Law of the Sea |
| ITU | International Telecommunication Union |
| JIU | Joint Inspection Unit of the UN system |
| juris | German legal database |
| LTC | Long-term care |
| MIGA | Multilateral Investment Guarantee Agency |
| NATO-SR | Civilian Personnel Regulations of NATO |
| NGO | Non-governmental IO |
| NJW | Neue Juristische Wochenschrift (German Law Journal) |
| NL/EPO agreement | Agreement between the EPO and the Kingdom of the Netherlands concerning the branch of the EPO at The Hague, NL, of 27 June 2006, NL Tractatenblad 2006, No. 155 |
| OAJ | Office of Administration of Justice of the UN |
| OASAT | Administrative Tribunal of the Organization Of American States (TRIBAD) |
| OECD | Organisation for Economic Co-operation and Development |

| | |
|---|---|
| ÖGBl. | Österreichisches Gesetzblatt (Austrian Law Gazette) |
| OJ | Official Journal |
| OLA | Office of Legal Affairs of the UN |
| OLAF | European Anti-Fraud Office |
| Old UNAT | UNAT before 31 December 2009 |
| OPCW | Organisation for the Prohibition of Chemical Weapons |
| OSCE | Organisation for Security and Co-operation in Europe |
| OSLA | Office of Staff Legal Assistance of the UNDT/UNAT |
| p. | page |
| para. | paragraph(s) |
| PF | Pension Fund |
| pp. | pages |
| PPI | Protocol on Privileges and Immunities |
| PS | Pension Scheme (Pension Regulation) |
| R. | Rule |
| Reg. | Regulation(s) |
| SG | Secretary-General |
| SR | Staff Regulations (Staff Rules), Service Regulations |
| StBl. | Bundessteuerblatt (German Federal Fiscal Tax Gazette) |
| SUEPO | Staff Union of the EPO |
| TEC | Treaty establishing the European Community |
| TEU | Treaty on European Union |
| TFEU | Treaty on the Functioning of the European Union |
| Triblex | Database of the ILOAT |
| UDHR | Universal Declaration of Human Rights |
| UN | United Nations |
| UNAT | Administrative Tribunal of the UN |
| UNBISNET | UN Bibliographic Information System |
| UN-CPI | Convention on the Privileges and Immunities of the UN |
| UN-CS | UN Common System |
| UNDP | United Nations Development Programme |
| UNDPI | UN Department of Public Information |
| UNDT | Dispute Tribunal of the UN |
| UNECOSOC | Economic and Social Council of the UN |
| UNESCO | UN Educational Scientific and Cultural Organization |
| UNFPA | United Nations Population Fund |
| UNGA | General Assembly of the UN |
| UNIDO | UN Industrial Development Organization |
| UNJSPF | United Nations Joint Staff Pension Fund |
| UNODC | UN Office on Drugs and Crime |
| UNOPS | United Nations Office for Project Services |
| UN-SG | Secretary-General of the UN |
| UN-SR | Staff Regulations and Rules of the UN |
| UN-WTO | UN World Tourism Organization |

| | |
|---|---|
| UPC | Unified Patent Court |
| USG | Under Secretary-General of the UN |
| v. | versus, against |
| VCDR | Vienna Convention on Diplomatic Relations |
| VCLT | Vienna Convention on the Law of Treaties |
| VCLT-IO | Vienna Convention on the Law of Treaties between States and International Organizations (not yet in force) |
| WB | World Bank |
| WBAT | Administrative Tribunal of the WB |
| WHO | World Health Organization |
| WIPO | World Intellectual Property Organization |
| WMO | World Meteorological Organization |
| YBIO | Yearbook of International Organizations |
| ZaöRV | Zeitschrift für ausländisches öffentliches Recht und Völkerrecht (German Law Journal) |
| ZBR | Zeitschrift für Beamtenrecht (German Journal for the Law of Officials) |

# Introduction

## A. The civil service law of international organisations – unity within diversity

The civil service law of public (intergovernmental) international organisations (IO) forms an integral part of the institutional law of IO and is within the sphere of public international law. The constituent instruments of IO are particular conventions by which each IO is endowed by its member states with a certain autonomy in order to ensure the unimpeded accomplishment of its tasks. The internal law of an IO is *particular* international public law since it is restricted in its effects to member states (Ipsen, p. 198: Given the different tasks of the IO one cannot speak of a self-contained law of IO). This is also the reason why the civil service law of IO does not constitute a uniform system of law applicable to all IO but, in principle, only refers to a specific IO. Nevertheless, the legal literature consistently refrains from using the plural form of the word "law" in the context of a description of the employment law of IO (e.g. Amerasinghe, The law; Schermers/Blokker; de Cooker). The use of the singular form shows that the law of the international civil service is a legal sphere in which largely uniform legal principles and similar structures and elements prevail justifying a coherent presentation.

In comparison with the other areas of institutional law of IO such as financing, general administration, internal legal order (Schermers/Blokker § 26 distinguish a total number of eleven areas of the institutional rules of IO) the employment law of IO is of enhanced coherence. A major reason for this lies in the jurisprudence of the international administrative tribunals. In constant case law the tribunals use the general legal principles common to member states and the principles enshrined in the international conventions and declarations on fundamental and human rights as a necessary complement to the service regulations (SR) of all IO. These general principles govern the employment relationship of all IO as a supreme value system (see, for example ILOAT Judgment 1118 para. 10: An IO "must at all times, and more particularly when amending the conditions of service, abide by those general principles").

This common set of rights which is laid down in only a fragmentary manner in the SR of IO supplements the SR as a kind of "shadow constitution". It provides the necessary judicial yardstick for the interpretation, gap filling and legal checks of the employment law of IO. The insular nature of the SR of an IO is thereby partly removed and the SR of IO are focused on common legal principles.

But even the structure and the elements of the SR of each IO show more converging than separating elements. Despite all the diversity of tasks IO are confronted with identical or similar problems in the field of their employment relationships.

Newly established IO do not reinvent their own SR but resort to existing and proven SR of functionally comparable IO.

During the operational phase of IO there is an ongoing exchange of experiences between the human resources and legal departments of IO. This often leads to an alignment of the SR. If there are new developments in the law of the international civil service, e.g. in the areas of data protection, social security systems (long-term care) or protection of dignity (harassment) the provisions drafted by one organisation are often used as a template by others.

Despite all the diversity in the SR of IO it, therefore, does seem justified to speak of a certain uniformity in this area (Schermers/Blokker, subtitle and § 22 et seq: "Unity within diversity"). The growing uniformity of the law of the international civil service is, however, not to be understood as goal, unlike e.g. the motto on the Great Seal of the United States: "*e pluribis unum*" (out of many, one), but as a working hypothesis for a comparative study of the law of the international civil service.

## B. Objectives

This book does not intend to supplement the series of monographs and commentaries on the SR of individual IO or of a group of IO. It intends to provide a general overview of the law of the international civil service, to disclose the substantial content of the SR and refer to their similarities and differences. Another purpose is the analysis of the general legal principles applicable to the law of the international civil service, notably derived from the case law of the international administrative tribunals. Given the multitude of IO a grouping of the IO in accordance with the similarities of their employment relationship is inevitable. For this purpose the law of the international civil service is subdivided into four civil service systems which show some degree of similarity in the structure and the elements of their SR.

For the purpose of this book the term SR is used in its broader sense, i.e. it also includes, in addition to the SR for active officials also the pension schemes (PS) and tertiary employment law (directives, circulars etc.).

*Part 1*

# Basic elements

*Chapter 1*

## The international organisations

### A. The legal nature of international organisations

The establishment of IO is based on the realisation that certain goals cannot be achieved by individual states on their own but only in cooperation with others. IO serve the purpose of achieving political, scientific, technical, humanitarian, social and economic objectives which exceed the national resources and opportunities (a good overview of the various objectives pursued by IO can be found in Seidl-Hohenveldern/Loibl § 2101 to § 4001).

The member states of an IO endow their organisation with the necessary legal status and functional sovereignty *sui generis* (Schermers/Blokker § 209; Seidl-Hohenveldern/Loibl § 0107) in order to achieve their common objectives.

In order to accomplish these tasks IO have legal personality in international law and in the national law of their member states. The status of legal personality was not expressly attributed to IO until some 40 years ago. The legal status was, however, derived by implication from the need to exercise its powers properly (see Schermers/Blokker § 1565 et seq. concerning the UN; but see Art. 5(1) and 5(2) EPO-EPC and Art. 47 TEU; Art. 335 TFEU).

The question of whether the individual organs, subsidiary organs, institutions or other bodies of an IO have their own legal personality in international and national law cannot be answered in general terms but only according to its constituent instruments (see Schermers/Blokker § 1571).

On the basis of their international legal personality, which is functionally limited and determined by their tasks (Schermers/Blokker § 1570), IO may enter into bilateral agreements with member states (see, for example, the headquarters agreements) and codify their entire internal legal system as particular international law (Seidl-Hohenveldern/Loibl para. 1513).

In national law, IO generally enjoy the most extensive legal capacity accorded to legal persons under the national law of each member state in order to act within the national legal order (e.g. rent buildings, buy equipment etc., Schermers/Blokker § 1559 et seq.; Wenckstern para. 447; Art. 335 TFEU; Art. 104 UN Charter; Art. 5(2) EPO-EPC).

IO are principally bound to respect the substantial municipal law of the member state (public law, civil law, criminal law) in which they perform their functions (Schermers/Blokker § 1602 et seq.; Wenckstern para. 37, 447). They are, however, not subject to the municipal law of member states for as far as they are acting within their own internal legal order based on the attributed power of organisational autonomy (Schermers/Blokker § 1196 et seq. § 1601 et seq.; Wenckstern para. 37). In addition, IO are exempt from the application of national law in some privileged areas (e.g. taxation) in order to guarantee the unimpeded functioning of the IO. Finally, IO are exempt from the enforcement of substantive national law and from national jurisdiction (Schermers/Blokker § 1605 et seq., § 1610 et seq.).

For the purpose of this book an IO means a public (intergovernmental) organisation (IGO). (For non-governmental organisations, NGOs, see below).

There is no universally accepted definition of an IO (Schermers/Blokker § 32). Art. 2 of the draft articles on the responsibility of IO adopted by the international law commission (ILC) in 2011 (UN doc. A/66/10, p. 6), however, "outlines certain common characteristics" of IO. This provision reads: "International organisation means an organisation established by a treaty or other instrument governed by international law and possessing its own international legal personality. International organisations may include as members, in addition to states, other entities".

These characteristics of public IO are generally accepted in the literature (Schermers/Blokker § 33; Seidl-Hohenveldern/Loibl § 0101 to § 0112; Stephen Bouwhuis, The International Law Commission's Definition of International Organizations; IOLR 2012 pp. 451 to 465). This definition of the term "IO" is also used in this book.

## B. The classification of international organisations

Depending on the purpose of the examination of the entity "IO", various methods of classification criteria can be applied in order to achieve a certain order and enhance transparency (Sands/Klein 1–031 to 1–033).

Most common is their classification according to the field and the geographical sphere of activities.

Depending on the substantive tasks enshrined in the constituent instruments, IO can be categorized in groups promoting, for example, international peacekeeping (UN), science and culture (EPO, ESA, ESO), social conflict solutions (ILO), health care (WHO), economy (FAO), trade (WTO), economic cooperation (EU), assistance to developing countries (World Bank, UNIDO), communication

(UPU, ITU), settlement of legal disputes (ICJ, Tribunal for the Law of the Sea). (See the detailed categorisation of IO according to their main tasks in Seidl-Hohenveldern/Loibl § 2101 to 4001).

The classification according to the geographical scope of activity of an IO differs between a universal (open) and a regional (closed) IO. Regional IO restrict their membership to a limited group of member states, such as the EU, ASEAN or the OAS, whereas universal organisations like the UN and its specialised agencies aim at attracting all states as members (see A. Duxbury, The Participation of States in International Organisations, 2013; Schermers/Blokker § 53).

According to the sovereign powers conferred on an IO by its member states a distinction can also be made between general IO and supranational IO.

Another classification of IO is based on institutional similarities, notably in the areas of their organisational structure, financing and in human resources. Under this classification IO may be assigned to "families" or "systems" of organisations. This applies primarily to the organisations of the "UN family" and the coordinated organisations (CO). Also the EU as an integrated union may be considered as a "family" of organisations, institutions and related bodies (see for more details Schermers/Blokker § 1691 to 1701).

For the purpose of this book a *pars pro toto* approach is indispensable in order to cope with the abundance of material and to reach a comprehensive presentation of the law of the international civil service. To this end the classification according to "families" of IO seems to be most appropriate. However, in order to take account of the various IO which are outside these "families" but have incorporated parts of their institutional components, a fourth ("mixed" or "hybrid") system of IO has to be added.

## C. Other types of international organisations

### I. Supranational organisations

IO may be called "supranational" if they are endowed with the power to enact rules which are directly binding on member states and their nationals without the need to transform regulations into national law by the parliament of a member state (Seidl-Hohenveldern/Loibl § 0113 et seq.; see, however, Schermers/Blokker § 61; they require in addition that IO should have the power to enforce their decisions and have some financial autonomy).

The EU is commonly referred to as the exemplary case of a supranational organisation (Seidl-Hohenveldern/Loibl § 0113). Another example of a supranational organisation is the EPO in Munich (Germany) which is an autonomous organisation "on the edge of the EU" (see also the order of the German Federal

Constitutional Court of 4 April 2001, case No. 2 BvR 2368/99: The EPO is a supranational organisation within the meaning of Art. 24(1) German Basic Law, which has the task of granting European patents. The European patent shall, in each member state for which it is granted, have the effect of and be subject to the same conditions as a national patent (Art. 2(2) EPO-EPC). The same classification applies to the European Union Intellectual Property Office (EUIPO) in Alicante (Spain) and the EU Community Plant Variety Office (CPVO) in Angers (France).

For the study of the international civil service law of IO the classification as a supranational organisation is of importance only insofar as the organisation performs permanent tasks (services) and, therefore, the SR provide mainly for a permanent employment relationship (officials) on a statutory basis (EU, EPO, EUIPO, CPVO).

## II. Non-governmental organisations

Non-governmental IO (NGOs) have to be distinguished from public (intergovernmental) organisations (IGOs) by their legal basis and their powers. They are not established by a treaty governed by international law and do not act with a legal personality under international law. Accordingly, it is not too difficult to distinguish between NGOs and IGOs. There is, however, no commonly accepted definition of NGOs (Schermers/Blokker § 47).

Among the most important characteristics of a NGO is its non-profit status which excludes all profit-oriented commercial enterprises and funds. (This criterium also applies to IGOs, but is usually not addressed as a budgetary principle because the member states determine the level of contributions to the budget of the IO in such a way that revenue and expenditure are in balance, see, for example, Art. 310(1) TFEU. Only service-oriented IO such as the EPO are endowed with the power to fix the level of their fees by themselves. In these cases, the level of fees has to be fixed at such a level that the revenue is "*sufficient*" for the budget to be balanced, Art. 40(1) EPO-EPC).

In 2015 the yearbook of international organisations (YBIO) included a grand total of 68,000 IO (38,000 active and 30,000 dormant IO).

Often NGOs co-operate with IGOs in fulfilling their tasks. The Economic and Social Council of the UN (ECOSOC), for example, grants a consultative status to NGOs (see Art. 71 UN Charter) and an associated status is granted by the UN Department of Public Information to NGOs which meet certain criteria (see the websites of UN-DPI and the YBIO).

## D. The number of public international organisations

In contrast to the number of states it is not possible to determine the precise number of public IO. There is also no official record of IO as is the case, for example, with the registration of international treaties (see Art. 102 UN Charter). The number of IO largely depends on how a public IO is defined. Although the YBIO records more than 7,000 IO this does include inactive or dissolved IO and is based on a definition of IO which is excessively broad and encompasses agencies, programmes, offices, funds, institutes, colleges, centres etc., of IO as separate entities. The relevant literature, therefore, estimates the number of IO to only about 500 to 700 (Schermers/Blokker § 33: more than 500 and fewer than 700; see more in detail: Amerasinghe, IOLR, p. 10 footn. 2).

*Chapter 2*

# The employment law of the international civil service

## A. Legal basis for the employment law of the international organisations

### I. The organisational sovereignty

IO can only properly fulfil the tasks entrusted to them by the member states if they are free from all influence and pressure of individual member states. The unimpeded functioning of an IO and the achievements of its objectives imply that power of autonomous organisational, administrative and financial sovereignty is attributed to IO (Schermers/Blokker § 209).

This sovereignty which today is even recognised under customary law (Kunz-Hallstein/Ullrich, Art. 13 para. 1) is nowadays the subject of express statements in the primary law of an IO (the convention, the charter). IO unlike states do not possess a general competence to create their own powers but are governed by the "principle of speciality", that is to say, they are invested by the states which create them with powers, the limits of which are a function of the common interests whose promotion those states entrusted to them" (Schermers/Blokker § 209). The organisational power of an IO includes the codification of the entire internal area of activity of an IO with a focus on its key activities, as well as the structuring and financing of the organisation and the implementation of its labour law.

In these areas IO act within their status as a personality of international law endowed with the power to provide a set of internal rules constituting "particular" public international law (Seidl-Hohenveldern/Loibl para. 1513; A. Gourgourinis in EJIL 2011, 993 ff); see, for example, Art. 47 TEU; Art. 5(1) EPO-EPC; see also Schermers/Blokker §§ 209, 1562).

In the national sphere of their member states IO enjoy the legal capacity accorded to legal persons under the national law (e.g. Art. 335 TFEU, Art. 5(2) EPO-EPC) in order to conclude contracts for the purchase of supplies, furniture, equipment or other goods and services for the acquisition of immovable property etc. (Kunz-Hallstein/Ullrich, Art. 9; Schermers/Blokker § 1591).

Demarcation problems may arise if a regulatory matter is assigned partially to the internal legislation of the organisation and partially to municipal legislation. Such interfaces, for example, occur in the areas of procurement (see Ullrich, procurement) and data protection (see Ullrich, data protection). IO, therefore, codify their procurement law autonomously as far as the internal phases of procurement are concerned. With the publication of the "prior information", but at the latest with the "invitation to tender", IO enter the national legal sphere. At this point of time IO are subject to national law. Similar interfaces occur in the area of data protection when internal data of an IO are externalised or data from external persons is stored and processed within the organisation.

Since, however, the adjudication of national laws of the member states is limited by the immunity of an IO from national jurisdiction and execution, national law is not in principle enforceable. The immunity from national jurisdiction is, however, not a privilege (Schermers/Blokker § 1612). If IO do not waive their immunity in a particular case (which rarely occurs in practice), they have to provide for a "friendly settlement or for arbitration" (Schermers/Blokker § 1613).

Apart from the functional powers expressly bestowed upon it in the constituent instruments, an IO must be deemed to have those powers which are conferred upon it by the necessary implication as being essential to the performance of its duties (advisory opinion of the ICJ of 13 July 1954 concerning the establishment of the UNAT p. 14: "The Charter contains no provision which authorizes any of the principal organs of the United Nations to adjudicate upon these disputes [between the UN and its staff members] ... It would, in the opinion of the Court, hardly be consistent with the expressed aim of the Charter to promote freedom and justice for individuals ... that it [the UN] should afford no judicial or arbitral remedy to its own staff for the settlement of any disputes which may arise between it [the UN] and them"). The power to establish the UN Administrative Tribunal "arises by necessary intendment out of the Charter" (see also the decision of the German Federal Constitutional Court of 10 November 1981 "Eurocontrol II" decision, case No. 2 BvR 1058/79; for an English translation see the website of the University of Texas at Austin, Institute for Transnational Law, Foreign Law Translations).

These "implied powers" must, however, not only be necessary for the performance of the duties of the organisation but must also respect "the balance of powers which is characteristic of the institutional structure" of the respective organisation (CJEU Judgment 9/56 "Meroni"; Schermers/Blokker § 232).

Another example of the implied powers of an IO is the establishment of the Pension Reserve Fund of the EPO in 1991 (Ullrich, Pension Schemes; ILOAT Judgment 1392). Owing to the lack of explicit powers in the constituent instrument of the EPO (the EPO-EPC), the Pension Reserve Fund was established as a new subsidiary body of the EPO based on those powers which were conferred upon the EPO by necessary implication in order to lend support to the Pension Scheme of the EPO by providing appropriate reserves. It was only in 2000 that the EPO inserted Art. 38(b) EPO-EPC as an express legal basis for the establishment of a Reserve Fund for Pensions and Social Security (EPO Codex) into its primary law, the EPO-EPC. Since then the EPO has, in addition, established a long-term care insurance Reserve Fund (EPO Codex), a Sickness Insurance Reserve Fund (EPO Codex) and a Reserve Fund to fund the Organisation's liability for lump-sum payments as partial compensation for the national tax on pensions (EPO Codex). All these funds are based on implied organisational powers since Art. 38(b) EPO-EPC does not presently provide an explicit legal basis for their establishment.

In their internal sphere of competences IO are exempt from the national sovereign powers of member states both *ratione personae* and *ratione materiae* (Wenckstern para. 993 et seq.).

### II. The autonomous sovereignty in personnel matters

The legal implementation of the autonomous regulatory area governing the staff members is aligned with the overall tasks of an IO. As "the backbone of every international organisation" (Schermers/Blokker § 491) its staff significantly contributes to the achievement of the results of an IO in pursuing the objectives set by member states. Thereby each organisation has its own codex of staff regulations to achieve them.

Despite the diversity of the civil service law of IO there is a continuous tendency "towards a certain rapprochement" (WBAT, Judgment 1 para. 28; Sands/Klein, 1–030). This is best illustrated by the subtitle of Schermers/Blokker's book on international institutional law: "Unity within diversity". This common approach to the law of the international civil service is not restricted to fundamental principles of law. It can be traced to the subtleties of the SR of IO which pay tribute to the phenomenon of complexification of all systems (Teilhard de Chardin, The Phenomenon of Man, 1955). IO are confronted with a large number of similar challenges concerning their personnel. All IO have, for example, to secure the recruitment on the broadest possible geographical bases from among nationals of the member states. The official duties of the staff members and their privileges and immunities have to be shaped in a way that guarantees the independence of the international civil service from any improper influence by individual member states. The working conditions have to be attractive enough to recruit staff on the broadest possible geographical basis from among nationals of the member states and must be directed to securing staff of the highest standard of ability, efficiency and integrity. The staff members must be guaranteed comprehensive legal remedies in disputes with their appointing authority.

Each IO is, therefore, confronted with a range of similar problems which can be solved by means of similar structures and elements in its SR. This trend towards standardisation of the SR (for an historical overview of the CO see Fürst/Weber) takes place in different stages and is influenced in different ways.

## III. The drafting of service regulations (secondary law) prior to the entry into force of the constituent instrument (primary law)

It is common practice to draft the SR of an IO already prior to the establishment of an IO in preparatory bodies like interim committees and working groups, these bodies are not reinventing the wheel. Their deliberations are regularly based on a synoptic overview of existing SR of functionally comparable IO. For example, the working group IV of the Interim Committee of the EPO mainly took the SR of the International Patent Institute in The Hague and of the EU as a basis for establishing the SR of the EPO and the pension schemes (PS) of the CO as a template for the PS of the EPO (see the documents of the working group IV (Personnel) of the Interim Committee of the EPO, publicly available from the EPO).

## IV. The development of the service regulations

Similar to national civil service law, the labour law of an IO is subject to an ongoing process of change. This process is inspired by developments in the national civil service law of the member states and is decisively influenced by numerous formal and informal contacts (panels of experts, task groups etc., see Schermers/Blokker § 507: there is "a harmonizing effect between organisations"), which exist primarily between human resources and legal departments of IO. In this way, new areas where a legal framework is required are detected at an early stage. This process has been made easier by modern means of communication. Recent examples include: rules on data protection, special procedures for the protection of dignity (psychological and sexual harassment at the workplace), ergonomic guidelines, rules concerning non-marital partnerships, rules concerning the use of the internet for private purposes and the establishment of funds designed to support appropriate resources for the organisation's long-term liabilities (pension funds, long-term care insurance and health care funds).

## V. The influence of the jurisprudence

The case law of the international administrative tribunals is of crucial importance for the interpretation and development of the SR of IO. The tribunals emphasise time and again that they are in no way bound by the case law of other tribunals (e.g. ILOAT Judgment 3138 para. 7: it may "however, carry persuasive authority", Judgment 1296 para. 7) or by the internal law of another IO (e.g. ILOAT Judgment 1099 para 9: "... the Tribunal's ruling turns solely on its interpretation of the Organisation's own texts"; 2420 para. 11: "the fact that an IO "belongs to the common systems does not enable it to decline or limit its own responsibility towards the member of its staff ..."). Despite this jurisprudence, the tribunals nonetheless apply the fundamental and human rights in a mostly uniform way to all IO under their jurisdiction without regard to their affiliation to a certain international civil service system.

In sum, it can be observed that the SR of most IO show increasing similarities in their structure and elements. The availability of the databases of the international administrative tribunals on the internet contributes to the harmonisation of the employment law of IO. The autonomy of IO in personnel matters is less relevant in relation to other IO than it is to national civil service law. The common legal principles of the international civil service as applied by the international administrative tribunals contribute to an ever-increasing degree of convergence of the employment laws of the IO. It, therefore, seems permissible, at least to some extent, to speak of one over-arching law of the international civil service.

## VI. The power to initiate proposals to amend the service regulations

During the operational phase of an IO all amendments of the SR are prepared by the administration of the organisation as the sole power to initiate these proposals and to forward them after due consultation of the staff (or an advisory committee with equal representation of staff members and management representatives) to the

legislative body is vested in the head of the secretariat (President, Director-General, Managing Director etc., e.g. Art. 17(2) TEU: "Union legislative acts may only be adopted on the basis of a Commission proposal, except where the Treaties provide otherwise").

This separation of powers corresponds to the "institutional balance" (CJEU Judgment C-40/10 para. 78: "the sole power to initiate proposals"), regularly provided for in the constituent instruments of an IO.

The head of administration is, of course, empowered to amend his proposal (as is the legislative body) after the proposal has been forwarded to him for deliberation and adoption, following consultation of the staff. If the proposal has however been "radically amended" by one of these bodies after the consultation of the staff it has to be considered as a new one it has to be resubmitted for a proper consultation (ILOAT Judgment 1618 para. 14).

## B. The four large civil service systems of the international organisations as *pars pro toto*

### I. General introduction

Among the various possibilities of classifying the IO it is appropriate for the purpose of this presentation to take that one which refers to the civil service system. This approach makes it easier to cope with the abundance of material by restricting the presentation to only one IO for each system.

Such classification of the SR of IO leads to the distinction between four civil service systems. Three of the systems follow a generally similar pattern whereas one system is more or less a *mixtum compositum* of the three others.

It has, however, to be noted that the affiliation of an IO to one of these systems does not enable it to decline or limit its own responsibility towards its members of staff or lessen the degree of legal protection (see, for example, ILOAT Judgment 2420 para. 11).

The international civil service system comprises:

- The conditions of service staff of those UN organisations which belong to the "Common System" (which is a specialised system within the "UN-family");
- The conditions of service of the EU institutions and bodies (the "EU-family");
- The conditions of service of the Coordinated Organisations (the Coordinated System", "CO");
- The conditions of service of those IO which do not adhere to the above – mentioned systems but have by and large adapted the service conditions of one or more of these systems (mixed or hybrid system), as represented here by the conditions of service of the EPO.

These four international civil service systems are discussed in more detail below.

### II. The systems

#### *1. The UN Common System*

With the approval of the statute of the ICSC by the UN General Assembly (UNGA) on 18 December 1974 (UN doc. A/RES/3357/XXIX) the UN established the ICSC as a common body for "the regulation and co-ordination of the conditions of service of the United Nations common system" (UN–CS). The ICSC performs its functions in respect of all IO participating in the UN-CS through having accepted the statute of the ICSC (for further details see the website of the ICSC). In conformity with Art. 9 of the statute of the ICSC, the Commission shall in the exercise of its functions "be guided by the principle set out in the agreements between the United Nations and the other organisations, which aims at the development of a single unified international civil service through the application of common personnel standards, methods and arrangements".

On January 2016, the UN-CS comprised the UN, 15 specialised agencies and IO, as well as ten affiliated programmes of the UN. This group of IO is not identical with the "UN family" which is much larger (see for more details the UN organisational chart on the UN website; Schermers/Blokker § 506, § 1692 to 1697 and the website of the ICSC).

The UN-SR can be considered as a prototype for the SR of the UN-CS's organisations (to some extent even for the SR of IO within the "UN family") and, therefore, serves as reference for the purposes of this book. The UN-SR are available on the UN website via the information system "UNBISNET" (UN doc. Symbol/Sales Number Keyword) and "UN Official Document Search under the keyword: "ST/SGB/2016/1"). Public access to UN documents is based on Rule 56 of the rules of procedure of the UNGA.

### *2. The civil service system of the EU*

The civil service system of the EU (the SR of the officials of the EU and the conditions of employment of other servants of the EU) applies in principle (some exceptions exist primarily in the salary structure, see, for example, the EUIPO) to all officials of one of the institutions of the Union (Art. 13 TEU, Art. 1a EU-SR; with the exception of the ECB, Art. 36 of the protocol on the statute of the European System of Central Banks and of the ECB) and to the European External Action Service (Art. 1b(a) EU-SR), the European Economic and Social Committee, the Committee of the Regions, the European ombudsman and the European data protection supervisor (Art. 1b(b) to (e) EU-SR). In addition, it is applicable in addition to more than 50 interinstitutional bodies, specialised agencies and decentralised bodies of the EU in so far as they refer in their constituent instruments to the EU-SR (see the website of the EU, institutions and other bodies).

The EU-SR do not in toto apply to the members of institutions (commissioners, parliamentarians) or judges (see, for example, Art. 243 TFEU) nor to the staff members of the EIB (see Art. 11(7) of the statute of the EIB, TEU Protocol (No. 5) due to its special tasks as a financial organisation (see the ECB referred to above). (There is some parallelism with the financial organisations of the "UN family", the WBG and the IMF, which also have SR system of their own. In contrast to the ECB and the EIB which are subject to the jurisdiction of the CJEU in staff disputes, they have, however, established their own administrative tribunals (WBAT and IMFAT) and are, therefore, not subject to the UNDT and UNAT.

On the whole the EU civil service system, to which reference is made in this book, is a very homogeneous set of rules (see Schermers/Blokker § 1698). A consolidated version of the EU-SR as of 1 January 2014 is available on the website of the European Commission Civil Service. Public access to EU documents is based on Reg. 1049/2001 of the European Parliament and of the Council.

### *3. The civil service system of the co-ordinated organisations (CO)*

In 1957 the Council of the OECD, the NATO, the WEU and the Committee of Ministers of the Council of Europe (CoE) established a common system of IO for the harmonized adjustment of salaries and allowances of their staff. Later on, the ESA and the ECMWF joined the system. In June 2011, the WEU was dissolved and ceased to be a co-ordinated organisation. On 1 July 2012 EUMETSAT obtained the status of a co-ordinated organisation.

In 1963, a conference initiated by the CoE was set up in order to draft model staff regulations for European IO. These regulations did not, however, prove to be a great success. For example, they were not used as a template for the EPO-SR by the EPO Interim Committee (1973 to 1977).

In 1987, the EPO withdrew its request to join the CO. The CO succeeded, however, in setting up a harmonised system of salary scales, uniform methods of adjusting remuneration, allowances and indemnities, and a uniform pension scheme (for more details on the history of the CO see: Fürst/Weber; the website of the ISRP provides technical assistance and information for the CO and about 25 other IO and offers services for the calculation and payment of pensions and tax adjustments; see also Schermers/Blokker § 506 and § 1724).

The civil service system of the CO is far less homogeneous than that of the UN and the EU. Nevertheless, the co-ordinated system contributes significantly to the harmonisation of the SR of the CO in general. This harmonisation is intensified by the frequent contacts between the staff of the CO responsible for legal matters and human resources.

Due to the better accessibility of the SR (the more technical CO do not grant general access to their internal documents), the CoE-SR are taken as reference for the purposes of this book. For the latest consolidated version of the CoE-SR of 9 September 2015 see the website of the CoE (rule of law, jobs) or the website of the CoEAT (texts). Public access is based on the Resolution 2001(G) of the Committee of Ministers.

### *4. The mixed (hybrid) civil service system*

Besides the three largely homogeneous international civil service systems of the IO a fourth system may be identified referred to for the purpose of this book as the "mixed" or "hybrid" system. This terminology mirrors the description of the national law of those countries which belong to a mixed (hybrid) legal system containing elements of various legal systems such as common law, civil law or muslim law (see, for example, J. Du Plessis, Comparative Law and the Study of Mixed Legal Systems, in: The Oxford handbook of comparative law, 2006). It comprises all other IO most with a smaller number of officials. The SR of these organisations do, however, not exist as independent blocks with totally different structures and elements. As already mentioned above, the SR of newly established IO are largely adapted to the SR of functionally comparable IO or "families" of IO.

For example, the SR of CERN, EMBL and ESO are based largely on the civil service system of the CO whereas the SR of Eurocontrol are very similar to those of the EU.

In this book the employment law of the EPO serves as reference organisation for this group of IO. In terms of manpower (7,000 officials in 2015) it is the 4th largest IO besides the UN-CS (2015: 84,000 staff members), the EU (2016: 45,000 staff members) and the World Bank Group (2013: 16,500 staff members). The EPO-SR are of particular interest because the EU-SR were to a large extent taken up word for word in the EPO-SR (see above) whereas the EPO-PS corresponds to that of the CO (see the document of Working Group V of the Interim Committee of the EPO (1973 to 1977) which is accessible in the archives of the EPO, see Singer/Geuß and the letter of the German Ministry of Finance (BMF) of 3 August 1998 (BStBl. I 1998, 1042). It is, therefore, interesting to note that the ILOAT and the CJEU as well as the tribunals of the CO have considerable opportunity to take position on SR with frequently identical wording.

However, until 2012 the internal civil law of the EPO was not publicly accessible.

As of 12 November 2012, the Administrative Council of the EPO adopted a new policy making most of its documents available to the public on the EPO's website. In addition, since 30 September 2015 the latest consolidated version of the EPO-SR, albeit without a large part of tertiary law, has been published on the EPO website (see EPO Codex).

### III. The unity of the employment systems of international organisations

Despite the above-mentioned classification of the SR of IO into four systems, the SR do not exist in isolation but have many similarities, not only in their basic structures but also in their specific elements (Schermers/Blokker § 540: "The law governing international officials does not substantially differ from one international organisations to the other"; see however the more sceptic approach of Seidl-Hohenveldern/Loibl para. 1512: A shared law of the SR of IO is only available to a limited extent today in the field of privileges and immunities). The reasons are manifold. As already mentioned, the starting point of alignment can be seen in the preparatory work prior to the establishment of an IO. At this stage the work of the "interim committees" is based to a large extent on the existing SR of functionally comparable IO.

During the operational stage of an IO there is an ongoing process of mutual cooperation between IO in the adaptation of their SR to new developments in the area of human resources (for example, the pension reserve fund of the CoE adopted by Resolution (2002)53 was modelled on the fund of the OECD, created in 2003 (CoE doc. CM(2005)152 of 12 October 2005). In preparing the pension reserve fund of the OECD this organisation in turn examined the pension funds of the UN, the ECB, CERN, ESA and the pension reserve fund of the EPO (OECD doc. BF/CB/PSWG(2000)1). This approach is based on the assumption that the delegations of the member states which have already agreed on a line of compromise in the council of one organisation will pursue this objective in the other organisation.

A further alignment of the SR of IO is to be found in the case law of the international administrative tribunals. Despite the fact that the SR of an IO are a source of law valid exclusively for the respective IO (similar to the municipal law of the member states; "particular international law", see Schermers/Blokker § 539; Joost Pauwelyn, Conflict of Norms in Public International Law, 2003; see also Seidl-Hohenveldern/Loibl para. 1504) the ILOAT applies common basic principles and methods of interpretation uniformly to all IO subject to its jurisdiction (in 2016: 62 IO). A significant number of these IO do not belong to the UN-CS but to the mixed civil service system. Since the SR of IO as a rule include neither a comprehensive charter of human rights nor specific principles of the international civil service, it is one of the main functions of the tribunals to fill the gaps in connection with the judicial review of administrative decisions concerning staff members.

In this respect the Noblemaire principle, can serve as a good example. It was born in the League of Nations days as a customary law which, at first, was only binding on IO belonging to the UN family (ILOAT Judgment 986 para. 7). Later on, it was extended to all other IO under the ILOAT's jurisdiction (see ILOAT Judgments 1912, 1913 (EMBL), 1791 (CERN)).

That is why the employment law of the IO already displays similar structures and elements to such an extent that there is "some unity within diversity" in the institutional law of the IO (Schermers/Blokker § 23 et seq.). This book aspires to contribute to this development.

## IV. The dual role of international organisations as an employer and a substitute state

IO have a dual responsibility towards their staff, "they must be both an employer and a substitute state" (H. Reichenbach, An administration at the services of half a billion Europeans, 2002, Staff Reforms at the European Commission, p. 39 accessible on the internet: ec.europa: eu/reform2002/documents/staff_reform_2002_en.pdf).

If states establish an IO in order to benefit from cooperation in certain fields and activities they attribute certain powers to the organisation. IO, unlike states are "not competent to determine their own competencies" but their power is functionally restricted to the competences indispensable for the functions of the IO (Schermers/Blokker § 209, Advisory Opinion of the ICJ of 8 July 1996, requested by WHO, ICJ Report, 1996, pp. 78–79). The states are thereby not absolved from their obligation to respect the fundamental rights enshrined in their national constitution and in the international conventions on human rights to which they adhere (*nemo plus iuris* principle (see the decision of the German Federal Constitutional Court of 4 April 2001, ref. 2 BvR 2368/99: there are bounds to the transfer of powers to an IO by the basic principles of the national constitution; Schermers/Blokker § 1575: "States that have founded an international organisation are bound by general principles of law. These principles will also be applicable in the legal order of the organisation"). The function of an IO "as a substitute state", therefore requires that the organisation assumes obligations under international law to respect and protect the fundamental rights of its staff members (see ECHR Judgment of 18 February 1999, "Waite and Kennedy v. Germany", Appl. No. 26083/94 para. 67).

In this function, IO have adopted their SR in order to provide an internal social infrastructure, internal means of settling labour disputes and an internal taxation system for their staff members on the salaries and allowances and other emoluments. (As far as the EU is concerned, the internal taxation rules are also applicable to retired staff; see, Art. 12 EU-PPI "emoluments" and Art. 2 Reg. No. 260/68). In the social area, the IO regularly provide for their own sickness, accident, invalidity, incapacity and death insurance schemes and for a pension scheme. Some IO even provide for a long-term care insurance (see, for example, Art. 83a EPO-SR) or offer temporary unemployment benefits (see, for example, Art. 28a EU-SR).

In addition, IO provide a variety of family-related benefits and allowances (see, for example, household allowance, child allowance, education allowances; Annex VII Art. 5 EU-SR). Some IO even provide for their own child care (kindergarten) and schooling (see, for example, the 13 European Schools which provide "a multilingual and multicultural education for nursery, primary and secondary level pupils" of children of the staff of the EU institutions, see more details on website eursc.eu). All IO grant family and parental leave (Art. 42a EU-SR) and maternity leave (Art. 58 EU-SR).

The function of an IO as a substitute state even extends to privileges for its staff such as the exemption from immigration restrictions, and from formalities concerning the registration of aliens, the right to import free of duty their furniture and motor cars for personal use, the inviolability of official papers and documents, the exemption from obligations in respect of military service and the immunity from national jurisdiction in respect of acts done in the exercise of their functions.

**The lack of a parliamentary control**

Although IO act towards their staff as substitute states they are not subject to a direct parliamentary control (an exception is the EU). This deficit of democratic accountability becomes clear where the SR are adopted or approved (UN) by a legislative organ (Council, General Assembly) of the IO which is composed of national officials or government members. This lack of parliamentary control exists throughout the existence of an IO. In order to promote democracy and the respect for human rights within their organisation, some IO have established parliamentary bodies (see, for example, the parliamentary assemblies of the CoE, the OSCE and NATO; the EU Parliament has a special status as an institution with legislative, supervisory and budgetary responsibilities) (see Seidl-Hohenveldern/Loibl § 1209 et seq.; for an overview on the history, structures and functions of the parliamentary assemblies, see Marschall).

## V. The numbers of staff members in international organisations

### *1. The numbers of staff members in organisations participating in the UN Common System*

The assumptions about the number of staff subject to the UN-CS differ considerably. The UN website "UN careers" quotes the number of 44,000 staff members (in 2015) as being subject to the UN-CS, whereas the UN website of the Dag Hammerskjöld Library quotes the number of 41,000 staff members (in 2014) working in the UN secretariat to which the staff members of the 15 specialised agencies and ten programmes of the UN-CS have to be added. The number of staff subject to the UN-CS as cited by the UN Systems HR Statistic Report 2012 of May 2013 on the UN Systems Statistic website (total staff by organisation) is thought to have been approx. 84,000 in 2013 for the UN and the agencies and programmes of the UN-CS. On the assumption that the most reliable data is that of the ICSC itself, which is competent to manage the UN-CS, the total number of active staff subject to the UN-CS is approximately 100,000 (see the salary booklet, introduction, of January 2014 on the ICSC website).

### *2. The number of staff members participating in the civil service system of the EU*

The staff establishment plan of the EU provides 39,687 budget posts in 2016 for the institutions (the European Parliament, the European Council, the Council, the European Commission, the Court of Justice of the EU, the Court of Auditors, the Committee of the Regions, the European Economic and Social Committee, the European ombudsman, the European data protection supervisor and the European external action service) and 6,016 budget posts in 2016 for the bodies set up by the Union and having legal personality (decentralised agencies, undertakings and institutions; see the EU database EUR-Lex, Budget online total revenue, Part C). This staff will be reduced by 5% spread evenly over the period 2014 to 2020 (see EU doc. SEC/2014/0615 final).

### *3. The number of staff members participating in the civil service system of the co-ordinated organisations*

In 2015 there were about 13,000 active staff members in the six CO (CoE, OECD, ESA, NATO, ECMWF and EUMETSAT). For more details see the website of ISRP.

### *4. The number of staff members participating in some organisations of the mixed system*

Approximate number of staff members in some selected IO: World Bank Group: 16,500 (2013); EPO: 7,000 (2015); CERN: 3,200 (2012); IMF: 2,400 (2015); EMBl: 1,570 (2015); Eurocontrol: 2,200 (2015); OPCW: 500 (2015); OSCE: 2,500 (2015); ESO: 700 (2012). The vast majority of the approx. 500 IO pertaining to this system are, however, rather small in terms of manpower and may not exceed 50 employees. The total number of staff will, therefore, be in the range of 60,000 staff members.

### *5. The total number of staff members employed by international organisations*

In addition to the difficulties in determining the number of IO, another uncertainty is the absence of a clear definition of the term "international civil servant". Frequently, the statistical information on the number of officials of an IO, if available at all, only relates to staff posts authorised in the budget and not to the actually occupied posts. In most IO there are additional staff members, not assigned to a budget post but financed out of other budgetary resources (local staff, auxiliary staff, temporary employment).

In these circumstances only a very rough picture can be given based on various resources, like the YBIO, the statistics of international administrative tribunals (calculation of the fees of the secretariat on the basis of the number of employees of the IO under its jurisdiction, e.g. the ILOAT), the ICSC and the websites of IO.

For the three mostly homogeneous families of IO, the UN, the EU and the CO a number of about 160,000 staff members can be derived. For the remaining approx. 500 IO a number of up to 60,000 staff members seem appropriate (see above), bringing the total number to about 220,000 active staff members.

### 6. *The number of retired staff members*

In addition to the active staff members there are a considerable number of retired staff (pensioners). These persons (including dependants and invalids) continue to derive various rights with regard to the IO. For illustration, reference is made to the UNJSPF. On 31 December 2014, this fund recorded a number of approx. 72,000 beneficiaries (see the annual report 2015 on the website of the UNJSPF).

At the EU, the projected number of beneficiaries (pensioners, survivors, invalids) amounted to about 22,449 in 2016 (see Commission doc. SEC (2010)989 final; Subject: Eurostat study on the long-term budgetary implications of pension costs of 18 August 2010 (projection years 2010 to 2026)).

At the CO, the number of beneficiaries is about 7,200 (2015), see the website of the International Service for Remunerations and Pensions (ISRP).

Assuming that there is approx. the same relationship between active staff and beneficiaries within the mixed system as in the EU-family and the CO System a total number of approx. 30,000 beneficiaries would appear as realistic. This would bring the total number of beneficiaries in all systems to approx. 130,000.

## C. The law of the international civil service and national law

The SR of IO belong to the core area of the organisational autonomy; they are the legal basis for the employment relationship between the IO and its staff, which may be called the "backbone" (Schermers/Blokker § 491) of every IO. The autonomy in personnel matters is indispensable for the unimpeded functioning and performance of an IO. In most IO, the authority to adopt and amend a comprehensive set of rules for the employment relationship can already be derived from the respective constitutional instrument (see, for example, Art. 336 TFEU, Art. 101(1) UN Charter, Art. 33(2)(b) and c) EPO-EPC). Even without any express codification, the power to adopt SR can be derived by implication from the organisational autonomy of IO (Seidl-Hohenveldern/Loibl para. 1524).

The autonomy in personnel matters is part of the international activity of an IO and is, therefore, also from the angle of "*ratione materiae*" protected against influence from member states (Wenckstern para. 995 et seq.). IO exercise their autonomy in personnel matters to the full extent. Only in some peripheral areas not part of the core functions of the IO may the SR refer to national labour law (see, for example, Art. 120 et seq. EU-CEOS (local staff), see also the hybrid conditions for auxiliary staff of the EPO, which are partly based on international and national labour law (see the EPO Codex; see also ILOAT Judgment 1450 and the Judgment of the Labour Court of Berlin of 12 September 1994, ref. 16 Sa 58/94).

In addition, IO engage other personnel on the basis of service contracts with companies (i.e. consultancies, security personnel or self-employed persons like IT specialists, interpreters and craftsmen). All these contracts are governed by national law. In recent years, this kind of contractual relationship has increased significantly and the problem of *de facto* employment relationships has gained a growing importance.

## D. The privileges and immunities of the international organisations and international civil servants

### I. Legal basis

#### *1. The privileges and immunities of international organisations*

IO are only able to achieve the tasks assigned to them in their constituent instruments by the member states if they are not fully exposed to national sovereign powers. This holds true particularly for the member states in which an IO has its headquarters, sub-offices or branches.

Member states are only willing to grant an IO particular sovereign rights with corresponding implications for their own sovereignty if the IO is endowed with the necessary functional sovereignty *sui generis* in order to ensure the accomplishment of its tasks without interference by individual member states. In addition, the principle of equality of member states requires that the host state of an IO which already benefits from the seat of the organisation on its territory, shall not in addition "receive a substantial income in taxes" from the organisation (Schermers/Blokker § 530; see also CoE Res (69)29 para. 58: "must not derive an undue fiscal advantage").

For these reasons IO as subjects of international public law are exempt to the extent required by their functions from the national substantive legal order of member states (autonomy in internal organisational, structural, financial and personnel matters and enjoyment of certain privileges, like exemption from national taxation). In addition, IO are exempt by their immunity from national jurisdiction and execution (Schermers/Blokker § 1610 et seq.; Wenckstern para. 37; Kunz-Hallstein, GRUR Int. p. 823; but see the restricted immunity of the EU under Art. 274 to 276 TFEU; for a comprehensive treatise of the privileges and immunities of the UN see Miller).

In literature there is a smooth transition between the terms "privileges" and "immunities". Often the terms are used as synonyms (see, for example, Kunz-Hallstein, Art. 8, para. 2). The following presentation is based on the "classical" differentiation by Schermers/Blokker (§ 1612: "Immunity from jurisdiction is not a privilege. It does not free the organisation from any obligation. The national laws remain applicable; it is only their adjudication in the courts which is prevented").

It would constitute a denial of justice if an IO were to just sit back and enjoys immunity from national jurisdiction and execution (Wenckstern para. 172, 494). The right to an effective legal remedy is the prevailing legal principle which remains unaffected. In the case of disputes arising under a contract or procurement, an IO will ordinarily provide for the legal remedy or arbitration. In staff disputes IO regularly provide a more formalised legal protection by an international administrative tribunal (but see, for example, ILOAT Judgment 2657).

Accordingly, "privileges" designates exemptions or modified applications of municipal laws whereas "immunities" may be defined as an exemption from the national jurisdiction and execution (see for more details Wenckstern para. 32 et seq.).

IO enjoy only such privileges in the territories of member states as are necessary for the unimpeded performance of their "official activity". The details under which an IO enjoys privileges and immunities are defined in the Protocol on Privileges and Immunities (PPI) annexed to the convention and forming an integral part thereof (see, for example, Protocol (No 7) to the TEU). The authorisation to establish PPI is regularly stipulated in the Convention itself (see, for example, Art. 343 TFEU and Art. 8 EPO-EPC). As a rule, the PPI is supplemented by headquarters and seat agreements.

In some PPI, an express definition of the term "official activities" may be found (see, for example, EPO-PPI Art. 3(4): "The official activities ... shall, for the purposes of this Protocol, be such as are strictly necessary for its administrative and technical operation as set out in the Convention"). IO are, however, by virtue of the principle of good faith, under an obligation to cooperate with the authorities of their member states in the application of the PPI (see, for example, Art. 20(1) EPO-PPI: "The Organisation shall co-operate at all times with the competent authorities of the Contracting States in order to facilitate the proper administration of justice, to ensure the observance of police regulations and regulations concerning public health, labour inspection or other similar national legislation, and to prevent any abuse of the privileges, immunities and facilities provided for in this Protocol".)

The immunity doctrine applicable to states prohibits the exercise of national jurisdiction on sovereign public acts (*acta iure imperii*) of another state (*par in parem non habet imperium*) but allows the exercise of jurisdiction in acts of a private (commercial) character (*acta iure gestionis*); see, Seidl-Hohenveldern/Loibl para. 1907; Schermers/Blokker § 210 et seq.; see also the Resolution adopted by the UNGA on 2 December 2004, doc. A/RES/59/38 and the Committee on Legal Affairs and Human Rights of the CoE, Report on the Accountability of international organisations for human rights violations, doc. 13370 of 17 December 2013, para. 30).

Unlike States which possess the power to create basically unlimited general competences IO are governed by the "principle of speciality". The powers conferred on them are limited by the promotion of those functions which the member states have entrusted to them (Advisory Opinion of the ICJ, ICJ Reports 1996 of 8 July 1996 pp. 66; see also Hailbronner, De Cooker/Süss, Gruber/Benisch, Schermers/Blokker § 209: "[IO] are not competent to determine their own competence").

Whereas the immunities of a state are geographically unlimited, the functional immunities of IO are restricted to the territories of the member states. On the other hand, the immunity of states is restricted to their public activities whereas the legally permissible acts of IO cover all functional activities, delimited only by the attributed powers. The categories "private activity" and "public activities" are therefore not suitable for characterising the activities of IO. It would be more appropriate to speak of "official" activities of IO (Kunz-Hallstein, Art. 8 para. 10, footn. 22, Crossing Frontiers, p. 602). This absolute immunity is granted by member states in order to ensure the independence of an IO in the entire field of its activities. Member states thereby even waive the judiciary powers which they would be authorised to exercise in regard of private acts of foreign states (e.g. rent of office space, purchase of working tools etc.).

Those states which are not a member of an IO are, however, not bound to grant immunity to an IO (see, for example, the Opinion of the US Court of Appeal 3rd Circuit, Nos 09–3601, 09–3640 of 16 August 2010 with regard to a licence contract on software tools with US-based company, see further Reinisch, Privileges).

Whereas the Vienna Convention of Diplomatic Relations (VCDR) of 18 April 1961 sets out the specific rules for the grant of privileges and immunities to the diplomatic missions of states, there is no generally applied international legal framework for the granting of privileges and immunities by the member states to IO. The only common denominator is the need of IO for those privileges and immunities which are indispensable for a full and unimpeded exercise of their tasks (see the CoE Resolution (69)29 of 26 September 1969, para. 188).

Often IO are granted some privileges in addition to those stipulated in the PPI. These special agreements (headquarters or seat agreements) are not always publicly accessible. These agreements basically take account of the special needs of an IO and its staff members in the host countries. Often, however, this may also be due to the fact that member states attempt to gain an advantage in the competition for the seat of an IO by offering additional privileges to the organisation and its staff. IO already in operation try, therefore, to counteract this unfavourable development by inserting a most-favoured clause into their seat agreements. Time and again there are (confidential) lengthy negotiations or even arbitration procedures and law suits before national tribunals, due to the restrictive stance taken by the host states on the interpretation of the rules on privileges (see, for example, the EMBL arbitration against Germany, Kunz-Hallstein, NJW 1992, p. 3069).

### 2. *The privileges and immunities of staff members, their family members, and other persons performing functions for the organisation*

#### a) The personal scope of privileges and immunities

The unimpeded functioning of an IO would not be fully ensured by the privileges and immunities granted to an IO, if its employees (the immunity continues even after they have ceased to hold office, see, for example, EU-PPI Art. 11(a)), national representatives, and experts performing functions for or on behalf of the organisation did not also enjoy some privileges and immunities. These privileges, immunities and other facilities are accorded to these persons solely in the interests of the IO; they are not designed to give these persons a personal advantage (see, for example, Art. 17(1) EU-PPI, Art. 19(1) EPO-PPI).

An organisation is required to waive the immunity of these persons where it considers that such immunity prevents the normal course of justice and the waiver is not contrary to the interests of the organisation (see, for example, Art. 17(2) EU-PPI, Art. 19(2) EPO-PPI). Due to the link between the immunity of an IO and its staff members ("accessoriness"), staff members may not waive this right by themselves. When privileges and immunities are in dispute the employee concerned must immediately inform the organisation (see, for example, Art. 23 EU-SR, Art. 27 EPO-SR).

The accomplishment of the tasks of an IO is entrusted to employees of the highest standard of ability, efficiency and integrity recruited on the broadest possible geographical basis from among nationals of the member states of the organisation (see, for example, Art. 27 EU-SR, Art. 5 EPO-SR). The employees will usually only be prepared to leave their home country with their family if they find adequate living conditions. A number of privileges and immunities are, therefore, also applicable to spouses, children and other family members forming part of the household of the official (for more details see the Protocol Guide for International Organisations of August 2015 issued by the Ministry of Foreign Affairs of the Netherlands, published on the website of the Government of the Netherlands).

Some PPIs provide for the possibility of a member state not to extend certain privileges, immunities and facilities to its own nationals or to persons who at the time of taking up their functions with the organisation had their permanent residence in that member state (see, for example, Art. 22(a) and (b) EPO-PPI). This applies, for example, to the exemption of officials and representatives while attending meetings of the organisation, in respect of military service, privileges in respect of money exchange regulations and the grant of diplomatic rights to the head of the organisation.

Representatives of member states taking part in the work of an IO, their advisers and experts enjoy certain immunities and facilities while attending meetings and in the course of their missions (see, for example, Art. 10(1) EU-PPI; Art. 12 EPO-PPI). Such persons enjoy *inter alia* immunity from arrest, detention and from seizure of their personal luggage, immunity from jurisdiction in respect of acts, including words written and spoken in the exercise of their functions and inviolability of their official papers and documents (see, for example, Art. IV UN-CPI, Art. 12 EPO-PPI).

Experts of IO are accorded immunities and facilities similar to those granted to representatives (see, for example, Art. VI UN-CPI, Art. 15 EPO-PPI).

International administrative tribunals are autonomous bodies of IO established on the basis of the international sphere of activity of an IO. In some cases, the tribunal and the judges derive immunities expressly from the respective provisions applicable to the organisation and its staff. They may also enjoy privileges (see, for example, Art. 3(4) statute of the CJEU, Art. IV.6 statute of the WBAT and Art. VIII statute of the IMFAT). In most cases functional immunities and privileges are granted at least in the seat state of the tribunal. The UN reform of Administration of Justice in 2009 did not provide for any privileges and immunities of the judges of the UNDT/UNAT. Despite ongoing requests by the Internal Justice Council (see, for example, UN doc. A/66/158 para. 24), it was not until 2015 that a formal request in this respect was presented to the UNGA. In its doc. A/70/187 of 31 July 2015 (p. 54 et seq.), the UN-SG requested the UNGA to confer on the judges the same immunities and privileges as are granted to staff members (see A. Megzari: Internal Justice of the United Nations: A Critical History 1945 – 2015, 2015, p. 531 et seq.). In quite a number of tribunals the question of immunity and privileges enjoyed by the judges is dealt with in internal arrangements which are not accessible publicly. Without this immunity, international judges could be exposed to actions for damages before national courts in respect of their official activities. They would even be worse off than their national peers whose liability is limited both by restricted state liability for damages in general and a restricted recourse against judges (Richterprivileg), which aims at ensuring legal certainty, *res judicata* and the independence of judges (as to the restriction of liability in case of infringement of EU law by national courts, adjudication at last instance, see CJEU Judgments C-173/03, C-224/01).

#### b) The geographical scope of privileges and immunities

Basically, the privileges and immunities of IO and their staff members are restricted to the territory of member states. IO may, however, try to extend their activities to third countries (see, for example, Art. 16 EU-PPI) and those countries often recognise the privileges and immunities of the IO of which they are not a member state (see more in detail: Aaron I. Young, Deconstructing International Organisation Immunity, Georgetown Journal of International Law, 2013, p. 311 et seq.; see also the US International Organisation Immunities Act of 9 December 1945 and the US Foreign Sovereign Immunities Act of 1976).

## II. Immunity of staff members and inviolability of official documents

### *1. The immunity of staff members in respect of official acts*

Staff members are fully subject to the applicable national law in their private legal relationship with other private persons (see, for example, Art. 23 EU-SR, CJEU, order T-394/02, Judgment T-497/93). Only in respect of all acts performed by them in their official capacity as staff members of IO do they enjoy immunity from legal proceedings (Schermers/Blokker § 534 et seq.). The question of the immunity of staff members towards the organisation itself, e.g. in cases of liability or recovery of undue payments, does normally not arise since the organisation may enforce its claims against staff members by a unilateral administrative act which may be appealed by the staff member. An organisation may, however, appeal a decision if there is a two-tier judicial system (see the UNDT/UNAT and the CJEU) and the staff member may not invoke immunity (see, for example, CJEU Judgment T-361/10 P). The same is valid for the informal review procedure of the ILOAT.

The immunity of staff members from national jurisdiction of the member states is, therefore, geographically more widespread than the immunity of diplomats which according to Art. 31 VCDR is restricted to the receiving state. On the other hand, the immunity of staff members is of a lesser degree of intensity than that enjoyed by diplomats; it is functionally restricted to the accomplishment of the tasks entrusted to them (Seidl-Hohenveldern/Loibl para. 1907).

Unlike diplomats, international civil servants take their residence in the host state of the organisation without the *agrément* of that state. A staff member may, therefore, unlike a member of the staff of a diplomatic mission, not be declared *persona non grata* (Art. 9 VCDR). However, unlike diplomats he does not enjoy immunity from the criminal jurisdiction of the state of his residence. If they commit a serious misconduct, international civil servants may, however, be immediately suspended from service. In such a case, a residence permit will be withdrawn. Unlike diplomatic staff (Art. 29 VCDR), an international civil servant is also liable to any form of arrest or detention.

The immunity of a staff member from national jurisdiction and enforcement in respect of his official activities is not a privilege. A staff member has (as in his private life) to pay due respect to the national law. Only the adjudication and the enforcement are excluded. The application of national substantive law is only excluded if privileges apply, for example in the field of taxation.

The immunity from adjudication is primarily applicable to civil and administrative law. In cases of doubt the IO decides for itself whether an act falls within the scope of official activities of a staff member. In the case of a dispute between the IO and a member state on this issue there will be recourse to arbitration (Kunz-Hallstein, Art. 8 EPC para. 6 and Art. 23 EPO-PPI). Criminal acts (e.g. sexual harassment, defamation, assaults and traffic offences) cannot be characterised as official activity. The exemption from jurisdiction also applies to staff members after they have ceased to hold office (for example Art. 11(a) EU-PPI).

The right of a staff member to refuse to give evidence in legal proceedings of information of which he has knowledge by reason of his duties may generally not be derived from the PPI but is stipulated in the SR (see, for example, Art. 19 EU-SR; CJEU Judgment C-54/90).

The immunity of international civil servants in respect of their official activities also applies to relations with colleagues and superiors (an example are incidents of harassment). In these cases, legal protection by international administrative tribunals is only provided indirectly. First of all, a staff member has to summit a request for assistance and protection to the administration of his organisation. If the organisation rejects the request he may proceed as usual in legal disputes with his appointing authority.

Also staff unions or staff associations enjoy collective immunity derived from their members and may, therefore, not be sued by staff members before national courts (see, for example, the decision of the Higher Regional Court Munich (OLG) of 30 September 2010, case No. 8 U 2029/10).

## 2. *The attachment of earnings*

The confiscation of the salary or the pension of an active or retired staff is generally considered as a legal issue since the amounts are paid from the budget appropriations of an IO which as an asset of the organisation are immune from any form of requisition, confiscation, expropriation and sequestration (e.g. Art. 1 EU-PPI; Art. 3(2) EU-PPI). It has, however, become standard practice in the law of the international civil service that an IO is deemed to have waived its immunity if a salary attachment order by a national administrative or judicial authority was served and the organisation did not forward any grounds for opposing the deduction from the salary (pension) of the (former) official.

The waiving of the immunity is as a rule deemed to have occurred after a certain deadline has elapsed without the organisation having notified the national authority to the contrary (e.g. Art. 3 DE/EPO Agreement, Art. 3 NL/EPO Agreement and Art. 4(1)(c) AT/EPO Agreement). In all these agreements, the EPO is granted a deadline of 14 days following the date of notification of the attachment of salaries to inform the competent authorities of its decision not to waive its immunity.

In consistent case law the CJEU interprets Art. 1 EU-PPI in such a way that no authorisation by the CJEU to serve an attachment to the EU administration is necessary if the institution does not intend opposing it (see CJEU Judgment T-497/93: "If the institution considers that it would not be contrary to the interests of the Community not to avail itself of its privileges and immunities it is bound, by virtue of its duty to cooperate in good faith with the national authorities, to give effect to the attachment order issued by the national court"; see also CJEU order T-394/02).

In the case of attachment of earnings under national law a certain amount of the salary is exempt from attachment for social reasons. An IO, acting as a substitute state may, to a certain extent, therefore, substitute the amounts exempt from attachment under national law, by its own rules.

## 3. *The assignment of earnings*

The assignment of salaries and emoluments of international staff members to third parties (banks, insurances etc.) is as a rule automatically recognised by an IO without further ado as being attributed to the staff member's private sphere of actions without involvement of the immunity of the organisation. After the deed of assignment is made known to the organisation the earnings assigned are retained and paid over to the creditors.

In case of divorce, IO will as a rule provide information on the accrued pension benefits pursuant to a national court order. IO will, however, ordinarily not provide a lump sum payment to the ex-spouse in accordance with a possible divorce settlement agreement. It is up to the official himself to fulfil this obligation from his own resources. Some IO allow to pay a portion of the monthly pension to be paid to the former spouse. For most pension issues, in the event of divorce the "Divorce" booklet available on the website of the UNJSPF may provide a useful guidance. See also CJEU Judgment C-430/97 and Annex VIII Art. 27 EU-SR.

#### *4. Inviolability of documents*

Official documents of IO are inviolable even outside the premises of an IO (see, for example, Art. 5 EU-PPI; Art. 2 and 12(1)(c) EPO-PPI). In order to prevent an investigation or confiscation of official documents outside the premises where the organisation exercises its special domicilary rights protected by the PPI (Art. 1 EU-PPI: "The premises and buildings of the Union shall be inviolable"), they shall be labled in an appropriate manner; see the Resolution (69)29 of the CoE on the Privileges and Immunities of IO of 26 September 1969, para. 49).

#### *5. Personal immunities of high officials*

The high officials of IO enjoy personal inviolability (Art. 29 VCDR) and immunity from criminal jurisdiction and extensive immunity from civil and administrative jurisdiction even in their private activities in the receiving but not in the sending state (Art. 31 VCDR). They retain their main residence in their home country and are accredited in the host state. According to the prevailing opinion they additionally enjoy the privileges and immunities accorded to other staff members in the interest of the unimpeded functioning of the IO. In contrast to the diplomatic status these general privileges and immunities are valid for all member states (even for the member state of origin if not withheld, see above). If, however, a high official would be declared *persona non grata* (Art. 9 VCDR), it is obvious that his activities in the IO would inevitably be terminated.

### III. Fiscal privileges of active staff members

#### *1. The exemption of salaries from national taxation*

The exemption of the salaries of the staff members of IO from national taxation (as for pensions, see below) is expressly stipulated in most protocols, conventions and agreements on privileges and immunities of IO (for example, Art. 12(2) EU-PPI; Art. V Section 18(b) UN-CPI; Art. 18(b) CoE-GAPI; Art. 16(1) EPO-PPI) and is constantly recognised in case law of international administrative tribunals as a general legal principle applicable to the international civil service (e.g. ILOAT Judgments 2257, 2256, 2032). It is an important guarantee of the equal treatment of the international civil servants, it strengthens their independence and objectivity and contributes to the principle of fiscal equality of member states (for more in details see Schermers/Blokker § 530). The tax exemption covers the whole "remuneration", i.e. the basic salary and all allowances (for example, Art. 62(3) EU-SR and Art. 12(2) EU-PPI).

### 2. *Internal taxation*

As the fiscal privileges of staff members are not designed to give them a personal advantage, most IO have set up their own internal tax regulations. Staff members are liable to this tax for the benefit of the organisation (e.g. Art. 12(1) EU-PPI in conjunction with Council Regulation No. 260/68 of 29 February 1968 laying down the conditions of procedure for applying the tax for the benefit of the EU countries; Art. V Section 18(b) UN-CPI in conjunction with the Tax-equalization Staff Assessment Plan of 18 November 1948 (UNGA Resolution 239 (III) (1948); for a historical survey on the Plan see the website of the United Nations System, Chief Executive Board of Coordination; for the current assessment rates see the ICSC Report A/66/30 of 20 August 2011 p. 74; Art. 16(1) EPO-PPI in conjunction with the Regulation of internal tax for the benefit of the EPO, not generally accessible). For this reason, it is argued in the literature that the tax exemption is basically not a real privilege but a measure to avoid double taxation. The competence to establish internal tax regulations applicable to staff members is either expressly stipulated or may be based on the power of organisational autonomy of an IO and its functions as a substitute state.

The form of taxation applied to staff salaries in an IO is the deduction at source, i.e. the salaries paid are net amounts after deduction of the internal tax. The tax (assessment) rates vary from IO to IO (see, for example, EU: Art. 4 of Council Regulation No. 260/68: progressive taxation between 8% and 45% and a "solidarity levy" until 2023, see Art. 66a EU-SR; UN: progressive assessment between 16% and 30% of the assessable income, see the salary scales on the website of the ICSC). The tax amounts normally appear as tax revenue for the IO. In the EU budget 2016 the proceeds from tax on salaries, wages, allowances and pensions amounted to about EUR 718 million (see the general budget 2016 of 24 June 2015, Title 4, Chapter 40, Item 400 in the Database EUR-Lex, Budget on-line).

The procedure of retention of tax at source permits no tax cuts of any kind.

There are no "internal revenue offices" at IO. (At the UN, the "staff assessment" is even expressly not considered as a withholding of tax but as "an amount deducted … from gross pay", …, "it cannot be reimbursed under any circumstances", UN doc. ST/IC/2014/6 point 2.).

Apart from the salaries the general tax liability of staff members of IO is principally based on the national taxation system in the country where the staff member has his fiscal domicile. Double taxation agreements may apply (there are no double taxation agreements between states and IO due to the fact that there is a lack of reciprocity). In deviation from the general rule, EU officials are considered in the application of income tax (apart from EU salaries), wealth tax, death duties and in the application of connections on the avoidance of double taxation, as having maintained their domicile in the country of origin. The official may not choose between his former tax residence and his tax residence in the country in which he is serving (Art. 13 EU-PPI).

In very few cases member states of the UN family organisations do not grant a tax exemption to their own nationals (e.g. US nationals). Similarly, French nationals working at CERN and having their domicile in France are subject to French income tax. Based primarily on the principle of equal treatment of staff members and on a fair balance of fiscal revenue of member states the UN and CERN compensate the officials concerned with a refund, placing them in the position in which they would be if their salary were not taxed by the home country (see UN doc. ST/IC/2014/6 and the website of the "Income Tax Unit of the UN"). The staff assessment amount is debited against the contributions to the "tax equalization fund" of the UN. Those member states who do not tax the earnings of staff members receive the staff assessment as a credit against their contributions to the UN. The method of calculation of the tax amount to be reimbursed has always been a source of conflict before the UN administrative Tribunals (see, for example, ILOAT Judgments 2296 (ILO), 2256 (OPCW), 2255 (UNESCO), 2032 (OPCW), 1224 (IAEA)). In its Judgment 2255 the ILOAT dealt with the reimbursement process in all detail. It adopted a method of calculation of the amount of reimbursement to ensure that the staff member's UN income remains totally free from national taxation (the so-called "last-income method", see UN doc. ST/IC/2014/6; see also ILOAT Judgment 1224).

### 3. *Progressive taxation*

From the reasoning of ILOAT Judgments 3020 (WTO) and 2255 (UNESCO) it may be derived that IO are under a duty not to tolerate progressive taxation in relation with tax-exempt salaries, i.e. not to calculate the applicable tax rate by hypothetically taking into account the tax-exempt internal salary. In Judgment 1491, the ILOAT explicitly endorsed the progressive taxation of the earnings of international officials. It held (para 6): "the French approach does not fully discount earnings from CERN for the purposes of taxation since they count towards the figure of total taxable income. But CERN is not to blame for the resulting increase in the rates of taxation .... It exerts control neither over the tax brackets and rates set by French law, nor over the method of reckoning their total income which is just a feature of the French manner of processing income tax".

Art. 12 EU-PPI, which exempts salaries and pensions paid by the EU from national taxation is interpreted by the CJEU as meaning that it excludes any national taxation, direct or indirect (CJEU Judgments C-558/10, 338/88, 260/86; see also Judgments C-229/98, C-333/88).

Art. 16(1) EPO-PPI third sentence explicitly provides that Contracting States may take into account the salaries and emoluments paid by the EPO when assessing the amount of tax to be applied to income from other sources. Art. 12 NL/EPO Agreement does, however, provide that payments which are exempt from national income tax shall not be taken into account when the amount of tax to be applied to income from other sources is assessed.

**Jurisprudence**

ILOAT Judgments

3020: The indirect taxation of the salary of an international official by its inclusion in the assessment of the spouse's rate of income tax violates the equality between officials by reducing the economic capacity from which the official's living with the spouse naturally benefits; 2450: The salaries of French nationals working at the International Federation of Red Cross and Red Crescent Societies and having their domicile in France are subject to French income tax. Since the Federation is not an IO but only an association under Swiss law whose international legal personality has been recognised by Switzerland, there is no tax exemption in France (see also Judgment 2178); 2296: The claim for tax reimbursement of an US citizen working for the ILO in Geneva was not time-barred since no limitation period instructions were publicly available. The right of the official to a tax reimbursement cannot be made contingent upon the right of the IO to recover the amount from the member state; 2256: Tax reimbursement agreements or SR which are not in conformity with the fundamental principle applicable to the international civil service that international officials enjoy a tax-exempt status as far as their salary is concerned, are simply unenforceable (see also Judgment 2255 above); 2032: The exemption of the salary paid by an IO from national taxation is a fundamental legal principle in the international civil service. It is a guarantee of independence of objectivity of IO and cannot be made dependent upon the whim of national tax authorities or the grace and favour of a member state; 1182: The salaries of the staff members of CERN holding French nationality are subject to French income tax. The tax amount paid is reimbursed by CERN in order to guarantee equal treatment of its officials and according to an agreement between CERN and France, CERN receives a refund from the French exchequer. Special arrangements for the payment of French taxes (partly by cash, partly by a set-off due to a tax credit) are irrelevant for the tax amount to be reimbursed by CERN; 1053: Based on an interpretation of the term "emoluments" in the UN-SR the UN-SG decided to reimburse national income tax levied on lump-sum payments from the UNJSPF. Based on this interpretation the IAEA reimbursed the national income tax until 1989 when this practice was discontinued. Since the IAEA followed this interpretation and its plain intent was to bind itself on that interpretation it became part of IAEA's policy. When the organisation chose to take a different view at a later stage, it was a violation of good faith to apply the new interpretation with retroactive effect; 177: No reimbursement of cantonal and local taxes paid by Swiss nationals on their international salaries paid by an IO located in Geneva. They could have settled in Geneva where they would have been exempt from those taxes.

CJEU Judgments/Orders

C-558/10: The division of reciprocal fiscal jurisdiction resulting from the EU-PPI prohibits the member states from imposing on an EU official any taxation, direct or indirect, on the salary paid by the EU. The exemption from national taxes on salaries paid by the EU forbids, therefore, the inclusion of these earnings in the calculations of the cap for a wealth tax (see also C-333/88); C-270/10: Art. 14(1) EU-PPI must be interpreted as meaning that the spouse of an EU official who established her residence because the husband joined the EU in the new country is regarded as having maintained her domicile for tax purposes in the former member state if she is not separately engaged in a gainful occupation (see also C-209/01, C-263/91); C-288/04: The decision of an EU institution defining the status of an official is binding on national authorities for the purposes of Art. 13 and 14 EU-PPI; C-229/98: Although Art. 13 EU-PPI precludes an official from being more heavily taxed (direct or indirect) in respect of his non-exempt income because he is paid a salary from the EU, this does, however, not mean that a member state which grants tax relief to household with an income below a certain index level is not allowed to take account of the EU salary for the calculation of the income of the household; C-333/88: Art. 13 EU-PPI does not preclude a member state from taking account of the salary paid by the EU when subsidizing interests on loans taken out for a main residence.

### 4. *Additional privileges for high officials*

The heads and high officials of IO regularly enjoy additional privileges. This practice corresponds to Resolution (69)29 of the CoE on the Privileges and Immunities of IO of 26 September 1969. Frequently they are even granted diplomatic status under the Vienna Convention on Diplomatic Relations of 18 April 1961. This applies for example to the UN-SG and all ASG, Art. V Section 19 UN-CPI; to the SG and the Deputy SG of the CoE, Art. 16 CoE-GAPI; to the President of the EPO, Art. 13 EPO-PPI; to the head of the EPO branch in the Netherlands, Art. 9(2) and to the staff members in a managerial position Art. 10(1) NL/EPO Agreement and to the head of the EPO sub-office in Austria, Art. 15 AT/EPO Agreement. In addition to the privileges and immunities granted to staff members under the EU-PPI, higher ranking officials of the EU Commission may enjoy wider privileges by bilateral arrangements with the host state (see, for example, the speech 99/118 of the Vice-President of the European Commission, Press Statements, Brussels, 29 September 1999: The Commissioners renounce some privileges granted by Belgium, for example exemption from VAT on consumer products and items for personal use, see the website of the European Commission, Press Release Database).

The judges, the advocates-general, the registrars and the assistant registrars of the CJEU enjoy the same privileges and immunities as the ordinary staff members (Art. 20 EU-PPI).

The members of the Executive Board of the ECB (Art. 19(1) of the Headquarters Agreement with Germany of 18 September 1998) enjoy a wider range of immunities and privileges than the ordinary staff members of the ECB (EU doc. SEC/GovC/4/98/07). Diplomatic status under the Vienna Convention is granted (for more details see Gruber/Benisch).

### *5. The privileges of other persons*

The conventions, agreements and protocols on privileges and immunities normally authorise the supervisory body of an IO to determine the categories of officials, consultants and experts to whom these privileges and immunities apply (see, for example, Art. 15 EU-PPI, Section 22 UN-CPI, Art. 17 EPO-PPI). Temporary agency workers and self-employed workers may not benefit from these rights because they are not in an employment relationship with the IO.

### *6. The exemption of invalidity benefits from national taxation*

The exemption of invalidity payments from national taxation depends on whether this benefit is equated with a salary payment or a pension. In the case of the EU this is not an issue since for EU staff both salaries and "emoluments" like pensions are exempt from national taxation and subject to the internal taxation of the EU institutions (Art. 12(2) EU-PPI in conjunction with Council Regulation No. 260/68 of 29 February 1968 laying down the conditions of procedure for applying the tax for the benefit of the European Communities).

At the UN, disability benefits (Art. 33 UNJSPF Regulations) paid by the UNJSPF are generally not exempt from national income taxation since the invalids are no longer officials of the UN and therefore not covered by Art. V Section 18(b) of the UN-CPI. UN invalids are, therefore, subject to national taxation in the same way as UN pensioners (for details see the UNJSPF Taxation Guide on the website of the UNJSPF and below).

At the CoE, the invalidity pension (Art. 13 et seq. Appendix V CoE-SR) is in the field of taxation equated with a retirement pension and, therefore, subject to national taxation (for pension taxation, see below).

At the EPO, the taxation of invalidity benefits ("invalidity pension" including a tax adjustment) was identical to that of CO invalidity pensions from its inception in 1977. On 1 January 2008, the invalidity system was changed. EPO invalids were no longer considered to have a retired status (pensioners) but the non-active status of a staff member. They had to contribute to the EPO Pension Scheme and their "invalidity allowance" was subject to internal taxation. This change in the legal nature of the invalidity benefits should have resulted in financial savings for the EPO since a tax adjustment was no longer due (for more details see ILOAT Judgments 3375, 3056). A large number of member states, however, maintained their view that the invalidity benefits were to be considered as pension benefits under Art. 16(2) EPO-PPI and, therefore, subject to national taxation of income. This prompted a series of disputes before national fiscal courts (see, for example, the Judgment of the Munich Fiscal Court of 4 December 2012, case No. 9 K 1741/10 accessible on the website of the "Finanzgericht München" and the Judgment of the German Federal Fiscal Court of 11 November 2015, case No. IR 28/14 which held that the invalidity allowance has to be equated with salary benefits and is, therefore, not subject to German income taxation in conformity with Art. 16(1) EPO-PPI. With effect from 1 April 2015, the EPO invalidity system was, nevertheless, replaced by an "incapacity system" (Art. 62b EPO-SR). The system provides for the payment of a proportion of the basic salary and the allowances if an official has reached the maximum of his sick leave entitlements. This system change meant that the question of national taxation on this kind of benefit became moot.

## IV. The taxation of pensions

The general legal principle recognised for the exemption of the salaries paid to international officials from national taxation does not include pensions. In contrast to the taxation of salaries, the taxation of pensions does not follow a uniform pattern but is dealt with in different ways in the various states and IO. "... the fact that in connection with pension rights different rules apply according to the place of residence of retired staff members constitutes neither a breach of property rights nor a violation of the principle of equality ..." (ILOAT Judgments 2292 para. 11, 2257 para. 20). The reason for this difference in treatment is to be seen in the legal assessment of pension rights. According to a prevailing opinion neither the independence and objectivity of former officials for the unimpeded functioning of an IO nor the fiscal equality of member states are arguments that justify the exemption of retired staff members from taxation on their emoluments by member states. This argument may be countered both by reference to some residual obligations which remain valid for retired staff (e.g. discretion, secrecy) and by the fact that most pensioners maintain their permanent residence even after retirement and are thereby contributing to preferential tax revenue of the host state of the IO. According to the prevailing opinion of experts in the law of the international civil service, the unconditional application of national taxation on pensions paid by IO would, however, have fatal consequences for the attraction and the retaining of staff of the calibre required (highest standard of ability, efficiency and integrity) and the recruitment on the broadest possible geographical basis from among nationals of member states.

It is, therefore, deemed necessary to cushion the impact of such a drastic change in taxation by adequate countermeasures. For this reason, various solutions may be envisaged, for example, to continue to subject the emoluments to the internal tax and exempting them from national taxation (EU, ESM, UPC (not yet in force in 2016)) or to moderate the impact of national taxation by raising the amount of pensions (UN) or to reimburse a part of the national taxes paid on pensions (CO, EPO for officials taking up their duties before 1 January 2009, Eurocontrol and various other IO).

Currently, the following picture emerges:

*– EU*

Based on Art. 1 EU-SR (the SR comprise the EU-PS as Annex VIII) in conjunction with Art. 2 of Council Regulation No 260/68 of 29 February 1968, the retirement pensions ("emoluments") are subject to internal taxation and are exempt from national taxation in accordance with Art. 1(a) of Council Regulation No. 549/69 of 25 March 1969 in conjunction with Art. 12(2) EU-PPI. The same holds good for the judges, advocates-general, registrars and assistant registrars of the CJEU (Art. 3 CJEU statute). Some EU-affiliated IO like the ESM (Art. 36(5) of the Treaty establishing the ESM) and the UPC (agreement not yet in force in 2016) have similar rules.

*– UN*

UN pensions are in general (see the UNJSPF 2010 National Tax Guide on the UNJSPF website) fully subject to the national taxation of the country where the pensioner has his fiscal domicile. In some countries there are, however, special rulings for tax exemption of UN pensioners having their fiscal domicile in that country (e.g. Austria, Hungary, India, Paraguay, Philippines, Singapore; see the AFICS Retirement Guide 2014, p. 13 et seq.).

For more in regard of Austria see Art. 37(d) Agreement between the Republic of Austria and the UN regarding the Seat of the UN in Vienna of 29 November 1995. UN pensions are not subject to taxation in Austria regardless of whether the beneficiary was a staff member of an Austrian-based organisation or not.

In order to safeguard a certain "net salary-to-pension ratio", a scale of "pensionable remuneration" was set up as basis for the contributions to be paid and the net pension the pensioner is entitled to. The pensionable remuneration amounts are calculated so as to achieve a service-to-pension ratio of 46.25% for professionals (corresponding to a fictitious length of 25 years of contributory service;

for details see the United Nations System, Chief Executive Board for Coordination on the UN website).

*– CO*

The pensions paid by the CO are subject to the national taxation of the country where the pensioner has his fiscal domicile. There is, however, tax exemption in the following countries (e.g. Andorra, Austria, Croatia, Hungary, Lithuania and Turkey, see CoE doc. GR-PBA (2013)6). The tax burden is cushioned by a partial tax adjustment. The aim of the tax adjustment is to moderate the national tax levied on pensions by 50%. This result would, however, not be achieved by simply granting a tax adjustment of 50% on national tax since the adjustment is also subject to national taxation and would, therefore, reduce the net pension by more than 50%. The right method to achieve the intended tax moderation level is, therefore, to calculate the theoretical national tax amount on the total of the pension and the amount of national tax and to compensate 50% of this amount. This compensation leads in fact to a compensation of somewhat over 50% of national tax since it does not take account of the effect of tax progression. The tax adjustment is financed out of the budget of the respective organisation. At NATO, the national tax burden is cushioned by a tax adjustment (see above). There is also the possibility to draw 2.5% of the total pension amount accumulated as a tax-free cash lump sum at the end of active employment.

The calculation and payment of the pensions, allowances and the tax adjustment and related services are carried out by ISRP (International Service for Remuneration and Pensions). ISRP also provides its services to 25 other IO (in 2015) (see for more details the website of the ISRP).

*– EPO*

The EPO Pension Scheme valid for staff members who joined the EPO since its inception in 1977 until 31 December 2008 is largely in line with that of the CO (see ILOAT Judgments 2689, 2292). The pensions paid by the EPO are fully subject to national income taxation (Art. 16(2) EPO-PPI). The tax burden was cushioned by a tax adjustment for national taxation of pensions identical to the tax adjustment of the CO (see above). As of 1 January 2009, the tax adjustment was replaced by a partial compensation which was subject to internal taxation and it was formally and unconditionally confirmed by the EPO administration to the individual pensioner that this partial compensation is to be exempt from national taxation.

Whereas some member states (e.g. France, Italy) agreed with this reasoning other countries continued to apply national income taxation.

In Germany, the fiscal courts did confirm the opinion of the tax revenue offices that the partial compensation is to be considered as a kind of pension payment to former EPO officials (Art. 16(2) EPO-EPC; see the Judgment of the Berlin-Brandenburg Fiscal Court of 19 December 2013, case No. 15 K 9035/11, confirmed by the German Federal Fiscal Court in its Judgment of 6 November 2015, case No. IR 38/14). As a consequence of these legal conflicts, the EPO decided to reintroduce the former system of the tax adjustment, in line with the CO as from 1 January 2015.

Tax exemption on EPO pensions is presently granted in Andorra, Austria, Croatia, Hungary, Lithuania, Monaco (except for French nationals), Slovakia and Turkey).

Since 1 January 2009 the EPO applies a new (hybrid) PS and a salary savings plan to all officials who joined the EPO on or after that date (see EPO Codex). This system comprises the traditional PS of the CO (see above) but with a maximum pension amount of twice the salary for Grade G1 step 4 (Art. 10(1) EPO-new PS, see EPO Codex) and without any tax adjustment. Amounts of pension contributions in excess of the contributions required for the pension entitlement are accumulated in a salary savings plan (Art. 65(3) EPO-SR) together with the contribution of the EPO. On termination of service the amounts owed are paid out as final salary.

The calculation and the payment of pensions and the tax adjustment are administered by the common service platform of the CO (ISRP, see above).

After the entry into force of the European unitary patent (European patent with unitary effect) EPO decisions regarding those patents may be appealed before the UPC. The EU-PPI will apply to the judges of the court (Art. 8(4) statute of the Unified Patent Court, see Annex I to the Agreement on a Unified Patent Court, Official Journal of the EU of 20 June 2013, 2013/C175/01). The pensions of these judges will, therefore, be subject to internal taxation and exemption from national income tax and tax progression, as is the case for the judges of the CJEU.

– *Eurocontrol*

The pensions paid by Eurocontrol are subject to national taxation of its member states. This tax is, however, compensated by an internal tax adjustment financed by the budget of Eurocontrol in order to even out the difference in the purchasing power of the EU pensions (ILOAT Judgment 1100).

### V. Other fiscal privileges

In addition to tax privileges on salaries and other emoluments some related fiscal privileges are often granted.

*– The acquisition of motor vehicles*

In general, staff members enjoy the privilege to import free of duty a motor car for their personal use at the time of taking up their post (for example, Art. 11(e) EU-PPI, Art. 14(1)(g)(ii) AT/EPO Agreement: not more than two motor cars). Owing to extremely high national taxation of the purchase of motor cars, some host countries provide in addition in the seat agreements with IO some fiscal relief to staff members for the purchase of duty-free motor cars during the duration of the employment in order to recruit and retain staff of a certain calibre and to facilitate the recruitment on a broad geographical basis (see the Protocol Guide for International Organisations of 20 November 2015 issued by the Ministry of Foreign Affairs of the Netherlands under point 9.5; in Austria most international officials may purchase a duty-free motor car every four years and higher ranking officials every two years (see the Information Circular of UNIDO for Austria, doc. UN/INF. 292 of 19 April 1991)).

*– Furniture and personal effects*

Staff members enjoy the right to import free of duty their furniture and personal effects (including consumer goods) at the time of first taking up their post and to export them on termination of their employment /Art. 11(d) EU-PPI, Section 18(g) UN-CPI, Art. 18(f) CoE-GAPI, Art. 14(g) EPO-PPI).

In practice, most seat states grant the duty-free import of goods up to several years after taking up the post. There may, however, be restrictions by national law of the host state relating to export prohibition (see Kunz-Hallstein, EPO-PPI Art. 14 para. 23). Usually, these privileges are handled generously.

*– Fiscal privileges in respect of currency and exchange regulations*

Customarily international officials enjoy broad privileges in respect of currency and exchange regulations (Art. 11(c) EU-PPI, Section 18(e) UN-CPI, Art. 18(d) CoE-GAPI, Art. 14(e) EPO-PPI). These privileges may be important in the case of the regular transfer of part of the remuneration by the IO to an account in another member state (for example, Annex VII, Art. 17(2) EU-SR). Practical problems are rare (see Kunz-Hallstein, EPO-PPI Art. 14 para. 20).

## VI. Exemption from compulsory national social security schemes

Most PPIs and seat agreements of IO contain provisions exempting the officials from compulsory contributions to the national social security schemes. Sometimes an exemption is granted on the condition that the IO has established its own social security scheme (e.g. Art. 18 EPO-PPI; but see Art. 10(3) EPO

Contract Staff Conditions, EPO Codex: Staff may opt for a national social security and pension scheme). Art. 14 EU-PPI stipulates that the EU shall lay down a social security scheme without expressly granting an exemption from national security schemes. Initially this caused difficulties in interpretation but finally the exemption was derived from Art. 16 EU-PPI which provides for the grant of customary diplomatic privileges. Also neither the UN-CPI nor the CoE-GAPI contain an explicit provision exempting staff members from compulsory contributions to a national security scheme. The social security of staff members of the UN is, therefore, not considered as an UN Common System matter under the control of the ICSC (UN doc. JIU/RE/2007/2 point 13, accessible on the website of the United Nations System, Chief Executive Board of Coordination).

The IO of the UN-CS have, therefore, wide disparities throughout their social security schemes.

The term "social security" is not specified in the PPIs or seat agreements. As in the national field, it includes at least health protection, sick leave, maternity and paternity leave, compensation in the case of illness or incapacity and insurance in the case of invalidity, accident, the occupational disease or death (Schermers/Blokker § 515 with further citations). Social security also comprises the pension scheme (pension benefit plan). Benefits granted under the social security schemes are as a rule exempt from national taxation by member states (but see the taxation of long-term care benefits, below).

The exemption from the compulsory contributions to national security schemes covers all kinds of social security schemes even if the internal system of the IO does not cover all social risks. For example, unemployment benefits are only provided by some IO (see, for example, Art. 28a EU-CEOS: a monthly unemployment allowance under very restrictive conditions; Part 6 para. 36 Conditions of Employment of the ECB: 60% of the last basic salary for six months and 30% of the subsequent six months and under special conditions a further allowance up to a maximum period of two years; CERN: 70% to 80% of basic salary up to a maximum period of 60 weeks (CERN Unemployment Insurance Scheme). Some IO grant an indemnity for loss of job; for example, CoE Appendix VI of the SR. In conformity with Reg. 9.3(d) and Annex III UN-SR the SG may, where the circumstances warrant, pay a termination indemnity (see also Art. 15b EPO Contract Staff Conditions, EPO Codex). In some countries, the employment period with an IO may count towards the unemployment cover granted under national law.

Also, a long-term care insurance is not yet generally accepted as a standard social security scheme in IO due to the absence of similar provisions in member states (see the document on "Long-term care in the European Union" published by the EU Commission (2008)). An increasing number of IO, however, provide for a long-term care insurance (see EU: Art. 72 EU-SR in conjunction with the

Joint Sickness Insurances Scheme of the European Institutions of 1 December 2005 (JSIS) and the Commission Scheme decision of 1 July 2007 laying down general implementing provisions for the reimbursement of medical expenses, Chapter 3 Services associated with dependence (permanent or long-term care in establishments, temporary or long-term home care). The EPO provides for a comprehensive long-term care insurance scheme, see Art. 83a EPO-SR and EPO Codex). Also ESO and CERN provide for a long-term care insurance scheme (see on the websites).

The taxation of benefits from a long-term care insurance by some IO remains controversial in some member states. Whereas most member states exempt long-term care benefits from national taxation some states equate such benefits with pensions and subject them fully to national taxation. This position is in contrast to the rulings of the CJEU in Judgment C-160/96 which held that long-term care allowance constitutes a sickness benefit in cash.

There are some PPIs where the exemption from compulsory national scheme is granted only if the IO has established an internal social security system which is "providing adequate benefits" corresponding to the national social security system (see, for example, Art. 18 ESO-PPI). This is hardly in line with the autonomy of IO in personnel matters. It may also be argued that the legislative organs of IO are well placed to consider whether the social security system equates with the standards applied by IO and those required by member states in general.

## VII. Various other privileges and facilities

### *1. General*

In addition to fiscal privileges and exemptions from compulsory national security schemes international civil servants enjoy various other privileges and facilities which are of lesser interest to the public. These principles and facilities, however, are of great practical importance for staff members and their families. Those facilities include *inter alia* the free entry into and the sojourn in the state concerned, the unimpeded duty travel to and from the respective state and repatriation on the termination of employment, the exemption from work permit and from military service, and a privileged treatment in time of international crisis, and the issue of identity cards by the host country.

Some member states grant additional facilities covering driving licences, the employment of domestic servants and the purchase of tax-free goods to a limited extent (see for more details in the Protocol Guide for International Organisations of August 2015 issued by the Ministry of Foreign Affairs of the Netherlands (see the website of the Government of the Netherlands)).

### 2. *Facilities concerning immigration, right of residence and repatriation*

Officials and their family members are not subject to immigration registration or to formalities for the registration of aliens (Art. 11(b) EU-PPI, Section 18(d) UN-CPI, Art. 18(c) CoE-GAPI, Art. 14(d) EPO-PPI). Exemption may also be granted from the registration of religious denomination (Art. 7(1)(c) NL/EPO Agreement). As a rule, international civil servants are, however, subject to the general requirement to register with local authorities. If visas are required they have to be granted promptly and free of charge (Art. 13(2) AT/EPO Agreement).

International officials receive identity cards issued by the organisation and identity cards issued by the Ministry of Foreign Affairs of the host country of the IO (see, for example, Art. 8 NL/EPO Agreement). These identity cards are neither diplomatic passports (official passports for higher ranking national officials) nor are they diplomatic identity cards issued by the host country recognising the status of the bearer under the VCDR (as for the grant of diplomatic rights to the heads and senior officials of IO). Difficulties with the facilities accorded to officials on their entry into the host country primarily occur in in relation to family members forming part of the household of the official (adult children in university education).

Upon termination of the employment the residence period in the host state is generally accepted as a legitimate stay for the purpose of acquiring residence rights in the host state (see, for example, Art. 7(4) NL/EPO Agreement).

In contrast to diplomats, employees cannot be declared *persona non grata* (Art. 9(1) VCDR). A substantial breach of the legal order of the host state (e.g. a serious crime) will, however, lead to summary dismissal and the loss of any preferential treatment by the host state, and criminal proceedings in the home country.

### 3. *Laissez-passer*

This document is issued by the respective organisation to staff members of some IO such as the UN and the EU, as a special travel document. It refers to the privileges and immunities granted to its holder (Art. 6 EU-PPI, Section 24 UN-CPI, see also the CoE Resolution (69)29 of 26 September 1969).

### 4. *Working permits for spouses*

Family members forming part of the household of an official enjoy the same facilities as the respective staff member as regards immigration and taking up residence in the host state of the IO. In contrast to the official, family members are, however, generally required to apply for a working permit in accordance with national law. This permit is regularly granted (for UN organisations see the survey in UN doc. JIU/REP/2004/2 p. 23 accessible on the website of the JIU of the UN System and the Guide to Employment of Spouses of the UN Secretariat Staff of June 2015 on the website of the UN HR portal, Working permit). Some member states even exempt family members from this requirement (e.g. Art. 7(2) NL/EPO Agreement). The grant of a working permit for spouses of international officials "is a very, if not the most important work/life concern for staff members" (UN doc. JIU/REP/2004/2 para. 31 ff). The refusal to grant working permits to spouses is "... a serious hindrance ... to recruit and retain qualified specialists ..." (UN doc. JIU/REP/2004/2 para 41).

### 5. *Private servants*

Some headquarter agreements of IO provide for the possibility of staff members to employ domestic or private servants without a residence or working permit being required (e.g. Art. 12 NL/EPO Agreement and the Protocol Guide for International Organisations of August 2015 issued by the Ministry of Foreign Affairs of the Netherlands (see the website of the Government of the Netherlands)).

### 6. *International crisis*

In times of international crisis officials and their family members enjoy similar facilities concerning repatriation to those of diplomatic agents (Section 18(f) UN-CPI, Art. 18(f) CoE-GAPI, Art. 14(f) EPO-PPI, there is no such provision in the EU-PPI).

### 7. *Exemption from military service*

The staff of some IO are exempt from all obligations in respect of military service (for example, Art. 14(b) EPO-PPI). A member state may, however, not be obliged to extend this privilege to its own nationals (e.g. Art. 22 EPO-PPI).

### 8. *Tax and duty-free purchase of goods*

Some IO operating world-wide still dispose of a "commissary" for staff members. These tax-free and duty-free stores are left over from the time when some consumer goods were not easily available in the host state. Such commissaries exist, for example, at the IAEA in Austria, at the FAO in Italy and the OPCW in the Netherlands (see ILOAT Judgment 3184, UNDT Judgment 2010/053, see also Art. 11(5) of the Headquarters Agreement between the Netherlands and the OPCW of 29 April 1997 and the Commissary of the IAEA in Vienna, see Section IV of the Supplementary Agreement on the establishment of an Agency Commissary of 4 June 1970).

# E. The liability for employment derived damages

## I. The liability of the organisation

Employment relationships are indispensable for the activities of an IO (Schermers/Blokker § 491). They, therefore, form an integral part of the official activities of an IO and are as such not subject to the national authority of a member state of the organisation. Also, national courts are not competent to settle disputes in this field by virtue of the immunity of IO *ratione personae*. Some doctrines also rely on the very nature of the matter *ratione materiae* (Wenckstern para. 993 et seq.).

The fact that national courts are not competent does not, however, release IO from respecting the rule of law and the fundamental rights of their employees to a fair trial safeguarded by all the international conventions on human rights.

Whereas IO do not usually waive their immunity with regard to outside contractual and non-contractual liabilities (see, for example, Art. 9 EPO-EPC) from the jurisdiction of national courts and instead provide for an arbitration procedure, in legal disputes with their staff IO regularly waive their immunity in favour of the jurisdiction of an international administrative tribunal either already based on primary law (e.g. Art. 270 TFEU; Art. 13 EPO-EPC) or on secondary law (e.g. Reg. 11(1) UN-SR; Art. 60 CoE-SR). In Judgment 2657 the ILOAT declared itself not competent to rule on the case of an external applicant for employment. It further held that it had no authority to order the organisation to waive its immunity but since the Judgment created a legal vacuum, it considered it highly desirable that the organisation should either waive its immunity or offer arbitration. Art. 122 EU-CEOS provides for an arbitration in disputes between an EU institution and a member of the local staff serving in a third country.

International administrative tribunals are either established by the respective IO itself or an IO may accept the jurisdiction of an international administrative tribunal which has already been established by another organisation. This is true mainly for the ILOAT (see Art. II(5) of its statute which permits other IO approved by the ILO's governing body to recognise the jurisdiction of the ILOAT).

Any proceedings between an official and an IO involving an action for compensation of damages originating in the employment relationship are governed exclusively by the SR and not by the general provisions of contractual or non-contractual liability of the primary law of an IO (Art. 340 TFEU; Art. 9(1) and (2) EPO-EPC; see CJEU Judgments F-50/09 para. 116; 17/85 para. 9; 9/75 para. 7; see also Kunz-Hallstein/Ullrich, Art. 9 para. 7).

There is no general provision in the SR of IO from which a liability for material or moral damages can be derived. Very few provisions provide for compensation of damages and these are scattered throughout the SR and implementing rules of IO (for example, on workplace-related invalidity or damages suffered in the exercise of official duties caused by third persons).

The general legal basis for the liability of an IO to material and moral damages is derived by the international administrative tribunals from the breach of a statutory or contractual employment relationship. International administrative tribunals do not usually disclose the details of the cognitive process by which they deduce this general legal principle, but only the legal prerequisite of a claim for damages, i.e. that the injury was caused by negligence or fault (for liability on a no fault basis for work place injuries, see ILOAT Judgments 2843, 2804, 2533, 435) on the part of the organisation and that there is a causal link between the unlawful act and the injury suffered (ILOAT Judgments 3215, 2471, 1942, 402; CJEU Judgments F-50/09, F-15/07, C-257/98, 169/83).

### II. The liability of the official

Claims against an official arising from the employment relationships are regularly governed by the provisions of the SR or by separate agreements. An official is personally liable towards his organisation in whole or in part for any damage suffered by the organisation as a result of a wilful or grossly negligent action in the course or in connection with the performance of his duties (Art. 340(4) TFEU in conjunction with Art. 22 EU-SR; Rule 10.1(b) UN-SR; Art. 9(3) EPO-EPC in conjunction with Art. 25 EPO-SR. Mostly the subject matter of the claim is an action for recovery.

The rules on disciplinary procedures are regularly applied to the recovery of the damage. The sums due are deducted from the salary of the official. This action may be appealed by the official with the competent Tribunal in the usual way.

If the damage suffered by the organisation is not the result of an action in the course or in connection with the official duties of the employee (e.g. intentional arson) the rules governing civil liability of the member states apply where the damage was caused (Rogalla, p. 149).

## F. The criminal responsibility of the officials

In order to safeguard the independence of the IO, its employees are exempt from national law in so far as their official activity is concerned and they also enjoy immunity from national jurisdiction to this extent. Outside this area of activity, international officials are subject to national law and jurisdiction like an ordinary citizen, this also holds good for criminal law. The organisation will forward the evidence of potential criminal acts of an employee to the competent national authorities.

Only certain senior officials enjoy extensive diplomatic immunity from the criminal jurisdiction of the receiving state in accordance with Art. 31(1) VCDR (for example, the Secretary-General and all Assistant Secretaries-General of the UN, Section 19 UN-CPI; the President of the EPO (Office) Art. 13 EPO-EPC, the head of the EPO (sub-Office) in Vienna Art. 15 AT/EPO Agreement).

With regard to the application of national criminal law in the area of malpractice, most IO have established internal administrative bodies empowered to conduct internal investigations safeguarding the financial interests of the organisation against fraud, corruption, embezzlement and other serious misconduct (see, for example, the European Anti-Fraud Office "OLAF" of the EU). In this respect reference is made to the OECD Convention on Combating Bribery of Foreign Public Officials in International Business Transactions of 17 December 1997 which also includes international officials (Art. 1(4)(a)). The improper act referred to in this Convention also covers transactions in cross-border cases between an IO and the host state.

*Part 2*

# The sources of international civil service law

*Chapter 1*

## Statutory employment law and general legal principles – basics and survey

It is generally recognised (see, for example, Schermers/Blokker § 1337; Amerasinghe, Principles, p. 234) that Art. 38(1) of the statute of the ICJ (although the provision has a binding legal effect on the court only) identifies the classical sources of international public law, namely:

- international conventions
- customary international law
- the general principles of law recognised by civilised nations
- judicial decisions and the teachings of the most highly qualified publicists of various nations.

In contrast to general international law, customary international law only plays a marginal role in the law of IO (Nettesheim, para. 29).

The law of an IO is derived primarily from an international convention, its founding treaty (the primary source of law). This treaty is governed by public international law and as a rule explicitly grants international and national legal capacity and a set of competences (see, for example, Art. 47 TEU and Art. 335 TFEU) to the IO derived from the sovereign powers of the founding member states. Expressly or by way of implication an IO is endowed with internal organisational autonomy including the competence to set up the SR and implementing rules (secondary and tertiary law). By virtue of its legal basis the law of the international civil service is also attributed to public international law. Because its impact is, however, confined to the member states of the respective organisation, it is generally referred to as a "particular" legal system within public international law (Seidl-Hohenveldern/Loibl, pp. 220, 224; Vitzthum, I § 39).

Based on the founding treaty of the organisation, the SR and implementing rules derived therefrom, the basic source of law of the respective IO is to be found in the staff rulings (and supplementary decisions) set up by the competent body (Art. 336 TFEU; Art. 101(1) UN-Charter; Art. 16 CoE-statute; Art. 33(2)(b) and (c) EPO-EPC).

In general, the legislative body of an IO may not act on its own motion in staff matters unless the head of administration (DG, President) has submitted an appropriate proposal for action. This "right to propose is an important safeguard of the stability of the staff's rights" (ILOAT Judgment 1369 para. 22, see also: CJEU, C-40/10 para. 78: "It is clear *inter alia* from Article 17(2) TEU that that situation is consistent with the institutional balance envisaged by the Treaties which, in principle, grant the Commission in respect of legislative procedures, the sole power to initiate proposals").

The secondary and tertiary law governing the employment relationship between the appointing authority and the staff member is sporadically supplemented by primary law provisions stipulated in the founding treaty of an IO (see, for example, the jurisdiction in staff disputes: Art. 270 TFEU, Art. 13 EPO-EPC; the personal liability of employees towards the organisation: Art. 340 TFEU; Art. 9(3) EPO-EPC; the general authority of the head of administration in staff matters: Art. 10(2)(f) – (h) EPO-EPC).

Of greater practical importance are, however, the rules, administrative instructions, circulars etc. adopted by the head of administration in the implementation of the SR. The authorisation to adopt these provisions and decisions is, as a rule, based on the SR (Art. 110(1) EU-SR; preamble of the UN-SR; Art. 62 CoE-SR; Art. 124 EPO-SR) or even on primary law (Art. 10(2)(a) EPO-EPC).

The totality of the codified civil service law of an IO does not, however, constitute the exhaustive legal system of the employment relationship. IO do not generally (see the exception below) dispose of a catalogue of fundamental rights (comprising as core values the human rights, see the CFREU), which is the case in the constitutions of most member states. Such fundamental rights have to be inferred "from the constitutional traditions common to the member states and from the guidelines supplied by international treaties for the protection of human rights" (CJEU Judgment C-274/99 P para. 37).

These general legal principles applicable to international civil service law are derived from the case law of the international administrative tribunals. As a rule, the details of this time-intensive and labour-consuming cognitive process are not disclosed in the judgment and the existence of a general legal principle applicable to the international civil service is expressed rather succinctly in the judgments. The legislative and executive bodies of the organisation are bound to observe these fundamental legal principles in all actions affecting the staff. In addition to the general legal principles applicable to the staff of IO, the international administrative tribunals have derived some specific general legal principles of the international civil service in order to take account of the specific legal position and the functions of IO.

Some general legal principles governing the employment relationship of all IO are already codified in the SR itself. For example, the right to equal treatment, to a fair trial and the freedom of association and assembly are to be found in most SR. Sometimes the reference to general legal principles even discloses the bounds of the respective freedom (see, for example, Art. 17a(1) EU-SR: "An official has the right to freedom of expression, with due respect to the principles of loyalty and impartiality").

The following 2nd Chapter of Part 2 of this book describes the general legal principles applicable to the international civil service as derived and applied by the international administrative tribunals. These principles are a primary source of law and represent a largely homogeneous canon of values which, despite being developed by the independent judicature of the various international administrative tribunals (see, for example, ILOAT Judgment 3138 para. 7: The Tribunal "is in no way bound by the case law of other international courts"; see also Art. 59 statute of the ICJ: "The decision of the Court has no binding force except between the parties and in respect of that particular case").

The 3rd Chapter of Part 2 of this book describes the essential structures and elements of the law of the international civil service as applied by the civil service systems of the EU, the UN, the CoE and the EPO. The SR, other rules and administrative instructions and circulars in staff matters of these systems provide a fairly representative overview of the institutional labour law of all IO.

*Chapter 2*

# The general legal principles of the international civil service law

## A. Introduction

The SR of IO "do not comprise a complete legal system" (Schermers/Blokker § 539). In particular there are only isolated references to some general legal principles applicable to the employment relationship between the appointing authority and the staff members. This does not mean, however, that IO are exempt from the observance of these fundamental rights in dealings with staff members. Member states of IO are bound (*nemo plus iuris*) to impose the respect of these principles on their organisation (Schermers/Blokker § 1575). In their dual function as an employer and a substitute state, IO are, therefore, under an obligation to respect the fundamental rights of their officials similar to the way that member states must respect them towards their citizens, especially for filling legal gaps and as a tool for interpretation.

The lack of a complete catalogue of fundamental legal principles in the SR of IO is generally explained by the fact that international officials are less likely to be at risk of falling victim to infringement of the full range of fundamental rights by the appointing authority (Schermers Address, p. 26: this is not so much because they are better than the states, but because their powers are limited). Due to the functional limitation of its powers, some fundamental rights are, as a rule, of no significance for the international civil service. This holds good, for example, for the prohibition of torture, slavery and forced labour (Art. 4 and 5 UDHR; Art. 3 and 4 EConHR; Art. 4 and 5 CFREU), the protection against removal, expulsion and extradition (Art. 9 and 13 UDHR; Art. 3 and 4 of the Prot. No. 4 EConHR; Art. 45 CFREU), the right to marry (Art. 1 UDHR; Art. 12 EConHR; Art. 9 CFREU), and the right to vote and to stand as a candidate at elections (Art. 39 and 40 CFREU). That finding should, however, not be invoked as a justification for not including a catalogue of fundamental rights of officials into the SR. In the event of an ultra vires act of the appointing authority towards an official, the competent court may make reference even to these remote principles.

## I. The concept of general principles of law

Among the general legal principle applicable to the international civil service (as well as in general public international law, Seidl-Hohenveldern/Loibl, para. 1515), fundamental rights form an integral part. The international administrative tribunals draw inspiration from the constitutional traditions common to the member states and from the guidelines supplied by international treaties for the protection of human rights on which the member states have collaborated or to which they are signatories (see, for example, CJEU Judgments C-274/99 P para. 37; F-80/08). The general legal principles of the international civil service are the result of a process of evaluative comparisons and cognition of the international administrative tribunals (Verdross/Simma, p. 387: In this respect, international law benefits from the more highly developed standards of national legal systems).

Apart from the general legal principles derived from generally accepted fundamental rights, the tribunals have developed a number of legal principles which can neither be derived directly from national principles nor from international treaties for the protection of human rights. The legal basis for these specific general legal principles of IO is to be found in the rationale for all IO. As most striking examples may be quoted:

- the acquired rights of staff members;
- the principles of independence of IO and its staff from individual interference by member states;
- the legal principles of Fleming and Noblemaire.

The general legal principles applicable to the international civil service, together with the founding treaty of an IO form its primary law standard in personnel matters. These core values are to be observed both in the exercise of legislative discretion by enacting secondary employment law (the SR) and in application of the SR by the administration. They also bind the administration in its interpretation of the SR, and in the exercise of value judgments and discretion.

Ultimately, it is up to the judicature of the respective tribunal exercising jurisdiction over the labour disputes within an IO to develop and illustrate the content of these general legal principles and to apply this value system as a basis for enforcing the law.

## II. The derivation of general legal principles applicable to the law of the international civil service

### *1. General*

In the founding treaties of IO, the member states divest part of their sovereignty to the organisation. This transfer of competences serves the purpose of strengthening their co-operation in certain fields of activities and ensures that the IO can carry out their functions without the interference of individual member states, above all the host country. IO are thus endowed with organisational autonomy including autonomy in personnel matters. As a consequence, the service law of IO is autonomous from national civil service law. This does not apply, however, to the obligation to respect the fundamental legal principles. Member states act within their respective constitutional powers when transferring specific competences as part of their sovereign powers to IO. By doing this, member states have duly to take into account the obligations imposed upon them by their own constitution and by international treaties they have entered into (*nemo plus iuris* principle). The competences transferred to IO are subject to these express and inherent limitations. This holds good even when the founding treaty contains no or only a limited reference to fundamental rights (ECHR, Appl. No. 26083/94, Judgment of 18 February 1999, Waite and Kennedy v. Germany, para. 67: "... where States establish international organisations ... there may be implications on the protection of fundamental rights. It would be incompatible with the purpose and object of the Convention, however, if the Contracting States were thereby absolved from their responsibility under the Convention in relation to the field of activity covered by such attribution").

In particular, the following international treaties and declarations on fundamental and human rights are taken as a primary source of law by the international tribunals even if they are (formally correct) declared as inapplicable to IO (see, for example, ILOAT Judgment 2662 para. 12 in relation to the EConHR):

- The Universal Declaration of Human Rights (UDHR) (see, for example, this keyword in the Triblex database of the ILOAT);
- The European Convention on Human Rights (EConHR) (see, for example, ILOAT Judgment 2292 para. 11);
- The European Social Charter (revised) of the Council of Europe of 3 May 1996 (see, for example, CJEU Judgments F-65/07, F-69/07 and 60/08).
- The Charter of Fundamental Rights of the EU (CFREU) (see Art. 6(1) TEU). The CFREU which has the same legal value as the EU treaties and is, therefore, in constant case law of the CJEU on staff matters referred to, see, for example, Judgments F-7/11 and F-60/11, F-43/10, F-42/10, F-86/09, F-33/08.

For other international instruments on human rights and labour rights referred to by international tribunals, see for example, ILOAT Judgment 2120 para. 10; CJEU Judgment F-1/05 para. 69).

As far as the specific general legal principles of the international civil service are concerned, the international administrative tribunals derive them from the purpose and objectives of IO.

The general legal principles applicable to the international civil service are derived from and applied by the international administrative tribunals in regard of the IO under their respective jurisdiction. This creative process of legal research and finding the law contributes to the development of the law of the international civil service.

International administrative tribunals that exercise their jurisdiction over several IO pertaining to more than one international civil service system, such as the ILOAT (among the approximately 60 IO under its jurisdiction there are members of the UN family and of the mixed civil service system like the EPO, CERN, ESO, Eurocontrol, EFTA, EMBL, Interpol and EUTELSAT), apply the general legal principles without any differentiation across the whole spectrum of IO. This, for example, holds good for the Noblemaire and Fleming principles, which originate from the UN civil service system and are applied consistently in the case law for IO in the mixed system.

This process is rather time-consuming (Amerasinghe, the Law, p. 157: "The question as to how in actual practice general principles are identified is not without difficulty"). International administrative tribunals increasingly derive the fundamental rights from international treaties and declarations which are already consensus-based. Despite the fact that international administrative tribunals are not bound by the rulings of other international tribunals they sometimes confirm that such other rulings may carry "persuasive authority" (see, for example, ILOAT Judgments 2794 para. 6, 1296 para. 7).

### 2. *Special derivations*

In the case of some IO, the derivation of fundamental legal principles is facilitated since treaties or declarations on human rights or other fundamental principles are enacted on the basis of the IO's own competences.

– The EU civil service system

The strict observance of fundamental rights in the EU has been underlined in constant case law by the CJEU since its beginnings (see, for example, CJEU Judgment 11–70 para 4 "[r]espect for fundamental rights forms an integral part of the general principles of law protected by the Court of Justice. The protection of such rights, whilst inspired by the constitutional traditions common to the member states, must be ensured within the framework of the structure and objectives of the Community").

This is also valid within the framework of the internal civil service of the EU (see, for example, CJEU Judgments C-274/99 P "Connolly", C-122/99 P and C-125/99 P, C-100/88, 75 and 117/82).

Without a list of fundamental rights in the Community law the CJEU has regularly made reference to the EConHR. This was done irrespective of the fact that the Community had no competence to become a party to the EConHR at that point of time (see in this respect the opinions of the CJEU 2/94 of 28 March 1996: "[a]s community law now stands, the Community has no competence to accede to Convention"). After the enactment of the CFREU the CJEU started, albeit with some hesitation (the Charter had not yet a binding effect), to refer to the Charter as an additional source of international law.

After its establishment at the end of 2004, the EU Civil Service Tribunal (CST) as a judicial body of the CJEU already referred to the CFREU even in the absence of an express legal basis (see, for example, CJEU Judgments/Orders F-7/11 and F-60/11, F-43/10, F-42/10, F-33/08, F-3/08, F-122/07, F-51/07, F-40/05). (The CST also referred in its judicature to the fundamental rights stipulated in the EConHR, e.g. CJEU Judgments F-86/09, F-80/08, F-40/05 and to the Code of good administrative behaviour of the EU, for example, CJEU Judgments/Orders F-96/09, F-3/08, F-122/07).

Upon the entry into force of the Treaty of Lisbon on 1 December 2009 the CFREU became legally binding (Art. 6(1) TEU: "...which shall have the same legal value as the Treaties; see also Art. 51(1) CFREU). Placed on this solid legal foundation, the judicature of the CJEU now regularly refers to the CFREU. As far as the EConHR is concerned, the new Art. 6(2) TEU together with Art 59(2) EConHR paved the way for the accession of the EU to the EConHR (but see the negative opinion 2/13 of 18 December 2014 of the CJEU). Art. 6(3) TEU stipulates that the fundamental rights, as guaranteed by the EConHR and as they result from the constitutional traditions common to the member states shall constitute general principles of the Union's law. This catalogue of written fundamental rights has confirmed and enlarged the sources of law hitherto applied in the case law of the CJEU.

For further details reference is made to the website of the EU Agency for Fundamental Rights which provides a case law database of the CJEU and the ECHR with direct references to the articles of the CFREU and the EConHR.

– The UN civil service system

The UDHR proclaimed on 10 December 1948 is one of the most cited legal instruments on human rights. Although it has no legally binding force on the member states of the UN, it provides a paramount programmatic approach.

In the internal employment relationship of the UN, however, the human rights stipulated in the UDHR have a binding effect. The UN administration is bound to respect the fundamental rights listed in the UDHR as fundamental principles of the international civil service (UNAT Judgment 15 (in relation to Art. 20 and

23 UDHR i.e. the right of association, Judgment 326 para II: "The Tribunal must uphold the principles embodied in the Universal Declaration of Human Rights and in the related International Covenants"; see also ILOAT Judgment 848; see, however: ILOAT Judgment 2611 para. 8: So far as concerns the UDHR and the EConHR "they apply, according to their terms, to member states not to international organisations").

The same binding effect holds good for the protection of fundamental rights stipulated in the UN Charter (advisory opinion of the ICJ of 13 July 1954 p. 57: "It would, in the opinion of the Court, hardly be consistent with the expressed aim of the Charter to promote freedom and justice for individuals" … that it [the UN] "should afford no judicial or arbitral remedy to its own staff for the settlement of any disputes which may arise between it and them." This opinion is, for example, referred to in UNAT Judgment 378 para. XII).

– The CoE civil service system

Within the internal employment relationship of the CoE, the EConHR and the European Social Charter (revised) of the CoE are of a paramount importance. In its Recommendation 856 (1979) the Parliamentary Assembly of the CoE stated (point 4): "Considering that the Council of Europe has always endeavoured to be in the forefront of social and economic progress, and that it would be unacceptable if the Council of Europe did not apply to its own staff the principles laid down in its Convention on Human Rights and the Social Charter". The CoEAT, therefore, may explicitly refer to the case law of the ECHR on the interpretation of the EConHR (see, for example, Appeal No. 114/1985 para. 31).

– The EPO civil service system

In conformity with its constitution (the EPO-EPC) the EPO is not competent to set up a treaty or to provide a declaration on fundamental rights. The EPO may, however, based on its internal autonomy in staff matters, establish an internal catalogue of human rights applicable to its employment relationship. In 1994 the Council of the EPO made a declaration which has been included in the EPO-SR (see EPO Codex) that the Council and the President of the Office (the secretariat of the EPO) note that the ILOAT considers the general legal principles, including human rights, when reviewing the law applied to EPO staff (see, for example, ILOAT Judgment 2292 para. 11). This statement by the internal bodies of the EPO does not, however, really confer any added value either to the EPO staff or to the jurisdiction of the ILOAT.

Rather it simply confirms the fact that the ILOAT in its case law consistently refers to general legal principles of the international civil service as a scale of primary values in its review process. It would be more pro-active to set-up a catalogue of human rights of the officials to be respected by the EPO as a substitute state or to refer to one of the treaties on fundamental and human rights explicitly.

## III. General legal principles as superior rules of law

The general legal principles of the international civil service are a primary source of law. They are overarching principles of the internal service law of IO (see, ILOAT Judgment 3046: "general legal principles form part of an official's term of appointment"; CJEU Judgment F-105/05 para. 138: "fundamental principles of the Community"). In practice, recourse by the international administrative tribunals is made to these superior rules of law if there is a need to fill gaps in the SR or if interpretation of these rules is deemed necessary or if the rules (secondary and tertiary law) or the administrative decisions conflict with these principles.

**Jurisprudence**

(See in more detail the judgments referred to in the following sections)

ILOAT Judgments

2912: Complaints are receivable even if they are based on a breach of general principles of law only; 2793: A methodology for determining salary adjustment may be lawfully used only if it permits stable, foreseeable and clearly understood results (a specific general legal principle of the international civil service) (1821, 1329); 1368: A staff member may challenge in an individual appeal the lawfulness of an underlying rule if he believes that the rule is at odds with a general legal principle of the international civil service; 986: The scale of pensionable remuneration was in conflict with the principle of acquired rights.

CJEU Judgments/Orders

F-40/05: Art. 17 EU-SR (version in force until 30 April 2004) must be considered in the light of the freedom of expression; T-94/01, T-152/01 and T-286/01: Art. 19 of the ECB-SR infringes the principle of equal treatment and is, therefore, illegal; 32/71: Art. 4(3) in conjunction with Art. 1(3) of Annex VII of the EU-SR is in conflict with the general legal principle of equal treatment in so far as it creates a difference of treatment between male and female officials.

## IV. The general legal principles as a basis for the incidental (indirect) review of staff regulations

International administrative tribunals are neither criminal courts nor civil courts (see, however, the exception in Art. II(4) ILOAT statute) nor courts of human rights. In relation to acts of general application (secondary and tertiary law) some competences which in various member states of IO are entrusted to constitutional courts (see, for example, the "European e-Justice Portal" for the judicial systems of the EU member states) are assured by international administrative tribunals.

The competences of the international administrative tribunals are primarily restricted to the complaints against individual decisions (or decisions affecting a class of officials) taken by any authority of an IO which the official accuses of having infringed the term of his appointment or the SR (see, for example, ILOAT Judgment 580: interpreting Art. II(1) of its Statute).

It is, however, constant case law of international administrative tribunals that an official may plead in support of an action against an individual decision also the illegality of an underlying general decision which affords the basis for the individual decision adversely affecting him (see, ILOAT Judgments 3146, 2793, 2655, 2615, 2410, 2129, 1786, 1451, 1368, 1329, 1265, 1000). He thereby runs no risk of being told that such challenge is time-barred (ILOAT Judgment 3146 para. 10).

Art. 277 TFEU even explicitly provides that any party in the proceedings before the CJEU may plead the inapplicability of an act of general application providing the basis in law for the individual decision notwithstanding the expiry of the time limit for instituting proceedings as laid down in Art. 263(6) TFEU. This incidental review is not an independent course of action but must be invoked in connection with an action of the official proceeding provided for in Art. 270 TFEU in conjunction with the EU-SR (CJEU Judgments F-128/12, F-26/10, F-29/09, T-64/92, 262780, 92/78).

Since the competences of international administrative tribunals in staff member's quashing actions are restricted to individual decisions under review (see, for example, ILOAT Judgments 1488, 1062: Only the individual decisions impugned were quashed not the underlying general decisions which were considered illegal for lack of consultation of the joint general advisory committee; 963 para. 5: The individual decisions are "the only ones the Tribunal may quash") international administrative Tribunals may not annul general decision but declare them as being "inapplicable" (*inter partes*).

The inapplicability of the respective rule does, however, urge the IO to correct the defective act of general application in order to restore legality *erga omnes* and to avoid further legal proceedings in similar cases.

According to case law in exceptional circumstances there is no need for an official to await an individual decision, he may directly challenge the lawfulness of a rule applicable to him. This concerns decisions "regulatory in character" (self-executing rules) like changes in the composition of a committee, changes of the appeals system or the jurisdiction or the introduction of new employment systems (see, for example, ILOAT Judgments 2244, 1660, 1618, 1451).

In contrast to the legal systems of other IO within the legal system of the EU the legality of acts of general application (also in the area of the civil service of EU institutions) is subject to legal review by the CJEU in conformity with Art. 263 TFEU (actions for annulment by the EU Commission).

In a much-noted decision (Judgment C-40/10), the CJEU annulled with effect *erga omnes* Art. 2 and 4 to 18 of Council Regulation No. 1296/2009 adjusting the salary scales of the officials following an action for annulment by the Commission.

**Jurisdiction**

ILOAT Judgments

1451: The decision to amend Art. 19 of the Provident Scheme of UPU in order to remove the jurisdiction from the ILOAT and to vest it in Swiss courts was not in line with the links of the scheme to international law (the basis in law, the international status of the organisation and its staff); 1265: The salary scale adopted was not in line with the rules governing the Common System (the Fleming principle) (1000); 986: The amendment of the scale of pensionable remuneration was in breach of an acquired right (with further quotations); 936: The retroactive application of a provision reducing staff pay infringed the rule against retro-activity.

CJEU Judgments/Orders

F-29/09: A provision of the SR properly adapted by the Council cannot be called into question on the grounds of an alleged breach of the principle of sound administration; T-94/01, T-152/01 and T-286/01: The restriction of the entitlement to the education allowance in Art. 19 ECB-SR infringed the principle of equal treatment; 91/85: The salary table infringed the general legal principle of equal treatment.

## V. The dynamic nature of general legal principles

Ever since their inception, the international administrative tribunals have derived numerous general legal principles as a source of law applicable to the law of the international civil service. This is an ongoing dynamic process necessary to cope with the dynamic nature of new challenges facing the employment relationship of the IO to their staff (Voigt, p. 11; Schermers/Blokker § 1338: "General principles of law are not static, but develop together with changing convictions in society").

International administrative tribunals take account, therefore, of the development of the general legal principles in the member states responding to change on social, moral and technical issues. As examples, the jurisprudence in the areas of data protection and same-sex marriages may be quoted.

Apart from the fundamental principles of law common to the constitutions of member states and enshrined in international conventions for the protection of human rights, the tribunals have disclosed various general legal principles which respond to the specific needs of IO. These principles arise from the aim of IO in pursuing the common interest of the member states specified in their founding convention.

Among those specific general legal principles the principle of acquired rights, the Noblemaire and Fleming principles and the principle governing the salary adjustment method may be quoted.

The dynamic nature of these principles can best be illustrated by reference to the general principle of acquired rights. In its Judgment 61 the ILOAT had first established the principle of acquired rights in relation to the balance of contractual obligations and fundamental terms of employment in consideration of which the official accepted an appointment. In Judgment 832 the ILOAT further applied this principle in relation to newly introduced fundamental terms of employment which subsequently induced him to stay on (for further references see ILOAT Judgment 3074). In Judgment 2632 the ILOAT applied the acquired right precept also in the case of pensioners of an IO.

## VI. The limitations of the general legal principles

### *1. The limitations in general*

Fundamental rights and freedoms are not without restrictions but must be considered with regard to their social function. Only the very essence of a fundamental right is untouchable.

Every limitation of a fundamental right which is recognised by the respective international administrative tribunal as a general legal principle applicable to the international civil service must be reasoned and justified. This means that the derivation of a general legal principle by the tribunal is no more than the first step in the finding of justice.

The mere succinct statement of the existence of a general legal principle is as a rule not sufficient to reach a judgment. Only the identification of the content and the limits of a general legal principle enables the tribunal to afford the requisite legal protection (Kokott, p. 855).

At the most general level it can be said that the limitations of the fundamental rights of international officials are to be determined by balancing them with the interests of the organisation in the unimpeded performance of its activities, with the rights and freedoms of others and with objective legal principles such as good faith and the principle of proportionality (see Art. 29(2) UDHR and Art. 52 CFREU).

The following examples are indicative in this context:

- The legal principle of equal treatment is limited by the principle of legality of administration ("equality in law is not equality in the breach of it", ILOAT Judgments 1536, 1194, 845, 769, 767; CJEU Judgments T-30/90, 134/84, 188/83).
- The freedom of speech does not absolutely prohibit prior authorisation of messages circulated by bodies representing the staff (ILOAT Judgment 3156; see however Judgment 496). International officials are under a special obligation not to abuse the freedom of speech by using expressions or resorting to behaviours incompatible with the appropriate decorum (ILOAT Judgments 1061, 1028 CJEU Judgment, T-146/94). The refusal to publish a corrigendum in the in-house magazine of an IO due to the immoderate nature of the article does not infringe the freedom of expression (ILOAT Judgment 2626).
- When its staff goes on strike, an IO has the right to order some staff members to perform their duties, provided it respects the principle of proportionality (ILOAT Judgment 805).
- According to the jurisprudence of the international administrative tribunals, the guarantee of unimpeded functioning of an IO requires some general limitations of the human rights of the staff in the international civil service which are generally stipulated in a code of conduct (or of ethics) of the respective organisation. As most pertinent examples of these obligations may be quoted the loyalty towards the organisation, the duty of moderation and the respect of confidentiality, the independence of any instructions from outside the organisation and the protection of the reputation of the organisation. (For more details see the "Standards of Conduct for the International Civil Service" of 2013 published on the website of the ICSC under "booklets").

### *2. The codified limitations of the general legal principles*

To the extent that general legal principles are codified in the SR they occasionally contain specific limitations. For example Art. 17a(1) EU-SR guarantees the right to freedom of expression "with due respect to the principles of loyalty and impartiality". Further limitations of this principle are valid for the publication of matters dealing with the work of the EU (Art. 17a(2) EU-SR) and the disclosure of work-related information in legal proceedings (Art. 19 EU-SR). Other restrictions are e.g. related to activities outside the organisation (Reg. 1(2)(f) UN-SR), to instructions from any Government or from any source external to the organisation (Reg. 1(2)(d) UN-SR), to any political activity (Reg. 1(2)(h) UN-SR) and to the discretion with regard to all matters of official business (Reg. 1(2)(i) UN-SR).

### *3. The guarantee of the very essence of a general legal principle*

The respect of the essence of a fundamental right or freedom is recognised by all international administrative tribunals. It is also enshrined in Art. 52(1) CFREU: "Any limitation on the exercise of the rights and freedoms ... must ... respect the essence of those rights and freedoms".

The ILOAT held in its Judgment 2493 that the request of an IO that staff members should obtain an authorisation before leaving their workplace to take part in a strike violates the essence of the right to strike and would "deprive" the right to strike "of all substance" (see, however, Judgment 2494: The special mission of Eurocontrol relating to the safety of air navigation must not lead to sudden stoppage of activity such as occur when shift work is abandoned (see also Judgment 2495).

The CJEU ruled in constant case law that fundamental rights may not be infringed upon their very substance (Judgments F-46/09, F-132/07, F-40/05).

Also the ECHR underlined in its case law the inviolability of the essence of human rights (e.g. ECHR Judgment of 9 April 2002, Podkolzina v. Latvia, Appl. No. 46726/99 para. 33 (with further references): "... do not curtail the rights in question to such an extent as to impair their very essence and deprive them of their effectiveness ...").

## VII. The guarantee of social security and participation rights

IO have a dual responsibility to their staff, "they must be both an employer and a substitute state, i.e. they must offer a specific social infrastructure" (EU Commission, Reforming the Commission, Reconciling family and career, September 2004 archived in the internet). These positive obligations ("status positions", Dröge) may already be partly derived from the fundamental general legal principles applicable to the international civil service which in addition to their priority function as "defensive rights" have a participatory approach. IO have, therefore, an obligation to provide *inter alia* for a joint staff-management machinery and for a safe, secure and harassment-free working environment (see, for example, ILOAT Judgment 2533: "It is common for a mature legal system to provide compensation on a "no fault" basis to employees who suffer work place injuries; the law of the international civil service can do no less"; ILOAT Judgment 3071: ".. the duty is a duty to investigate claims of harassment promptly and thoroughly"). This obligation for positive actions already fundamentally guarantees the setting up of a social security system and of participation rights for the staff of IO (Dröge, Kirchhof). It is also underpinned by the provision enshrined in international conventions providing for the protection of social security and participation rights (Art. 27 et seq. and Art. 34 CFREU: solidarity and entitlement to social security benefits and social services providing protection in cases such as maternity, illness, industrial accidents, dependency or old age; Art. 12 et seq. and Art. 21 et seq. ESC (rev) and Art. 10 et seq. CCFSR).

In assuming this responsibility as "substitute states" IO have the right to establish their own social security scheme even without being explicitly authorised to do so by their conventions (Art. XII para. 175 et seq. of the CoE Resolution (69)29 of 26 September 1969 referring to the CoE and the UN). In most conventions of IO the right to establishing their own social security scheme is explicitly stipulated with the proviso that the organisation and its staff are exempt from all compulsory contributions to national social security schemes in the event of the organisation establishing its own social security scheme (Art. 14 EU-PPI, Art. 18 EPO-PPI).

Some PPI of IO even provided for a say of their host state in setting up a social security scheme (see, for example, Art. 18 ESO-PPI): "... providing adequate benefits, subject to agreements to be concluded with the States concerned". It may even be generally assumed that the host state assumes the position as a guarantor of the establishment of an "adequate" internal social security scheme by the organisation in order to avoid subsidiary liability.

Some smaller IO or IO with short-term contract staff or IO with locally employed staff may subject their staff members to the social security scheme of the host state (e.g. Art. 121 EU-CEOS) or offer the possibility to opt for a national security scheme (e.g. EPO contract staff, see EPO Codex; see also the agreement between the Republic of Austria and the International Atomic Energy Agency of 7 August 1973).

### VIII. The doctrine of special status

The fundamental rights enshrined in the constitutions of member states and in international conventions for the protection of human rights form an integral part of the general principles of law. International tribunals draw inspiration from these sources of law in order to develop the general legal principles applicable to the employment relationship in the international civil service (see CJEU Judgment C-274/99 P, "Connolly", para. 37).

In a democratic society it is, however, legitimate to subject public servants, on account of their particular close relationship with the state and the exercise of official functions, to specific obligations including additional limitations of certain fundamental rights (see, for example, Art. 10(2) EConHR concerning the freedom of expression).

The same principle applies to the fundamental rights enjoyed by the international civil servants (CJEU Judgments C-274/99 P, "Connolly", para. 44; F-40/05, summary, para. 11; Kokott, p. 881).

Specific limitations of certain fundamental rights apply to the international officials because of their official activities entrusted to them by the respective organisation. A fair balance must be struck between the fundamental rights of the officials and the legitimate concern of the organisation "to ensure that its officials and agents observe the duties and responsibilities implicit in the performance of their tasks" (CJEU judgment C-274/99 P, "Connolly", para. 48).

These restrictions must correspond to the objectives pursued by the organisation and must not be a "disproportionate and intolerable interference which infringes upon the very substance of the right protected" (CJEU Judgment F-40/05, summary, para. 11).

In general terms, the fundamental rights of international officials are limited by the standards of integrity, loyalty, independence and impartiality (see ILOAT Judgment 1061 para. 5). In this respect, special attention has to be paid to the confidence of the member states in the independence and the reputation of the IO.

The restriction of certain fundamental rights applicable to the international staff is *sui generis*, i.e. it does not necessarily correspond to that of national officials. This holds good, for example, for the right to strike which is considered in contrast to several member states as being lawful in all IO (ILOAT Judgments 2493, 2342, 615, 566; as to the CJEU see below under "The right to strike").

In most IO, the limitations of certain fundamental rights of staff members are stipulated in the SR (see, for example, Reg. 1(1) and 1(2) UN-SR) and in a separate Code of Conduct (Ethics) (see, for example, ICSC: Standards of Conduct for the International Civil Service of 2013 published under "booklets" on the website of the ICSC; ILO: Principle of Conduct for Staff of the ILO, 2009; Code of Conduct for Commissioners of the EU, Document C(2011)2904 of 20 April 2011). The core ethical rules applicable to the EU staff in relation to their appointing authority are contained in the EU-SR. The Code of Good Administrative Behaviour of 13 September 2000 is applicable only in the relation of the officials with the public.

In the EU-SR the following essential specific limitations of fundamental rights are codified:

Art. 11

Obligation to seek neither nor take instructions from any authority or person outside the institution. The duties shall be carried out objectively, impartially and in keeping with the duty of loyalty to the Union;

Art. 11a

An official shall not deal with a matter in which he has any personal interest;

Art. 12

Obligation to refrain from actions and behaviour harmful to his position;

Art. 12a

An official shall refrain from psychological or sexual harassment;

Art. 12b

Limitation of activity outside the organisation;

Art. 13

Legal consequences of gainful activities of the spouse of an official incompatible with that of the official;

Art. 15

Limitation to stand for public office;

Art. 17

Limitation of unauthorised disclosure of information received in the line of duty;

Art. 17a

Freedom of expression restricted by the principles of loyalty and impartiality;

Art. 18

All rights in any writings or other work done by an official in the performance of his duties shall be the property of the European Union;

Art. 19

Restriction to disclose information received in the line of duty in any legal proceedings;

Art. 20

Obligation to reside in the place of employment or at no greater distance there from as is compatible with the proper performance of his duties.

## IX. Methods of interpretation in public international law

The secondary and tertiary law of IO is characterised by a lower degree of regulation in comparison with the national labour law systems. The resulting increase of abstract terms in which the SR are drafted in order to cover various cases and the relatively high number of legal lacunae impose a particular high demand in interpretative skills on the judges of the international administrative tribunals.

The rules of interpretation have to be derived primarily from internationally customary law (see Art. 38.1(b) statute of the ICJ). In addition, some guidance may be drawn from Art. 31 to 33 of the VCLT which may be qualified as rules "reflecting customary law" (Villiger, p. 24) and are also applicable in matters concerning statutory interpretation (Amerasinghe, Jurisdiction, p. 509).

International administrative tribunals explicitly refer to the "customary methods of interpretation" (ILOAT Judgments 2006 para. 10; 742 para. 8; 493 para. 5: "it construes such texts by the accepted methods of legal interpretation") without disclosing the details of their finding of justice.

Traditionally, five methods of interpretation may be discerned (Villiger, p. 421, 422) whereby none of the methods takes precedence.

- The historical method, referring to the preparatory documents of the rules.
- The textual (literal, grammatical) method, interpreting the text in accordance with the ordinary meaning of the relevant terms.
- The systematical method, appreciating the meaning of a term in its context.
- The teleological (functional) method, interpreting the text in the light of its object (aim) and purpose.
- The logical method, interpreting the text by taking reference to rational principles.

Other doctrines apply a different number of methods (see, for example, Schermers/Blokker, § 1346 et seq.; see also ILOAT Judgment 2258 para. 5(b): Statutory provisions must be interpreted in such a way that their true meaning is preserved, taking into account, *inter alia*, the actual letter of the provision, its origin, its aim and its place within the legal frame work .."). Within every process of interpretation the general legal principle of good faith (*bona fides*) prevails (Villiger, p. 426; Art. 31(1) VCLT). In the area of the employment law of IO the method of interpreting legal texts authenticated in two or more languages has to be added (Art. 33 VCLT).

## X. The methods of interpretation applied by the international administrative tribunals

It is trite law that "When the text is clear there is no call for any interpretation" (*in claris non fit interpretatio*); (ILOAT Judgment 1125 para. 4; see however Seidl-Hohenveldern/Stein, § 333: such a statement may be assessed as a circular argument in case of dispute).

The historical method refers to the preparatory documents of a text (ILOAT Judgments 2258: Communication from the organisation to a staff member must be interpreted according to the meaning that their addressee can reasonably ascribe to them; 1299 para. 7: "The obscurity of the text prompts reference both to the preparatory work on the rule and to the Organisation's practice in applying it").

The textual method of interpreting a term starts from its "ordinary meaning" (Art. 31(1) VCLT). In this context, attention has to be paid to formulations of a text granting a broad degree of discretion ("can", "may") or if it is of a binding force ("must", "has") (ILOAT Judgment 1222 para. 4: "The primary rule of interpretation is that words are to be given their obvious and ordinary meaning").

The systematical method interprets a term in the context of the whole set of regulations within a legal act (UNAT Judgment 4: ".. the whole system of conditions and guarantees ... in the Staff Regulations ... is ... very clear indicating ...").

The most commonly applied interpretation methodology by international administrative tribunals is the teleological method. ILOAT Judgments 3154 para. 6: "This interpretation is consistent with ... and that the express purpose ...."; 2362 para. 4: "Had that been the purpose of the Rule ..."; 1618: The purpose of Art. 38 EPO-SR is such that the need for further consultation of the general advisory committee would be understandable if the proposals of a change in the SR forwarded by the President to the Council had been so radically amended as to be really new ones.

The principles of effectiveness and of implied powers are primarily derived from the teleological method of interpretation (CJEU Judgment C-84/95 para. 13 "context and aims"). They may be interrelated (UNAT Judgment 4 p. 17).

According to the principle of effectiveness (effet utile) an interpretation may not impair the full effect of a provision (CJEU Judgments C-223/98, 48–75, 9/70) or even "a great part of its values" (UNAT Judgment 4 p. 17: "the legal text must remain effective rather than ineffective: Res magis valeat quam pereat").

The implied-power-doctrine is an interpretation method which expands the explicitly stipulated powers conferred upon an IO if they prove insufficient for the fulfilment of its official activities. This doctrine takes account of the fact that IO need to have a legal basis for their activities (principle of attributed powers) and it is "never possible to lay down an exhaustive list of powers of the organisations in a constitution" (Schermers/Blokker § 232, see also Art. 352 TFEU).

The following examples can be mentioned: In 1993 the EPO created a Pension Reserve Fund without an explicit legal basis in the EPO-EPC. Only seven years later the explicit authorisation for the establishment of the Fund was inserted in Art. 28(b) EPO-EPC. (In the meantime, three other Reserve Funds have been established by the EPO based up to now on the implied power doctrine, see EPO Codex: long term-care insurance fund, sick insurance fund, and fund for the organisation's liability for payment of the tax adjustment on pensions).

A classical example is the establishment of the UNAT. The ICJ confirmed in an advisory opinion of 13 July 1954 (p. 57 et seq.) that the UN General Assembly had the power to establish the UNAT even without express provision for it in the UN Charter. It found that to do justice to the UN officials in a legal dispute with the secretariat it would "hardly be consistent with the expressed aim of the Charter to promote freedom and justice for individuals … that it should afford no judicial or arbitral remedy to its own staff …" (see also UNAT Judgment 4 p. 17).

The use of implied powers may, however, not infringe the institutional balance of the organisation (CJEU 9/56 ("Meroni")) and must be concordant with the fundamental principle of international law (see Schermers/Blokker § 226).

Also, the logical method of interpretation is frequently referred to by the international administrative tribunals. It comprises a set of rational principles traditionally drawn from Latin.

Most commonly used Latin terms by international administrative tribunals are:

*a fortiori* argument (a maiore ad minus): inference drawn from the truth value of a statement that another is even more true. (At present, there are references to this principle in about 90 judgments of the ILOAT; see, for example, Judgments 3542 para. 5; 3428 para. 13).

*per analogiam* ("by analogy" argument): Things (cases) being similar in some respects are also similar in others. (At present, there are references to this principle in more than 100 ILOAT judgments; see, for example, Judgment 3524 para. 5, 2967 para. 9; see also the advisory opinion of the ICJ of 1 February 2012 to ILOAT Judgment 2867 and CJEU Judgments F-46/09 para. 92, 94: Applicability of a rule by analogy and of another judgment; F-23/05 para. 99: Reference to another judgment by analogy).

*a contrario* reasoning, an interpretation to the contrary. (There are some dozen references by the ILOAT to this principle, see, for example, Judgment 3424 para. 6).

*contra proferentem*: where a regulation is ambiguous it is interpreted to the detriment of its author and in favour of the staff. (There are about a dozen references to be found in the jurisprudence of the ILOAT, see, for example, Judgments 3434 para. 4, 1755 para. 12).

*expressio unius exclusio alterius*: "Express mention in a text of one or more things belonging to a category excludes by implication all other things in a category" (ILOAT Judgment 975 para. 7).

*lex specialis*: A special rule takes precedence over a general one (*lex generalis*) (CJEU Judgments F-96/09, F-121/07).

*Tempus regit actum*: the rule in force on the date on which the decision was taken is applicable (principle of no retroactivity, CJEU Judgment T-532/08).

In accordance with Art. 33 VCLT the ILOAT in particular held in a number of rulings that if a difference in meaning of equally authenticated texts appears which cannot be resolved by the usual interpretation methods the meaning shall be adopted which best reconciles the texts having regard to the intent of the drafter taking into account *inter alia* the actual letter, the opinion, the aim and the systematical place of the provision (ILOAT Judgments 1820, 1450, 1032, 853, 537).

**Jurisprudence**

ILOAT Judgments

3339: The principle of *lex specialis* cannot be applied to laws which are not at the same level of hierarchy; 3189: If an interpretation is sound the duty of care does not imply a duty always to interpret texts in the staff's favour; 3154: The ordinary meaning of "gross salary"; 3080: A passing reference to husband and wife in the SR does not warrant an interpretation of all the relevant provisions thereof as denying same-sex spouses the entitlements concerned (2590); 3003: Execution of a judgment by an organisation does not divest the organisation of its right to submit the judgment to the ICJ for an opinion (82); 2959: The SR provide no explicit and specific exemption from the requirement of competition. The expression "so far as possible" cannot be referred to a certain post but to circumstances of the vacancy; 2882: A staff member who appeals to the wrong body does not on that account forfeit the right to appeal. Rules of procedure must be construed with common sense and not set traps for the official (1832, 1734); 2868: An "interpretative clarification" cannot validate an earlier decision taken without authority; 2643: The SR as they stand bar the UN-SG from giving the term "spouse" the broad interpretation requested (see, however, the interpretation in Judgment 2590: same-sex marriages and Judgments 2550, 2549: registered same-sex partnerships). The decision was nevertheless quashed for lack of reasoning; 2567: In case of doubt the text should be interpreted to the detriment of the author (*contra proferentem*); 2315: It is a rule of interpretation that a provision has no retroactive effect unless that is clearly intended; 2258: Communications to staff members must be interpreted according to the meaning that their addressee can reasonably ascribe to them; 2006: There is no presumption of retroactive effect of a provision; 1717: Interpretation of the term "payment"; 1618: Interpretation of a rule according to its purpose (here: further consultation of a joint advisory board in case of radical changes of draft SR, Art. 38 EPO-SR); 1456: In construing the rules the tribunal is bound to take an objective view and pay heed to their wording, context, purport and purpose; 1450: In the interpretation of various authentic text versions the language of the original in the preparatory work does not prevail; 1299: The obscurity of a text prompts reference to both the preparatory work on the rule and the practice in applying it; 1296: Although the ILOAT is not bound by decisions of the CJEU in case of identical wording the court's decision do carry persuasive authority; 1222: The primary interpretation method is that words are to be given their obvious and ordinary meaning; 1125: A clear text does not require interpretation; 1099: The unclear authentic version of a text is to be interpreted in a way that reconciles all other authentic versions (1032, 926, 853); 975: It is a principle of interpretation that the explicit mention of things in one category excludes by implication all other things in the category (*expressio unius exclusio alterius*) (here: illness during maternity leave); 742: According to the customary methods of interpretation any action prescribed in a text is deemed to be of immediate effect. There is no presumption of retroactive effect; 608: The intent of a regulation is to be found in its nature, its purpose and also in its history and the manner in which it has been applied; 537: The interpretation of authentic legal texts in various languages is incumbent on the Tribunal. It cannot be maintained that it is for each staff member to choose the language version which suits him best, but considerations of equity remain important; 507: Interpretations by the supreme court of a state are not binding on the tribunal but great weight may be attached to its observations; 256: If a literal interpretation is not conclusive, it is necessary to consider the purpose of the provision; 77: For contractual employment the generally accepted methods of interpretation apply. In particular the mutual intention of the parties at the time the contract was concluded is to be inquired.

CJEU Judgments/Orders

T-415/06 P: The SR employ precise wording and there is no reason to extend the scope of the EU-SR to a new category of contract staff by analogy (T-298/02 and further case law cited); 79/82: The SR in force must be interpreted with regard to their context and purpose and not in the light of rules which have been repealed; T-43/89: The SR are an independent instrument of the Communities and must be interpreted in their own context and according to their own rules without reference to national laws; T-42/89: Interpretation of a term of the SR ("taking-up of duties") authenticated in more languages; 342/82: The SR must be interpreted as not conferring an entitlement to an invalidity pension at the maximum rate if the invalidity arises from a public-spirited act performed prior to the entry into service.

## B. The application of human (fundamental) rights in the international civil service

### I. The protection of human dignity at work

#### *1. General*

The notion of human dignity is generally referred to in the case law of the international administrative tribunals of the national constitutional courts and in the doctrine as the "heart", the "cornerstone" or the "overarching principle" of all human (fundamental) rights. It is enshrined as a core value in various national constitutions and international conventions on human (fundamental) rights (Preamble of the UDHR: "Whereas recognition of the inherent dignity …"; Art. 1 of the CFREU: "Human dignity is inviolable. It must be respected and protected." The EConHR does not explicitly refer to the human dignity. Nevertheless, the ECHR recognises the respect for human dignity as the "very essence of the Convention", see, for example, ECHR, Judgment of 11 July 2002, I. v. The United Kingdom, Appl. No. 25680/94 para. 70; see also Art. 1(1) German Basic Law (Grundgesetz)).

The human dignity is not only inherent to the very essence of all human rights but is considered as a fundamental right in itself.

Human dignity must also be respected and protected in the employment relationship between an IO in its capacity as a substitute state and its staff.

The notion of "human dignity" is, like "all basic moral and legal principles (justice, freedom, autonomy etc.", Adorno pp. 228–229) neither explicitly defined in the international conventions on human rights nor in national constitutions. There is also no definition to be found in the case law of the international administrative tribunals, which, as usual, do not disclose their cognitive process but only announce the final outcome. The same is valid for the notion of "dignity" in the SR of IO (Art. 12a(3) EU-SR; Reg. 1.2(a) UN-SR).

The idea of "human dignity" may therefore be best illustrated and shaped by the case law of the international administrative tribunals.

In constant case law the international administrative tribunals deal with human dignity issues (in the ILOAT Triblex database more than 100 extracts relate to the "respect for dignity"). The term "human dignity" is thereby frequently used, together with related ethical principles like: honour, reputation or dignity (ILOAT Judgment 3366); dignity and reputation (ILOAT Judgment 2861); dignity and privacy (ILOAT Judgment 2741); dignity and respect (ILOAT Judgment 3193; CJEU Judgment F-40/05); dignity and good name (ILOAT Judgment 2324); dignity and duty of care (ILOAT Judgment 3104); dignity and integrity (ILOAT Judgment 1614); personality, dignity or physical or psychological integrity (CJEU Judgment F-58/10). The idea of human dignity in the workplace may also be elucidated to some extent by the following terminology used by the tribunals in defining unacceptable behaviour which violates the dignity of staff members. To this end the following terms are frequently used in this context: to "demean, humiliate, belittle" (ILOAT Judgment 3115); to "discriminate" (ILOAT Judgment 1436); "insult, threat, defamation or attack" (ILOAT Judgment 3158) "stigmatised or victimised" (ILOAT Judgments 2973, 1376); "sexual and psychological harassment" (ILOAT Judgment 2973); "humiliated, offended or intimidated" (ILOAT Judgment 2553); "humiliating, belittling, offending, intimidating, discriminating" (ILOAT Judgment 2861); to "intimidate, insult, harass, abuse, discriminate or humiliate" (ILOAT Judgment 2524); "mobbing or harassment" (ILOAT Judgment 2594); "bullying mobbing", "harassment" (ILOAT Judgment 3071).

### 2. *Psychological (moral) and sexual harassment*

Psychological (moral) and sexual harassment are among the most common forms of violation of human dignity in the workplace of international staff.

Harassment has been an issue in the case law of the international administrative tribunals since their inception, albeit under another terminology like incompatibility with the "professional dignity" or with the "good name and dignity" (e.g. ILOAT Judgments 30, 361, 781). The number of complaints against harassment before the international administrative tribunals has steadily grown in recent decades (e.g. nearly 40 ILOAT cases in the years 2011 to 2015 and only two cases from 1996 to 2005).

In the last decades, a considerable number of IO have tried to promote the respect of dignity at the workplace and strengthen the means of legal protection against harassment by amending the SR and adopting specific rules against harassment.

The addressee of legal remedies against harassment is primarily the appointing authority, which may have violated its duty of care to staff members and may be in breach of its duty of good governance (ILOAT Judgments 2973 para. 17, 2654 para. 7). The harasser is susceptible to disciplinary measures.

The organisation is under a duty to provide a safe and adequate environment for its staff and both to investigate claims of harassment "promptly and thoroughly" and accord full due process and protection to the person accused (ILOAT Judgments 3337 para. 11; 3071 para. 36; 3065 para. 10; 2642 para. 8; CJEU Judgment F-52/05 para. 25: "with all the necessary vigour and respond with the rapidity and solicitude requested by the circumstances of the case"). The duty extends to both the staff member alleging harassment and the colleague against whom a complaint is made.

Staff members of the EU institutions may in addition claim assistance and damages on the basis of Art. 24 EU-SR (obligation to assist a staff member in particular in proceedings against any person perpetrating threats, insulting or defamatory acts etc.). This duty also exists in relation to acts of another official (CJEU Judgment 18/78), whereas the ILOAT (Judgment 1489) held that Art. 28 EPO-SR (which is formulated similarly) is not applicable in the internal employment relationship of the EPO.

Where a pattern of harassment exists, the date to be taken into consideration with respect to the receivability of a complaint against harassment is the date on which the last event occurred (ILOAT Judgments 3485, 3347, 2100).

– *The definition of psychological and sexual harassment*

Art. 12a(3) and (4) EU-SR and its interpretation by the case law of the CJEU (e.g. Judgment F-95/09, F-138/06 and F-37/08) may serve as the generally agreed standard of the notion "harassment" in international civil service law. It also corresponds to the definition of harassment in Art. 2(3) of Council Directive 2000/78/EC of 27 November 2000 establishing a general framework for equal treatment in employment and occupation.

*Psychological harassment*, therefore, means "any improper conduct that takes place over a period, is repetitive or systematic and involves physical behaviour, spoken or written language, gestures or other acts that are intentional and that may undermine the personality, dignity or psychological integrity" of a person.

The case law of the CJEU has consistently held that the adjective "intentional" applies to the first condition and not to the second. The first condition of harassment relates to the "improper conduct" which must be intentional. That excludes all reprehensible conduct which arises accidentally. Secondly, it is not a requirement that the acts are committed with the "intention" of undermining the dignity of a person. It is therefore sufficient that the intentional acts objectively have the aforementioned effects (see also ILOAT Judgment 2370 para. 8: harassment need not necessarily be intentional).

If the improper conduct does not amount to harassment, it may nevertheless constitute a violation of the general duties of the organisation to treat staff members with dignity and to avoid causing them undue and unnecessary injury (ILOAT Judgment 2067). Such a behaviour may also trigger disciplinary measures. Harassment may also include an intrusion on privacy (ILOAT Judgment 3299).

*Sexual harassment* means, in conformity with Art. 12a(4) EU-SR, "conduct relating to sex which is unwarranted by the person to which it is directed and which has the purpose or effect of offending that person or creating an intimidating , hostile, offensive or disturbing environment".

A single incident may amount to sexual harassment if it is sufficiently severe (see ILOAT Judgment 3085 para. 29 and Art. 2.9(b) of the Collective Agreement on the prevention and resolution of harassment-related grievances between the ILO and the ILO Staff Union of 26 February 2001).

Similar definitions of psychological and sexual harassment are to be found in the Decision of the European Commission of 26 April 2006 on the policy on protecting the dignity of the person and preventing psychological harassment and sexual harassment (Doc. C(2006) 1624/3).

Rule 1(2)(f) UN-SR prohibits harassment without defining this term. There is, however, a definition of the term "harassment" to be found in Sections 1(2) and 1(3) of the Bulletin of the UN-SG of 11 February 2008, doc. ST/SGB/2008/5 on the Prohibition of discrimination, harassment, including sexual harassment, and abuse of authority.

In accordance with the definition of harassment in this document, an intention to harass a staff member is not necessary, a causal link is sufficient ("might reasonably be expected or be perceived to cause offence or humiliation to another person").

At the CoE, Rule No. 1292 of 3 September 2010 on the protection of human dignity at the Council of Europe contains in Art. 1(2) definitions of psychological and sexual harassment which correspond in essence to the definitions given in Art. 12a(3) and (4) EU-SR.

At the EPO, definitions of harassment are given in Art. 2 of Circular No. 341 on the Policy on the prevention of harassment and the resolution of conflicts at the EPO (see the EPO Codex).

**Jurisprudence**

ILOAT Judgments

3485 (3347): see above; 3318: An allegation of harassment must be borne out by specific facts, the burden of proof is on the person who pleads it. An accumulation of events over time may be cited in support of such an allegation; 3250: Institutional harassment (2642); 3173: An employee may be exposed to conduct which objectively would not be characterised as harassment but may be perceived by the employees as harassment and induce work-related stress; 3166: Intimidation by a senior manager may be considered as harassment even if the subordinate exceeds his role by challenging decisions of the manager; 3142: An organisation is under a duty to investigate the complainant's claim of harassment independently of any question as to the renewal of the contract of employment; 3106: An organisation has a duty of care to ensure that material that injures the dignity of its staff members is not communicated; 3104: Dignity offended by humiliation and marginalisation (not enough work given); 3099: Dignity violated since no accurate record was taken of the interviews; 3085: A single incident may amount to sexual harassment (lewd remarks at a condom demonstration); 3071: Duty to investigate claims of harassment promptly and thoroughly. The duty extends both to the complainant and the alleged harasser (3065). Criticism should be done in a manner that ensures respect for the dignity of the official; 3069: Actions of a subordinate may constitute harassment; 3064: Investigation on harassment delayed, moral injury redressed; 2982: Replacement of the complainant under circumstances amounting to harassment; 2973: Failure to fully investigate allegations of harassment in a timely manner; 2938: After leave on personal grounds there is a duty to reinstate the official promptly and with due regard to the dignity of the staff member; 2931: To expect the complainant to work at a post that was graded below the level of duties actually being performed is an affront to dignity; 2879: Presumption of innocence; the organisation bears the burden of proof (the standard of proof is beyond a reasonable doubt), violation of dignity; 2861: Acts of retaliation, the official was not involved in the reorganisation, was excluded from professional activities and isolated from colleagues and ignored by the superior, dignity not respected, harassment; 2856: Transfer to a grade without conferring the commensurate duties violates the dignity (2819, 2229); 2839: No harassment but affront to dignity; 2795: Failure by the organisation to investigate allegations of harassment, bullying and mobbing; 2771: Sexual harassment and harassment by superior, upon his complaint against the disciplinary measure the matter was remitted to consider an appropriate penalty; 2750: The respect of dignity requires that notice be given in the case of expiry at the due date of a fixed-term or a short-term appointment; 2745: An administrative decision cannot be characterised as harassment simply because it is based on a "honest mistake" (2370); 2720: Violation of the dignity and the free exercise of the right to file a complaint if an organisation challenges the findings of fact made in a judgment, which had *res judicata* authority; 2706: Sexual harassment by superior (2645, 2642, 1619); 2654: Obligation to initiate an objective inquiry into the validity of accusations; 2647: An allegation of harassment must be borne out by specific facts to be delivered by the official alleging harassment (2577, 2406, 2370, 2067); 2626: The refusal to publish in an in-house magazine the corrigendum of an article may violate the dignity of the staff member concerned; 2594: In exceptional cases a single incident can amount to harassment. It is up to the person alleging that he has suffered harassment to prove the facts, this burden of proof cannot be reversed (2409, 2370, 2100); 2587: No harassment if there is a reasonable explanation for behaviour (2524); 2553: Whether an act amounts to harassment is a question of facts, the facts and the surrounding circumstances must be carefully examined; 2552: Accusation of harassment is a serious matter and requires a thorough investigation of the matter and full due process and protection has to be accorded to the person accused; 2524: An organisation is under a duty to provide "safe and adequate environment" for its staff. It is liable for all inquiries caused by superiors (or colleagues) if their treatment is an affront to personal or professional dignity of others (2067, 1875, 1609); 2414: Dignity of the official requires a timely information of unsatisfactory aspects of the service delivered (2170); 2394: Hasty termination of a contract and careless advertisement of a post without giving a chance to comment on the termination violates dignity; 2373: Humiliation of a staff member being escorted by a security officer when handing in his request for review of the decision not to review the contract; dignity impaired; 2324: Violation of dignity by placing a senior officer on leave pending review of his performance; 2306: Violation of dignity when terminating a contact; 2222: Waiving immunity without prior information of the staff member injures his dignity; 2191: In a transfer the organisation must carefully take into account the dignity of the employee concerned (1972, 1757, 1726, 1496, 1234, 942, 476); 2100: see above; 1609: Violation of dignity by a superior addressing women in coarse and lascivious language.

CJEU Judgments/Orders

F-43/10: Whereas the impact of the behaviour on the recipient is important that perception must nonetheless be capable of being objectively confirmed; F-42/10: The physical behaviour must objectively be intentional in character, which excludes reprehensible conduct arising accidentally. On the other hand, it is not necessary that the harasser has the intention to undermine the personality, dignity or physical or psychological integrity of a person (no malicious intent needed); F-95/09: In case of harassment the reasonable period to request assistance from the Commission under Art. 24 EU-SR starts from the last act of harassment. The request must be submitted within a reasonable period (a five year period in analogy to the limitation period for claims for damages in the case of non-contractual liability (Art. 46 Statute of the CJEU) seems reasonable); F-1/09: No psychological harassment by a negative appraisal report (F-31/05); F-5/09: Psychological harassment constitutes non-decision-making conduct. It is only the express or implied rejection of the request for compensation that constitutes an appealable decision; F-35/07: The obligation to provide assistance under Art. 24 EU-SR includes the duty to examine seriously, expeditiously and in total confidentiality a complaint of psychological harassment; F-61/06: Jokes about the colour of skin of one of the colleagues, regardless of whether or not that reprehensible and unacceptable conduct is repeated, cannot as such be classified as psychological harassment if the jokes ceased when the colleague concerned requested that they should stop; T-486/04:

An official who claims to have been the victim of mental harassment must put forward evidence proving that he has been subject to conduct aimed, from an objective view, at discrediting him or impairing his working conditions.

## II. Protection of privacy

The respect for workplace privacy of international officials is recognised by the tribunals as a general principle of law applicable to the international civil service. It is derived from the constitutional traditions common to the member states and from the human rights enshrined in international conventions. The most pertinent examples are: Art. 12 UDHR: "No one shall be subject to arbitrary interference with his privacy, family, home ..."; Art. 8(1) EConHR: "Everyone has the right to respect for his private and family life, his home ..."; Art. 7 CFREU: "Everyone has the right to respect for his or her private and family life, home ...".

The respect for privacy "embraces a wide variety of matters" (CFREU, Commentary, Art. 7 point I). It includes workplace privacy (ECHR Judgment of 16 December 1992, Niemetz v. Germany, Appl. No. 13710/88). As far as the international civil service is concerned the right to privacy safeguards the official against interventions by the organisation in his private sphere (right to defence) and requires the organisation to provide a safe and adequate workplace environment for its staff (ILOAT Judgment 2524 para. 30).

Violations of workplace privacy are often interrelated with an act of harassment or a violation of data protection.

The main areas in which workplace privacy of international staff members is endangered by invasion are:

- Information on personal behaviour;
- Confidentiality of documents;
- Information about officials to authorities outside the IO;
- Electronic workplace surveillance and access to personal e-mail accounts.

As with all other general legal principles applicable to the international civil service, the right to "respect of privacy" is not absolute but has to be balanced with other fundamental rights (see Art. 52 CFREU and e.g. CJEU Judgment F-46/09 para. 113: In accordance with Art. 8(2) EConHR an interference by a public authority in private life "may be justified provided that (i) it is in "accordance" with the law, (ii) it pursues one or more of the – exhaustively listed – objectives and (iii) it is necessary in order to achieve that (those) objective(s)").

**Jurisprudence**

ILOAT Judgments

3520 (3513): A group assessment of applicants by an assessment centre does not constitute a breach of privacy; 3260: No violation of privacy if an organisation threatens disciplinary measures if an official does not comply with his private financial obligations; 3160: Breach of confidential information (3004); 3106: Conduct of private life; 3077: A candidate in a competition is not entitled to know the identity of other candidates for reason of confidentiality; 3071: An intrusion of privacy may be regarded as a harassing behaviour; 3055: IO should refrain from passing on damaging information about a staff member. If the outside recipient has a legitimate interest the information should not be passed on without giving the official an opportunity to challenge it and give his own account (256); 3031: The organisation's refusal to remove the references to the medicine from its submissions before the internal appeals board does not violate the complainant´s right to privacy; 2879: The respect for privacy is violated if an organisation is stating in an e-mail to all staff that sanctions were applied to a certain staff member who was not named but could easily be identified; 2861: A publication that reflects adversely on a person infringes privacy; 2766: The participation of a staff representative as an observer at the assessment centre does not unreasonably affect the privacy of the official concerned; 2529: It is a breach of privacy when a review panel shares details of a performance appraisal report with subordinates or peers; 2396: Consulting outside authorities about the professional behaviour of an official; 2350: Access by the organisation to the e-mail account of an official on sick leave (2183); 2271: It is both necessary and legitimate from an organisation to investigate requests for sick leave, to examine medical certificates and to check the health of staff members. The information should, however, be gathered and processed on a fully confidential basis; 1843: Compulsory medical examination on termination of appointment does not violate the respect for privacy; 1547: The refusal to deliver invitations to a union meeting is a breach of the privacy of mail.

CJEU Judgments/Orders

F-46/09: Transfer of a medical opinion to a third party in disregard of the respect for privacy of an official; F-130/07: Restricted use of medical data compromising privacy of a staff member; T-165/03: The right to respect for private and family life embodied in Art. 8 EConHR and Art. 7 CFREU forms an integral part of the general principles of law. It is, however, not an unfettered prerogative and may be restricted, provided it corresponds to objectives of general interest, is not disproportionate with regard the objectives pursued and does not infringe the very substance of the right; T-66/98: Disclosure of medical records to the settlement office of the sickness insurance scheme; T-90/95: Limitations of the right of a staff member that his health status is kept confidential; T-10/93: The requirement that a candidate should undergo a pre-recruitment medical examination is in no way contrary to the fundamental principle of respect for private life (C-404/92P).

### III. Data protection

The protection of personal data of the staff of IO is recognised by the international administrative tribunals as a general legal principle applicable to the international civil service which takes precedence over the internal guidelines on data protection of an organisation (see Ullrich, data protection). In the absence of common constitutional tradition of the member states this general legal principle is primarily derived from international conventions. Among those to be mentioned are: Art. 8 CFREU (Protection of personal data); The UN-Guidelines for the regulation of computerised personal data files (Doc. A/RES/45/95) adopted by the UNGA on 14 December 1990, the CoE Convention No. 108 for the Protection of Individuals with regard to Automatic Processing of Personal Data of 28 January 1981 and the EU Regulation 45/2001(EC) of 18 December 2000.

The core elements of data protection are contained in Art. 8(2) CFREU, in Chapter II of the CoE Convention No. 108 and in point A of the UN Guidelines.

It must, therefore, be ensured that personal data are:

- collected and processed fairly and lawfully (with the consent of the person concerned or on a legal basis);
- stored for a specific and legitimate purpose and not misused;
- adequate and not excessive in relation to the purpose for which they are stored;
- stored with the knowledge of the person concerned;
- accurate and securely stored;
- not stored longer than necessary.

The staff member has a right to access the data concerning him and to have it rectified.

At the dawn of modern information technologies, in the early 1970s, IO followed the example of their member states and adopted specific provisions for the protection of personal data of their staff members in order to address the specific risk to respect for privacy posed by automatic processing of data.

These "third generation fundamental rights" (see the introductory remarks to the EU Commission Report 2012 on the application of the EU Charter of Fundamental Rights) are derived from the principle of respect for privacy (Report of the Centre for European Policy Studies by Irion/Luchetta, Brussels, April 2013, p. 11, point 2.1.1).

As far as can be seen, the OECD was the first IO to adopt provisions on data protection for its staff, on 1 June 1988, followed by the CoE, on 17 April 1989 and by the EPO, on 1 July 1992 (for details see Ullrich, data protection, II.12). Due to their very specific technical nature, the rules on data protection in the employment relationship of IO are usually not embodied in the SR themselves but referred to in supplementary rules to the SR. Within the internal hierarchy of norms the guidelines for the protection of data of most IO are only tertiary law (but see the EU).

The data protection rules adopted by IO regularly apply to automated personal data files and automatic processing of personal data (see Art. 3 CoE Convention No. 108).

The extension of the protection for the processing and storage of personal files partly by automatic means is provided for in Art. 3(2) of the EU Regulation No. 45/2001 (EC). At the CoE personal data collected, stored and used manually are covered by the internal regulations on data protection. In other IO one will have to resort to the underlying principle for the respect of privacy in order to justify a broader interpretation of the protection of personal data processing.

Nowadays, the number of internal databases of an IO is difficult to estimate. The automated storage and processing of personal data comprises not only the files relating to personnel administration in the traditional sense, such as the capture of duty travel, sickness leave, flexible working hours, etc. Increasingly the actual work performance of staff members, e.g. data relating to their use of electronic media, is stored and processed. This may trigger conflicts if the data are used for evaluating individual behaviour at the workplace. Additional conflicts may arise in relation to the widespread tolerance of the use of these facilities for private purposes, if private data is searched.

The following provisions on the protection of personal data of staff members can be cited with respect to the four international civil service systems.

The proposed new General Data Protection Regulation of the EU (GDPR), which is likely to enter into force in 2018, will not cover the processing of personal data by the EU institutions which will remain subject to Regulation No. 45/2001 (EC) (Preamble para. 14(a) of the GDPR). This regulation will, however, be adapted to the GDPR in order to allow an application at the same time as the GDPR (Preamble para. 14(a) of the GDPR).

The Secretary General of the UN promulgated on 29 November 2004 the bulletin for the "Use of information and communication technology resources and data" (UN Doc. ST/SGB/2004/15) and on 12 February 2007 the bulletin on "Record-keeping and the management of United Nations archives" (UN doc. ST/SGB/2007/5).

On 17 April 1989, the Secretary General of the CoE promulgated the regulation for a system of data protection for personal data files at the CoE. The regulation is mainly based on the CoE Convention No. 108. The regulation applies to all personal data collected, stored and used by the CoE, automatically or manually (Art. 1). The respect of data protection principles is supervised by an independent data protection commissioner (Art. 4). On 7 October 2011, the Parliamentary

Assembly of the CoE adopted Recommendation 1984/2011 on "The protection of privacy and personal data on the Internet and online media". In Art. 2.9 of the Recommendation, the Secretary General of the CoE is asked to ensure, through the adoption of specific internal rules and regulations, the protection of privacy and personal data of members of the Council of Europe's bodies as well as Council of Europe's staff, and to reinforce the position of the Council of Europe's commissioner for data protection.

On 19 March 2014, the EPO adopted a revised version of the Guidelines for the protection of personal data in the EPO (Office) (see EPO Codex).

The EPO Guidelines are supplemented by Art. 8 AT/EPO Agreement. On the basis of this, Art. 8 the EPO ensures that persons whose data is processed electronically are able to enforce their rights vis-á-vis the EPO in matters of data protection at least to the extent provided for in the CoE Convention No. 108. This guarantee applies to both staff members of the EPO and external persons.

There should be an independent supervision (data protection officer) and there must be sanctions for an employee who is in breach of the data protection guidelines. The transfer of data to recipients other than within the organisation (data export) is a particularly sensitive area. A transfer is, therefore, subject to the consent of the employee concerned or to permissibility by virtue of international law or by the law of the organisation (see, for example, Art. 15(2) EU-PPI: "The names, grades and addresses of officials ... shall be communicated periodically to the governments of the member states"; Art. 9 EU Regulation 45/2001 (EC) and Art. 8 EPO Guidelines for the protection of personal data in the EPO (Office) (EPO Codex).

Occasionally, there is a specific grievance redress mechanism for staff members in the case of an alleged breach of the protection of their personal data by the organisation. Under Art. 33 EU Regulation 45/2001 (EC), a staff member may lodge a complaint with the European Data Protection Supervisor (EDPS) without acting through official channels. In conformity with Art. 25 of the EPO Guidelines for the protection of personal data in the EPO (Office), a staff member may apply to the Data Protection Officer for advice on data protection matters or if he thinks that an office department has infringed his rights on data protection.

Any failure to comply with the obligations under the data protection provisions makes a staff member liable to disciplinary actions (Art. 49 EU Regulation (EC) 45/2001) or for damages (Art. 22 EU-SR and Art. 26 EPO Guidelines for the Protection of Personal Data in the EPO (Office) in conjunction with Art. 20 EPO-SR).

The international administrative tribunals and the internal appeals committees of IO form an integral part of the internal legal system of an IO in resolving disputes with regard to their employment relationship with staff members. As such they are also subject to the principle of data protection when storing and processing the names of complainants electronically in their case law databases. Since May 2002 the ILOAT anonymises the names of complainants in its case law database Triblex. Since September 2005 the UNAT maintains its case law database in the same way. Its successors, the UNDT and the UNAT, as well as the CJEU (CST) do, however, in principle publish the full name of the complainant in their case law databases (see further on this topic Sobotta, para. 129).

**Jurisprudence**

ILOAT Judgments

3338: Award of EUR 100 for breach of data protection by forwarding information to an external recipient without a legal basis; 3120: Reference to Art. 8 CFREU, right of a staff member to have full and unfettered access to his medical files and to have them rectified; 2933: In a reassignment process the organisation is right to refuse information regarding another candidate on the grounds that personal data are confidential; 2576: The data protection guidelines of the EPO apply only to automated personal data file and automated processing of personal data. Nevertheless, the rules protecting documents and information contained in the personal files of employees must be strictly applied. However, the disclosure within the framework of cooperation with national authorities for legitimate reasons is not prevented; 2516: The use of electronic data processing for the calculation of a staff member's remuneration is duly authorised under EPO's data protection guidelines; 2183: Protection of private data in a professional e-mail account of the organisation. If official access becomes necessary for reasons of urgency or because the account holder is on prolonged absence, the access to any data which may be confidential must be assessed with the utmost care; 2073: Infringement of the data protection provisions by automated individual performance checks; 1756: As to the confidentiality of data, an organisation may not deny an employee access to any significant information which it has about him and which is or may later be put in his personal file. He also must have the opportunity of challenging or adding to it (see also: 1732, 1716 and 1684).

CJEU Judgments/Orders

F-46/09: A decision based on medical data collected for another purpose more than one and a half years before the transfer of the data to the decision-taking institution without the consent of the employee is unlawful; F-30/08: Leak of personal data, disclosure of the applicant's name contained in the Commission's press release and enabling the press to identify him as being one of the officials who were subject to disciplinary proceedings and giving the impression that he was involved in a financial scandal (EUR 90,000 damages); F-130/07: The provision of Art. 10(2)b of Regulation No. 45/2001 on data protection does not require an explicit statement of the precise purpose of the processing of data; C-404/92P: A refusal in relation to a specific aids screening test for the pre-recruitment medical examination comprises any other test with might merely point to the possible presence of the aids virus irrespective of the fact that the institution cannot be obliged to take the risk of recruiting the person concerned.

## IV. The principle of equal treatment and non-discrimination

This principle is one of the key principles guaranteed by most member states of IO and incorporated in international conventions on human rights. Constant case law of the international administrative tribunals recognises this as a general legal principle applicable to the international civil service. The following international instruments may serve, in particular, as a source of law for the derivation of the right to equal treatment and non-discrimination:

- Art. 20 CFREU: Equality before the law and Art. 21 CFREU: Non-discrimination;
- EConHR Art. 14: Prohibition of discrimination and Protocol No. 12 to the Convention Art. 5: Equality between spouses (see ILOAT Judgment 2193);
- Art. 20 of the European Social Charter (rev. 1996): Right to equal opportunities and equal treatment in matters of employment and occupation without discrimination on the grounds of sex (see also Art 4.3 and Art. 27);
- Art. 26 of the International Convention on Civil and Political Rights: Equality before the law (see ILOAT Judgment 2193);
- ILO Equal Remuneration Convention 1951 (No. 100) (see ILOAT Judgment 2097);
- UDHR Art. 1: Equal in dignity and rights; Art. 2: Equal rights without distinction of any kind (see ILOAT Judgment 2193); Art. 7: Entitlement to equal protection of the law and to equal protection against any discrimination in violation of this Declaration and against any incitement to such discrimination; for special aspects of equality see Art. 10 (fair and public hearing), Art. 16 (equal rights as to marriage), Art. 21(2) (equal access to public service) and Art. 23(2) (right to equal pay for equal work).

The terms "equal treatment" and "non-discrimination" are mostly used as synonyms (see, for example, CJEU Judgment C-619/11 para. 26: "the principle of equal treatment and non-discrimination"), (see also the opinion of the advocate general, CJEU Judgment C-236/09 para. 29 and CJEU Judgment T-6/92 and T-52/92 para. 103).

The principle of equal treatment requires "that similar situations should not be treated differently and that different situations should not be treated identically unless such a differentiation is objectively justified" (CJEU Judgment C-217/91 para. 37; see also F-83/07 para. 2; C-110/03 para. 71; C-442/00 para. 32).

The standard formula on equal treatment used by the ILOAT is worded as follows: The principle of equality requires that situations (positions in fact and in law) which are identical or comparable be governed by the same rules and the rules that govern dissimilarity must be appropriate and adapted to the dissimilarity (ILOAT Judgments 2704, 2194, 2066, 1990).

"In most cases involving allegations of unequal treatment, the critical question is whether there is a relevant difference warranting the different treatment involved" (ILOAT Judgment 2313 para. 5).

The principle of equality is breached if the different treatment is not appropriate and adapted to that difference (ILOAT Judgment 2313 para. 5). The authority which is required to give equal treatment to dissimilar situations has a broad discretion in adapting rules that take into account that dissimilarity (ILOAT Judgments 2194 para. 6(a) and 1990 para. 7). There is no breach of the principle of equality where the treatment is a fair, reasonable and logical outcome of circumstantial differences (ILOAT Judgment 754 para. 6).

The SR of the EU contain the most comprehensive provisions to ensure equal treatment of staff. Art. 1d(1) EU-SR prohibits any discrimination based on any ground such as sex, race, colour, ethnic or social origin, genetic features, language, religion or belief, political or any other opinion, membership of a national minority, property, birth, disability, age or sexual orientation. Non-marital partnership shall be treated as marriages if certain conditions are fulfilled. Art. 1d(2) EU-SR guarantees full equality between men and women in working life but allows corrective measures for the under-represented sex. Art. 1d(5) EU-SR even shifts the onus of proof to the institution if an official considers himself wronged because the principle of equal treatment has not been applied to him.

The Secretary General of the UN is required by the Staff Regulations to provide and enforce the Staff Rules, consistent with the broad principles of human resources policy enshrined in the UN Charter (see Secretary General's Bulletin, doc. ST/SGB/2014/1 of 1 January 2014). Under Art. 8 of the UN Charter the eligibility of men and women to participate under conditions of equality in the organs of the UN is guaranteed.

Art. 3 CoE-SR entitles staff members to equal treatment without direct or indirect discrimination, in particular on grounds of racial, ethnic or social origin, colour, nationality, disability, age, marital or parental status, sex or sexual orientation, and political, philosophical or religious opinions.

Art. 5 EPO-SR is about the general criteria for recruitment and contains similar guarantees of equal treatment similar to those of the CoE-SR.

The principle of equal treatment and non-discrimination is one of the general legal principles most frequently referred to by the international administrative tribunals. For example, the Triblex database of the ILOAT contains (as of 2016) about 200 judgments containing the keyword "equal treatment".

The principle of equal treatment and non-discrimination is binding on all organs of an IO in the entire employment relationship. Violation of this principle occurs most frequently in the areas of recruitment, gender and pay.

With regard to administrative decisions, there is a close interrelationship between the principle of equal treatment, the exercise of discretionary power and arbitrary considerations. The principle of equal treatment forbids arbitrary and/ or unjustified distinction between individuals or groups in similar or identical positions, not the differentiated or graduated treatment of situations which are intrinsically and objectively different (ILOAT Judgment 2979 para. 4). Also any discretionary power must conform to the principle of equality of treatment (ILOAT Judgment 572 para. 1) but otherwise an organisation is free in the exercise of discretion to have regard to all relevant considerations, general or particular and it may differentiate so long as the differentiation is not arbitrary.

**Jurisprudence**

ILOAT Judgments

3575: The principle of equal treatment cannot be invoked to protect misconduct; 3340: Internal and external candidates in a competition are in a different situation in fact and in law and they may therefore be subject to different methods of calculating professional experience without breach of the principle of equal treatment (2859); 3157: Unequal treatment when establishing a short-list; 3073: The principle of equal opportunity among candidates is violated if the qualifications required were altered after the recruitment procedure had begun; 3071: If different treatment is allowed in principle, the second issue is whether the different treatment is appropriate and adapted to those differences (2915); 3032: A competition must be objective and transparent in order to guarantee equal treatment; 3020: Unequal treatment, if the salary paid by the IO exempt from national taxation is indirectly taxed, because it is included in the rate of the husband's national income tax; 3006: In the case of a retroactive upgrade of a staff report the question of promotion has to be reassessed; 3003: The request of an IO for the stay of execution of a judgment until the ICJ renders its opinion (Art. XII ILOAT statute) arises in the context of a procedure which is already fundamentally imbalanced to the detriment of the staff member. The Tribunal does not in any way amplify the consequences of this inequality; 2980: To add candidates to a short-list after the evaluation has begun is against equal treatment of all candidates; 2979: The principle of equal treatment requires the adoption and implementation of impartial reasonable and objective rules which provide the same treatment in law for similar cases (prolongation of service beyond the statutory retirement age); 2936: Trifling differences do not justify different treatment; 2931: A post graded below the level of duties violates the principle of equal pay for work of equal value; 2925: It is not discriminatory to require particular residential requirements for the grant of an expatriation allowance; 2906: A decision which stems from a factual (clerical) error (promotion without the necessary qualifications) and is not consistent with its author's intention can be reversed at any time. The opposite would be liable to conflict with the principle of equal treatment of officials; 2870: The conditions for the payment of the education allowance to non-national staff members is in conformity with equality if the rules are appropriate and adapted to their general circumstances, even if their application in individual cases is less than perfect; 2869: Violation of equality if a member of the staff union is not promoted simply because no appraisal report could have been established for the period of his mandate; 2834: Preferring candidates with potential managerial skills over those with greater seniority or higher ratings as examiners does not constitute unequal treatment; 2725: The complaint of an official is receivable if a decision confers benefits to third parties which may result in unequal treatment to his detriment; 2706: Principle of equal pay for work of equal value violated; 2704: Discrimination because of activities within a staff association; 2649: No provision in the SR requires equal remuneration between permanent staff members and temporary workers; 2638: Benefits such as home leave or education allowance are designed to restore a degree of equality; 2637: The grant of an education allowance is not intended to discriminate but to restore equality for staff members having their closest material or personal ties to other countries; 2619: The grant of special leave on a case-by-case basis is in conformity with the equality until it is proved that officials in identical situations are treated differently; 2597: Equal treatment demands that the right to an expatriation allowance takes fair and reasoned account of different situations. A period of three years, residence in the country prior to taking up duties in the organisation is not unreasonable to exclude the right to an expatriation allowance; 2556: The principle of equality requires the equal application of the relevant law not its equal misapplication (equality of the law does not embrace equality in the breach of it, 1536, 1369, 1366, 1321, 1194, 845, 769, 767, 614); 2549: Unequal treatment of same sex partners in a registered partnership; 2527: No unequal treatment if a member country does not allow the transfer of pension rights despite the efforts made by the organisation; 2520: Equality is not *prima facie* violated if a staff member participates in the selection of candidates having a professional relationship with or even supervisory responsibility for one or more of the candidates; 2513: Arbitrary decision not to extend an appointment beyond the normal retirement age; 2498: Discriminatory treatment, but retroactive effect limited by the SR; 2418: The application procedure was in breach of the principle of equal treatment; 2393: The fact that not all candidates were asked the same questions does not, in itself, demonstrate unequal treatment; 2314: After having been transferred the complainant continued to perform the duties of the preceding post. The grant of a special post allowance has to be continued until a proper evaluation of the work is performed (equal pay for work of equal value); 2313: Different treatment in relevantly different situations may breach the principle of equality if the different treatment is not appropriate and adapted to that difference; 2296: All staff members in like cases have to be similarly advised on fundamental conditions applicable to all staff (e.g. time limits concerning claims); 2292: Even if the EPO is not a member of the CO and is not bound by the EConHR in the same way as the signatory states, the general principles enshrined in the EConHR (including the principle of non-discrimination) apply to relations with staff. The fact that different rules apply to retired staff members according to their place of residence does not violate the principle of equality; 2256: International staff members cannot be deprived of their tax exempt status either by the organisation or by one of its member states (2032); 2210: The requirement among other things of equal treatment places the organisation under an obligation to provide a clear and precise definition of the concept of a "similar" post; 2193: Same-sex partnership. Entitlement to benefits for a dependent spouse. Even in the context of a culture of tolerance compatible with changing moral beliefs the DG cannot be compelled to deviate from the clearly defined SR by referring to the principle of equal treatment (but see Judgments 3203, 2860, 2549 and the dissenting opinion of Justice Hugessen in Judgment 2193); 2138: The award of long-term contracts was exceptional and wholly discretionary and the fact that a contract is granted to one staff member creates no rights for any other staff member; 2120: Discrimination of staff members in a marital or intimate personal relationship with other staff members; 2097: Paying lower salary rates to a person doing temporary work on a short-term basis is not discriminatory; 2066: Equal treatment does not preclude amendment of a rule or the way in which it is applied; 2023: Step increases within a grade are not contrary to the principle of equal pay for work of equal value; 2004: It is open to the interpretation of unequal treatment if one candidate is given the potentially unfair advantage by flying him across the ocean to be interviewed while another one is interviewed at a video conference; 1990: Equal treatment in a competition by introducing a corrective factor for languages; 1866: No violation of equal treatment if staff members residing outside the headquarters have no right to compensation if they do not wish to place their child in a subsidised nursery; 1804: Violation of equal treatment by promoting a staff member on the basis of a promise contrary to the SR; 1789: Violation of equal treatment by rejecting an application on the grounds that the applicant is overqualified; 1600: A decision to promote based on considerations other than ability and record of performance is in violation of equal treatment; 1549: Equality in a competition demands scrupulous compliance with the rules announced beforehand; 1491: The fact that CERN's staff members holding French nationality are not exempt from French income tax but are entitled to repayment by CERN of tax actually paid is not in violation of equality. The difference in treatment (higher tax rates for their other income) is due solely to the working of French tax law, not to CERN's working; 1461: The payment of interest on arrears restores parity between someone who received an allowance at the due date and someone who received it later; 1420: Discrimination because the parity in the purchasing power of staff in different duty stations was violated; 1333: Docking of wages for strike action. No unequal treatment if the family allowance paid by the EPO is deducted but some officials in receipt of the Dutch children allowance fared better; 1324: It offends against the principle of equal treatment when the determination of the place where an official takes home leave is made according to different criteria for the original designation and the review; 1268: At every stage of a competition including the arrangements made, the conduct of the tests and the evaluation of their results, every candidate must be treated equally (1071, 107); 1194: A special leave is ordinarily granted on individual application it would have been a pointlessly formal approach to demand that every single German official applied for special leave for the declaration of 3 October 1990 as a public holiday in Germany; 1196: No breach of equal treatment if different categories of staff are treated differently (1119, 845); 656: It is a breach of the principle of equality to treat examiners and translators more favourably than lawyers in the counting of prior experience; 551: In unusual circumstances and for a strictly limited period, different conditions for promotion according to nationality are permitted, e.g. in order to satisfy quotas for recruitment for the purpose of developing the international character of the body of staff.

CJEU Judgments/Orders

F-155/12: Choice of the subject for a written test of a competition, no infringement of the principle of equal treatment; F-20/08, F-34/08 and F-75/08: Cancellation of a problematic question in a recruitment competition without prejudicing equal treatment of candidates; F-19/08: The preference given to one or more languages of the community does not infringe equal treatment if the linguistic knowledge is of relevance for performing the duties of the post; F-83/07: No indirect age discrimination by requiring a certain diploma of secondary education; F-115/07: Refusal to grant a fixed allowance to an official even though other officials in a comparable situation receive it (presumption of lawfulness of a decision); F-4/07: An official may not rely on an unlawful decision to allege an infringement of equal treatment (the principle of legality prevails); F-148/06: The allocation of merit points must be undertaken on a basis of equality; F-122/06: Unequal treatment of the spouse of an official who is in a registered stable non-marital partnership in relation to his sickness insurance cover; F-54/06: The abolition of weightings for pension rights acquired after the entry into force of revised SR on 1 May 2004 does not violate equal treatment, since European integration made weightings less and less necessary; F-52/05: Under Art. 12a(4) EU-SR sexual harassment shall be treated as discrimination based on gender; T-219/02 and T-227/02: Imposing age limits in recruitment procedures is reasonable and proportionate and does not violate equal treatment; C-122/99 P and C-125/99 P: Under Community legislation household allowance is granted only to married couples in conformity with the definition of the term "marriage" generally accepted by member states. The principle of equal treatment cannot apply to other partnerships (see, however, now Art. 1d(1) EU-SR which entered into force on 1 May 2004); T-35/96: There is no breach of equality if the appointing authority makes nationality a prevailing criterion in order to maintain or restore a geographical balance, provided the qualifications of the candidates are essentially equal; T-66/95: No infringement of equal treatment if an official at the end of his term of office does not engage in any gainful employment and continues to be affiliated to the sickness insurance of the organisation, but his ex-spouse does not; T-60/92: The prohibition of overqualified candidates (university degree) from entering a competition (category C post) violates equal treatment in conjunction with Art. 27 EU-SR which provides that recruitment shall be directed to securing the services of officials of the highest standard of ability, efficiency and integrity; T-6/92 and T-52/92: No disguised unequal treatment if retired officials who incur higher expenses resulting from illness are not regarded as a separate category of sickness insured persons; T-30/90: No person may plead in his own cause an unlawful act committed in favour of another.

## V. Freedom of association, assembly and trade union matters

### *1. General information*

The freedom of association and assembly and freedom in trade union matters is recognised in Art. 20 and 23(4) UDHR; Art. 12(1) CFREU and Art. 11(1) EConHR. It is also one of the few labour law principles of the international civil service explicitly guaranteed by the SR of most IO (Art. 24b EU-SR; Rule 8(1)(g) UN-SR; Art. 47 CoE-SR; Art. 30 EPO-SR). International administrative tribunals may have recourse to those principles where the SR fall short of the legal protection due under them (see UNAT Judgment 15 para. 11: "the principle of the right of association to which the United Nations solemnly pledged is admitted on all sides to be a principle which must prevail also inside the organisation's own Secretariat.").

The freedom of association includes the right to form and to join all types of staff associations regardless of their denomination, internal structure and legal form, e.g. staff committees, staff councils, trade unions and other groupings representing and promoting the interests of the staff of an IO. The terminology used in the SR does not provide a uniform picture. The creation of staff associations is left to the discretion of staff members. Only the setting-up and the functions of the staff committees (staff councils) as the standard internal bodies of an IO representing the interests of staff are dealt with in the SR (Art. 9 and Annex II EU-SR; Art. 6 to 9 and Appendix I CoE-SR; Art. 33 et seq. EPO-SR). The UN-SR deviate from this pattern providing for "staff representative bodies" (Rule 8(1) UN-SR) as a *mixtum compositum* of a staff committee and trade union elements ("hybrid system").

The freedom of association only guarantees the basic features of the staff committees/staff councils which are internal bodies of an IO, i.e. their internal structure (statute), the election of staff representatives etc. The freedom of association does not extend to the type of staff-management relations. The participatory rights of staff committees/staff councils have been developed by the international administrative tribunals as a special general legal principle.

The freedom of association and freedom in trade union matters guarantees the right of staff members to freely form and join trade unions of the international civil service. This freedom includes the right to represent, to protest and to promote the interests of union members.

Staff associations (staff committees and trade unions) of IO have a special calling to protect the common interests of the staff members of IO. There are two main reasons for this. IO dispose of a dual character. They are not only employer but also a "*substitute state*". In addition, the legislative function of this "substitute state" is not in the hands of a democratically legitimated legislator. The delegates of the legislative bodies of an IO (Council, General Assembly) are generally national civil servants appointed by the respective central or federal ministries. It is apparent that this composition of the organ of an IO authorised to adapt the SR may cause a conflict of interests between the international staff and their national counterparts or even competitors (see, for example, the EUIPO or the EPO and the national patent and trademark offices of the member states). In addition, national delegates are primarily concerned with their national administrative functions in their home countries and meet as a rule only once or twice a year at the premises of the IO to fulfil their mandate in the legislative and supervisory organ of the IO.

Furthermore, the heads of IO are regularly exposed to disguised exertion of influence by individual member states (see, for example, ILOAT Judgments 1821 para. 15 and 448 para. 8(b)).

The democratic deficit (as far as the external action of IO are concerned, see Stein, HJIL 64 (2004) p. 563–570), the concentration of power in the hands of the head of an IO and the hidden pressure by interested national circles calls not only for an effective legal protection *ex post* by the international administrative tribunals. There is also a need for powerful staff associations (staff committees, trade unions) which are able to promote the common interests of staff by aiming for an effective social dialogue which goes beyond mere consultation rights.

The freedom of association not only protects the right of individuals to form and to join staff committees and trade unions but also the collective rights of these groupings in general.

In most IO, the SR provide for an internal joint staff-management machinery (joint advisory committees, general advisory committees, staff regulation committees, joint committees, staff-management coordination committees etc.) to cooperate between the administration and the staff in all matters concerning the revision of the SR, the conditions of work, staff welfare and all matters of a general nature concerning the staff. In addition to these internal joint bodies, staff members may also set up external associations (trade unions, professional associations or similar groupings) which exert their influence on the administration from the outside. At some IO, the administration has entered into a framework agreement (recognition or co-operation agreement).

As far as the exercise of the freedom of association (staff committees and unions) by staff members and the underlying bounds of this freedom are concerned, all actions of the staff associations and its members fall under the immunity protection enjoyed by the individual staff members of the organisation.

### 2. *Staff committees*

The staff associations most closely involved in the staff-management relations are the staff committees/staff councils. The structure, function and mandate of these bodies are to a varying comprehensively stipulated in the SR (as regards the peculiarities of the UN system see below) of the organisation. As a rule, these bodies are internal bodies (Art. 9(3) EU-SR; Annex I Art. 4 CoE-SR; Art. 34 EPO-SR) of the organisation without their own personality in law (ILOAT Judgment 2827 para. 4) and with the mandate to represent the interests of all staff members in issues relating to the SR and all matters of a general nature concerning the staff. Staff committees are generally elected direct via secret ballot by the staff-at-large (see, for example, Art. 33 EPO-SR, but see the UN system below). The staff committees elect or appoint their representatives to all joint committees, panels, working groups etc.. As to the internal organisational structure, see, for example, Annex II Art. 1 EU-SR.

Staff members must have complete freedom to choose their representatives in accordance with the established rules concerning the democratic principles and the principle of equal treatment (CJEU Order T-396/03). In conformity with the jurisprudence of the CJEU, the EU, however, has a supervisory function with regard to the election of the staff representatives (CJEU Judgment 146 and 431/85). It is under a duty to intervene of its own motion if it has doubts as to the regularity of an election (CJEU Order 146/85 R). Any complaint in this connection must be examined with the necessary assiduity (CJEU Judgment 54/75).

The ILOAT follows a rather formalistic approach in relation to the powers of the head of administration to supervise the elections of the staff committee. Whereas the tribunal underlines the interest of the organisation in a stable and functioning staff committee, it has held that it has no jurisdiction as to any claim for annulment of the election of a staff committee or any order to conduct new elections (ILOAT Judgments 2636 para. 15, 78). This reasoning seems rather doubtful. An internal staff body in an organisation represents the staff's broad band of interests within the joint staff-management machinery. It must, therefore, be within the overall responsibility of the organisation that the mandate of the staff representatives is based on proper elections which respect the general principles applicable to the international civil service. It cannot be that there is a legal vacuum left in this area.

The participation rights of staff representatives in the process of shaping opinions of the management and taking decisions is generally rather limited.

The staff councils/staff committees of the UN organisations diverge from the standard pattern of staff committees of the IO. The staff councils/staff committees of the UN organisations form an integral part of the staff unions/staff associations which are hybrid participation bodies. They are composed of elements of trade unions and of internal staff committees. The staff councils/staff committees are elected direct by the staff-at-large. All candidates for election must, however, be duly paying members of the staff union (see, for example, Rule 13(3) UNSU Statute). The staff council elects the representatives to joint and other bodies. Those representatives must be contributory members (see, for example, Reg. 1(2) UNSU Part II – Regulations).

### 3. *Trade unions*

International trade unions may be set up, formed and joined by staff members of an IO in the exercise of their freedom of association and in trade union matters (a definition of the staff trade union is given, for example, in ILOAT Judgment 2672 para. 9). The unions are the most powerful representatives of the common interests of their members. They are in principle (but see below, the UN) entities outside the internal structure of the organisation and legally independent of the organisation. As a matter of principle, they do not depend on a formal "recognition" by the organisation (collective agreement, memorandum of understanding). Nevertheless, a recognition will entail a preferential treatment (see below). They are formed under the law of a member state. However, due regard has to be given to the special calling as a trade union representing international civil servants and to the immunity accorded to their members. The staff unions as voluntary associations of international staff members act under national law and, as a rule, enjoy the legal capacity accorded to legal persons under the national law of a member state and, in particular, may be a party to national legal proceedings (Judgment of the Landgericht Berlin, EPO trade union v. Germany of 8 December 2014; Judgment of the Appeal Court of the Hague (NL), EPO trade union v. the EPO of 17 February 2015). In order to avoid legal uncertainty they need to have some rules incorporated in a charter, a statute or other document (ILOAT Judgment 2672 para. 9) which are consistent with the provisions of national civil law as a prerequisite for legal transactions under national law. As far as the distinction between internal and external relationship of actions of the trade unions is concerned, see, for example, the Judgment of the German Federal Constitutional Court, BVerfG, case No. 2 BvR 1458/03 of 3 July 2006 (English version available).

International trade unions primarily protect, represent and promote the interests of their members. In virtually all IO there is at least one staff union set up by staff members. At the EU institutions more than a dozen unions are active. This plurality of unions in an organisation may lead, however, to a complexification of the political dialogue with the management and to a reduction of effectiveness. The aims, objectives and activities of international unions do not depend on a formal recognition by the organisation. Unions that have entered into a recognition of co-operation or framework agreement with the organisation (recognised unions, see, for example, Art. 10c EU-SR and the framework agreement of the EU Commission, see also below, the UN system) may, however, enjoy some preferential treatment.

In contrast to the objectives and activities of staff committees, those of the staff unions are not specified in the SR and additional rulings. A clear demarcation of competences is contained in Art. 10b EU-SR (trade unions shall act without prejudice to the statutory powers of the staff committees).

A non-exhaustive list of objectives and activities of trade unions includes the following key elements:

- safeguarding and promoting the working conditions and the welfare of staff, ideally through collective bargaining, ultimately by strike;

- providing assistance and legal advice to staff members in employment – related matters;
- giving financial and legal support in appeals and disciplinary procedures of staff members;
- (in the furtherance of the above objects) maintaining regular contacts and engaging in discussions with the staff and the administration, informing staff members, issuing publications, political activities like lobbying during the meetings held by national delegates, and organising all kinds of industrial actions.

As with all other freedoms, the freedom of association and freedom in trade union matters have their bounds. These are defined by the rights of others (including those of the organisation) of equal fundamental value and are determined by the balancing of interests in the individual case, having regard to the generally accepted principle that no fundamental right may be violated in its essence. Unions may, therefore, be prohibited from holding general assemblies of their members during working hours, from having time off for trade unions activities or from using additional office space for their activities. The access to modern facilities for communicating with staff may be restricted (CJEU Judgment C-193/87 and C-194/87: no obligation to make the messenger service available to trade unions; ILOAT Judgment 2228: no obligation to grant access to the internal e-mail system, but see Judgment 1547 concerning the constant practice to distribute invitations to attend a meeting of the unions). Unions also have to observe the negative freedom of association (no compulsory membership) and respect the principle of non-discrimination of staff members. Despite some prerogatives concerning the freedom of speech, the staff union must respect the dignity of all staff members and of the organisation. On the other hand, the trade unions benefit from the immunity enjoyed by their members.

It would, however, be an infringement of the essence of the freedom of association, if an organisation would "starve a union" and "harass" its members so that they would be "driven willy-nilly out of the association" (ILOAT Judgment 403). Unions must, therefore, have the right to communication and to a dialogue with their members and to the general exchange of information with staff. There must also be the possibility to attract new members and to prepare and execute all kinds of industrial actions (CJEU Judgment C-193/87 and C-194/87).

As a corollary to the wider range of objectives and because they have their own assets and represent primarily the interests of their members and not of all staff (ILOAT Judgment 2228 para. 11), staff unions' right to assistance by the organisation is restricted. Nevertheless, unions "must clearly be provided with sufficient facilities within the framework of negotiated agreements or if need be, administrative regulations, to enable them to carry on their activities" (CJEU Judgments

C-193/87 and C-194/87; ILOAT Judgment 2228 para. 11). If an organisation has granted some facilities to a staff union explicitly or in line with constant practice, it is legally bound and may not withdraw them as it pleases (ILOAT Judgments 911, 494, 403).

Whereas IO will be more readily prepared to grant extensive facilities to staff unions with which they had entered into a framework agreement, trade unions may be hesitant to conclude such an agreement for fear of a curtailment of their activities.

The establishment of branches of national trade unions in an IO would conflict with the obligation of a staff member to carry out his duties and conduct himself solely with the interests of his organisation in mind (e.g. Art. 11 EU-SR, see also ILOAT Judgments 1269, 1244). A staff member may, however, belong to a national trade union as long as his duties as a staff member remain unaffected.

The channel of appeal provided for under the respective provisions of the SR and the status of the international administrative tribunals is generally (but see the CoE and the OECD) available to staff members only (individual disputes, see, for example, ILOAT Judgment 1547) and not to trade unions. Within the legal system of the EU, however, there is the possibility for international trade unions of the staff of the EU to institute legal proceedings against an act of an EU institution under the conditions laid down in Art. 263 TFEU but not under Art. 90 and Art. 91 EU-SR (CJEU Judgment 18–74). Since the unions are set up under the national law of a member state their legal capacity and *locus standi* under national law are to be assessed under those provisions.

The staff unions/staff associations of the UN organisations diverge from the usual patterns of trade unions of IO. The "staff representative bodies" (Rule 8(1)(a) UN-SR) assume a double function as a trade union and an internal staff council/staff committee. In this hybrid function the unions levy fees from the staff members (see, for example, Rule 3(1) UNSU Statute: All staff members assigned to the UN secretariat in New York are members of the union). The amount of the fees is within the range 0.01% to 0.5% of net salary (UN doc. JIU/REP/2012/10 p. 13).

A staff union may enter into a recognition/cooperation agreement with the administration (UN doc. JIU/REP/2012/10 p, 28 et seq.) which may include consultation and collective bargaining.

More than 50 staff unions of the UN organisations are belonging to one of the three federations of UN unions/associations (FICSA, CCISUA, UNISERV). These federations pursue the general interests of the international staff and assist the individual staff unions in their daily work (UN doc. JIU/REP/2011/10 and the websites of the federations).

### 4. *Other groupings*

In addition to the staff committees and trade unions, there are also associations (clubs) that safeguard and promote cultural, social and sporting interests. These bodies depend on the allocation of funds made available by the organisation. These clubs are set up by the staff members and are subject to statutory provisions. Their activities do not constitute an official activity of the organisation and do, therefore, not enjoy the privileges and immunities granted to the respective organisation.

Occasionally, there are professional associations and trade union divisions specifically for some categories of employees. On the one hand, they are of no great importance and on the other hand they can cause serious social tensions among the staff (Busch, p. 239 f).

### 5. *Collective bargaining*

The right to collective bargaining between the social partners is guaranteed in several international conventions (see, for example, Art. 28 CFREU and Art. 11 EConHR which must be interpreted as including the right to collective bargaining and to conclude collective agreements; see ECHR, case Demir and Baykara vs. Turkey, Appl. No. 34503/97 of 12 November 2008). The term "collective bargaining" is defined in Art. 4 of ILO Convention No. 98 on the Right to Collective Bargaining of 1949. Bargaining in the strict sense is characterised by negotiations between partners of equal bargaining power (economic strength may be unequal, see ILOAT Judgment 380 para. 21) in order to reach a compromise. Negotiations would, however, be frustrated if either party would begin negotiations with the determination "not to make any concession in any circumstances" (ILOAT Judgment 380 para. 21).

The exercise of the right to collective bargaining must, however, not prevent the imposition of lawful restrictions by the EU law and national legislation and practices (see Art. 28 CFREU). The limits of collective bargaining are further illustrated by Art. 11 EConHR (see, for example, EU network of independent experts on fundamental rights of the CFREU, 2006, Art. 28 point IV). The exercise of the right to collective bargaining may, therefore, be restricted *inter alia* for members of the administration of the state. Along the same lines ILO Convention No. 98 on Collective Bargaining stipulates: "This Convention does not deal with the position of public servants engaged in the administration of the State".

In many states, the SR for national officials are unilaterally decided by law without any collective bargaining. In 28 European countries surveyed by the ILO, five governments take these decisions by law and 23 countries use some form of negotiation to determine the working conditions for the public service (ILO

Working Paper No. 309 of 2015, see also ILO General Survey concerning labour and collective bargaining in the public service, ILO International labour Conference 102nd Session 2013, doc. ILC 102/III/1B).

Because IO exercise public competences assigned by member states the lawful restrictions applicable to the right of collective bargaining are also applicable to the law of the international civil service. Generally, IO adopt their SR by unilateral decisions of the legislative body of the IO (see, for example, Art. 336 TFEU and Art. 10c EU-SR: agreements concerning its staff with representatives of trade unions and staff associations "may not entail amendments to the Service Regulations ...", see also Art. 10b EU-SR; Art. 101 UN Charter, see also UN doc. JIU/REP/2011/10 para. 130; Art. 33(2)(b) EPO-EPC).

This does, however, not preclude that trade unions may be consulted on proposals for the amendments of the SR (see Art. 10b(2) EU-SR), in addition to the consultation of the staff committee or the internal bodies which may extend to some type of negotiations.

The collective bargaining between IO and trade unions is, therefore, as a rule restricted to reaching framework, recognition and cooperation agreements concerning the prevention of labour conflicts, the procedures to be followed in the case of strike and the grant of facilities to the union. There are, however, some efforts at an extension of the right to collective bargaining (see, for example, the Copenhagen Declaration of FICSA of February 2012, para. c) ii) and UN doc. JIU/REP/2011/10, recommendation 5). See in this context also the Judgment of the Appeals Court of The Hague (NL) of 17 February 2015, appeal in a case of the EPO trade union v. EPO. The Court held that the trade union should be admitted to collective bargaining with the EPO. The Court thereby explicitly referred to Art. 11 EConHR but not to the limitations of the right stipulated therein).

In its judgment of 20 January 2017, the Supreme Court of the Netherlands sets aside this judgment and held that the Netherlands Courts have no jurisdiction to hear the unions claims against the EPO (for more details see below under Excursus: Immunity of IO from national jurisdiction in staff matters). It will finally be up to the ILOAT to decide on these issues.

**Jurisprudence**

ILOAT Judgments

3084: An IO must ensure that a staff member is not disadvantaged on the grounds of his participation in staff union activities (e.g. FICSA); 2672: Definition of the terms "staff association" and "union". National law which requires formalities like registration cannot apply since its members are only international civil servants, nevertheless, the general principle of legal certainty requires some sort of legal structure of the association; 2636: The claims for annulment of the election of the staff council and for new elections are outside the jurisdiction of the Tribunal. They do not concern the terms of appointment or general principles of law but derive from the statutes of the staff association. A staff member's conduct of his private life or his trade union activities are not, apart from exceptional cases, the concern of the administration (274: an act of misconduct at a meeting of the Council); 2459: The freedom of association is not violated if an organisation distinguishes between recognised and representative associations. Only the latter have a right to participate in the decision – making process. This restriction observes the principle of proportionality between the participation rights of staff and the interests of the organisation in the smooth operation of its administration; 2228: The access to the internal electronic mail system may be made available to the staff committee only, i.e. not to trade unions; the staff unions should, however, not be hampered (see 1547). They must be provided with "sufficient facilities" to enable them to carry on their activities. The organisation may, however, ensure that the facilities made available to the staff committee representing the staff as a whole are not misused for the benefit of a trade union having its own assets and representing only part of the staff (see also the order of the German Federal Constitutional Court of 3 July 2006, BvR 1458/03, English version available); 1806: The decision to offer the president of the staff association/ staff union a post in the personnel unit on the condition that he resigns from his post in the staff association is incompatible with the independence of the staff association; 1547: Even without a formal agreement with the staff union, the staff had in accordance with consistent practice the plain expectation that a summons to a meeting would be delivered without let or hindrance. The refusal to deliver invitations to a union meeting is a breach of the privacy of mail and of the freedom of speech that is part and parcel of the freedom of association. Members of the staff union have a standing in alleging a violation of the freedom of action of a staff association; 1542: A complaint is not receivable about the collective interests of trade unionists, e.g. seeking the grant of staff union facilities (critical remark: this reasoning seems rather doubtful since an organisation could hamper the collective rights vested in a staff union without providing legal remedy); 1437: A transfer attributable to the work for the staff union would not be in line with the freedom of association; 1392: A collective agreement with a staff union does not divest the staff member of the safeguards he enjoys under the SR. A collective agreement is "a basic vehicle of social process, justice and peace" and a source of law. A staff member, even if not a member of the union, may rely on a collective agreement on the basis of the freedom of association and the principle of equal treatment. The Tribunal will apply any material rule of international law or any body of law, but no national law save where there is express recourse thereto in the SR or in the individual contracts of employment; 576: The mere coincidence of a transfer and the attendance of a meeting as a staff representative does not suffice to establish a misuse of authority; 520: The lack of success in a selection procedure was not due to staff activities but to a lack of minimum requirements for the post; 496: Freedom of association is destroyed if communication between the members is permitted only under supervision by the administration on the grounds of accuracy of information (the standard excuse for censorship from time immemorial). The grant of facilities to the staff association cannot be withdrawn at will (see Judgment 911); 495: In accordance with the principle of freedom of association representatives and members of the staff association may act in furtherance of their common interests without the risk to be penalised for proper actions; 450: Salary deduction for participating in a demonstration; 403: It is for the staff, and not for the DG, to organise itself. What is not described in the SR are the facilities offered to staff associations. It is, however, now customary for the administration to guarantee or provide them, since an efficient working of staff associations is in the interest of the administration. Most important are the permission to take time off within reasonable limits, the provision of office space and the deduction of membership from the salary; 87: Staff representatives have special responsibilities but also special rights, in particular a significant freedom of speech and the right to criticise. This includes the right to criticise the head of administration subject to the duty to observe the moderation incumbent on any official and the strict duty to observe the decorum appropriate to his status as an international civil servant; 78: None of the regulations empower the DG to invalidate elections held by the staff committee or a staff union to form its executive committees on the ground that such elections were irregular.

CJEU Judgments/Orders

F-121/10: Neither Art. 28 CFREU nor Art. 10 EConHR oblige an EU institution to enter into collective bargaining with a staff union. There is also no right of co-determination in relation to amendments of the SR or to an agreement with the trade unions on salary matters; T-396/03 (T-368/94): EU institutions have a duty to ensure that their employees have complete freedom to choose their staff representatives in accordance with the established rules, in particular the principle of representativeness (representation of all function groups), the democratic principles and the principle of equal treatment; T-191/02: The operational rules in a framework agreement between an EU institution and the staff unions do not confer any right or impose any obligation on the individual staff member; T-349/00: Violation of the framework agreement between the EU Commission and the staff unions providing for the participation of all staff unions which signed the agreement in the social dialogue process; T-203/99: Special leave for union members based on the framework agreement between the EU Commission and the staff unions; T-33/91: The freedom of trade union activities means not only that officials have the right without hindrance to form unions of their choosing, but also the collective right of the union to protect the interest of their members as employees, in particular by means of bringing court proceedings (see Art. 263 TFEU; see, however, Judgments 18/74, 175/73); T-28/89: Calculation of the time-limit for changes to the electoral rules. The duty to ensure the freedom of elections is not confined to penalizing irregularities committed or preventing from occurring. The institutions have the right to intervene of their own motion if they have doubts as to the regularity of an election; C-193/87 and C-194/87 (leading judgment): The freedom of trade union is, in addition to an individual freedom, a collective right of the association itself. An organisation may not prohibit officials from joining a union or participating in union activities or impose any penalty whatsoever on them by reason of such membership or activities. There is no general principle which obliges an organisation to make the messenger service available for the distribution of union communications to their members. An administration is, however, obliged to grant the necessary facilities to enable a staff union to participate in the preparation of common proposals to be submitted to the Council; 146/85 R: EU institutions have the duty to intervene of their own motion when they have doubts as to the legality of elections of the staff committee; 146 and 431/85: The Court has jurisdiction in electoral disputes concerning the appointment of staff committees on the basis of provisions laid down in the SR. Actions of staff members may be brought against the EU institutions concerned regarding the acts or omission of the appointing authority arising out of the exercise of its supervisory function; 54/75: EU-institutions are obliged to supervise the organisation and conduct of elections to the staff committees and to examine with the necessary assiduity any complaints which may be submitted in this connection. If the elections are vitiated by illegality, the administration is entitled and required to disband the improperly elected committee.

### 6. *The right to strike*

#### a) The principle

Like in the national laws of many countries, the right to strike is not expressly referred to as a fundamental right in some of the most international legal renowned instruments. The relevant provisions only refer in general terms to the freedom in trade union matters (see, for example, Art. 23(4) UDHR and Art. 11 EConHR). The right to strike is, however, generally deduced as a corollary to the freedom of trade unions in literature and in case law.

As an appropriate example, reference may be made to the decision of the ECHR, Appl. No. 68959/01, Eerji Yapi-ol Sen v. Turkey of 21 April 2009. In this decision the ECHR held that under Art. 11 EConHR the right to strike is indissolubly linked as a corollary to the freedom and protection of trade unions.

In addition, the ECHR quoted ILO Convention No. 87 (Freedom of Association and Protection of the Right to Organise of 7 July 1948) and the European Social Charter (revised 3 May 1996).

In other international legal instruments, the right to collective actions (strike) is explicitly recognised. The most prominent examples are: the CFREU (Art. 28: "... to take collective action to defend their interests, including strike action ..."), the European Social Charter (Art. 6.4: "... including the right to strike ...") and the International Convenant on Economic, Social and Cultural Rights (of 16 December 1966; Art. 8.1(d): "...The right to strike ...").

Irrespective whether the right to strike is explicitly guaranteed or deduced as a corollary to the right of association the exercise, of that right is subject to certain restrictions (see, for example, Art. 28 FREU, the right to strike action is subject to "... union law and national laws and practices ...")., In recent judgments, the CJEU (C-341/05 and identical wording in C-438/05) held that the right to strike is a fundamental right, which has, however, "to be reconciled with the requirements relating to rights protected under the Treaty and in accordance with the principle of proportionality" (C-341/05 para. 94). In its decision of 21 April 2009 (Application No. 68959/01 Enerji Yapi-Yol Sen v. Turkey) the ECHR held that the fundamental right to strike is not absolute but subject to certain restrictions and conditions. A general ban applied to all public servants is, however, incompatible with the exercise of this right (para. 32).

Similar to the right to collective bargaining, many countries have restricted the right to strike for members of armed forces, police and other public servants (see Gernigon/Odero/Guido p. 17 et seq. and p. 49 et seq.). However, unlike the right to collective bargaining, the right to strike in IO has been more influenced by those member states of IO where civil servants may strike (see Schermers/Blokker § 541).

In some IO the right to strike is even expressly guaranteed. At the EU, the right to strike is not provided for in the SR but in the framework agreement between the EU Commission and the trade unions and staff associations. The CJEU Judgments 44, 46 and 49–77 of 18 March 1975 which held that the Judgment in no way implies "any decision in relation to the exercise of an official's right to strike ..." may therefore not be used as a pretext to call into question the legal basis for the right to strike of EU officials. The right to strike is expressly guaranteed in Art. 47bis CoE-SR, in Art. 30a EPO-SR and in Part 1 para. 8 Conditions of Employment of the ECB and Part 1 para. 1(2) ECB Staff Rules.

Of special significance for the guarantee of the right to strike is the jurisprudence of the ILOAT. According to its case law, a strike is lawful "as a matter of principle" (Judgments 2342, 566).

Like all other legal principles, the right to strike is not guaranteed without any implied or explicit limitations. There is a broad consensus that the right to strike is subject to a reasonable period of notice before a strike actually starts (see, for example, Art. 37 EU framework agreement; Art. 30a(5) EPO-SR; Part 1 para. 8 Conditions of Employment of the ECB and Part 1(2)(3) ECB Staff Rules). There is also widespread agreement that a reasonable number of staff members in essential services must not strike in order to guarantee the survival of the organisation (for more details, see ILOAT Judgment 805). In its judgment 2494 the ILOAT stated that the right to strike must not lead to sudden work stoppages at Eurocontrol due to its special mission relating to the safety of air navigation.

Any limitation of the right to strike must, however, respect its very essence as it is the case with other fundamental principles. The right to strike may, therefore, for example, not be made subject to a discretionary decision by the head of administration. It is a matter for the international administrative tribunals to establish the permissible limits of the right to strike.

For lack of international judicature, reference is made to the judgment of the Appeal Court of the Hague (NL) of 17 February 2015. In a dispute between the trade union (SUEPO) of the EPO and the EPO the court held that the restrictive definition of the term "strike" in Art. 30a(2) EPO-SR ("concerted work stoppage") and the "limited duration of a strike" (Art. 30a(2) EPO-SR) violates the right to strike which allows other collective actions such as go-slow actions and strikes of general duration. In its judgment of 20 January 2017, the Supreme Court of the Netherlands set aside this judgment and held that the Netherlands Courts have no jurisdiction to hear the Union's claims against the EPO (see below under Excursus: Immunity from IO from national jurisdiction in staff matters). It will finally be up to the ILOAT to decide on these issues in the context of international civil service law if the dispute is brought before it.

#### b) Content and scope of the right to strike

– Definition of the right to strike

The SR of IO do not contain a definition of strike actions (but now see Art. 30a(2) EPO-SR inserted in 2013 in the EPO-SR). There exists also no commonly agreed definition of strike in the case law of the international administrative Tribunals. The Committee of Experts on the application of Conventions and Recommendations of the ILO has come to the conclusion that: "Any work stoppage, however, brief and limited may generally be considered as a strike if the action is conducted in a peaceful manner." The definition includes actions which are not a work stoppage in the strict sense but have the same paralysing effect as a work stoppage (go-slow-strike, work-to-rule) (Gernigon/Odero/Guido, p. 12).

– Types of strike actions

As at national level, the international civil service faces with a wide range of types of strike actions which are continuously being expanded by the resourcefulness of staff unions. As some of the most frequently used strike actions the following types may be quoted:

- discontinuous strike
- partial or selective strike (strike of employees in key positions only, in order to disrupt the function of the whole organisation, see ILOAT Judgment 805);
- stop-work meetings
- go-slow-strike
- work-to-rule
- demonstration strike
- blocking of dossiers (see ILOAT Judgment 2440)
- sit-down strike
- wildcat strike (strike without prior authorisation by the staff union, if it is retroactively authorised).

The most important examples for illegal strike actions which may trigger disciplinary actions are:

- strike actions which are not peaceful (e.g. offensive actions at picket lines)
- refusal of individual employees to work without due notice of strike by the staff union (see ILOAT Judgment 2342)
- sudden stoppage of work in a sensitive area (e.g. air navigation control, see Judgment 2494)
- strike action infringing the freedom to work for non-strikers.

For more details, see Gernigon/Odero/Guido, p. 25 ff.

- Actions by the organisation

In the case of a strike an organisation may only dock the corresponding remuneration. No lockouts are permitted in IO (see ILOAT Judgment 616).

- Objectives of a strike

The objectives of a strike in an IO are to furthering and defending the interests of the staff (Art. 10 of ILO Convention No. 87). Political and sympathy strikes are generally of no concern to the law of the international civil service.

- Legal consequences of a strike

A strike does not break the obligation of the employment relationship. Only those provisions of the SR are suspended which are incompatible with the strike action, all others remain in force (ILOAT Judgment 615). Salary is withheld by virtue of the provision contained in all SR that salary is only due for service rendered (e.g. ILOAT Judgment 615 para. 6). In addition to the docking of salary for days of strike an organisation may also withhold the respective amount of allowances if the SR so provide (ILOAT Judgments 1333, 1041). If an organisation did not set up special rules on salary deduction, different from those for absence from service for other reasons, then those general rules are applicable to strikes (ILOAT Judgments 615, 566: The deductions for a strike were obtained by dividing the number of strike days by the number of working days in the respective month, multiplied by the amount of salary. This was not line with the general rule in the SR that the deductions in case of absence from service had to be calculated on the basis of the "thirtieths" rule).

When a strike comes to an end, the administration frequently enters into an agreement with the staff union in order to reach an amicable settlement in respect of the docked salary in order to restore good working relations (ILOAT Judgment 2440).

– Framework agreements

Some IO have entered into framework or recognition/co-operation agreements with staff trade unions (see, for example, UN doc. JIU/REP/2012/10 p. 28 et seq.) The most prominent example is the EU Commission, which entered into continued agreements with staff unions and associations in 1974, 2003 and in 2008. These agreements provide for rules in the case of collective actions (strike) and comprise the service obligations of staff members in essential services, the obligation to give notice, wage deductions and the resumption of work, and regulate the provisions of facilities for the trade unions.

**Jurisprudence**

ILOAT Judgments

3369: Strike-related docking of salary in the case of part-time working; 2494: Participating in an industrial action by a sudden stoppage of activity and by abandoning the workplace may be subject to disciplinary measures under the special mission of Eurocontrol relating to the safety of air navigation; 2493: To make the exercise of the right to strike conditional or obtaining a prior authorisation to be absent from duty would deprive this right of all substance; 2440: An IO cannot presume the participation of a staff member in an industrial action. It can withhold salary only for those periods for which it has proof of his participation; 2342: According to settled case law, that as a matter of principle a strike is lawful (see Judgment 56), the work stoppage of two staff members without corresponding due notice by the trade unions is not a collective action; 1333: The deductions for one day's strike included *inter alia* the family allowance. The fact that staff members posted in the EPO branch in the Netherlands suffered no loss since they received the Dutch child allowance is not a breach of the principle of equal treatment since staff members posted in another member state are not in the same position in law; 1041: Remuneration in Art. 65(1) EPO-SR denotes both salary and allowances, deductions from pay in the case of a strike may therefore comprise both payments; 805: In the case of a strike the requisitioning of staff members in essential services (survival of the organisation) must respect the principle of proportionality, i.e. the proper balance between the rights and duties of the organisation and the staff union in the event of an industrial action. When the strike is paralysing a section of the organisation not only the total number of staff in this section but in the whole organisation has to be taken into account in order to evaluate the proper bounds of requisitioning staff members; 616: If in the case of a strike someone stays at home and asserts that he is at the disposal of his superior he is deemed to be on strike. There is a generally accepted principle that payment is due only for service rendered. A lockout or a compulsory unemployment to get through a spell of financial stringency are unknown in IO; 615 (566): As a matter of principle a strike is lawful. In principle, all provisions of the employment relationship continue to apply. Only those provisions of the SR which are incompatible with the work stoppage are suspended. An organisation is entitled to make special rules on salary deductions in case of a strike. A dispute over the calculation of salary deductions in case of a strike is not tantamount to an impediment of the right to strike.

CJEU Judgments/Orders

C-341/05 (identical wording: C-438/05): as reaffirmed by Art. 28 CFREU, the right to collective action (strike) is recognised as a fundamental right which forms an integral part of the general principle of the EU law. The exercise of that right is, however, subject to certain restrictions. It must be reconciled with the requirements relating to the rights protected under the EU law, national law and practices; 44, 46 and 49–74: According to a recognized principle in the labour law of the EU member states, wages and other benefits pertaining to days of strike are not due to employees who have taken part in a strike. That statement does, however, not imply any decision in relation to the existence of a right of EU employees to strike. The present strike has nevertheless been considered by all concerned to be a method of defending collective interests of the staff and was, therefore, described as a strike action.

ECHR decision

Decision of 21 April 2009 (Enerji Yapi-Yol Sen v. Turkey, Application No. 68959/01): A general ban applied to all public servants is incompatible with the right to form and join trade unions as guaranteed under Art. 11 EConHR. The right to strike is indissolubly linked as a corollary to the freedom and protection of trade unions under the ILO Convention No. 87 of 9 July 1948 (Freedom of Association and Protection of the Right to Organise) and of the ESC (rev. 3 May 1996). The right to strike is, however, subject to certain restrictions and conditions as stipulated in Art. 11(2) EConHR.

### 7. *The freedom of assembly*

The fundamental right to freedom of associations is closely linked with the freedom of assembly. In the field of the international civil service the freedom of assembly, however, plays a more subordinate role. In practice, it mainly protects the participation of staff members in general assemblies and in industrial actions. In this context there is, therefore, no need to dwell on this freedom in more detail.

## VI. The freedom of expression

The freedom of expression (sometimes also denoted as freedom of speech or freedom of discussion and debate, see, for example, ILOAT Judgment 3106 para. 9 and 10) constitutes "one of the essential foundations of a democratic society, one of the basic conditions for its progress and for the development of every man" (CJEU, Judgment C-274/99 P, "Connolly", summary para. 1; see also ECHR Judgment Gündüz v. Turkey, Application no. 35071/97 para. 37: "Freedom of expression constitutes one of the essential foundations of any democratic society and one of the basic conditions for its progress and for each individual's self-fulfilment").

The international administrative tribunals draw inspiration from the constitutional tradition of the member states and from international conventions like the UDHR, the EConHR and the CFREU to confirm in settled case law the importance of the fundamental right to freedom of expression for the international civil service. Special reference is made to Art. 6(1) TEU in conjunction with Art. 11(1) CFREU: "Everyone has the right to freedom of expression. This right shall include freedom to hold opinions and to receive and impart information and ideas without interference by public authority and regardless of frontiers" (see also the identical wording of Art. 10(1) sentences 1 and 2 EConHR and see Art. 19 UDHR: "Everyone has the right to freedom of opinion and expression…"). The right to freedom of expression is often associated with other fundamental rights like that of the freedom of assembly and association. (For more details see the "human rights handbook", No. 2 of the CoE: "Freedom of expression").

The particular importance of the freedom of expression for the international civil service is borne out by the fact that a number of IO explicitly refer to it in their SR. For example, the right to freedom of expression was embodied in Art. 17a EU-SR on the occasion of the revision of the EU-SR on 1 May 2004. Likewise Reg. 1(2)f UN-SR guarantees the inviolability of the right to expression: "… personal views and convictions … remain inviolable …". The fundamental right to freedom of expression as applicable to the international civil service extends "to the free expression, orally or in writing, of opinions that dissent from or conflict with those held by the employing institution" (CJEU Judgment C-274/99 P "Connolly", summary para. 2; see also ILOAT Judgments 1061, 911, 87).

As in national law the freedom of expression in the international civil service is not without bounds. Restrictions are justified where they protect the rights of others. It is legitimate to subject international public servants on account of their status to restrictions on the exercise of the freedom of expression such that an IO is not impeded in carrying out the official tasks assigned to it by the member states (see, for example, CJEU Judgment C-274/99 P, "Connolly", summary para. 2). The duty of loyalty is incumbent upon every international civil servant. He may not resort to behaviour incompatible with the decorum appropriate to his status and must not impair the dignity of the international civil service (ILOAT Judgment 1061 para. 3). There is a general obligation of reserve and moderation incumbent on every official (CJEU Judgment T-146/89 para. 80). The IO and the courts have to find a "fair balance" (CJEU Judgment C-274/99 P, "Connolly", summary para. 2) between the rights of the employee to freedom of expression and the legitimate interests of the IO by taking into account all the circumstances of the case, including the nature of the duties performed by the official and his place in the hierarchy.

The EU-SR, for example, contain the following explicit restrictions on the freedom of expression: Art. 11: Carry out duties and conduct himself solely with the interest of the Union in mind; Art. 12: General behavioural obligations; Art. 12a: Psychological or sexual harassment; Art. 17: Unauthorised disclosure of information; Art. 17a: Respect of the principle of loyalty and impartiality; Advance information of the intention to publish a matter dealing with the work of the organisation; Art. 19: Permission to disclose information in legal proceedings with the exception of proceedings before the CJEU and before the Disciplinary Board. (But see Art. 22a and 22b information on possible illegal activity, fraud and corruption.)

**Jurisprudence**

ILOAT Judgments

3156: To prevent abuse of the right of free speech prior authorisation of messages may be permitted (but see Judgment 2227); 3106: A defamatory statement made in circumstances that afford a defence. An organisation must be neutral when differences of opinion emerge within a staff union; 2705: Statements made in legal (court or internal appeal) proceedings are privileged ("court privilege"). Even if defamatory they cannot be the subject of legal proceedings or sanctions; 2656: Deliberately false allegations of misconduct against another staff member are not protected by the freedom of expression; 2626: The refusal to publish a corrigendum in the organisation's in-house magazine may infringe the freedom of expression; 2228: The freedom of expression of the staff union should not be hampered by the organisation by not providing any facilities. The access to the internal e-mail system may, however, be restricted to the statutory Staff Committee which represents the staff as a whole and has no own assets (see also the Order of 3 July 2006 of the German Federal Constitutional Court, case No. 2 BvR 1458/03 (available in English) relating to this ILOAT Judgment); 2227: The staff representation enjoys a broad freedom of speech and the right to take to task the administration. There is no right of an organisation to a prior censorship over the communication of written information produced by staff groups or associations; 2114: The complainant sent a letter to the Dutch Parliament which contained remarks suitable to damage the relations inside the Council and towards the secretariat of the organisation. These discrediting statements were not protected by the freedom of expression and could have been detrimental to the reputation of the organisation; 2048: Sending a threatening letter to a colleague is not covered by the freedom of speech; 1547: The refusal to deliver invitations to a union meeting is unquestionably a breach of the freedom of speech, that is part and parcel of the freedom of association; 1391: The mere failure to prove the truth of allegations in court proceedings does not mean that a complainant has either abused his freedom of speech or forfeited the privilege of court proceedings; 1061: Freedom of expression must be protected particularly for staff representatives. Airing of grievances in a radio interview, however, may jeopardise the reputation of the organisation and warrant dismissal; 1028: The freedom of speech affords no excuse for insulting remarks about a superior on the staff report (endorsement of the assessed staff member in the staff report: "Does getting a rating of 1 ("outstanding") depend on the number of drinks colleagues are stood and the value of presents directors get ?"). The sanction was, therefore, wholly warranted; 911: (leading judgment): A staff association enjoys special rights that include broad freedom of speech and the right to take to task the administration. The freedom of speech is wider than that allowed to a staff member and only gross abuse will be inadmissible; 496: Freedom of speech of a staff association is destroyed if communication between the members is permitted only under supervision. It is from time immemorial the standard excuse for censorship not to suppress the truth but just to make sure that only the truth is told; 274: Freedom of association necessarily involves freedom of discussion and debate and this freedom, when feelings run strong can spill over into extravagant and even regrettable language. The staff has its own rules for dealing with such misdemeanours (87); 63: Accusing a colleague of incapacity and subversion in statements addressed to national authorities, institutions and outside persons harmed the interest of the organisation and is incompatible with the duties of a staff member in the international civil service as specified in the SR.

CJEU Judgments/Orders

F-41/10: The exercise of the freedom of expression in relation to the report of alleged illegalities under Art. 22 EU-SR; F-28/06: The freedom of expression does not entitle an official to make unfounded allegations against his superiors which are likely cast discredit on their honour; F-40/05: The right to freedom of expression is not a unfettered prerogative but may be subject to restriction. Art. 17 EU-SR which restricts unauthorised disclosure by officials of information received in the line of duty is not an unwarranted restriction of their rights; C-340/00 P: The refusal to publish must be interpreted restrictively. It is only permissible if publication could represent a real risk of serious prejudice to the interests of the organisation; C-274/99 P: ("Connolly", leading judgment): The freedom of expression includes the scope of activities of the EU institutions. It extends to the expression orally or in writing of opinions that dissent from or conflict with those of the employer. The right is, however, subject to specific restrictions which are justified by the legitimate aim to protect the rights of the organisation charged with the responsibility of carrying out tasks in the public interest. Citizens must be able to rely on their doing so effectively. There must be a fair balance between the freedom of expression of staff members and the observance of their duties and responsibilities. The publication of the book entitled: "The Rotten Heart of Europe, The Dirty War for Europe's Money" without prior permission whilst on leave on personal grounds violates the required duty of loyalty and seriously prejudiced the legitimate interests of the organisation. The requested prior permission does not entail unlimited censorship which infringes upon the very substance of the freedom of expression. The complainant remained subject to the obligation to request prior permission even during the period of leave on personal grounds; T-146/89: The applicant was not criticised for having made inaccurate statements but for insulting members of the Court of Auditors and his failure to observe his duty of loyalty and the obligation of reserve and moderation incumbent on every official.

## VII. The right to property

The right to property as a general legal principle of the international civil service derives both from the constitutional traditions of most member states of IO as well as from international conventions on human rights. Particularly worth mentioning is Art. 1 of the Protocol No. 1 to the EConHR: "Every natural or legal person is entitled to the peaceful enjoyment of his possessions"; Art. 17 CFREU: "Everyone has the right to own, use, dispose of and bequeath his or her lawfully acquired possessions"; Art. 17(1) UDHR: "Everyone has the right to own property alone as well as in association with others".

As a general principle, providing legal protection against an IO as a "substitute state" the right to property is not limited to the term "property" in a restricted sense but comprises all legal positions similar to ownership like intellectual property, acquired rights or other entitlements, e.g. pension claims and social benefits (see the "human rights handbook", No. 4 of the CoE: "The right to property"). Nevertheless, the right to property plays only a minor role in the law of the international civil service. There is a relatively low potential threat of infringement of the property of staff members in the restricted sense of ownership under the domestic law on the one hand, and on the other hand the international administrative tribunals have derived specific general legal principles to protect legal positions of staff similar to ownership, like the doctrine of acquired rights and the entitlement to damages caused to staff members. In such cases the tribunals regularly base their judgments on these specific principles without referring to the right of property at all.

The SR of IO do not generally provide for the protection of the property of staff members. There are, however, provisions which provide for the entitlement to compensation in the event of loss or damage to personal property of staff by third parties attributable to the performance of official duties.

The compensation is restricted to cases where the staff member was not able to obtain full compensation from the person who caused the damage and the official did not either intentionally or through grave negligence cause the damage (e.g. Art. 24(2) EU-SR). At the UN secretariat Rule 6(5) UN-SR providing for compensation for loss or damage to personal effects attributable to service is implemented by an administrative instruction (UN doc. ST/AI/149/Rev. 4). No compensation is due for loss or damage caused by the negligence or misconduct of the claimant. The scheme excludes a number of effects from compensation and sets maximum limits for the compensation of others. The claims are examined by a claims board (see also Art. 40 CoE-SR and Art. 28 EPO-SR).

The SR of most IO contain provisions on the restriction of intellectual property rights (e.g. patents and copyright) of staff members on work performed as part of their official duties (Art. 18 EU-SR; Rule 1(9) UN-SR). All such rights are vested in the respective organisation. In appropriate cases, the institutions of the EU may award a bonus to an official who is the author of a patented invention (Art. 18(3) EU-SR).

**Jurisprudence**

ILOAT Judgments

2843: The organisation assumed liability for transportation costs, telephone expenses, costs incurred in the course of the internal appeal proceedings and all future material damages causally linked to the accident in the car park of the organisation. To extend the liability of the organisation beyond its liability under this no-fault regime, a claimant must prove negligence or the intentional breach of duty (2804, 2533, 435); 2403: An organisation is under an obligation to take proper measures to protect its officials from financial loss suffered in the course of employment. In particular if the loss is directly associated with compulsory participation in a provident fund established by the organisation (no proper system of monitoring and analysis in place); 2292: It is not in breach of property rights that in connection with pension rights different rules apply according to the place of residence of retired staff members.

CJEU Judgment

C-274/99 P ("Connolly"): The right to property may be subject to restrictions (e.g. prior permission for the publication of any matters dealing with the organisation), provided that the restrictions correspond to objectives of general interest pursued by the organisation and are neither disproportionate nor infringe the essence of the right to property.

## VIII. Freedom of thought, conscience and religion

The international administrative tribunals acknowledge the freedom of thought, conscience and religion as a general legal principle of the international civil service. Apart from national laws the freedom can be based on Art. 6(1) TFEU in conjunction with Art. 10 CFREU; Art. 9 EConHR and Art. 18 UDHR (see also the "human right handbook" of the CoE on protecting the right to freedom of thought, conscience and religion).

Despite the codification of this freedom in the SR of most IO (Art. 1d(1) EU-SR; Reg. 1.2(f) UN-SR; Art. 3(1) CoE-SR) the risk of potential conflict with this freedom in the international civil service is far less than in the member states of IO.

There are, however, the areas of recruitment and the personal files where the legislative of IO deemed it necessary to set up specific rules, for the protection of this freedom (see, for example, Reg. 4.3 UN-SR: Selection of staff member shall be made *inter alia* without distinction as to religion; Art. 26 EU-SR: The personal file of an official shall *inter alia* contain no reference to his political, trade union, philosophical or religious activities and views or the sexual orientation, Art. 46(4) CoE-SR: The file shall not refer to the political, philosophical or religious views of the staff member.

**Jurisprudence**

ILOAT Judgments

24: Staff members enjoy entire freedom of conscience in respect both of their philosophical considerations and their political opinions but they have the duty to abstain from all acts capable of being interpreted as associating them with propaganda or militant proselytism in any sense whatsoever. The refusal of an official to participate in measures of enquiry as to his loyalty to which his national government considers it necessary to subject him is justified by the freedom of conscience. Otherwise this would result in a state of uncertainty and insecurity prejudicial to the performance of the duties of staff members whose responsibilities are exclusively international in character (23 to 21, 19 to 17).

CJEU Judgment

130–75: If a candidate participating in a competition test informs the organisation in good time of difficulties to take part in the competition on a certain date due to religious reasons the organisation should endeavor to avoid such date.

## IX. The right to a safe and healthy working environment

The right to safety and health at work is recognised by the international administrative tribunals as a general legal principle applicable to the international civil service. It may be derived from coherent national laws of member states and from international conventions like Art. 31(1) CFREU: "... right to working conditions which respect his or her health, safety and dignity"; point 19 CCFSR: "... satisfactory health and safety conditions ..."; Art. 3 ESC: "The right to safe and healthy working conditions".

The SR of some IO explicitly stipulate the duty of the organisation to ensure a safe and healthy working environment (see, for example, Art. 1e(2) EU-SR: "Officials in active employment shall be accorded working conditions complying with appropriate health and safety standards at least equivalent to the minimum requirements applicable under measures adapted in these areas pursuant to the Treaties". This provision was implemented by the decision of 26 April 2006 (decision C(2006)1623/3) by the Commission establishing a harmonised policy for health and safety at work for all European Commission staff, see CJEU Judgment F-50/09 para. 127; see also Art. 38a EPO-SR).

– Safety measures

Within their internal organisational autonomy, IO have discretion to adopt all measures they consider necessary to ensure a safe working environment. Nevertheless, in contrast to other areas of organisational autonomy, the safety at the workplace of an IO has close links with the safety of clients and the prevention of fires at the place of employment. Similar to the administration of justice the provision on privileges and immunities (protocols, general agreements, conventions, seat agreements) regularly provide for an obligation of the organisation to cooperate with national authorities in the area of safety of the premises of the organisation (see, for example, Art. 20 EPO-PPI: "The organisation ... shall ensure the observance of police regulations ... or other similar national legislation ..."; Art. V, Section 21 UN-PPI: "... secure the observance of police regulations ..."; Art. 2 CoE-PPI: with the same wording). The applicable safety guidelines are, therefore, as a rule agreed with the local fire police and technical inspection associations. The procedures and guidelines include the regular inspection of all working areas and equipment of the premises and car parks as well as the setting up of evacuation plans and the holding of fire drills. All larger organisations have a safety unit responsible for providing a safe and secure workplace.

– Healthy working environment

IO are under a duty to ensure the welfare of their officials at workplace. As in the area of the social security of staff members, the host country of an IO has a vital interest in ensuring that the conditions at the workplace of an IO are comparable with its national labour inspection system (see, for example, Art. 20 EPO-PPI: "... to ensure the observance of ... regulations concerning public health, labour inspection or other similar national legislation"). Similar to the internal social security system IO are, as a rule, reluctant to allow the interference of national authorities in their organisational autonomy. As a rule, IO dispose of internal regulations on occupational health and ergonomics. All larger IO have a separate medical advisory unit advising staff members in all work-related medical questions and representing the administration in medical committees competent, among other things, for issues of sick leave and invalidity.

– Physical and mental health

The duty of an organisation to provide a safe and healthy working environment extends to guaranteeing a working place free from harassment, retaliation and hostility (ILOAT Judgment 2524 para. 6: Harassment and mobbing are "extreme examples of the breach of the duties to provide a safe and secure workplace"). In this context, the right to a safe and healthy working environment will regularly overlap with other general legal principles like that of the duty of care (see, for example, ILOAT Judgment 2973), the respect for dignity (see, for example, ILOAT Judgments 2839, 2795), of due process (see, for example, ILOAT Judgment 2524) and the precept of good faith (see, for example, ILOAT Judgment 2524).

– The liability of the organisation

As a rule, the SR of IO provide for lump-sum compensation in the case of total invalidity (in some cases even for partial invalidity, e.g. the EU) and for entitlement to an invalidity allowance or invalidity pension.

The lump-sum compensation is deemed in principle to be an adequate compensation also for workplace injuries suffered based on a no-fault regime (ILOAT Judgment 2533: A mature legal system provides compensation for work place injuries on a "no-fault" basis). If the invalidity arises from an occupational accident or an occupational disease, a minimum amount of invalidity allowance or pension may be guaranteed and the staff contributions to the retirement pension may be paid by the organisation (see, for example, Art. 78 EU-SR). Additional compensation is due in the case of material or moral damages caused by negligence on the part of the organisation. The legal basis for such additional compensation is derived from the general liability of IO to third parties.

**Jurisprudence**

ILOAT Judgments

3145: The tribunal ordered the appointment of a medical expert to determine whether the health problems of the complainants were work-related; 3096: Having regard to the nature of investigation the complainant could not help but think that the investigation was directed at her. In addition, other acts of harassment like verbal attacks/aggression in retaliation of the Director in charge of the investigations were detected; 3025: An IO has a duty to provide a safe and adequate environment for its staff and they in turn have the right to insist on appropriate measures to protect their health and safety (2524); 2910: The investigation to ensure a workplace environment free from any form of harassment was not carried out properly and promptly (2642); 2843: The physical injury as a result of slipping on liquid in the car park of the organisation is covered by the no-fault regime. Moral damages are due only if there is negligence (failure to take reasonable steps to prevent a foreseeable risk of injury) on the part of the organisation, which was not proven; 2804: The complainants received in addition to an invalidity pension under a no-fault regime for work-related invalidity (repetitive strain injury) a lump-sum payment. They sought additional compensation for damages caused by negligence and breach of the duty to safeguard their health and safety. Since negligence was not proven, the tribunal rejected the complaints without considering whether in the case of gross negligence, the liability of the organisation would justify additional compensation; 2795: It is the duty of an organisation to provide for an acceptable working environment and carry out investigations both promptly and thoroughly to determine whether the facts prove that harassment has taken place; 2706: The organisation failed to provide a safe and adequate work environment since the complainant was the victim of sexual harassment. The verbal reprimand was clearly not commensurate with the seriousness of the misconduct; 2594: The organisation was not in breach of the duty to protect the complainant from physical injury; 2403: An organisation is under an obligation to protect its staff members from physical injury in the course of their employment. The same is true with respect to loss of or damage to personal property; 1609: An organisation is liable for injury a staff member may cause to other members of staff in the context of employment. The organisation has a duty to ensure a safe and healthy working environment free from harassment and intimidation; 1486: Illness due to an assignment exposing the staff member to an area of special hazard to his health (hepatitis B); 402: If an employer has failed to exercise due skill and care in arriving at a judgment on the safety of the place of work, the employee is entitled to compensation in full against the consequences of the misjudgment.

CJEU Judgments/Orders

F-92/09: There is a duty of the organisation to have regard to the welfare of officials (here: psychological problems after a transfer) which reflects the balance of reciprocal rights and obligation between an official and the organisation; F-50/09: Right that the working conditions respect health, safety and dignity of staff members as recalled in Art. 31(1) CFREU. Duty to ensure safety in the specific living and working conditions of an official posted outside the member states. Duty to assess the risk, take preventive measures and inform the staff member; T-377/08 P: The case law on the restricted judicial review of medical opinions does not apply in the case of a purely technical question (here: repair or purchase of a wheelchair). Under the duty to have regard to the welfare of its officials, the organisation should also take into account the interest of the official concerned (T-48/01); F-30/08: When faced with an incident of alleged harassment, an organisation is required to intervene with all the necessary vigour and respond with the rapidity and solicitude required by the circumstances of the case with a view to ascertaining the facts and taking the appropriate actions to restore a safe working environment; T-57/99: The duty to have regard for the welfare of officials obliges the organisation to provide healthy working conditions (here: no exposure to asbestos); T-36/89: Under the SR officials are to undergo a medical check-up every year. The medical service is under a duty to warn the official of the existence of any illness revealed and to alert him to a behaviour posing a threat to his health. The failure constitutes a service-related fault and renders the organisation liable; 169/83 and 136/84: Traffic accident on an authorised mission in car of the organisation. Negligence on the part of the organisation in the maintenance of the car was established. Entitlement to additional compensation not covered by the organisation's invalidity scheme.

## X. The right to an effective remedy and to a fair trial

The immunity of IO from individual national jurisdiction and execution within the scope of their official activities (functional immunity) does not release them from the fundamental right to an effective legal remedy and to a fair trial as enshrined in international conventions (Art. 8 UDHR; Art. 47 CFREU; Art. 6 and 13 EConHR) (for more details see the "human rights handbook" of the CoE on protecting the right to a fair trial under the EConHR).

In the view of the ECHR the right to a fair trial which comprises the right of access to the courts holds a "prominent place" in a democratic society (Judgment Waite and Kennedy vs. Germany, Application No. 26083/94, point 67). It is the "keystone in the arch of the legal community" (Rengeling, para 947: "Schlußstein im Gewölbe der Rechtsgemeinschaft").

The right to an independent and fair trial forms an integral part of the general legal principles of law applicable to the international civil service (see, for example, CJEU Judgment F-40/05 para. 122, 124). It is also stipulated in the SR of IO (Art. 90 et seq. EU-SR; Reg. 11.1 and Rule 11 UN-SR; Art. 59 et seq. CoE-SR; Art. 106 et seq. EPO-SR), sometimes it is even codified in the primary law of an IO (see, for example, Art. 270 TFEU; Art. 13 EPO-EPC).

Since IO do not as a rule waive their immunity from national jurisdiction they have to provide for another effective legal remedy, i.e. arbitration (for more details see under "immunity").

In disputes with their staff, IO not only enjoy immunity but also act like a substitute state based on their sovereignty in personnel matters. This is why IO provide for legal remedy in disputes with their employees through their own judicial bodies, the international administrative tribunals (in some smaller IO sometimes referred to as "appeals boards", not to be confused with the internal appeals boards competent for giving a preliminary legal opinion). The final responsibility for the efficiency of the judicial remedy remains, however, with the IO as a legal entity. The legislature of the IO, acting on a proposal by the secretariat, has an obligation to ensure effective legal protection.

The following (non-exhaustive) areas of possible deficiencies in providing effective legal remedy to the staff may be identified.

– Limited jurisdiction

International tribunals are courts of limited jurisdiction. They are bound in their judicature by the mandatory provisions of their respective statute set up by the legislative organ of the IO (ILOAT Judgments 2657, 1964, 1554, 803, 621, 339, 67).

It is constant case law that the ILOAT, based on its statute excludes candidates participating in a general competition for a vacancy from its jurisdiction (Judgments 2657, 933). In Judgment 2657 para. 6 (case *Klausecker*), the Tribunal held that the EPO "should seek a solution affording the complainant access to a court either by waiving its immunity or by submitting the dispute to arbitration" (see under Excursus below). It may be added that the CJEU holds in constant case law that complaints lodged by candidates for a vacancy at an EU institution are admissible.

A similar gap in the legal protection of staff members by the ILOAT results from the absence of a provision for the suspending of operations or enforcement (application for interim measures, ILOAT Judgment 2623 para. 2: The Tribunal has no authority to issue interim injunctions) whereas the CJEU may adopt interim measures (Art. 156 et seq. rules of procedure of the GC).

– Execution of judgments

The final rulings of international administrative tribunals (for one-tier and two-tier justice systems, see below under CJEU, UNDT and UNAT) carry the authority of *res iudicata* and the organisation has to give effect to the judgments. This is an obligation assumed by recognising the jurisdiction of the tribunal. If an organisation does not give immediate effect to the judgment the only means of ensuring execution of its judgments is to order payment of penalties (e.g. ILOAT Judgment 2806: EUR 10,000 per month of delay; 1362: CHF 10,000 per month of delay) since international administrative tribunals do not dispose of their own institutions to enforce their judgments and are not empowered to avail themselves of the enforcement bodies of the member states.

– Excessive delays in court proceedings

Art. 6(1) EConHR guarantees the right to a fair trial "within a reasonable time" considering all circumstances of a case (above all its complexity). In July 2015, the ILOAT was facing 450 pending cases. The ILOAT delivers about 100 judgments per year. In 2015 it rendered, however, a total of 167 judgments (see more in detail ILO doc. GB.325/PFA/9/1 (Rev) of 15 October 2015). (For more details see under Excursus below, Judgment of the Hague Regional Court, Appeal of 30 September 2014 in case Verveer v. EPO). It remains to be seen whether the ILOAT will take measures to avoid excessive delays in court proceedings with the financial and logistic support by the IO concerned. (See also the draft decision of the Governing Body of the ILO in point 13 of ILO doc. GB.325/PFA/9/1 (Rev)).

## XI. Excursus: Immunity of international organisations from national jurisdiction in staff matters

For more than a decade the immunity of IO from national jurisprudence has been a topic of international public law doctrine and addressed by the ECHR and several national Supreme Courts. This especially holds good for the jurisdiction in staff matters (see, for example, Hailbronner, de Cooker/Süss, Reinisch/Weber, Reinisch: The Immunity, Reinisch: Challenging Acts).

### *1. The jurisprudence of the ECHR*

IO are not a party to the EConHR (an exception is now provided for the EU in Art. 59(2) EConHR as amended by Art. 17(1) of Protocol No. 14). The EU is required under Art. 6(2) TEU to accede to the EConHR. The negotiation process for the accession started mid-2010. A draft agreement has, however, been declared incompatible with EU law by the CJEU (Opinion 2/13 of 18 December 2015).

Staff members of IO cannot, therefore, directly impugn the decision of an IO or its judicial organ before the ECHR. Such complaints are declared by the ECHR as incompatible *ratione personae* with the provision of the EConHR (see the decision *Boivin v. 34 Member states of the CoE*, Application No. 73250/01 of 9 September 2008, a complaint directed against a judgment of the ILOAT concerning an individual labour dispute with Eurocontrol).

Only if a member state of the EConHR has been "involved directly or indirectly in a dispute" between an IO and an official can an act or omission of a member state be considered as engaging its responsibility under the EConHR (case "Boivin", cited above). This is primarily the case if the official has exhausted "all domestic remedies" against a member state (Art. 35(1) EConHR) for not having assumed its responsibilities under the Convention when transferring part of its sovereignty to the IO as regards both the protection of fundamental rights of the official and the judicial "mechanisms controlling their observance" (case "Boivin", cited above).

Unlike in the *Boivin* case in the leading judgments *Waite and Kennedy v. Germany* (Judgment of 18 February 1999, Application No. 26083/94) and *Beer and Regan vs. Germany* (Judgment of 18 February 1999, Application No. 28934/95) both applications were declared admissible but unfounded.

In the Waite and Kennedy case the applicants argued that under German Labour Law they had acquired the status of employees of ESA after their contracts as temporary employees had expired. The German labour courts and the German Federal Constitutional Court rejected the applicant's appeal for adjudication. They held that the internal acts of ESA in staff matters could not be regarded as the acts of a public authority within the meaning of Art. 19(4) of the German Basic Law (Grundgesetz) and that ESA enjoyed immunity from jurisdiction in staff matters. The ECHR assumed jurisdiction and declared that the right to a court which is embedded in Art. 6(1) EConHR was not absolute, but may be subject to limitations. The immunity from national jurisdiction "is a long-standing practice established in the interest of a good working" of an IO free from unilateral interference of individual governments. This is a "legitimate objective" for the "limitation placed on Art. 6" EConHR. To read Art. 6(1) EConHR "as necessarily requiring the application of national legislation in such matters ... would ... thwart the proper functioning of international organisations ..." (Waite and Kennedy, cited above, para. 72). The limitations may, however, not impair the very essence of the right to a fair trial, they must pursue a legitimate aim and there must be a reasonable relationship of proportionality between the means employed and the aim sought to be achieved.

In the present case the court found that the applicants had reasonable alternative means available to protect their right to a fair trial. They could have recourse to the appeals board of ESA or could seek redress as temporary workers from their employer before German labour courts. The court did, however, not provide a detailed analysis as to whether the appeals board conforms with the international standard of procedural justice.

In the Beer and Regan case the ECHR reached the same conclusion on the merits as in the case of Waite and Kennedy. In this case, however, the appellants, after having appealed before the ESA's appeals board without success, seized the ECHR again which declared the application irreceivable (Beer and Regan v. Germany and the member states of ESA, Application No. 70009/1, decision of 15 May 2003) because the application was manifestly ill-founded (Art. 35(3) EConHR) since other means of legal process were available to the applicants as they had been made aware in the previous judgment rendered in this regard.

In the decision A.L. v. Italy (Application No. 41387/98) delivered on 11 May 2000 the court was of the opinion that the possibility offered to NATO staff members to file an appeal with the appeals board of NATO was a reasonable means to protect the right to a fair trial as stipulated in Art. 6 EConHR. The findings of the court were based on the following considerations:

- the members of the appeals board are independent, they are neither members of the secretariat nor of the Council;
- the members are appointed for a term of three years among the persons of recognised competence;
- the procedure before the board is contradictory;
- the decisions of the board are motivated;
- in the proceedings before the board the complainant was represented by three attorneys and he did not call the proceedings into question;
- holding the deliberations of the Board *in camera* may be justified in the interest of public order and national security, because the activities of NATO are in the military field.

The court, therefore, concluded from this analysis that the requirements of Art. 6 EConHR were met. It declared the application as manifestly ill-founded (Art. 35(3) EConHR and rejected it as inadmissible (Art. 35(4) EConHR).

In the *Boivin* decision (cited above) the complaints were essentially directed against the relevant ILOAT Judgment 2035 concerning a labour dispute with Eurocontrol. This dispute emanated from the internal legal order of Eurocontrol which enjoys a legal personality separate from that of its member states. Since the member states of the EConHR had not been involved directly or indirectly, their responsibilities under the Convention could not have been engaged. The ECHR, therefore, declared the complaints as incompatible with the EConHR and rejected the application as inadmissible.

In the decision *Connolly v. 15 Member states of the ECHR* of 9 December 2008 (Application No. 73274/01), the court found that the protection of fundamental rights by community law can be considered to be "equivalent" to that of Art. 6 and 13 EConHR.

In the decision *Rambus Inc. v. Germany* of 16 June 2009 (Application No. 40382/04; see also *Lenzing AG v. Germany* of 9 September 1998, Application No. 39025/97) relating to a company's complaint about the denial of a fair trial in the appeals procedure regarding its patent rights before the EPO, the Court explicitly referred to its jurisprudence concerning a labour law conflict between international civil servants and an IO.

In the decision *Perez v. Germany* of 6 January 2015 (Application No. 15521/08 the complainant, a former staff member of the UNDP, lodged an application about the unfair proceedings in UN staff disputes (Internal Appeal Board, UNAT). She held Germany responsible for breach of her right to a fair trial (failure of a public hearing and impartiality) under Art. 6 EConHR. She considered prior legal action before the German Federal Constitutional Court as futile and brought the case directly before the ECHR. The court held that it would be incompatible with the purpose and object of the EConHR if the contracting states by attributing immunities to an IO were absolved from their responsibility under the convention. The applicant was, however, not estopped from claiming access to the German courts and holding Germany responsible for its alleged failure to grant her access to the domestic courts. This was an effective remedy which she would have had to exhaust in accordance with Art. 35(1) and (4) EConHR.

In the decision *Klausecker v. Germany* of 6 January 2015 (Application No. 415/07) the complainant was refused employment with the EPO despite having passed all tests as a patent examiner, as he did not meet the physical requirements of the post. In its Judgment 2657 of 11 July 2007 the ILOAT declared his appeal as irreceivable based on a lack of jurisdiction since applicants for a post in an IO who have not been recruited are barred from access to the ILOAT. The tribunal noted, however, that the judgment "creates a legal vacuum" and considered it highly desirable that the organisation seeks a solution affording the complainant access to court "either by waiving its immunity or by submitting the dispute to arbitration".

The EPO did not waive its immunity and no agreement could be reached regarding the establishment of arbitration proceedings. In these circumstances, the complainant filed a complaint with the German Federal Constitutional Court. In an order of 22 June 2006, the Court declared the complaint as inadmissible since the decision of the EPO remained an internal act of the IO with no consequences for the German legal order. In addition, the applicant had at his disposal reasonable alternative means to protect his right to an effective legal remedy (ILOAT and arbitration offered by the EPO). On 22 December 2006 Mr Klausecker lodged an application against Germany before the ECHR (Application No. 415/07). This application was dismissed on 6 January 2015. The Court held that the right to a fair trial under Art. 6 EConHR was sufficiently safeguarded by the availability of the arbitration offered by the EPO as a reasonable alternative means to the proceedings before domestic courts.

### *2. The German Federal Constitutional Court (Bundesverfassungsgericht)*

In its leading decision „*Eurocontrol II*“ of 10 November 1981 (BVerfG E 59, 63–95; for an English translation see the website of the University of Texas at Austin School of Law, Institute for Transnational Law), the German Federal Constitutional Court had to decide whether the judicial protection of the staff of Eurocontrol in labour disputes with the organisation warranted by the ILOAT met the minimum standards of the rule of law as enshrined in the German Basic Law (Grundgesetz) and the international minimum standard of elementary procedural justice as derived from the developed system of the rule of law and from the procedural law of international courts.

The court found that actions by Eurocontrol in staff matters were not matters of (German) public authority in the sense of Art. 19(4) German Basic Law. These acts remain within the autonomous internal sphere accorded to IO in order to fulfil their tasks without interference by individual member states. German courts have no international subsidiary competence (Auffangszuständigkeit) if the judicial protection appears inadequate as compared with national requirements. In such a case, however, the authority under Art. 24 German Basic Law to transfer part of its sovereign powers to IO might have been transgressed.

In the present case, the court came to the conclusion that the status and the Rules of Procedure of the ILOAT corresponded to the international minimum standards of elementary procedural justice and did not altogether contradict the minimum standards of the rule of law embedded in the German Basic Law.

The court further ruled that the ILOAT was a genuine judicial organ. It was set up by an act of international law and its decisions in relation to the objects of a complaint are taken on the basis of powers established by law and in accordance with lawful proceedings based exclusively on codified law and legal principles. Its judges are bound by independence and impartiality.

All these conditions were met in the case under scrutiny. The access to the tribunal was not made unreasonably difficult. The distance of the tribunal from the working place of the complainant and the limitation of the languages of procedure were reasonable for an international staff member of a European-based

IO. The right to a hearing and a minimum degree of procedural equality were guaranteed.

In its order of 3 July 2006 (case No. 2 BvR 1458/03, see the publication website "Juris") the Constitutional Court had to adjudicate on the complaint of members of the EPO trade union challenging a decision about unimpeded access to the internal e-mail system of the EPO. In its Judgment 2228 of 16 July 2003 the ILOAT had already dismissed an appeal filed by the same complainant concerning the same facts as being without merits.

In its order, the Constitutional Court further refined its position adopted in the Eurocontrol II decision with respect to the legal protection of EPO staff provided by the internal appeal proceedings and by the ILOAT. It reaffirmed that those proceedings correspond essentially to the standards of German basic law and the international minimum standards of elementary procedural justice. The proceedings before the ILOAT were independent of the proceedings before the internal appeals committee. The tribunal decided "on the basis of its legally defined powers and under rules of due process" and on the subject matter of the proceedings submitted to it only in accordance with legal rules and principles. The judges of the tribunal were obliged to be independent and impartial.

Against this background the complainants had failed to substantiate their claim that there was a structural deficit as far as legal protection was concerned, which should have been dealt with by the federal organ responsible for foreign issues.

### 3. *The Supreme Court of the Netherlands (Hoge Raad)*

In its Judgment of 23 October 2009 (*Anonymous v. EPO*, case No. 08/00118, Nederlandse Jurisprudentie 2009, 527), the Supreme Court ruled on the immunity of the EPO from national jurisdiction in a labour law dispute with one of its former officials. The complainant was employed by the EPO as a patent examiner. When his permanent invalidity was established the EPO paid him a lump sum equal to 2.75 times his annual basic salary and a monthly pension.

Not satisfied with the amounts paid he filed an internal appeal and requested moral damages for work-related invalidity. The EPO finally rejected his request based on the unanimous recommendation of the internal appeals committee. He then brought an action against the EPO before the Hague District Court. The court declared by Judgment of 3 August 2006 that the Netherlands courts had no jurisdiction on this case. By Judgment of 28 September 2007 the Hague Regional Court confirmed the Judgment of the District Court.

The Supreme Court held that the EPO, not being a party to the EConHR, was not directly bound by Art. 6 EConHR. Being, however, founded by member states which are bound by the Convention when transferring part of their sovereignty to an IO, the EPO is indirectly bound to offer comparable means of judicial protection to their staff members (*nemo plus iuris* argument), "which implies a less rigorous test".

The right under Art. 6 EConHR to a public hearing is not absolute. The prior hearing during the internal appeals procedure is also relevant in deciding whether a written procedure is sufficient.

Art. 6 EConHR "requires only one judicial body with full jurisdiction in a system of legal redress". The ILOAT is "an independent and impartial judicial body which even reviews cases in the light of fundamental human rights". The ILOAT exercises its jurisdiction effectively, it is "readily accessible" and its proceedings do not take so long as to deny effective judicial protection.

The Supreme Court, therefore, found that the complainant had an effective judicial protection available within the autonomous structure of the EPO which was equivalent to that required under Art. 6 EConHR and that the functional immunity of the EPO must be upheld.

#### *4. The Belgian Supreme Court (Cour de Cassation)*

In the *"Siedler"* case the Supreme Court decided on the immunity of the WEU (an IO with a very small number of staff which ceased its operations in 2010 and was closed in 2011) from Belgian jurisdiction (Judgment case No. S.04.0129F of 21 December 2009). Mrs. Siedler who was employed by the WEU in Belgium requested compensation for the termination of her employment without notice. Not satisfied with the judgment of the appeals board (the international administrative tribunal of WEU) she lodged an appeal with the Labour Court of Brussels. The court held that the internal judicial protection by the WEU did not come up to the standards required by Art. 6 EConHR and decided on the merits of the case. The Brussels Higher Labour Court upheld the judgment under appeal. It confirmed that the grant of privileges and immunities to IO is generally accepted in the interest of an unimpeded functioning of IO from the unilateral interference of individual governments. IO remain, however, subject to the rule of law and they are *inter alia* bound to respect the right to a fair trial. The court examined whether Mrs. Siedler had reasonable alternative means of effectively protecting her right.

The court recognised the functions of WEU's appeals board as being to some extent compatible with the requirements of Art. 6 EConHR. The board did perform judicial functions, it was competent to hear disputes, it could annul decisions and order the grant of damages and its producings were adversarial. On the other hand, there were no provisions for the enforcement of decisions, the hearings were secret, the decisions were not pronounced in public and the judges were, appointed for a term of two years only. In view of the appointment procedure and the short term of office, their independence and impartiality was doubtful. The court concluded that the immunity of the WEU was not accompanied by an effective means of legal redress. The court, therefore, assumed its jurisdiction and applied Belgian Labour Law.

The WEU appealed to the Supreme Court. The court partially annulled the judgment of the Higher Labour Court based on the reason that Belgian Law instead of the SR of the WEU, which takes precedence over provisions of national law, was applied. As to admissibility of Belgian jurisdiction, the Supreme Court did not enter into a detailed analysis of the requirements of a judicial protection for WEU staff members equivalent to that provided for in Art. 6 EConHR. It simply reiterated one of the findings of the Higher Labour Court that the power to appoint the members of the appeals board was delegated to the Intergovernmental Committee which appointed them for a period of two years only and, therefore, their independence was not sufficiently secured and Belgian jurisdiction had to be applicable. These findings have been heavily criticised for "overzealously" applying the criteria of Art. 6 EConHR to international administrative tribunals (see P. Schmitt).

### 5. *Other Supreme and Appeal Courts*

The French Supreme Court (Cour de Cassation) recognised the immunity from national jurisdiction in staff disputes, e.g. in cases of the OECD and the WEU (for details see *de Cooker/Süss* and *Reinisch*, The immunity, p. 296 et seq.). The Italian Supreme Court (Corte di Cassazione) recognised the immunity from national jurisdiction in staff disputes e.g. in the cases of the FAO and the MFO (for details see *de Cooker/Süss* and *Reinisch*, The immunity, p. 296 et seq.)

On 16 July 2013 (case No. 1223887/12–31860) the District Court of the Hague (NL) had ruled that in the case Verveer v. EPO, the EPO did violate the right to afford a legal remedy in conformity with Art. 6 EConHR. The Judgment was essentially based on an e-mail from the registrar of the ILOAT stating that in view of the high workload of the tribunal it would take around 15 years before the case of the complainant would be heard. In its Judgment of 30 September 2014 (case No. 200.136.028/01) the Regional Court of Appeal set this Judgment aside on the presumption that the ILOAT would do what was needed to prevent unacceptable delays.

In a Judgment of 17 February 2015 the Appeal Court of the Hague (NL) (case No. 200.141.812/01) adjucated in a case of the EPO v. the EPO trade union (SUEPO) that the Appeal was receivable since the protection of rights of SUEPO guaranteed by Art. 6 EConHR was "manifestly deficient". SUEPO had no access to the ILOAT (undisputed) and the EPO did not afford arbitration. Thus the right of SUEPO to an effective legal remedy to enforce collective rights was impaired. As to the merits, the court held that the actions of SUEPO were restricted (restrictive definition of the term "strike", no right to collective bargaining). In its judgment of 20 January 2017, the Supreme Court of the Netherlands set aside the judgment of the Hague Court of Appeals and declared that the Netherlands courts had no jurisdiction to hear the union's claims against the EPO (case No. 15/02186).

## C. Objective legal principles of the international civil service law

### I. The derivation

In addition to the recognition of fundamental human rights there are also objective legal principles which are applied by the international administrative tribunals as a source of law of the international civil service.

These principles are, as a rule, not stipulated in the SR of IO (for exception see, for example, Art. 85 EU-SR: undue payment; Art. 25 EU-SR: stating the grounds of a decision).

The international administrative tribunals derived these legal principles from the "rule of law" which is enshrined in international conventions (e.g. Art. 2 TEU, Recitals in the preambles of the UDHR, the EConHR and the CFREU), is provided for in most national constitutions and applied by national courts, and is considered as anathema to arbitrariness (see, for example, ILOAT Judgment 759 para. 3; UN doc. S/2004/616; Elliott, p. 101).

These principles have to be respected by all organs of an IO *inter alia* in the setting-up, the implementation and the application of the SR. Among these principles are the principle of legality of the administration, the principles of legal certainty, of proportionality, of good faith, and of good administration.

The objective legal principle and the fundamental human rights of staff members are to be understood as forming an integral part of the rule of law in a broader sense (Rengeling, p. 63 with references to the jurisprudence of the ECHR).

### II. The principle of legality

#### *1. The administration*

##### a) General

Although the principle of legality is binding for all actors of an IO it is of particular importance for the head of the secretariat, as the appointing authority of most staff members of the organisation and the responsible authority for all administrative decisions in their employment relationship. It basically results from the balance of power of an IO that the administration is bound to respect the SR set or at least approved by the legislative organ of the organisation and by the general legal principles applicable to the international civil service law as a whole, whereas "the suitability or efficiency" of a decision is not subject to a legal review (Schermers/Blokker, § 915).

Within the field of objective legal principles applied by the international administrative tribunals, the principle of the legality of administration is characterised by a specific feature. In contrast to other legal principles applied by the international administrative tribunals the principle of legality of the administration is rarely referred to explicitly in their rulings (for exceptions see, for example, ILOAT Judgment 825 para. 18: "The rule is that an Administration is bound to comply with the law", likewise: ILOAT Judgment 2252 para. 2; the CJEU stated in Judgment 42 and 49/59 that the principle of respect for legal certainty could not be applied in an absolute manner but its application "must be combined with that of the principle of legality"). The obvious reason for this is to be seen in the competence (or even the "raison d'etre") of international administrative tribunals which is to pass judgments on the legality of an administrative act adversely affecting the appellant. This legal principle is, therefore, already enshrined in the constituent instruments of the international administrative tribunals on the primary law of the IO (see, for example, Art. 263 TFEU: "The Court of Justice of the European Union shall review the legality … of acts … of the Commission …"; Art. II.1 ILOAT Statute: "… alleging non-observance, in substance or in form, of the terms of appointment of officials … and of such provisions of the Staff Regulations as are applicable to the case"; Art. 2(1)(a) UNDT Statute: " … alleged to be in non-compliance with the terms of appointment or the contract of employment. The terms "contract" and "terms of appointment" include all pertinent regulations …"; Art. II(1) IMFAT: "… challenging the legality of an administrative act …"). It would, therefore, be redundant, if the tribunals were to make reference to the principle of legality in their rulings.

The principle of legality of administration is, however, regularly referred to explicitly by the international administrative tribunals, if the case under review involves a margin of discretion, or a value judgment or if a decision is based on a misuse of authority (below b) and c)). In cases of discretion and value judgments, the judiciary power is restricted to scrutinising whether the administration observed the bounds of latitude vested in it.

### b) Reasonable discretion and value judgments

In the exercise of his administrative powers the head of administration of an IO is in most cases not legally bound to take one specific action or decision but he can choose between several potential courses of action. The authorisation is to be found either in the explicit wording of the rulings set up by the legislature of the organisation or results from the intrinsic nature of the administrative action.

The administrative discretion or value judgment is not in principle precluded from appellate review (see ILOAT Judgment 2312: The fact that a decision is discretionary does not take it outside of the tribunal's jurisdiction). However, the international administrative tribunals may exercise only a limited review, since the administration is normally better placed to evaluate the interests involved. The review of the judicature is restricted to verifying that the administration did not commit a "manifest error of assessment or misuse of powers" (see, for example, CJEU Judgment T-7/01, para. 50, 62) or to the question of whether the administration "has remained within reasonable bounds and has not used its power in a manifestly incorrect way" (CJEU Judgment F-57/06 para. 44). If the administration used its discretionary power the tribunal will ordinarily not substitute its assessment for that of the organisation (see, for example, ILOAT Judgment 2762 para. 17; see also CJEU Judgment T-120/01 and T-300/01 para. 219: not put itself in the place of the administrative authority).

The general legal principle that warrants the exercise of a reasonable administrative discretion and value judgment is probably the principle most frequently relied upon by international administrative tribunals. The thesaurus of ILOAT's Triblex database shows 581 (as of the year 2015) extracts registered under the keyword "discretion".

Each tribunal has developed a standard clause to be used as yardstick for the judicial review of discretionary decisions and value judgments taken by the administration of an IO.

The ILOAT's standard clause reads (see, for example, Judgment 3372 para. 12): "The Tribunal will interfere with such a decision only if it was taken without authority or in breach of a rule of form or of procedure, or if it rested on an error of fact or of law, or if some essential fact was overlooked, or if there was abuse of authority, or if clearly mistaken conclusions have been drawn from the evidence".

The standard clauses applied by the CJEU have a more abstract reading. The review is confined to establishing that there has been no "manifest error of assessment" or "misuse of powers" (Judgment F-112/06 para. 86, 92 and similarly C-3/84 para. 25). A measure "is vitiated by misuse of powers only if it appears, on the basis of objective, relevant and consistent evidence, to have been taken with the exclusive or main purpose of achieving an end other than that stated or evading a procedure specifically prescribed …" (Judgment F-104/09 para. 95 and Judgment F-105/05 para. 11 and Judgment T-146/89 para. 88).

The breach of the principle of reasonable discretion regularly involves the violation of other general legal principles of the international civil service law, such as the principles of equal treatment, of hierarchy or norms or of *patere legem* (see the jurisprudence below).

International administrative tribunals do not ordinarily distinguish between "discretionary decisions" which are mostly characterised by using the words "may" or "should" in the operational part of the ruling and the "value judgment" in the factual part of the ruling (see ILOAT Judgment 608 para. 6; CJEU Order F-155/12 para. 58).

The ILOAT held in Judgment 3006 para. 7: "Assessment of merit is an exercise that involves a value judgment". It is usual to refer to decisions or recommendations involving a value judgment as "discretionary … because of the nature of a value judgment, the grounds on which a decision invoking a judgment of that kind may be reviewed are limited to those applicable to discretionary decisions". (See also ILOAT Judgment 2976 para. 8: "… a value judgment akin to that involved in a discretionary decision"; ILOAT Judgment 2357 para. 4: "It is not strictly accurate to describe a decision as to the application of Article 71(2) [EPO-SR] as discretionary. The question whether a particular school or university corresponds to "a child's educational stage" is essentially a question of fact, albeit one that may, in some circumstances permit a value judgment. However, because of the nature of that question, a decision under Article 71(2) is subject to limited review on the same grounds as a discretionary decision properly so called". Only in a limited number of rulings does the ILOAT, therefore, use the term "value judgment" (see ILOAT Judgments 2826, 2393, 529). The ILOAT'S Triblex database does even not contain the keyword "value judgment".

Also in the judgments of the CJEU the terms "discretion" and "value judgment" are used inter-changeably and review by the judicature is restricted to manifest errors (see, for example, CJEU Judgments F-114/07 para. 111: staff report; F-34/07 para. 69, 71: career development report; T-285/04 para. 99: career development report).

If discretion is granted to the head of administration by a rule or by the intrinsic nature of a decision the latitude given must be exercised. The failure to exercise discretion is a manifest error of assessment which invalidates the action taken (see, for example, ILOAT Judgments 1371 para. 11 and 608 para. 7).

The exercise of discretion without a discretionary power leads to a decision tainted by illegality (see, for example, ILOAT Judgments 1616, 271).

The fact that the judicial review of a discretionary decision or a value judgment is limited does not exempt the administration from its general obligation to state the reasons for its decision (ILOAT Judgment 1235). The Tribunal must be put in a position to evaluate whether the administration has remained within reasonable bounds and did not use its powers in a manifestly incorrect way (see, for example, ILOAT Judgment 2125 para. 5).

### c) Areas of judicial discretion

Due to the large number of decisions on discretion and value judgments the presentation of cases is sorted into groups extending both to Judgments of the ILOAT and to Judgments/Orders of the CJEU.

#### *aa) Appointment, promotion, selection board*

ILOAT Judgments

3084: It is constant case law that an *ad personam* promotion lies at the discretion of the DG. The failure to exercise discretion was a legal flaw as was the involvement in FICSA; 3043: A promotion should not be granted as redress for an alleged injury; 3006: The grounds for review of a value judgment (promotions) are limited to those applicable to discretionary decisions. The principle of equality requires that all candidates are assessed by reference to the staff reports of the same period; 3005: Wide discretion to convert a fixed-term contract appointment to a permanent one (see also similar discretion in relation to the following conversions; 2308: Short-term to fixed-term; 2138: Fixed-term to long-term; 1349: Fixed-term to indefinite); 2978: Correct exercise of discretion, the complainant's profile did not match the advertised post; 2884: The use of an assessment centre was not included in the vacancy notice, flawed discretion in the determination of the selection procedure; 2869: Abuse of discretion, all decisions regarding promotion or non-promotion of staff union representatives must be and must appear to be, taken impartially; 2835: The change in the composition of the selection board did not change the terms of the competition; 2834: Discretion not flawed if candidates with higher potential in managerial skills were preferred over those with higher seniority and higher rating but fewer managerial abilities; 2706: The promotions are given at discretion but are governed by strict procedure; the dilatory attitude to the long-standing request for promotion based *inter alia* on the missing of job descriptions for several years obliges the organisation to review the application for promotion; 2393: A selection process requires a high degree of judgment with which the Tribunal will interfere only if a serious defect is demonstrated (1827); 2272: Promotion disregarding the higher ranking rules approved by the Council is an error of law and an abuse of authority; 2221: A promotion is a discretionary decision, the mere satisfaction of the necessary criteria does not ordinarily confer a right to promotion (see, for example, 2173, 1973, 1827, 1355, 1179, 1137); 2074: Discretion in the determination of equal competence by the selection board; 2040: The members of a selection board are best placed in assessing the ability of candidates. A decision to make an appointment is a discretionary one (see also, for example, 1730, 1185, 1184); 2004: The gender cannot be a factor in the choice of a candidate. Unequal treatment (discretion flawed) if one candidate is interviewed by video and another in person; 1968: The organisation had committed itself only to making promotions which had been approved and recommended by the promotion board; this qualifies the discretion of the President; 1827: In a selection process the tribunal will interfere only if a serious defect is demonstrated; 1771: No right to an external expert enquiry to determine qualifications for a post; 1733: Failure to exercise discretion, decision based on the veto of a member state; 1564: Generally to the discretion of a selection committee; 1355: Promotion wholly or mainly based on considerations of sex would unquestionably be unlawful; 1204: By exercising discretion in a promotion procedure an organisation must abide by its own rules and whatever decision it takes it will be subject to judicial review.

CJEU Judgments/Orders

F-104/09: A decision not to promote an official is vitiated by misuse of powers only if it appears, on the basis of objective, relevant and consistent evidence, to have been taken with the exclusive or main purpose of achieving an end other than that stated or evading a procedure specifically described by the Treaty for dealing with the circumstances of the case (see also F-105/05; C-310/04; C-342/03; T-282/03); F-82/08: The appointing authority has a wide discretion for the purpose of finding candidates for an appointment (see also C-121/01 P); F-145/06: Discretion of the selection board. In the review of legality the judicature must confine itself to ascertaining whether the decision of the selection board was free from manifest errors (see also T-145/02; T-332/01; T-214/99; 417/85); F-73/06: The assessment of a selection board that a candidate has failed constitutes the expression of a value judgment. It is subject to a judicial review only in the event of a manifest error (see also T-336/02; T-193/00); F-57/06: Wide discretion when considering the comparative merits of officials eligible for promotion. The judicial review is confined to the question of whether the administration "has remained within reasonable bounds and has not used its power in a manifestly incorrect way" (see also F-95/06; T-132/03; C-58/91); F-123/05: The exercise of discretion with respect to the holding of competitions for appointment must be compatible with the mandatory provisions of the SR; T-156/89: Wide discretion of the appointing authority and the staff committee in assessing the abilities of the persons to be appointed as members of the selection board.

### *bb) Benefits/allowances*

ILOAT Judgments

2357: Education allowance, the decision as to whether a school or university corresponds to a "child's educational stage" is in some circumstances a value judgment. It is, therefore, subject to the same limited review as a discretionary decision (see also 1837, 1836, 1835); 2193: Benefits and allowances for a dependant spouse of the same gender are discretionary decisions (but see now: 3080, 2860, 2760, 2550, 2549); 1814: Dependent allowance; discretion as to who may be considered as a dependent child, the staff member must, however, be made aware of any criteria the administration is applying; 485: Travel expenses for a locally recruited staff. The administration cannot exercise unfettered discretion (see also: 484, 483); 422: The question of whether a child is *de facto* fully dependent on the complainant falls within the discretionary authority of the administration.

### *cc) Disciplinary measures*

ILOAT Judgments

3295: Proportionality of a disciplinary measure; 3035: The suspension from duties in a case of serious misconduct lies within the discretion of the DG. The duration was beyond a reasonable time limit (see also 2365, 1927); 2944: Discretion to determine the severity of a disciplinary measure; 2899: Disciplinary measure flawed, right to be heard must be respected in an especially rigorous manner; 2845: Refusal to extend employment beyond the statutory age was a hidden disciplinary action; 2773: A disciplinary authority has discretion to determine the severity of a disciplinary measure. The measure adopted must not manifestly be out of proportion to the offence (see also 1984, 207); 2752: Warning and reprimand are illegal actions in case of performance-related matters (see also 1405); 2698: Suspension from duties beyond a reasonable time; investigations not conducted with the dispatch required by the case law; 2659: Reassignment as a hidden disciplinary sanction; 2656: In determining whether a disciplinary action is disappropriate to the offence, both objective and subjective features are to be taken into account; 2496: In disciplinary proceedings the right of the staff member to a fully adversarial procedure must be scrupulously respected; 2494: The special mission of Eurocontrol in air navigation justifies a penalty for a sudden stoppage of activity (but see 2493: measures must not restrict the exercise of collective rights of staff in such a way as to deprive them of all substance); 2391: The disciplinary sanction was set aside since the statement of the appeals board that the principle of proportionality was infringed was ignored by the administration; 2351: Uncertainty of a diploma was not established, the cancellation of the disciplinary sanction entails that of the decision of non-renewal of contract; 2261: Disciplinary measure; the DG failed to give reasons for disagreeing with the proposal of the appeals committee; 2229: A transfer which is also disciplinary in nature must comply with the safeguards applicable to disciplinary actions; 2190: Discretion in the lifting of the immunity of a staff member; 2114: The imposition of a mild disciplinary measure like a reprimand is a discretionary decision; 1724: The tribunal exercises its power of review and decides whether the reason for the dismissal were the interests of the fund or the conduct of the complainant. In the latter case disciplinary proceedings should have been initiated; 1445: The choice of a particular sort of disciplinary measures is at the discretion of the DG.

CJEU Judgments/Orders

T-120/01 and T-300/01: In the case of a manifest error of assessment as regards the appropriateness of a disciplinary measure it is not for the court to put itself in the place of the disciplinary authority; C-252/97: It is for the appointing authority to choose the appropriate disciplinary measure to be imposed and this choice is subject to censure only in the event of manifest error or misuse of powers (see also: 228/83); T-146/89: Since there is not a fixed relationship between the various sorts of failure by the officials to comply with their obligation and the disciplinary measures available, the penalty imposed must be based on an appraisal by the appointing authority (see also F-106/11; 403/85); T-26/89: The determination of the sanction to be imposed in each individual case must be based on a comprehensive appraisal by the appointing authority of all the particular facts and the aggravating or mitigating circumstances; 13–69: The court cannot criticise the discretionary power of the appointing authority to choose the adequate disciplinary measure, unless the measure imposed is disproportionate to the facts found against the official.

### dd) *Dismissal/termination of contract*

ILOAT Judgments

2232: The decision of the plenary organ to terminate the appointment of the DG must be viewed as an administrative decision and is, therefore, receivable. The internal appeals board is, however, not competent to hear the complaint of the DG. To concede that the plenary organ has unfettered discretion to terminate the appointment would constitute an unacceptable violation of the principle of due process; 1724: There is discretion vested in the President to end an appointment in the organisation without resort to a disciplinary process. The discretion is, however, not unfettered. The reasons must be given to enable a judicial review. The organisation's interests are paramount but mutual confidence must be respected and staff treated fairly (see also; 1496, 1234, 901); 1583: No termination for poor performance without proper warning and giving an opportunity to do better; 1441: Misconduct, disciplinary measures; 1250: Summary dismissal for misconduct; 1249: Error of discretion, decision influenced by a member state; 1238: Error of discretion, reinstatement ordered; 475: Unauthorised absence, the dismissal is justified; 351: Dismissal in case of confinement; 349: Dismissal out of proportion with the offence.

CJEU Judgments/Orders

F-74/06: Broad discretion to conclude contracts of engagement justifying dismissal in the case of wrongful conduct without the obligation to initiate disciplinary proceedings (case law cited); T-7/01: The authority has a wide discretion in respect of a dismissal of a temporary staff member in the case of a failure to comply with his obligations. The judicial review is restricted to verifying that there has been "no manifest error or misuse of powers" (case-law cited).

### ee) *Extension of retirement age limit*

ILOAT Judgments

2915: The decision to extend the retirement date beyond the normal retirement age is a value judgment which can be challenged on the same grounds as a discretionary decision (see the standard clause applicable to discretionary decision, see also 2669, 2513, 2377); 2845: The DG used this discretionary authority to refuse the extension of the age limit beyond the statutory age limit for purposes other than those for which it was intended. This is an abuse of authority; 2125: Discretion to extend the contract beyond the normal retirement age. The reason of the refusal based on "rejuvenation of the staff" is too general to constitute sufficient justification since it could be used systematically to circumvent the possibility of extending employment beyond the normal retirement age (see also: 267, 223, 204); 1143: The discretionary decision not to extend the employment relationship beyond the statutory retirement age was flawed. The DG should have taken into account the complainant's financial situation provided that that was not the exclusive factor and that the interests of the organisation were also taken into account (see also 358).

### *ff) Facilities granted to staff union*

ILOAT Judgments

1547: Latitude in affording facilities to the staff union may not hamper the freedom of speech or privacy of mail as an integral part of the freedom of association; 496: Discretion to alter the scope of the facilities extended to the staff association, but the modification must be properly justified. Illegality of censorship imposed by the administration.

### *gg) Leave*

ILOAT Judgments

2619: Discretion to grant special leave; 2052: Discretion to grant sick leave outside the place of residence; 1969: According to the SR the review of the home address for the purpose of home leave is a discretionary decision (see also: 1324, 1217, 525, 335); 1855: Discretion to grant special leave to attend a training course; 1680: Discretion to grant special leave does not stretch to the breach of rules or the general legal principles that safeguard the dignity of staff members (see also 809); 1472: Setting the home address for granting home leave is a discretionary decision.

### *hh) Immunity*

ILOAT Judgments

2190: The lifting of immunity from legal process is at the discretion of the head of administration and beyond the jurisdiction of the Tribunal since it involves relations between the organisation and a third party (see also: 3297, 1543, 933, 70, but see 2222: The complainant did not challenge the lifting of his immunity in itself but the circumstances in which the decision was taken, i.e. the right to be informed, his dignity and reputation); 1292: Discretion of the DG to determine whether a staff member should qualify as a diplomatic agent within the meaning of the instructions of the host state and whether he fits the given quota.

### *ii) Organisational measures*

(Change of career path, post classification, grading, assignment, job description, redefinition of functions, abolition of post, redivision of duties).

ILOAT Judgments

3589: Grading of a post is a matter of discretion (see also: 3082, 2927, 1281, 1067, 929); 2975: Decisions taken in relation to restructuring a reclassification of posts are discretionary ones (see also: 2856, 2807, 2742, 2562, 2510, 1779 with further references); 2514: Grading of staff members involves a value judgment as to the nature and responsibilities of the post (see also; 1495, 1281); 2373: The redefinition of a post and the modification of a job description and the qualifications required for a particular post are discretionary decisions (see also 2080); 2365: Suspension is at the discretion of the DG; 1729: Decisions on funding and reorganisation and abolishing a post are discretionary ones (see also 1231);

1614: Reforming the structure and abolition of posts are discretionary decisions; 1590: In the determination or alteration of the duties to be performed on a given post the organisation enjoys the widest discretion in matching duties to needs; 1495: A decision determining a career path is a discretionary one (see also 1415, 1412); 1398: Wide discretion of the organisation over the organisation of work; 1371: Reduction-in-force procedure; failure to exercise discretion (see also 608); 1152: Grading requires close familiarity with conditions in which a staff member works. The tribunal will not substitute its own assessment or direct that a new one be made unless it is satisfied on the evidence that there is a fatal flaw (see also 1067); 968: The attribution of duties, the nature of duties and the grading of posts are matters of discretion to appoint, transfer and promote staff; 648: Whether a candidate qualifies is a matter of discretion; 594: The totality of enumerated duties, taken in the light of the everyday functioning of the post, in all the circumstances surrounding such functioning, is decisive for the grading of the post; 529: The assessment of the type of work performed and the level of responsibility is a value judgment.

CJEU Judgments/Orders

F-16/12R: Reorganisation and reassignment, there is a wide discretion (see also: C-12/05P); F-4/09: Wide discretion in reassigning a staff member; T-572/08P: The grading of a post is a discretionary decision; F-90/07: Wide discretion of the appointing authority not to fill a vacant post but to reassign an official with his post (see also: 316/82 and 40/83); F-119/06: Wide discretion in the organisation of departments according to the tasks and the assignment of staff (see also: F-76/03; T-325/92); F-122/05: It would be a misuse of discretion to decide the level of a post after the notice of vacancy had been published (see also: T-10/94); T-82/95: Retirement of a high-ranking official in the interest of the service, wide discretion; T-108/89: The discretion in organisational measures is infringed if, taken together, after a change or reduction of responsibilities the remaining ones fall clearly short of those corresponding to grading of the post, taking account of their character, their importance and their scope; 280/87: A reassignment of duties is a managerial decision which does not oblige the administration to give the official concerned a hearing or to state the grounds on which the decision is based.

### *jj) Patere legem*

ILOAT Judgments

1968: The President committed himself in an instruction only to making promotions which have been approved and recommended by the promotion board. This discretionary power is, therefore, limited by this commitment; 1204: The exercise of discretion in promoting staff members is limited by the obligation of the organisation to abide by the rules (see also 1025); 1053: The interpretation of a provision by an organisation becomes binding if it has been followed over several years. When changing such an interpretation the principle of good faith has to be respected (see also 421).

### *kk) Probation*

ILOAT Judgments

3085: The decision not to confirm the appointment for unsatisfactory performance is a discretionary decision (see also 2558). Three principles have, however, to be respected: information about the evaluation criteria and the deficiencies, assistance to the staff member to improve and a clear warning that continuation of employment is in jeopardy; 2883: If a probationary period was flawed the tribunal will ordinarily order reinstatement as a probationer. If, however, a long time has elapsed since the termination of appointment, the tribunal will order compensation for loss of a valuable opportunity; 2845: Discretionary power abused for an act of retaliation; 2728: An organisation has the widest discretion to find out whether a probationer has the mettle to make a satisfactory career in an organisation (see also: 1386, 1246, 1161); 2646: A high degree of deference ought to be accorded to the organisation in the exercise of discretion regarding decisions in probationary matters (see also 1418, 1352, 1052); 2172: Based on a recommendation of the appeals board that the extension of the probationary period was flawed and that the complainant's appointment should have been confirmed. The tribunal will even substitute the discretionary decision and confirm the appointment.

CJEU Judgments/Orders

The CJEU Judgments/Orders follow the same line of discretion and judicial review as the ILOAT in cases of probationary decisions. See, for example, F-61/06; T-56/01 and 69/01; C-17/88; CJ 290/82.

### *ll) Renewal/extension of contract*

ILOAT Judgments

3257: Extension/renewal of contract is within the discretion of the administration but there is an obligation to state reasons; 2916: Discretion in establishing unsatisfactory performance, but principle of due process, i.e. warning, opportunity to do better must be respected; 2513: Extension of contract refused for undisclosed or purely arbitrary reasons; 2414: An adverse decision cannot be based on unsatisfactory performance if the organisation did not respect its own rules established to evaluate that performance (see also: 1298); 2350: The extension of an appointment is a matter of discretion. An organisation may not get rid of a staff member as it pleases, it has to give reasons. The tribunal may exercise only a limited power of review over such a decision (see also: 2175, 1290, 1273, 1128, 1052, 1047, 1044); 1730: Application of the normal selection procedure to staff members previously privileged by a special arrangement with a member state, as a precondition for the renewal of contract; 1617: Discretion, unfavourable appraisal justifies a shorter extension of contract; 1546: Non-renewal justified, sufficient warning; 1335: No fatal flaw shown by the decision not to renew a contract (see also 1332); 1317: Even where the SR say that a contract is *ipso facto* extinguished on expiry, non-renewal is to be treated as a distinct and challengeable administrative decision (see also 1040, 17). This requirement is an indispensable safeguard of security of employment in the international civil service which commonly only grants fixed-term appointments; 1312: Circumstances of private life are relevant only in so far as they may affect the performance of official duties. A decision not to renew a contract is illegal if the staff member was held against his will in his home country because he had started divorce proceedings.

CJEU Judgments/Orders

F-8/10: The renewal of a contract falls within the broad discretion of the competent authority and the review by the judicature is, therefore, limited to ascertaining that there has been no manifest error in the assessment of the interests of the service or misuse of powers (see also: F-35/07; F-38/06; T-7/01).

### *mm) Salary adjustment*

ILOAT Judgments

2632: A practice of salary adjustment, even where repeated, does not bind the organisation; 2095: Salary adjustment is discretionary, but a methodology which ensures a stable, foreseeable and clearly understood adjustment must be used; 2081: An organisation is bound by the rules it has adopted in determining the salary adjustment; 1912: The periodic adjustment of salaries is within the discretion of the organisation subject to the general principles of the law of the international civil service. There is no right to an automatic indexing but the salary adjustment rules must not bring about an erosion of salary that could be regarded as substantially jeopardising the contractual balance between the organisation and its staff members (see also: 1118); 1821: An organisation must choose a methodology or standard of reference which meets all general legal principles of the international civil service and the results must be stable, foreseeable and clearly understood. If the methodology grants discretion to depart from a standard, proper reasons must be given. The mere desire to save money at the staff's expense is not in itself a valid reason; 1713: In choosing figures of local pay there is no single hard and fast approach. The ICSC must be allowed some discretion; 1682: Misuse of discretion, the salary adjustment of the Coordinated Organisations did not serve "as a guide"; 1519: Neither the organisation nor the ICSC went beyond the bounds of discretion; 1498: The tribunal will not interfere in the drafting of the salary policy but it has power of review in that area (see also: 1265, 1000).

CJEU Judgments/Orders

C-40/10: The discretion of the EU Commission to make proposals and the discretion of the EU Council resulting from Art. 65 EU-SR to decide on salary adjustments is restricted by the adjustment procedure stipulated in Annex XI EU-SR. It is justified *inter alia* in order to avoid discussions and recurrent difficulties between the staff union and the institutions. As to the discretion of the EU Council in the case of a sudden deterioration in the economic and social situation within the EU ("Exception clause" in Art. 10 of the Annex XI EU-SR; see below under "Limited right of the organisation to bring an action").

### *nn) Seniority (prior experience)*

ILOAT Judgments

818: The organisation has wide discretion in setting up rules for calculating the seniority of staff members acquired previous to their appointment; 598: The president of the organisation is free to exercise discretion as to whether a form of co-operation service counts in the calculation of seniority (see also: 597); 572: The system for reckoning seniority gives the President of the organisation a discretionary power, he must, however, comply with the principle of equal treatment (see also 571).

CJEU Jugements/Orders

T-91/98: Discretion to allow additional seniority by taking into account experience prior to the appointment (Art. 32 EU-SR; see also T-19/90 with further references).

### *oo) Staff (appraisal, performance) reports*

ILOAT Judgments

1617: There is no fatal flaw of discretion if a procedural flaw relating to the due reporting period is corrected retroactively (see also: 1610, 1179, 1144, 1115, 806, 724, 723, 599, 565); 1463: The tribunal will not replace the performance appraisal of a staff member by its own. It will exercise only a limited review and will not interfere unless it finds one of the fatal flaws announced in its standard clause on discretion (see also: 1137, 868); 1179: The tribunal is generally satisfied if the staff member is offered the possibility in the reporting form to give his comments in order to remedy a possible error of appraisal (see also: 973); 1136: An assessment will not stand if there is an obvious mistake of fact or failure to show the sort of objectivity that ought to govern reporting (see also 973: if there is a "fatal flaw" of the reporting officer's assessment); 880: Performance reports serve no purpose unless the superior has full freedom in commenting on performance. If the rules governing the staff reports stipulate a choice of whole marks from 1 to 5 in-between ratings ("a 3, albeit inclining to 2") are inadmissible for the sake of proper comparing of staff members' reports. A reporting officer may, however, add comments in order to qualify a given marking.

CJEU Judgments/Orders

F-114/07: A reporting officer has wide discretion in judging the work of the official upon whom he must report. The report's annulment is only justified if an inconsistency is manifest (see also: F-34/07; T-178/00 and T-341/00); F-27/08: It is not for the tribunal to substitute its assessment for that of the reporting officer. He enjoys wide discretion in the appraisal of the work of the official. Value judgments relating to the career development reports are subject to judicial review only as regards irregularities of form or manifest errors of fact vitiating the assessment made by the administration or any misuse of power; F-46/06: A career development report is a value judgment (see also T-144/03, T-33/91, T-33/90).

### *pp) Transfer/reassignment*

ILOAT Judgments

2839: In the exercise of the discretion to reassign, the organisation must take into account the interest and dignity of the staff member, the former level of duties, the matching of qualification; the decision must be transparent and reasons must be given; 2819: Transfer of a principal director to a post without commensurate tasks, lack of respect for the official's dignity, reassignment ordered by the tribunal within 28 days; 2635: Transfer motivated by a desire to resolve relational difficulties; 2191: Discretion flawed, interests and dignity affected; 1757: In processing, ordering and notifying transfer an organisation must heed the staff member's dignity and good name and not cause undue injury; 1556: No reasons that the transfer was wrong or improper; 1496: Abruptness of transfer, new job not on a par with the old one and not in keeping with the qualifications of the staff member; 1496: Transfer as a hidden disciplinary action; 1234: Discretion flawed, two transfers within 18 months without stating the reasons for the transfers and giving an opportunity for responding (see also: 1078, 1076, 1050, 1018); 1146: No transfer but merely a redivision of tasks, 939: Transfer may even be ordered against the wishes of the staff member concerned.

CJEU Judgments/Orders

C-294/95 P: In the case of tensions prejudicial to take the proper functioning of the service the organisation has a wide discretion in reassigning a staff member; T-80/92: There is only a misuse of discretion if the discretionary powers are used for a purpose other than that for which it were conferred; T-59/91 and T-79/91: The principle of equivalence of grade and post calls, in the event of a change of the duties, not for a comparison between the present and the previous duties but for a comparison between the present duties and the grade which the official occupies.

### *qq) Vacancy notice*

ILOAT Judgments

1595: Though the qualifications in a vacancy note are not absolutely binding and the DG may exercise some discretion, he may not utterly discard them or flout the rules; 1357: Discretion to withdraw a vacancy notice at any time, even at an advanced stage of the selection process. However, any modification of a qualification criteria after the publication of the vacancy notice would vitiate the selection process (see also: 3073 and the Judgments referred to).

CJEU Judgments/Orders

F-46/07: Also the procedural rules adapted by an organisation for its appointment procedure must be scrupulously observed (see also the case law cited therein); F-39/07: The wide discretion regarding appointment presupposes that the appointing authority has meticulous regard to the requirements laid down in the vacancy notice (see also: F-44/05 and the case law cited therein).

*rr) Miscellaneous*

*Actuarial methods*

ILOAT Judgment 1392: Discretion in the choice of an actuarial method used for the foreseeable costs of a pension fund.

*Assistance*

Despite an almost identical wording of Art. 24 EU-SR and Art. 28 EPO-SR (assistance by the organisation) the CJEU applies Art. 24 EU-SR also in the case of insults, threats etc. from colleagues whereas the ILOAT restricts the application of Art. 28 EPO-SR to attacks from outside the organisation (see, for example, CJEU Judgments T-136/03 and ILOAT Judgment 1489). CJEU Judgment T-59/92: The administration has discretion in the choice of the ways and means of providing assistance to staff members; C-137/88: The obligation to exercise discretion in a case which requires granting assistance to a staff member is particularly pressing in matters of the transfer of national pension rights.

*Certificate of service*

ILOAT Judgment 509: The administration enjoys discretion in this matter but the certificate must contain all the information set out in the SR (see also 211).

*Correction of an unlawful action*

ILOAT Judgment 2371: Discretion as to the form and terms of a communication to the recipients of a report of the ombudsman which was unlawfully circulated.

*Duty travel request*

ILOAT Judgment 3088: Misuse of discretion by rejecting the duty travel request of the acting chairman of the staff committee to the meeting of the Council.

*Entry date*

ILOAT Judgment 2865: Discretion to set a date for entry. The date was not calculated in order to deprive the complainant of his entitlement to an expatriation allowance.

*Fleming principle*

ILOAT Judgment 1280: Discretion of the organisation in carrying out the review of salary scales for the staff of the general service; 1279, 1266, 1265: In the exercise of discretion the ICSC is bound to respect the rules of a chosen method.

*Internal appeals board*

ILOAT Judgment 2558: An internal appeals board enjoys broad discretion in rejecting an offer of additional evidence.

*Long-term care benefit*

ILOAT Judgment 2976: The decision to grant an exceptional long-term care benefit is based on a value judgment akin to a discretionary decision.

*Medical opinion*

ILOAT Judgment 2361: The tribunal may not replace the finding of medical boards with its own, it has full competence as to whether there was due process and as to whether the findings show any material mistake or inconsistency or overlook some essential fact, or plainly misread the evidence (see also 1284, 1248). CJEU Judgment T-10/93: The court cannot, in the exercise of its judicial review criticise an assessment of an exclusively medical nature. It is, however, its task to ascertain whether the refusal to recruit is based on a reasoned medical opinion establishing a comprehensible link between the medical findings which it contains and the conclusion which it draws.

*Non-referral to the internal appeals board*

ILOAT Judgment 1541: Discretion of the administration in not referring a case to the internal appeals board if the appeal would overload the administration with pointless work and expenditure. The internal proceedings are deemed to be closed and a complaint before the tribunal is receivable.

*Original of a bill*

ILOAT Judgment 1783: Discretion to accept any other proof instead of the original of a bill.

*Over-qualification*

ILOAT Judgment 1789: It is a discretionary error if an application has been rejected on the grounds of over-qualification for the job advertised.

*Penalty*

ILOAT Judgment 349: The selection of an appropriate penalty is a discretionary one but the principle of proportionality must be respected.

*Per diem*

ILOAT Judgment 2129: Even in exercising discretion the administration must base its decisions on objective considerations and avoid breaching any of the guarantees protecting the independence of the international civil service.

*Recovery of undue payment*

ILOAT Judgment 1111: The decision to claim back a mistakenly paid sum is a discretionary one.

*Resignation*

ILOAT Judgment 856: Discretion in accepting resignation at shorter notice.

*Special compensation*

ILOAT Judgment 1334: The tribunal will not interfere in the discretion of the organisation to grant special compensation for special duties, save in obviously anomalous cases.

*Step increase, extension of contract*

ILOAT Judgment 2350: Discretion of the administration in granting not a two-step but only a one-step salary increase, and not a three-year but only a two-year extension of contract.

*Time frame*

ILOAT Judgment 1367: Stating no reasons for a deadline to remove household effects is an arbitrary exercise of discretion.

### d) Misuse of authority (non-discretionary decisions)

Misuse of authority in the case of non-discretionary decisions involves more than a simple infringement of the SR or of a general legal principle (a simple "error of law" or an "abuse of power", see ILOAT Judgment 675 para. 8). It presupposes that the decision taken is influenced by improper motives (ILOAT Judgment 1392 para. 35: Where the administration uses its powers for some purpose other than that prescribed by law, see also Art. 7 European Code of Good Administrative Behaviour: The power is used for purposes other than that for which it has been conferred).

A misuse of authority is not presumed. The burden of proof is on the party that pleads it (ILOAT Judgment 3032 para. 24). Personal prejudice is often concealed and must be inferred from surrounding circumstances (ILOAT Judgment 1775, para. 7).

**Jurisprudence**

ILOAT Judgments

2803: The decision vested on considerations extraneous to the interest of the organisation (476); 2540: Acts of retaliation; 2283: Intimidation or threat of reprisal; 1496: Suddenness and secretiveness of a transfer; 1376: Allegations of victimisation against a superior; 535: If an organisation had appointed an obviously less well qualified candidate than the complainant the plea of misuse of authority would succeed; 495: Victimisation of staff members because of their activities in the staff association.

CJEU Judgments/Orders

F/105/09: Abuse of power arising from the use of successive fixed-term employment contracts or relationships (F-69/07 and F-60/08; F-65/07); F-46/06: There is no misuse of power unless there is objective, relevant and consistent evidence that the contested act pursued an aim other than that ascribed to it by the SR (T-111/99; T-35/96).

### *2. The legislative power*

The constituent instruments of IO provide for a certain balance of power which resembles to some extent to the separation of powers that characterises democracies. It is the plenary body of an IO which assumes, *inter alia*, the function of the law-maker in the field of the internal SR of an organisation (Art. 336 TFEU; Art. 101(1) UN Charter; Art. 16 CoE Statute; Art. 33(2)(b) and (c) EPO-EPC).

In the legislative process the member states unified in the plenary body, dispose of a wide legislative discretion which is framed only by the respective primary law of the organisation and the general legal principles of the international civil service law as developed by the international administrative tribunals.

Since the judicial review by the tribunal is in general restricted to complaints alleging the infringement of individual rights, there is mostly no direct legal control over general rulings adapted by the legislature. Constant case law has it, however, that officials may challenge in each case the lawfulness of the general ruling underlying an individual decision. This incidental legal review comprises the questions whether the legislative body exercised its discretion within the bounds referred to above (see, for example, ILOAT Judgments 1368 para. 11; 1329 para. 6: using an index "as a guide" for the adjustment of salaries).

**Jurisprudence**

ILOAT Judgments

2439: Any authority which has to apply the right to equal treatment to dissimilar situations enjoys considerable discretion when adopting rules that take into account such dissimilarity; 2244: The competent bodies may repeat or modify rules they have established but their discretionary powers are limited by the general legal principles of the international civil service law; 2232: The termination of appointment of a DG is a decision taken by the legislative power of the organisation but that decision must be reviewed as an administrative decision; 1963: It is generally within the discretion of the executive organ to propose or not to propose the amendments to the SR; 1912: An organisation has discretion in establishing regulations for the periodic adjustment of salaries provided that these regulations do not violate the principles of the international civil service law; 1682: The Council paid only perfunctory heed to its obligation to take the salary adjustments of the C.O. "as a guide" (see also 1368); 1641: An organisation has a broad discretion to amend its SR; 1450: Discretion to use the possibility of granting fixed-term contracts instead of permanent employment; 1199: Exercise of discretion in using the United States as the "comparator" in determining the pay in the UN common system; 1118: The tribunal may not review the reasons of policy underlying a general decision by a legislative power of the organisation; 986: The bounds of discretionary authority were violated by the further reduction of the pension entitlements (breach of an acquired right); 963: Any authority is bound by the rules it has itself issued until it amends or repeals them; 936: Adoption of salary adjustment in breach of the rules adopted (see also 899); 532: The discretionary power of the legislative organ of an IO to set rules for the internal dispute procedure is limited by the statute and rules of the tribunal whose jurisdiction has been recognised by the organisation.

CJEU Judgments/Orders

C-40/10: The discretion conferred on the Council in the annual review of remuneration is restricted by the regulatory acts adopted by the Council to implement Art. 65 EU-SR. The salary adjustment method shall ensure a degree of medium-term stability and avoid discussions and recurrent difficulties; C-496/08 P (see also C-443/07 P): The legislative body enjoys a considerable degree of latitude to make amendments to the SR; F-105/05: A measure is vitiated by misuse of powers only if it appears, on the basis of objective, relevant and consistent evidence, to have been taken with the exclusive or main purpose of achieving an end other than that stated or evading a procedure specifically prescribed by the treaty.

## III. Legal certainty (stability in law)

### *1. General*

The general principle of legal certainty guarantees the stability of legal relations and protects against arbitrary actions by public authorities. The principle is primarily derived from the corresponding general principle common to the majority of member states. Its application requires an appropriate balance with the principle of justice (H. Leawoods, Gustav Radbruch: An extraordinary Legal Philosopher, Washington University Journal of Law & Policy (2000), p. 489). Based on these considerations, the legislative organs of the IO have adopted rules in the SR and the statutes of the international administrative tribunals which provided time-limits for the filing of complaints and appeals (e.g. ILOAT Judgments 2722, 2463, 2003, 1466, 1279, 1106, 602: The receivability of a complaint filed out of time would impair the stability of legal relations that the staff and the organisation require; CJEU Judgment 34–65: The principle of legal certainty requires that the decisions of an organisation cannot, forever, be called in question). This established legal balance between legal certainty and justice may, however, be corrected by the principle of good faith (e.g. ILOAT Judgments 2722, 1466, 1315: The stability in law which is the purpose and the whole point of time-limits may, however, not be used by an organisation in breach of the complainant's good faith).

The principle of legal certainty is also the underlying principle for the doctrine of *res judicata* which concerns the rules governing the revocation and alteration of administrative acts of the organisation, the recovery of undue payment and the precepts governing the delegation of powers of the head of administration. Other aspects of law in relation to the principle of legal certainty are the requirement for clear and precise legislative and administrative acts and the principle that acts taken by an organisation which may adversely affect an official may, as a rule, not take effect before their publication or notification.

The confidence of staff members in the legal certainty of their legal relationship with the organisation is the basis for a substantial judicature on specific general legal principles governing the international civil service, such as the doctrine of acquired rights and assurances.

Another aspect of the principle of legal certainty which may in addition to corresponding to national law in most member countries be derived from the term "security" in Art. 6 CFREU and Art. 5 EConHR are guarantees protecting against arbitrary remand and detention. This aspect of legal stability is of no relevance for the law of the international civil service.

### 2. *Deadlines for complaints and appeals*

The principle of legal stability implies that administrative decisions of organisations cannot be called in question by staff members forever (e.g. CJEU Judgment 34–65, ILOAT Judgment 2722). The legislature determines the proper time-limit available to the staff member to assess the lawfulness of the administrative decision allegedly affecting him (and possibly seek judicial review) and the legal stability which requires that after a reasonable time period the decision becomes final (see, for example, CJEU Judgment T-192/99). The time lines laid down in the SR or the statutes of the tribunals have to be strictly complied with by all parties concerned and the tribunal itself in order to achieve stability in law and avoid discrimination or arbitrary treatment in the administration of justice (e.g. ILOAT Judgment 3059, 1832 para. 6; CJEU Judgment T-109/98). There may be no derogation from the time-limits unless there is a quite exceptional case of unforeseeable circumstances or *force majeure* or if the organisation sets traps or if the rules of procedure are construed too pedantically (e.g. ILOAT Judgments 2882, 1376, 1247, 602, 522; CJEU Judgment T-109/98).

**Jurisprudence**

ILOAT Judgments

3059: It is fundamental to the law governing legal relations between a staff member and his organisation that adverse decisions must be challenged in a timely manner in accordance with the relevant SR; 3053: Where the only body competent to hear an appeal (in the present case the Council) declines jurisdiction and mistakenly forward it to the secretary of the organisation (the President), that decision is a final one; 2907: Exception from time limits when an organisation by misleading the complaint or concealing some paper from him is deprives him of the possibility of exercising the right of appeal in breach of the principle of good faith (2821, 752); 2882: A staff member who appeals to the wrong body does not on that account forfeit the right of appeal. The wrong authority has to forward the appeal to the right authority (1832, 1734, 607, 522); 2863: The conditions for receivability are governed exclusively by the provisions of the statute of the tribunal and not by the SR of the organisation (90 days limit instead of three months to file an appeal); 2831: Precise calculation of the time limit for an internal appeal (date of reception of the decision, expiration date extended until the next working day); 2823 (1798): Payslips are individual decisions that may be challenged. They cannot be challenged, however, if they merely confirm an earlier decision. The determination of seniority or reckonable experience can only be challenged within three months of its original determination; 2715: It would excessively formalistic if a complaint registered within the time limit were to be irreceivable merely because the translation of an appended item of evidence was supplied later; 2424: An organisation may not plead its own failure to act with regard to the complainant if the complainant was not informed about the opinion of the appeals board; 2345: The organisation should have realized that the complainant was mistaken in believing that he needed to wait for the authorisation of the organisation to file his complaint with the tribunal. The failure to give guidance conflicts with the requirement of good faith, the complaint is, therefore, receivable; 2282: If the integrity of an appellate process is corrupted at its very source by an attempt to keep the staff members from exercising their legal rights by means of intimidation or threats of reprisal, the tribunal will order severe sanctions; 1897: If an organisation did not contest the receivability of a premature appeal during the internal procedure the principle of good faith prevents it from doing so subsequently; 1247: The organisation may not plead that a complaint is time-barred if the SR provide for a prior amicable settlement procedure which has not yet come to an end.

CJEU Judgments/Orders

F-72/08: If an administration sends a holding reply shortly before the expiry of the time-limit for filing an appeal this does not produce any legal effect and is not capable of extending the time-limits under Art. 90 and 91 EU-SR ("not a pardonable confusion"; see also T-14/03: Time limits are a matter of public policy and are not subject to discretion of the parties or the Court; F-27/06 and F-75/06: The principle of legal certainty requires that a complaint is "lodged" when the institution receives it; T-192/99: If the SR (e.g. Art. 41 EIB-SR) provide for an optional conciliation procedure the limitation period for filing an appeal does not start to run before this procedure has been concluded; T-109/98: There is no derogation from the rules on procedural time-limits unless there is a quite exceptional case of unforeseeable circumstances or force majeure; T-15/91: The time-limits under Art. 90 and 91 EU-SR for bringing complaints and appeals are mandatory and not a plea to be raised at the discretion of the parties or the court (F-123/06; F-79/07; F-105/07); T-129/89: The time-limits under Art. 90 and 91 EU-SR ensure legal certainty and clarity, they are of a binding nature for all parties and the court (T-58/89; 161/87; 232/85); 127/84: The grading of a colleague in a position similar to the complainant must be regarded as a new fact which is sufficiently substantial to allow him to request a review.

### *3. Limitation periods for claims*

In order to safeguard the stability of legal relations a number of IO have laid down limitation periods for claiming the payment of damages, allowances and the reimbursement of costs in their SR (see, for example, Rule 3.17 UN-SR).

In the absence of any statutory rule for bringing such claims within a set period, it is for the judicature to set a reasonable time limit in the light of the circumstances of the case in order to safeguard legal certainty (ILOAT Judgments 2411, 322: a six-year period is unreasonable; CJEU Judgment T-433/10 P). In Judgment 53 the ILOAT held that in order to determine whether a reasonable time has elapsed account has to be taken of all the circumstances of the case "including *inter alia* the *bona or mala fides* of the official, the nature of the error, the degree of negligence of the Organisation and of the official and the hardship caused …".

Along these lines the CJEU held that a claim for compensation must be brought before the organisation within a reasonable period after the official became aware of the situation. In the appraisal of the reasonableness of the limitation period the CJEU referred to Art. 46 of its statute which stipulates that an action for non-contractual liability against the Union is time-barred after a period of five years from the occurrence of the event giving rise thereto (see CJEU Judgments T-433/10 P; F-103/09; T-16/09 P; F-5/09; F-87/07; T-144/02).

In Judgment 2411 concerning the EPO the ILOAT confirmed its judicature that without an explicit time-bar in the SR there is a "right" of the staff member to a retroactive payment of allowances (ILOATJudgment 322). The tribunal considered that the claims for the retroactive payment of a dependent's allowance which was delayed for a period of two and a half years was not time-barred. The complainant was inadvertently late in submitting his claims and he provided substantial continuous financial help for his parents.

In the meantime, the EPO has drawn the consequences of this ruling and included limitation periods (with the exception of *vis major*) for the payment of allowances and the reimbursement of costs (Art. 65(1)(e) and Art. 76(3) EPO-SR: granted retroactivity only for the six months preceding the month in which the request was submitted).

See also the recovery of undue payment and the related topic of decisions with recurring effects and the claim of arrears and default interests.

**Jurisprudence**

ILOAT Judgments

3080: The complainant may not claim an allowance retroactively after he failed to do so as soon as his entitlement arose, this entitlement is due only as from the date of his initial claims and not the date on which he became entitled to the benefit (2860, 2550); 2411: There is a right to a retroactive claim for an allowance (here: dependent child allowance) if no time-limit is laid down in the SR and the claim is not unreasonably delayed. In the present case (a not-wilful delay of two and a half years) the delay was not unreasonable; 2282: The two year's limitation period for the claim of an allowance in the IAEA-SR is not applicable since it cannot be invoked by the organisation which has by its own actions prevented the timely exercise of the claim; 322: A delay of six years for claiming the dependant's allowance for a child whose birth had not been notified in time to the organisation is an unreasonable delay.

CJEU Judgments/Orders

T-433/10 P: A claim for damages based on a misconduct of the EU must be brought within a reasonable period from the date on which the official became aware of the potentially unlawful event; T-16/09 P: A claim for compensation from the organisation for loss has to be submitted within a reasonable period of time (three and a half months is a reasonable period).

### *4. Res judicata and stare decisis*

(see below in Part 3, the system of legal protection)

### *5. Clarity and precision of acts, rules and applications*

A sub-principle of legal certainty requires that administrative acts of an IO, the rules adapted by the legislative organ of an IO on the pleas and applications in legal proceedings are sufficiently clear and precise (intelligible and coherent) so that the parties concerned may draw the necessary legal consequences on that basis alone.

**Jurisprudence**

ILOAT Judgments

3033: Decisions terminating the employment relationship must be clear and precise; 2210: Obligation to provide a clear and precise definition of the concept of a "similar post" in order to enable interested staff members to take an informed decision on the prospects of an application; 1864: Rules should contain notions which are precisely defined.

CJEU Judgments/Orders

F-98/09: The principle of legal certainty requires administrative authorities to adopt rules that are sufficiently clear, so that individuals may be able to ascertain unequivocally what their rights and obligations are and may take steps accordingly; F-1/08: The pleas and arguments of fact and law relied on in an appeals procedure must be sufficiently clear and precise (intelligible and coherent) to enable the defendant to prepare his defence and to enable the tribunal to give judgment (F-8/10; F-76/09; F-15/09; F-4/08; F-108/07; F-5/07).

### 6. *Revocation or alteration of decisions*

The adoption of an administrative decision creates a presumption as to its validity (CJEU Judgment 7/56, 3/57 to 7/57; see also 15/85). The principle of legal certainty and stability in law requires that the withdrawal of an administrative decision conferring individual rights for a staff member is not at the unfettered discretion of an IO. Since the SR of an IO generally do not contain conditions upon which such administrative decisions may be revoked retroactively (*ex tunc*) or in respect of the future (*ex nunc*), the international administrative tribunals have to take "reference to the rules acknowledged by the legislation, the learned writing and the case law of the member countries" (CJEU Judgment 7/56, 3/57 to 7/57).

– Unlawful administrative decisions conferring individual rights

The withdrawal of an unlawful (wrong or erroneous) measure conferring individual rights is in principle permissible with retroactive effect (*ex tunc*) provided the withdrawal occurs within a reasonable period of time and provided the organisation has sufficient regard to how far the applicant might have been led to rely on the lawfulness of the measure (CJEU Judgment 15/85). (As to the evaluation of a reasonable lapse of time, see in detail CJEU Judgments 7/56, 3/57 to 7/57 with a survey of the national law of some member states).

The revocation of a wrong or erroneous decision conferring individual rights with effect for the future (*ex nunc*) is always possible (this results by implication from the provisions in the SR making recovery of payment subject to well-defined conditions; CJEU Judgment 54/77). Such decisions "... cannot create vested rights such as to prevent revocation" (CJEU Judgments 54/77; 15–60). But see the special case of appointments, below.

– Lawful administrative decisions conferring individual rights

A lawful decision conferring individual rights cannot be unilaterally withdrawn with retroactive effect since it would impair the protected confidence of the staff member concerned in the stability of the legal relationship. This confidence prevails over the interests of an organisation to reverse a decision. In principle, such a decision also creates a vested right for the future. This holds good especially for the appointment of a staff member. On the other hand, an IO must have some latitude to adjust its SR to enable it to meet the challenges in an evolving world. This inevitably entails the revocation or alteration of rules which confer individual rights to staff members. In order to reconcile the interests involved in this process international administrative tribunals have developed the doctrine of acquired rights (see, for example, ILOAT Judgments 2682, 986, 832, 61).

– Partially unlawful decisions conferring individual rights

Partial unlawfulness of a decision conferring individual rights does not entail the revocability of a decision in its entirety unless the decision is deprived of its *raison d'étre* if the unlawful part is removed (CJEU Judgment 7/56, 3/57 to 7/57). If a decision is dissociable only the unlawful part is revocable.

– Unfavourable decision being unlawful

An unfavourable decision of an organisation which is unlawful has, of course, to be withdrawn with retroactive effect *(ex tunc)* without delay after the administration has become aware of it. The staff member may be entitled to damages accorded to settled case law if a number of conditions are satisfied as regards the illegality of the decision (see, for example, CJEU F-5/05 and F-7/05, F-6/07; C-17/07 P).

– Special case: appointments

If a selection procedure was tainted with a legal flaw, the public interest in maintaining legality leads to the cancellation of the decision. The organisation has, however, the duty to shield the staff member irregularly appointed from any injury he may suffer from the quashing of the appointment he accepted in good faith.

**Jurisprudence**

Except appointments

ILOAT Judgments

3021: Unlawful withdrawal of commissary privileges; 1927: Lawful suspension revoked, no damages accorded; 1394: Damages for the alleged unlawfulness of a decision which has been withdrawn after the filing of the complaint; 1130: The grant of incremental steps on a provisional basis may be withdrawn with retroactive effect; 1111: A wrongfully granted termination indemnity may be claimed back under the provision of the SR relating to recovery of undue payment; 1006: The reversal of a decision granting the complainant non-local status after nine years is not allowed even if the decision was based on an error of fact or law; 994: A lawful decision on grading may not be retroactively worsened by the organisation; 986: An administrative decision may be replaced by a more favourable one so long as it does not thereby offend against the rights of any third party; 618: As a rule an organisation may alter or reverse a decision unless it is expressly forbidden to do so and provided that vested rights are safeguarded. In the present case, no right to an appointment had been conferred to the complainant; 587: An administration may revoke a decision provided that it has not violated a vested right (here: removal of the complainant from the Medical Benefit Fund for failure to pay his contributions); 123: The retroactive withdrawal of an unlawful decision conferring the right to repatriation travel expenses based on the erroneous assumption that the complainant was internationally recruited is lawful.

CJEU Judgments/Orders

T-123/89: The retroactive withdrawal of a legal decision which has conferred individual rights is contrary to the general principle of law. The communication of an incorrect interpretation of rules (here: entitlement to an expatriation allowance) cannot give rise to a legitimate expectation since an organisation cannot give a valid undertaking not to apply the SR (162/84, 137/79, but see the recovery of undue payment); 159/82: In the special circumstances of the case the court considered the admission of the appellant to the competition as lawful. The retroactive withdrawal of the admission which has conferred individual rights is contrary to the general principles of law; 54/77: The retroactive withdrawal of a wrong or erroneous decision (here: payment of an expatriation allowance) conferring individual rights is generally subject to very strict conditions. The revocation of such a decision as regards the future is always possible; 15–60: The decision granting a separation allowance was the result of a wrong interpretation of a legal provision. Even if in certain cases in view of a vested right a retroactive withdrawal would be excluded. A withdrawal with effect for the future is always possible; 7/56, 3/57 to 7/57: The decision to bring the applicants within the ambit of the SR was valid and irrevocable, whereas the grading and the classification in a certain step was unlawful. This partial unlawfulness does not entail the revocability of the measure in its entirety, but is restricted to the unlawful part.

**Jurisprudence**

Appointments

ILOAT Judgments

3206 (3073): Irregular competition cancelled. The successful candidate is shielded from any injury that might result from the cancellation of an appointment which she accepted in good faith; 2959: The rights of employees to impugn a decision regarding appointment do not depend on their chances of successful appointment (1549, 1272). Irregular appointment cancelled without prejudice to the appointed candidate; 2884: The selection process was flawed. Exceptionally this did not result in the impugned decision and the underlying selection being set aside, since a link between the breach of the SR and the outcome of the process was not proven. The complainant was entitled to moral damages only; 2769: The selection process was flawed. The appointed candidate and the complainant had already left the organisation. The complainant was compensated for losing a valuable opportunity; 2712: The management goal to increase the proportion of women in senior management positions or that of geographical distribution of the officials could not override the required qualifications and the experience initially stipulated. The successful candidate was in good faith and must, therefore, be shielded from any injury resulting from the ordered revocation of his appointment; 2620: Unlawful direct appointment instead of a competitive appointment. The appointment was quashed and a competition ordered. The tribunal did not make an order to shield the directly appointed staff member from the consequences of quashing his appointment; 2457: The selection procedure was flawed by the absence of one member of the promotion board. The competition procedure was set aside and complainant restored in his position prior to the meeting of the board. The tribunal took no decision with regard to the successful candidate; 2336: The selection procedure was unlawful. The decision was quashed and the resumption of the procedure ordered. The successful candidate being in good faith must be shielded from any injury from the ordered revocation; 2210: The selection procedure was unlawful and must be resumed. The appointed candidate was in good faith and must be shielded from any injury resulting from the annulment of the impugned decision; 2051: The selection procedure was flawed for failure to give reasonable notice and by refusing to take into account the family circumstances (arrangements for wedding). The successful candidate must be shielded from any injury resulting from the quashing of his appointment accepted in good faith; 1158: The complainant claimed the quashing of a decision based on the outcome of a promotion procedure which adversely affected him. The tribunal quashed the decision without any further ruling and ordered compensation for damages (further related Judgments: 1646, 1477, 1359, 1315, 1223).

CJEU Judgments/Orders

T-10/94: A procedure for filling a post and deciding the level of the post only after the authority has received the candidatures, is illegal for lack of objectivity. The court annulled the procedure and the appointment of the candidate. The shielding of the incumbent was not ordered; T-58/91: The reservation of posts for candidates of a predetermined nationality was a legal flaw justifying the annulment of the appointment of the persons concerned. Since the complainant knew of the reservation the court did not order shielding the incumbents from any injury resulting from the cancellation of their appointments; T-37/89: In principle a competition is vitiated by an unlawful refusal to admit a candidate. This is not the case where one or more candidates have been wrongly admitted. In this case the posts which are irregular may be separated from those which are not; 188/73: The discretion of the appointing authority in a vacancy procedure must be exercised within the self-imposed limits contained in the vacancy notice. The procedure was considered to be illegal and appointment of the successful candidate quashed and his shielding not ordered.

### *7. Unjust enrichment, recovery of undue payment*

As a sub-principle derived from the cardinal principle of stability in law, undue payment is in principle recoverable. The recovery falls within the discretionary power of the organisation. The recovery must be brought – even in the absence of a ruling in the SR – within a reasonable period and all circumstances must be taken into account, *inter alia* whether the official was in good or bad faith and the responsibility for the mistake.

Most IO provide for a specific ruling in the SR explicitly authorising the administration to the recovery of undue payments (Art. 85(1) EU-SR; UN Administrative Instruction ST/AI/2009/1; Art. 38 CoE-SR; Art. 88 EPO-SR). The general legal principle is, therefore, applicable only as a corrective factor which contributes to solving a legal conflict. As a rule the SR provide for the recovery of an undue payment if the recipient was aware that there was no due reason for the payment or if the fact of the overpayment was patently such that he could not have been unaware of it (for example Art. 85(1) EU-SR). The last part of the phrase is the legal paraphrase of the legal term "negligence". Whether an official was by negligence not aware of the fact of overpayment has to be determined by taking into account the ordinary case exercised by a normally diligent official in accordance with his grade and level of experience (see, for example, CJEU Judgment T-180/02 and T-113/03, 310/87).

Some SR of IO provide for the preclusion of the request for recovery of undue payment after a specific lapse of time (EU: Art. 85(2) SR: The request is invalidated five years after the date on which the sum was paid and if the recipient did not deliberately mislead the administration; UN: Administrative decision ST/AI/2009/1, Section 3.1 provides for an even shorter period of two years under certain conditions).

The recovery of undue payment is assimilated to a statutory right and is, therefore, also valid for erroneous payments made by an official to the organisation (ILOAT Judgment 81).

**Jurisprudence**

ILOAT Judgments

3201: Recovery of overpayment. The complainant did not exercise ordinary diligence in the management of his pension matters; 3167: An unfortunate error of the organisation was not grave enough to negate the right to recover overpayments: 2899: The recovery of undue payment falls within the discretionary power of an organisation. Case law has it that in case of an overpayment by mistake an organisation must take all circumstances into account which would make it unfair or unjust to require repayment – at least in full. Relevant circumstances are the good or bad faith of the official, the sort of mistake made, the respective responsibility for the mistake and the inconvenience for the official in the case of repayment (1849, 1111, 53); 2847: The recovery of undue payment is not imprescriptible and must be brought – even in the absence of a ruling in the SR – in reasonable time. Because of the concealment on the part of the complainant (no declaration of a parallel drawing of the family allowance from the national authority) the tribunal held that a retroactive recovery of five years was not an unreasonable length of time (53); 2565: The recovery of the terminal allowance was not extinguished by prescription within a period of two years; 2230: The complainant was aware that there was no due reason for the payment of a part of medical costs. A lapse of three years does not exclude the recovery of overpayment; 1849: In the case of recovery of overpayment all circumstances should be taken into account. Wrong calculation of the post adjustment received from UNIFIL to which the complainant was seconded by the WHO. Since WHO has been fully reimbursed by UNIFIL there is no indebtedness by the complainant to the WHO; 1366: Overpayment of an education allowance. The complainant must have been aware of the patent disproportion between the advances and the actually incurred expenses. Since the organisation did waive some of the sum due and did not demand interest, the complaint was dismissed; 1347: Recovery of the part of the tuition fees paid by the organisation for which the complainant got financial aid from the university. The recovery of the payment in twelve monthly instalments provided for in the SR did not constitute an improper disciplinary action; 1195: The time between the payment and the request for repayment was not long enough to extinguish the obligation by extinctive prescription; 497: The education grant was paid by mistake and *prima facie* is recoverable. The extent to which it is recoverable depends on the circumstances of the case (repayment of half was considered to be sufficient).

CJEU Judgments/Orders

T-195/03: It is not necessary for the official concerned in the exercise of his duty of diligence, to be able to determine the precise extent of errors made by the administration. The fact that he has doubts about the validity of the payment is sufficient (T-14/03, T-205/01, T-122/95; 252/78); T-180/02 and T-113/03: An official exercising ordinary care, with a high grade and level of experience cannot be unaware that the payment of the expatriation allowance attaches to expatriation in the meaning of the SR (T-235/94); T-107/92: A lapse of time of eight years is not unreasonable if the complainant has been particularly negligent; 310/87: The term "patently" in Art. 85 EU-SR does not mean that the official needs to make no effort to reflect or check, but rather that the recovery is due where the error is one which does not escape the notice of a normal diligent official *a fortiori* one of the applicant's grade and seniority; 36/72: The vouchers issued to the complainant did not allow the complainant exercising normal diligence to recognise the undue payment of the household allowance. The overpayment was, therefore, not patent.

### *8. The principle of non-retroactivity*

The rule against retroactivity is derived from the general legal principle of legitimate expectation which itself is a specific configuration of the precept of stability in law. It is recognised by the national law of most member states. The rule applies both to the SR and to individual decisions. Its purpose is to protect the confidence of staff members in the retention of an acquired favourable legal position for the past. The rule against retroactivity may be viewed, therefore, as the *alter ego* of the general legal principle of acquired rights which safeguards a favourable legal position for the future.

A rule or decision is retroactive, if it affects some change in existing legal status, rights, liabilities or interests form a date prior to its proclamation (ILOAT Judgment 2315 para. 23 in relation to a retroactive provision).

The rule against retroactivity may frequently overlap with the principles of good faith and the *patere legem* rule.

**Jurisprudence**

ILOAT Judgments

3214: Decision must be based on the provisions in force at the time the decision is taken and not at the time the claim was submitted. Exceptions: requirements of good faith, principle of non-retroactivity and protection of acquired rights (3034, 2985, 2459); 3033: An unfavourable decision cannot take effect before the date of notification; 2986: A provision is retroactive only if it affects some change in existing legal status, rights, liabilities or interests from a date prior to its proclamation, but not if it merely affects the procedures to be observed in the future with respect to such status, rights, liabilities or interests (2315); 2702 (leading judgment): The rotation policy was not retroactively applied to the complainant; 2637: Exceptionally, retroactive effect may be granted to a decision where the effect is favourable to a staff member (1130). In this case retroactivity would not confer any benefit on the complainant; 2315: A change in the nature of discretion to be exercised in deciding on the renewal or extension of a contract cannot be regarded as to have retroactive effect. This holds good even if the seven-year period introduced by the seven years policy (non-career organisation) is computed from a time prior to the proclamation of that policy; 2006: There is no presumption of retroactive effect (742); 1979: The rule of non-retroactivity prevents an organisation from applying retroactively an unfavourable rule to the staff. In order to determine whether the rule is unfavourable its overall effects must be assessed; 1669: The principle of non-retroactivity requires that a decision (here: the grant of an invalidity pension) may not work to the staff member's detriment before the date at which he has notice of it; 1604: A mistake in the calculation of the post adjustment by the ICSC (in favour or to the detriment of the staff member) may not be corrected with retroactive effect taking into account the lack of practicability, but the calculations have to be corrected reasonably soon after the defects do emerge; 1589 (leading judgment): The retroactivity of the termination of appointment did not observe the period of notice; 1531: No decision unfavourable to an official may take effect before the date at which he gets notice of it; 1186 (Interlocutory order): The abolition of a free after-service health insurance has no retroactive effect on the earlier coverage (as to the issue of acquired rights, see Judgment 1226); 1130: The rule against retroactivity is, though a general principle, not absolute. Favourable retroactive decisions are admissible as is the retroactive replacement of a provisional decision (e.g. incremental steps on a provisional basis until a new salary scale came into force) by a definitive one; 1117: The salary adjustment system is perforce retroactive according to criteria applied *a posteriori*. The claim for interest, therefore, fails; 1053: The interpretation of a rule followed over several years becomes part of the organisation's personnel policy and cannot be changed retroactively (Reimbursement of national taxes levied on the partial lump-sum payment of pensions); 986: The principle of non-retroactivity is also binding on tribunals, however, an administrative decision taken after the one impugned may, if more favourable, repeal it with retroactive effect; 792: The change of the construction of a provision in the SR must be properly made known and may not be retroactive (767); 742: There is no presumption of retroactive effect of a legal text; 51: The retroactive reduction of the expatriation allowance is unlawful. Being of a different nature it cannot be offset against the benefit of a retroactive salary increase.

CJEU Judgments/Orders

T-260/09 P (F-27/08): An administrative measure may exceptionally be retroactive where the purpose to be achieved so demands and where the legitimate expectation of those concerned are duly respected. An administration may, therefore, take a decision with retroactive scope following the annulment of a decision by the judicature provided that those conditions are satisfied. In the present case, however, the administration did not comply with the grounds of the Judgment and unlawfully withdrew the merit points of the applicant retroactively without any legal basis; F-80/08 R: A judicial decision ordering the suspension of operation of a measure is a provisional measure designed to preserve the future. A suspension, unlike an annulment, cannot have retroactive scope; C-443/07 P: The annulment of SR applies, unless otherwise provided, to the future consequences of situations which arise under the previous legislation (C-60/98); T-58/05: Since the date on which the Regulation took effect does not precede the date of its publication, the Regulation cannot be held to be retroactive (T-177/95).

### *9. Delegation of authority*

The delegation of authority is generally considered as a prerequisite for successful implementation of results-based management in IO (see UN doc. JIU/REP/2004/7).

The normal method of exercising authority within an IO has it that the DG (the President) takes the decision and the responsible staff member signs the notification on his behalf (e.g. ILOAT Judgment 805). The head of administration may, however, delegate his authority to take decisions to staff members either by a rule or by an explicit decision.

**Jurisprudence**

ILOAT Judgments

3494: A delegation of authority must have some basis in the rules; 3177: The authorised decision-maker does not have to be signatory to the final decision; 2896: No published delegation of the authority to take decisions (decision on prolongation of service); 2871: Mere notification of a decision taken by the DG (decision on renewal of contract); 2558: The delegation of authority must be proven either by virtue of a statutory provision or by virtue of a lawful delegation. Extension of a probationary period taken *ultra vires* in the absence of any formal delegation; 2028: At the request of a complainant proof of delegation of authority is required; 1834: Termination of appointment on behalf of the DG and with his prior approval; 1696: Appointment not confirmed since there was no rule to delegate authority to the chairman of the advisory committee; 1375: The want of proper delegation of the right to sign will not necessarily be fatal to a decision if the letter refers to the authority which took the decision.

CJEU Judgments/Orders

F-89/07: The delegating authority must take an express decision transferring its powers. The delegation can relate only to clearly executive powers; C-301/02 P: A delegating authority cannot confer powers different from those it has itself received. The delegation must be taken by an express decision and can only relate to clearly defined executive powers. The body to which the powers are delegated must be subject to the same conditions as those to which it would be subject if the delegating authority exercised them direct (e.g. obligation to state reasons and to publish).

### IV. The principle of proportionality

The principle of proportionality is recognised as a general principle of law in the national laws of the member states of IO and is enshrined in international conventions (see, for example, Art. 6(1) TEU in conjunction with Art. 49(3) CFREU regarding criminal offences and severity of penalties) and recognised in the settled case law of the international administrative tribunals as a general legal principle applicable to the law of the international civil service. It is explicitly stipulated in Art. 1(d)(4) EU-SR (reasonable accommodation for a disabled official unless it would impose a disproportionate burden on the employer) and Art. 1(d)(6) EU-SR (general application of the principle of proportionality).

Acts imposing a financial burden on the official must not exceed what is appropriate and necessary to attain the objective pursued. If there is a choice of measures, the least onerous measure must be chosen (CJEU Judgment T-6/92 and T-52/92).

The main area of application of the rule of proportionality in the law of the international civil service is to be found in the field of disciplinary law. A disciplinary decision is qualified by the international administrative tribunals as a discretionary decision. The infliction of a disciplinary measure is subject, therefore, to a limited judicial review.

**Jurisprudence**

ILOAT Judgments

3295: A disciplinary measure must not be out of proportion to the offence (2944, 2773, 1984, 207); 2849: Despite the fact that unsatisfactory conduct and unsatisfactory performance are different matters with different administrative consequences, an exemplary prior service may be a mitigating factor in the determination of a proper sanction (2656, 937); 2745: A behaviour disproportionate to the matter which is said to have prompted the course followed may be taken into account in the evaluation of harassment-related aspects (2524, 2370); 2719: The summary dismissal cannot be regarded as disproportionate to the misconduct of which the complainant was guilty; 2656: In determining whether disciplinary action is disproportionate to the offence, both objective and subjective features are to be taken into account (1445, 937, 203); 2601: Demotion as a proportionate disciplinary action for blows with a subordinate and a strike in his face (1725); 2555: Dismissal for alteration to the configuration of his computer in order to visit pornographic sites and download software and music is not a disproportionate measure; 2391: The SG did not state reasons why he disregarded the opinion of the appeals board that the decision was taken in breach of the principle of proportionality. The decision was quashed; 2365: The suspension of employment as a precautionary measure must be in accordance with the principle of proportionality (2262, 1927); 2324: A decision to place a senior officer on leave for bad performance must respect the principle of proportionality; 1977: The penalty of dismissal for fraud against the organisation was not disproportionate but amply warranted (1831, 1828, 1070); 1878: The summary dismissal was out of proportion since the complainant who called his superior a fascist but twice offered an apology which was accepted in writing by the superior; 1599: The sanction of a written reprimand was not disproportionate to the misconduct (striking someone in the face at work); 1584: The creditors of the official approached the organisation many times after the complainant had received several prison sentences. The sanction of dismissal was proportionate; 1447: The dismissal for professional incompetence was disproportionate; 1363: The dismissal for the pursuit of private business (preparing and filing patent applications in a law firm during leave on personal grounds as a patent examiner) is not a disproportionate disciplinary measure; 1346: Dismissal for wilful and repeated insubordination is not disproportionate; 1250: Dismissal after refusing transfer to a post outside the headquarters was proportionate; 1238: The award of a compensation instead of reinstatement ordered by the tribunal (999) was, in the present circumstances, disproportionate; 1210: The dismissal for misappropriation of funds was proportionate in the circumstances of the case; 805: To order staff members to perform their duties during a strike action in order to ensure the survival and continuance of work was proportionate in the circumstances of the case (29 staff members out of a total of 1880 staff members were ordered to work); 349: The summary dismissal was out of proportion with the offence committed; 237: To come on duty smelling of alcohol does not amount to misconduct serious enough to justify dismissal; 210: A disciplinary sanction must not give adequate weight to the nature of the conduct only, but must take into account all circumstances of the case, including mitigating factors.

CJEU Judgments/Orders

F-135/07: The applicant was reappointed after the first appointment has been annulled by the court for administrative mistakes in the selection procedure. Because of changes to the SR in the intervening period the applicant was awarded a minor classification. The tribunal quashed the decision *inter alia* for infringement of the principle of proportionality; T-94/01, T-152/01 and T-286/01: Art. 19 ECB-SR infringes, among other legal principles, the rule of proportionality in that it excludes officials who are not entitled to the expatriation allowance from the grant of an education allowance; T-197/00: The removal from his post is a proportionate disciplinary measure in the case of acts of corruption (T-12/94, 46/72); C-274/99 P ("Connolly"): The refusal to publish interferes with the freedom of expression. It must be interpreted restrictively and applied in strict compliance with certain requirements such as that it be proportionate to the aim pursued; T-203/98: The dismissal was disproportionate to the facts proven on which the disciplinary measure was based; C-252/97 P: When the truth of the facts alleged against the official is established it is up to the appointing authority to choose the appropriate disciplinary measure. The court cannot substitute its own judgment for that of the appointing authority except in the case of manifest error or misuse of powers; T-183/96: The disciplinary measure of demotion was disproportionate to the facts (aggressive tone and lack of the necessary decorum's in the comments on the appraisal reports); T-146/94: Distribution of a document containing views regarded as insulting to the Court of Auditors. The disciplinary measure of dismissal was considered to be proportionate; T-549/93: Proportionality of a dismissal for sexual harassment.

## V. The principle of good faith (*bona fide*), fairness, equity and estoppel

The legal principle of good faith (*bona fide*) is generally recognised in national and international law as one of the cardinal legal principles of law derived from the rule of law. It is also embedded in Art. 2(2) of the UN Charter (see also: ICJ Judgment of 20 December 1974 New Zealand vs. France, p. 49: "... one of the basic principles governing the creation and performance of legal obligations, whatever their source, is the principle of good faith"). The principle is also referred to in the preamble and Art. 26 (*pacta sunt servanda*, every treaty in force must be performed in good faith), and Art. 31(1) VCLT (see also Art. 31.1 of the VCLT-IO which is, however, not yet in force, status as at May 2016).

In the area of the international civil service the principle of good faith means that the legal relations between the organisation and its staff members are not only governed by the SR and implementing rules but that these rules must be applied in a way which does not conflict with the principles of justice and ethics. The exercise of rights both by the organisation and the staff members may not lead to an abuse of rights (The requirement of good faith dealings "is a two-way street", ILOAT Judgment 2152 para. 11).

The exercise of rights may be modulated by the principle of good faith in different aspects. The most important are: limitation (e.g. setting no traps), modification (e.g. a consultation procedure must be open minded) and completion (e.g. keeping a promise, care and assistance). The principle of good faith eludes *a priori* a precise definition (Cheng, p. 105; Lindemann, p. 173) and can be better illustrated by means of application, i.e. judgments of the international administrative tribunals. In this respect the terminology is not always consistent. Sometimes similar terms like: fairness, equity, estoppel (*venire contra factum proprium*) or *pacta sunt servanda* are used, whereby questions of dogmatic subtleties are not addressed. In case law these principles play an important role (see, for example, in 2016 there were a total of 175 judgments in the ILOAT Triblex database referring to the term "good faith", 147 judgments to "fairness", 122 judgments to "equity" and 26 judgments to "estoppel").

In conformity with the nature of the principle of good faith, it is applied mostly as an *ultima ratio* remedy in order to reach a verdict complying with the principles of justice and ethics. The rule of good faith frequently overlaps with other legal principles, in particular the principles of legitimate expectation, the *patere legem* principle, the prohibition of abuse of powers, the duty of care and the respect of dignity.

The following overview shows that the judicature of the ILOAT more frequently refers to the principle of good faith than the CJEU. One reason may be that the scope of jurisdiction of the CJEU is limited to the uniform structure of the EU civil service system whereas the jurisdiction of the ILOAT extends to 62 IO (in the year 2017) comprising organisations connected with the UN and to the mixed international civil service systems.

**Jurisprudence**

ILOAT Judgments

3353: Good faith requires an organisation to inform an official in advance of any action which may impair his rights or rightful interests; 3264 Good faith requires the IO to give guidance and support during the extension of the probationary period: 3234: Refusal to submit evidence to the appeals panel, violation of good faith; 3204: Good faith requires that a promise is kept; 3188: Failure to respond to a request may involve a breach of good faith; 3157: The successful candidate who accepted his appointment in good faith must be shielded if the flawed selection process was set aside; 3099: The duty of good faith requires that there is an accurate record of an interview; 3069: Actions taken in good faith by a subordinate that serve the function of protecting his legitimate interests (e.g. statements made in response to criticism or attack) do not constitute harassment; 3038: Inordinate delay and the conduct of the organisation in reaching an agreement on the amount of a compensation; 3005: A substantive promise by the competent person of an organisation must be kept in accordance with the rule of good faith (782); 2996: The principle of good faith requires that an appeal is not deemed irreceivable if the organisation did not abide by the requisite formalities enabling the submission of the appeal (formal obligation in the SR to inform about legal remedies); 2935: A claim for punitive damages may be allowed only in exceptional circumstances, *inter alia* if the organisation is in gross breach of its obligations to act in good faith; 2916: Employment may not be terminated for poor performance without giving a warning and an opportunity to do better (2861, 2515, 2337); 2907: Except for cases of *vis major*, time limits for filing a complaint lose their validity if the organisation has misled the complainant or concealed some paper from him so as to do him harm, in breach of good faith (2821, 752); 2906: The promotion to a director's post resting on a pure factual clerical error was unlawful. The reversal is possible if the principle of good faith is respected, i.e. the decision must be reversed as soon as the error was noticed and the complainant is shielded from unfavourable consequences (no reimbursement of the higher salary received); 2899: In the case of overpayment the repayment must not be unfair and unjust, *inter alia* the good or bad faith of the recipient must be taken into account (see overpayment); 2882: Rules of procedure must be strictly complied with, but must not be construed too pedantically or set traps (appeal sent mistakenly to the wrong body) (2722, 2017, 1832, 1734, 1502, 1466, 1393, 1375, 1279, 1247, 1106, 647, 607, 603, 522); 2869: The promotion or non-promotion of staff union representatives must be made in good faith and also must appear to be made in good faith; 2865: No breach of good faith if a staff member fails to request an expedited procedure since the organisation has to ensure, without being prompted, that procedures are properly conducted; 2817: A number of matters pointing to the conclusion that the reorganisation of the department was not taken in good faith; 2800: Relations between an organisation and its staff must be governed by good faith. Bad faith cannot be presumed, it must be proven and requires an element of malice (2293); 2798: The principle of good faith requires that the deadline for filing an appeal does not start before the recognition of the tribunal's jurisdiction was brought to the complainant's attention; 2768: The principle of good faith and the concomitant duty of care demand that the organisation informs the staff member of any action that may imperil his rights or harm his rightful interests; 2762: If there are no special rules for the recruitment of spouses, friends or close associates of the highest ranking officials it will take very little to establish improper motive or bad faith; 2750: Even if the SR provide that no notice is necessary in the case of expiry at the due date of an appointment limited in time, the principle of good faith requires that reasonable notice be given; 2745: Harassment does not require bad faith, prejudice or other malicious intent; 2729: The offer of a donor government to fund a post must be considered in good faith; 2584: If an organisation participates in settlement discussions the duty of good faith requires that, unless it expressly states otherwise, the time for taking further steps is extended (2066: reconsidering a decision); 2540: The duty of good faith requires that a subordinate has an opportunity to answer a criticism made and his answer or explanation be fairly considered; 2524: Serious allegations against an official that have not been properly investigated violate good faith; 2515: Any decision departing from the obligation to inform the official of the aspects of performance or conduct that are said to be unsatisfactory and to provide an opportunity for remedy is considered as not taken in good faith; 2475: Good faith requires a staff member to answer the charge made against him and to test the evidence; 2458: Good faith is not a one-way street, this includes the duty to collaborate with the medical board and to allow its effective functioning; 2414: Good faith requires that the staff member be informed in a timely manner as to the unsatisfactory aspects of his performance (2337, 1583); 2408: The decision not to renew the contract was based on improper reasons and demonstrates want of good faith; 2345: Violation of good faith since the organisation should have realised that the complainant had mistakenly presumed that he should wait for authorisation before filing a complaint; 2325: A delay of 15 months in informing the complainant about the result of a selection process is in breach of good faith (2116); 2304: Violation of good faith by the staff member by not replying to a request of the administration; 2163: The application for a post must be considered in good faith and the basic rules of fair and open competition; 2081: Any change in salary levels will ordinarily have a "knock on" effect for the level of salaries used as a basis for the following years. It would be a want of good faith requiring staff to challenge each new determination of salaries. The successful challenge of the level of salaries for the previous year is automatically carried on for the subsequent years; 2060: The selection process applications must be considered in good faith and in keeping with the rules of fair competition. If the process is flawed the resulting appointments are quashed (but see ILOAT

Judgment 2884 para. 19). The organisation must, however, shield the successful candidate (1497, 1315); 1924: An offered settlement proposal which is accepted by the staff member cannot be withdrawn (good faith, *pacta sunt servanda*) (1530); 1897: If an organisation does not contest receivability of a premature appeal during the internal appeal, the principle of good faith prevents it from doing so subsequently (1393); 1848: A staff member must deal in good faith with his sickness insurer and allow the insurer direct access to his physician to seek information; 1328: It is a breach of good faith to demand of a staff member that he refiles a complaint against a refusal to enforce a judgment. A request for execution of the judgment is sufficient; 1125: The rule of good faith requires that the construction which an organisation wilfully and consistently puts on a rule for years becomes binding (1053, 421); 1082: It is bad faith to enter a new objection in the surrejoinder when the complainant may not reply; 810: Good faith requires proper notice of transfer and details as to the nature of the post and the duty station; 380: The object of a consultation would be frustrated and the principle of good faith infringed if the decision-maker were determined from the outset not to be influenced by anything that might be said. The same holds good for negotiations if either party determines to make no concession under any circumstances; 339: A clause in a contract of employment which provides for premature termination without reasonable grounds is forbidden by the principle of good faith.

CJEU Judgments/Orders

F-19/08: The principle that contracts should be performed in good faith applies to the contracts for temporary staff; T-390/07 P: Time limits for appeals are binding except where the conduct of the institution gives rise to a pardonable confusion of a complainant acting in good faith (T-127/07P, T-12/90); F-25/07: The principle of good faith was not infringed since the organisation did not give any assurance of grading irrespective of the statutory changes envisaged; T-324/04: Good faith in the case of recovery of undue payment (T-312/02); T-288/04: Even if a staff member thought in all good faith that an agreement would be reached with the administration on the change of his basic salary without a claim being brought, the complainant has to comply with the time limits for bringing a claim; T-192/99: Consultation with staff must be such as to have an influence on the substance of the measure adapted, which implies that it must be timely and *bona fide*; 156/80: If an implied decision of rejection is followed by an explicit decision having the same substance, it is irrelevant to establish which of both decisions is formally contested if the complainant filed his complaint within the time limit which started to run from the date of the implied decision. It would be contrary to good faith to require a complaint against the explicit decision; 43/59, 45/59 and 48/59: Good faith requires that decisions of dismissal must be justified on grounds relevant to the interest of the service and without arbitrariness (T-223/99).

## VI. Good administration and due process

### *1. General*

The principle of good administration is a collective legal term ("umbrella provision", see Kanska, p. 312) used in the Continental-European legal system, whereas the principle of due process belongs to the Anglo-American legal system. Both terms resemble each other to a certain extent and comprise a bundle of sub-principles to the rule of law (see Kanska, p. 306: the right to good administration mirrors the principles of fair trial (or due process)).

In the context of the international civil service these principles may be broken down into the sub-principles of the obligation to state the grounds of an administrative decision, the right of the staff member to be heard before any individual measure which would adversely affect him is taken and the right that his affairs be dealt with in a reasonable time.

The principle of good administration referred to in Art. 41 CFREU also includes some customer-related rules of behavior, the right to damages caused by the EU and the right of language, which are not *per se* applicable to the employment relationship between the IO and its staff.

– The principle of good administration

The principle of good (sometimes referred to as "proper" (CJEU Judgment C-255/90 P) or "sound" (CJEU Judgment F-137/14) administration is derived from constant case-law of the CJEU and has been codified (albeit not exhaustively) in Art. 41 CFREU (see the explanations in Art. 41 CFREU in the OJ 2007/C303/02; see also Labayle). It is enshrined in the European Code of Good Administrative Behaviour (see the website of the European ombudsman). The Code entered into force on 1 November 2000 and aims at explaining in more detail the meaning of the right to good administration in practice. Although the Code does not directly apply to the relations between the EU institutions and its officials (see the "scope" of the Code) it nevertheless contains a near-exhaustive list of fundamental rights and principles (Rengeling, para. 1089) determining the legal relationship between an IO and its staff (see the briefing notes of the workshop on EU Administrative Law, 2011, p. 157: "The principle of good administration requires the administration to exercise its powers under the Staff Regulations in a particular way and to take special care in the application of legislation"; for more details see Laubinger).

The principle of good (sound) administration "... does not, in itself, confer rights upon individuals, except where it constitutes the expression of specific rights such as the right to have affairs handled impartially, fairly and within a reasonable time, the right to be heard ... or the obligation to give reasons for decisions ..." (CJEU Judgment, T-193/04; see also CJEU Judgment F-99/06).

The principle of good administration frequently overlaps with other objective legal principles which are dealt with separately in this book (see *inter alia* the principles of legality, of legal certainty, of proportionality and good faith).

The following jurisprudence refers to the principle of good administration in general. The jurisprudence in relation to the individual rights derived from this principle is dealt with under items 2, 3 and 4 below.

**Jurisprudence**

CJEU Judgments/Orders

T-641/11 P: The principle of good administration does not have a binding effect greater than that of a regulation (F-25/07, F-70/05, F-43/05); F-7/07: In conformity with the principle of sound administration the organisation has a duty to all candidates in a competition to ensure that the tests are conducted as smoothly and properly as possible; F-73/07: The principle of sound administration obliges the administration when taking a decision concerning an official to take into consideration all the factors which may affect its decision, it should take into account not only the interests of the service but also those of the official concerned (F-99/06, T-11/03, T-7/01, 417/85). The principle of good administration does not, in itself, confer rights upon individuals, except where it constitutes the expression of specific rights, such as the right to be heard and others (T-193/04); T-231/97: In conformity with the principle of sound administration the organisation must, when taking a decision which may have serious financial consequences for certain individuals, check all the information which might have a bearing on the results; C-255/90 P: The principle of proper administration cannot transform the mere possibility of the selection board to request additional information from a candidate into an obligation.

– Due process

The principle of due process is embedded in the United States Constitution ("Due Process Clause"). It is also recognised under this term as a general legal principle applicable to the civil service system of the UN family. In the context of the law of the international civil service it refers both to fair administration and judicial proceedings before the internal advisory boards of an IO and the administrative tribunals of the UN family.

The principle of due process is frequently referred to in the case law of the ILOAT (in 2016 about 141 extracts in the Triblex database) whose judges are regularly committed to the Anglo-American legal system, whereas the CJEU abstains from having regular recourse to this legal principle.

The principle of due process frequently coincides with other general legal principles like the principle of equality or the *patere legem* principle. It is, as with the principle of good administration, regularly broken down into its sub-principles. Of great significance in practice are the right to be heard, the duty to state the grounds of a decision and the duty to act within a reasonable time.

**Jurisprudence**

ILOAT Judgments

2940: Due process requires that a staff member is entitled to be apprised of the composition of an advisory body which is competent to give a reasoning on his claim; 2916: Performance appraisal procedures must be transparent and adversarial; 2757: It is a fundamental aspect of due process that a person should not take a decision in a matter in which he has a personal interest; 2667: The duty to act independently and impartially is incumbent also on advisory bodies; 2605: It is not a requisite element of due process in every case to inform an official in advance that an investigation into certain allegations will be undertaken; 2524: It is a failure of due process to put serious allegations before the advisory panel unless they have been properly investigated and the complainant is given an opportunity to answer the allegations; 2432: In view of the seriousness of the complainant's illness the principle of due process requires that the Invalidity Committee should have met before issuing a final decision; 2414: Due process requires timely information about unsatisfactory aspects of performance so that steps can be taken to remedy the situation (1386); 2315: An official must get all information material pertinent to the outcome both in internal proceedings and before the tribunal (here: names of the members of the advisory body) (1815); 2282: There is a positive obligation of an IO to assist staff in the exercise of their recourse and to place no obstacle in their way (2197; 2072); 2083: The decision to stop reimbursing medical bills was not based on an independent expert medical opinion and was, therefore, not in line with due process; 2014: The organisation did not disclose the identity of an accuser and had no other evidence, due process flawed; 1814: It is a breach of due process if the rule says that the Joint Committee "shall meet" but its members rather than gathering conferred by correspondence; 1796: Breach of due process by a hidden disciplinary sanction; 1763: Serious breach of due process. The chairman of the Joint Disciplinary Board should have refrained from personal involvement in the investigation; 1384: The denial of the alleged misconduct shifts the burden of proof to the organisation. The investigations showed many flaws of due process (concealing evidence, incomplete and inaccurate summary of the investigation); 1350: The termination of the fixed-term appointment before the date of expiry based on poor performance must scrupulously observe due process.

### 2. *The duty to state grounds of decisions*

The administration of an IO is legally bound to state the reasons when taking a decision affecting its staff members. This obligation is recognised as a general legal principle of the international civil service by all international administrative tribunals. It is to be found explicitly codified in some SR (Art. 25(2) EU-SR; Art. 59(4) CoE-SR) and is also stipulated in Art. 41(2)(c) CFREU, Art. 296 TFEU and Art. 18 European Code of Good Administration Behaviour. In contrast to the objective principle of good administration itself, the principle to state grounds is recognised as a principle conferring individual rights to staff members.

Even if the duty to state reasons for a decision does not stem from the SR an organisation is obliged to act in compliance with the general principle.

In settled case law the ILOAT held that the purpose of the obligation to state the reasons for an administrative decision is to provide the official with details sufficient to allow him to ascertain whether a decision is well-founded to assess whether he should bring an action and, secondly, to enable a judicial review by the appeal bodies and tribunals.

The CJEU despite the explicit obligation in Art. 25(2) EU-SR to state the grounds of decision concerning the officials, has held in constant case law that the principle cannot be extended to the dismissal of staff members holding a contract for an indefinite period (see, for example, T-471/04). Based on "the development of the law concerning the protection of workers against dismissal and the abusive recourse to successive fixed-term employment contracts" the CJEU changed its former case law. In its extensively reasoned Judgment F-1/05, the CST held that temporary staff members holding a contract for an indefinite period may not be dismissed without stating reasons. This decision was confirmed by the General Court in the Judgment (appeal) T-404/06 P albeit with a more formalistic approach based on Art. 11(1) EU-CEOS which provides for an application of Art. 25 EU-SR by analogy and by interpretation of this article for members of temporary staff.

This decision joins the mainstream of international administrative tribunal's jurisprudence by trying to shield staff members of the international civil service, at least in a rudimentarily way, against the risk of job loss. It is not surprising that the largest number of cases before the ILOAT relate to the non-renewal or non-extension of fixed-term contracts.

The duty to state reasons for terminating an employment relationship was confirmed by the ILOAT even in a case where the SR explicitly provided for an *ipso facto* termination of contract without an obligation to state any reasons. The tribunal held that the non-renewal is considered as a distinct and challengeable administrative decision which must be reasoned (ILOAT Judgments 1317 para. 23, 675 para. 9 and 10). The tribunal further pleads in constant case law that under the conditions in which an IO carries on its work, there arises an expectation that normally a contract will be renewed.

In recent jurisprudence, the ILOAT extends this commitment of IO to the reasoning of decisions taken after a consultative body (e.g. the internal appeals committee, the grievance panel or the disciplinary committee) has delivered its advisory opinion. Whenever the head of administration intends to deviate from this opinion, he has to give clear and cogent reasons, otherwise the decision is considered flawed (ILOAT Judgments 2811, 2807, 2699, 2391, 2355, 2261, 2092).

A lack of adequate reasoning for a decision may be remedied at the internal appeal stage if the principles of due process are respected (ILOAT Judgments 3148, 2668). It is, however, not permissible for an organization to introduce new arguments to justify a dismissal for misconduct that go beyond the grounds specified in the notice of dismissal since that would entail infringing the right to be heard before a disciplinary measure is imposed (ILOAT Judgment 3126).

**Jurisprudence**

ILOAT Judgments

3586: The non-observance of the principle of equality of arms constitutes a breach of due process; 3485: The failure of the Board to hear witnesses violates due process; 3264: In general access to all documentary evidence in the selection process does not extend to the reports regarding the results of the selection process (2899, 2700); 3200: Due process rights in the context of investigation. All relevant facts must be ascertained and the employee must be given an opportunity to test the evidence put against him and to answer the charge made (2771, 2475); 3172: Refusal to produce documentation or identify potential witness was in breach of due process rights; 3162: The complainant was deprived of an opportunity to defend himself against various allegations, egregious breach of due process; 3158: No prior information on the substitution of a member of the appeals committee violates due process; 3148: The lack or inadequacy of an explanation can be remedied at the appeals stage provided the staff member is given a full say (2668, 2180; but see 2877, 2339); 3041: When abolishing a post or terminating an appointment proper reasons for the decision and an opportunity to contest the decision must be given as well as assistance in finding a new assignment; 2991: It is a general principle of the international civil service that valid reasons must be given for not renewing (or extending) a fixed-term contract (2414, 1911, 1544, 1154, 946, 675); 2978: The reasons for the choice of candidates in a competition may be disclosed at a later date, even in the context of appeal proceedings (2194, 2016, 2035, 1787, 1550); 2924: An error of reasoning does not establish ill will or a breach of the duty of care; 2877: A decision to the detriment of an official must be fully and adequately motivated. The reasons must be sufficiently clear, precise and intelligible (2339); 2869: The reasons for not promoting or not appointing a candidate must be revealed (1365); 2839: Obligation of the organisation to inform a staff member of the reasons for a reassignment (2229, 2191, 2067, 1757); 2834: The right to information does not extend to access to the merit considerations of a selection board; 2811: When deviating from the recommendation of an internal appeals board the head of administration has to give clear and cogent reasons to all counts of the opinion (2807, 2699, 2391, 2355, 2347, 2261, 2092); 2803: Obligation to state reasons for a transfer; 2802: Restructuring is a valid reason for the abolition of a post, provided that it is not motivated by extraneous considerations like bias or ill will; 2668: The reasoning may consist simply of a reference to some other document; 2645: The decision not to renew the appointment was taken for reasons other than that invoked by the organisation; 2392: Giving reasons for not selecting the complainant for a post after the internal appeal proceedings had been exhausted is in breach of the duty to state reasons (2124); 2354: The obligation to consult the Staff Committee when abolishing a post presupposes that this body is fully informed in order to give a reasoned opinion (2352); 2312: No right to give reasons for not renewing a contract prior to the decision being taken; 2229 (leading judgment): As a general rule a staff member must have access to all the evidence on which the decision is based or is intended to be based. This applies *a fortiori* if the information is used in legal proceedings. Only in special cases might confidentiality preclude disclosure (1756); 2125: The desire to rejuvenate the staff is too general to constitute a sufficient justification for the refusal of extending a contract; 2124: The obligation to give grounds for a decision serves the purpose of giving the staff member the possibility to evaluate whether he should challenge it. It is also indispensable for the judicial review body (1817, 477); 2121: The failure to cite a reason for not renewing a contract cannot be remedied by simply referring to another body without stating why; 2035: When the result of a competition is announced the reasons for the choice need not be notified at the same time as the decision (1787); 1990: How ample the explanation of a decision need be will turn on circumstances; 1289: Even if a decision is not reasoned a staff member may still be able to defend his rights. He may, for example, discern from earlier correspondence between the parties or in the last resort from the brief of the organisation in reply to the complainant the reasons of the decision impugned; 1154: The mere information that a fixed-term appointment carries no expectancy of renewal is rather a reason of form than of substance and as such not sufficient to justify the refusal to extend a fixed-term appointment; 771: No obligation to state reasons for general decisions of the Council; 24: Any unmotivated decision would not be subject to the general review which is vested in the tribunal and would be liable to become arbitrary (23 to 21, 19 to 17).

CJEU Judgments/Orders

F-8/10: The obligation to state reasons is applicable by analogy to contract staff for auxiliary tasks. A decision refusing to renew a fixed-term contract must be reasoned; F-16/09: The administration is obliged to state in a sufficient and detailed manner the reasons on which a career development report is based; F-73/06: In the case of decisions taken by a selection board in a competition the obligation to state reasons must be reconciled with the observance of the secrecy surrounding the proceedings of selection boards; C-150/03 P: In the case of a choice between several candidates the organisation has a duty to state reasons, at the very least when rejecting a complaint made by an unsuccessful candidate. The extent of the duty is to be determined by the particular facts of the case; C-316/97 P: The requirements of a statement of reasons must be assessed in the light of the circumstances of the case, in particular, the measure at issue and the nature of the reasons relied on (T-11/03), C-254/95 P: The obligation to state the reasons on which decisions of a selection board in a competition involves as a rule two stages. In the first phase, the applications are examined on the basis of objective factors, those may be communicated to the candidates concerned. In the second phase, the markings of the competition tests are comparative in character and covered by secrecy; T-13/95: The duty to state grounds requires that sufficiently precise and coherent reasons are given. Summary referral to the interests of the service does not satisfy these requirements; T-92/91: Failure to refer to the legal basis for a decision is not harmful to its legality if there can be no doubt as to the legal basis in the mind of the official concerned; T-22/91: The reasons given by the selection board did not take account of the notice of competition and are, therefore, flawed; C-343/87: No obligation to give reasons to candidates who have not been promoted. Reasons must be given, however, for the decision to reject the complaint of such a candidate.

### 3. *The right to be heard (right to reply)*

The right to be heard (*audi alteram partem*) in administrative proceedings (for court proceedings see below under part 3, procedural matters) is recognised in settled case law by all international administrative tribunals as a general legal principle of the law of the international civil service (see, for example, ILOAT Judgment 987; CJEU Judgment F-51/07). The right to a hearing has, therefore, to be respected in all administrative proceedings concerning staff members regardless whether it is stipulated or not in the SR. This cardinal principle is derived from the basic legal principle valid in most contracting states of IO and in international conventions (Art. 41(2)(a) CFREU, see also Art. 16 European Code of Good Administrative Behaviour: "Right to be heard and to make statements"). In the ILOAT Triblex database the case law for this principle is to be found under the keyword "right to reply". The EU often refers to the collective term "rights of the defence".

**Jurisprudence**

ILOAT Judgments

3148: The lack or inadequacy of an explanation can be remedied at the appeal stage provided that a full say is given (2668); 3126: The right to be heard before a disciplinary measure is imposed; 3126: The staff member has a right to ensure the accuracy of personal information and data of his medical file (2047, 2045, 1684); 3065: The adversarial principle was flawed by not letting the complainant see the testimonies of the witnesses and by not offering an opportunity to comment; 2916: Withholding reports and reassigning the complainant without an opportunity to respond is in breach of the right to reply; 2899: In disciplinary proceedings the official must be given an opportunity to refute the content of all essential documents (1881, 69); 2893: General principles do not require that a complainant is offered an opportunity to put his case before an appeals board both in writing and orally. All the right to a hearing requires is that the complainant is free to put his case even without invitation to do so (1127, 623, 428, 232); 2786: An official accused of misconduct must be given the opportunity to test the evidence and to produce evidence to the contrary; 2605: If through a routine review and audit or an investigation irregularities have been identified, the staff member concerned must be notified with sufficient precision to enable him to defend himself against such allegations (2524, 2515, 1639, 1484, 1395, 1386, 1384, 1082, 922, 907, 901, 888); 2599: Termination of the probation period in breach of the right to be heard; 2598: The internal appeals board infringed the right to a fair hearing since the complainant was not offered the possibility to submit a rejoinder to the organisation's reply (2513); 2558: Discretion of the appeals board to reject a request for additional evidence; 2540: Right of a staff member to express an opinion about his subordinates (442); 2496: Right to fully adversarial proceedings (hearing, establishing evidence, gathering testimonies) (2475, 1675, 1673); 2424: Breach of the right to be heard by the dispute committee (refusal to reschedule the hearing); 2394: Opportunity to comment before a decision is taken; 2365: Suspension without a hearing was lawful. The right to be heard was safeguarded in the disciplinary proceedings (2262, 1927); 2254: Unlawful disciplinary proceedings. Information was not gathered in the context of adversarial proceedings guaranteeing the complainant's right to be heard (1251, 1221, 1212, 1133); 2229: A transfer of a disciplinary nature must afford the staff member the safeguards available in the case of disciplinary sanctions (1972, 1556, 1496); 2222: Waiver of the diplomatic immunity of a staff member in violation of the right to a hearing; 2062: The tribunal will not use confidential documents to the detriment of the complainant unless he had an opportunity to see them beforehand (1815); 1977: Waiver of a complainant to exercise his right to a hearing; 1817: Omissions in the reasoning of a decision may be repaired in the course of appeal proceedings provided that the staff member is given his full say (1484); 1741: After an appraisal the official must have at least an opportunity of adding any timely comments of his own for entry in his personal file; 1518: The decision was made on the strength of internal correspondence which neither the complainant nor the appeals board had seen. This is a gross breach of the right to be heard (1228, 1188); 1344: Amendment of a patent search report without giving the examiner who has signed it an opportunity to comment; 1234: Opportunity to correspond to the reasons of a transfer must be given; 1228: The Appeal Committee had a duty to communicate the content of the report which was submitted to it, to the complainant and afford him the opportunity of challenging it or commenting on it; 1176: Discounting a new material fact supplied by the organisation too late for the complainant to be able to comment; 987: Right to a hearing must be given before the notification of the termination of appointment and not at the same time; 585: Scope of the right to be heard if a decision is based on a multi-stage procedure.

CJEU Judgment/Orders

F-42/10: The right to be heard does not entail that the applicant should have access to the inquiry report nor that he should have been heard on the content of an inquiry document before the contested decision is taken; F-46/09: An appellate medical committee under Art. 33 EU-SR is intended to provide an additional guarantee for candidates and relates to the principle of observance of the right to a fair hearing (F-95/05); F-51/07 (Appeal case T-491/08P): Withdrawal of an unlawful act. The infringement of the right to be heard is not penalised by the annulment of the contested measure, if the unlawfulness did not influence the content of the measure. Such an unlawful act may, however, give rise to compensation (T-48/05); C-344/05P: The right to a hearing is not breached if the administration does not give prior warning during the preparation of an appraisal report (T-157/04 in part annulled); F-95/05: The right to a fair hearing, in particular through the intervention of a doctor of the staff member's choice (Art. 33 EU-SR) was infringed; F-65/05: Right to be heard in an assessment procedure (periodical report) under Art. 43 EU-SR; F-5/05 and F-7/05: The European Anti-Fraud Office (OLAF) forwarded to the Italian authorities information about officials in order to open investigations into the existence of possible criminal crimes. This was not a preparatory act but a decision which adversely affected the officials concerned. The officials should have been heard and had the possibility to defend their case prior to the information being forwarded; T-82/95: Breach of a hearing due to the failure of the appointing authority to take note of the comments of the staff member prior to his retirement in the interests of the organisation (Art. 50 EU-SR, senior official); 125/80: An official should be heard, as far as possible, before there is a decision on his reassignment; 75/77: Possibility for a candidate to express his point of view if he is declared physically unfit for appointment (121/76); 124/75: An official charged does not have the right to be assisted in his defence by a person of his choice in respect of a hearing by the appointing authority; 32–62: An official must have the opportunity of replying to allegations before any disciplinary measure is taken.

### *4. Reasonable periods for decisions*

The principle of good administration requires that the administration of an IO handles the affairs with its staff within a reasonable period of time (Art. 41(1) CFREU; Art. 17 European Code of Good Administrative Behaviour).

The administrative tribunals recognise a general legal principle conferring the right to international staff members that decisions are taken within a reasonable time limit. The notion of a reasonable time limit is, of course, "not a defined concept" (Kanska, p. 314). There is, however, a comprehensive judicature of the ILOAT. This case law primarily focuses on delays in internal appeal proceedings. The principle is not a one-way street and the complainant "cannot sit back and do nothing when an appeal is lodged" (ILOAT Judgment 1970 para. 9).

The principle under consideration, which derives from the principle of good administration, has to be seen in the context of the objective legal principle of legal certainty and stability in law. For the sake of legal certainty, the time limits set in the SR and statutes of the tribunals for staff actions (e.g. requests for allowances, complaints, appeals) have to be strictly observed.

**Jurisprudence**

ILOAT Judgments

3510: The administration must respect the need for expeditious appeal proceedings as the necessary prelude for judicial review; 3374: Appeal proceedings delayed by 20 months, damage awarded; 3302: The meaning of "reasonable time" varies to the particular circumstances of each case. A delay is not unreasonable if the complainant is responsible for a failure to exhaust the internal means of redress (2811). An appeal is unreasonably delayed if the complainant can show that the proceedings are unlikely to end within a reasonable time (2939): 3130: A two-tiered appeal process of less than two years is not considered as an unreasonable delay; 3114: A delay of a year and a half to take a decision following a recommendation of the appeal board is manifestly unreasonable; 3023: An appeal process of 17 months is unreasonably delayed if the only issue is receivability; 3035: The suspension of the complainant for a period of 13 months is unreasonably long (2698: investigation unduly delayed); 3026: The opportunity to improve performance requires that a reasonable time be given for that improvement to occur; 3016: More than four years for the post classification-exercise is egregiously long; 2975: The case law allows a complainant to file a complaint direct before the tribunal if the organisation fails to take a decision within sixty days from the notification of the claim to it (Art. VII.3 ILOAT Statute); 2904: Duty to maintain a fully functional internal appeals body; 2902: An appeal process of 19 months is unreasonably long; 2878:

An appeal process of 21 months is unacceptable: 2844: Four months to consider the report of an appeals board are unreasonably long (2170, 1968); 2768: A delay of three years is unacceptable; 2626 (leading judgment): Settled case law has it that if internal appeals proceedings are unreasonably delayed resulting from malfunctioning of that body or from the inadequate resources at its disposal, the staff member concerned may file a complaint direct before the tribunal. The duty to take quick action is reinforced where the dispute must be resolved rapidly to serve any purpose; 2522: Hampering internal appeal proceedings by not providing the results of the review in due time; 2392: The fact that the complainant did not come direct to the tribunal when the internal proceedings took too long cannot be held against him; 2325: A delay of 15 months between the selection of the successful candidate and the notification was unreasonably long; 2197: Positive obligation that internal appeal proceedings move forward with reasonable speed. Damage for an unreasonable delay of 20 months between filing the appeal and the start of the hearings; 2116: Appeal proceedings of 30 months are unreasonably long; 2072: Appeal proceedings of 24 months are too long; 2039: The requirement to exhaust internal remedies may not paralyse the exercise of rights; the complainant may, however, only make use of the argument of unreasonable delay if he has to no avail done its utmost to accelerate the proceedings. In general, a request for information of the state of proceedings is enough; 1970: No unreasonable delay because the complainant did not pursue his appeal diligently; 1968: The argument of the organisation that there is a heavy backlog may be a reason but it is not an excuse (a year after the appeal was filed the administration was unable to predict when the position paper would be ready); 1829: Appeal proceedings of three months are not unreasonably delayed; 1684: Appeal proceedings of 19 months are too long; see also: 1674, 1534, 1486, 1433, 1404, 1344, 1243 and the cases cited therein); 857: Reasonable time of notice of non-renewal of a contract (703).

CJEU Judgments/Orders

F-103/09: A request for compensation must be brought before the organisation within a reasonable period running from the point in time where the official becomes aware of the situation he is complaining about (by analogy the period of five years laid down in Art. 46 of the statute of the CJEU for non-contractual liability applies (T-144/02)); F-95/09: Time limit for submitting a request for assistance in respect of psychological harassment. The time starts to run from the last act of harassment. As a rule a request for assistance in respect of psychological harassment is submitted within a reasonable period if it is forwarded within a period of five years (analogy to Art. 46 of the statute of the CJEU); F-42/08: Failure to comply with a reasonable period for lodging a claim for compensation. The five years period taken in analogy from Art. 46 of the statute of the CJEU is not a hard and fast limit but depends on the circumstances of the case (F-125/05, T-144/02); F-51/07: The withdrawal of an unlawful administrative measure must take place within a reasonable period. As a general rule a period corresponding to the three-month period for bringing proceedings is reasonable; F-124/05 and F-96/06: The abnormal length both of the period preceding the initiation of disciplinary proceedings and of the proceedings, themselves is unreasonable; F-40/05: In disciplinary proceedings the organisation is under the duty to act diligently and to observe reasonable time requirements (T-307/01, C-270/99 P); C-326/91 P: Considerations to assess whether disciplinary proceedings have been conducted within a reasonable period.

# D. The specific general legal principles of the international civil service

## I. The introduction

The general legal principles of the international civil service as applied primarily by the international administrative tribunals are, in general, identical with those recognised in the member states, in international conventions and declarations on fundamental and human rights.

There are, however, some legal principles that have been acknowledged by the tribunals in order to safeguard the specific reason of existence of an IO. Some of these principles can easily be recognised as having been derived from other, more general, legal principles, like that of acquired rights or the protection of legitimate expectations in the renewal of fixed-term contracts. Others, like the Noblemaire principle and the exemption of salaries paid by IO from national taxation have been specifically developed in order to protect the unimpeded functioning of IO and the complete independence of its staff in order to achieve the synergetic effect of added value intended by the member states. The staff of the IO is in total in a far weaker and isolated position in comparison to national civil servants. There is, in principle, no entrepreneurial co-determination and the staff unions of IO have no negotiation rights on salaries and working conditions, and may hardly rely on the solidarity of national staff unions. Finally, the national delegates in the legislative and supervisory boards (Council, General Assembly) are, as a rule, staff members of the national civil service and as such in a certain competitive relationship. They may also sometimes fall short in their supervisory functions with respect to the head of the administration during their sporadic meetings. All these issues have led to the development of some specific general legal principles.

## II. The principle of the protection of legitimate expectation

### *1. The principle in general*

The principle of the protection of legitimate expectation which is "the corollary of the principle of legal certainty" (CJEU Judgment F-105/05 para. 139) has been explicitly declared in the case law of the CJEU to be "a superior rule of law" and one of the "fundamental principles of the Community". Its purpose is "to ensure that positions legitimately acquired … are protected" (see CJEU Judgment F-105/05 para. 138 et seq. with further references). This principle may also more specifically be referred to, for example, as the principle of protection of an assurance or as an acquired right (see the following section).

In the field of the law governing the EU civil service the CJEU has regularly recourse to the general principle of (acquired) legitimate expectation without seeing the need to develop an extensive doctrine on sub-categories of this general principle, like the protection of acquired rights which is referenced regularly in the case law of the ILOAT. This may be primarily because the statutory system of permanent officials of the EU is characterised by more stability than the contractual employmentship of the most other IO.

In contrast to the CJEU the ILOAT in most cases of this kind only implicitly refers to the general principle of legitimate expectation as such. Its case law is primarily based on the doctrine of acquired rights. Even if the Triblex database of the ILOAT quotes 35 judgments as of 2016 as taking reference to the principle of legitimate expectation, most of these judgments are explicitly based on other principles like good faith and duty of care (see, for example, Judgments 2729, 2337).

**Jurisprudence**

ILOAT Judgments

1427: Entitlement to moral damages for the inquiry due to the thwarting of the legal expectation of prompt and correct executions of the Tribunal's Judgment; 1351: A decision not to renew a fixed-term contract disappoints expectation of further employment (1232); 1090: Alleged breach of a promise, payment for moral injury; 687: Expectation of confirmation of the probationary period.

CJEU Judgments/Orders

F-41/15: Change of the seat of the IO, no legitimate expectation; F-116/14: Legitimate expectation in an offer of employment; F – 29/09: An official cannot rely on the principle of legitimate expectation in order to challenge the legality of a provision of the SR; C-496/08 P: (see also under acquired rights): Individuals cannot rely on the principle of protection of legitimate expectations in order to oppose the application of a new legislative provision, especially in a sphere in which the legislature enjoys a considerable degree of latitude (F-70/05; C-284/94); F-51/07: A beneficiary cannot rely on "acquired legitimate expectations" if he has provoked the adaptation of the measure by means of false or incomplete information or if the illegality justifying the withdrawal of a decision could not escape the notice of a normally diligent official, who, in view of his ability to carry out the necessary checks, cannot be absolved from the duty to make every effort to be attentive and verify (T-127/07); F-45/07: Recognition of two persons as surviving spouses, reduction of the survivor's pension to 50%, no legitimate expectation to receive the full amount of pension; C-213/06 P: An uncertain contractual situation of a staff member cannot form the basis of precise assurance on the part of the administration, which is necessary to give rise to legitimate expectation; F-105/05: Since the Council of the EU is the only EU institution which has power to adopt the SR, the EU Parliament could not give statements on the reform of the pensions for EU staff which gave rise to a legitimate expectation (but see now Art. 336 TFEU, the EU-SR are laid down by the European Parliament and the Council); F-43/05: No infringement of legitimate expectation if SR are changed in an area whose adaptations to changes in economic circumstances is frequent (travel expenses for home leave); T-471/04:

Legitimate expectation in a contractual commitment restricting the discretionary power of the administration in case of a temporary staff member; T-324/04: The organisation did not detect the irregularity of the entitlement to an expatriation allowance. The organisation was, nevertheless, right in recovering the allowance since the error was obvious and could have been noticed by the complainant having regard to his grade and experience; T-25/03: No breach of the principle of legitimate expectation unless the administration has given precise assurances (T-205/01).

### 2. *The assurance (promise)*

The principle of protection of legitimate expectation also ensures compliance with assurances (CJEU Judgment T-471/04). On occasion, the ILOAT also relies on the principle of good faith according to which anyone to whom a promise is made may expect it to be kept (see, for example, Judgment 2945).

The ILOAT case law requires that:

a) The promise must be *substantive* (e.g. Judgment 3362),

b) The promise must come from someone *competent* or *deemed to be competent* to make it (e.g. Judgment 3204),

c) Its breach should *cause injury* to the person who relies on it (e.g. Judgment 3204), and

d) The *position in law must not have changed* between the date of the promise and the date at which fulfilment is due (e.g. Judgment 3005).

If an IO makes a statement that some emoluments paid to staff members are to be considered as exempt from national taxation, employees are protected by the principle of tax exemption as one of the fundamental principles of the international civil service (ILOAT Judgments 2256, 2032).

The CJEU case law applies a three-step approach as a precondition for invoking the legal protection of an assurance (see Judgment F-114/07 and the case law cited):

a) The assurance given by the competent authority must be *precise*, *unconditional* and *consistent.*

b) The assurance must have led the official to entertain reasonable expectations. Thereby the official has the duty corresponding to his grade and experience to check and verify the correctness of the assurance (Judgment F-51/07, Judgment T-324/04).

c) The assurance must be consistent with the SR.

**Jurisprudence**

ILOAT Judgments

3362: The promise to renew a contract was not substantive; 3204: Firm commitment to pay a certain sum to an official; 3005: Promise by someone who did not have the authority nor were they deemed to have authority to make a promise; 2945: No legitimate expectation (promise) of contract renewal if an organisation makes an incorrect statement to a third party (e.g. a bank); 2779: A promise by a non-authorised official to extend a contract beyond the statutory retirement age is illegal. Moral damages were awarded since the Secretary-General did not correct the false promise; 1924: If an offer for a settlement proposal is accepted, no party can then withdraw from it; 1804: Fulfilment of a promise made to a staff member on recruitment to promote him under certain conditions which was not in accordance with the requirements of the SR. Promotion upheld (good faith) but award of moral damages to the complainants (staff representatives); 1781: Verbal promise to receive three-step increments; 1667: The announcement that success in liaison work should serve the advancement of the employee's career is not a direct promise; 1481: Promise to convert the complainant's appointment within a certain period; 1278: It does not matter what form (written, oral, express or implied) the promise takes; 1090: Belated correction of an interview given by the Executive Director in which the complainant had good reasons to believe that a promise had been made; 1040: The promise was neither substantive nor did it come from someone competent or deemed to be competent; 956: No firm promise or commitment for the extension of contract; 892: The mere reference to a common practice is not a substantive promise; 782 (leading judgment): Preconditions for a promise; promise on an indefinite appointment.

CJEU Judgments/Orders

T-175/03: Legitimate expectation of a staff member that the organisation respects contractual provisions which restrict its power to terminate a contract; T-145/04: The acknowledgement of exceptional qualifications is not a promise for an appointment to a higher grade; T-398/03: There is no valid assurance if an institution has no competence to deviate from an explicit rule in the SR, from the implementing rules, administrative instructions or documents of general information; T-329/03: There is no valid assurance to be appointed if the complainant is put on a reserve list, he also may not rely on purely internal documents. There is also no assurance to be inferred if the administration does not reply to a request for information; T-25/03: The assurance as to the appointment was not sufficiently precise; T-205/01: No promise to the entitlement to the household allowance; T-319/00: No precise promise to be appointed as official or as temporary staff member for an indefinite period; T-22/99: A promise of promotion must be in accordance with the SR; T-235/94: The mere information by the administration regarding the change of employment of the promoted spouse and the confirmation of the right to the household allowance without asking the official to inform the administration about the higher income of his spouse which exceeds the limit for the entitlement to the household allowance is not a precise promise for granting the household allowance; T-123/89: The silence of the administration to a request for information on an entitlement is not a precise assurance. An incorrect application of the EU-SR by the administration cannot create a legitimate promise; 162/84: A promise which does not take account of the SR cannot give rise to legitimate expectation.

### 3. *The principle of acquired rights*

The freedom of the IO to modify the SR and implementing rules is not unlimited and must in particular take into account the general legal principle of acquired rights. The doctrine of acquired rights for the staff of the international civil service has been developed by the international administrative tribunals since their inception (see, for example, ILOAT Judgment 61, old UNAT Judgment 202, CJEU Judgments C-443/07, 68/69).

This general legal principle has even been codified in the UN-SR (Reg. 12(1) UN-SR) and in the statutes of most UN specialised agencies (see, for example, Reg. 93 UNESCO-SR; Art. 12(1) WHO-SR). These provisions do, however, not contain a definition of the principle of acquired rights but leave it to the judicial power to determine its content. Reg. 12(5) UN-SR states that the "staff rules shall not give rise to acquired rights within the meaning of regulation 12(1) while they are provisional" (Reg. 12(3) and 12(4) UN-SR state that the provisional staff rules and amendments shall be reported annually to the UNGA and shall enter into full force and effect on 1 January following the year in which the report is made to the UNGA).

The principle of acquired rights (or vested rights) means that such rights must be respected "notwithstanding any amendment to the rules" (see, for example, ILOAT Judgment 365). It is applied in a very large number of judgments of the ILOAT (in 2016, 154 extracts can be found in the Triblex database) whereas there are only a few cases of the CJEU with reference to this general principle. Apparently the CJEU prefers to have recourse to the more general principle of (acquired) legitimate expectation.

The extensive case law of the ILOAT has led over the years to a well-developed doctrine of acquired rights. The relatively small number of successful complaints by staff members in relation to the huge number of total complaints may indicate that there is a trend to overestimate the violation of this principle. It may, however, also be due to the fact that the administration takes the judicature on acquired rights into account more and more when preparing changes of the SR for their legislative bodies.

### a) The doctrine of acquired rights as applied by the judicature of the ILOAT

#### *aa) General introduction*

According to the jurisprudence of the ILOAT, which has contributed most in this area, an acquired right is:

A fundamental or essential term of the official's contract, of the SR or of a decision (Judgments 2972, 2696) which was likely to induce an "ordinary" (Judgment 1446) staff member "reasonably" (Judgment 365) to enter (Judgment 61) or to "stay on" in the service of an IO (Judgments 2089, 832).

In the three leading judgments 61, 832, 2089 the ILOAT recognised, elaborated and consolidated its doctrine on the general principle of acquired rights (see also Judgment 3074).

In Judgment 61 ("Lindsey") of 1962, the ILOAT established the basic criteria for the doctrine. It held that the change of the contractual obligations or terms of appointment to the detriment of the staff member amounts to the breach of an acquired right when the structure of the contract of appointment is disturbed or there is impairment of any fundamental term of appointment in consideration of which the official accepted the appointment.

In Judgment 832 the ILOAT stated (para.13): "A somewhat broader framing of the doctrine is wanted so that it will cover not just terms of appointment that were in effect at recruitment but also terms that were brought in later and were calculated to induce the staff member to stay on". It went on to state that an objective three-tests standard has to be applied in order to determine whether the altered term is fundamental and essential.

In Judgment 2089 (and most recently in Judgment 3074) the ILOAT summarised and confirmed the doctrine of acquired rights applied by the tribunal.

#### *bb) Details*

– Ambit

The doctrine of acquired rights is broader than the rule against retroactivity. Whereas the latter rule prohibits the amendment of a legal position which has existed in the past, the doctrine of acquired rights looks to the future as well as to the past (Judgment 2089 para. 13).

– Personal rights

Only personal rights of staff are covered by the principle of acquired rights. Benefits which are granted to the IO itself are "*res inter alios acta*" and can, therefore, not generate an acquired right of a staff member (Judgments 372, 369).

Staff members may benefit at best indirectly (as a legal reflex from privileges and immunities granted to the organisation in the Protocol of Privileges and Immunities and in seat agreements).

Only as far as privileges and immunities are part of the employment contract, are based on an individual decision, are incorporated in the SR (or a higher ranking rule) or are based on a general legal principle, they may provide the legal basis for an acquired right. For example, the exemption of international salaries from national taxation may be explicitly stipulated in the primary law of an IO (see, for example, Art. 16(1) EPO-PPI) or at least result from the general legal principle of the exemption of international salaries from national taxation.

– The three tests approach

In its fundamental Judgment 832, the ILOAT has developed the doctrine of acquired rights further by applying a three tests approach. This three tests method has since then being confirmed in several Judgments (see, for example, 3074, 2986) as a firm standard.

The first test applied by the tribunal concerns the nature of the altered term. The tribunal distinguishes between the contract of employment (there is also the possibility that a practice becomes the source of an acquired right, see ILOAT Judgment 2089, para. 14), a decision and the SR. In the case of an employment contract the acquired rights are obvious (the same result will be achieved by the general law principle of "*pacta sunt servanda*"). In this respect the tribunal notes, however, that, *inter alia*, owing to the increasing complexity of employment the conditions of service mainly do not appear amongst the stipulations in the contract of appointment but in the provisions of the SR incorporated by reference (Judgment 61 para. 12). The jurisprudence of the ILOAT in relation to acquired rights is therefore mainly concerned with changes to the SR. The tribunal hereby distinguishes basically between two types of provisions.

On the one hand, there are *provisions* which appertain to the structure and functioning of the organisation. These are *of an impersonal nature* and are subject *per se* to variation. On the other hand, there are *individual terms and conditions* in consideration of which a person has accepted appointment.

The *impersonal provisions* may be altered at any time in the interests of the service having regard to the general principles governing international service.

Conversely individual terms are to a large extent assimilated to contractual stipulations. Such terms may only be modified without the consent of a staff member if there is no impairment of any fundamental and essential term in consideration of which the official *accepted appointment* (Judgment 61) or (if the terms were brought in later) induced him to stay on (Judgment 832).

In some rare cases an acquired right may even arise under an express or implied provision which the parties intend to be inviolate (Judgment 368) or which is explicitly referred to as an acquired right (Judgment 1020: Appendix VII Interpol-SR, an acquired right to keep the duty station).

In its Judgment 832 the tribunal clarified that this test step is not based on any subjective reflection of whether this term or that did actually "make the staff member sign on or decide to stay". It is sufficient that the term was of the sort "that might sway his decision".

The second test relates to the *reason* for the disputed change to the SR. The organisation has a duty to state proper reasons. The *mere desire* to save money at the staff's expense is not by itself a valid reason (Judgment 1912). On the other hand, financial considerations are a legitimate reason (Judgment 2089). The stated reasons must not be a simple "screen to hide an ulterior motive" (Judgment 2089). By applying this test the tribunal considers whether the term by its very nature is subject to variables of life, like cost-of-living index or the value of currency or the financial situation of the organisation (Judgment 832).

The third test laid down by the tribunal refers to the effect *(the impact, the consequences)* of the changes on the staff pay and benefits (Judgment 2089). Here the tribunal conducts a detailed examination. Not every financial decline is a violation of an acquired right. The reduction of merely supplementary or marginal benefit ("fringe benefits") is not considered to be of such an effect (Judgments 429, 323).

A term which gives a right that is remote or contingent is less likely to survive an amendment of the rules than one that is direct and immediate (Judgments 1446, 429). An important and fundamental decline in an acquired position can even be triggered when the impairment is gradual and due to an accretion of financial decisions which are no longer open to challenge and each of which, taken simply, would not itself have been deemed unlawful (Judgments 1917, 1514, 986).

In this context reference is made to the doctrine of revocation of decisions lawfully (unlawfully) conferring benefits. In Judgment 1006 the complainant pleaded a violation of the principle of acquired rights when the organisation revoked an alleged unlawful decision which had conferred him benefits. The tribunal decided in his favour since the organisation did not abide by the rules for almost nine years, however, without disclosing the type of general principle it was applying.

**Jurisprudence**

ILOAT Judgments

*No violation* of an acquired right was established in the following Judgments:

3524: No acquired right to an age-50 rule for promotions; 3375: The change from the invalidity pension system to an invalidity allowance system does not violate an acquired right;

3373: A particular model of organising a service cannot constitute an acquired right (but duty of care must be respected); 3358: The withdrawal *ex nunc* of a legally unfounded decision does not violate an acquired right but re-establishes a situation in conformity with the law; 3251: No acquired right to a promotion exercise; 3074: The conditions for the payment of a household allowance are not fundamental and essential terms within the meaning of an acquired right; 2986: The possibility of transferring pension rights which was subject to the existence of provisions authorising the transfer in member state's national law, was purely hypothetical. The new provisions did not call into question but only altered the method of calculating pensionable years. Therefore, fundamental terms of employment were not adversely affected; 2972: An organisation has the right to assign new different shift patterns. The official must expect those changes. There is no acquired right on the actual amount of the shift allowance or the continuation of any particular method of reckoning. There may, however, be a duty of care to cushion against financial hardship; 2696: Amendment of a reduction-in-force procedure. Given the remote and contingent nature of the prior procedure there is no infringement of an acquired right; 2682: Lowering of the retirement age from 65 to 60 violates no acquired right; 2632: A practice of salary or pension adjustment even where repeated does not constitute an acquired right to the adjustment of pensions being identical to the adjustment of salaries. The adjustment of pensions may be restricted to the adjustment in relation to the cost of living (inflation) thus not taking into account a standard-of-living adjustment of salaries; 1917: No acquired right to a specific system of health insurance; 1912: No acquired right to an automatic indexing of salaries; 1886: No acquired right to the amount and the conditions of the payment of the expatriation allowance; 1791: No acquired right if salaries are slightly reduced for one year due to a financial crisis; 1660: No breach of an acquired right since there was no written rule or practice entitling staff to full indexing of pensions to the cost of living; 1515: The trend of a declining of purchasing power which was not offset by rises in pay does not amount to the breach of an acquired right; 1446: The prospect of increases in emoluments after 20, 25, 30 and 35 years of satisfactory service is too remote to influence seriously the mind of the ordinary applicant in deciding to accept appointment; 1392: A pension contribution is by its very nature subject to variations. The raising of the pension contributions from 7 to 8 percent is warranted for sound actuarial reasons; 1334: Only benefits that have some basis in law may be protected under the doctrine of acquired rights (no breach of an acquired right in the case of the loss of an on-call duty allowance based on management practices); 1330: No breach of an acquired right if the competence for disputes is conferred to the UNAT instead of the ILOAT; 1241: No breach of an acquired right in the case of the removal of an unfair advantage under the health insurance scheme even if the advantage was enjoyed for a long time; 1239: A particular benefit (differential benefits) may not indefinitely preclude reforms that are in the general interest; 1226: Abolition of free after-service medical cover. The change was moderate (max 4% of full pension, dispensation for low pensions and transitional measures), no violation of an acquired right; 1199: The new pensionable remuneration scales took account of shifts in economic trends and tax rules in the US. The reasons for the change were not intrinsically unlawful; 1196: The repeal of a staff regulation which had potential for an undue increase in pay is not in breach of an acquired right; 1123: No acquired right to a *de facto* alignment of pay with the scales of the EU; 1084: A change in the title of an official is not a breach of an acquired right; 1026: The particular arrangements for the grant of promotion confer no acquired right because on recruitment staff cannot foretell what their career prospects will be; 1020: Officials had an explicitly stipulated acquired right with regard to the location of their duty station. When the whole organisation moved to a new location, the organisation dealt with the transfer of the complainant in a way which did not breach an acquired right; 952: A change in the SR restricting the possibility of having adopted relatives treated as dependents does not breach an acquired right; 751: No acquired right in relation to hours of work, incidental benefits, fixed elements of expatriation allowance and frequency of salary surveys; 726: Introduction of a temporary salary levy of 1.5 per cent with a guarantee of nominal basic salary is no breach of an acquired right; 666: No acquired right to the actual amount of an allowance (indemnity) or to a particular method of reckoning it (368, 366); 596: Rules on reckoning seniority and provisions on the conditions of promotion do not create acquired rights; 514: Reimbursement of tax on lump-sum payments from the UNJS-PF may not be construed as an acquired right; 462: The possibility of obtaining a language allowance is not ordinarily a matter of decisive importance to a new recruit and, therefore, no acquired right; 429: The rate of contribution to the pension scheme by the organisation is a matter of lesser importance and does not give rise to an acquired right; 426: A reduction of fringe benefits of a little more than USD 6,000 (tax payable) has to be compared with the total amount the staff member would expect to be receiving in salaries and emoluments over the next 21 years. There is, therefore, no infringement of an acquired right; 391: The reduction of salary by 2.2 per cent over a period of six months does not infringe an acquired right; 372: Privileges deriving from headquarters agreements are granted in the interest of the organisation and are not personal rights of staff, they do not create an acquired right (369); 371: No acquired right to the continuance of the career patterns and grading structure; 368: No acquired right to the amount and the conditions of payment of the education, expatriation and leave expense allowances, since staff members should expect amendments prompted by changes in the cost of living, reforms of the structure of the organisation or financial difficulties; 365: No acquired right to the method of a salary adjustment or a certain salary increase on promotion or to a certain amount or method of calculation of allowances; 357: The modification of a provision on compensation for accumulated leave does not infringe an acquired right; 293: No acquired right on the description of an employment as "permanent" instead of "continuing".

*Violation* of an acquired right was established in the following Judgments:

2089 (leading judgment): The Tribunal did not have to decide whether the periodic adjustment of pensions should be viewed as an acquired right. It nevertheless held that, even assuming that the periodic adjustment of pensions should be viewed as an acquired right, such a right could go no further than the maintenance of the purchasing power of the pensions paid at the time of entitlement; 1912 (dissenting opinion): The erosion by inflation of the purchasing power of salaries substantially impairs the contractual balance of employment; 1886: The outright abolition of the expatriation allowance would violate an acquired right, although there is no acquired right to the amount and the conditions of payment of the allowance (see 666, 371, 368, 366, 365); 1514: A fall in the purchasing power of salaries below some critical point may be a breach of an acquired right. This is so even where impairment is gradual and due to an accretion of final decisions which are no longer open to challenge and each of which, taken simply, would not itself have been deemed unlawful (a cumulative loss of 10% of the purchasing power was however not to be considered as to be below a critical point) (1368); 1392: The right to a pension is inviolable but not the amount of pension contributions; 1025: Rules on promotion only confer an acquired right insofar as they offer an expectation of advancement; 986: A cumulative loss in the scale of pensionable remuneration of about 20% is an important factor of the acquired pension and amounts to a breach of an acquired right; 441: The reimbursement of travel expenses for home leave is a considerable advantage to the official and may have prompted him to accept the appointment, its abolition, therefore, constituted the loss of an acquired right; 365: The substance of the acquired right to promotion is merely the possibility of advancement because it is only on the strength of such a possibility that a staff member may have accepted appointment; 292: The change of the character of the payment from an allowance (which is characterised by the fact that the recipient cannot be made to account for what he does with the money) to a reimbursement may be treated as a change of an essential term of the employment contract which is safeguarded by the principle of acquired rights; 323: When an organisation has calculated a payment of salary and announced it the officials entitled to it acquire a right which the organisation has no power to destroy; 61 (leading judgment): The cumulative decline of the pension system (barely higher contribution for employees, but remarkably lower contributions by the organisation and the reduction of the maximum amount of pensions from 60 to 54.5 per cent of insured earnings and the abolition of guaranteed termination benefits) is an infringement of acquired rights.

#### b) The doctrine of acquired rights as applied by the judicature of the CJEU

As has already been stated above, there is only very restricted case law of the CJEU on vested rights. The court has not even developed a real doctrine in relation to this general principle. It simply refers to it or gives a purely formal description without any guidance on how to evaluate in detail the criteria for its application. (See, for example, Judgment T-30/02 para. 55: There is no acquired right to the unchangeability of existing rules on promotion Judgment C-496/08 P para. 84: "A right is considered to be acquired when the event giving rise to it occurred before the legislative amendment").

CJEU Judgments/Orders

C-496/08 P: Officials who advanced in their careers because they passed the internal competition, have acquired rights to have the advance thus made under the old SR acknowledged. However, such right merely implies the right to the same treatment as all the officials of the new grade that they have just obtained; C-443/07 P: Candidates who are successful in a competition and are included in a list of suitable candidates have no acquired right to be appointed, but are merely eligible to be so. Their classification in grade was dependent on their appointment which could be subject to certain recruitment conditions of the new SR which in the meantime entered into force. This consideration holds good for officials recruited on a probationary status before the new SR entered into force; F-126/06: The principle of acquired rights is applicable only within the same career group (officials, temporary staff); T-135/05: No acquired right to the method of calculation of the coefficients safeguarding the purchasing power of pensions (see also T-116/96 and joint cases); F-103/05: An official has no acquired right to the inviolability of the SR as they have been at the date of his recruitment provided that there is sufficient transitional period; T-58/05: An official cannot claim an acquired right unless the facts giving rise to that right arose by virtue of a particular status prior to the amendment of the provisions of the SR; 54/77: The irregular grant of continued payment of elements of remuneration cannot create a vested right as to prevent revocation; 56/75: The immediate withdrawal of a benefit based on a situation which is not in conformity with the SR cannot infringe the principle of vested right; 28/74: An EU official can only derive vested rights from statutory provisions.

### *4. The protection of legitimate expectation in the renewal or extension of fixed-term contracts*

Although a fixed-term contract carries no right to renewal (ILOAT Judgment 2678, CJEU Judgment T-160/04 para. 30) it is a general principle of international civil service law that valid reasons must be stated for any decision not to renew or extend a fixed-term (including short-term and probationary contracts; ILOAT Judgments 2991, 1817, 1418; CJEU Judgments F-63/11, F-85/10, F-38/06). Valid reasons must also be stated in case an employment contract of indefinite duration is terminated (CJEU Judgment F-74/11; for a period of notice see Art. 47(c)(i) EU-CEOS).

The decision of the administration on an extension or renewal of a fixed-term contract is a discretionary one (e.g. ILOAT Judgment 2991 para. 9, CJEU Judgment T-160/04 para. 30), therefore the case law governing discretionary decisions applies.

When exercising its discretion, the organisation has to take into account not only the interests of the service but also those of the staff member (CJEU Judgment F-124/12). The ILOAT very clearly states that inevitably “there arises an expectation” of the staff member concerned that normally a contract of temporary employment will be renewed (ILOAT Judgment 675 para. 10). Accordingly, when exercising its discretion the organisation is under an obligation to take a reasoned decision on the non-renewal of a fixed-term contract and to communicate it to the staff member (ILOAT Judgment 2499 para. 6, 2104, 1911, 1544, 1154, 1128, 675; CJEU Judgments F-63/11, F-85/10, F-38/06). This holds good even if the SR provide that no notice is necessary in the case of expiry at the due date of a fixed-term contract. This obligation arises from the principles of good faith and the respect for the dignity of the staff member concerned (ILOAT Judgments 2750 para. 27, 2531, 2104, 675).

The notice must be based on valid reasons and the notification of the non-renewal is to be treated as a distinct and challengeable administrative decision (ILOAT Judgments 3286, 2573, 1317, 1298, 1159, 1154).

The most important reasons given for the non-renewal of a contract are: the elimination of tasks performed by the complainant (ILOAT Judgment 2708), if the extension would be beyond the normal retirement age (ILOAT Judgments 2377, 2125), if the qualifications of the complainant are not sufficient for the increased requirements of the post (ILOAT Judgment 1335), if the organisation is faced with financial difficulties (ILOAT Judgment 3586; CJEU Judgment F-63/11), as consequence of a written reprimand (ILOAT Judgment 956) or the abolition of the complainant's post because of cuts in the expenditure on staff (ILOAT Judgment 954).

Fatal errors in the exercise of discretion in contract-renewal matters are for example: non-renewal based on unsatisfactory performance without taking into account all appraisal reports due (ILOAT Judgments 3417, 2573, 1351), if the organisation bases the decision not to renew a contract on the wishes of a member state (ILOAT Judgments 1249, 1230).

The reasons justifying the non-renewal of the contract must be given to the staff member within a reasonable period of notice in order to exercise his rights and to take whatever steps he sees fit (ILOAT Judgments 2104, 1983). The case law of the ILOAT requires a minimum period of notice (ILOAT Judgments 2531, 2162, 1145). A mere reference to a letter sent to the staff member years ago cannot ordinarily be considered as the statement of valid reasons for the non-renewal of a fixed-term contract (ILOAT Judgment 1911).

A failure to observe the notice period does not invalidate a non-renewal decision as a whole. In such a case, the notice period is replaced by an admissible one. If the notice period ends after the expiry of the contract, the notice requirement is met by extending the contract respectively (ILOAT Judgment 2162). In Judgment 1040 the ILOAT ruled, however, that "if due notice is not given there will be implied renewal for a further period".

If the non-renewal or the termination of a contract for an indefinite period is based on unsatisfactory performance the organisation is under a duty give the staff member a timely warning so as to allow him to improve (ILOAT Judgments 2678, 2573, 2414, 1617, 1583). An express threat of non-renewal is not necessary (ILOAT Judgment 2162). If the official failed to improve in respect of other shortcomings the contract may nevertheless be terminated since on the whole he is not up to standard (ILOAT Judgments 1583, 1546).

Regarding the issue whether a fixed-term appointment may be terminated during sick-leave see ILOAT Judgments 3175, 1494, 938, 607.

If a decision on the non-renewal of a fixed-term contract is set aside by the tribunal it does not normally order the renewal of the contract since a fixed-term contract carries no right to renewal. Since, however, the complainant has lost a valuable opportunity to a valid discretionary decision for renewal, the loss of the opportunity warrants the award of material damages (ILOAT Judgments 2678, 2306). In Judgment 1154 the ILOAT held that the organisation "must do its utmost to reinstate the complainant by granting him an extension of appointment". Only if that proves impossible has the organisation to pay him damages. In Judgment 1298 the ILOAT exceptionally ordered the reinstatement of the complainant: "... in view of his length of service, loss of pension entitlements if he is not reinstated and the difficulty he would no doubt face in finding other employment at his age ... since it would not be fair just to award him financial compensation".

In contrast to the jurisprudence of the ILOAT, the case law of the CJEU primarily concerns officials on a statutory basis which warrants in principle a stable employment relationship up to retirement. This is the reason why there is a somewhat restricted jurisprudence on the non-renewal of the appointment in relation to EU staff members holding limited appointments under the EU-CEOS.

**Jurisprudence**

ILOAT Judgments

3626: The organisation bears the onus of proof that a contract is not renewed because there is a practice or policy to phase out a post; 3596: Reasonable notice of the non-renewal of a fixed-term appointment must be given (3448): 3586: Failure to disclose all documents proving that no funds were available for the extension of the contract (3295, 2700); 3444: The non-renewal must be done on objective grounds and not on a pretext for removing an undesirable staff member; 3299: The decision on whether to extend or renew a fixed-term appointment is a discretionary one; 3286: The unsatisfactory performance procedure was not followed, this may have had an influence on the decision not to renew the contract; 3282: Assessment of performance flawed, non-renewal decision set aside; 3166: The non-renewal of the contract of the alleged harasser did not involve a vindication of the complainant's rights. The task of the organisation is to determine a response to the grievance and to award compensation to the aggrieved person; 3090: The complainant worked under 24 successive short-term contracts over more than seven years. This long relationship was considered as equivalent to that of a permanent staff member; 2991: A decision not to renew a contract is a discretionary one. It is a general principle of the international civil service laws that there must be a valid reason for any decisions not to renew a fixed-term contract. If a non-renewal is based on unsatisfactory service and there is no performance appraisal report drawn up the decision is tainted with a legal flaw (2916); 2867: The decision not to renew the complainant's fixed-term contract on the ground of the abolition of the post is quashed since the appointing authority had no authority to abolish the post; 2750: A reasonable notice must be given even in the case of an expiry of a fixed-term or short-term contract where the SR stipulate an automatic ending without notice. The principle of good faith and respect of dignity require that the staff member may exercise his right to appeal and take whatever action necessary; 2729: The absence of agreed funding of the post of an associate expert is a valid reason for the non-renewal of the contract; 2678: The simple notification of the non-renewal of a contract is treated as a decision having legal effect for the purposes of Art. VII(2) of the Statute of the ILOAT (2573). The decision is a discretionary one. An organisation must not in good faith end someone's appointment for poor performance without first warning him and giving him an opportunity to do better (1583). A decision may not be based on unsatisfactory performance if the organisation has not complied with the rules to evaluate that performance (2414); 2162: A fixed-term contract must not be terminated for unsatisfactory performance without a prior clear warning and a chance to improve. An express threat of non-renewal is not necessary. In the case of failure to improve, the shortcomings need not be the same as those pointed out in the warning (1546); 1817: Before ending a probation period on the grounds of poor performance the organisation must ordinarily give a fairly prompt warning so as to allow for improvement. If the probationer still proves unsatisfactory dismissal, will be in order even if founded on new shortcomings; 1617: Renewal of a fixed-term contract for only one year in order to allow for an unfavourable appraisal report to improve rests within the discretionary power of the organisation; 1596: Manipulation of renewal in order to avoid the payment of a termination indemnity; 1583: In the case of the non-renewal of a fixed-term contract for poor performance prior warning is needed, giving the staff member the chance to improve. The shortcomings need not to be the same as those identified later. All that is needed is that the official should realise that on the whole he is not up to standard; 1544: The true reason for the decision on the non-renewal of the appointment must be communicated to the staff member; 1526: The organisation may base its decision not to renew a contract on the fact that there is no adequate post available. In such a case the organisation has nevertheless to avoid undue hardship by e.g. extending the contract for a limited period; 1525: No valid discretionary decision to terminate a fixed-term contract since the principle of due process was infringed; 1494: No right to extended sick leave after expiry of a fixed-term contract if other social protection is provided; 1351: Failure to consider the latest appraisal report when refusing the renewal of the fixed-term contract because of unfavourable performance. Damages awarded; 1342: Decision not to renew a contract was based on personal prejudice; 1317: Even if the SR stipulate that a fixed-term contract is *ipso facto* extinguished on expiry, the non-renewal is to be treated as a distinct and challengeable administrative decision. It is a general principle of the international civil service that there must be a valid reason for any decision not to renew a fixed-term contract and that the reasons must be given to the staff member; 1249: Non-renewal of a contract in conformity with the wishes of a member state. The decision is outside the power of discretion, it infringes the general principle of independence of the organisation and its staff; 1232: Application for early retirement was made under the duress of a member state. The organisation has a duty to renew the official's contract based on a later application by the complainant since no valid reason would have warranted a deviating discretionary decision; 938: Right to extended sick leave after termination of a fixed-term appointment; 607: Decision not to grant extended sick leave to a staff member beyond the end of a fixed-term appointment was unlawful; 427: A "solid" expectation for a contract renewal.

CJEU Judgments/Orders

T-368/12 P: When deciding on the renewal of a fixed-term contract the organisation is under a duty to have regard to the welfare of the staff member; F-124/12: The organisation is under a duty to have regard to the interests of an employee to continue his employment relationship (F-35/07, F-38/06); F-74/11: Termination of a contract of indefinite duration. No manifest error of assessment, budgetary appropriations had been exhausted; F-63/11: Since the organisation did not base its decision not to renew the contract on valid reasons the decision was annulled; F-1/05 (confirmed by T-404/06 P): Termination of a contract of indefinite duration. The decision to terminate the appointment was vitiated by a manifest error of assessment of the applicant's performance; F-8/10: The complainant explicitly requested the renewal of his fixed-term contract. The court held that the refusal by the organisation had to be motivated. The complaint was nevertheless rejected since the organisation referred to Art. 29 EU-SR which provides that the organisation may apply privileged procedures to fill the post of the complainant by another staff member; F-72/09 and F-17/10: The complainant holding a fixed-term contract was informed by the organisation in a letter that his appointment will not be renewed (Art. 8 EU-CEOS) at the expiry of the term. The tribunal rejected the appeal as being without merit since the complainant did not provide any proof that the discretionary decision was based on a fatal flaw; F-88/08: When terminating a contract of indefinite duration the organisation has to state valid reasons, on the one hand to allow the staff member to ascertain whether the decision is well-founded or is vitiated by an error allowing its legality to be contested and, on the other hand, to enable the tribunal to review the legality of the decision; F-54/08: It is settled case law that a temporary agent holding a fixed-term appointment has no right to have this appointment renewed. The discretionary decision of the organisation may, however, be restricted by its internal rules; F-38/06: The tribunal stated that the information given to the staff member holding a fixed-term contract that his contract would expire did not contain any written motivation. An oral motivation had been given, however, and additional information had been supplied by the organisation when rejecting the complaint.

### *5. The principle of stability, foreseeability and a clear understanding of the results of a salary adjustment method*

An IO is ordinarily free to determine an adjustment method or a standard for the salaries and pensions provided that the general principles of the international civil service law are respected (ILOAT Judgments 1912 para. 13, 1821). It may, however, not depart from rules granting rights in relation to a salary adjustment method without amending it in accordance with the general principles (ILOAT Judgment 2081 para. 8).

In addition, the ILOAT has developed general principles of the international civil service law warranting specific substantive and procedural guarantees for the salary adjustment.

Besides the Noblemaire and Fleming principles, which refer to the level of salary, the tribunal has developed the general legal principle of the international civil service law that the results of a salary adjustment method must be "stable, foreseeable and clearly understood" (ILOAT Judgments 2420, 2095, 2081, 1913, 1912, 1821, 1419, 1265). As usual, the ILOAT has not disclosed the details of the derivation of this unwritten precept from other sources of law, like fundamental principles underlying the national legal systems or international conventions, but simply determines its existence. Ultimately, the principle may be qualified as a special aspect of the principles of legitimate expectation and good administration in order to moderate the specific danger to which the interests of the international staff are exposed during the implementation of the salary adjustment processes. This danger results from the dependency of the IO on the financial contributions from member states, on the varying development of the costs of living and the purchasing power in the member states and a certain (unspoken) conflict of interest between the international staff and the national delegates, who as a rule are national ministry officials, in relation to their salaries.

The case law of the CJEU (Judgment C-40/10 para. 68) follows an approach similar to that of the ILOAT. The Court found that the salary adjustment procedure restricts the Council's discretion and was justified *inter alia* in the light of the need to ensure a degree of medium-term stability and avoid discussions or recurrent difficulties.

The annual remuneration (salaries and pensions) adjustment procedures of the EU, the CO and the mixed international civil service systems are based on the principle of parallelism with the evolution of the purchasing power of remuneration of the national civil servants in the central government services of representative member states.

The adjustment methods contain express reservations to depart from the regular adjustment procedure in the case of an economic crisis in member states or if the financial obligations and essential operating requirements of the organisation so require (affordability moderation clause, expectation clause). If these conditions are met, the legislative body of the organisation may reduce or postpone the annual adjustment.

The annual adjustment system of the UN-CS is fundamentally different from that of the other civil service systems. It is not based on the evolution of the purchasing power of remuneration in the member states but takes account of the Noblemaire and Fleming principles. The salaries are adjusted by the result of periodic salary studies to determine the best-paid national civil service used as a comparator for the professional and higher categories of staff and similar surveys of the conditions of service in the country of service for the general civil service staff.

In contrast to the moderation and exception clauses, which are based on statistical data and are determined in accordance with arithmetical terms, the affordability clause grants broad discretion to the legislative body. It is very doubtful how such a clause can be reconciled with the general principle governing the salary adjustment procedure as developed by the case law of the ILOAT. Up to now the ILOAT has had no opportunity to express its view on this issue. Such an affordability clause may even result in a kind of double counting of elements justifying a reduction of salary adjustment if the adjustment method is based on the development of salaries of national officials in some reference countries.

There are some doubts as to the consistency of ILOAT's jurisprudence in the application of this general principle of the international civil service. In his dissenting opinion in ILOAT Judgment 1912 Judge Hugessen qualifies the majority opinion as "paying lip service" to the principle of stability, foreseeability and clear understanding of a salary adjustment system. He questions whether the adjustment of salary can be described as a "methodology, system or standard" if the adjustment is left to the sovereign appreciation of the employer. The majority opinion he states reduces this principle to "mere empty words".

In connection with the principle of stability, foreseeability and clear understanding of a salary method, the most important findings of the ILOAT are:

- a deviation from an external index serving as an "orientation" must be objective, adequate and known to the staff (Judgments 2057, 1912);
- an organisation has the duty to check the lawfulness of any decision by another body outside the organisation on which it bases its own decision (Judgments 1765, 1265);
- the mere desire to save money at the staff's expense is not in itself a valid reason to depart from a standard (Judgments 1821, 1682, 990).

**Jurisprudence**

ILOAT Judgments

3180: Late payment of salary adjustment, interests are due; 2782: The salary adjustment forms an integral part of the salary, staff members not party to the proceedings leading to Judgment 2560 are nevertheless entitled to receive the salary arrears, since the organisation breached the provisions; 2632: A practice of salary and pension adjustment, even where repeated, does not bind the organisation that adopted it. It is at liberty to abandon the practice provided that it does so lawfully; 2610: An organisation does not have to confine itself to ensuring that the methodology (e.g. the Fleming principle) recommended by the ICSC had been followed. It is competent to check whether the rules applied in the chosen methodology and the ensuing results did not breach the chosen methodology or a general principle of law; 2533: Risk of "spoliation" of a disability pension without indexation clause. Exceptionally the complainant may apply by way of a request for the execution of the judgment if the purchasing power of the payment has been reduced by at least 10%; 2420: A salary adjustment methodology which has to satisfy the requirements of stability, foreseeability and transparency cannot be applied without a degree of flexibility and without leaving some room for interpretation by the competent authority, e.g. by restoring the margins applied by the UN common system; 2410: The position advocated by the Governing Board of the Pension Fund of CERN that it could not give its backing to the extraordinary pension adjustment requested by the President of the Pensioner's Association is not a legislative act which could implicitly be challenged; 2303: The Fleming principle is not flawed if without taking into account the "language factor" the conditions of service including the salaries are "among the best in locality without being the absolute best" (1713); 2252: If the level of the salary adjustment is set by a body external to the organisation, the latter must ensure that the figures proposed comply with the law; 2129: The principle of stability, foreseeability and transparency which governs the adjustment system of the salaries is not entirely applicable to the determination of allowances granted for specific purposes, e.g. travel expenses. Nevertheless, even such a decision must be based on objective considerations and guarantee protecting the independence of international civil servants; 2095: The organisation neither developed nor used a methodology able to ensure that the results of a salary adjustment are stable, foreseeable and clearly understood; 2081: The new salary adjustment procedure did not respect the rule in force as it might reasonably be understood by the staff; 2089 (leading judgment for the principle of acquired rights): The change in the practice for adjusting pensions in line with the adjustment of salaries to reflect change in both cost of living and standard of living is not in breach of an acquired right; 2057: There is not an acquired right to an automatic indexing of salaries (1682, 1329). To apply an external index as a simple "orientation" for the adjustment is in itself not a breach of any right, even if it is regrettable that there is not a more precise methodology of adjustment. Any deviation from the suggested orientation must be objective, adequate and known to the staff (1912; see the dissenting opinion of Judge Hugessen in this judgment where he qualifies this adjustment "methodology" as an act of "arbitrariness"); 1915: The phasing out of the language factor for the UN General Service staff in Austria was in conformity with the ICSC's salary survey method; 1821: An IO is free to choose a methodology, system or standard of reference for determining salary adjustments in line with all other principles of international civil service law. The results must be stable, foreseeable and clearly understood. If discretion is granted to depart from a standard, proper reasons have to be stated. The need to save money may be one valid factor to be considered, provided the method adapted is objective, stable and foreseeable. The mere desire to save money at the staff's expense is not in itself a valid reason to depart from a standard; 1765: An organisation has the duty to check the lawfulness of any decision by another body on which it bases its own decision (wrong post-adjustment multiplier delivered by the ICSC); 1682: If the salary adjustment system of another IO is serving "as a guide" (1514), the organisation has a certain discretion but is not free to apply only part of the other system. It has at least a duty to state proper reasons for any departure from the system. The mere desire to save money at the staff's expense is not in itself a valid reason; 1641: The suspension of an interim adjustment for a period of six months is a tenable compromise between the interim indexing of pay to the local market and the closest possible match between international and local pay on the strength of general surveys; 1420: A salary adjustment is intended to maintain or restore parity in purchasing power between staff whatever their duty station may be, is an essential feature of international pay schemes. The refusal of such an adjustment result is a discrimination of the staff concerned; 1329: It may be a pity that, despite this seemingly strict method, the organisation had to resort to the compromises that the financial strains of its members demanded but the tribunal, nevertheless, held that there was no breach of any legal obligation (1368); 1265: The salary adjustment methodology is an important factor in ensuring that the results are stable, foreseeable and clearly understood; 1199: United States federal civil service is the "comparator" for determining the pay and pension in the UN common system for staff in the professional and higher categories. It was justified to base the adjustment only on the economic trend in just one country; 1160: Salary adjustment was not carried out in accordance with the approved methodology; 1123: The *de facto* alignment to the salary scales of the EU in the past confers no right on the staff for the continuance of parity (but see the dissenting opinion); 1001: The "Commissary benefits" are not relevant for a comparison with the typical pay in the local employment market in order to apply the ICSC methodology for the salary adjustment of the General Service staff in the UN-CS; 990: An organisation is bound by its own SR as long as they remain in force. Having put the pensionable remuneration into its own SR, the organisation has an obligation to compensate the amount of pensions due under its SR and not the inferior pension amount paid by the UNJSPF; 936: The organisation followed the rule of thumb applied by the CO of not letting pay get out of line with the broad trend in national civil services. Since the Dutch levy did not fall under the CO rules for the calculation of the salary adjustment its application infringes the stability of legal relations and the legitimate expectations of staff; 365: There is no acquired right to a certain method of salary adjustment.

CJEU Judgments/Orders

C-40/10: Under Art. 65a EU-SR the rules in Annex XI EU-SR governing the annual adjustment of the level of remuneration are characterised by a precise and limited framework for the method of the annual salary adjustment which restricts the Council's discretion from Art. 65 EU-SR. This ensures medium-term stability and avoids discussions and is intended to maintain a harmonious management-staff relationship. In the case of an economic crisis the Commission would have to consider submitting a proposal for misapplying the normal adjustment. Under the Treaties, in principle, the Commission is granted the sole power to initiate proposals in respect of such legislative procedures. Since the consequences of the economic crisis had been noticeable during the reference period, the Council could have acted already at that earlier date for the purpose of the submission of a corresponding proposal by the Commission. The Council was precluded from deviating from the Commission's proposal on account of the economic crisis (see in this context C-63/12, C-66/12, C-196/12); 59/81: The stability of the salary adjustment method excludes the taking into account of factors other than those mentioned in the methodology (81/72).

### *6. The withdrawal of an administrative decision*

This issue has been dealt with in the context of legal certainty.

### *7. The recovery of undue payment*

This issue has been dealt with in the context of the objective general legal principles.

### *8. The right to information*

The ILOAT has acknowledged in settled case law the right of an official to be informed of any action that may affect his legitimate expectations (Judgment 2116: "an organisation must inform employees" in advance of any action that may imperil their rights or rightful interests"). The tribunal derives this general principle of law from the principles of good faith, the concomitant duty of care (Judgment 2768) or the requirements of due process (Judgment 1319).

The duty to inform the staff member extends to actions in a broad sense (Judgment 1756: the term "action" is defined "quite broadly"; see in this respect Art. 27 CFREU "Worker's right to information and consultation within the undertaking).

The duty of information may be restricted in "special cases in which higher dictates preclude disclosure" (e.g. reason of state, criminal proceedings, see ILOAT Judgment 1756 para. 10(b)). In those cases, however, material information may not be withheld merely to strengthen the position of the administration or one of its officers in a dispute with the employee (ILOAT Judgment 1756). No duty of information exists for the organisation in trifles without impact on the rights or legal interests of the staff member (ILOAT Judgment 1756).

Frequently overlaps occur between the right to information and other general legal principles, in particular the right to be heard, the principles of good faith, due process, the obligation to state reasons for a decision and the protection of legitimate expectation in the renewal of fixed-term contracts.

The duty of information also exists in relation to the staff committees and the advisory committees (see more in detail under "consultation"). These bodies can only fulfil their tasks if they are informed by the appointing authority in conformity with the relevant provisions and general principles of law. In practice, this duty has a high priority in an employment relationship in which the employer is at least to some extent in a position of a "substitute state".

In contrast to the jurisprudence of the ILOAT the CJEU has not acknowledged a special right to information as a general legal principle of law. The court takes recourse in cases of like issues to other general legal principles such as the duty of care (see, for example, Judgment T-90/95: information as to state of health).

**Jurisprudence**

ILOAT Judgments

3414: No right to be on an e-mail distribution list after having been released from the position as President of the Staff Council; 2940: Right to be informed about the composition of an advisory body (see due administrative process); 2921: Content requirements for a vacancy notice: minimum information needed to reach an informed decision; 2907: Concealing from the complainant some paper needed to exercise the right to appeal; 2884: Information on the use of an assessment centre is needed in the vacancy note; 2837: Non-publication of the promotion list deprived the complainant of information useful in filing a request for review; 2817: The complainant was not informed in a timely manner on the restructuring of his unit and the negative consequences for his post; 2768; Obligation to inform an official especially in opaque legal situation like the transfer of pension rights acquired under of a public or private scheme prior to recruitment; 2605: Informing a person in advance that an investigation will be undertaken is not a requisite element of due process (in certain circumstances alerting a person may compromise the investigation). Once irregularities are identified, precise information must be given to enable the official to respond adequately; 2531: Breach of the duty of information in the case of belated information on the reasons for not renewing a contract of employment; 2529: Duty of giving a timely and specified warning as to the unsatisfactory aspects of service and the consequences (2414, 2170, 2104, 2007, 1911, 1872, 1386, 1212); 2515: The advertisement of the complainant's post was an implicit decision to dismiss him without giving him a warning or stating reasons; 2392: Failure to give timely information as to the reasons for recommending external candidates in preference to internal ones; 2354: Lack of precise information on the reasons for the termination of appointment; 2315: To ensure due process both in internal proceedings and before the tribunal the staff member must get any item of information material to the outcome; 2229: Staff members are entitled, even outside the context of a dispute, to have access to significant information concerning them, that is in the possession of the administration; 2222: Duty to inform the staff member about the reasons for the waiving of his diplomatic immunity; 2116: The organisation was cavalier in the way in which it informed the complainant about the outcome of the selection process; 2047: The staff member is entitled to get copies of all medical reports about him from the organisation's health insurance (2045); 1815: Duty to inform a staff member about the names of the members of the selection board; 1764: Duty to inform the official about the charges against him (here: forgery of airline tickets) does not extend to the kind of penalty he may be incurring; 1756: Right to information as to whether the organisation has prompted the police to act and, if so, how (search of private premises); 1684: The organisation must disclose an internal medical report to the official concerned even if the doctor has requested confidentiality for risk of trouble; 1526: The right to information requires each party to a contract to let the other have beforehand any material information on points that may reasonably be seen as decisive; 1319: Denying the board of appeal the information needed for a timely and complete opinion is an infringement of the requirements of due administrative process; 1245: The information was enigmatic in the extreme, the complainant did not receive a proper notification; 946: Failure to inform the complainant of the reasons for a decision.

## III. The principle of unimpeded accomplishment of tasks of the organisation

### *1. The privileges and immunities*

(see above under "Legal basis")

### 2. *The independence of the organisation and its staff*

IO can achieve the goals entrusted to them by member states only if the organisation and its staff enjoy full independence in the accomplishment of their duties from any improper influence of individual member states and other external third parties. All member states are to have equal confidence in the independent discharge of duties of their organisation.

One important pillar for the protection of independence of IO from national sovereign power are the privileges and immunities accorded to them and its staff by the member states. They provide for exemption from national jurisdiction, enforcement and to some extent from the application (or a modified application) of national law.

There is, however, still an open flank of independence of IO from the improper influence of certain member states. The basis of this phenomenon is the fact that member states are not only the founding fathers of an organisation but they remain the masters of the destiny of their organisation throughout their existence. IO depend on the political support, the good will and in most cases of the financial contributions of their member states. That is why IO have a vital interest in being on good terms with all member states. This does not exclude the perception of particular interests of a member state within the activities of an organisation. These interests must, however, be brought into the competent bodies and organs of the organisation in conformity with the statutory proceedings and inside the system of democratic participation pursued in an open dialogue with the representatives of the other member states. IO are, however, in some danger that their synergetic value will be usurped unilaterally by individual member states in an improper way. This impairment of independence may be called the Achille's heel of IO. It is a large "grey area where it is difficult to make absolute judgments about right and wrong" (Ali, p. 11). Since the unimpeded functioning of an IO depends to a large extent on the decisions taken by the delegates of the member states in its legislative and supervisory organs, an IO is particularly vulnerable to unilateral pressure by individual member states. This improper influence is most noticeable in the area of employment of international staff. member states show a tendency to regard the employment of their citizens as a matter of national interest (Schreuer/Ebner, para. 9). They exert "more or less subtle pressures" (Schreuer/Ebner, para. 55) in order to favour their nationals in relation to recruitment, transfer, career prospects, extension of fixed-term contracts and termination of contracts (Ali, p. 6). All this covert influence, especially from the most powerful member states, is not easy to establish and almost impossible to document (Schreuer/Ebner, para. 70).

The independence of IO and their staff is not only jeopardised by the improper pressure exerted by individual member states, it may also be exposed to the failure of some staff members to respect their exclusively international calling. International staff members must in the discharge of their duties remain independent of any authority outside the organisation, they may under no circumstances be perceived as a representative of his or her home country. Despite this obligation some staff members seek the support of national delegations for their career prospects by frequently lobbying during the sessions of the plenary committee or by directly communicating their wishes to the competent national authorities.

Most SR or even conventions establishing IO contain provisions which are intended to protect the independence of IO from improper influence.

Art. 11 EU-SR, Reg. (1)2(d) UN-SR, Art. 25(1) CoE-SR and Art. 14 EPO-SR codify the obligation of staff members neither to seek nor to take instructions from any government, authority, organisation or person outside the organisation. In some organisations this obligation is even subject to the signature of a corresponding declaration (Reg. 1(1)(b) UN-SR, Art. 25(1) CoE-SR).

Art. 100(2) of the Charter of the UN even explicitly enshrines the obligation of the members of the UN to respect the exclusively international character of the responsibilities of the UN-SG and the staff and not seek to influence them in the discharge of their responsibilities.

Some international administrative tribunals (in particular the ILOAT) have developed in constant case law the general legal principle of the independence of IO from member states in order to ensure the confidence of the member states in the unimpeded performance of their duties. This principle acts as an objective principle of law which is binding on the member states, the executive head of the secretariat of the organisation and the staff members.

As will be shown below in the jurisprudence of the ILOAT, the ideal concept of independence of IO often falls short in reality (see more in detail the articles of Ali and Martin).

**Jurisprudence**

ILOAT Judgments

2232: The independence of international civil service servants is an essential guarantee for the proper functioning of the IO. In the case of heads of IO this independence is protected, *inter alia*, by the fact that they are appointed for a limited term of office. To concede that an early termination would lie in the unfettered discretion of the appointing authority would deprive them of the necessary legal protection; 2129: The administration of an IO must avoid breaching any of the guarantees protecting the independence of international civil servants; 2032: The exemption from national taxes is an essential condition of international employment and is a guarantee of independence; 1821: It is perfectly proper for member states to try to exert influence over an organisation by proper democratic means such as a debate, discussion and persuasion within the committees and the governing body; 1791: There is not a shred of evidence to suggest that the organisation was yielding to the insistence of one member state; 1733: To allow a member state a veto on the appointment of a staff member is tantamount to receiving instructions from outside the organisation and is therefore a breach of the independence of the organisation; 1730: The decision of the organisation was not influenced in any way by the wishes of a government; 1475: It is inadmissible that a staff member involves government officials in questioning the internal work of the organisation; 1456: An IO remains free by virtue of its administration and financial autonomy to discard any figure given by a national authority for the purpose of the internal pension scheme of the organisation if that figure was worked out on a basis that offends against internal prescriptions of the organisation; 1312: An IO has the duty to safeguard the right of its employees to work in full independence for the organisation. (The complainant was held against his will in his home country and could not return to his duty station at the end of home leave); 1249: Member states are not allowed to interfere in the area of personnel management; 1232: The complainant applied for early retirement under duress from his home country. The principle of independence of international civil servants means, that a staff member may not be put on early retirement where a member state has ordered him to apply for it; 1230: The organisation must have known that the government of the member state of the official wanted him to go back. That being so, it ought to have paid special heed, for the sake of independence of the international civil service, and his own in particular, to find out just what he really intended; 448: The organisation cannot bow to governments' wishes not to extend the appointment before making sure that they are compatible with its own interests; 431: The head of the organisation may not forgo taking a decision not to renew the contract of a government official of a member state in the organisation's interest for the sole purpose of satisfying a member state; 127: The technical advisor induced the national authorities to take steps which led to the dismissal of the complainant. He is entitled to damages; 122: A member state objected to the appointment of the complainant to a permanent post. Such objection cannot be reconciled with the fundamental principle of the independence of an IO in relation to its member states; 21: The head of an organisation cannot associate himself with the execution of the policy of a government. This conflicts with the *erga omnes* principle of independence of the organisation; 15: The order of the organisation that the complainant has to respond to the subpoena addressed to him by a national court is in clear conflict with the independence of IO and its staff.

### *3. The Noblemaire and Fleming principles*

It is one of the basic principles of the human resources policy of IO to recruit staff on as wide a geographical basis as possible (Art. 27 EU-SR; Reg. 4(2) UN-SR, Art. 12(1) CoE-SR, Art. 5(1) EPO-SR). In some IO the recruitment is as a rule limited to nationals from among the member states (EU, EPO). The distribution of staff members by nationality is regularly (see, for example, the website of the EU Commission, staff figure) forwarded for information purposes to the national delegations in the plenary organ of the IO. It is generally tolerated for obvious reasons that host countries are over-represented in the lower staff grades.

The principle of a proportional (as a rule in relation to the financial contributions of the respective member state) geographical distribution of staff can only be observed if the salaries offered by the IO are commensurate with the highest salaries paid to national officials in one of the member states. This is also a precondition for securing for the IO the services of staff members of the highest standard of ability, efficiency and integrity (see, for example, Art. 27 EU-SR).

Since its inception, the level of salaries of the professional and higher categories of the League of Nations in 1920 is determined on the basis of the Noblemaire principle, named after the chairman of a committee of experts appointed by the Council in order to consider the basis for setting the salaries of the international civil service (for a historical review see ICSC doc. ICSC/59/CRP.5 of 5 May 2004). The Noblemaire principle does not bestow a privilege on international civil servants but its purpose is to draw some of the best qualified people from every member state into the service of the IO (ILOAT Judgment 986 para. 7).

In parallel to the salaries of the professional and higher categories of the UN-CS the level of salaries of the General Service category of the UN-CS is determined in accordance with the Fleming principle named after the chairman of a committee of experts appointed by the UNGA in 1949 (see, for example, ILOAT Judgment 1519 para. 2).

In accordance with the Noblemaire principle the salaries of the professional and higher categories of the UN-CS are set each year by reference to the salaries of the national civil servants of equal rank in the country where those salaries are the highest (see, for example, ILOAT Judgment 2420 para. 2 and UN docs. A/RES/44/198 and A/RES/59/268 and on the website of the ICSC). From 1921 to 1946 the comparator civil service was the British civil service and since then the US federal civil service in Washington DC was served as the comparator. To give full effect to the Noblemaire principle, additional measures have been taken by the ICSC (see in detail ILOAT Judgment 831 para. 2 et seq.). These are the "post adjustment" allowances which take account of the difference in purchasing power of salaries between New York and Washington DC and safeguard that the salaries of all staff members of the UN-CS in the professional and higher categories have equal purchasing power with New York irrespective of the duty station. In addition, there is a "margin" added to the salaries which may be compared with an allowance for a quasi-diplomatic service.

The application of the Noblemaire principle has frequently been confirmed by the UNGA (see docs. A/RES/44/198 and A/RES/59/268 and the website of the ICSC).

Based on the Fleming principle the totality of the terms of service, i.e. not only the salaries of the General Service category of the UN-CS, are established by comparison with the best prevailing conditions at each duty station for similar work, without being the absolute best (see Annex I(6) UN-SR).

The Noblemaire principle covers both pay and pension since the legal relations of staff with the IO do not end when they leave its employ (ILOAT Judgment 986 para. 7; see in this context section 5.40 of the Compendium of the ICSC in the internet portal. There may be a different comparator service for the pensions from that for the pay).

Nowadays, the Noblemaire principle is considered in the jurisprudence of the ILOAT not only as a general principle of the UN-CS (see, for example, ILOAT Judgment 986 para. 7) but as a general principle of international civil service in general (see ILOAT Judgment 1912 para. 18 and 1913 para. 17 with references to EMBL and 1791 para. 15f with reference to CERN). It is not a principle derived from national precepts but an independently developed general legal principle for the international civil service).

As to the scope of applications of the Fleming principle, the ILOAT had until now no opportunity to rule on the application of this principle outside the UN-CS as a general principle of the international civil service. It is, however, to be expected that the purpose of this principle would be susceptible for such a general application.

As far as can be seen, the application of the Noblemaire principle in the civil service systems of the EU and the CO has not been an issue up to now. It may, however, be referred to in case of a further lowering of the salaries and pensions.

**Jurisprudence**

ILOAT Judgments

a) Noblemaire principle

3360: The basis for the calculation of the post adjustment index for Vienna did not violate the Noblemaire principle; 2420: The Noblemaire principle must be applied with a certain degree of flexibility leaving some room for interpretation by the competent authority. The fact that budgetary considerations may be taken into account does not, in itself, invalidate the decision setting the salary scale, provided that other reasons justifying the decision are correct; 1913: The Noblemaire principle is not applicable since the pay slips did not contain a reduction in remuneration; 1912: The tribunal recognised the Noblemaire principle as a general principle of the international civil service not only of the UN-CS, but applicable to EMBL and to CERN (1791: No breach of the Noblemaire principle by the exceptional application of a "crisis levy" for a limited period); 1356: The current practice of applying the Noblemaire principle by the ICSC is not to take account of different working hours in duty station; 1199: The US federal civil service is the "comparator" for determining the pay and pension in the UN-CS under the aegis of the Noblemaire principle. It was, therefore, reasonable to take economic trends in the US alone into account for the determination of the pensionable remuneration; 986: The Noblemaire principle also covers pensions; 831 (leading judgment): The definition of the Noblemaire principle and the measures taken for its implementation; 498: Justification of the difference in the application of the Noblemaire and Fleming principles on the pay scales of the staff in professional and higher categories and in the General Service category.

b) Fleming principle

2303: The application of the Fleming principle is not flawed if without taking into account the "language factor" the conditions of service including salaries are among the best in the locality without being the absolute best; 1915: As concerns the relevance of the language factor under the Fleming principle there must not be a perfect match between outside jobs and those in the UN-CS; 1713: The dropping or the phasing out of the language factor in the present case amounts to a breach of the Fleming principle which ordains that General Service staff shall have pay and other terms of employment that match the best in the locality without being the absolute best. In choosing the figures of local pay for the purpose of applying the Fleming principle there can be no single hard-and-fast approach (1265); 1641: Preserving accrued benefits is not the aim of the Fleming principle. It requires no more than alignment with the best conditions at the duty station; 1519 (leading judgment): Definition of the Fleming principle, the history of the principle and the revision of this general methodology by the UNGA in 1992. The reduction of fringe benefits such as recreation facilities and employer sponsored events was not unlawful. The cost of training need not be taken into account in the comparison with outside pay. Difficulties to compare the internal scheme of staff health insurance with the national social security scheme; 1334: The Fleming principle does offer a guide for setting general levels of pay for local staff but not for any particular component of such pay; 1279: Discretion in the application of the Fleming principle in the selection of comparator for local employers for the salary survey (1280); 1265: Infringement of the Fleming principle if benefits improperly granted to staff of some organisation of the UN-CS (here: extra within-grade step increments) are counted to inflate artificially the comparative figures of pay of staff in organisations that do abide by the rules of the UN-CS; 1086: There is no breach of Fleming principle when the organisation takes account in its salary system of the end-of-service allowance of the host country; 1001: The tax relief of a "commissary" bestowed by the host country at no cost to the organisation may not count in comparison of pay under the Fleming principle. The organisation's decision to reduce salaries on that account is unlawful (1000); 323: The text of the Fleming principle stipulated in para. 301.13.4 FAO-SR will be considered by the tribunal broadly and it will be careful not to put the discretion of the Director-General into a legal straitjacket.

### *4. Facilitating the possibility for staff members to retain personal links with the place of origin*

The case law of international administrative tribunals (in particular the ILOAT and the CJEU) has developed a general legal principle of the law of the international civil service which obliges IO to facilitate the possibility for staff members to retain personal links to the place of origin (see, for example, ILOAT Judgment 271 and CJEU Judgment T-49/89, but see F-43/05). The primary purpose of this principle is not to make money concessions to staff, but the interest of an IO in safeguarding an international workplace environment. The confidence of the member states in the independent accomplishment of the duties of an IO is underlined by the multinational character of its workforce.

There is a wide legislative discretion as to the facilities granted to staff members for strengthening their bonds to the respective home station. There is no right of staff members to a specific kind of facility offered by the SR of an IO (CJEU Judgment F-43/05). In most cases there is a periodic (annual, biannual) reimbursement of travel expenses or a flat-rate payment (Art. 8 Annex VII EU-SR) for the staff member and his family to travel to the home country. In addition, the necessary travelling time is granted (EU, UN, CoE, EPO). The SR of some IO provide for additional home leave (CoE, EPO).

**Jurisprudence**

ILOAT Judgments

2638: The benefits for home leave are designed to restore equality between officials serving in a foreign country and those who are working in a country where they normally have their home (2637); 2389: The purpose of the home leave is to enable staff members who, owing to their work, spend a number of years away from the country with which they have the closest personal and material ties to return there in order to maintain those connections; 937: The primary purpose of home leave is not to make money concessions to staff but it is an advantage for an IO that staff members should maintain links with their home countries; 271: The principle of home leave has from the earliest time been justified by the interest of an IO that its staff members should maintain links with their home countries.

CJEU Judgments/Orders

F-43/05: The reimbursement of the annual travelling expenses to the place of origin of an official is based solely on a discretionary decision of the legislative organ of the EU. There is no general principle of the EU legal system or of international public law from which an obligation may be derived for the legislator to grant such a reimbursement; T-49/89: The possibility for an official to retain his personal links with the place where his principal interests are situated constitutes a general principle of law governing the European public service.

## IV. Other specific legal principles

### *1. Participation rights*

#### a) The right of the staff associations to consultation

##### *aa) General introduction*

Whereas the freedom of association guarantees the basic features of the staff committee as an association as such (approval of its statute, election, general activities etc.), the principle of participation rights concerns the minimum scope and content of the activities of the staff committee within the staff-management machinery.

In addition to the modest collective participation rights of the staff associations in IO there are some framework agreements of IO with international trade unions which provide for some features of a social dialogue, like negotiations, concerted actions and conciliation procedures with recognised trade unions. Most important examples are the EU Commission and the ILO. However, also in these cases the decision-making authority is vested in the legislative and executive bodies of the organisation.

International administrative tribunals have developed a general legal principle of the employment law of IO in all general matters concerning the legal relationship between the staff and the organisation. The staff committees of the organisation (either directly or as staff representatives in advisory bodies) must be informed and consulted (ILOAT Judgment 911 para 17: "... one of an executive head's duties is to consult the staff association in keeping with the general principles set forth above ..."; CJEU Judgment T-192/99 para 89: "The consultation of staff representatives which the Bank is obliged to organise under a general principle of labour law common to all the Member states ...").

As usual the tribunals do not disclose in detail the internal deliberations on how they arrive at this principle. Apart from the already mentioned general principle common to the labour law of member states reference may be made to Art. 21 ESC (revised 1996) which reads: "With a view ensuring the effective exercise of the right of workers to be informed and consulted ... in accordance with national legislation and practice: .... b) to be consulted in good time on proposed decisions which could substantially affect the interest of workers, particularly on those decisions which could have an important impact on the employment situation ...". Other international treaties and charters contribute even less to the derivation of this general principle since they are "empty rules" without any guarantee as to the scope and content of the right to information and consultation (see Art. 27 CFREU: " ... be guaranteed information and consultation in good time in the cases and under the conditions provided for by Union law and national laws and practices"; see also Art. 153(1) TFEU: "... the Union shall support and complement the activities of the Member states in the following fields ... e) the information and consultation of workers").

The rights of the staff committee to information and consultation do not extend to the right of the trade union to collective bargaining (comprising negotiations in the strict sense). Nevertheless, some type of negotiations may also be applied by the joint consultative bodies with a view to promoting social peace (see below).

The duty to consult obliges the organisation to give timely notice and information to the staff representatives in the advisory bodies in all matters concerning the employ of staff in general and to assure that the consultation process is such "as to have an influence on the substance of the measure adopted" (CJEU Judgment T-192/99 para. 90). (For details see below).

Consultation "is one of the modest forms of participation in a decision-making process, since in no circumstances does it involve any obligation for the administration to act upon the observations made by staff committee in the course of the consultation" (CJEU Judgment T-63/02 para. 23 and Judgment T-192/99 para. 89: The consultation process "in no way implies that those representatives have a right of co-decision ..."). The managerial prerogative of the employer is left intact. Staff committees and the administration do not dispose of "equality of bargaining power" (ILOAT Judgment 380 para. 21). (But see below, the right to co-decision in the area of pension funds of IO.)

Consultation implies only a hearing and an opportunity to comment on intended changes to the general legal relations between the staff and the organization, primarily the SR (ILOAT Judgments 1020 para. 2 and 380 para. 21: "The decision-maker's duty is to listen or at most exchange views". Nevertheless, it must be in the interest of the head of administration to reach a well-reasoned opinion of the staff committee or the consultative body. This may imply giving the other side the opportunity to assent to the proposed decision maybe at the cost of some concession which then shifts into a kind of negotiation (ILOAT Judgment 380 para 22).

The consultation requires a proper consultation process and both sides must show good faith (ILOAT Judgment 1200).

In practice the consultation process does not take place in the form of a questionnaire addressed to the staff committee. As a rule, the SR of IO provide for "joint advisory bodies" in all employment matters of general concern (e.g. general advisory committees, recruitment, promotion and disciplinary committees).

The involvement of such bodies (Art. 10(2) EU-SR: staff regulations committee; Reg. 8(2) UN-SR and Rule 8(2)(a)(ii) UN-SR: staff management coordination committee; see also UN doc. JIU/REP/2011/10; Art. 6 and Appendix I CoE-SR: staff committee; Art. 38 EPO-SR: general consultative committee) represents an enhanced consultation in the interest both of the staff and the management. These bodies are "joint" i.e. they consist of members appointed in equal numbers by the administration and the staff committee (e.g. Annex II Art. 2 EU-SR and Art. 38 EPO-SR) and a "neutral" chairperson. It is the obvious goal of such general consultative committees not simply to deliver separate statements of both parties but, as far as possible, to reach a unanimous reasoned opinion in the interest of social peace. This implies, however, that both sides are prepared to engage in an open discussion, to dwell on the arguments of the other side and to be open-minded to a compromise solution in the organisation's best interest.

### *bb) The activities of staff committees*

The activities of staff committees are protected by the participation rights and by the freedom of discussion and debate with respect to all lawful matters to protect the interests of the employees (see, for example, Art. 9(3) EU-SR). An organisation must refrain from doing anything which might impede this freedom of activity of a staff committee (ILOAT Judgment 2636 para. 28, see also the similar approach for the activities of the trade unions in CJEU Judgment C-193/87 and C-194/87). An organisation may, therefore, not exercise censorship by requiring that all communication to and from the staff committee should be submitted for inspection by the organisation (ILOAT Judgment 496 para. 37). On the other hand, the participation rights do not extend, for example, to "intimidation, offensive behaviour or aggression". The duty of an IO "to provide for a safe and secure workplace extends to ensuring that such conduct does not occur in relation to Staff Association affairs" (ILOAT Judgment 2636 para. 28).

A staff committee exists not only in the common interests of the staff but also partly in the interests of the organisation (ILOAT Judgment 496 para. 17). The staff committee (in contrast to trade unions of IO) represents all staff and is not financed by contributions from the staff members and depends fully on the support from the organisation (but see the different UN system).

Whereas the jurisprudence of the ILOAT (e.g. Judgment 496 para. 19) can be interpreted as recognising a right of the staff committees to the grant of some basic facilities allowing them to the discharge of their functions, the case law of the CJEU seems more restrictive (CJEU Judgment C-193/87 and C-194/87 para. 26). According to this doctrine an organisation has only to grant the necessary facilities to enable staff representatives to participate in the meetings of the consultative bodies, i.e. time off work for that purpose (CJEU Judgments/Orders C-194/87 para. 36, 37; F-39/08; F-54/09 and Judgment T-52/10 P). This legal position seems too restrictive to perform the role assigned to it by the law of the international civil service.

### *cc) Facilities provided to staff committees*

The effective accomplishment of the functions of staff committees requires the availability of various facilities. The grant of such facilities is "not just a goodness of heart" but is in the broad interest of the organisation to have the committee perform its responsibilities fully and efficiently (ILOAT Judgment 911), otherwise there would be no place for it in the SR (ILOAT Judgment 496). The activities of the staff representatives are as a consequence deemed to be part of the normal service (see, for example, Art. 1(6) Annex II EU-SR). Staff representatives thus exercise official duties prescribed in the SR (ILOAT Judgment 1147).

With the general provision that an IO has a wide discretion in determining the extent of the facilities granted to staff committees, the following facilities provided for staff representatives in the staff council of the UN may serve as a guidance (for details see UN doc. ST/AI/293: Facilities to be provided to staff representatives; see also UN doc. JIU/REP/2012/10 p. 14 et seq. and ILOAT Judgments 3449, 496, 403, 382). A general clause provides that staff representatives and the staff committees shall be afforded such facilities as may be required to carry out their functions promptly and efficiently. More specifically the following facilities are generally provided:

- facilities for the holding of meetings convened by the staff committee,
- secretarial assistance, office space,
- communication facilities,
- facilities for the reproduction and distribution of notices,
- release from official duties (full or partial, depending on the function of the representative, number of represented staff),
- application of official duty status for participation in intra-organisational, international and intergovernmental meetings.

In most organisations there are also written arrangements between the organisation and the staff committees on the grant of facilities to the committee and its representatives (see, for example, ILOAT Judgments 911, 496; CJEU order F-54/09). At the EPO, the facilities granted to the staff committee are stipulated as Annex 3 of doc. CA/4/14 available on the EPO website.

Facilities granted cannot be withdrawn by the organisation at will. A complete withdrawal of the facilities might even amount to a violation of the right to associate (ILOAT Judgment 496 para. 19). Changes facilities which have been unilaterally granted do not have to be negotiated or agreed. Abrupt, drastic or comprehensive changes would be illegal. Other changes must be properly motivated and are subject to the standard scrutiny of the international administrative tribunals in the cases of discretionary decisions (ILOAT Judgment 496 para. 34).

### *dd) The details of the right to consultation*

IO have a wide discretion to implement the general principle which ensures that staff committees must be informed and consulted in all general matters concerning the legal relations between the staff and the organisation. This covers first and foremost all changes to the SR and the implementing rules. Often excluded from the requirement for consultation are general measures relating to the organisation of work (ILOAT Judgment 1398), the introduction of new means to increase staff efficiency (computer program, ILOAT Judgment 1398) and the recruitment of staff not covered by the SR (ILOAT Judgment 2036, but see ILOAT Judgment 2875).

In most IO this core right of consultation is supplemented by optional consultation on questions of a more general nature, like staff welfare, general conditions of life or human resource policies (see Art. 9(4) EU-SR; Reg. 8(1) UN-SR; Appendix I Art. 5(3) CoE-SR; Art. 38 EPO-SR). The details of the respective consultative machinery of the four international civil service systems is dealt with under "Collective rights of staff", see below).

It is a precondition of any consultative proceedings that the members of the consultative body have at their disposal all the information necessary to form a reasoned opinion (ILOAT Judgment 2615 para. 5, 1062). The necessary information must be delivered by the organisation on its own motion without having been explicitly requested to do so by the members of the consultative committees (obligation to deliver, see ILOAT Judgment 1065 para. 5).

A further consultation is required if the document under consideration by the consultative body has subsequently undergone a radical change either by the head of the administration or by the legislative organ (ILOAT Judgment 1618; CJEU Judgment C-443/07 P). Other discussions between the administration and the staff representatives on the subject matter do not replace proper consultation in the consultative body (ILOAT Judgment 1488).

The document on which consultation is required must be available to the members of the consultative body in such time that the goal of the consultation can be achieved. In practice, a time limit of about two weeks seems adequate.

The duty of consultation is not violated if the staff representatives fail to participate in a meeting of the consultative body despite being invited (ILOAT Judgments 1839, 1838, 1565).

The duty of information and consultation must be carried out in compliance with the general legal principle of good faith (ILOAT Judgments 1618, 1062, 380; CJEU Judgment T-192/99 para. 87: "*in bona fide*" and has to be "fair and just"). This implies that the consultation process may still be influenced by arguments put forward by the staff representatives. The object of the consultation is that the decision-maker "will make the best decision and the assumption is that he will not succeed in doing that unless he has the benefit of the views of the persons consulted". In practice, the difference between consultation and negotiation is not entirely clear cut. There may be a middle way between consultation and negotiation (ILOAT Judgments 380 para. 21 and 2827). The head of administration is well advised to aim for a compromise solution in the interest of social peace. He may not exercise his unilateral power to decide until all possibilities to achieve a compromise within the joint advisory bodies have been exhausted (ILOAT Judgment 380 para. 23). The object of consultation "would be frustrated if the decision-maker began with a determination not be influenced by anything that might be said to him" (ILOAT Judgment 380 para. 21).

There may, however, be cases where it would be advisable if the chairman of the consultative committee were to have recourse to secret voting in order to reach the best reasoned opinion, since committee members on both sides may be under pressure by the other members and therefore refrain from stating their personal opinion.

### b) Co-determination

In the area of pension funds of IO the staff representatives have voting rights on all decisions taken by the supervisory bodies.

The most important pension funds of IO are:

- The UNJSPF

One third of the members of the UNJSP Board and the staff pension committees are elected representatives of participants in service in the UN or in another UN member organisation (Art. 5 and 6 Reg. of the UNJSPF respectively).

- The EPO-RFPSS

In the Supervisory Board of the EPO-RFPSS one third of the voting members are appointed by the central staff committee (Art. 5(1)(c) and Art. 6(2) statute of the EPO-RFPSS, see Ullrich, Pension Schemes).

- The CERN/ESO Pension Fund

The Governing Board of the Pension Fund consists (in addition to four members appointed by the Councils of CERN and ESO and the management, and two professional expert members) of four members appointed by the CERN and ESO staff associations and pensioner associations (Art. I 2.06.1 Rules of the Pension Fund). Each member has the right to vote (Art. I 2.06.6 Rules of the Pension Fund).

**Jurisprudence**

ILOAT Judgments

3346: Dispute between the administration and the staff committee on the interpretation of the opinion given by the general advisory committee; 2877: The adoption of a new specimen contract for Vice-Presidents of the secretariat of the EPO which introduces special provisions for the pension claims of previously serving staff members without prior consultation (Art. 38 EPO-SR) is unlawful (2876, 2875, 2036); 2874: The introduction of the office-wide pilot project BEST (Bring Examination and Search Together) for EPO examiners needs consultation in conformity with Art. 38 EPO-SR (1488); 2615: Bodies to be consulted with the task of formulating an opinion before a decision is taken must be informed as objectively and fully as possible about the interests involved. This should contribute to the smooth implementation of the decision. Advisory bodies can play their role only if they have access to all relevant information for forming their opinion; 2562: The use of "on loan" staff does not amount to a "proposal" in the meaning of Art. 38 EPO-SR and does not need consultation; 2457: Based on the SR of the organisation the tribunal considered that the absence of one member of the selection board did constitute a procedural flaw, despite the fact that the board's opinion was unanimous; 2422: Relevance of an *amicus curiae* brief even if the staff representation expresses views deviating from earlier ones; 2288: The safeguard available to international civil servants in the form of the mandatory consultation of an advisory body prior to any disciplinary measure cannot legally speaking be said to be complied with unless that body held an official meeting, discussed the matter and issued minutes; 2196: Under Art. 38 EPO-SR there is an obligation to consult the general advisory committee if a productivity norm changed; 2110: Quality of data delivered by the administration for consultation on an increase of premium for permanent invalidity; 2036: Guidelines for the recruitment procedure of Vice-Presidents of the secretariat of the EPO are not a matter which falls under the consultation process provided for in Art. 38 EPO-SR; 1978: The execution of the judgment did not raise any problem of a general nature concerning staff as a whole. There was, therefore, no need for consultation under Art. 38 EPO-SR; 1839: No breach of the duty to consult the staff representation if staff representatives were invited but refused to take part in a consultation committee. The refusal does not have the effect of disqualifying the committee or invalidating its recommendation (1838, 1565); 1672: Appeal of a member of the general advisory committee of the EPO against the failure to consult the committee in conformity with Art. 38 EPO-SR. The plea failed since the draft document of final job descriptions was for information purposes only and had no legal effect; 1618 (leading judgment): The purpose of consultation of a joint committee in Art. 38 EPO-SR is that enough information is delivered by the administration to enable it to come to a reasoned opinion based on a real exchange of views, and both sides must show good faith. The poor drafting of a proposal does warrant delaying discussion or rejecting the proposal but it does not warrant a complete refusal to formulate any opinion whatsoever. A further consultation would be necessary if the proposals had been so radically amended as to be really new ones; 1565: If no staff representative chooses to attend the meeting of the selection committee that cannot have the effect of invalidating its recommendations (1839); 1488 (leading judgment): The rule on the consultation of staff representatives in Art. 38 EPO-SR "casts a wide net" that goes beyond mere changes in legal provisions. It applies to cases where any proposal is made which concerns the whole or part of the staff (e.g. changes of a point system to rate patent examiners). A formal consultation procedure is necessary. It does not matter that management may have consulted the staff on the subject in other ways; 1398: the President of the EPO has wide discretion in the organisation of work and he is not bound to consult the staff representation or the joint advisory bodies before introducing new means of improving the staff efficiency (here: patent examiners are required to use a certain computer program); 1369: No duty to state again the reasons for a decision which had already been revealed in the consultative process; 1291: Art. 38 EPO-SR requires proper consultation on the insurance premium for permanent invalidity; 1200 (leading judgment): What the rules on consultation plainly require is cooperation between staff and management. Though it is not to take the form of bargaining there must be a real exchange of views and, if it is to work, both sides must show good faith; 1131: Failure of the organisation to abide by the consultation rules of a separation procedure caused by serious financial constraints; 1062 (leading judgment): The increase of staff contributions to the costs of the compulsory death and invalidity insurance was a proposal under Art. 38 EPO-SR which needed consultation. Consultation entails that the administration has to deliver enough information to enable the joint advisory committee to come to a reasoned opinion (obligation to deliver). Merely telling it that the administration would give it more details and provide data if it so wished does not comply with a proper consultation procedure; 1020: Consultation does not require negotiation let alone approval; 975: No consultation of the general advisory committee under Art. 38 EPO-SR needed for a mere interpretation of the EPO-SR; 911: The grant of facilities (e.g. use of printing materials) to staff is not a privilege the organisation may withdraw as it pleases. It is not just out of the goodness of heart to provide such facilities, but it is in its own broad interest to have the association perform its responsibilities fully and efficiently. Even if there is no explicit legal obligation, the administration has a duty to consult the staff association in keeping with the respective general principle if it intends to withdraw some of the facilities entirely or in part; 380 (leading judgment): Where there is an obligation to consult, the duty of the organisation is to listen and to exchange views in order to benefit from the views of the persons consulted. This object would be frustrated if the representatives of the organisation in the consultative committee would begin with a determination not to be influenced by anything that might be said to them. In this case there would be no good faith consultation. The consultation has also the purpose to give the representatives of the organisation the opportunity of obtaining the assent of the other party to the proposal, maybe at the cost of some concession.

CJEU Jugements/Orders

F-96/08: The right to be consulted under Art. 46 ECB-SR (now Part 1 para. 49 Conditions of Employment of the ECB) does refer to the modest form of consultation only; T-63/02 para. 30: The possibility that consultation of the staff committee might have an influence on the substance of the salary adjustment cannot be excluded; C-165/01: The reference to national law where local staff is employed cannot include the rules concerning the staff representation. Those arrangements are governed exclusively by Art. 9 EU-SR and Art. 7 EU-CEOS; T-192/99 para. 89 et seq.: The consultation of staff representatives which the EIB is obliged to organise under a general legal principle of law common to all the member states must be such as to have influence on the substance of the measure adapted, which implies that it must be timely and *bona fide*.

### 2. *The right to receive care and assistance*

#### a) General introduction

International administrative tribunals have developed the general legal principle of the international civil service that international officials have a right to receive care and assistance from their organisation. Taking into account the principle of correspondence of rights and duties, the case law of the tribunals mostly deals with this principle under the heading of the duties of an organisation to provide care and give assistance to its staff members.

The derivation of this general legal principle by the international administrative tribunals, as far as it is disclosed at all, depends on the nature of the employment relationship.

For IO with staff employed on a statutory legal basis (e.g. EU, EPO), the principle is derived from the mutual trust of a life-long employment, in principle, and the balance of reciprocal rights and obligations created by the SR. It is interrelated with the principles of good management and justice and overlaps with the protection of dignity and reputation of the staff member (CJEU Judgments F-95/09, T-76/03, T-39/93, T-133/89, 229/84, 53/72).

For IO with contractual staff the ILOAT seems to derive the duty to provide care and assistance from the principle of good faith (Judgments 2345, 2017, 1734) which includes the duty of the organisation to avoid causing its staff unnecessary injury and undue hardship (Judgments 1756, 1734, 1496, 367).

Although the duty to provide care is not identical with the duty of assistance (CJEU T-67/99 para. 66) both principles are often interrelated (see, for example, ILOAT Judgments 3104, 2204). The duty to provide care is also addressed under the terms "to have regard to the welfare" of the official (see, for example, CJEU Judgments T-76/03, F-92/09) or "to have regard to the interests" of the official (see, for example, CJEU Judgment T-76/03, C-298/93 P).

### b) The duty to provide care (solicitude)

The SR of IO do not generally contain an express provision stipulating the duty of an IO to provide care to its staff. It is, however, well-settled case law of all international administrative tribunals that an IO is under an obligation to provide care to its staff based on a general principle of law. Extensive case law has clarified its scope and content. The duty of having regard to the welfare of officials cannot, however, lead the administration to giving the SR an effect contrary to the clear and precise wording. An official cannot therefore rely on this right in order to obtain advantages which he cannot be granted under the SR (see, for example, CJEU Judgment T-14/03).

### c) The duty of assistance

The obligation of an IO to assist its staff is fragmentarily codified in most SR (Art. 24 EU-SR; implicitly in Reg. 1(2)(c) UN-SR; Art. 40 CoE-SR; Art. 28 EPO-SR) as an obligation to assistance if by reason of his office or duties a staff member or his family living in his household is subject to insult, threat, defamation or attack to his person or property. Such acts may also trigger compensation for damages suffered by a third party, in as much as the staff member may not obtain compensation from the perpetrator.

The duty to assist (protect) has to be provided against criminal acts by third parties, colleagues and superiors (CJEU Judgments T-80/09 P, T-254/02, T-5/92, 18/78). In contrast to this jurisprudence of the CJEU, the ILOAT declares the duty to assistance as being not applicable against the treatment by a superior (Judgments 1489, 1270). This does not, of course, relieve the organisation from its duty to treat staff members with dignity and avoid them unnecessary injury, e.g. in case of harassment by a superior or colleague (e.g. Judgment 2706).

There is no duty of assistance against acts of the IO itself (CJEU Judgments T-95/04, T-45/91, 191/98, 98/81). The duty also exists towards retired staff members (CJEU Judgment 229/84).

The duty to assist requires the organisation to intervene: "... with all the necessary vigour and respond with the rapidity and solicitude required by the circumstances of the case ..." (CJEU Judgment T-136/03).

The codified duty to provide assistance is not exhaustive. Based on the general legal principle international administrative tribunals have developed an obligation for IO to provide assistance and give guidance to staff, especially probationers, in the performance of their duties and to warn them in specific terms if they are not giving satisfaction and are at risk of dismissal (see, for example, ILOAT Judgment 2982 and CJEU Judgment T-248/08. The same holds true in the case of the abolition of a post. Here, IO are obliged to assist their staff in finding a new assignment by putting proper institutional support mechanisms in place (see, for example, ILOAT Judgments 3041, 3038).

An IO is also obliged to assist and protect its staff against the violation of the privileges and immunities granted to them in the interest of the unimpeded functioning of the organisation. Here the ILOAT held that if an organisation does not contest the exemption of emoluments paid from national taxation it is its duty "... to protect him against the claims of the authorities of the member state, to reimburse him the amount of tax he has paid to the state and to employ its own considerable power, authority and influence to have the .... authorities change their position" (ILOAT Judgment 2032 para. 17).

**Jurisprudence**

ILOAT Judgments

3586: Duty of care violated. Failure to disclose all documents on which the organisation bases its decision. New funds were available before the expiry of the contract (3295, 2700); 3485: Allegation of harassment not taken seriously, violation of the duty of care; 3422: Moral damages for breach of the duty of care to treat the official with dignity and respect;

3409: Not to renew the contract was in violation of the duty of care; 3376: Duty of care towards permanent staff in the case of outsourcing of work (3373); 3365: The organisation neglected its duty of care towards the complainant and its duty to investigate allegations of harassment promptly and thoroughly; 3336: A period of three and a half years between the request and the decision violates the duty of care; 3188: By any standard a delay of nearly 19 months to complete the internal appeal process violates the duty of care; 3041 (3038): Violation of the duty of care by not giving prior notice to the staff member of the decision to abolish her post and failure to put to a proper institutional support mechanism in place to assist the staff member in finding a new assignment; 2997: Request for the transfer of pension contributions into national insurance schemes, duty of care fulfilled; 2986: The duty of care does not mean that an organisation must take special steps to exempt a staff member from the normal application of rules which are unfavourable to him (no invitation to submit a transfer application for pensions before the entry into force of a new text); 2983: The duty to assist a staff member against threats, insults or defamation includes, for example, not to divulge an e-mail with a confidential content; 2924: An error of reasoning establishes neither ill will nor a breach of the duty of care, particularly when the actual decision is correct; 2878: No breach of the duty of care since the time limit for submission of a request to review the decision (appeal) was not extended by the settlement negotiations between the complaint and the organisation. He could have filed the appeal and withdrawn it later if the negotiations were successful; 2768: The duty of care demands that the organisation treats its staff with due consideration in order to avoid causing them undue injury. This duty of care is greater in a rather opaque or particular complex legal situation, for example in the case of the transfer of pension rights; 2654: By failing to conduct an inquiry into psychological harassment thoroughly and accord full alleged due process to the validity of accusations, the organisation breached its duty of care (2642); 2594: An organisation is under an obligation to take proper means to protect its staff members from physical injury occurring in the course of their employment (e.g. work-place harassment); 2522: Breach of the duty of care. The organisation made every effort to hamper the legal proceedings (belated information on the outcome of the internal appeal, belated reply to the complainant's request for review); 2403: An IO is under an obligation to protect its staff members from loss or damage of their personal property (for example the obligation to take adequate measures to ensure regular monitoring of the performance of the provident fund; 2345: An organisation must interpret the statement of a staff member in good faith. This comprises the duty to spare the staff member unnecessary injury, to give guidance and help to put right a mistake (information that he needs not to wait for an authorisation before filing a complaint) (2017, 1832, 1734); 2280: No duty of an organisation to assist a staff member in a national taxation dispute if the organisation considered in good faith that he was not entitled to tax exemption; 2258: Duty of care to express its decisions clearly so as to remove from its actions any potentially harmful ambiguity; 2254: Duty of the organisation to assist a staff member faced with procedural problems in a legal dispute (2017); 2204 para. 7 (leading judgment): An IO owes a duty of care and assistance under the general principle of law of the international civil service; 2032 (leading judgment): Obligation to protect a staff member against the illegal (the organisation did not contest the tax exempt status of the complainant) claims of authorities of a member state by reimbursing him the amount of tax he has paid to the state and to employ its own considerable power, authority and influence to have the national authorities change their position; 1832: Obligation of the organisation to forward an appeal which was addressed to the wrong internal organ to the competent one; 1756: It is the duty of care which obliges an organisation not to cause its staff undue injury even in private life (information whether the organisation had prompted the police to act in order to have the opportunity of challenging or adding to it); 1752: The successor in title of a staff member may only claim damages if the staff member himself may have suffered in his employ, e.g. because of failure of the organisation to respect the duty of care; 1623: The duty of care does not extend to staff grievances about the application of national law which bestows an option on a member state (here: clause on progressive taxation); 1496: Duty of care in a transfer (1234, 943, 631, 367); 1489: Art. 28 EPO-SR (corresponding to Art. 24 EU-SR), which obliges the organisation to assist staff members in the case of attacks related to their status or duties is not applicable for a claim to help from the organisation against treatment by a superior (1270) (but see CJEU Judgments T-80/09 P, 18/78 where this provision is declared applicable if the perpetrator is another official of the organisation); 946: The need for savings afford no proper excuse for breach of the principle that protects staff against arbitrary decision-making; 730: The breach of the obligation to render the necessary assistance had the effect that the delay in filing did not render the complaint irreceivable.

CJEU Judgments/Orders

F-116/10: It is normally incumbent upon the official who is seeking the assistance and protection under Art. 24 EU-SR to provide at least some evidence of the reality of attacks of which he claims he was the victim (F-30/08, 229/84); F-62/10: The duty of care is substantially increased if the health of an official is affected; F-45/10: Duty to assist in a case of psychological harassment (F-100/09, F-26/09, F-2/09, F-86/07, F-63/06, T-154/05, T-486/04); F-95/09: Requirement for a reasonable period to apply for assistance under Art. 24 EU-SR; F-92/09: The duty to have regard to the welfare of officials requires the administration, where there is doubt as to the medical origin of the difficulties encountered by the official in performing his tasks, to take all necessary steps to dispel that doubt before a decision dismissing that official is adopted; T-80/09 P: Also Art. 24 EU-SR is devised primarily to protect officials against attacks by third parties, the duty to provide assistance laid down in that provision also exists in a case in which the perpetrator of the act referred to by that provision is another official of the organisation (T-254/02, T-5/92, 178/80, 18/78; but see ILOAT Judgments 1489 para. 9 and 1270 in regard to Art. 28 EPO-SR); F-75/09: Duty to provide assistance against the newspaper publication: “Revealed: how Eurocrat leaked trade secrets over lavish dinners” referring to three dinners in which the complainant took part; F-50/09: No duty to assist, since the alleged attack to the person was not by reason of the position or duties of the official; F-2/09: The obligation to assist laid down in Art. 24 EU-SR is not against acts emanating from the institution itself (T-95/04, T-45/91,191/81, 98/81); F-116/07: Under the duty to provide care an organisation is committed to delivering to a staff member a reasoned opinion in an official language of the organisation in which he has a sound knowledge (F-13/08 and F-31/08); F-30/08: Duty to render rapid assistance in the case of a press article of defamatory nature; F-124/05 and F-95/06: The duty to provide care does not prevent an organisation from bringing disciplinary proceedings against the official (T-156/05, T-236/02); T-136/03: By virtue of the duty to render assistance to an official against any act in the sense of Art. 24 EU-SR, the administration must intervene with all the necessary vigour and respond with the rapidity and solicitude required by the circumstances of the case with a view to ascertaining the facts. It is sufficient that the official concerned provides at least some evidence of the reality of attacks (T-136/98, T-5/92, 224/87); T-76/03: The duty to have regard to the welfare of officials reflects the balance of reciprocal rights and obligations created by the SR. The organisation shall take into consideration all factors which may affect its decisions, also the interests of the individual concerned (T-55/03, T-203/97, C-298/93 P); T-14/03: The duty to have regard to the welfare of officials cannot lead the administration to giving the SR an effect contrary to their clear and precise wording; T-387/02: Limits of the duty to assist in the case of legal proceedings before a national court; T-166/02: The refusal of a transfer because of pending disciplinary proceedings is not contrary to the duty of care; T-67/99 para. 66: The duty to assist under Art. 24 EU-SR and the duty of care are not completely identical (T-114/98 and T-115/98); T-90/95: The duty of care requires informing a staff member completely about the outcome of a medical examination important to his health; C-62/94 P: It is not inconsistent with the duty of the administration to have regard for the welfare of an official if he has been reassigned to another post, even a few months before retirement; T-59/92 (leading judgment): In the case of public and personal defamation of an official, the organisation must defend him publicly and by name. The non-material damages suffered may not be fully compensated by an express declaration of the fault in the judgment or the publication of that part of the judgment in the Official Journal; C-137/88: The obligation to provide assistance is particularly pressing with respect to complex litigations concerning pension rights; 55/88: Scope of the duty of assistance against another official; C-193/87 and C-194/87: The duty for care does not apply to resolving problems concerning collective relations between the organisation and trade unions; C-180/87: No duty to assist in case of coercive measures by the national police as a result of the personal conduct of the official; 229/84: The obligation to provide assistance also extends to retired staff.

### *3. The patere legem principle*

According to settled case law of international administrative tribunals an IO is bound by the rules it has itself laid down until it repeals or amends them (*tu patere legem quam ipse fecisti* principle, see, for example, ILOAT Judgment 867). This holds good for rules which have been adopted both by the legislative and executive body of an IO. The general principle is derived from the corresponding national legal orders of the member states and the more general ("supreme", Alpa, p. 14) principles of good faith and mutual trust (ILOAT Judgment 2712 para. 5).

The *patere legem* principle also applies to rules of practice, internal directives and other measures of an internal nature (CJEU Judgments 80 to 83/81 and 182 to 185/82). If it is the plain intent of an IO to bind itself by the interpretation of a provision of the SR, the general principle of *patere legem* applies (ILOAT Judgments 1461, 1403, 1053, 421).

The principle does not apply to individual decisions (CJEU Judgment F-25/07).

**Jurisprudence**

ILOAT Judgments

3601: Where an organisation decides to fill a post by competition it must comply with the *patere legem* principle (3032, 2163); 3073: Modifying the criteria for appointment during the selection process violates the *patere legem* principle (2712); 2562: The organisation did not abide by the timelines for the internal appeals procedure, it cannot, therefore, be heard to argue that the complainant has failed to exhaust internal means of redress; 2414: The organisation cannot base an adverse decision on a staff member's unsatisfactory performance, if it did not comply with the rules it had established to evaluate the performance; 2316: An organisation cannot deprive an official of his incremental step to which he is entitled when the performance and conduct have been satisfactory, if the organisation did not abide by the necessary preliminary procedure for cases of unsatisfactory performance (2170); 2125: Obligation of an organisation to respect its own detailed criteria for the extension of the age limit of staff; 1821: Failure of the organisation to show compliance with the SR requiring the use of the Coordinated Organisations' index as an "orientation" for its own salary adjustment procedure (1419, 1265); 1696: A delegation of authority must have some basis in the rules otherwise it infringes the principle of *patere legem*; 1671: No violation of the *patere legem* principle since the criteria of "fair contribution" criterion was not a retroactively introduced new promotion criterion but a means of determining the relative merit of candidates; 1549: The *patere legem* principle demands a scrupulous compliance with the rules announced beforehand by the organisation until they have been repealed or amended (1463, 1359); 1419: An organisation may change its salary adjustment methodology, but as long as the present methodology holds good the organisation is bound to it by the *patere legem* principle; 1204: An organisation must not go beyond the duly published rules and resort to secret provisions that change the thrust of the ones it intended to treat as binding; 1200: When the organisation wishes to amend its SR it must abide by the rules of its own making; 1158: An organisation must abide by the conditions it has itself set for the competition procedure to fill vacancies; 425: Post descriptions have to be respected by the organisation as long as they remain in force.

CJEU Jugements/Orders

C-40/10 para. 64: The Council, by adopting a method of adjusting remuneration under Art. 3 of Annex XI of the EU-SR, assumed obligations which it has bound itself to observe for the period it has defined; 56/75: The immediate withdrawal of a benefit which is not in conformity with the SR is legal; C-304/97 P: Commitment to required qualifications and knowledge in a vacancy note; T-576/93 to T-582/93: An official is only subject to the SR and related provisions. An agreement between the organisation and the trade unions and staff associations is intended only to govern collective labour relations and does not give rise to rights of an individual official; 70/74: The Council cannot, in order to escape an obligation plead that it has discretion, the exercise of which it has itself determined; 148/73: An internal directive is a rule of conduct indicating the practice to be followed from which the administration may not depart without giving the reasons which have led it to do so.

### *4. The hierarchy of norms*

The internal legal order of an IO is based on a hierarchy of norms in order to cope with the diversity of employment issues and the different hierarchical layers. This hierarchical phenomenon is sometimes, metaphorically speaking, referred to as a "pyramid of rules" (Schermers, § 1341, see also Nettesheim Art. 249 para. 26 et seq.). At the apex of this pyramid of rules is the constitution of the respective organisation (primary law) which is implemented by the SR (secondary law) and administrative instructions, circulars etc. (tertiary law) (Schermers § 1341).

The lower-ranking legal rules may not deviate from the prevailing rules in content and scope. Internal administrative instructions are null and void if they cannot be interpreted as being in accordance with the prevailing SR (see, for example, ILOAT Judgment 1733 para. 17, see also Seidl-Hohenveldern/Loibl, para. 1611).

Most constitutions (primary law of the organisation) of IO explicitly provide for the power of the legislative body of the organisation to adopt the SR (Art. 336 TFEU; Art. 101(1) UN-Charter; Art. 16 Statute of the Council of Europe; Art. 33(2)(b) and (c) EPO-EPC).

The authorisation for the head of the administration to set up implementing rules to the SR is normally laid down in the SR (Art. 110 EU-SR: Adoption of general implementing rules). In addition, internal administrative instructions may be adopted, based on the general organisational power vested in every institution in the interest of efficient working, see CJEU Judgment 791/79 and the implied-power doctrine; Reg. 12(1) and 12(2) UN-SR: Rules supplementing the SR or amendments to the Reg. are set up by the UN-SG but they are provisional until the requirements of Reg. 12(3) and 12(4) UN-SR have been met; Art. 62(1) CoE-SR; Art. 10(2)(a) EPO-EPC.

The legislative body may also adopt at its discretion implementing provisions to the SR (right of initiative by the head of administration to be respected), see, for example, Art. 128 EPO-SR and Art. 52 EPO-PS.

For the ranking of the general legal principles governing the law of the international civil service, see above under "General legal principles as superior rules of law".

**Jurisprudence**

ILOAT Judgments

2863: An organisation which has recognised the jurisdiction of the tribunal may not depart from the rules in the statute of the tribunal which it has accepted (the deadline for filing an appeal is 90 days and not 3 months as stipulated in the SR) (2312, 1096, 1095, 852, 786, 762, 533, 532); 2760: If the SR grant dependency benefits to "spouses" the administration cannot adopt a more restrictive definition in tertiary law ("husband" and "wife") to deny same-sex spouses the benefits; 2628: The rules of application infringes the higher-ranking rule in the SR and thus breach the principle of hierarchy of rules; 2120: The tertiary rules did not implement or clarify the SR but extend its reach substantially and cannot, therefore, stand. They are also in conflict with general legal principles of law and those which govern the international civil service, as well as international instruments on human rights; 2082: The failure to draw up lower-ranking implementing rules despite the mandatory wording of the higher-ranking SR results simply in the condition being treated as not having been required; 1634: The terms of the contract of employment do not prevail over the SR. The head of administration is bound to abide by the SR; 1631: There is a hierarchy under which the Rules may not derogate from the Regulations, nor the Manual from the Rules; 1258: Regulations take precedence over the text on internal policy issued by the Director-General.

CJEU Jugements/Orders

C-40/10 para. 29 and 61: Art. 65 EU-SR (normal annual salary adjustment) and Art. 10 of Annex XI EU-SR (version prior to 1 January 2014, exception clause) have the same rank in the hierarchy of norms; F-86/08: Internal directives may not deviate from the higher-ranking provisions of the EU-SR (T-43/04, 791/79); 32/71: By rendering the retention of the expatriation allowance after a marriage subject to the acquisition of the status of "head of household", the EU-SR have created an arbitrary difference in treatment between male and female officials. The provision in the EU-SR was, therefore, in conflict with the higher-ranking general legal principle of equal treatment.

### *5. The right to material and moral damages*

#### a) General introduction

On the basis of their legal personality, IO enjoy – in addition to their international legal personality (Schemers, §§ 1562 et seq., for codification see, for example, Art. 47 TEU and Art. 5(1) EPO-EPC) – also the most extensive legal capacity accorded to legal persons under the national law of each member state (Schermers §§ 1591 et seq., for codification see, for example, Art. 335 TFEU and Art. 5(2) EPO-EPC). IO can, therefore, enter into contractual and non-contractual liabilities and are responsible for their actions under private law (Schermers §§ 1613 et seq.). "The laws remain applicable, it is only their adjudication in the courts which is prevented (Schermers § 1612).

Since general agreements on the liability of IO towards third parties do not exist the issue of liability of IO must be settled by reference to national law. Contractual liability of IO is normally governed by the law of the country referred to in the contract between the organisation and the contracting party (see, for example, Art. 340(1) TFEU and Art. 9(1) EPO-EPC). The non-contractual liability is normally governed by the general legal principles common to the laws of the member states (see, for example, Art. 340(2) TFEU) or by the law of the member state in which the organisation or its branch or sub-office has caused the damage (see, for example, Art. 9(2) EPO-EPC).

Whereas the jurisdiction governing a dispute between the organisation and a staff member is explicitly laid down in the constitution of the organisation and/ or the SR (Art. 270 TFEU and Art. 90, 91 EU-SR; Reg. 11(1) UN-SR; Art. 59 et seq. CoE-SR; Art. 13 EPO-EPC and Art. 106 et seq. EPO-SR), the liability of the organisation towards staff members is, as a rule, neither codified in general terms in the constitutions nor in the SR. The SR provide only for specific entitlements of officials, especially in the area of social protection (sometimes including occupational disease and accidents at work, see, for example, Art. 73, Art. 78(5) EU-SR; Rule 6(4) UN-SR; Appendix XII Art. 14 CoE-SR) and in case of damage suffered in their official function by third parties (see under duty of assistance).

As far as the general non-contractual liability of the organisation towards staff members is concerned, the international administrative tribunals and the doctrine apply by analogy the principles of general law governing the liability of the organisation towards third parties (see, for example, Art. 340(2) TFEU; Art. 9(2) EPO-EPC) with the proviso that the organisation is fully responsible for a breach of duties owed to staff members under the SR and in respect of the general principles governing the international civil service and especially under the obligation to provide a safe and healthy workplace environment (see Karpenstein, para. 62; Kunz-Hallstein/Ullrich, Art. 9 EPO-EPC; CJEU Judgments T-41/01, C-257/98 P, C-259/96 P; ILOAT Judgments 2804 para. 23, 435).

An IO is obliged to protect its staff members from physical and moral injuries occurring in the course of employment and from losses of damages to personal property and financial losses suffered in the course of employment. The liability of an IO towards its staff members, therefore, provides *overall protection* against damages occurring in the course of employment. The liability must not be "attributable to any decision – be it lawful or not – or to mismanagement but may be based on an irrational behaviour extraneous by its very nature to the performance of duty such as, say, an act of violence, or sexual harassment or theft" (ILOAT Judgment 1609).

Areas where claims may arise most frequently are: Unlawful dismissal, dilatory appeals procedures, an unsafe or unhealthy workplace environment, misuse of power, affront to dignity, violation of data protection, physical or moral harassment or failure to protect from attacks of third parties. There are also more remote areas of liability like the mismanagement of a provident fund (ILOAT Judgment 2403).

In all cases where the SR include specific entitlements (mostly lump-sum payments) in the case of workplace-related damages, based on a non-fault regime, these claims are deemed, in principle, to provide a final settlement. International administrative tribunals may, however, award additional compensation if the lump-sum payments are insufficient for the injury suffered (see explicitly Art. II(2) statute of the ILOAT: "The Tribunal shall be competent to settle any dispute concerning compensation provided for in cases of invalidity, injury or disease incurred by an official in the course of his employment and to fix finally the amount of compensation, if any, which is to be paid").

The degree of negligence on the part of the organisation has an impact on the assessment of the quantum of damages (ILOAT Judgments 2843, 2804, 2533, 435, 402; CJEU Judgments T-401/11 P, F-50/09, F-15/07, C-259/96 P, 169/83 and 136/84). Lump-sum compensation cannot, however, lead to double compensation (CJEU Judgment C-257/98 P para. 20 to 23).

There are a huge number of cases in which IO grant material or moral damages to staff members (e.g. 269 ILOAT extracts of judgments in the ILOAT Triblex database in 2016). In addition, there are probably a large number of damages payment to staff on a confidential basis in order not to compromise the reputation of the organisation.

#### b) The competences of international administrative tribunals

The rescinding of the administrative decision in itself constitutes appropriate and, in principle, sufficient reparation for any non-material harm which the official may have suffered (see, for example, CJEU Judgment F-6/07 para. 151).

The jurisprudence of the tribunals accepts, however, that an adequate reparation for damages suffered by unlawful actions of an IO by staff members is not always possible solely through the annulment (rescission) or the replacement of an administrative decision. In order to restore full justice damages have often to be awarded in addition. To this end the tribunals did not only had to derive a general legal principle of law allowing them to award material and moral damages, but also to permit actions within the limited competence vested in them by their statutes and/or the SR.

– Types of admissible actions

The types of actions generally admissible before international administrative tribunals are: action for annulment (rescission) of an administrative decision and action for damages. The action most frequently applied is the action for annulment (rescission) which is explicitly stated in the statutes of the tribunals or the SR.

At the ILOAT, however, an action for damages had to be declared generally admissible by way of interpretation of the statute. Article VIII second sentence of the statute of the ILOAT stipulates that, if the "rescinding of a decision or execution of an obligation is not possible or advisable, the tribunal shall award the complainant compensation for the injury caused to her or him". In Judgment 69 the tribunal held that it could not base itself on Art. VIII of its statute in order to grant an indemnity, the quashing of the decision impugned not being impossible or not seeming inappropriate. The tribunal indicated however, that the award of damages would nevertheless be possible. In its Judgment 1419 the tribunal declared that Art. VIII second sentence of its statute "does not preclude the tribunal's determining in the exercise of the competence conferred by the first sentence, the financial consequences of an organisation's failure to abide by its staff regulations or to discharge its contractual obligation".

The complainant is at liberty to choose either an action for annulment (rescission) of the administrative decision or for damages or both together. This ruling corresponds to Art. 10(5)(a) and (b) statute of the UNDT and Art. 9(1)(a) and (b) statute of UNAT.

The CJEU held in Judgment 9–75 that according to Art. 91 EU-SR the court has jurisdiction in proceedings relating to the legality of an act adversely affecting the official, whatever the nature of the action may be. The question of admissibility of the action is based on Art. 270 TFEU (Art. 340 TFEU does not apply). Actions for annulment of a decision and actions for damages are distinct types of action but Art. 90 and 91 EU-SR make no distinction between them as regards the legal procedures to which they may give rise. The official is, therefore, at liberty to combine both actions. If the compensation sought results from a decision of the administration it is for the official to submit within the time-limits a complaint for annulment. If the action for annulment is declared inadmissible, so is the action for compensation which seeks reparation exclusively for the "closely linked" consequences of the measure contested in the action for annulment. Otherwise an official could circumvent the obstacle of inadmissibility of the application for annulment by bringing an action for compensation for which no strict deadlines apply (CJEU Judgments T-249/04, T-27/90, T-5/90).

If the compensation sought results from a non-decisional conduct of the administration, the official must commence with a request for compensation and after the explicit or implicit dismissal of the request which constitutes a decision, he may submit an action for damages (CJEU T-23/05).

Actions for a *declaratory order* are, as a rule, inadmissible (see, for example, CJEU Judgment T-146/95 para. 23: "... claims which only seek declarations in respect of matters of fact or matters of law cannot, of themselves, be considered valid"; see, however, ILOAT Judgment 684). Such claims are, however, admissible in the context of an action for damages, e.g. for a service-related fault, such as the duty to provide assistance (Art. 24 EU-SR) or the belated establishment of appraisal reports (CJEU Judgments T-59/92, T-73/89, 10/72 and 47/72). The ILOAT may in exceptional cases make a declaratory order to restore the honour and reputation of the complainant (Judgments 2720, 684), e.g. by ordering that the text of the judgment to be circulated to the whole of the staff (see also Judgment 2861 para. 93).

Where the administration has failed to take an explicit decision upon a claim, its inactivity is assimilated into a negative decision. A complaint is, therefore, receivable in the same manner as a complaint against an explicit decision (see, for example, Art. VII(3) ILOAT statute).

### c) Actions for annulment and damages in detail

#### *aa) Action for annulment*

If an international administrative tribunal is satisfied that the complaint challenging the legality of a decision is well-founded, the ordinary consequence is that it orders the rescission of the decision impuged (Art. 91(1) EU-SR; Art. XIV(1) IMFAT). Some statutes even explicitly provide that instead ("or") of rescinding the decision, the performance of the obligation relied may be ordered (Art. VIII statute of the ILOAT, Art. 10(5)(a) statute of the UNDT, Art 9(1)(a) statute of the UNAT and Art. XII(1) WBAT).

This wording does, therefore, not preclude the power of the tribunals to rescind an illegal decision, but empowers a tribunal to order all necessary measures to correct the effect of the flawed decision (see above the similar reasoning of the ILOAT in regard of its competence under Art. VIII second sentence of its statute to grant damages). If a tribunal quashes a flawed decision it has full discretion as to the relief it grants (ILOAT Judgments 2636 para. 16, 1783 para. 4). It will either decide on its own, or if the execution calls for the play of administrative discretion, leave it to the organisation to give full effect to the reasoning and wording of the judgment (ILOAT Judgment 1419 para. 23). The tribunal is, however, not empowered to order apologies or to require undertakings as to the performance of obligations in the future (ILOAT Judgment 2636 para. 16).

Examples:

In the case of an unlawful dismissal, the tribunal will quash the flawed decision and order reinstatement if there is a vacant post and the complainant is qualified for it (e.g. ILOAT Judgments 3437, 2034, 1447, 1246, 1238, 90). However, reinstatement of an employee on a fixed-term contract is only ordered in exceptional cases (see, for example, ILOAT Judgments 3417, 3353, 3299, 1317).

If a decision to terminate a probationary period is quashed and it is not clear whether the appointment would have been confirmed, no reinstatement is ordered but material damages for the loss of a valuable opportunity are awarded (e.g. ILOAT Judgment 2732). If an unlawful decision concerns financial benefits which could easily be calculated, the tribunal will of its own volition order compensation (see Art. 91(1) second sentence EU-SR). A successful action for annulment does, therefore, encompass remedies of specific performance.

If a decision not to renew a fixed-term appointment is set aside, the tribunal may order the organisation to take a new decision or, if a renewal be only fair, order reinstatement or, if a reinstatement is not possible or advisable award, compensation for the injury caused.

The performance required is inadvisable *inter alia*, if the circumstances of the dismissal were such that it would no longer be reasonably possible for the employee to perform his duties effectively and harmoniously (see ILOAT Judgment 1238) or if practical difficulties would be expected because of the time that has elapsed since the termination of employment (ILOAT Judgments 2883, 2854, 2742, 1548, 1246).

In case of a great damage the tribunal not only annulled the impugned decision and ordered reinstatement, it even ordered the grant of employment for a longer period, since the renewal of short-term employment did not suffice (ILOAT Judgment 1376). The tribunal may also grant the organisation an option between the reinstatement of the complainant and the payment of damages (e.g. LOAT Judgments 1629, 1553, 1132).

*bb) Action for damages*

For the liability of the organisation to be incurred in the case of a claim for damages a number of conditions must cumulatively be met. According to settled case law of the CJEU (Judgments T-396/03, T-165/03, T-120/01 and T-300/01, C-257/98 P, C-259/96 P, C-136/92) for the liability of the organisation to be incurred in a claim for damages the illegality *of the conduct* (act or omission) of the organisation, the actual damage suffered and the existence of a causal link between that conduct and the damage alleged to have been suffered must be satisfied. If one of those conditions is not satisfied, the entire action must be dismissed. It is first and foremost for the party seeking to establish the liability of the organisation to adduce conclusive proof for the existence of the alleged damage and the causal link between the damage and the conduct complained (CJEU Judgment C-401/96 P).

Other international administrative tribunals like the ILOAT apply the same conditions in the case of a claim for damages.

– The illegality of the action or omission

IO are under a duty to provide a safe and healthy work environment. They are under an obligation to implement adequate health and safety measures (e.g. ILOAT Judgment 2804). The duty to provide a safe and secure workplace extends to ensuring that intimidation, offensive behaviour or aggression do not occur in relation to staff associations' affairs (ILOAT Judgment 2636 para. 28).

It is common for a mature national legal system to provide for a compensation on a no-fault basis to employees who suffer a workplace injury, so "the law of the international civil service can do no less" (ILOAT Judgment 2533 para. 6). The risks are covered as a rule by an insurance on a no-fault regime and in general considered by the tribunals as an adequate compensation for the injury suffered (see Art. 73 EU-SR, Rule 6(4) UN-SR, Appendix XII Art. 14 CoE-SR, Art. 62b, 83, 83a, 84 EPO-SR).

In order to get additional benefits over and above those awarded under the SR, the official must prove negligence on the part of the organisation (ILOAT Judgments 2843, 2533, 435; CJEU Judgments F-50/09, T-40/11 P, C-257/98 P, C-259/96 P, T-20/89, 169/83 and 136/84).

In exceptional circumstances compensation for moral damages may even be awarded in a case where the conduct of the organisation was held to have been lawful. Such exceptional cases may be found, for example, in the suddenness of the implementation of a lawful decision violating the dignity and reputation of the staff member (ILOAT Judgments 1294, 447, 396, 361).

– The causal link

There must be a causal link between the action or conduct of the organisation and the alleged injury. The ILOAT, for example, did not acknowledge sufficient causal link in Judgment 732. The belated receipt of the payment of the organisation to a staff member was found to be due to technical difficulties within the bank system and the organisation was not held liable for injury to "business, profession and reputation" of the staff member. In CJEU Judgment T-144/02 the Court awarded material damages for loss of remuneration. The complainant should have been recruited as a temporary staff member and not left as a staff member of a joint undertaking. The direct causal nexus between the unlawful act and the damage sustained was established with a sufficient degree of certainty.

– The damage suffered

Finally, the official must have suffered material or moral damage. The complaint must provide evidence for this injury. Save in special circumstances, the annulment of the decision contested by the official, is in itself appropriate and, in principle, adequate compensation for the moral damage suffered by the applicant. The annulment is not adequate compensation if the action caused injury to the reputation or dignity of the official. In this case, moral damage is awarded (ILOAT Judgment 1481; CJEU Judgment T-307/01).

As regards the typology of damages resulting from the murder of an official a distinction must be drawn between: non-material "*ex haerede*" damage suffered by the victim himself, material damage suffered by close relatives depending on the deceased's income and non-material damage suffered by the close relatives, see CJEU Judgment T-401/11 (F-50/08).

Under very special circumstances the ILOAT did not even quash an unlawful decision since the complainant could not demonstrate a link between the breach of the SR and the outcome of the selection process, but it awarded a considerable amount of moral damages (ILOAT Judgment 2884).

Staff members are under an obligation to avoid or mitigate the damage suffered. The official owes a duty of good faith to collaborate actively and not to impede or prevent the functioning of internal remedies like proceedings of the medical board or the internal appeals board (ILOAT Judgment 2458).

– Special features of the award of damages

The general principle of law governing the liability of IO toward their officials for unlawful actions in the course of employment does not provide for any restriction of the amount of damages to be awarded.

This is, in principle, also valid for the decision-making power of the international administrative tribunals.

The statutes of the UNDT (Art. 10(5)(b)) and the UNAT (Art. 9(1)(b)), however, restrict the award of compensation normally to the equivalent of two year's net base salary of the applicant. Only in exceptional cases may these tribunals order the payment of a higher compensation and have to provide reasons for that decision.

Apart from the general notion of material and moral damages international administrative tribunals may award *nominal (token)* damages, i.e. small damage are awarded to show that the complainant is in the right but did not suffer a sufficient injury (e.g. ILOAT Judgments 2575: one Euro; 2356, 2073).

*Exemplary or punitive damages or a penalty* are only awarded in exceptional circumstances, for instance, where there was a gross breach of legal principles (e.g. violation of good faith) or in cases of gross abuse of power (ILOAT Judgments 3152: A penalty of EUR 25,000 for each month of delay in executing the Judgment; 2806: A penalty of EUR 10,000 for each month or part month of delay in executing Judgment 2575; 2540: Exemplary damages of CHF 25,000 for a retaliatory action simply because an official had pursued an internal appeal; 2418: Punitive damages for a serious breach of legal principles; 1620: A penalty of CHF

25,000 for each month of failure to execute a judgment; 1362: CHF 10,000 for each further month of failure to execute a judgment).

In conformity with their statutes (Art. 10(7) UNDT and Art. 9(3) UNAT) the UNDT and the UNAT do not award exemplary or punitive damages.

– The award of *moral damages*

Whereas the award of material damages does not, as a rule, give rise to particular difficulties (see, for example, ILOAT Judgment 1251), the award of moral damages does not follow rigid rules, but is based on a considerable judicial discretion.

Moral damages are awarded by the tribunal on request by the complainant if the rescission of the decision or the performance of the obligation or the material or moral damages awarded are not deemed to be sufficient to compensate the injury caused by the organisation. Save in special circumstances, the CJEU holds that the annulment of the decision impugned is in itself appropriate and, in principle, adequate compensation for the moral damage suffered (CJEU Judgments T-307/01, T-89/01, T-368/94). Although the ILOAT seems, in principle, to share this view (ILOAT Judgment 1481 para. 8), it considers, in constant practice, the annulment of a decision to be an insufficient redress for the injury caused.

It is not enough for a successful claim for moral damages to allege emotional distress. What is required is that the effect on the feelings is appreciably greater than that of the ordinary fortunes of everyday life (ILOAT Judgment 565). Frictions to a greater or lesser degree, are the inevitable adjunct of life and to award damages for this sort of emotional distress would be to invite ceaseless litigation. Only exceptional circumstances warrant compensation for such distress (ILOAT Judgments 1380, 1131, 550).

Moral damages are most frequently awarded in the following areas: due process, duty to provide a safe and healthy working environment, equal treatment, harassment, hidden disciplinary action, humiliation and injury to feelings and reputation, misuse of power, right to defence, undue delay in the internal appeals and medical procedures, victimisation and false allegations, violation of dignity and good name.

In measuring the quantum of moral damages, the tribunals take all aspects peculiar to a case into account, such as the age and the record of the complainant, the type of injury, the seriousness of the injury, the professional status of the official responsible for the injury and, where appropriate, the degree of negligence.

The amount of moral damages cannot, of course, be ascertained by using mathematical methods. The ILOAT, for example, awarded moral damages ranging from one euro nominal damage up to one year's salary (Judgments 2575 and 2891). Combined material and moral damages are also awarded (ILOAT Judgments 2861: exemplary, material and moral damages of CHF 190,000; 1251: two years' salary and allowances "under the other heads of injury"; 1317: three years' salary and allowances "for all forms of injury"); 1231: two years' gross salary for injury "under all heads". In the case of undue delay in the internal appeals procedure, the ILOAT normally awards a small amount of moral damages (e.g. ILOAT Judgments 2851, 2820: EUR 1,000; 2841: EUR 1,500).

Jurisprudence on material and moral damages

**ILOAT Judgments**

*Due process*

3485: EUR 30,000 moral damages for breach of due process (3347: CHF 2,500; 3172: EUR 15,000); 2839: Moral damages awarded, appeals board failed to make a mandatory referral to the grievance panel; 2524: Material and moral damages of EUR 35,000 for harassment by absence of due process; 1741: No appraisal report after the probation period *ex aequo et bono* USD 40,000 in damages under all heads of injury; 1525: Breach of due process caused moral injury but no damages awarded, since the official had sufficient redress in the award of full pay without having to provide any service in return; 1434: Moral damages, the organisation denied the appeals board access to information and documents; 1370: Moral damages due to malfunctioning of the appeals board (1317); 999: Moral damages for breach of due process in the internal appeals proceedings.

*Duty to provide a safe and healthy working environment*

2843: In order to extend the liability beyond the organisation's liability under a no-fault regime for workplace injury, the complainant must prove negligence (slipping on liquid in the underground car park); 2804: The liability of the organisation for work-related invalidity may be extended beyond the lump-sum compensation in the case of a breach of a duty by negligence. No causal link between the failure of the organisation and the alleged injuries was proven; 2533: It is common for a mature national legal system to provide compensation for a workplace injury on a no-fault basis. The same is valid for the international civil service. Negligence could, however, have an impact on the assessment of damages; 2524: Moral damages awarded, harassment and mobbing are extreme examples of the breach of the duties to provide a safe and secure workplace and to ensure that the employee is treated fairly and with dignity; 435: Loss of hearing, but the organisation did not expose the appellant to a degree of danger incompatible with the normal performance of his duties; 402: If an organisation is at fault, the limited compensation in the case of illness, accident or death under the SR does not apply.

*Harassment*

2982: Moral damages for actively damaging the personal and/or professional reputation (immediate replacement without a hearing or giving a warning); 2973: Moral damage, no investigations in the case of alleged sexual and moral harassment; 2706: Moral damages for sexual harassment by superior; 2524: Moral damages for harassment (open hostility, isolation, humiliation); 1637: Moral harassment and injury of health; 1619: False allegations of sexual harassment, the organisation failed to carry out a full and proper inquiry, moral damages awarded; 1376: Moral damages for not taking proper actions against sexual harassment and abuse of authority.

*Hidden disciplinary action*

2854: Decision to terminate a contract as a disguised disciplinary measure; 2845: Moral damages for an act of retaliation for filing complaints, 2659: Definition of a hidden disciplinary sanction; 2232: Termination of appointment as a hidden disciplinary action; 2229: Transfer as a hidden disciplinary action; 1929: Transfer in a brutal manner as a disguised disciplinary measure; 1496: A transfer out of the blue as a disguised disciplinary measure; 1234: Moral damages for a transfer being a reduction in grade and offence to dignity; 631: Moral damages for downgrading (relegation to a post of lower responsibility and declining importance).

*Humiliation, injury to feelings and reputation, violation of dignity and good name*

2861: Substantial moral and material damages for illegal dismissal and publications, dignity and reputation injured; 2839: Moral damages for reassignment without due regard to the interests and the dignity of the staff member; 2819: Transfer to a post which did not match with the qualifications and the level of work of the previous post, violation of dignity; 2819: Moral damages for dignity injured; 2779: Breach of the duty to respect dignity, moral damages awarded; 2416: Moral damages for the hurt of feelings and mental distress as a result of actions by the organization, including the threat of disciplinary proceedings; 2394: Harm of legitimate interests and impairment of dignity since the organisation advertised the complaint's post before he had a chance to comment on the termination of his contract; 2372: Infringement of dignity by improper placement on special leave and excluding the official from access to the premises; 2222: Violation of the dignity and the right to be informed that the official's diplomatic immunity had been waived; 2090: Failure to observe dignity; 1875: Material and moral damages are due if a superior violates the dignity of an employee. If a third party makes false allegations the organisation is under a duty to communicate its view that the allegations, are false; 1742: Moral damages awarded for violation of dignity and imposing a disciplinary sanction without a due disciplinary process; 1726: Moral damages for a transfer without a hearing which is an affront to dignity; 1496: Abrupt transfer, offence to dignity, moral damages awarded; 1395: Humiliation by telling the complainant that she does not need to be present at the premises until the end of her contract, no hearing; 1384: Moral damages for a flagrant disregard of the right to defence against a presumptive evidence of theft, damage to career and reputation; 1340: Untrue criticism of superior, failure to protect and vindicate the good name; 942: Flawed transfer and violation of the dignity and the good name; 843: Moral damages for humiliation and anguish; 781: Moral damages for an unwarranted sanction and attack on the good name; 630: Injury to feelings and reputation by *inter alia* not giving the complainant any real work; 447: Injury to the feelings and reputation of the complainant due to unaccountable transfer.

*Misuse of power*

2540: A retaliatory action simply because an internal appeal is filed is a gross misuse of power; 1609: A subordinate is entitled to damages if his supervisor commits an abuse of authority (rough language, rough behaviour). On that account the organisation is liable; 21: Wrongful exercise of power, unlawful decision not to renew an appointment.

*Undue delay in the internal appeals and medical procedures*

3038: Moral damages for the delay in implementing a decision with respect to an appeal; 3023: Undue delay of approximately 17 months of an internal appeal with the only issue being receivability, entitlement to moral damages; 2904: Moral damages for undue delay of 16 months of an internal appeal which hinged on a simple question of receivability and the entire process lasted over eight years; 2891: Moral damages for an unacceptable delay in the appeals procedure (42 months); 2878: Moral damages for an excessive delay of 21 months (simple receivability question) in the internal appeals procedure; 2851: An internal appeals procedure of two and half years is much too long, moral damages awarded; 2841: Moral damages for an appeals procedure of 18 months (simple question of receivability); 2744: Moral damages for excessively long (three years) appeals procedure; 2522: Moral damages since the internal appeal proceedings were not conducted with due diligence; 2392: Moral damages for undue delay and defects in the appeals procedure; 2325: Moral damages for an excessive delay between the selection of the successful candidate and the information to the complainant thereof; 2197: Moral damages due to the delay of 20 months between filing of the appeal and the start of the hearings; 2196: Moral damages for excessive delay of internal appeal proceedings. The heavy volume and a backlog of internal appeals may be a reason, but they are not an excuse for the delay. Lack of resources can never justify depriving employees of their right to a speedy and just resolution of their grievances; 2116: Moral damages for a delay in appeal proceedings (two and a half years between filing and final decision); 2072: Moral damages for undue delay of appeal proceedings (a simple case was for before the appeals board for two years); 1873: Damages for injury caused by delay in executing a judgment (1771); 1620: Award of a penalty for each month of delay in the execution of a judgment; 1516: Moral damages due to years of dilatoriness in establishing the degree of invalidity; 1427: Moral damages for the injury due to the thwarting of the official's legitimate expectation of prompt and correct execution of a judgment; 1394: Moral damages for undue delay (six years) in the rating of performance; 1365: Moral damages for defective execution of a judgment; 1362: Penalty payment of CHF 10,000 for each month of delay of execution of a judgment; 1361: Damages for the failure to give effect to the rulings of the tribunal; 1338: After award of a specific sum by the tribunal the organisation must pay within one month after the judgment has been notified, otherwise interest is due; 1331: Moral damages for excessive delay in the selection process; 1328: Obligation to pay compound interest for the delayed execution of judgment; 1284: Moral damages due to delay in the proceedings of the medical committee; 1026: Damages for the injury caused by the dilatoriness of the appeal proceedings; 724: Moral damages for excessive delay in approving the appraisal report; 388: Moral damages for belated attempts to find another employment for the complainant and inordinately long internal appeal proceedings; 82: Indemnity for the delay in giving effect to a part of the judgment.

*Breach of Service Regulations*

2884: Moral damages for the breach of the SR (not including the use of an assessment centre in the vacancy note); 2742: Substantial material and moral damages as consequence of an unlawful decision to reassign the complainant to another post at the same grade but with significantly diminished duties, responsibilities and status; 2170: Moral damages for not complying with internal rules requiring an annual appraisal report; 2073: Failure by the organisation to follow its own rules on data protection, nominal award of damages; 1782: Moral damages for incorrect termination of appointment; 1553: Material and moral damages for the failure to give the complainant, as a staff member, priority for a vacant post; 1251: Material and moral damages for the wrongful termination of appointment and injury to the professional career and prospects; 1043: Damages for all forms of injury sustained by unlawful dismissal; 1017: Moral damages awarded for improper termination of the probation; 809: Unlawful decision as to the creation of an unclassified post and compulsory special leave, decision not quashed but moral damages awarded; 565: Moral damages for injury caused by irregularities in an appraisal report; 494: Damages for wrongful dismissal since reinstatement has not been applied for; 480: Where a decision not to extend an appointment is improper the tribunal generally awards compensation less than the amount of remuneration which the complainant would have received up to the end of a further appointment (431, 427; obligation to seek other employment); 393: Moral damages for being improperly rejected in selection proceedings; 359: Refusal to renew an appointment was not based on decisive facts, compensation instead of reinstatement which was not desirable in the present case; 223: Material and moral damages for refusing to renew the appointment on mere suspicions; 172: Material and moral damages due to a dismissal on unproven grounds of misconduct; 133: Damages for the whole of the injury the complainant suffered as a result of the illegal decision to terminate his indeterminate appointment without taking all appropriate steps to find him other employment.

*Other important moral damage cases*

3013: The obligation to pay compound interest is always an exception; 2935: A claim for punitive damages may be allowed only in exceptional circumstances, e.g. if the organisation is in gross breach of its obligation to act in good faith; 2931: Moral damages for a breach of the principle of equal pay for work of equal value; 2867: Moral damages for the violation of the duty of care; 2678: Renewal of contract denied without proper evaluation, material and moral damages awarded for loss of a valuable opportunity (2306); 2558: Moral damages for extending the probationary period without delegation by the head of administration; 2457: A claim for damages is receivable if the request had been made in the course of the internal appeals procedure, albeit only orally and in general terms (2416, 2360); 2418: Punitive damages since the decision was irregular and the organisation's attitude showed a distinct lack of even-handedness; 2371: Moral damages for breach of confidentiality by the ombudsman and defamatory remarks; 2356: Moral damages for documents which should have been removed from the personnel files; 2314: Moral damages for failure to observe the principle of equality; 2190: Moral injury due to the inactivity of the organisation to investigate whether an accident revealed any administrative failure; 1904: If the Judgment gives an organisation the choice between reinstatement and the payment of damages, and the organisation chooses to pay damages, it does not have to pay the contributions to the pension fund and the sickness insurance, since the separation took place at the date at which reinstatement was applied for; 1878: Moral damages due to a disciplinary measure which was out of proportion; 1804: Moral damages for violation of the principle of equality (promise of irregular promotion); 1547: The organisation broke with a consistent practice to deliver notices of a non-recognised union to staff members, moral damages awarded; 1407: Moral damages awarded for taking away the title of an employee; 1386: Moral damages for premature dismissal after probation without written warning and guidance. Material damages instead of a further probation after the long time that had elapsed since the date of dismissal; 1351: Moral damages for disappointment of the expectation of further employment; 1313: Moral damages for not executing a judgment properly; 1090: Moral damages for not keeping a promise; 939: Damages for a procedural flaw of lesser importance instead of quashing the decision; 972: Material damages since reinstatement was not advisable and moral damages for serious mistakes of facts; 675: Moral damages due to assuming that a fixed-term contract expired automatically on the specified expiration date and for not stating any reason; 665: Moral damages due to the overlooking of an essential fact and drawing clearly mistaken conclusions from the evidence when setting up the evaluation report; 640: Damages for unlawful dismissal since the charge of attempted theft was not proven; 620: Damages since the medical experts should have consulted each other not just in writing and by telephone, but by meeting together; 448: Compensation instead of reinstatement if mutual trust has diminished considerably; 436: Investigation by the tribunal under Art. 11 of its Rules will merely be ordered in aid of some relief, such as reinstatement or compensation but not for the sake of ascertaining the facts (no inquisitorial principle); 431: Damages for the expectation of further employment are less than the restitution of salary and pension rights in the case of an illegal dismissal; 396: For serious wrong likely to prove damaging to a staff member's career the organisation is obliged to pay compensation even if there is no decision to be set aside; 382: Moral damages for faulty transfer giving the impression that the complainant had been edged out of his position; 373: Damages for improper transfer and loss of professional standing since a position of equal grading may differ considerably in status and prestige (367, 311); 203: Damages for a disciplinary sanction out of all proportion and for loss of salary, since reinstatement was not advisable; 135: Moral damages for the prejudice caused to the complainant by the state of uncertainty as a result of a rescinded decision (122).

CJEU Judgments/Orders

F-104/10: It is not for the tribunal to issue directions to the administration; F-46/09: The annulment of an act may in itself constitute appropriate and, in principle, sufficient reparation for the injury suffered. Exceptionally, non-material damages are awarded, if the annulment of the act cannot constitute full reparation, i.e. if the illegality committed was particularly serious (F-42/06, T-328/01); F-30/08: Considerable moral damages are awarded for various faults of the organisation (e.g. delay in information about assistance; instituting disciplinary proceedings without having relevant information available, no offer of apology or regrets, leak of personal data); F-124/05 and F-96/06: Moral damages *inter alia* since the decision to institute disciplinary proceedings was taken more than seven years after the accused conduct and the proceedings continued for three years; F-5/05 and F-7/05: Moral damages for violation of the right to defence; T-48/05: Moral damages for feelings of injustice and frustration, a slur on the honour and professional reputation on the complainant on account of the unlawful conduct of the organisation; T-166/04: If there are objective circumstances preventing the administration from implementing a judgment (applicant for a vacant post retired after the first judgment), the organisation has a duty to explore a possible settlement. Moral damages awarded; T-309/03: Award of non-material damage for impairment of honour and reputation; T-76/03: Moral damages for a transfer which was published by using the expression: "relieved of his duties" with an obvious disciplinary connotation; T-16/03: Moral damages for the refusal of a fair hearing and for an incorrect evaluation in the notation report; C-284/98 P: Obligation of the staff member to show reasonable diligence in limiting the extent of the damage; C-180/87: Moral damages for providing the police of a member state information relating to the service extraneous to the subject-matter of the investigation; C-207/81: Moral damages for an excessively long period to establish the report of an official.

*Chapter 3*

# The typical structures and elements of employment rules

## A. The legal nature of employment

Today the vast majority of IO employ their staff on a contractual basis (based on bilateral acts of consensus). Only EU and EPO staff are appointed on a statutory basis by means of a unilateral act of appointment. The employment contracts are limited nowadays to a few basic elements of a mainly formal nature, in particular the date at which the staff member is required to take up his/her duties, the nature and the period of appointment, the period of probation and the category and level the staff member is assigned to. The substantial part of the employment relationship is based on the provisions of the SR (staff regulations, staff rules) to which the letter of appointment refers (see, for example, Annex II of the UN-SR). The SR determine the whole employment relationship (rights and obligations of staff, career, working conditions, social security, legal protection etc.). The "dichotomy" (Priess, p. 51) of the contractual relationship between the contract of employment and the unilaterally standardised rules of employment which are not negotiable is therefore of a more formal nature. The substantive difference between the statutory relationship of permanent officials in the EU or the EPO service law systems and the contractual relationship in the other IO is mainly characterised by the impossibility to terminate a permanent official's relationship by notice.

In the civil service systems of all IO, including the EU and the EPO systems, there are special contractual arrangements for the filling of most senior management positions like UN-SG, USG, ASG, Presidents, Vice-Presidents, Principal Directors etc. For these cases staff specimen contracts apply. They deviate from the general civil service provisions concerning the appointment and terms of employment (e.g. appraisal, remuneration, representation allowance, pension provisions and end of contract).

The following sections give a survey on the different types of employment relationship in IO.

### I. Permanent staff

In the civil service system of the EU the employment relationship with the "institutions" and the "agencies" (see Art 1a(1) and (2) EU-SR) for the "officials"

(Art. 336 TFEU) and the employment relationship in the EPO for "permanent employees" (see Art. 33.2(b) EPO-EPC) is, for the vast majority of staff, provided solely on a statutory basis. In both organisations it was the aim of these statutory relationships with staff to secure the independence and the stability of the organisation. At the EU, this legal form of employment relationship was also influenced by the supranational character of the organisation. At the EPO, the decision in 1977 to adopt statutory staff rules similar to the EU was based on the consideration that most patent examiners were going to be taken over from national patent offices and an employment status comparable to national civil service employment needed to be offered. Moreover, there was concern that the high degree of specialisation of a patent examiner in the various fields of technology would constitute a major barrier for future alternative employment.

The legal differences between statutory and contractual employment of a permanent nature in an IO is ultimately limited, since in both cases the employment relationship is characterised almost always by the statutory provisions unilaterally adopted by the IO. In the case law of the ILOAT there is no difference in principle (e.g. in the meaning of the terms "loyalty" and "care" owed respectively by the staff and the organisation) between the permanent employees of the EPO and the contractual relationship of the staff of all other IO which accept the case law of the tribunal (see also Seidl-Hohenveldern/Loibl consistently using only the term: international civil servant). The only significant difference between statutory and contractual relationship lies ultimately in the generally easier termination of contractual relationships (even for permanent/continuing contractual staff). If the post of an EU official becomes supernumerary (Art. 41(2) EU-SR) the staff member concerned receives an allowance decreasing gradually from 85% to 60% of his basic salary for a period varying with the age and length of service (Annex IV of the EU-SR) and has priority for reinstatement for a period of two years (Art. 41(3) EU-SR).

In the EU and the EPO, only statutory permanent staff are employed for core activities.

## II. Contract staff

### *1. Continuing appointments*

IO use different types of employment contracts. Closest to the permanent officials of the EU system and the EPO are the "continuing appointments" of the UN-CS (Rule 4(14) UN-SR) which replaced the former term "permanent appointments" in 2009 (see doc. A/63/694). In contrast to the contract for permanent staff of the EU and the EPO, the continuing appointments can be terminated more easily to take account of the financial dependency on member states for contributions. If, in the interest of the service the abolition of a post or a reduction of staff becomes necessary (Reg. 9(3)(a)(i) and 9(3)(b) UN-SR) a termination indemnity is paid which is much lower than at the EU or the EPO if a permanent official's employment relationship is terminated. In accordance with a schedule the UN pays between three and twelve months gross salary for one to 15 completed years of service or more (Annex III UN-SR).

Continuing appointments are "open-ended" appointments (Rule 4(14)(a) UN-SR). A continuing appointment is granted after the successful completion of a competition examination, a minimum period of uninterrupted, active service on fixed-term appointments and certified satisfactory performance (Rule 4(14)(b) UN-SR: two years).

The EU provides for this type of employment (engagement for a fixed or indefinite period) under its "temporary staff" and "contract staff" terms (see below; Art. 1, Art. 8 et seq. and Art. 79 et seq. EU-CEOS).

The CoE (and other CO, see, for example, Reg. 9 OECD-SR) uses contracts of employment of an indefinite duration ("permanent staff members", Art. 1(1) CoE-SR).

The EPO does not provide for indefinite contractual employment (Art. 2 Conditions of employment for contract staff).

### 2. *Fixed-term and temporary staff*

This type of employment is the most widespread in IO. It varies, however, in terms and content.

In the EU civil service system, the Conditions of Employment of other Servants of the EU (EU-CEOS) provide for servants engaged under contract (Art. 1 EU-CEOS). They comprise: temporary staff, contract staff, local staff, special advisers and accredited parliamentary assistants. Whereas temporary agents as a rule either fill a temporary post in the budget or temporarily fill a permanent post Art. 2 EU-CEOS), contract agents are paid from appropriations for this purpose provided for in the budget (Art. 79 EU-CEOS). (For details, see below.)

The UN-SR provide for fixed-term appointment (Rule 4(13)) for, in principle, up to five years and a temporary appointment (Rule 4(12)) for, in principle, up to one year. (For details, see below).

The CoE-SR staff regulations provide for fixed-term and indefinite-term contracts (Art. 6, Art. 15A and 15B CoE-SR). (For details, see below).

The EPO provides for employment of contract staff ("other employees" in the meaning of Art. 33(2)(b) EPO-EPC) for non-core activities and for a limited term). (For details, see below.)

In all IO, the most senior management staff is appointed on a contract basis, the most widespread term being five years (e.g. Reg. 4(5)(a) UN-SR; Art. 17(3) TEU) which in some IO may be renewed for a further period.

### III. Local staff

For simple manual or auxiliary duties in IO local staff are often recruited under national law (see, for example, Art. 4 and 120 et seq. EU-CEOS: staff engaged in places outside the EU). The application of national labour law within the IO is at the discretion of the organisation (see, for example, Art. 120 EU-CEOS: "... in accordance with current rules and practice in the place where they are to perform their duties"). In so far as the organisation refers to the application of national law the international administrative tribunals have no jurisdiction. The legal protection of this staff is guaranteed by the organisation, either through the waiver of its immunity, thus permitting a legal process before a national labour court, or by offering arbitration. Usually IO provide for an arbitration clause in disputes with local staff (see, for example, Art. 122 EU-CEOS).

The EPO has a statute comparable to local staff (Statute for the "auxiliary staff" of 17 January 1986). This provides for a hybrid system, partly referring to the organisation's and partly to the national labour law system. Accordingly, the legal protection is divided between the national labour courts and the jurisdiction of the ILOAT (see Kunz-Hallstein/Ullrich, Art. 13 EPO-EPC, para. 21 and ILOAT Judgment 1450 referring to the judgment of the Labour Court of Berlin and the Appellate Labour Tribunal of Berlin and ILOAT Judgment 1555 referring to auxiliary staff at the EPO sub-office in Vienna). Since this mixed system did not prove practical due to demarcation problems it has not been applied further.

### IV. Non-staff personnel

#### *1. Contractors*

IO, due to their organisational power and financial autonomy in personnel matters, conclude contracts with self-employed workers (service or work contracts), consultants, experts, special advisers, national experts etc. It is not always clear in each case whether these contracts are with freelancers or employment contracts (see Seidl-Hohenveldern, IPRax 1995, p. 14 et seq.). This "grey area" of the employment relationship is known under the term "disguised" employment. It is characterised by typical elements of employment, such as monitoring of working hours, the supply of material and equipment needed and the financial risk being taken by the organisation (see ILOAT Judgment 701: lease of work or relation of subordination).

A disguised employment relationship often coincides with the outsourcing of tasks in specific areas like catering, cleaning, security and maintenance services. A preferred area is also the IT department, where specific and permanently up-to-date external expertise is needed. This disguised employment relationship carries the risk of inferior working conditions, the loss of rights and benefits compared with a permanent employment relationship and the denial of effective support by the staff representation (see in this context ILOAT Judgment 2919). (For a critical review on this issue in the UN system see Cihan Terzi, UN doc. JIU/REP/2012/5.)

At the EU, there is a special kind of "outsourcing" of tasks to executive agencies with their own legal personality, established by the Commission in order to implement EU programmes. This externalisation process was the subject of a critical report by the European Court of Auditors in 2009 (Special Report No. 13: Delegating implementing tasks to executive agencies: a successful option?), mainly focused on the limited supervision of the agency's work and an insufficient cost-benefit analysis.

### 2. *Temporary agency staff*

Another problem is the use of temporary agency staff hired from agencies by IO (in order to avoid confusion with the contracting staff the EU agency EPSO (European Personnel Selection Office, see below) prefers the expression ("interim staff"). Such staff are used in order to improve flexibility of manpower (meeting the peaks and troughs). In contrast to the "temporary staff" of IO (e.g. Rule 4(12) UN-SR and Art. 2 EU-CEOS), temporary agency staff are not employed by the IO itself but by an intermediary agency ("triangular employment relationship"). Unfortunately, the terms "sub-contracting staff", "temporary staff" or "external contractors" are also used where hired agency staff is meant.

With regard to the legal protection of temporary agency staff, see the Judgments of the ECHR of 18 February 1999, application no. 26083/94, Waite and Kennedy v. Germany and application no. 28934/95 Beer and Regan v. Germany concerning the legal protection of temporary agency staff of ESA. In its Judgments 2919 and 2649 the ILOAT dealt with the employment relationship of "external contractors supplied by third-party agencies" at the EPO in its headquarters in Munich and its sub-office in Vienna.

### 3. *Trainees*

Most IO offer trainee programmes for persons having completed their first university degree. In general, these programmes last several months. At the EU institution, trainees are paid up to EUR 1,000 per month (see the website of EPSO).

#### *4. De facto employment relationship*

This issue may arise when an employment relationship is illegal *ab initio* or if the true legal relationship is not that of a self-employed contractor or temporary agency staff but of an employee of the organisation. An *in extenso* examination of this issue is contained in IMFAT Judgment No. 1999–1, see also ILOAT Judgment 2183 (illegality of employment relationship did not exclude jurisdiction) and ILOAT Judgment 701 (self-employment or relation of subordination). The conditions set in the case law of the ILOAT for the recognition of a *de facto* employment relationship are rather high (ILOAT Judgments 3051, 2926).

### V. Structures of employment

The appointment of a staff member by the administration of an IO generally presupposes that an appropriate budget unit (post) is approved by the decision-making body responsible for the decision on the budget or that adequate budget appropriations for "external staff" (local staff, agency staff, freelance staff, trainees etc.) are available.

Each functional post for an international staff member is assigned to function groups (job groups) and each group comprises several grades. The same applies for staff members not assigned to a post but paid from respective budget appropriations (e.g. EU contract staff). The specific category and the grades are determined by the required qualifications, the nature of the duties and the extent and level of responsibility (see, for example, Art. 5 EU-SR; Reg. 2(1) UN-SR). For each grade these quantitative and qualitative characteristics are often defined in an abstract job description. If the actual duties exercised and confirmed by a job specification do not comply with the job description, compensation payments may be triggered (see, for example, ILOAT Judgments 2819, 2431).

The career development of a staff member, i.e. his promotion to the next higher grade, is based on merits (appraisal reports) and experience in conformity with implementing rules on promotion. These rules are set up in order to guarantee a fair and consistent promotion procedure and the equal treatment of staff. The procedure is supervised by harmonisation or promotion boards. The grades comprise a certain number of steps in grade, through which the staff member usually advances automatically in intervals of one or two years, unless his performance is unsatisfactory.

**Details**

EU

Until the large reform of the EU-SR on 1 May 2004, the posts of EU civil servants were grouped in the categories A, B, C, D and LA and divided up into to eight grades, each of which included up to eight steps of seniority levels (for details see "Reforming the Commission", employment conditions up to this date, see the website; ec.europa.eu/reforms).

According to the aim of this reform of the SR in force since 1968, human resources management in the EU institutions had to be revised in order to produce a civil service "that listens to the public, and which is efficient, permanent, transparent and independent" (Reforming the Commission, p. 1). Beside the introduction of a lifelong learning and mobility policy a new career structure for officials was adopted, based on proven ability and performance, rather than on length of service. The previous service categories were merged into "function groups" – administrator ("AD") and assistants ("AST"). A third function group – secretaries and clerks ("AST/SC") – was added on 29 October 2013 (Regulation No. 1023/2013). For the AD and AST function group a single pay scale (Art. 66 EU-SR) with 16 grades (each with only up to five steps) was introduced. The AD took the place of the categories A and LA, comprises grades 5 to 16 of the pay scale (see Art. 5 and Annex I EU-SR). AD staff is typically engaged in drafting policies, implementing EU law, analysing and advising. The AST function group is employed in a supporting function (secretarial, administrative, financial etc.) and comprises grades 1 to 11 of the pay scale. This replacement of the horizontal career system (higher pay due to a higher step) by a vertical one (promotion to a higher grade) results in a more merit-based promotion and less automatic progression in terms of pay.

A separate pay scale applies to the secretaries and clerks function group AST/SC groups which comprises six grades (Art. 66 EU-SR).

AD, AST and AST/SC officials basically perform core tasks in the EU institutions. This is the reason why in the EU Commission over 98% of staff on budget post are AD, AST and AST/SC staff.

In addition to its permanent officials the EU engages temporary staff for a fixed or indefinite period (Art. 8 EU-CEOS). These staff generally fill budget posts classified as temporary or temporarily fill a permanent post. Most provisions of the EU-SR apply by analogy to temporary staff (see Art. 8 et seq. EU-CEOS).

EU's contract staff are not assigned to budget posts but paid from budget appropriations (Art. 3a and 3b EU-CEOS). They perform manual or administrative support services tasks (Art. 3a EU-CEOS) or auxiliary tasks (Art. 3b EU-CEOS). They are divided in four function groups and 18 grades corresponding to their duties (Art. 80, 86 and 89 EU-CEOS). A special salary scale applies (Art. 93 EU-CEOS).

Art. 120 et seq. EU-CEOS contains special provisions for local staff serving in a third country and for parliamentary assistants (Art. 125 et seq. EU-CEOS).

There is also an agreement on working conditions and the pecuniary regime for auxiliary conference interpreters by the Institution of the European Union (AIIC-EU Convention.aii.net July 14, 2008. Accessed May 29, 2017, <http://aiic.net/p/3540>).

The establishment plan staff 2016 of the EU includes 37,312 permanent posts (officials) and 2,375 temporary staff posts, of which 23,612 officials and 427 temporary staff posts are attributable to the EU Commission. The decentralised agencies and other bodies with legal personality comprise 171 permanent and 5,845 temporary posts (see the EU database EUR-Lex, Budget online, total revenue, Part C).

In addition, there are EU bodies with autonomy over budgetary and staffing matters. The ECB, for example, has about 1,300 permanent posts (2016) and the EUIPO comprises some 510 permanent and about 300 temporary posts (2016).

UN

Employment with the UN-CS is based on a purely contractual relationship. The contract of employment (letter of appointment), however, only outlines some basic characteristics of the employment, including the type of employment, the date of entry, the period of probation and the category and the level of salary (see UN-SR Annex II). For the substance of the employment relationship reference is made to the UN-SR (Staff Regulations) which are unilaterally adopted by the UNGA (Art. 101(1) UN-Charter) and the UN-SR (Staff Rules) promulgated by UN-SG, consistent with the UN-SR provided, and enforced by the SG of the UN (see the preamble of UN doc. ST/SGB/2016/1 by which the UN staff regulations and rules effective as from 1 July 2016 were promulgated).

The present UN-SR replace the 16 different contract types by three employment relationships. Instead of three different sets of staff rules (the 100-, 200 – and 300-series appointment types are being phased out, see Rule 13(4) et seq. UN-SR) there is only one single set of staff rules.

The UN-SR provide for three types of contractual employment, depending on the duration of service: continuing, fixed-term and temporary appointment (Reg. 4(5) and Rule 4(11) UN-SR). In addition, there are special arrangements for the appointments of USG and ASG (Reg. 4(5)(a) first sentence UN-SR).

The "continuing appointment" is an open-ended appointment, replacing the former "permanent appointment" (Rule 4(14)(a) UN-SR, as to the difference see the UN Inspira website: "continuing appointments" FAQ, ed. 2015). As to the implementing rules, which are still under consideration by the UN-SG, see UN doc. A/67/816.

The fixed-term appointment is granted for a service period of between one and five years. It does not carry any expectation of renewal or conversion, but a continuing appointment may be granted under certain conditions (examination, satisfactory service of two years, Rule 4(13)(c), 4(14)(b) UN-SR).

A temporary appointment is granted for a service period of less than one year to meet seasonal or peak workloads. It may be extended for up to one year under certain conditions (Rule 4(12)(a), (b) UN-SR). It does not carry any expectation of renewal and may not be converted into any other type of appointment (Rule 4(12)(c) UN-SR).

All posts are classified in categories and levels in accordance with the standards promulgated by the SG and related to the nature of duties, the level of responsibilities and the qualifications required (Rule 2.1(a) UN-SR). Each post is assigned to one of the three main categories: professional and higher categories ("P-staff"), field service staff ("FS-staff") and general service staff ("GS-staff") (Rule 2(1)(b) UN-SR).

The professional and higher categories include the grades P1 to P5, D1 to D2 (directors) and at the senior managerial level the grades ASG and USG. The field service category comprises the grades FS-1 to FS-7 and the general service category the levels 1–7. UN staff members belonging to the field service category are as a rule recruited internationally for a duty outside the duty station for a limited period of time. They are paid in conformity with a special salary scale and a scale of pensionable remuneration (see Appendix A to the UN-SR). The adjustment of salaries follows the same pattern as for P-staff (Noblemaire principle, see the website of the ICSC).

Staff in the GS category may be locally recruited (Rule 4(4) UN-SR) on the best prevailing conditions (Fleming principle) at the place of employment. The methods by which the best prevailing conditions should be applied are determined by the ICSC (Art. 11(a) statute of the ICSC). The allowances and benefits available to GS-staff members are published for each duty station (Rule 4(5) UN-SR).

As of 1 January 2015, the total number of UN staff was 32,094 employees with a contract of one year or more (thereof 4,057 P-staff and 4,193 GS-staff without a time limit and 6,527 P – staff and 17,217 GS-staff with a fixed-term appointment and in addition project staff). The UN-CS had a total of 83,618 staff members, thereof 8,905 P-staff and 10,699 GS-staff without a time limit and 22,657 P-staff and 39,885 GS-staff with a fixed-term appointment and, in addition, project staff (for more details see the extensive personnel statistics document CEB/2015/HLCM/HR/19 of the chief executive board for coordination: www.unsystemceb.org).

### CoE

The staff regulations of the CoE (CoE-SR) provide employment for an indefinite duration and for a fixed-term (Appendix II Art. 6 CoE-SR). Each post is assigned to a grade. The grades are classified into four categories: A (senior civil servant, responsible for administrative, planning and research duties), B (staff for executive and supervisory duties, secretarial and clerical duties), C (staff for technical, manual or service duties) and L (interpreters and translators), see Art. 4 CoE-SR).

The category A staff comprises the grades A1 to A7, the other categories being: LT1 to L5, B1 to B6 and C1 to C6. The grades include up to eleven incremental steps of seniority level, through which the staff member at regular intervals advances of two to four years if he has fully satisfied the requirements of his post (Appendix IV, Art. 3 CoE-SR).

As of 2017 the CoE employs about 2,200 people.

### Mixed system/EPO

The functional structures of employment in the IO adhering to the mixed system are similar to those of the contractual employment in the UN-CS and the CO system. Only the EPO has a statutory employment system of permanent employees, similar to that of the EU. The EPO-SR for active staff were taken over from the EU-SR in 1977 and the EPO-PS reflects that of the CO, which was also adopted in 1977.

With effect from 1 January 2015 the EPO adopted a new career system and redesigned its grading and salary structure (see EPO doc. CA/D 10/14 available on the EPO website). The former A, B and C categories of staff post were replaced by six job groups split into 17 grades (Annex I EPO-SR). The steps in grade were reduced to a maximum of five. The career system is characterised by two career paths, a technical and a managerial one (Art. 47 EPO-SR). Professional development is based on appraisal reports made at least once a year (Art. 47a EPO-SR). A bonus system has been introduced in the form of a lump-sum payment for exceptional performance. The bonus is neutral as regards pension (Art. 48a EPO-SR). The job description and the job specification of the former EPO-SR were deleted. The minimum qualifications for the assignment to the different job groups and grades and the recognition of prior experience are regulated by implementing rules (not publicly available). The conditions of employment for contract staff at the EPO were adapted to the new EPO-SR as far as necessary.

In addition to the statutory permanent employees (in 2016 about 7,000 budgetary posts) for its core activities, the EPO may fill up to a maximum of 5% of the budgetary posts with contract employees for a limited service period. There are also specimen contracts for senior management staff (principal directors, Vice-Presidents) and the temporary employment of interpreters.

## B. Recruitment, development and termination of employment

### I. Recruitment

#### *1. General introduction*

The recruitment of an international employee is based on a recruitment procedure having regard to the SR of the respective IO and to the general principles of law governing the international civil service. The availability of a vacant budget post (see, for example, Art. 4 EU-SR: "No appointment ... shall be made for any purpose other than that of filling a vacant post ...") or at least the necessary budget appropriations is a precondition for the opening of a recruitment procedure. The conditions for appointment are regulated in very similar terms in the SR of the IO of all international civil service systems. The applicant may be appointed only if he meets a number of personal conditions (see, for example, Art. 28 EU-SR and Art. 14 CoE-SR). The most common qualifications required for appointment are:

- the possession of the citizenship of a member state of the IO (exceptions possible);
- the production of appropriate character references;
- the fulfilment of obligations concerning national military service;
- the physical fitness to perform the duties;
- the production of diplomas and qualifications required;
- having successfully participated in a competition based on qualifications or tests or on both.

The act of appointment itself is different between officials appointed on a statutory basis and staff members in a contract relationship. The officials (EU, EPO) are appointed by a unilateral sovereign act of the appointing authority: the handover of the certificate of appointment ("an instrument issued by the Appointing Authority", see Art. 1a(1) EU-SR). The handover of the certificate has no constitutive effect (Rogalla, Art. 283 para. 29). Employment based on a contract relationship is established by a "letter of appointment" signed by the appointing authority and countersigned by the employee. It usually stipulates the nature and duration of the employment, the classification, the starting salary and a reference to the application of the SR (see, for example, Rule 4(1) and Annex II UN-SR).

Today the contractual employment relationships are also, almost entirely, determined by SR which have been unilaterally established by the IO. (Only for the employment of the senior managerial staff are specific specimen contracts used which deviate from the provisions of the general SR.). Ultimately the difference between staff appointed on a statutory or on a contractual basis is essentially limited to protection against dismissal.

In general, recruitment is a very time-consuming and expensive process. For this reason, most IO nowadays use an online-based recruitment system. In addition, the EU has established a centralised inter-institutional recruitment procedure by setting up a "European Personnel Selection Office" (EPSO) which became operational in January 2003 (EU doc. OJ L 197, 26.7.2002, pp. 56–59).

The UN has established "Inspira", the electronic support tool which replaced the former "Galaxy" system in 2010. Up to now this system only applies to job openings and recruitment within the UN Secretariat. Other organisations of the UN family do have online recruitment systems of their own.

### 2. *The recruitment procedure*

The recruitment procedure of IO basically follows the principle of competition (Annex III EU-SR, Rule 4(16) UN-SR, Appendix II Art. 15 CoE-SR) on the basis either of tests or qualifications or both (Art. 29(1)(b) EU-SR, Rule 4(16) UN-SR, Appendix II Art. 15 and 16 CoE-SR; for the definition of the term "competition" see also Art. 1(1) of the Administrative Procedures of EPSO, EU doc. OJ C 41, 26 February 2009, p. A/1). The aim of the procedure is to secure for the IO the services of officials of the "highest standard of ability, efficiency and integrity" (Art. 27 EU-SR). The selection procedure is either ruled in the SR (e.g. Annex III EU-SR) or in administrative instructions (see, for example, the UN staff selection system in UN doc. ST/AI/2010/3).

At some organisations, before the opening of a general (external) selection process, which is open to internal and external applicants, the organisation is obliged first to consider, whether the post can be filled by the transfer or promotion within the organisation (see, for example, Art. 29(1)(a) EU-SR). There is no right to fill a vacancy without a selection process (CJEU Judgments C-121/01 P, C-174/99 P). In Judgment 1527 the ILOAT stated that having regard to the SR the organisation was not free to bypass a competition to a post by promotion. At the UN Reg. 4(4) UN-SR provides that "fullest regard shall be had, in filling vacancies, to the requisite qualifications and experience of persons already in the service of the United Nations". At the CoE there is almost the same ruling (Art. 12(2) CoE-SR). In some IO, in the event of equal merit, preference is given to the candidate of the sex which is under-represented in the grade and category to which the vacancy belongs (see, for example, Appendix II Art. 22 CoE-SR: under-representation is assumed if the proportion of staff of that sex is below 40%).

For the recruitment of senior-officials (Presidents, Vice-Presidents, Directors General, Secretaries General etc.) special competition procedures may apply (see, for example, Art. 29(2) EU-SR). Often only proposals from delegations of the plenary organ or at least applications which are supported by a delegation are permitted. It cannot be excluded that within these recruitment procedures political considerations take precedence over professional and linguistic skills.

The selection process as the centrepiece of the recruitment procedure is in the hands of a selection committee (Art. 30 EU-SR; Art. 2(1), Art. 7 EPO-SR: selection board; Appendix II Art. 9 CoE-SR: appointment board, at the UN there is an *ex post* examination of the selection by central review bodies which assume the functions of a selection committee (Rule 4(15) UN-SR). The selection committee is responsible that the applicable procedures were followed correctly and all candidates considered in a fair, transparent, objective and non-discriminatory manner.

The recruitment procedure is generally divided in the following phases:

- the publication of the vacancy notice;
- the admittance to the selection process (pre-selection);
- the selection process;
- the appointment.

#### a) The publication of the vacancy notice

The vacancy note is drawn up by the appointing authority. As a rule, the staff representation is consulted (see, for example, Annex III Art. 1(1) EU-SR).

A vacancy notice (at the UN "job opening") must be sufficiently precise since the underlying rationale of the publication of the notice is to provide all information regarding the main duties of the post and the required qualifications such that possible applicants can make an informed decision as to whether they should apply or not.

In addition to the nature of competition (internal or open, see, for example, Annex III, Art. 1(a) EU-SR), the type of the activity required (job description), the necessary qualifications and the kind of competition (based on qualification and/or tests) must be indicated, see, for example, Annex III, Art. 1(b) EU-SR.

If a competition is based on tests it must be stated what kind they will be and how they will be marked. If an assessment centre is involved, this information must be contained in the vacancy notice (ILOAT Judgment 2884, see also Judgment 2210: the candidates admitted shall be informed of the nature of the tests).

The vacancy notice must contain an invitation to all qualified internal candidates to apply (ILOAT Judgments 2921, 2920; see also CJEU Judgments T-145/02, C-119/96 P, T-132/89). A notice of competition to recruit candidates for similar posts which will become vacant later on will be in conflict with the requirements of equal treatment, objectivity and transparency if it does not contain a clear and precise definition of the concept of a "similar" post. Otherwise staff members will not have sufficient information to enable them to exercise their rights without hindrance (ILOAT Judgment 2210).

An organisation is not bound to ensure that the notice of vacancy should actually reach everyone. Its duty goes no further than to issue the notice by some suitable means and with suitable promptness (ILOAT Judgment 729).

If a vacancy announcement is withdrawn, the applicants must be informed without delay (ILOAT Judgment 2116: the organisation was cavalier in the way it informed the complainant only four months later of the withdrawal of the vacancy notice – compensation was awarded).

A vacancy notice may not contain a reference to sex, race, colour, ethic or social origin, genetic features, language, religion or belief, political or any other opinions, age, disability or sexual orientation (see, for example, Art 1d(1) EU-SR and Art. 13 CoE-SR). Age limits in a vacancy note violate, according to the European ombudsman the principle of non-discrimination rule of the CFREU (see also in the internet directory: "Reforming the Commission" and Rogalla, Art. 283 para. 35). Nevertheless, some SR of IO allow age limits under certain conditions (see, for example, Art. 13(2) CoE-SR; "provided that such limits have an objective and reasonable justification").

The reference in a vacancy notice to marital status and family relationship violates the general principle of law against discrimination (ILOAT Judgment 2120). In Judgment 2762 the ILOAT ruled, however, that if SR do not preclude, the recruitment of spouses it is imperative that special procedures be put in place to ensure the integrity and transparency of the selection process. Under Circular No. 666 of the ILO of 4 April 2007 (Art. 6) the recruitment of close relatives is only permissible if no other equally qualified person is available.

#### b) The admittance to the selection procedure (pre-selection, pre-screening)

The application file is examined as to compliance with the requirements laid down in the vacancy notice. At the EU, the compliance with the objective general conditions (see Art. 28(a), (b) and (c) EU-SR: citizenship, citizen rights, character requirements, fulfilment of military service) is examined by EPSO (see EPSO Administrative Procedures of 27 February 2015). Special conditions which require a degree of evaluation (diplomas, degrees etc) are examined by the selection board (Art. 1(3) EPSO Administrative Procedures and Art. 28(d) and (f) EU-SR). It is obvious that a candidate who does not fulfil these minimum requirements for the pre-selection phase does not qualify to be admitted to the selection process (ILOAT Judgments 1497, 1383, 564; CJEU Judgments 34/80, T-145/02). The selection board is bound by the text of the vacancy notice, it cannot refuse admittance to the selection procedure by changing the terms of the vacancy note *sub rosa* in breach of the duty of trust and fairness the organisation owes its staff (ILOAT Judgment 1223). The admissibility of a candidate after the application deadline violates not only the principle of *patere legem* but also the principle of equal opportunity among candidates and may give the impression of preferential treatment (ILOAT Judgment 2712, 1549).

The UN only accepts applications to job openings electronically (see the Applicant's Manual "inspira", available on the UN website <HR Portal>). At the UN, the pre-screening is executed by the human resources management and subject to an *ex post* examination by central review bodies (Rule 4(15) UN-SR). At the CoE the examination is done by the appointments board (Appendix II Art. 13 CoE-SR).

At the EPO, the appointing authority draws up a list of candidates who satisfy the conditions laid down in Art. 8 EPO-SR and sends it to the selection board (Annex II Art. 4 EPO-SR).

A candidate may not be excluded from a competition solely on the grounds that he has a higher level of education than that to which the competition relates (CJEU Judgment T-60/92). The deletion from the list of candidates who were invited by telephone to attend an interview within two days and who were unable to attend for family reasons constituted a legal flaw (ILOAT Judgment 2051). The restriction of simultaneous electronic applications at EPSO for a number of competitions conflicts with the objectives of Art. 27(1) EU-SR to recruit candidates of the highest standard of ability, efficiency and integrity (CJEU Judgment F-99/08). The organisation is obliged to inform a candidate who is rejected already at the stage of the pre-selection and to state reasons at least in a summary form (CJEU Judgment 225/82).

### c) The selection process

The selection process is governed by the respective provisions of the SR or administrative rules and the general principle of law for the international civil service, in particular the principle of a fair competition and of equality. After the selection process has begun, i.e. starting with the publication of the vacancy notice, the terms of competition may not be modified (ILOAT Judgments 3073, 2712, 1549, 1359, 1223, 1077, 1071, 729, 107). The selection process must be held under satisfactory conditions of objectivity and transparency (ILOAT Judgments 3032, 2520, 2210, 1990, 179; CJEU Judgments F-22/05, T-165/03, T-290/03, T-336/02).

#### *aa) The selection committee*

At most IO, the selection committee consists of a chairman appointed by the appointing authority and an equal number of members designated by the appointing authority and the staff representation (Annex III Art. 3 EU-SR: Selection Board; Rule 4(15) UN-SR: Central Review Board, Central Review Committee; Appendix II Art. 10 CoE-SR: Appointments Board; Annex II Art. 1 EPO-SR).

The selection committee members are chosen from staff members whose grade is at least equal to that of the post to be filled (Annex III Art. 3(1) EU-SR). At the EU, there is even an obligation that the committee shall comprise members of each gender (Annex III Art. 3(5) EU-SR).

The composition of the selection committee must remain stable so that the marking criteria are uniform and applied in a consistent manner (CJEU Judgments F-22/05, T-290/03, T-165/03, T-336/02, T-92/01, but see the exception in CJEU Judgment 24/78).

Whereas in most IO the selection committee is the master of the selection process, at the UN the selection bodies have been replaced in 2002 by review bodies. These central review bodies (Rule 4(15) UN-SR) are responsible for monitoring the procedural aspects of the selection process and ensuring that the evaluation criteria have been observed. The assessment itself is left to the individual programme managers who determine the selection criteria and are leading the assessment without an independent selection body (see UN doc. A/C.5/63/3/Add. 2 Annex, para. 29). The selection body (assessment panel, expert panel) itself is composed of at least three members (two being experts of the subject matter and one from outside the work unit), see UN doc. ST/AI/2010/3, Section 1(c) and (g)).

The absence of a member of the selection committee remains a mistake of law even if there would have been no different conclusion if all board members would have been present, it can also not be corrected through subsequent consultation of the absent member (ILOAT Judgment 2457). The composition of the selection committee must include at least one member who guarantees an objective assessment of the candidate's professional qualities (CJEU Judgments T-290/03, T-32/89, T-31/89). The nomination of a committee member who has a professional relationship or even a supervisory responsibility is not harmful if it does not go beyond the proper bounds of such a relationship (ILOAT Judgment 2520). The refusal of a staff representative to take part in the selection cannot make the boards choice void since he does not have a veto (ILOAT Judgment 1767). The members of the selection committee are completely independent in the discharge of their duties and the proceedings are secret (Annex III Art. 6 EU-SR).

#### *bb) The assessment*

The assessment is a process of evaluating applicants to determine whether they meet all, some or none of the requirements of the position under recruitment (see, for example, the definition in Section 1(b) of the administrative instructions on the staff selection systems of the UN Secretariat, UN doc. ST/AI/2010/3).

According to consistent case law, selection committees have to examine meticulously the candidate's files and observe scrupulously the requirements set out, *inter alia*, in the vacancy note (CJEU Judgment T-116/03; ILOAT Judgments 2712, 2584, 1787, 1646, 1331, 1158). A modification of the criteria for appointment to the post during the selection process violates the principles of *patere legem* and of mutual trust, fairness, equal treatment, objectivity and transparency (ILOAT Judgment 2712).

The assessment is a competitive examination (Annex III EU-SR; Rule 4(16)(b) ii UN-SR; Appendix II Art. 15 and 16 CoE-SR and Art. 7(1) EPO-SR). It is generally based on written and oral tests (interviews) or on qualifications, or on both (Art. 29(1) EU-SR; Section 7(5) of UN doc. ST/AI/2010/3; Appendix II Art. 15 and Art. 16 CoE-SR; Annex II EPO-SR). The evaluation mechanisms may include the involvement of assessment centres (see, for example, Section 7.5 of UN doc. ST/AI/2010/3; EPSO: doc. EPSO/TF/2008/public of 11 September 2008). For IO with fewer staff there may nevertheless be some risk as to the evaluation of internal candidates by the assessment centres. As a rule, the selection committee itself should be best placed to assess in an objective manner the qualifications based on appraisal reports. Leaving the assessment to an external body which is contracted by the HR department of the organisation may risk a breach of objectivity and transparency and even a disguised influence on the assessment process.

On completion of its proceedings, the selection committee draws up the list of suitable candidates (generally in order of merit) together with a reasoned report (Art. 30 and annex III Art. 5 EU-SR; Appendix II Art. 13(2) CoE-SR; Annex II Art. 5(IV) EPO-SR). At the UN, the "hiring manager" prepares the reasoned and documented record of evaluation of the proposed candidates (Section 7(6) of UN doc. ST/AI/2010/3). The organisation has a wide discretion in relation to selecting a proposed candidate out of the list of suitable candidates. Candidates on a list of suitable candidates have no unconditional right to be appointed to the vacant post, even if they are placed first (CJEU Judgments T-58/05, 26–68).

#### d) Legal review of the selection process

The opinion of the selection committee on the outcome of the selection is a value judgment. Decisions based on such assessments are subject to legal review only where there is a flagrant breach of the rules governing the selection board's work or general legal principles such as equal treatment, objectivity and transparency. The general principle for the limited review of discretionary decisions applies and, therefore, a court may not replace the assessment of a selection board by its own or rule on the organisation's choice (CJEU Judgments T-371/03, T-267/03, T-277/02, T-17/90, T-132/89; ILOAT Judgments 3669, 3209, 2834, 2809, 2457, 2210, 2060, 2040, 2020, 1990).

Whereas the duty of confidentiality applies to all meetings of the selection committee (see, for example, ILOAT Judgment 556) the court may order the submission of the deliberations of the selection board (ILOAT Judgment 1177: "An item that forms part of the decision may not be withheld from the Tribunal's scrutiny"; see also 1637, 1406, 1115, 556). (As regards the dissenting case law of the CJEU and the ILOAT in respect of the *locus standi* of unsuccessful external applicants see below).

The composition of the selection committee must, if possible, remain the same during the course of the selection procedure. In particular, the exchange of the chairman of the committee by the vice-chairman may only take place at his resignation or for reasons which are independent of the will of the administration (CJEU Judgment T-193/00).

Further ILOAT Judgments

3542: The tribunal cannot hear complaints relating to the recruitment procedure (2657); 3206: Selection procedure flawed (3157); 2712: The principle of fair geographical distribution of staff or the goal of increasing the proportion of women in senior management positions is decisive only if the opposing candidates were of equal merit; 2647: Even if the SR of an IO oblige the appointing authority "to have full regard to the qualifications and experience of persons already in its service" this does not automatically give a right of precedence over other candidates (107); 2299: The selection committee may not grant an interview to a candidate who appears unsuitable *a priori*; 2054: There is no right to preferential treatment of a disabled applicant in the recruitment procedure if there is no provision in the SR in this respect;
2004: Flying a person across the ocean to be interviewed while leaving a competitor from the same area at home is open to the interpretation of unequal treatment (but see 2897: generally a video conference is an acceptable method for conducting interviews); 1331: A period of ten months between the issue of the vacancy notice and the meeting of the selection board is an undue delay and gives entitlement to damages; 521: It does not violate the legitimacy of the recruitment process if the application is rejected because the required university degree is missing, even if the appellant has many years of experience in the field of the vacant post; 238: It does not violate the impartiality of the selection board, if, with the result of the written examination, the names of candidates were made known to the selection board in order to assess their general suitability under further criteria (degrees, professional experience etc).

Further CJEU Judgments/Orders

F-135/12: Selection procedure flawed by instability due to large fluctuation in the composition of the selection committee; F-115/11: Impartiality of the members of the selection committee; F-50/08: The composition of the selection board. Failure to comply with the necessity that a board of more than four members had to include at least two members of each gender; F-7/07: Malfunctioning of the computer during the selection procedure; F-22/05: Stability of the composition of the selection board, equal treatment of candidates; 40/86:

Not all test papers must be marked by the same examiner; 144/82: The selection committee must proceed on the basis of objective criteria which are known to the candidates and must state adequately the grounds on which its decision is based; 89/79: The proceedings of the selection boards are covered by the obligation to secrecy; 130/75: Written tests and the date of the test should be the same for all candidates. There is a necessity for a candidate to inform the appointing authority in good time if a certain date is impossible for him, e.g. for religious reasons.

### e) Excursus: The European Personnel Selection Office (EPSO) and the "inspira" system of the UN secretariat

#### *aa) EPSO of the EU*

EPSO was established on 25 July 2002 by a common decision of organs and institutions of the EU (OJ L 197, 26 July 2002 p. 53). It became operational as of 1 January 2003. EPSO serves to more economical recruitment and ensures the application of the following standardised principles (see in the internet "Reforming the Commission"):

- to monitor best practice and development in recruitment techniques;
- to plan competitions on the basis of a jointly approved scheme;
- to standardise selection procedures and make them more professional;
- to ensure equal treatment of all candidates with particular emphasis on geographical balance;
- to speed up the recruitment procedure;
- to introduce computer-based testing at the pre-selection stage.

EPSO's recruitment task extends to most institutions and agencies of the EU (but not to the ECB, EIB and EIF). It is reserved for the recruitment of officials (administrators and assistants). Procedures for temporary staff are generally organised by the institutions and agencies themselves. On request, it provides assistance for organising the selection procedures in EU agencies not adhering to the system. In March 2010, a new selection procedure was introduced by EPSO in order to allow a quicker competition and a competency driven rather than a knowledge-based testing (see the "epso eu-career portal").

The selection procedure under EPSO is subject to the higher-ranking recruitment provisions of Art. 27 et seq. and Annex III EU-SR. It is computer-based admission testing. The applicant must create an EPSO account (online registration), serving as electronic interface between EPSO and the applicant. Only English, French and German will be used for the invitations, tests and correspondence between the applicant and EPSO. After the examination of the compliance of the application with the general conditions (citizenship, full citizen's rights, character requirements and fulfilment of military service obligations) and the specific conditions (diplomas, professional experience, knowledge of languages – if required by the competition notice), a pre-selection procedure (computer-based tests) takes place. Successful candidates have to take part in the assessment phase and oral testing. Following the competition procedure, the selection board draws up a reserve list of successful candidates. The reserve lists for generalist competitions are valid for one year, for other profiles they are valid for a longer period. Candidates on the list may be contacted by the interested institution and invited for an interview. If successful, a job will be offered.

On 15 June 2010, the CJEU (Judgment F-35/08) decided on an interpretation of Annex III EU-SR by EPSO. It held that only the selection board and not EPSO has the competence to choose the questions for the pre-selection tests (computer-based tests). The tasks of EPSO remain essentially organisational. The decision of EPSO not to put the complainant on the reserve list was annulled and all other candidates who were excluded on the basis of the pre-selection test results were invited for a new competition under the responsibility of the selection board.

*bb) The "inspira" system of the UN secretariat*

The application process at the UN secretariat is also based on an online recruitment system. The former "Galaxy" system was replaced on 22 April 2010 by "inspira" (see in the internet <careers.un.org> and the Applicant's Manual 2015 (Instruction Manual for the Applicant on the Staff Selection System inspira)).

After registration and completing a profile, the applicant has to select the vacancy (job opening) he is interested in and has to submit his job application. If he is deemed by a pre-screening exercise to be eligible for the job, he is admitted to the assessment exercise based on written examinations, case studies etc. If he is short-listed, a competency-based interview takes place (via telephone, video conference or in person). Recommendations are evaluated by a review body and the selected candidate is notified. Candidates who have successfully been vetted but are not selected are included in a roster of candidates recommended for selection. If a candidate is in a group of recommended candidates for selection and was not actually selected, he remains on the roster indefinitely (Section 9(5) of UN doc. ST/AI/2010/3 Amend. 1). He may either be automatically selected or apply for positions on his own initiative if he thinks himself to be qualified.

#### f) The obligation to give reasons to unsuccessful candidates

It is a general principle of law, anchored in most of the SR, that a decision adversely affecting an employee shall state the grounds on which it is based (see, for example, Art. 25 EU-SR). This is equally valid for decisions taken on the basis of a selection procedure adversely affecting the unsuccessful candidates. A general reference to the poor quality or performance of the candidate is not enough (CJEU

Judgment T-289/94). On the other hand, the requirement to state reasons must not place an intolerable burden on the functioning of the selection board especially in a competition with many candidates. The communication of the marks obtained in the various tests therefore constitutes an adequate statement of reasons (CJEU Judgments F-127/07, T-294/03, C-254/95 P). Only where special circumstances exist (e.g. if the applicant only narrowly failed the oral phase), must intermediate remarks, marked scripts and general marking criteria be delivered (CJEU Judgment F-74/07).

The obligation to state reasons must be reconciled with the observance of secrecy governing a selection process (see, for example, Annex III Art. 6 EU-SR), which protects the independence of the members of the selection committee, particularly with regard to their future work in such committees, but also warrants the confidentiality of personal data of the competitors (CJEU Judgment C-254/95 P; ILOAT Judgment 1513: "As a general rule a complainant may not be entitled to consult any records that may have been made of discussions by a selection committee: members of such committees would not feel free to discuss candidates independently in future if they felt at risk of having their own views divulged"; see also ILOAT Judgments 2834 and 556).

If the appointing authority appoints a candidate appearing on a list of suitable candidates arranged in order of merit and follows that order it is not required to give the reasons for its decision to the lower arranged candidates. If the list is, however, not arranged in order of merit, but, for example, in alphabetical order, grounds must be given to the unsuccessful candidates (CJEU Judgment T-1/90).

A delay of 15 months before a candidate is informed of his unsuccessful application does not constitute a fatal procedural flaw of the selection process but it may justify a claim for damages (ILOAT Judgment 2325).

### g) The appointment

The appointing authority selects the most suitable candidate from the list established by the selection committee. Hereby it is not bound by the suggested order of merits of the candidates. If the appointing authority, however, deviates from this order or if the list of suitable candidates is drawn up without reference to the order of merit, sound reasons connected with the interest of the service have to be given to the unsuccessful candidates (CJEU Judgments T-1/90, T-37/89, 246/84).

The appointing authority is not obliged to give effect to the result of the recruitment procedure. However, if it decides to start a new competition by reasons of irregularities during the previous procedure it has to indicate the character or nature of those irregularities. The same reasoning is valid if an organisation terminates the recruitment procedure relying on an internal transfer without stating sound reasons for not appointing one of the candidates who had been successful in the competition (CJEU Judgment T-37/89). Candidates who have not been found suitable by the selection committee may not be appointed according to the meaning and purpose of the selection process (CJEU Judgment 246/84, see also Art. 30 EU-SR: The selection board draws up a list of suitable candidates. "The appointing authority shall decide which of these candidates to appoint to the vacant posts").

The SR of some IO provide for rules restricting the appointment of candidates who have a family relationship with a staff member (see, for example, Rule 4(7) UN-SR; see also ILOAT Judgment 2762, concerning the recruitment of the spouse of the President of the EPO (Office), the tribunal found that if the recruitment of spouses, friends and other close associates of staff members is not excluded from recruitment "it is imperative that special procedures be put in place to ensure the integrity and transparency of the selection process"). An appointment procedure may involve a promotion (ILOAT Judgment 3194).

The employee is, as a rule, recruited at the first step in the grade set out in the notice of competition they have passed (Art. 32 EU-SR; Rule 3(4) UN-SR; Art. 16 CoE-SR; Art. 11(2) EPO-SR). Additional seniority, however, may be granted by taking into account previous professional experience (see, for example, the EU Commission decision of 16 December 2013, doc. C (2013) 8970 concerning the criteria applicable to classification in step based on Art. 32 EU-SR). The additional seniority is restricted (see, for example, Art. 32 EU-SR, a maximum up to 24 months applies).

The appointment takes place either based on the handover of a "letter of appointment" (Reg. 4(1) and Annex II UN-SR; Art. 15 CoE-SR) confirmed by the employee, which constitutes the contract of employment or by a unilateral act of appointment (Art. 1a EU-SR: "an instrument" issued by the appointing authority) (As to the legal differences between a contract of employment and an act of appointment, see above).

#### h) The probationary period

The SR of IO, as a rule, provide for a probationary period after appointment (Art. 34 EU-SR; Art. 48 EU-CEOS; Art. 17 CoE-SR; Art. 13 EPO-SR; see ILOAT Judgments 2646, 2558, 1386, 1352, 1175, 1153, 736, 687, 503). At the UN, the former type of probationary appointment was repealed with effect of 1 July 2009 (see Rule 13(3) UN-SR). The first year of fixed-term appointment functions as a probationary period. Staff with temporary and continuing appointments are not required to serve probationary periods. Most IO of the UN-CS provide, however, for a probationary period (see UN doc. CEB/2010/HLCM/HR).

The probationary period is a testing phase which serves the purpose of enabling the organisation to make a more concrete assessment of the candidate's suitability for a particular post, the manner in which he performs his duties and his efficiency in the service (CJEU Judgments T-26/91, 290/82).

The probationary period is generally lasts between six and twenty-four months, the length is sometimes depending on the type of appointment (for example, at the EU there is a nine – month probationary period for all officials).

It is settled case law that the appointing authority has broad discretion both in determining its own needs and in saying whether someone is fit for employment. An international court therefore only has limited power of review (ILOAT Judgments 2883, 2724, 2646, 1817, 1418, 1386, 1052; CJEU Judgments C-17/88, 75/85, 3/84, 347/82).

An IO has the duty to comply with the principles of proper administration, equal treatment and to have regard to the interests of the probationer. Although the probationary period is not a training period, the organisation must ensure adequate physical working conditions, and give instructions and advice enabling the probationer to demonstrate his abilities during that period. The organisation has to identify any unsatisfactory aspects of the performance in a timely fashion so that remedial steps may be taken. The organisation has to give a specific warning that continued employment is in jeopardy (ILOAT Judgments 2788, 2732, 2646, 2529, 1817, 1386, 1212; CJEU Judgment T-26/91). Poor performance does not warrant ending a probationary period unless there is no hope of reasonably early improvement, usually by the expiry of the probation (ILOAT Judgment 1817).

The existence of doubts as to the ability of a probationer can justify an extension of the probationary period for a (limited) additional trial period (CJEU Judgment C-301/02 P; see Art. 34(3) and (4) EU-SR). If an illness occurs during the probationary period, an extension of the probationary period is not necessary (discretion) if the remaining period provides a sufficiently broad basis for assessment (CJEU Judgment C-17/88). The extension of a probationary period is in itself not a sufficient reason for the non-confirmation of an appointment. Ways and means of improving the performance of the probationer must be suggested (ILOAT Judgment 2883).

The deadline for submission of the probationary report ensures that the decision on the confirmation of the appointment can be made before the end of the probationary period. A delay in drawing up the report is not such as to affect adversely a probationer where the decision was taken after the expiry of the period, if he remains in his post and is paid during that period (CJEU Judgments 290/82, 98/81, 175/80, 99/77).

Dismissal at the end of the probationary period requires an adversarial process, i.e. the probationer must have the opportunity to comment on all objections that led to the dismissal (CJEU Judgments 206/81, 175/80).

## II. The development of employment

Employment with an IO is subject to various changes in the course of the professional life of a staff member. The following categories of employment development should be mentioned:

- career development;
- change in the administrative status;
- transfer;
- conversion of appointment.

### *1. Career development*

#### a) General introduction

The most important development of employment is based on the careers systems established by the IO. EU officials, EPO permanent employees and almost all IO offer their staff with a longer-term employment have the prospect of an increase in their level of responsibility, combined with an appropriate increase in salary. There are only very few "non-career" organisations, like the OPCW (see ILOAT Judgments 2981, 2980, 2690, 2456, 2315), the OPEC and the OSCE which are committed to the principle of staff rotation within a maximum period of service.

The career system usually provides for a periodic move in the step in grade ("career move") based on satisfactory service and at longer intervals, depending on the performance appraisal, for the promotion to a higher pay grade ("career jump"). The number of service years necessary for a promotion depends on the ranking of the staff member in the periodic appraisal reports. In some IO there are career bands (average career, rapid career) for promotion. Staff members under-performing or who have been subject to a disciplinary measure are as a rule excluded from promotion for a certain period of time. The careers system normally ends at the managerial level (middle and higher management).

#### b) Advancement in incremental steps

The SR of IO provide for an advancement to the next higher step in a grade (incremental step, Art. 44 EU-SR; Rule 3(3)(a) UN-SR; Appendix IV Art. 3 CoE-SR; Art. 48 EPO-SR). As a rule, grade increments are awarded automatically on the basis of satisfactory service (appraisal report) or by special decision (EPO: up to two steps in case of excellent performance). It is a continuous advancement following a certain period varying from organisation to organisation and depending on the category of staff, the grade and the step already held. The time span for progressing from one step to the next is between 12 and 48 months. For senior staff incremental steps are reduced (see, for example, Annex III EPO-SR) or eliminated (see, for example, Annex I UN-SR, no-step increments for USG and ASG).

### c) Promotion

#### *aa) General information*

The term "promotion" in the SR of IO is not used uniformally. In some organisations promotion means the advancement to a post in a higher grade (level) (see, for example, Rule 3(4)(b) UN-SR; Art. 21 CoE-SR). Other organisations restrict the term to the advancement of the staff member to the next higher grade in the function group (Art. 45(1) EU-SR; Art. 49(2) EPO-SR). A promotion may exceptionally result from a reclassification of the post (see, Art. 49(4) and Art. 3(a) EPO-SR). The filling of a higher post outside the career system is generally reserved to successful applicants of an external and/or internal (open) competition (ILOAT Judgments 2906 and 1204: out-of-career promotion; CJEU Judgment T-88/04: promotion by appointment). In all IO staff members have the right to participate in a general open (external and internal) competition, particularly where this would lead to an appointment to a higher grade outside the normal career system. Internal candidates are subject to the same selection criteria as external candidates (see, for example, CJEU Judgment 255/90 P). The participation in an internal competition is sometimes restricted to a certain category of staff holding a special type of contractual relationship (see, for example, Art. 29(3) EU-SR).

At some IO, the administration must examine, prior to a general (external and internal) competition, the possibility of an internal transfer, a promotion or a purely internal competition (Art. 4(3) and 29 EU-SR, see also ILOAT Judgments 1359, 1223 and Judgment 21–70).

Career promotion is done after consideration of comparative merits on the basis of the merit rating in the appraisal reports, based on ability, efficiency and conduct in the service (see, for example, Art. 43 EU-SR). In addition to the report, further requirements may be defined, such as a minimum time in the previous grade (Art. 45(1) EU-SR) or a minimum age (ILOAT Judgment 2221 concerning the EPO), a certain period of reckonable experience, a certain level of record of performance for an average or rapid advancement in career (ILOAT Judgments 1968, 1804, 1029, 908, 884) or other pertinent elements (CJEU Judgment F-51/08). A promotion may be refused for disciplinary reasons (ILOAT Judgment 1439).

The appointing authority has a wide scope of discretion in the selection and promotion procedure, and international civil servants do not have a right to promotion (ILOAT constant case-law, see Judgment 2944 with extensive further references; CJEU Judgments F-53/08, F-7/08, T-311/04, T-330/03: the judicature must be confined to the question of whether, having regard to the methods and processes by which the administration may have arrived at its assessment, it kept within proper bounds and did not use its power in a manifestly incorrect way. The judge cannot substitute the tribunal's assessment of the qualifications and merits of officials for that of the appointing authority (Judgment C-277/01 P quashing Judgment T-99/00 where the Court substituted his own assessment for that of the appointing authority).

*bb) The appraisal report*

As in most national public administration the legal systems of the IO also provide for performance appraisal (notation) systems (see, for example, Judgment T-233/01 para. 29: the notation report is an indispensable instrument for a promotion procedure). An untypical appraisal report is the probationary report which in most IO is a precondition for the appointment (see, for example, Appendix II Art. 19 CoE-SR).

Appraisal reports are set up periodically (usually annually) and are decisive for the rate of advancement through the incremental steps and in the career grade or for a change in the functional group or type of employment. Most appraisal systems of IO tend to lead to an inflation of above-average ratings of staff members. For this reason, some IO promulgate guiding principles on appraisal in order to ensure that the reporting officers comply with a certain percentage of ratings. The EU expects 15% of the staff to be above and 10% to be below average (see on the EU website: "Reforming the Commission"), other organisations expect a rate of above-average box markings of up to 30%).

Since appraisal reports represent a discretionary decision, in which subjective evaluation elements cannot be excluded completely, they are often the subject of complaints. In order to prevent, if possible, a flood of legal appeals most IO provide for an internal conciliation procedure prior to legal proceedings (see, for example, at the UN: rebuttal process, section 15 of the Admin. Instruction in UN doc. ST/AI/2010/5 and at the EPO Art. 110a SR: Objection procedure for appraisal reports).

– EU

On 23 December 2004, in connection with the reform of SR on 1 May 2004, the EU Commission has adopted a new annual performance appraisal system for its staff. The system is based on a merit ranking (point system) of the officials concerning ability, efficiency and conduct in service. The essence of the appraisal procedure is published in "Reforming the Commission" (see on the EU website). Other EU organs are deviating, however, in some other aspects.

Under the EU Commission appraisal system, up to 20 merit points are awarded to staff members. The appraisal is split up in three categories; up to ten points are awarded for the performance rating, up to six points for the ability rating and up to four points for the conduct in service rating. The ranking is based on a target which is established at the start of the reference year in the light of a dialogue between the line manager and the official on the agreed job description, the assignment of tasks and the objectives.

In addition to the merit points up to twelve priority points can be awarded, i.e. up to ten priority points for special services to the directorate general which has a point account depending on the level of staffing. A promotion committee can award up to two more priority points for activities performed in the interests of the Commission. If a directorate general exceeds the Commission's average number of merit points for the previous year by more than one point, a corresponding reduction of the quota of priority points is carried out for the next year in order to achieve a uniform point assignment within the Commission. All points are continuously accumulated on an account. If an annually fixed number of points (depending on the available budget points) is achieved, a promotion is triggered, independent of age and seniority of the official. Points accumulated over and above the threshold necessary for a promotion remain on the account for a further promotion.

Staff with a scoring under ten points are not eligible for promotion. If an official consistently underperforms, corrective measures (administrative inquiries) may be initiated. When an official drops between 9.5 and 7.5 points a supportive and remedial programme is drawn up in order to solve the difficulties. If the overall score is below 7 points, immediate remedial actions are initiated. The official has six months to improve his performance otherwise the procedure provided for a dismissal or downgrading (Art. 51 EU-SR) may be initiated. (For more details see "Reforming the Commission", '"Appraisal and promotion" on the EU website; see also *inter alia* the following CJEU Judgments: T-58/11 P: Withdrawal of merit points and priority points; F-82/09: Deletion of merit and priority points; F-36/08: Priority points; F-27/08: Deletion of merit points; F-7/08: Granting of merit points; F-102/07: Priority points; F-148/06: Procedure to grant merit points at the EU Parliament; F-116/06, F-113/06, F-83/06, F-104/05, F-99/05, F-98/05: Priority points; T-250/06 P, T-311/04: Priority points; see also the decision of the European ombudsman in complaint 2007/2008/ELB of 25 August 2009.) In conformity with Art. 43 EU-SR the official who refuses to accept the annual report may lodge an appeal within the reporting procedure (Art. 6 Implementing Rules to Art. 43 EU-SR). If the report has become final, it constitutes a decision within the meaning of Art. 25 EU-SR and the official may lodge a complaint provided for in Art. 90(2) EU-SR.

– UN

At the UN, the former performance appraisal system (see UN doc. ST/AI/2002/3) was replaced by the performance management and development system with effect of 1 April 2010, see UN doc. ST/SGB/2009/4 section 4(2) and UN doc. ST/AI/2010/5 hereinafter referred to as: "Administrative Instructions" pursuant to Rule 1(3)(c) UN-SR.

The new system does not apply to staff with temporary appointments (section 1 Administrative Instructions). The system is supported by an electronic tool (e-Pas or e-performance, see E-PAS User Guide at www.unescap.org) that captures the main stages of the performance process (section 2(3) Administrative Instructions). The performance cycle is normally twelve months (section 3 Administrative Instructions). The overall performance appraisal comprises four ratings: "exceeds performance expectations", "successfully meets performance expectations", "partially meets performance expectations" and "does not meet performance expectations" (section 9(3) to 9(9) Administrative Instructions). Staff members who receive one of the two latter overall ratings may initiate a rebuttal process (section 15 Administrative Instructions). A performance rating that has not been rebutted is final and may not be appealed, however, an administrative decision based on that appraisal may be appealed by the normal justice mechanisms (section 15(7) Administrative Instructions).

An appraisal report that does not meet performance expectations warrants the refusal of a salary increment (section 16(4) Administrative Instructions and Rule 3(3)(a) UN-SR). If performance expectations are partially met the increment will be withheld pending improvement (section 16(5) Administrative Instructions).

– CoE

At the CoE the appraisal report system is based on Art. 22 and Art. 22 bis CoE-SR and implementing conditions laid down by the Secretary General (not published).

– EPO

The EPO's notation system was revised as of 1 January 2015. It is now based on Art. 47a EPO-SR (appraisal reports) and extensive implementing rules (not published). The former system was the subject of some 80 judgments (as of 2016) available on the ILOAT'S Triblex case law database under the keywords "performance report" and "promotion". Appraisal reports are subject to an objection procedure (Art. 110a EPO-SR) and are excluded from the internal appeal proceedings (Art. 110(2)(e) EPO-SR).

*cc) The joint promotion committees and review bodies*

Decisions of the appointing authority of an IO on promotions are taken on the basis of the selection of comparative merits of officials eligible for promotion. In some IO this is done with the involvement of a joint promotion committee. The task of the joint promotion committees is to give advice to the appointing authority. The appointing authority must respect the general legal principles of the international civil service as well as pertinent rules in the SR, in particular those of comparative merits in relation to ability, efficiency and conduct in the service (see ILOAT Judgments 1600, 1355).

At the EU, the Directors-General communicate to the staff members the list of officials they wish to propose for promotion (Art. 5 General Implementing Rules to Art. 45 EU-SR, see Commission decision doc. C(2013)8968 of 16 December 2013 and CJEU Judgment F-112/15). If a jobholder is not on the list, he may lodge a complaint within 5 working days with the joint promotion committee. The committee must compare the merits of the officials eligible for promotion on the basis of the list of officials proposed for promotion by the DG and take account of the complaints against non-inclusion on the list. It issues its recommendation regarding the official to be promoted, addressed to the appointing authority which carries out a final comparison of the merits of eligible officials and publishes the list of officials promoted. If an official is not on the final list of officials promoted, he may file an appeal in conformity with Art. 90(2) EU-SR.

At the UN, the recruitment and promotion procedures are similar despite the different denomination of the joint boards advising the appointing authority on the exercise of the recruitment and promotion procedures (Rule 4(15)(b) UN-SR: central review bodies sometimes called: appointment and promotion boards, see UN doc. JIU/Note 2012/1Annex I).

At the CoE, promotion panels are involved in the internal competition (Appendix II Art. 21 CoE-SR, the detailed rules governing internal competition are not publicly accessible).

At the EPO, the provisions on the promotion boards were deleted in connection with the adoption of the new career system in January 2015. The redesigned promotion process is exclusively in the hands of the administration. If an official is dissatisfied with his appraisal report, he may start an objection procedure with the appraisal committee (Art. 110a EPO-SR). Appraisal report decisions are excluded from the internal appeals procedure (Art. 110(2)(e) EPO-SR). An official may request a review procedure against a non-promotion decision (Art. 109 EPO-SR) and, if he is dissatisfied, lodge an internal appeal (Art. 110 EPO-SR).

### *dd) The judicature on promotion*

There is an extensive case law from the ILOAT and the CJEU on the issues of promotions. The following overview is limited to important decisions. In addition, reference is made to the judgments under the "appraisal report" section and the general legal principles of equal treatment and the exercise of discretion.

ILOAT Judgments

2944: No right to promotion (settled case law, see, for example, Judgments 2006, 1207, 1016), the organisation has a wide discretion in relation to promotion, there is only a limited power of judicial review; see, for example, Judgments 2835, 2834, 2272, 2221, 2173, 2060, 1973, 1827, 1670, 1556, 1137, 1109; 2906: Promotion caused by a purely factual error does not establish a right to promotion; 2869: Promotion refused, appearance of an abuse of discretion; 2859: Promotion to a higher grade with a higher salary of one cent; 2837: Failure to publish a list of officials who were granted a personal promotion; 2770: Decision to deny retroactive effect of the promotions is quashed; 2706: Mishandling of an application for promotion, moral injury, no promotion for compensation of injuries; 2535: The lack of budgetary allocations is not a reason which can be validly invoked to deny promotion to which a staff member would have a right and to deny him the commensurate salary; 2457: The absence of a member of the promotion committee in its deliberations constituted a flaw, despite the fact that the board's opinion was unanimous; 2272: Decision on promotion was flawed by abuse of authority and an error of law since a hierarchically higher-ranking rule was infringed; 2053: Art. 49 EPO-SR does not provide for a promotion as a result of experience gained while on unpaid leave; 2006: No retroactive promotion since the new circular on promotion is deemed to be of immediate and not retroactive effect; 1968: If an organisation has committed itself only to make promotions which have been recommended by a promotion board, a promotion without that recommendation is irregular (1600); 1827: The tribunal is interested only in a selection process if a serious defect is demonstrated; it is not enough simply to assert that someone is better qualified than the selected candidate; 1804: A promise to promote someone in breach of the rules infringes the general legal principle of equal treatment (1667); 1733: It violates the independence of an organisation if a promotion is made dependent on the outside instructions of a member state; 1600: A promotion is flawed if necessary information is withheld from the promotion committee or if the promotion is due to evidence other than ability and record of performance; 1565: There is no general principle of law which would require the participation of a staff representative in a promotion committee; 1527: Promotion quashed for by-passing the promotion procedure; 1370: Receiving the acting allowance shows that there is no promotion; 1355: The Director-General is not bound by the promotion committee's recommendations (but see Judgment 1968) and in particular need not to appoint the candidate the committee has put first, but he has to give reasons (1235, 1223); 1223: The denial of a promotion by appointment is an appealable decision; 1204: Also in the case of out-of-career promotion the organisation must abide by the published rules and not resort to provisions that change the thrust of the ones it intended to treat as binding. If the organisation refers to performance, it has to provide evidence of comparative and analytical assessment; 1177: If the decision to promote a staff member is not based upon the assessment of an independent body the Director-General has to disclose to the tribunal all items necessary to appraise the background of the impugned decision and determine whether it shows any flaw; 1025: The rules on promotion do confer an acquired right insofar as they offer staff an expectation of advancement. But the particular arrangements for the grant of promotion confer no such right.

CJEU Judgments/Orders

F-26/13: Application for annulment of an appraisal report; F-66/10: Appraiser's grade lower than that of the holder of the post, failure to fix objectives for the holder of the post; F-53/08: Promotion exercise, balance of interest; F-14/09: Misappraisal of the comparative merits of all administrators being eligible for promotion; F-53/08: the judge will quash the whole promotion procedure only if it is substantially flawed, otherwise it will annul only the specific decision concerning promotion; F-51/08: Misappraisal of comparative merits (grade and responsibility of the complainant); F-16/08: Missing motivation concerning a decision on merit points; F-125/07: Discriminatory promotion procedure; F-93/07: Decision refusing promotion was based on non-applicable provisions; F-81/07: Obligation to motivate a negative decision on promotion before a complaint is filed; T-502/04: Action for annulment of the decision awarding priority merit points; T-435/04: Annulment of a decision disallowing merit points under the preceding appraisal system has no legal basis; T-394/04: The award of priority merit points is not limited to the current promotion exercise, but may influence several promotion exercises. An official may therefore bring an action before the court against the only act awarding points which entails binding and definitive legal effects in regard to him irrespective of whether he is promoted or not (F-110/06, F-107/06); T-88/04: Promotion by appointment, procedural error in the evaluation; T-437/04 and T-441/04: The promotion exercise violated the principle of equal treatment; T-177/03: No obligation to give reasons for a promotion decision in respect of non-promoted candidates, but there is an obligation to state reasons rejecting the complaint of such candidates. The reason must be stated before a complaint is filed. The failure to state any reason at all cannot be remedied during the proceedings before the court. Besides the annulment of the decision, an additional compensation for non-material harm may be justified (T-117/01, T-25/92, 343/87); T-172/03: Incomplete reasons in respect of non-promoted candidates may be supplement during the legal proceedings; T-132/03: Non-inclusion on the list of officials promoted, duty to state reasons, misappraisal of merits; T – 4/03: The negative decision on promotion was based on incomplete motivation and did not take into account the relevant appraisal reports; T-134/02: The promotion was vitiated by illegality, since the assessment of the promotion committee was based on a provisional appraisal report which could not serve as a basis for the refusal of a promotion; C-277/01 P: Judgment T-99/00 is quashed for substituting its own assessment of the merits for that of the appointing authority; T-378/00: Absence of an appraisal report falsifies the promotion assessment; C-68/91 P (T-233/01): The periodic appraisal report constitutes an indispensable criterion for assessment. If the promotion board is unable to consider the comparative merits of candidates for promotion because of a substantial delay on the part of the administration in drawing up the reports of one or more candidates, the promotion procedure is tainted with irregularity; C-255/90 P: In an open (internal and external) appointment procedure there is no obligation of the promotion board to ask an internal candidate to complete his application files (T-133/89); C-21–70: The (promotion) appointment of an official to a vacant post which takes place on the basis of a document containing negative assessments of a non-successful candidate which were neither in his personal file nor brought to his knowledge, is vitiated by illegality.

#### d) Temporary posting

Occasionally, the SR provide for the possibility to assign a staff member temporarily with the performance of duties of a higher grade. Frequently, this concerns the replacement of another staff member on protracted sick-leave or seconded to another post (see, for example, Art. 7(2) EU-SR). The temporary posting may be restricted in time. The staff member will receive an acting allowance (Art. 7(2) EU-SR: from the beginning of the fourth month of temporary posting). In some organisations, a staff member may be called upon to perform (for a certain period) the duties of a post classified in a higher grade with a view to acquiring the prescribed qualifications. If, by the end of that period, he cannot be promoted to the higher grade there will be a retroactive grant of an acting allowance (see, for example, Art. 12 EPO-SR).

#### e) The transition from one category of grade (functional groups) to the other (vertical transition)

Within each type of employment relationship there is generally a hierarchical order of grades classified into categories or functional groups (vertical classification) for career prospects. A staff member is as a rule appointed in the starting grade of the category or functional group to which he is assigned in conformity with the required qualifications in the vacancy note. As a rule, his career ends when he reaches the top end of the grade of his category or the functional group. In most IO there is, however, in exceptional cases, the possibility for outstanding qualified staff members to a transition into a higher category or functional group of staff.

At the EU, an administrator's career covers grades AD5 to AD16. AD5 is the entry grade for university graduates, the recruitment/promotion to a higher grade requires previous experience (for more in detail on types of employment, permanent officials, examples of qualifications required see the EPSO website). An EU official in the function group AST is able to move into the higher AD function group (see "Reforming the Commission" in the internet directory). The appraisal report of an official in the AST5 function group may contain an opinion on whether the incumbent has the potential to carry out the functions of an AD post (Art. 43(2) EU-SR). An official in the AST function group at grade 5 may be appointed to a post in the AD function group under certain conditions (taking part in a compulsory training programme, passing an oral and written examination, see Art. 45a EU-SR).

At the UN, the entry level in the professional and higher categories is P2 (two years' work experience), P3 (five years' work experience), P4 (seven years' work experience), P5 (ten years' work experience), P6/D1 (15 years' work experience) or P7/D2 (more than 15 years' work experience). There is, therefore, only one category of career grade for the continuing appointments (professional level and D level).

At the CoE, there are rules on promotions within the A, B and L grades as well as internal competition procedures for C grade staff becoming eligible for appointments to category B posts and for L and B grade staff becoming eligible for appointment to category A posts (see Appendix II Art. 24(e) and (f) CoE-SR).

At the EPO, the former distinction of posts in the three categories A, B and C was replaced as of 1 January 2015 by six job groups divided into 17 grades and two career paths, technical and managerial, see Annex I EPO-SR). In principle, transition to the grade in a higher job groups or a change in the career path is possible.

### *2. Change of the administrative status*

#### a) General information

The administrative status of a staff member may undergo several changes during his employment relationship with the IO. Starting from the normal administrative status in active employment, i.e. performing the duties pertaining to the post to which the staff member has been appointed (see, for example, Art. 36 EU-SR), he may be on secondment, on leave on personal grounds, on leave for military service, on parental (paternity) or family leave, or on leave in the interests of the service (Art. 35 EU-SR sets out 6 statuses besides the active status). At the EPO, the term "non-active status" includes all other statuses apart from active status and reserve status (see Art. 42 EPO-SR).

A special case among the forms of administrative status of an official is retirement because upon it service terminates (see, for example, Art. 47 EU-SR). Retirement either takes place automatically when the staff member reaches the retirement age or at his own request when he reaches a certain age (see, for example, Art. 52 EU-SR). At the EU, an official is also automatically retired if total permanent invalidity prevents him from performing his duties (Art. 53 EU-SR).

#### b) Special leave

As has already been pointed out in the introductory part of this book, an IO not only has the function of an employer, but it is also, at least to some extent, a "substitute state". In this function it has to provide its own social infrastructure. This is especially important in the IO with lifelong employment (EU and EPO officials). IO must provide working conditions which allow for the reconciliation of work and family.

Contrary to the entitlement to annual leave, home leave, maternity leave, sick leave and short-term time off for special reasons (serious illness of relatives, marriage, participation in national elections etc.; see more in detail under social security), the entitlements to leave discussed below are considered by the organisation with officials (EU and EPO) on a statutory basis as a change of the active administrative status of employment. In the two other international civil service systems, similar leave is granted, but the question of administrative status is thereby not an issue.

As a rule, entitlement to the salary is discontinued during special leave.

*aa) Secondment*

Staff members of IO may, in the interest of the service or at their own request, be directed to serve in another organisation or in another institution of the organisation. At the EU, a secondment is restricted (for more details, see Art. 37 EU-SR). At the UN, there is an Inter-Agency Mobility Accord of 10/11 October 2005 (UN doc. CEB/2005/5 Annex V) between the member organisations of the UN-CS, based on Rule 4(9) UN-SR). This "inter-agency mobility" allows for a "transfer" (without a right to return to the releasing organisation) or for an "exchange" (right to return granted). The mobility of staff is meant to strengthen the cohesiveness and the effectiveness of the UN system and is rooted in the desired principles of greater harmonisation, precision and flexibility in order to engender responsiveness to the diverse needs and requirements of the organisation of the UN common system (see the preamble of the Inter-Agency Mobility Accord).

In addition to the mobility accord, the SG may second staff members to serve in a specialised agency or another IO (Rule 4(9) UN-SR).

At the CoE, staff members in employment for an indefinite duration may be seconded to work in another IO or national, local or regional administration (Appendix II Art. 5 B CoE-SR).

At the EPO, secondments in the interest of the service may be granted to a public or private body. The secondment may not normally exceed two years (Art. 43 EPO-SR).

As far as the secondment from a national civil service to an IO is concerned, see, for example, ILOAT Judgments 2413, 2239, 2238, 2012, 1826.

*bb) Leave on personal grounds*

Under Art. 40 EU-SR leave on personal grounds may be granted at the request of the official in exceptional circumstances for periods of up to one year with the possibility of an extension up to a total duration of 15 years in the course of the entire career of the official. The entitlement to salary is discontinued during the leave, as is the increase in seniority for the advancement in the step and the promotion in grade.

At the UN, the entitlement to special leave for fixed-term and continuing appointment under Rule 5(3) UN-SR includes the family leave. Special leave is normally without pay but the SG has discretion to grant leave with full or partial pay.

At the CoE, there are extensive provisions governing unpaid leave for family events or for personal reasons (Appendix VII CoE-SR).

At the EPO, unpaid leave on personal grounds is for a period of one year which may be extended for two further years. Special rules apply for the membership to the social security scheme and the pension scheme. There is a right to reinstatement under certain conditions (Art. 45 EPO-SR).

*cc) Leave for military service*

The organisation of the EU civil service system and the EPO-SR provide for leave if an official is called up for military service (Art. 42 EU-SR; Art. 44 EPO-SR).

*dd) Assignment to non-active or reserve status*

In the EU civil service system, if an official has become supernumerary by reason of a reduction in the number of posts, he is assigned to non-active status (Art. 35(d) and 41 EU-SR) (see more in detail under "Termination of employment").

At the EPO, the situation is more or less identical even if the term "assignment to reserve status" is used (Art. 46 EPO-SR, see more in detail under "Termination of employment").

The service law systems of the UN and the CO with no staff appointed by unilateral act on a statutory basis do not provide for such an administrative status but instead terminate the service. The staff member receives a severance grant or a retirement pension.

*ee) Parental (paternity) leave*

(See under "Social security")

#### *ff) Family leave*

(see under "Social security")

### *3. Transfer and reassignment within the organisation*

A staff member may either be transferred to a vacant post of equivalent grade at his own request or at the initiative of the appointing authority (see, for example, Art. 7 EU-SR).

A transfer in the interests of the organisation is a discretionary decision (ILOAT Judgments 2803, 1050; CJEU Judgments T-325/02, T-51/01, T-100/00). The international courts may not therefore ordinarily interfere in the assessment of the organisation, which is the best judge itself of what is in the best interests of the organisation. The courts will, however, exercise their power of review and determine whether the organisation transcended the normal bounds of discretion and decided in flagrant breach of a general principle of law. The staff member's dignity and reputation, in particular, must be protected (see, for example, ILOAT Judgments 2819, 2229).

Case law has it, that the staff member be given a hearing beforehand when the transfer may harm his dignity or private interests and is not a matter of urgency (ILOAT Judgments 1496, 810).

At the EU, there is a difference between the terms "transfer" and "reassignment". In the case of a transfer in the strict sense of the term the official is transferred to a vacant post, whereas in a case of reassignment the official is transferred together with his post, i.e. only the duties assigned are changed (see, for example, CJEU Judgment T-80/92). It is only in case of a transfer that the formalities provided for in Art. 4 and 29 EU-SR have to be observed. The material rules of the right and legitimate interests of the official concerned under Art. 7 EU-SR (principle of equivalence of post and grade) are identical for transfer and reassignment (CJEU Judgment F-4/09). This difference in terminology is not always consistently applied in the judicature of the ILOAT (see Judgment 2839 para. 19, see also Judgment 1146: no transfer but redistribution of duties by rotation).

At the UN, the transfer of staff members is dealt with in Reg. 4(2) UN-SR and indirectly in Reg. 1(2)(c) and Rule 1(2)(a) UN-SR. An explicit authorisation to transfer a staff member is to be found in the Admin. Instruction doc. ST/AI/2010/3 of 21 April 2010 under Section 2(5). There is, however, no explicit authority to reassign staff (see CJEU Judgment F-4/09).

The transfer rules of the CoE are contained in Appendix II Art. 5 A CoE-SR.

The EPO has transfer rules similar to the EU in Art. 4 EPO-SR. The reassignment is provided for in Art. 11a EPO-SR.

**Jurisprudence**

The jurisprudence of the CJEU and the ILOAT is not fully coherent in the methods applied by their judicial review. The CJEU consistently requires that the responsibilities of the official in the new post must correspond to the grade and requires no comparison between the present and previous duties (see CJEU Judgment T-325/02). The ILOAT on the other hand underlines that the transferred official has to be provided with work at the same level as in his previous post and matching his qualifications (see ILOAT Judgments 2839, 2819). Since the decisive criterion is the matching of the responsibilities of each post to attributed grade (specified as a rule by the job description) the method followed by the CJEU is the more precise method of comparison.

ILOAT Judgments

2839: No reasons given for reassignment (transfer) is a disregard of dignity (2833); 2819: A transfer must show due regard, in both form and substance, for the dignity of the official, particularly by providing him with work of the same level as in his previous post and matching his qualifications (Judgments 2229, 1757), no adequate post as a principal director was offered, the tribunal set 28 days or a deadline for reassignment to an adequate post; 2803: Transfer violated the dignity of the complainant since no commensurate post was offered; 2792: In the absence of explicit requirements in the SR there is no participation right for staff representatives in a transfer board; 2646: An official on probation who underperforms is not entitled to a transfer; 2635: In a case where the interests of the organisation and the staff member in a transfer decision are at odds, the greater weight may be accorded to the interests of the organisation (883). The transfer decision is flawed since the complainant had no opportunity to respond to the issues prompting the decision; 2229: Transfer may be motivated by the need to eliminate tensions compromising the functioning of the service; transfer as a hidden disciplinary measure (1929); 2191: The organisation must carefully take into account the interests and the dignity of an official opposed to a transfer; 2027: Even a simple measure of an internal reorganisation like a transfer may sometimes impair the staff member's rights and legitimate interests, and is therefore appealable; 2025: Transfer decision based on incomplete or wrong information; failure to assess the complainant's circumstances in the case; 1972: A transfer can be justified as a means of settling a conflict situation (1018); 1929: A transfer as a hidden disciplinary action (1496); 1726: Consultation on transfer between duty stations; 1590: No transfer but rotation of duties within the same post; 1343: Whether the new post after a transfer is commensurate with the former post and grade depends on an objective test, namely the level of duties; 1234: Transfer offended against dignity since it was taken without explaining the interest of the organisation and without giving a reason for moving the official for the second time in eighteen months; 1161: No right to a transfer; 1146: No transfer but a redivision of duties; 996: The requirement in the ESO-SR that the staff member's consent is necessary for a transfer is in marked contrast to other IO; 939: If the organisation's best interests so require the transfer may be ordered even against the wishes of the staff member.

CJEU Judgments/Orders

F-4/09: Even if the SR do not provide for a reassignment it is a change of duties which is safeguarded by the principles which are to be observed under Art. 7 EU-SR (the new post of the official must correspond to his grade); T-76/03 (C-12/05 P): Reassignment caused by significant and irreversible tension with management is strongly justified by the interests of the service. As a mere measure of internal organisation taken in the interests of the service the organisation must not state the grounds on which a decision is based, provided that the position of the official under the SR is not affected and the principle of equivalence of grade and post is not infringed by an effective decrease in the responsibilities, taking account of their character, their importance and their scope. A communication to the entire staff using the expression that the official is "relieved of his duties" had a disciplinary connotation and causes a non-material damage to the official (see also T-118/04, T-134/04, T-339/03); T-325/02: Reassignment, the responsibilities (taking account of their character, importance and their scope) in the new post should correspond to the grade. There is no comparison between the present and the previous duties (T-59/91 and T-79/91); C-294/95 P: Justification of a transfer in the interests of service, as a means of settling internal relationship difficulties.

### *4. Conversion of appointment (horizontal transition)*

Each IO usually has several types of employment relationship. It is clear that staff in a short-term employment relationship will generally seek a conversion to a permanent appointment.

At the EU, staff in the AST function group may pass to the AD function group by successfully participating in a certification procedure for certain categories of temporary staff and for fixed-term appointments there are conversions to appointments for an indefinite period (Art. 8 and 85 EU-CEOS).

There is no conversion from a temporary or contract employment to the status of official (permanent employee). Staff interested in this kind of employment relationship have to participate in an open (external or combined internal-external) competition for those posts. If they are successful they can expect that their professional experience acquired at the organisation in the previous employment will be taken into account for the incremental steps. Temporary staff members retain the step in grade acquired in that capacity if they are appointed officials (Art. 8(2) EU-CEOS) in the same grade immediately following the period of temporary service (Art. 32(2) EU-SR, see the decision of the European ombudsmen in complaint 3199/2007/(WP)(VL) BEH of 22 December 2009 and references).

Contract staff in general may not participate in internal competitions for permanent posts. Participation in an internal competition is open for a special category of temporary staff (Art. 29(3) EU-SR).

At the UN, a fixed-term appointment can be converted into a continuing appointment after two years' service and the successful completion of a competition examination (Rules 4(13) and 4(14)(b) UN-SR), whereas a temporary appointment may not be converted to any other type of appointment (Rule 4(12)(c) UN-SR).

The "probationary appointment" as a special type of appointment under the UN-SR has been deleted in the new UN-SR, effective 1 July 2009. (For transitional measures in relation to staff members holding a probationary appointment as at 30 June 2009, see Rule 13(3) UN-SR). A two-year fixed-term appointment and a satisfactory record of service are preconditions for continuing appointment (Rule 4(14)(b) UN-SR) and may be considered as a kind of probationary period even if a general probationary period is not provided for in the UN-SR. Most other IO of the UN-CS do provide provisions for a probationary period (see UN doc. CEB/2010/HLCM/HR para. 44 et seq.).

At the EPO, there is the possibility of conversion of a contract relationship into a permanent employment on a statutory basis in restricted cases. Art. 15a EPO conditions of employment for contract staff provides for such a conversion under very strict conditions. They apply especially to patent examiners who have not acquired the necessary language skills of the job description (see in the EPO internet portal, under "Required profile for EPO Patent examiners").

#### *5. Downgrading (demotion)*

In some special cases, the SR of most IO provide for a transfer of the staff member to a lower grade (downgrading, demotion).

- A staff member who, on the basis of consecutive periodical appraisal reports, continues to underperform may be downgraded (Art. 51(1) EU-SR; Art. 22bis(2) CoE-SR; Art. 52(1) EPO-SR); at the UN other administrative actions may ensue (see UN doc. ST/AI/2010/5, Section 10).
- As a result of a disciplinary procedure a staff member may be (temporarily or definitely) downgraded (Annex IX Art. 9(1)(e)(f) EU-SR; Rule 10(2)(vii) UN-SR: demotions with deferment; for a specified period, eligibility for considerations for appointment, Art. 54.2(e) CoE-SR; Art. 93(2)(e) EPO-SR).

### III. The termination of employment

#### *1. General introduction*

Termination of employment in IO is done, despite a sometimes varying terminology under similar circumstances.

The main reasons for the termination are:

- the termination of employment on the grounds of age or invalidity, or in the interests of the service (high-ranking political officials) or by reason of a reduction in the number of posts or of staff,

- termination on request,
- death,
- dismissal (termination of appointment) for incompetence, removal from post for disciplinary reasons.

There are major differences between employment on a statutory basis (EU and EPO officials) and contractual employment. There is no general termination of appointment for officials as in the case of temporary or fixed-term appointments, or appointments for an indefinite period. There is also no termination of service for EU and EPO officials if they have become supernumerary by reason of a reduction in the number of posts (see more in detail below).

Special provisions apply in general in case of termination of employment during the probationary period.

The general principle of the prohibition of arbitrary use of power is of particular importance for the termination of contractual employment. Such decisions must be based either on unsatisfactory performance or must lie in the interests of the service. There must also be no breach of an adversarial procedure, or an error of fact or of law, nor any abuse of authority or obvious misappraisal of the facts (see, for example, ILOAT Judgment 2090). Extensive case law has been developed on the protection of legitimate expectations in the renewal or extension of fixed-term contracts.

The following sections outline the most important cases of termination of service in the four civil service systems as well as the assignment to non-active status in the case of EU and EPO officials.

### 2. *EU*

#### a) Officials

##### *aa) Termination of service*

The service is terminated by resignation, compulsory resignation, retirement in the interests of the service, dismissal for incompetence, removal from post, retirement or death (Art. 47 EU-SR).

- Resignation (Art. 48 EU-SR)

The official has to state unequivocally in writing his intention to resign. No period of notice applies, but the organisation may postpone resignation by a certain period.

- Compulsory resignation (Art. 49 EU-SR)

This provision applies, for example, in the case of loss of full citizen rights or the loss of nationality of a member state (Art. 28(a) EU-SR) or if the official declines a post offered twice at the end of a secondment or leave on personal grounds (Art. 39 and 40 EU-SR). The joint committee has to be consulted.

- Retirement in the interests of the service (Art. 50 EU-SR)

Applicable to high-ranking political posts only.

- Dismissal for incompetence (Art. 51 EU-SR)

("idiot clause") Besides the downgrading or classification in a lower grade dismissal is possible after a procedure before the joint advisory committee.

- Removal from post (Art. 47(e) and Annex IX Art. 9(1)(h) EU-SR)

On the basis of an opinion of the disciplinary board the official may be removed from his post.

- Retirement (Art. 52 and 53 EU-SR)

The official is automatically retired on the last day of the month in which he reaches the retirement age. He is also automatically retired after the organisation recognises his total permanent invalidity under Art. 78 EU-SR.

If an official has not yet reached the pensionable age (66 years, Art. 77 EU-SR) and his service terminates otherwise than by reason of death or invalidity and he is not entitled to an immediate or deferred retirement pension (Art. 9 EU-PS), he will receive a severance grant under Annex VIII Art. 12 EU-SR.

*bb) Assignment to non-active status and resignation*

If an official has become supernumerary by reason of a reduction in the number of posts, his appointment is not terminated but he will be assigned to non-active status (Art. 35(d) and 41 EU-SR). For a period of two years he has priority for reinstatement in a post corresponding to his grade and his qualifications (Art. 41(3) EU-SR).

During the period of non-active status, he is entitled to a monthly allowance according to his age and length of service (Annex IV (3) EU-SR) (three months full basic salary, further three months 85% of basic salary, next five years 70% of basic salary and thereafter 60% of basic salary). Income from new employment is deducted from the allowance if it exceeds, together with the allowance, the last remuneration received (Art. 41(3) EU-SR). The staff member is also covered by the sickness insurance during the period of entitlement to the allowance. At the end of the period of entitlement to the allowance he is required to resign. Where appropriate he may receive a retirement pension (Art. 41(4) EU-SR).

This non-active status (reserve) regime provides an important distinction between contractual employment and the employment of an official whose "security of tenure" is guaranteed by the SR (see, for example, CJEU Judgment T-45/90 para. 90).

#### b) Temporary staff

Temporary employment ceases (apart from cessation on death), on reaching the retirement age (Art. 47(a) EU-CEOS), during or at the end of the probationary period in accordance with Art. 14 EU-CEOS, or being unable to resume service after paid sick-leave (Art. 48 EU-CEOS), for disciplinary reasons (Art. 49 and 50 EU-CEOS) or in the case of total invalidity (Art. 33 EU-CEOS), at the date stated in the contract (fixed-term contract) or at the end of a period of notice (Art. 47 EU-CEOS). Specific rules apply in the case of a contract for an indefinite period (Art. 47(c) EU-CEOS).

#### c) Contract staff

The termination provisions for temporary staff apply by analogy (Art. 119 EU-CEOS).

#### d) Unemployment allowance for temporary and contract staff

In the case of termination of appointment, a former member of the temporary or contract staff may be entitled to a retirement pension or to a severance grant if he meets the respective conditions (Art. 39 and 109 EU-CEOS). In the case of total invalidity, he receives an invalidity allowance for as long as the invalidity lasts (Art. 33(1) EU-CEOS) and, if applicable, additional compensation for the termination of the contract (Art. 33.3 EU-CEOS).

If a former temporary or contract staff member becomes unemployed and is not in receipt of a retirement pension or invalidity allowance and the service is not terminated by resignation or by cancellation of the contract for disciplinary reasons and he has completed a minimum of six month's service and is resident in a member state, he is entitled to a monthly unemployment allowance under certain conditions and for a maximum period of three years. The allowance decreases over time (from 60% to 30% of the former basic salary, see Art. 28a and 96 EU-CEOS).

### *3. UN*

A separation from service is triggered by resignation, abandonment of post, expiry of appointment, retirement, termination of appointment or death (Rule 9(1) UN-SR).

– *Resignation (Rule 9(2) UN-SR)*

In the case of a separation initiated by the staff member a notice of three months is generally required but resignation is normally accepted at shorter notice.

– *Abandonment of post (Rule 9(3) UN-SR)*

Separation initiated by the staff member other than by way of resignation. This is not regarded as a termination of appointment.

– *Expiration of appointment (Rule 9(4) UN-SR)*

Temporary and fixed-term appointments expire automatically without prior notice.

– *Retirement (Rule 9(5) UN-SR)*

This is not regarded as a termination of appointment.

– *Termination of appointment (Rule 9.6 UN-SR)*

Reasons for separation from service initiated by the appointing authority on other grounds are:

- abolition of post or reduction of staff,
- unsatisfactory service,
- health reasons,
- disciplinary reasons.

In addition, it is possible to terminate an appointment in the interests of the organisation under certain conditions (see, for example, Rule 9(6)(c) vi and (d) UN-SR). A written notice of termination has to be given to the staff member. The period of notice depends on the type of appointment (Rule 9(7) UN-SR).

Termination indemnity

A termination indemnity is paid in accordance with Rule 9(8) and Annex III UN-SR depending on the type of appointment (temporary, fixed-term, continuing appointment) on the number of completed years of service up to a maximum of twelve months gross salary, less staff assessment, where applicable. The indemnity is not paid if the staff member is in receipt of a retirement benefit or compensation for total disability (Rule 9(8)(c) UN-SR). There are also special provisions for staff members who are near the age above which they may apply for early retirement benefits (Rule 9(8)(d) UN-SR).

### *4. CoE*

All employment contracts are terminated at the end of the month in which the staff member reaches the age limit (Art. 23(1) CoE-SR). Fixed-term contracts terminate on expiry, unless renewed (Art. 23(2) CoE-SR). Contracts for a fixed term or indefinite period can be terminated by resignation (period of notice is three months) or by the organisation in the case of the abolition of the post (consultation of the joint committee is required), for disciplinary reasons, for manifest unsuitability or unsatisfactory work (under-performance procedure), or in the case of permanent invalidity (Art. 23(3) CoE-SR).

A termination indemnity for the loss of the job may be awarded (Art. 44 and Appendix VI CoE-SR) if the service is terminated for specific reasons (for example, suppression of a post, staff cuts, withdrawal of the member state of which the employee is a national). The calculation of the indemnity differs between fixed-term and indefinite contracts and depends on certain conditions, above all on the length of service. The maximum indemnity is ten months' pay for fixed-term and twenty-four months' pay for indefinite contracts.

### *5. EPO*

At the EPO, the provisions for the termination of service of permanent employees on a statutory basis are largely identical to those of the EU-SR. The same is applicable to the assignment to non-active status (irrespective of the use of the term "reserve status" in Art. 46 EPO-SR instead of "non-active status" in the EU-SR), to the receipt of an allowance after a post has become supernumerary by reason of a reduction in the number of posts, and to resignation (see Art. 46 and 114 EPO-SR).

The termination of contract employment largely corresponds to the provisions on temporary and contract staff of the EU. It is however noteworthy that in very restricted cases (primarily concerning patent examiners) it is possible to convert a contract relationship into permanent employment on a statutory basis. If a contract ends at the contractually specified date a termination indemnity of one month's basic salary multiplied by the number of years of service is paid. (In contrast to the EU, no unemployment allowance is granted).

### *6. The termination of service due to age*

Upon reaching the retirement age (Art. 52 EU-SR: 66 years; Reg. 9(2) UN-SR: 65 years; Art. 24 CoE-SR: 65 years; Art. 54 EPO-SR: 65 years) a staff member is automatically retired and the employment of EU temporary and contract staff "ceases" (Art. 47 and 119 EU-CEOS) at the age of 66 years; at the EPO, the contract for contract staff expires at the age of 65 (Art. 2(4) Conditions of employment for contract staff of the EPO).

A differentiation has to be made in some organisations between the compulsory retirement age (see, for example, Art. 52 EU-SR as applicable until 1 January 2014: age of 65) and the pensionable age (see, for example, Art. 77 EU-SR as applicable until 1 January 2014: age of 63). The retirement age is the age at which an official is retired automatically. The pensionable age is the age at which his entitlement to the payment of the pension arises. As of 1 January 2014, the retirement age and the pensionable age were laid down uniformally at the age of 66. At the UN, the pensionable age is the compulsory retirement age (65 years, see Art. 28(a) Statute of the UNJSPF). At the CoE, the compulsory retirement age and the pensionable age are uniformally set at 65 years (Art. 24(1) CoE-SR and Art. 8(1) Third PS). At the EPO, the retirement age is 65 years and the pensionable age is 60 years (Art. 8(1) EPO-PS).

Due to the adverse impact on the financial balance of the pension schemes caused by the increase in life expectancy, there is a general trend in IO to raise the pensionable and compulsory retirement ages (see Art. 77(6) EU-SR: The pensionable age may be reassessed every five years, taking into account the evolution in member states and the evolution in life expectancy).

In many IO, meanwhile, employment beyond the normal retirement age is possible on an exceptional basis at the request of the employee and in the interests of the service (Art. 52 EU-SR: until the age of 67 or exceptionally until the age of 70; Reg. 9(2) UN-SR: The UN-SG may extend the age limit of 65 years in exceptional cases; Art. 24bis (1) CoE.SR: a staff member may be retained in service up to the age of 67 years at most; Art. 54 EPO-SR: until the age of 68). The extension of employment beyond the regular retirement age is a discretionary decision (ILOAT Judgments 2896, 2845, 2779, 2669, 2513, 2377, 2125; 1143). At the EPO, there is a list of criteria for evaluating the interests of service relating to the prolongation of employment (see ILOAT Judgment 2896). The first step in a two-step approach is the assessment of the needs of the service and only if a need has been established is the suitability of the employee to fulfil these needs assessed.

### *7. The protection of legitimate expectation in the renewal or extension of fixed-term contracts*

(This topic is dealt with in section "general legal principles")

# C. Rights and obligations of staff

## I. The rights

### *1. Introduction*

The rights of staff of IO result (apart from the general principles of law) mainly from the SR, the tertiary law regulations (administrative directives, circulars, guidelines and other lower ranking provisions), the PPI and seat agreements. Occasionally, some rights of the staff members are even ascertained by the primary law (the "constitution") of the organisation (see, for example, Art. 270 TFEU and Art. 13 EPO-EPC: legal protection of staff and Art. 33(2)(c) EPO-EPC: increases in existing pensions to correspond to increases in salaries). It is only to a limited degree that staff member's rights are the result of individual contracts, and such cases are primarily reserved to staff members in leading positions.

The core areas of staff rights relate to remuneration, social security, pensions and collective rights.

### *2. Entitlement to remuneration*

Staff members are entitled to a remuneration that corresponds to their grade, step and their individual family and personal burden.

For staff employed on a statutory basis (EU and EPO officials), the SR explicitly state that their entitlement to remuneration may not be waived (Art. 62(2) EU-SR and Art. 64(1) EPO-SR). This provision became particularly important when the EPO reached a "compromise settlement" with its staff on the increase of salaries. In order to allow for such a settlement, the EPO Council amended the text of Art. 64(1) EPO-SR by adding that "this provision shall not invalidate the individual declaration concerning decision CA/D 4/96" (ILOAT Judgment 1980 para. 7c, see also ILOAT Judgments 1979, 1978, 1967, 1932, 1931, 1663). The entitlement to a pension may be temporarily waived (deferred pension, until reaching the pensionable age; see, for example, Annex VIII Art. 9 EU-SR).

#### a) The basic salary

The remuneration comprises basic salary and related allowances (Art. 62(3) EU-SR; Reg. 3(1) to 3(4) UN-SR; Art. 41(1) CoE-SR; Art. 64(2) EPO-SR).

##### *aa) The amount of salaries in general*

The amount of the salaries of international staff is occasionally subject to critical debates in the plenary organs of the IO, the national parliaments and the press. The following arguments may be invoked against this criticism.

- The salary system must be sufficiently attractive to nationals of all member states, even for those with the highest salaries (see the "Noblemaire Principle") in order to secure for the organisation the services of employees of the highest standard of ability, efficiency and integrity, recruited on the broadest possible geographical basis from among nationals of all member states of the organisation (Art. 27 EU-SR; Reg. 1(1) and Reg. 4(2) UN-SR; Art. 12 CoE-SR; Art. 5 EPO-SR).
- Staff of IO must meet increasingly specialised requirements. In addition to the multilingualism, the staff work in the organisation's own legal and administrative system (in a "substitute state").
- Staff work in an international work environment and are exposed to increased flexibility requirements regarding the country of service.
- A cross-comparison with the level of salaries of national staff working in the permanent missions of member states of IO and in the diplomatic missions justifies to a large extent the level of pay in IO.

*bb) The salary scales*

The basic structures of the salary systems of the staff of IO largely follow a similar pattern. The SR contain the modalities for granting salaries to varying degrees of comprehensiveness. The details are given in implementing rules. The salary scales, usually broken down into grades and steps (as well as the allowances), are generally to be found in annexes to the SR (but see Art. 66 EU-SR). Most salary scales are available on the internet (see the internet portals of the EU, the ICSC, CoE and the EPO). The salary scales display the basic salaries, i.e. after deduction of the internal tax (at the UN-CS called the "staff assessment"), and sometimes the gross salaries are also displayed (e.g. UN scales, EPO scales). As a rule, the vertical layout of the salary scales is based on grades, the horizontal on the steps.

At the EU, a special "solidarity levy" of between 6% and 7% has been applied since 1 January 2014 and will continue until 31 December 2023 (Art. 66a EU-SR).

The salary scales of the UN-CS do not reflect the total amount of salary entitlement. The net base salaries are to be supplemented by the "post adjustment" (Rule 3(7) UN-SR). This adjustment ensures that the remuneration of staff in the P and higher categories have the same purchasing power at all duty stations as in New York. In addition, it allows for regular adaptation of the local net base salaries in New York itself to the development of the cost of living.

The amount of the post adjustment is different from duty station to duty station. It is a significant percentage of the total remuneration. On 1 January 2015, the post adjustment multiplier (percentage of the net base salary) in the following countries and duty stations was as follows: New York 66.7, Switzerland 80.8, Berlin 36.4, Afghanistan 54.6, Beijing 69.0, Rome 48.1 and Japan 70.3. The figures are regularly updated (if possible, monthly) (see the post adjustment circulars on the ICSC internet portal under "cost-of-living"). The post adjustment is composed of four elements:

- the difference in prices between the location where the staff member works and New York,
- the local inflation,
- the exchange rate of the local currency to the US dollar,
- the average expenditure pattern (shopping basket).

For the calculation of the post adjustment multiplier an advisory committee of the ICSC, the ACPAQ (advisory committee on post adjustment questions) assists. One point of the post adjustment multiplier corresponds to one percent of the staff member's net base salary. From time to time a part of the adjustment multiplier points is incorporated into the base salaries (consolidation of post adjustment). The consolidation is in itself not a salary increase but a restructuring measure. The consolidation moderates the increase of the post adjustment index. A negative post adjustment index is not possible. A detailed presentation of the post adjustment system is to be found on the ICSC internet portal (the post adjustment system booklet). For the consolidated post adjustment effective on 1 January 2015, see the ICSC Circular ICSC/CIRC/PAC/481 available on the ICSC website.

The salary scales of the UN-SR (Annex I UN-SR, the actual effective scales are to be found on the ICSC internet portal) contain – in addition to the net base salary (i.e. gross salaries after application of the internal tax (the "staff assessment") – separate figures for staff members with and without dependents (spouse or child) and the gross salaries).

Another specific characteristic of the UN-CS salary system for the P and higher categories is the "pensionable remuneration" (Rule 3(5) UN-SR). While in most IO, pension contributions and benefits are based on the basic salaries (see, for example, Art. 77(2) EU-SR), the contribution and the benefits in the UN-CS pension system are calculated on the basis of the pensionable remuneration scale. This scale serves as a fictitious salary scale for the calculation of pension contributions and as the real pension scale for the calculation of pension benefits.

The reason for this complexity is the fact that the post adjustment is not part of the salary scales (and also not subject to the internal staff assessment). Using the salary scales as the sole basis for calculating the pension contributions and benefits would result (in addition to the 70% maximum rule of pensions) to a significant loss in the amount of the pension due to the high percentage of post adjustment in the total remuneration of the staff. For this reason, the ICSC sets up a table of pensionable remuneration that is valid worldwide (see the ICSC

Internet portal). The amounts set in the pensionable remuneration scales are calculated on the basis of the gross salaries and some additional elements (non-pensionable component, see UN doc. A/65/30 para. 85). On average, the amounts in the pensionable remuneration scales are considerably higher than the amounts in the gross salary scales. This has the effect of substantially compensating for the national income tax on the UN pensions. The pensionable remuneration is regularly updated, in conformity with the up-dating of the salary and post adjustment scales.

The salary system for the UN general service and other locally recruited categories of staff is less complicated. In conformity with the Fleming Principle the remuneration of staff is in accordance with the best prevailing conditions of service in the locality. There is therefore no single global salary scale, but there are local salary scales. The ICSC establishes and reviews, pursuant to Art. 11(a) ICSC Statute, the methodology for headquarters and non-headquarters salary surveys. The ultimate responsibility for non-headquarter surveys is assigned to the respective UN-CS organisation. An overview of the salary scales is given on the ICSC internet portal.

#### *cc) Examples of the amount of salaries of the international civil service (after deduction of internal tax)*

EU (effective 1 July 2015)

Monthly net salary

- Officials in functional groups AD and AST, Officials in an initial position (grade 5): EUR 4,489 to EUR 5,079;
- Experienced official (grade 8): EUR 6,502 to EUR 7,357.
- Officials in a top management position:
  - grade 9 (head of unit): from EUR 7,357 to EUR 8,324;
  - grade 14 (director): from EUR 13,641 to EUR 15,435;
  - grade 16 (Director General): from EUR 17,463 to EUR 18,962.
- Functional group AST/SC: grade SC1 step 1: EUR 2,400; grade SC6 step 1: EUR 4,453.
- Contract staff (other servants):
  - Function group I (manual and administrative support): from EUR 1,907 to EUR 2,760;
  - Function group II (clerical and secretarial tasks): from EUR 1,980 to EUR 3,246;
  - Function group III (executive tasks): from EUR 2,536 to EUR 4,702;

– Function group IV (administrative, advisory, linguistic and equivalent technical tasks): from EUR 3,246 to EUR 6,811.

UN (effective 1 January 2015)

P and higher categories

A distinction is made in the salary scale between the net salary of a staff member with or without a dependent spouse or child (see Annex I UN-SR).

– For a single staff member in an initial position (grade P2, step I) total annual net salary: USD 47,292 plus post adjustment (for example, New York 64.9% of base net salary);
– For an experienced professional (with a dependent) (grade P5, step V) total annual net salary: USD 94.563 plus post adjustment (for example, New York 64.9% of base net salary).

The fictitious salary scale for the calculation of the contributions to the pension scheme (pensionable remuneration as of 1 February 2013) for professionals in grades P3 – P4 step XI is between USD 148,264 and USD 178,387, for professionals in grade P5 step XIII is USD 219,569. (The pension is subject to the national income tax in the country of residence in conformity with the legislation applicable to pensioners of the respective IO).

General service category

The annual base net salary taking the example of Austria (1 November 2015) for:

– an official in an initial position (level 1 step I): EUR 24,156;
– an experienced staff member (level 7 Step VI): EUR 67,185.

CoE (effective 1 January 2016)

Monthly net base salary

– support staff unmarried (grades B2-B4): between EUR 2,943 and EUR 3,858;
– an experienced (unmarried) professional (grade A2): EUR 5,821;
– a head of section (unmarried) (grade A4): EUR 8,347.

EPO (effective 1 July 2015)

The monthly net basic salary in Germany (headquarters) for:

– an administrative employee (grades G1 – G9): between EUR 2,731 and EUR 7,175;
– an examiner, administrator, lawyer (grades G7 – G13): between EUR 5,223 and EUR 11,934;

– a director, boards of appeal member (grades G13 – G15): between EUR 11,423 and EUR 14,003.

Other IO adhering to the mixed civil service system align their salary scales in varying degrees with the salaries of the functionally most comparable salary system of the EU, the UN-CS or the CO. The salaries paid by CERN and ESO (see ILOAT Judgment 2133) and EMBL are more or less aligned with the salaries paid by the CO. The OPCW has the salary structure of the EU.

*dd) Adjustment of salaries*

(This topic is dealt with in section "general legal principles", see above and in section "rights and obligations of staff", see below).

*ee) The salary increase*

A staff member is entitled to the salary carried by his grade and step (see, for example, Art. 62(1) EU-SR). He is recruited at the first step in the grade specified in the vacancy note (see, for example, Art. 31(1) and Art. 32(1) EU-SR). Additional seniority steps may be granted to take account of previously acquired professional experience (see, for example, Art. 32(2) EU-SR and ILOAT Judgments 962, 957, 953, 895, 886, 884, 881, 861, 851).

During his service, a staff member whose performance has been evaluated as satisfactory generally advances "automatically" (see, for example, Art. 44(1) EU-SR) to the next step in his grade). Salary increments are awarded annually or biannually, the intervals may sometimes be reduced (see Annex I item 4 UN-SR) and it is even possible for an advancement of up to two steps to take place every year (Art. 48(1) EPO-SR). In the higher grades, the number of incremental steps is generally reduced.

Promotion is normally to the first step in the new grade. This holds good for the IO whose salary scale systems provide for at least the same amount of salary as the last step of the previous grade (see, for example, the EU salary scales and Art. 46 EPO-SR). Some SR of IO even explicitly state that a promotion may under no circumstances result in a reduction of the total net remuneration (see, for example, Art. 49(5) EPO-SR). In such cases, a compensatory allowance is therefore granted (ILOAT Judgment 2624).

*ff) Payment arrangements*

Salaries are paid on a monthly basis (monthly instalments) even if the salary scales, like in the P and higher categories of the UN-CS (see Annex I UN-SR) show the annual amounts. The salary is normally due at the end of the month. At the EU, payment of remuneration is made on the 15th day of each month for the current month (Annex VII Art. 16(1) EU-SR).

Special payments such as a 13th month bonus, holiday or Christmas bonuses are unknown throughout IO.

Salaries are generally paid at the place and in the currency of the country where the staff member carries out his duties (see, for example, Annex VII Art. 17(1) EU-SR). The staff of some IO can have a part of their remuneration transferred to another member state (country of origin) of the organisation on a regular basis (see, for example, Annex VII Art. 17(2) to (5) EU-SR).

*gg) Forfeit or reduction of salary*

In certain cases the salary can be forfeited or reduced. The most important cases are:

– Unauthorised absence from service

In the case of an unauthorised absence from service, the staff member must forfeit his remuneration for the respective period (Rule 5(1)(e)(ii) UN-SR; Art. 31 CoE-SR; Art. 63(1) EPO-SR; at the EU, the annual leave is reduced accordingly and, if it has been used up, the remuneration is forfeited, Art. 60 EU-SR).

– Strike

An IO may deduct remuneration corresponding to the strike period.

The SR of most IO are mute on the issue of the right to strike (e.g. the EU-SR and the UN-SR). The right to strike is explicitly provided for in the CoE-SR (Art. 47bis), the ECB-SR (Art. 8) and the EPO-SR (Art. 30a). The right to strike is, however, recognised in all IO. Based on a general principle, recognised in the labour law of the member states, remuneration is not due to persons who have taken part in a strike and generally a deduction of one thirtieth of remuneration is applied for each day of strike (CJEU Judgment 44, 46 and 49/74; see also the old UNAT Judgment No. 249: "... salary is the essential counterpart to work performed ..."; see also old UNAT Judgment No. 692).

In the CoE-SR and the ECB-SR, the amount of salary to be deducted in the case of strike is not specified. Art. 65(1)(c) EPO-SR provides the deduction of one twentieth (before 1 July 2013 one thirtieth, see doc. CA/D 5/13 and CA/57/13 available on the EPO website, under "organisation", "Council") for each day of strike on a working day. (See also ILOAT Judgment 3691: The employee on strike must be considered to be in service with regard to the social insurance coverage and the pension entitlement; ILOAT Judgment 3369: In the case of part-time work the deductions from the remuneration are not calculated on a strict proportionate basis if the SR provide for a deduction on the basis of lump-sum fractions per day).

Nevertheless, in a non-negligible number of cases, IO forgo a reduction in the remuneration, at least partially (allowances, social benefits) by way of a compromise in order to not further deteriorate the working atmosphere.

– Disciplinary measures

The SR provide for a reduction of the salary by relegation in step or downgrading. Some IO provide for a reduction of a certain amount of the retirement pension and the invalidity allowance (Annex IX Art. 9(2) EU-SR: for a given period and not extending to dependants; at the UN, disciplinary measures cannot be imposed on retired staff members, see UN doc. ST/IC/2014/26 para. 15; the same holds true for the CoE; at the EPO, the retirement pension may be reduced (Art. 93(2) (f) EPO-SR).

– Long-term illness

For contract staff, the duration of paid sick leave is determined according to the nature and duration of the appointment (Art. 16 EU-CEOS; Rule 6.2 UN-SR; Art. 45(6) CoE-SR and Rule No. 1331 of 24 March 2011; Art. 9(3) EPO Conditions of employment of contract staff.

For statutory staff (EU, EPO), after a certain maximum period of sick leave with full pay which is considerably longer than for contract staff, the official may be entitled to an invalidity allowance (Art. 59(4) EU-SR; Art. 78 EU-PS) or a reduced salary during extended sick leave and during incapacity (Art. 62a(7)(b) and Art. 62b EPO-SR). (For more in detail see below).

– Non-active (reserve) status

Staff on a statutory basis (EU, EPO) who have become supernumerary are assigned to non-active (reserve) status. In lieu of his salary the staff member is entitled to a special allowance.

#### b) Allowances and reimbursement of expenses

In addition to the basic salary, the employees of IO may be entitled to allowances, which provide financial compensation for special family and personal burdens. They are also entitled to the reimbursement of expenses which occur by reason of their duties.

Despite differences in the various conditions for the entitlement and the amount of an allowance their basic structures are broadly similar in all four civil service systems.

The annual update of the remuneration includes the allowances (see, for example, Art. 62(3) and 65 and Annex XI 3(1) EU-SR).

It is necessary to distinguish between the allowances as part of the remuneration or the pensions and any benefits granted under the social security system of an IO.

*aa) Family allowances*

Family allowances serve as the financial compensation for staff's additional costs due to family burdens or obligations to furnish assistance. They comprise household allowance, dependent (child) allowance and education allowance (Art. 67(1) EU-SR; Appendix IV Art. 4, 5 and 7 CoE-SR; Art. 67(1)(a) EPO-SR: including a child care allowance). At the UN, the SR do not use the term "family allowances", since only the dependency allowances (Rule 3(6) UN-SR) and the education grant (Rule 3(9) UN-SR) are explicitly dealt with. A kind of household allowance is already integrated in the salary scale (see Annex I UN-SR: Net "D" rate applicable to staff members with and Net "S" without dependents).

(1) The household allowance

A married staff member or a staff member with a dependent child or an official who is registered as being in stable non-marital partnership is under certain conditions entitled to the household allowance (see, for example, Art. 67(1)(a) and Annex VII Art. 1(2)(a), (b) and (c) EU-SR). Occasionally, an entitlement exists in other cases, if the staff member actually assumes family responsibilities (Annex VII Art. 1(2)(d) EU-SR; Appendix IV Art. 4 CoE-SR; Art. 68 EPO-SR).

The amount of the household allowance is generally of the order of about 6% of the basic salary (at the EU it is composed of a basic amount of (1 January 2014) EUR 170,52 plus 2% of the official's basic salary (Annex VII Art. 1(1) EU-SR), at the CoE it is 6% of the basic salary, or 6% of the basic salary for grade B3 step 1 whichever is the greater (Appendix IV Art. 4(1) CoE-SR), for the EPO see Art. 68 EPO-SR.

If the spouse of the employee (without a dependent child) is gainfully employed with an income exceeding a certain level, there is normally a reduction of the household allowance (see, for example, Annex VII Art. 1(3) EU-SR). If both spouses are staff members of the same IO only the spouse with the higher basic salary is entitled to the allowance (see, for example, Annex VII Art. 1(4) EU-SR).

There is almost no case law of the ILOAT on household allowance since in the organisations of the UN-CS an additional amount of salary corresponding to the household allowance has already been included in the salary scales. The only case worth mentioning is Judgment 927. Here, the tribunal held that the "trial separation" of the spouses prior to the divorce decree under French law is neither a "legal separation" nor a "similar situation" within the meaning of Rule VI 1(13) CERN-SR. The complainant was therefore entitled to the family allowances.

The judicature of the CJEU on household allowance is consistently associated with the principle of "no duplication of benefits" cases. But see CJEU Judgment F-86/09: Entitlement to the household allowance for officials registered as being in stable non-marital partnerships (Judgment F-153/12).

(2) Dependency benefits

Staff members with a dependent child are entitled to dependency benefits (in some SR of IO like the EU-SR, the dependency benefits are called "dependent child allowance"). The definition of a dependent child is not uniform across the four international civil service systems.

The EU-SR require that the legitimate, natural or adopted child of an official or of his spouse is "actually being maintained by the official" (Art. 67(1)(b) and Annex VII Art. 2(2) EU-SR). In addition, there are some special cases where a child may be recognised as a dependent child.

At the UN, a "dependent child" is a child for whom the staff member "provides main and continuing support" (Rule 3(6)(a)(iii) UN-SR). The dependency allowance is, however, not paid for a staff member with no dependent spouse in respect of the first dependent child since in this case there is already entitlement to an increased basic salary (Reg. 3(4)(a)(i) UN-SR and Annex I footnotes D and S UN-SR). There is, however, entitlement to the dependency rate of the staff assessment (tax). In the CoE-SR the child must depend "on the staff member's household or on the staff member alone for main and continuing support" (Appendix IV Art. 5(1)(ii) CoE-SR). At the EPO, a dependent child is basically a legitimate natural or adopted child of a permanent employee, or of his spouse, who is "mainly and continuously" supported by the permanent employee or his spouse (Art. 69(3)(a) EPO-SR). As in the EU-SR there are some specific additional cases where a child may be recognised as a dependent child.

IO have set up rules in internal instructions and guidelines in order to determine whether the financial support of the child is sufficient to justify the qualification of dependency (see, for example, ILOAT Judgment 2532 concerning the respective guidelines of the EPO).

The allowance is generally paid for children under 18 years of age. On application, with supporting evidence, the allowance is paid up to the age of 26 years for children in educational or vocational training (Annex VII Art. 2(3)(b) EU-SR; in the UN, the allowance is paid for a child between the age of 18 to 21 years attending university or the equivalent full-time, Rule 3(6)(a)(iii) UN-SR; Appendix IV Art. 5(1)(iii) CoE-SR and Art. 69(4) EPO-SR: up to the age of 26 years).

The amount of the dependent child allowance is, for example, at the EU EUR 372,61 per dependent child (1 January 2014) (Annex VII Art. 2(1) EU-SR).

In case a child is prevented by serious illness or invalidity from earning a livelihood the allowance is paid on a continuous basis irrespective of the age of the child, for the duration of the illness or invalidity (see, for example, Annex VII Art. 2(5) EU-SR). Some organisations grant an additional amount of the dependency allowance if the mental or physical handicap of the child puts a heavy financial burden on the official (see, for example, Art. 67(3) EU-SR).

In exceptional cases (broad discretion) and under very restrictive conditions (mostly: main and continuing support) most IO provide for the granting of the dependency allowance for other persons (EU: Annex VII Art. 2(4) EU-SR: for any person for whom the official has a legal responsibility and whose maintenance creates a heavy financial burden; UN: Rule 3(6)(a)(v) UN-SR: for the father, mother, brother or sister of the staff member; CoE: Appendix IV Art. 5(2) CoE-SR: for an ascendant of the official or his spouse if there is a legal obligation; EPO: Art. 70 EPO-SR: for the parents and other relative, by blood or marriage of the employee or his spouse by virtue of a legal or juridical obligation).

In addition to the dependent child allowance, some IO provide for subsidised pre-school care (kindergarten, crèche). If no free places are available, staff members receive a pre-school allowance (childcare allowance) which is paid as a lump sum or covers a part of the costs of the childcare (see, for example, Annex VII Art. 3(2) EU-SR). At the EPO, officials entitled to the dependent's allowance may request a child care allowance under Art. 70a EPO-SR to cover the costs of preschool care and a crèche.

**Jurisprudence**

ILOAT Judgments

3533: A child by definition, cannot simultaneously be the dependent child of two permanent employees; 2847: Concurrent family allowances paid by other sources; 1866: A staff member who prefers to reside in a location where there are no crèches subsidised by the organisation and does not wish to place his child in a subsidised crèche cannot invoke unequal treatment; 1814: Treating the mother of the complainant as a dependent person under the SR presupposes a "heavy" maintenance expenditure. The organisation failed to establish its own rules to put this criterion into concrete terms; 1715: The staff member has the burden of proving the legal nature and the consequences of a particular form of marriage under national law as a precondition for the entitlement to dependency payments for his wife; 1397: Consideration of a national rental income for the calculation of the complainant's parents' own income in order to decide on their dependency; 1333: There is no violation of the principle of equality if, in the event of a strike, besides the salary the dependency allowance is also reduced proportionately; 1176: Treating a person as a dependent child confers health insurance coverage *ipso facto* of that person. The organisation may, therefore, not transfer the burden of proof that there is no other coverage for the complainant; 1142: Dependent's allowance for the parents of the official. The parents are not required to let a flat they own in Rome during their visit (for whatever length of time) to the complainant in the NL; 1072: Calculation of the limit of occupational earnings of the spouse as a precondition for the entitlement to the dependency allowance; 952: The revision of the conditions to treat adopted children as dependents does not violate an acquired right; 743: In the case of a divorce the spouse who is granted custody for a child is entitled to the dependency allowance; 498: The differences in the family allowance between the P and higher categories and the general service category is based on different circumstances and therefore the principle of equality is inapplicable; 426: No acquired right to every item making up the dependency allowance and every detail of the process of calculation of the dependency allowance; 422: Both parents are staff members. It is up to the discretion of the Director-General to interpret the SR as to whether the step-daughter was fully dependent on the complainant; 322: For personal reasons the complainant waited six years before claiming a legitimate child allowance. He lost the right to retroactive payment because of the purpose of the provisions on family allowance.

CJEU Judgments/Orders

F-65/12: The entitlement to a dependent allowance is not excluded if the spouse is also an EU official; F-22/12: Appropriate documentary evidence of actual maintenance. No evidence of a transfer of money by postal services needed; F-60/09: Payment of the dependent child allowance in respect of a child prevented by serious illness from earning a livelihood. Application of an internal instruction on the calculation of the amount of own income of the child which reduces or excludes the entitlement; T-85/91: The concept of "a legal responsibility to maintain" used in Annex VII Art. 2(4) EU-SR makes it necessary to determine whether the national legal system to which the official is subject imposes a responsibility on the official;
C-70/91 P (T-75/89): Annex VII Art. 2(4) EU-SR which permits in exceptional cases the treatment of a person, for whom the official has a legal responsibility, and whose maintenance involves "heavy expenditure" as a dependent child, must be interpreted such as not to exclude a child from the scope of the provision; T-41/89: A child is not actually maintained by the official (Annex VII Art. 2(2) EU-SR) if he performs his military service, and this provides for all his basic needs. This is also valid for the provision of Annex VII Art. 2(3)(b) and Art. 2(4) EU-SR since rules that create a right to financial benefits must be given a strict interpretation; 6–74: It is in accordance with Annex VII Art. 2(4) EU-SR that the official should first utilise his non-EU resources before applying for this exceptional benefit. This benefit has to be taken into account for the calculation of the "heavy expenditure" which is a precondition for the entitlement. There are objective and justified criteria which are compatible with the principle of equal treatment and all other general principles of law cited by the applicant.

(3) The education allowance

Children of international civil servants, who are not nationals of the country of their duty station, are confronted with disadvantages when visiting a school or university at the duty station, especially in respect of the language or of the recognition of the graduation diploma in their home country. IO endeavour, therefore, to provide their employees with adequate relief from this additional burden. Occasionally, IO offer the opportunity for free schooling in the respective language section of a school established by them or at least co-funded (see, for example, the 14 European Schools at the duty station of large EU institutions and the European School of Munich, which was established at the initiative of the EPO as an IO at the edge of the EU, see in the internet www.eursc.eu). If this opportunity is not provided, employees are regularly entitled to an education allowance.

The rules governing the eligibility for this allowance are quite variable in detail between the four international civil service law systems. This is especially true for the commencement of entitlement (child's age), the requirement for proving the existence of direct and indirect school costs, the reimbursement of the costs of school transport, the maximum amount (ceiling) of the refund and the type of settlement (monthly lump-sum payment and final settlement at the end of the school year (see for details; Art. 67(1)(c) and Annex VII Art. 3 EU-SR; Rule 3(9) UN-SR; Appendix IV Art. 7 CoE-SR; Art. 71 EPO-SR).

In some IO, even staff members who are nationals of the country of employment are, under certain conditions, exceptionally entitled to the education allowance (Appendix IV Art. 7(2) CoE-SR; Art. 71(2) EPO-SR).

**Jurisprudence**

ILOAT Judgments

3523: Payment of the education allowance was discontinued. A practice that is inconsistent with the SR cannot obtain legal force; 3358: Legally unfounded decision reversed (dual nationality); 2638: The main justification for the education allowance is the fact that the duty station of the employee is not in his home country. The allowance is designed to restore a degree of equality between officials (2637); 2357: An official who seeks to bring himself within an exception to a general rule (e.g. an education allowance is generally not payable to an official serving in his home country) has to establish that he falls within the exception (1837, 1836, 1835); 2016: The SR provide only for the reimbursement of costs actually incurred and not for costs on a hypothetical basis; 1784: In the absence of original documents as evidence for the educational costs, the IO decides, subject to review by the tribunal, whether the proof offered is satisfactory; 1366: The obligation to recover overpayment of the education allowance may lapse with time; 1347: The recovery of overpayment of the education allowance and the change of responsibilities are not disciplinary actions; 1118: The education allowance is a component of the remuneration and may be adjusted; 1051: There is no discrimination if the amount of the allowance is conditional on different contingencies such as whether or not a school provides board; 963: Prohibition of the retroactive reduction of the refundable amount of educational expenses; 743: The spouse who is granted custody in the event of divorce should be entitled to the child allowance; 666: The education allowance may be offset by direct subsidy to the school; 518: At the EPO, the provisions concerning the education allowance only cover the fees charged by a school and not the reimbursement of kindergarten fees; 497: The regulation providing for an education grant refers to a scholastic year not exceeding twelve months; 472: According to the SR, the education allowance is payable for a child regularly attending an educational establishment on a full-time basis. It is not payable for a training course prior to taking up employment; 371: There is no acquired right to the amount and the conditions of payment of the education allowance. Its abolition, however, would, in principle, constitute a breach of an acquired right; 292: Invalid amendments to the rules granting entitlement to the education allowance.

CJEU Judgments/Orders

F-22/12: Appropriate documentary evidence for the educational costs borne by the official; T-188/03: Granting the education allowance on an exceptional basis is not an act adversely affecting an official. Only if the exceptional nature of the decision were put forward subsequently as a ground for refusing to grant the allowance would the decision adversely affect the official concerned. In the absence of any criteria in the SR, reference should be made to the type of schooling provided, as defined by the national authorities; T-66/00: The complainant was obliged to state the income of her son during his vocational training which should have been taken into account for the calculation of the education allowance; T-86/91: The distinction between educational and vocational training (Annex VII Art. 2(3)(b) EU-SR) allows the payment of the education allowance to be withheld where the dependent child in respect of whom the allowance is sought receives vocational training with no connection to an educational establishment; T-10/90 and T-31/90: The grant of the education allowance does not require that the attendance of a primary educational establishment is compulsory under the national legislation. Education allowance cannot be refused therefore, where the child attends the establishment before the age of compulsory school attendance; C-145/90 P: The criteria for the grant of the dependent child allowance and the education allowance are different. The entitlement to the education allowance may vary month by month;

T-34/89 and T – 67/89: The "regular full-time attendance" at an education establishment in Annex VII Art. 3 EU-SR means that the student must actually follow the programme of instruction laid down by the rules of the establishment; T-152/81 and joined cases: The second indent of the third paragraph of Art. 3 of Annex VII EU-SR restricting the entitlement to the double education allowance to officials entitled to the expatriation allowance is an objectively justified differentiation; T-43/79: Definition of the term "actual education cost" in Annex VII Art. 3 EU-SR.

(4) No duplication (overlapping) of benefits

In order to avoid double payment of allowances (grants) to staff members, the SR of IO provide for clauses prohibiting to duplication (overlapping) of benefits (non-duplication clause). Allowances paid from other sources are deducted from those paid by the organisation if the allowances are "of like nature".

At the EU and the EPO, the non-duplication clause applies to all family allowances (Art. 67(2) and (4) EU-SR; Art. 67(2) EPO-SR, even if the allowance is paid to the spouse of the official or to his dependants, see ILOAT Judgment 1297). Rule 3(6)(c) UN-SR contain a non-duplication clause for the dependency allowances. The CoE-SR provide for such a clause in regard to the household and the dependency allowance for the staff member or his spouse (Appendix IV Art. 4(6) and Art. 5(1)(v) CoE-SR).

In the event that a husband and his wife are employed in the service of the same IO and both are entitled to the household allowance, only the spouse who receives the higher salary is entitled to it (Annex VII Art. 1(4) EU-SR). Reg. 3(4)(b) UN-SR stipulates that if both husband and wife are staff members only one may claim for a dependent child allowance. If a husband and wife are employed by the CoE or by the CoE and another CO and both are entitled to a household allowance, the allowance is paid only to the person whose basic salary is the higher (Appendix IV Art. 4(5) CoE-SR). Art. 67(3) EPO-SR conforms with the EU rules.

Besides the non-duplication clause there are sometimes provisions which exclude or reduce the entitlement to the household allowance of an official without dependants, if the spouse has his or her own income and it is above a certain ceiling (see, for example, Annex VII Art. 1(3) EU-SR; Appendix IV Art. 4(3) and 4(4) CoE-SR; Art. 68(3) EPO-SR).

**Jurisprudence**

ILOAT Judgments

2847: The complainant's spouse received family allowance (household allowance and dependent child allowance) from France and the same allowances at the full rate from Eurocontrol. This payment conflicted with the rule against concurrent benefits. Requirement to reimburse the full overpaid amount (five years). No extinctive prescription applies; 1333: Deduction of the family allowance as well as the corresponding basic salary during a strike period is lawful. There is no breach of the principle of equality if other staff members who are also on strike continue to receive family allowances of like nature from a member state during the strike period since they are not in the same position in law; 1297: The child allowance under Netherlands' law is an allowance of like nature to the EPO dependent's allowance under Art. 67(2) EPO-SR. The purpose of both allowances is to contribute to the costs of child maintenance. The tribunal exceptionally relied in its ruling on the persuasive authority of a ruling of the CJEU (Judgment 14/77) since the wording and even the Article of the EPO-SR are identical with the one of the EU-SR.

CJEU Judgments/Orders

F-42/14: Overlapping of national allowances and allowances under the EU-SR; F-84/10: Overlapping of national education allowance and the allowance under the EU-SR; F-83/10: Education allowance, deduction of an allowance of like nature from other sources; C-135/06 P: The dependent child allowance paid by Luxembourg and the double dependent child allowance paid under Art. 67(3) EU-SR are not "of like nature" within the meaning of Art. 67(2) EU-SR; F-62/06: The Belgian orphan's benefit is not of like nature to the dependent child allowance paid by the EU;
T-147/95: The household subsidy paid by the employer (a beer brewery) to the husband of an EU official is not of like nature to the household allowance paid under the EU-SR; T-141/95: It is for the EU institutions to examine as early as possible whether or not an allowance paid by another source is of like nature within the meaning of Art. 67(2) EU-SR. If the organisation decides to discontinue to apply the rule against overlapping since it has failed to classify correctly the national allowances declared by the official concerned, the decision to discontinue the false application of the rule on overlapping takes effect when the improper deduction was first made; T-167/89: Application of the provision of overlapping (Art. 67(2) EU-SR) in the case of payment of a national study grant in another country. The principle of equal treatment restricts the application of the actual purchasing power coefficient of the amount of the national allowance in addition to the exchange rate. The official concerned may not be placed in a worse position than a staff member who gets his EU family allowances in full, regardless of where they are spent; 189/85: The EU-SR are binding in their entirety and are directly applicable in all member states. They are also binding in so far as the cooperation of member states is necessary in order to give effect to administrative measures resulting from the EU-SR. Since the entitlement to a family allowance (as part of "remuneration"), however, is linked to gainful occupation, the non-duplication clause of Art. 67(2) EU-SR prevails over a national non-duplication clause in so far as the spouse has a comparable link, i.e. paid employment in a member state and is entitled to an allowance of like nature under national law; 186/85: The non-duplication clause of Art. 67(2) EU-SR is applicable only if there is a comparable link with the circumstances conferring entitlement to family allowances, i.e. if the spouse of the official is in paid employment ("remuneration") and not if he is self-employed; 142/78: Art. 67(2) EU-SR established a general principle in every case, to prevent a married couple from drawing two household allowances since they are of like nature and paid for the same purpose; 106/76: Art. 67(2) EU-SR applies only to regular allowances which effectively constitute a part of the remuneration but not to an *ex gratia* payment granted on extraordinary grounds (family holiday allowance).

### (5) Excursus: Benefits for staff members in a union of two persons (same-sex marriage, registered partnership, cohabitation agreement etc.) equal to married hetero-sexual staff members

In the late 1980s there was, based on changes occurring in society, a national trend to open up the institution of marriage for persons of the same sex and to introduce other forms of partnerships for persons of the same or opposite sex (e.g. registered partnerships and non-registered cohabitation agreements). Based on this national legislation in member states, IO were confronted with requests by their employees in a status other than a traditional marriage to grant them the benefits of the household allowance, the marital increment to the expatriation allowance or to include their partners in the internal health insurance and to grant them the survivor's pension.

Subsequently the recognition of partnerships outside traditional marriage was subject to detailed legal scrutiny by the international administrative tribunals on the basis of the law governing the international civil service. After a period of legal uncertainty there is now a clearer approach in dealing with these issues.

EU

Within the reform of the EU-SR effective 1 May 2004, the EU council took account of the change in the legal assessment of same-sex partnerships in EU member states. Ever more member states recognised other forms of partnership outside traditional marriage such as same-sex marriage, registered partnerships and cohabitation agreements between same-sex and opposite-sex partners. Giving legal recognition to such other forms of union between persons meant that the official and his partner were no longer barred from receiving a number of family benefits like the household allowance, coverage by the internal sickness insurance and the survivor's pension (see Art. 1d(1), Art. 72(1) and Annex VII Art. 1(2)(c) EU-SR). This EU legislature therefore also drew the consequences from CJEU Judgment C-122/99 P and C-125/99 P of 31 May 2001 which held that it was the intention of the Community legislature to grant the entitlement to the household allowance only to married couples (Annex VII Art. 1(2)(a) EU-SR old version). The EU administration was therefore prevented from extending the benefits for married couples to an official and his partner by a "mere interpretation" of the EU-SR. Only the legislature could alter this legal situation.

UN

At the UN, the SG decided (see the SG's bulletin ST/SGB 2004/4 of 20 January 2004) that the family status for the purpose of entitlements under the UN-SR should be determined in all cases on the basis of the long-established principle that matters of personal status are determined by reference to the law of nationality of the staff member concerned. Marriages and legally recognised domestic partnership contracts by a staff member under the law of his nationality thus qualify for benefits provided for family members.

The organisation requests the permanent mission of the respective country to confirm the existence and validity of the domestic partnership.

In Judgment 1183 the UNAT was confronted with the question as to whether a registered same-sex partnership under French law (PACS) qualify a staff member concerned to receive the entitlements provided for a family member. The tribunal, while reminding that delegations in the General Assembly had divergent views as to whether there was a need for a decision of the legislator or an interpretation of the UN-SR would be sufficient considered that certain legal aspects of the UN-SR were not static but could be interpreted with consideration to social changes in the member states. Since the UN-SR give no definition of the term "couple" and "marriage", the UN-SG could interpret them in an administrative decision (see the bulleting quoted above), taking account of the radical transformation in social behaviour and changes in social perceptions. This interpretation confirmed a long-standing practice of the organisation to determine the family status according to the law of the country of nationality of the staff member. The UN is not a body for determining the societal choices of various communities existing throughout the world. The UN is a forum of tolerance and for showing respect for diversity, since it accepts both polygamous unions and same-sex unions.

The tribunal confirmed its jurisprudence that "the administrative instructions and information circulars" of the UN-SG "have the same force and effect as the staff rules unless inconsistent with the staff regulations". The tribunal was therefore obliged to apply the rules contained in the bulleting as "existing positive law". Since the French registered domestic partnership between same-sex partners was covered by the decision of the UN-SG the tribunal ordered that the applicant be paid all spousal benefits and entitlements.

CoE and EPO

The CoE, the EPO and most other IO follow the concept of the UN, not to insert explicit provisions in the SR for extending the entitlement for family benefits to staff members in other unions of partnership, but to achieve the same result by way of interpretation of the SR. This concept presupposes of course that the SR do not contain a definition of the terms "couple" or "marriage" in the sense of a traditional marriage.

**Jurisprudence**

ILOAT Judgments

Judgment 3203 of 4 July 2013

In this Judgment the complainant pursues the explicit recognition of his same-sex partnership (Civil Solidarity Contract under French law) by the ITU. In earlier proceedings resulting in Judgment 2643, the SG of the ITU stated that he was barred by the explicit definition of "spouse" as denoting "husband and wife" from giving the term "spouse" a broader interpretation so as to include registered same-sex partnerships (see also Judgment 2826). In consequence of the earlier Judgment in this matter, the SG referred the issue of domestic partnerships to the ITU Council for decision. There was, however, no consensus in this body on the recognition on same-sex partnerships and it was decided not to consider the matter further. The tribunal acknowledged that the Council was free to make such a decision and it has no authority to compel it to modify the SR (see Judgment 1118 para. 10).

Judgment 2860 of 8 July 2009

In this Judgment the tribunal deviated from its ruling in Judgment 2193 of 3 February 2003 and decided that a same-sex partnership based on the Civil Solidarity Contract (PACS) under French law must be assimilated to a marriage. The term "spouse" in the FAO-SR has to be interpreted as to include partners under a "PACS" or a similar form of registered partnership. The new "PACS" concept which was developed after profound amendments to French law was confirmed by the permanent representative of France to the FAO Judgment 2193 pre-dated these changes in the French law.

Judgment 2760 of 9 July 2008

Under the law of Canada persons are permitted to marry a person of the same sex and the Federal Civil Marriage Act confers them the full status of a marriage of opposite sex. Since the IAEA-SR do not contain a definition of the term "spouse", the tribunal interpreted this term as to include the marriage between two persons of the same-sex. The staff member was therefore entitled to claim the dependent spouse benefits as well as any other benefits linked to his status as a married person.

Judgment 2590 of 7 February 2007

The complainant, a staff member of the FAO, was married under the same-sex marriage law of the Netherlands. The Council of the FAO, while recognising the principle that the personal status of a staff member for the purpose of FAO's entitlements is determined by reference to the law of the nationality of the staff member concerned, decided to examine the issue of same-sex partnerships further.

Since the SR did not contain any definition of the term "spouse" the tribunal did not wait for the outcome of these deliberations but ordered that the term should be interpreted as including the spouse of a same-sex marriage under Dutch law.

Judgment 2550 of 12 July 2006

In this judgment directed against the ILO, the tribunal confirmed its considerations in Judgment 2549 of the same day as to same-sex partnerships under German law. In doing so it referred to the ruling of the German Federal Constitutional Court of 17 July 2002 (see NJW 2002, 2543 et seq.) which declared that same-sex life partnerships were a status equal to that of a traditional marriage. This reasoning was confirmed by a testimony of the German Counsel General in Geneva, and a decision by the German Federal Labour Court: life partnership is "a new *sui generis* marital status". The tribunal, therefore, considered that the term "spouse" in the SR included life partnerships under German law.

Judgment 2549 of 12 July 2006

In this judgment directed against the ILO, the tribunal noted that the ILO unlike the UN (see UNSG's bulletin ST/SGB2004/4) had not adopted an administrative provision (see bulletin of 1 February 2004 issued by the SG of the UN) for the assimilation of a registered partnership to a traditional marriage and that the involvement of the ICSC and the UNJSPF to address the issue of recognition of domestic partners had not yet been settled. Since, however, a statement by the Danish Ministry of Justice had indicated that a registered partnership had the same legal effect as the contracting of a marriage subject only to some minor exceptions (e.g. concerning adoption), the tribunal considered the term "spouse" in the SR to include registered partners under Danish law.

Judgments 2444 and 2443 of 6 July 2005

The EPO had initially rejected the request of the applicants for an assimilation of same-sex marriage under Dutch law to a traditional marriage under the EPO-SR due to lack of a legal basis.

The administration of the EPO found itself bound (in accordance with the legal opinion of the CJEU, see above) to a traditional concept of marriage, based on the SR which were effective as of 1977. During the proceedings before the tribunal (the internal appeals procedure had not been completed after two years and the tribunal therefore considered the direct filing of a complaint to the tribunal as receivable), the Council of the EPO interpreted the term marriage in the EPO-SR as to include same-sex unions if they were formally recognised according to the law of the staff member's nationality.

CJEU Judgment

In Judgment T-58/08 P of 5 October 2009, the court held that the term "unmarried partner of an official" used in Art. 72(1) EU-SR which provides for the sickness insurance coverage referred solely to the first three conditions laid down in Annex VII Art. 1(2)(c) EU-SR and not to the first sentence, which referred to a "registered" non-marital partnership. The word "registered" referred solely to certain formal aspects set out in the first condition laid down in Annex VII Art. 1(2)(c) EU-SR. The concept of a "non-marital partnership" does not need to be comparable to a marriage. The partnership needs neither be regulated by law nor subject to a specific registration requirement; it merely implies a union between two persons and the presentation of a document recognised by a member state, acknowledging their status as a non-marital partner. The EU-SR do not even require verification as to whether the consequences of the partnership concluded by the official concerned are similar in numerous respects to those of a marriage (but see the appealed Judgment F-122/06). The "cohabitation agreement" under Dutch law which, in contrast to a traditional marriage and a "registered partnership", has no consequence laid down by law, nevertheless meets the requirements under Art. 72(1) and Annex VII Art. 1(2)(c) EU-SR due to the term used in the agreement. (For Judgments C-122/99 P and C-125/99 P of 31 May 2001 relating to the repealed version of the EU-SR, see above).

Conclusions

Thanks to the above-mentioned judicature of the international administrative tribunals the legal issues of same-sex marriages and other same-sex or opposite-sex unions in the field of the law of the international civil service have been clarified to a large extent. Since IO have no legislative power in the field of family law, the different forms of unions between persons have to be established by national law. If the national authorities confirm that the rights and obligations deriving from such unions are similar with those under a traditional marriage, equal treatment under the law of the international civil service is required. The interpretation of the respective provisions of the EU-SR by the CJEU (General Court) (see Judgment T-58/08 P, dealt with above) goes even further and does not demand that the rights and obligations of such unions be similar to those of a traditional marriage.

It can be stated that most IO will not have to adapt their SR to this social evolution of human partnerships in their member states. In most cases, the desired results may be inferred by mere interpretation or by administrative decisions. Legal uncertainty may, however, arise in some specific areas, for example the participation in the internal health insurance cover or the entitlement to a survivor's pension. For this reason, it is preferable that an explicit ruling be introduced in the SR.

The EU-SR may serve as the best example among IO of explicit provisions that under certain conditions non-marital partnerships are to be treated as marriage (see Art. 1d(1); Art. 72(1) and Annex VII Art. 1(2)(c) EU-SR).

*bb) The expatriation allowance*

Under their SR, IO are bound to recruit staff on the broadest possible geographical basis from among nationals of member countries. Staff members must also be willing to be transferred to offices of the organisation in a country other than that in which they are serving. Similarly, to accredited staff of diplomatic missions, staff of IO are granted an expatriation allowance (non-residence allowance, "margin") in order to compensate for certain burdens and disadvantages suffered by staff members who are obliged because of their work to leave their country of origin and settle abroad. The conditions and amounts of the allowances differ significantly across the SR of IO.

It is of course natural that the allowance is not granted if the staff member concerned already has links with the country of his duty station prior to his expatriation and therefore suffers fewer disadvantages. Circumstances arising from work done for another State or for another IO are not be taken into account for this purpose. At some IO there is a yearly decrease in the allowance.

(1) EU

The EU grants its civil servants an expatriation allowance (Art. 69 EU-SR and Annex VII Art. 4(1)(a)) equal to 16% of the total of the basic salary plus household allowance and dependent child allowance, of at least a basic amount of EUR 505,39 (Art. 69 EU-SR). An expatriation allowance is paid to staff members who are not and have never been nationals of the state of employment, and, for a period of five years (which ends six months prior to recruitment in order to prevent that by a short-term change of residence before entering the service an entitlement may arise) did not habitually reside or carry on their main occupation within the European territory of that state. Activities for another state or an IO are not taken into account. A reduced allowance (foreign residence allowance, equal to one quarter of the expatriation allowance) is paid to those foreign nationals who do not fulfil the other criteria for the payment of an expatriation allowance (Annex VII Art. 4(2) EU-SR).

Officials who are or have been nationals of the state in whose territory they are serving but who for a period of at least ten years prior to the date of entering the service had their habitual residence outside the European territory of that state for reasons other than the performance of duties of the state concerned or an IO are also granted an expatriation allowance (Annex VII Art. 4(1)(b) EU-SR).

(2) UN

At the UN, the basic idea of the expatriation allowance is already taken into account when determining the salary for the staff in the professional and higher categories. In conformity with the Noblemaire principle (the so-called "margin", see the ICSC booklet on "Salaries and Allowances", 2014, Section I.C. and the annual reports of the ICSC on the internet portal). UN-CS staff in the general service category is entitled to an expatriation allowance (non-resident's allowance) at some duty stations (see the ICSC internet portal, "Decisions and Recommendations", Compendium, Section 3.50).

(3) CoE

The CoE grants an expatriation allowance under substantially similar conditions to those at the EU (Appendix IV Art. 6, Art. 6bis, 6ter CoE-SR). When any point on the frontier of the country of which the staff member is a national is at a distance of less than 50 km from the place of employment, the expatriation allowance is only granted under certain conditions. The allowance equals 16% of the basic salary and 20% if there is entitlement to household allowance. Staff recruited on or after 1 January 1996 or 2012 are subject to stricter conditions for entitlement to the allowances. In addition, the rate of the allowance is gradually reduced over time (Appendix IV Art. 6bis, Art. 6ter CoE-SR).

(4) EPO

The EPO conditions for eligibility to the expatriation allowance are essentially comparable to those of the EU (Art. 72 EPO-SR). However, the entitlement of a staff member who is not a national of the country of employment to the allowance is already lost with a prior three-year permanent residence in the country. The period does, however, not end six months prior to recruitment, as in the case of the EU-SR (the omission of this restriction has given rise to some disputes, see the case law below). The amount of the expatriation allowance is 16% of the basic salary and, for staff with entitlement to the household allowance, 20% of the basic salary.

**Jurisprudence**

ILOAT judgments

2893: No entitlement to the expatriation allowance if the staff member has worked for an IO before recruitment as an employee of a private company and therefore had his main occupation within the state of employment; 2866: The onus of proof is on the complainant to adduce cogent evidence for permanent or continuous residence abroad; 2865: Change of residence between accepting the job and starting to work does not confer entitlement to expatriation allowance; 2864: Entitlement to expatriation allowance in the case of a change of nationality with retroactive effect before the date of taking up duties; 2653: It cannot be inferred from the circumstances that the complainant intended permanently to leave the country where he should start to work, and to settle in another country for some length of time; 2611: Condition of permanent residence in the ten years preceding appointment in another country is not met if the complainant hired and worked, albeit for short periods, in the country of the duty station; 2597 (2596, 1864, 1150, 1099): Change of residence to another country at the date of receipt of the offer of employment at the IO does not interrupt the long-term residence in the state of the IO; 2214: The purpose of the expatriation allowance is to provide compensation for the lack of affinity with the country of employment and certain disadvantages due to the establishment of a new residence. The term "permanent or continuous residence" in Art. 72(1)(b) EPO SR means that the official has objective and factual links with the country of employment. It is of no relevance whether he paid taxes there or retained a home address at his former place of residence; the legal status of the permanent residence is also irrelevant; 1886: The complainant was offered, after several temporary contracts, a permanent contract with a reduced expatriation allowance. The tribunal dismissed the appeal because there was no acquired right to the amount and the conditions of payment of the allowance, only outright abolition would violate that right; 1864: The provisions of Art. 72(1) EPO-SR according to which there is entitlement to the expatriation allowance only if in addition to a foreign nationality, the staff member did not have in the host country residence for the last three years prior to his appointment, does not exceed the limits of legislative discretion; 1150: The expatriation allowance is paid to staff who have no affinity with the host country. For such a factual link, only simple residence is required, a low income or another residence abroad are irrelevant in this respect; 1099: According to Art. 72(1)(b) EPO-SR the previous activity in the country of employment does not remove eligibility to expatriation allowance if the official was in the service of his home country's administration. This requires a contract of service which made him an employee of that country; 927: The temporary separation of a spouse under French law does not change the marital status and therefore has no impact on the entitlement to the expatriation allowance; 926: According to Art. 72(3) EPO-SR, there is also an entitlement to the expatriation allowance for nationals of the country of employment if the staff member had continuously resided in another country for at least ten years before entering the service. An interruption of this period by nine months excludes the claim since it restored the affinity with the home country; 371: The total abolition of the expatriation allowance would infringe an acquired right, but amendment to the amount and conditions of payment would not (366); 51: A retroactive reduction of the expatriation allowance cannot be set off against a retroactive increase in salary, as the two payments serve different purposes.

CJEU Judgments/Orders

F-33/09: An official loses the entitlement to the expatriation allowance only if he has habitually resided or carried on his main occupation within the state of employment for the total period referred to in Annex VII Art. 4(1)(a) EU-SR (188–83, C-452/93, T-205/02, C-7/06 P); F-12/08: An episodic and brief absence from the country to which the official is posted, at the beginning of the reference period preceding his entry into service cannot be regarded as terminating his habitual residence in the country; F-6/08: Professional activity and personal relations are the decisive criteria for residence. If the only reasons to stay in a country are to complete university studies or practical training, a change of residence cannot be presumed; T-390/07: the official's "place of origin" is a technical term and is not to be confused with the term "habitual residence". A change of the "place of origin" after recruitment has no effect on the entitlement to the expatriation allowance. The object of granting an expatriation allowance is to compensate the official for the extra expenses and the inconvenience of taking up employment and thereby being obliged to change the place of habitual residence (201/88, T-123/89); F-129/06: Habitual residence corresponds to the place where the official had established the permanent or habitual centre of interest with the intention for it to be of lasting character. For the purpose of determining habitual residence all the factual circumstances which constitute such residence must be taken into account. Important indications are the place where the person carried out his occupation, where he paid national insurance contributions and taxes on earnings and where he owes any property (T-368/03, T-299/02, T-205/02, C-452/93 P, T-90/92); C-424/05 P: "Work done for another state" in the meaning of Annex VII Art. 4(1)(a) EU-SR includes work done within a permanent representation of a state; F-7/06: Refusal of the expatriation allowance in the case of double nationality; F-120/05: Employment in a private company that acts on behalf of the EU is not a period that is disregarded for the eligibility to the expatriation allowance in term of Annex VII Art. 4(1)(a) EU-SR (T-43/93); T-473/04: Employment as assistant of the European Parliament is to be disregarded for the eligibility to the expatriation allowance; T-379/04: The term "member state" in Annex VII Art. 4(1)(a) EU-SR refers only to government authorities and does not include governments of regions or autonomous communities (T-342/04, T-190/03, T-299/02); T-324/04: The mere maintenance of a sickness insurance and the fiscal residence at the place of origin are formal aspects and not sufficient to establish a permanent centre of interests at this place; T-259/04: To reside for a limited period at the place of employment for the execution of a working contract of a limited duration does not correspond to a habitual residence; T-72/04: Work done for another state or an IO within the meaning of Annex VII Art. 4(1)(a) EU-SR requires a legal relationship to this state or organisation, work done for a permanent representation to the EU is sufficient (T-283/03, T – 83/03); T-190/03. The activity for another state or for an IO according to Annex VII Art. 4(1)(a) EU-SR must be a main occupation; T-99/03: Definition of the term "international organisation" in Annex VIII Art. 4(1)(a) EU-SR; T-251/02: The distinction in Annex VII Art. 4(1)(a) EU-SR between the work done for an IO and a private employer is justified by the fact that while serving in an IO the official cannot be deemed to have established a lasting tie with the country in which he is employed; T-127/00: Working for a subcontractor of an IO is not work done for an IO in the meaning of Annex VII Art. 4(1)(a) EU-SR; T-60/00: In the case of work done for an IO preceding the EU employment, the calculation of the five years period preceding the work for the IO includes the six months period stipulated in Annex VII Art. 4(1)(a) EU-SR (201–88); T-18/91: The fact that a future staff member resided as a student outside the member state where he is employed does not preclude him from receiving the expatriation allowance even if he maintained regular contacts with his parents, made occasional visits and took part in practical training periods during university vacation in that state; T-123/89: No legitimate expectation if a promise does not take account of the provisions of the SR, no vested rights if different criteria were applied to the concept of "international organisation" in the meaning of Annex VII Art. 4(1)(a) EU-SR; 201–88: The fact that an official was in the country of employment merely as a student is not sufficient to preclude his having habitually resided there; 211–87: No right to the expatriation allowance if the official already had lasting ties with the country of employment (habitual residence, main occupation) prior to the period in which he was doing work for another state within that country; 330–85: The official, a national of his country of employment, did not break his social and professional ties with this country for the required period of ten years; 246–83: The general principle of equal treatment between men and women does not require differing interpretations of the precondition for the granting of the expatriation allowance in order to offset any domestic or social expenses or obligations; 185/80: The performance of compulsory military service is not a valid reason for interrupting the ten year period of habitual residence; 147–79: It does not violate the principle of equality to make the entitlement to the foreign residence allowance depend on the single criterion of nationality; 21–74; the concept of "nationals" contained in Annex VII Art. 4(1)(a) EU-SR must be interpreted in line with the principle of equal treatment between male and female officials. Nationality imposed by law on a female official upon her marriage with a national of another state and which she was unable to renounce, is therefore not to be taken into account.

*cc) Rent allowance (rental subsidy)*

Some IO provide for the granting of a rent allowance for employees of the lower and middle grades. The purpose of this allowance is to enable this group of staff to acquire an appropriate residence at the duty station at a level of rent, which does not exceed a certain percentage of the salary (see, for example, Art. 74 EPO-SR). At the UN, a supplement to the post adjustment is paid ("rental subsidy" if the rent is substantially higher than the average rental costs (Rule 3(7)(d) UN-SR). The entitlement depends on the production of evidence (see ILOAT Judgments 2475, 2470, 2038, 1783, 1458). At the EU, a temporary accommodation allowance may be paid to officials serving in a third country in accordance within the provisions of Annex X EU-SR. At the CoE, the provision for a rent allowance, Appendix IV Art. 11 CoE-SR, was deleted in 2011.

*dd) Service allowances*

In addition to the allowances predominantly justified by family or personal reasons, there are a number of allowances and compensation payments granted by IO for service reasons. These include in particular, the language allowance, compensation for overtime, night work, shift work, on-call duty, work on Sundays and public holidays, compensation for temporarily performing the duties of a post in a higher grade, the termination indemnity and the compensatory allowances or the basis of the protection of confidence. The post adjustment at the UN-CS (which guarantees that at all duty stations the net remuneration has a purchasing power equivalent to that at the base of the system, New York) is dealt with in connection with the base/floor salary (see above). (Unemployment benefits are dealt with under the social system (see below)).

(1) Language allowance

In a number of IO, a language allowance is granted for language skills of staff in the lower and middle grades. In the general service of the UN the allowance is granted for skills which go beyond the requirements in the job description. The knowledge of the languages must be proven (Rule 3(8) UN-SR; Art. 75 EPO-SR).

The language allowance does usually not form part of the basic salary, but it is in most organisations part of the total net remuneration, which is decisive at the promotion to a higher grade (for example Art. 49(5) and 64(2) EPO-SR).

(2) Overtime compensation/remuneration

International employees even if they are not permanent employees like at the EU and the EPO, are at the disposal of the organisation usually at all times. Entitlement to compensation for overtime does therefore generally not exist for the higher career categories (EU: Art. 56(2) EU-SR: function groups AD and AST 5–11; UN: Rule 3.11 UN-SR: professional and higher categories), but in the case of substantial or recurrent periods of overtime, compensatory time off may be granted; CoE: Appendix IV Art. 10 CoE-SR: categories B4 and above, grades A, L and above; EPO: Art. 57(2) EPO-SR: grade 7 and above). Time taken to the place of work or to make an official journey is generally not considered overtime (see, for example, Appendix VIII Art. 10(1) CoE-SR).

(3) Compensation for night work, shift and on-call duty, work on Sundays, Saturdays and public holidays

For extra duties performed by staff in the lower and middle career groups compensatory time off or additional remuneration is granted:

Examples:

- Art. 56a EU-SR: shift work,
- Art. 56b EU-SR; stand-by duty (on-call duty),
- Art. 56c EU-SR: compensation for particularly arduous working conditions,
- Rule 3(12) UN-SR: night duty (night differential),
- Art. 56 EU-SR: work on Sundays and public holidays.

(4) Compensation for temporarily performing duties of a post in a higher grade

A higher salary or an allowance is granted for temporarily performing the duties of another post in a higher grade or additional duties (EU: Art. 7(2) EU-SR: differential allowance; UN: Rule 3(10) EU-SR: special post allowance; CoE: Appendix IV Art. 13 CoE-SR: extra duty allowance; EPO: Art. 12 EPO-SR: a higher basic salary or a functional allowance).

In practice, these are cases where the duties of a post need to be performed by another person because of extended sick leave or leave on personal grounds, parental leave or family leave of an official. According to ILOAT Judgment 2563, the temporary occupation of a post in a higher grade at the EPO was not permitted if the post had not been occupied before by another staff member. ("One cannot be called upon to do duties of another person if that person does not occupy any post to which those duties are attached.").

The special post allowance is meant to reward a staff member financially for carrying out the duties of a higher-level post, and the payment of the allowance cannot be equated with a positive assessment of the service provided (ILOAT Judgment 2356). The special post allowance payable before a post was abolished remains the yardstick for measuring the value of the work. If the official continues to perform those duties, he is entitled to the special post allowance based on the principle of equality (equal pay for work of equal value, ILOAT Judgment 2314). The compensatory allowance is of a temporary nature and there is no longer a legal basis for it if the staff member is assigned the duties of the higher grade because of promotion. The general rules governing promotion (no lower remuneration than before promotion) must, however, be observed (ILOAT Judgment 460).

(5) Early termination indemnity

In some IO there is an entitlement to some compensation for early termination of an employment.

Under the EU-SR, there is entitlement to a monthly allowance for officials assigned to non-active status (becoming supernumerary by reason of reduction in the number of posts, Art. 41 EU-SR) or in the event of retirement in the interests of the service (Art. 50 EU-SR). An allowance decreasing from 85% to 60% of the basic salary is paid for a period determined by multiplying the length of service by a percentage of the official's age (see Annex IV EU-SR). Similar rules apply to the "reserve status" for officials of the EPO (see Art. 46 EPO-SR).

At the UN, there is entitlement to a "termination indemnity" (Rule 9(8) and Annex III UN-SR). "The purpose of the payment is to compensate the staff member for the loss of expectation of employment" (ICSC Report for 2009, doc. A/64/30 para. 40(a)). The ICSC examined the harmonisation of this indemnity among the organisations of the UN-CS (ICSC Report from 2015, doc. A/70/30 para. 194).

At the CoE, an "indemnity for loss of job" is paid if the service of a staff member has been terminated for special reasons (e.g. suppression of the post, refusal of a staff member to be transferred permanently to the duty station in another country, Art. 44 and Appendix VI CoE-SR).

All these entitlements or compensations find their justification in the early termination of a legal position of a staff member originally acquired for a longer period, or even up to retirement. In contrast to these "compensatory entitlements" the "unemployment benefits" are not a compensation but a form of social insurance cover (see below). Nevertheless, the differences are not always clear-cut (see also the ILOAT Judgment 2842 (ESO), 2587 (Red Cross and Red Crescent), 2380 (CERN).

(6) Compensation for protection of confidence (compensatory allowance)

In addition to the entitlement to service allowances and compensations explicitly defined in the service regulations, an entitlement to a compensatory allowance may be also derived from the general legal principle of protection of confidence (acquired right). This is the case, for example, if there is a change of the service regulations in connection with the integration of one IO into another (see, for example, the integration of the International Patent Institute into the EPO, see ILOAT Judgments 441, 372, 371, 368; see also the following case law).

**Jurisprudence**

ILOAT Judgments

2314: The entitlement to allowance for temporarily carrying out duties of a higher-level post remains despite the abolition of the post, if the higher-value services are continuously provided (principle of equality); 1677: Unlawful extension of the conditions for granting the compensatory allowance for carrying out duties of a higher-level post; 1334: Changes in the allowance for on-call duty are not covered by the general principle of acquired rights, no application of the Fleming Principle. The decision may, however, be set aside for the infringement of other general principles of administrative law; 1107: Binding promise of a compensatory payment for loss of shift-work; 897: By virtue of the guarantee of the net salary on promotion the compensatory allowance must also take into account the possible loss of a language allowance (737); 460: No acquired right to the continued payment of a duty allowance over and above the salary increase on promotion but remuneration after promotion may not be lower than before; 371: Granting of a compensatory allowance on the basis of the protection of confidence (integration of the International Patent Institute into the EPO; 265: No violation of an acquired right if a temporary lump-sum bonus is lost due to reorganisation.

CJEU Judgments/Orders

T-325/00: Unemployment benefits for temporary staff of the EU. The purpose of the unemployment benefit is financial support, in case of the staff member becoming unemployed when his service has been terminated. The benefit is not due if the service was terminated by resignation or by cancellation of the contract for disciplinary reasons (Art. 28a EU-CEOS) or if the staff member rejects a contract extension to a post with identical working conditions; 198 to 202/81: No right to a temporary posting allowance since the official was not performing higher ranking duties.

*ee) Reimbursement of expenses*

Staff members are entitled in many cases to the reimbursement of expenses in a lump-sum settlement or against itemisation. Most common are the following reimbursements: travel expenses and daily subsistence allowances for official travel and relocation costs related to recruitment, expenses for transfers and termination of service, expenses for travel to place of origin (home) and expense allowances. Some IO also grant an installation allowance and an allowance for returning home.

(1) Expenses for official journey

For official journeys, the travel expenses include: transportation expenses, daily subsistence allowance and miscellaneous expenses (see, for example Rule 7(5) to 7(8) and 7(10) to 7(11) UN-SR). The transportation expenses are usually reimbursed for the most economic means of transport in accordance with detailed rules. The miscellaneous expenses include necessary additional expenses, such as communication expenses for official purpose, costs for space, equipment and services required for official use, etc. In many cases there are special arrangements for the use of private cars for an official journey and the reimbursement of taxi costs. The daily subsistence allowance is paid as a lump-sum *per diem* according to different rates for each country (see, for example, Annex VII Art. 13 EU-SR and Art. 78 EPO-SR) or up to a maximum ("hotel ceiling") on production of supporting documents. There are frequently also arrangements for missions of long duration and additional reimbursements for particularly high accommodation costs, and arrangements with airlines and the obligation to book the travel via the travel agency of the organisation.

(2) Removal costs and travel expenses related to recruitment, transfer and termination of service

On recruitment, transfer and termination of service removal costs and travel expenses are reimbursed (EU: Annex VII Art. 9 EU-SR: removal expenses; Annex VII Art. 7 EU-SR: travel expenses; UN: Rule 7(15) and (16) UN-SR: removal costs; Rule 7(1) UN-SR: travel expenses; CoE: Art. 42(1)(b) CoE-SR and Rule No. 1212 of 30 November 2005 on the reimbursement of travel expenses, subsistence allowance and removal expenses; Art. 80 EPO-SR: recruitment, transfer, termination of service; Art. 81 EPO-SR: lump sum compensation for removal expenses). In some IO, there is additionally an entitlement to a daily subsistence allowance if change in the place of residence is required in order to comply with the residence obligations (see, for example, Annex VII Art. 10 EU-SR).

(3) Travel expenses to the place of origin

Staff is frequently entitled at certain intervals (yearly or every two years), to the reimbursement of travel expenses to visit the place of origin (to the underlying general legal principle, see above) in order to maintain the family, social and cultural ties (see, for example, Annex VII Art. 8(1) EU-SR). The expenses are reimbursed as a flat rate or according to the regulations for missions. There are disputes relating to a change in the place of origin subsequent to taking up duties (see, for example, ILOAT Judgments 1324, 854, see below).

(4) Residence allowance and accommodation expenses

In many IO, representation and (partly) accommodation expenses are reimbursed to senior management staff (President, Secretaries General, EU-Commissioner etc.; see, for example, Art. 71 and Annex VII Art. 14 and 15 EU-SR). The residence allowance of a member of the Commission amounts to 15% of the basic salary (EUR 20,667) and the representation allowance to EUR 607 per month (EU doc. Ares (2013) 698607 of 15 April 2013).

(5) Installation allowance, resettlement allowance

In the international civil service systems, the following allowances are usually granted on taking up appointment, on transfer and on leaving the service:

EU: Annex VII Art. 5 and 6: installation allowance, resettlement allowance; UN: Rule 7(14): settling-in grant; CoE: Appendix IV Art. 8: installation allowance; EPO: Art. 73: installation allowance.

(6) Other expenses

In most IO, there are specific rules for granting an allowance if an official incurs expenses by reason of his duties (see, for example, Art. 71 and Annex VII Art. 14, 15 EU-SR). (For reimbursement of costs incurred in the course of appeal proceedings against the organisation, see below.)

**Jurisprudence**

Official journey expenses – ILOAT Judgments

2129: The adjustment system for salaries is not entirely applicable to the determination of allowances granted for specific purposes, such as that covering expenses incurred by officials on travel status; 1977: Declaring the costs of a flight in business class, despite the use of economy class, fraud, dismissal.

Official journey expenses – CJEU Judgments/Orders

T-22/01: Administrative competence to grant a specific reimbursement in travel costs; T-28/98: The place of origin and the place of recruitment are not necessarily identical; T-71/89: Lump-sum reimbursement for short journeys within the area of employment without production of supporting documents.

Removal expenses, daily subsistence allowance – ILOAT Judgments

3429: Right of the organisation to set a reasonable maximum amount for the reimbursement of the removal costs; 3086: The organisation did not become a party to the removal contract; 3074: The conditions for payment of removal expenses do not have the character of an acquired right; 1950: Reinstallation indemnity is contingent upon the complainant being entitled to claim reimbursement of removal expenses. This is not the case if the residence is maintained at the duty station; 1846: Reimbursement of removal costs is only for expenses actually incurred, dispute over the outstanding sum must be settled between official and removal firm prior to reimbursement; 1367: Misuse of authority in setting deadline for move; 1108: Waiver of subsistence allowance at recruitment by contractual agreement; 976: Reimbursement for luggage transportation during home leave; 933: Return of original documents regarding removal costs; 761: Entitlement to the return of removal documents for corrective purposes.

Removal expenses, daily subsistence allowance – CJEU Judgments/Orders

F-131/07: No entitlement to daily subsistence allowance after receiving part of the installation allowance; F-126/05: Change of residence after secondment, entitlement to subsistence allowance; T-473/04: Coexistence of a second residence for a certain period for the purpose of granting a subsistence allowance; T-180/02 and T-113/03: Daily subsistence allowance granted; T-104/00: An entitlement to the daily subsistence allowance due to the change in the place of residence exists only if special costs or inconveniences are proven; T-132/97: Daily subsistence allowance of officials on probation; 280/85: Reasons for entitlement to the daily subsistence allowance.

Travel expenses on recruitment, transfer and termination of service –
ILOAT Judgments

485: No entitlement to travel expenses incurred on initial appointment of locally recruited staff members (484, 483).

Travel expenses on recruitment, transfer and termination of service –
CJEU Judgments/Orders

F-126/05: No travel expenses on recruitment when taking up appointment since the official was already in the place of his future posting; T-28/98: The place of origin and the place of recruitment are not necessarily identical.

Expenses for travel to home country/place of origin – ILOAT Judgments

2389: The home country is not necessarily identical with the nationality of a staff member. In exceptional circumstances it may be another country provided that he maintained his normal residence there for a prolonged period preceding his appointment and that he continues to have close family or personal ties in that country; 1364: Criteria for the review of the original place or origin; 525: The place of home is not necessarily identical with the place of origin, it need not be the country of nationality of the staff member, nor does he have to live there, decisive is the place the staff member is most connected to (1324); 441: Reimbursement of travel expenses to the home country as an acquired right; 270: No reimbursement of travel expenses for family members who live in the place of origin.

Expenses for travel to home country/place of origin – CJEU Judgments/Orders

F-49/08: The need for the production of documents that the travel has taken place is inherent in the provision; F-43/05: Wide discretion to modify the technical rules for travel in accordance with higher rules of international law or community law, no specific motivation necessary; T-354/03: Sharing of costs for the annual travel to the place of origin for the children of divorced spouses in the case of disagreement between their parents; T-221/02: Calculation of the cheapest and shortest routing for the reimbursement of travel costs for the annual trip home; T-52/89: There is a general legal principle governing the European public service that it must be possible for an official to retain his personal links with the place where his principle interests are situated. Staff members and their family members, understood in the wider sense, should be able to maintain social and cultural ties to the place of origin; T-44/89: In order to determine the centre of an official's interest, which forms the basis for determine the place of origin, it is necessary to establish that the person retains a permanent link with a certain place having regard *inter alia* to the main family ties, heritable interests or essential civic interests both active and passive.

Installation allowance – ILOAT Judgments

3293: Conditions of payment of a higher amount of the installation allowance (length of service) are not fulfilled (3292); 1820: The additional installation allowance for the family members is only due if they are not already resident at the employee's new duty station; 1744: No reimbursement of removal expenses in the absence of proper vouchers in support of the claim; 363: Grant of an extended installation allowance.

Installation allowance – CJEU Judgments/Orders

F-2/15: Obligation to change residence (Art. 20 EU-SR) after diplomatic secondment recruitment by an EU institution; F-131/07: Installation allowance for temporary agents; F-126/05: A precondition for the right to the installation allowance is a change of the habitual residence which must be construed as referring to the centre of interests of the official concerned (T-132/95); T-195/03: The installation and the transfer of habitual residence are questions of fact; T-384/02: Definition of habitual residence, calculation of the annual period in Annex VII Art. 9(3) EU-SR; T-180/02 and T-113/03: Change of residence in the case of secondment; T-13/02: Installation allowance in case of change of place of employment, T-104/00: The second half of the installation allowance is due only if the change of the family's residence is a direct consequence of the residence requirement of the official; T-42/89: Calculation of the refund of the installation allowance if the official leaves the service less than two years after entering it.

Resettlement allowance, repatriation grant – ILOAT Judgments

3018: No resettlement allowance is due if the official was recruited by another IO in another country when his employment ended; 2828: No entitlement to the repatriation grant, if the employee does not prove his repatriation (2582); 2103: Deferment of the payment of the repatriation allowance until national court's decision on damage claim of the organisation.

Resettlement allowance, repatriation grant – CJEU Judgments/Orders

T-69/03: Actual transfer of habitual residence as a condition for the resettlement; 79/82: The resettlement allowance of two months' basic salary will not be granted if the official does not resettle together with his family.

(7) Extinctive prescription

A number of service regulations provide for a preclusion period (extinctive prescription) for the entitlement to allowances and reimbursements. The deadlines are usually between three months and one year (see, for example, Rule 3(17) UN-SR: "...Retroactivity of payments"; EPO: Art. 65(1)(e) and 76(3) EPO-SR: deadline of six months; see ILOAT Judgment 2411; for details and the legal position in the case of absence of an explicit provision in the SR, see under limitation periods for claims).

### *3. The remuneration adjustment systems*

#### a) The adjustment systems of the EU, the CO, the EPO, CERN and ESO

The job requirements and selection criteria for the recruitment of staff specified in the service regulations are directed to securing the services of staff of the highest standard of ability, efficiency and integrity and ensuring the broadest geographical basis from among nationals of the member countries. This aim can only be achieved by attractive salaries, allowances and pensions which comprise a continued adjustment methodology. All salary systems of the IO therefore provide, in one form or another, remuneration adjustment procedures (ILOAT Judgment 1420). In most SR or implementing rules a regular (usually annual) review of the level of remuneration is explicitly defined. The adjustment of remuneration comprises the salaries and allowances. (As for the adjustment of pensions see below.)

In order to avoid time-consuming negotiations with the staff associations and to ensure social peace in the international civil service systems of the EU, the CO, the EPO and other organisations of the mixed mode system, detailed adjustment procedures have been developed. As regards the EPO and other organisations of the mixed mode civil service system, they are even obliged to adopt adjustment procedures which are stable, foreseeable and clearly understood.

The annual adjustment procedures of the EU, the CO and most organisations of the mixed civil service system adhere to the principle of parallelism with the evolution of the weighted average purchasing power of the net remuneration of the national officials in the central government services of representative member countries. To this end, calculations are based on statistical data and the results are determined in accordance with arithmetical terms. The national salary evolution is deflated by local inflation in order to obtain the real increase in purchasing power. The local inflation is calculated by Eurostat using a "Harmonised Index of Consumer Prices" (HICP) based on the same basket of goods and services in each member state. The weighted average of percentage changes in the purchasing power is called the "specific indicator" (EU, EPO) or "reference index" (CO). The amount of the salary adjustment is obtained by multiplying the specific indicator/reference index with the changes of the cost of living (inflation) for Belgium (for the EU Luxembourg is included). For other countries, the salary adjustment is obtained by applying the respective "Purchasing Power Parity Coefficient" (PPPC) for the country in order to guarantee equalities of purchasing power of officials in all places of employment of an IO.

Intermediate updates of remuneration in the case of substantial changes in the cost of living are provided for in the EU-SR (Annex XI Art. 4) and the CO Rules on the Remuneration Adjustment Procedure (Art. 7) but not in the EPO-SR.

The EU adjustment procedure applies from 1 January 2014 to 31 December 2023 (Annex XI Art. 15 EU-SR) and may continue to apply provisionally beyond this date. The CO adjustment procedure is effective from 1 January 2017 to 31 December 2020 but may be prolonged in the absence of a proposal for amendment (see Annex I Art. 1 Rules on the Remuneration Adjustment of the co-ordinated organisations on the OECD website). The EPO adjustment procedure applies with effect from 1 July 2014 and will be revised in 6 years (Art. 10(1) and Art. 11(1) Implementing Rules to Art. 64(6) EPO-SR). The Council will, however, decide on the implementation of the Rules every year on the basis of an assessment of whether the prevailing circumstances allow the procedure to apply (Art. 11(1) Implementing Rules to Art. 64(6) EPO-SR). There may be some doubts as to the compatibility of this clause with the general legal principle of foreseeability and transparency of the remuneration adjustment procedure.

### b) Exceptions from the regular adjustment procedure

The EU, the CO and the EPO civil service systems contain express reservations to depart from the regular adjustment procedure if the increase in purchasing power of officials exceeds a certain margin if there is a serious economic crisis in the member states, or if the financial obligations of an organisation so require (affordability clause, moderation clause, exception clause). If the conditions are met the legislative body of the organisation may reduce or postpone the annual adjustment of remuneration.

#### *aa) The EU*

Up to 2013, the EU-SR contained a broad exception clause (Annex XI Art. 10) concerning the possibility of taking account of a "serious and sudden deterioration in the economic and social situation of the community" when determining the annual adjustment of salaries of the officials.

In November 2009, the EU Commission proposed the annual salary adjustment for July 2009 based on the regular adjustment procedure. In December 2009, the Council considered applying the exception clause and reducing the adjustment accordingly. In consequence of an action brought by the Commission against the proposal of the Council, the CJEU held in its Judgment C-40/10 (see also the Press Release No. 114/10) that the Council could have been aware of the economic crisis in member states and should have acted in accordance with the duty of loyal cooperation among EU institutions already in summer 2009 in order to allow the Commission based on its exclusive right to initiative, to forward a proposal to adjust the salaries based on the exception clause. The CJEU annulled the articles of the regulation that fixed the reduced amounts for the adjustment.

In 2011, the EU Commission was required to submit to the Council a new salary adjustment proposal based on the exception clause taking into account the serious and sudden deterioration in the economic and social situation identified by the Council. In this case, the action by the Commission to apply the regular adjustment procedure was dismissed (CJEU Judgment C-63/12, see also Judgments C-66/12 and C-196/12 and Press Release No. 148/13).

In 2013, the Council adopted a revised exception clause and inserted a new moderation clause in the SR (Annex XI Art. 10 et seq. EU-SR). Both clauses provide for a precise mathematical procedure based on official statistical information.

The moderation clause provides an upper and lower limit of the "specific indicator" (see above under a)) of ±2%. If the value of the "specific indicator" exceeds this limit, the value of the limit is used to calculate the update value. The remainder is applied for an adjustment as form 1 April of the following year.

The exception clause applies if there is a decrease in the Gross Domestic Product (GDP) in the member states of the Union.

If the value of the GDP in the Union is between -0.1% and -1%, only 33% of the value of the specific indicator is used to calculate the value of the update. The remainder of the update value is to be taken into account on 1 April of the following year (Art. 11(1) Implementing Rules, Annex XI EU-SR). If the GDP in the Union is between -1% and -3%, 100% of the value of the specific indicator is to be taken into account on 1 April of the following year. If the GDP is below -3% the applied specific indicator is 0%. The value of the specific indicator shall, however, form the basis of the calculation of a future update once the cumulative increase of the Union GDP becomes positive (Art. 11(4) Implementing Rules, Annex XI EU-SR).

*bb) The CO*

At the CO, the CCR recommended in its 211th Report (2011) that the Councils of the CO adopt exceptions to the regular adjustment if salaries are not financial affordable by the organisation if exceptional or unforeseen circumstances so warrant (affordability clause) or if the purchasing power increase falls outside a predetermined range (moderation clause). This Report had to be adopted by each Council of the CO (see, for example, Annex I OECD-SR and Annex II NATO-SR).

Appendix 2 Art. 1(4) Rules of the Remuneration Adjustment Procedure of the CO contains a moderation clause which restricts the regular adjustment of remuneration of staff members. If the product of the "reference index" and the harmonised index local consumer price (HICP), corrected if necessary by the purchasing power parities coefficient (PPPC), falls outside a pre-determined "purchasing power reference curve" (this curve is obtained by enlarging the purchasing power parity by a margin of plus or minus 2% to the salary scale for Belgium, see Art. 4(5)(1) of the Rules), the adjustment is reduced accordingly.

In addition to the moderation clause, the rules provide for an affordability clause (Art. 8 of the Rules). If exceptional or unforeseen circumstances so warrant or if the organisation could not otherwise reasonably expect to meet its financial obligations the salary adjustment could be reduced to the national consumer price index or the adjustment could be awarded in part only or not at all.

There is some probability that this affordability clause would be inconsistent with the case law of the ILOAT as to the foreseeability and transparency of the adjustment procedure. It remains to be seen whether the administrative tribunals of the CO will follow this case law.

*cc) The EPO, CERN and ESO*

In 2014 the EPO adopted a new annual salary adjustment procedure (see doc. CA/80/14 accessible on the EPO website) with the inclusion of moderation and exception clauses similar to the EU (Art. 8 and 9 Implementing Rules to Art. 64 EPO-SR). Differences exist, however, as regards some details of the clauses.

The moderation clause limits any salary increase to ±2% of the HICP in any contracting state if the overall result of the adjustment procedure, i.e. the specific indicator multiplied by the HICP for Belgium and the PPPC relating to the country concerned would exceed this limit (Art. 8(1) Implementing Rules to Art. 64(6) EPO-SR). Any remainder of the adjustment is included in the adjustment of the following year (Art. 8(2) Implementing Rules to Art. 64(6) EPO-SR). If the adjustment would lead to a lower salary than that in force in the previous year an express nominal guarantee clause applies (Art. 8(3) Implementing Rules to Art. 64(6) EPO-SR).

The exception clause refers to the collective decrease of the GDP in all 38 member states of the EPO. It applies if the decrease is between 1% and 3%. In this case the adjustment is paid on 1 April of the following year. If the decrease is greater than 3% there is no adjustment, but the value shall form the basis of a future adjustment when the GDP becomes positive.

There are additional interpretative comments on the interaction of the moderation and exception clauses which are, however, not publicly accessible.

The CERN salary adjustment procedure is split into a yearly review procedure taking account, among other factors, of the cost of living in Geneva and the movement of the salaries of Swiss civil servants and a five years' review. This review follows the UN-CS (see below).

As to the salary adjustment system followed by the ESO, see ILOAT Judgment 3408.

### c) The adjustment system of the UN-CS

The salary adjustment procedure of the UN-CS differs significantly from the adjustment procedures of the EU, the CO and the EPO civil services. Since its founding in 1974 by the UNGA the ICSC is engaged in the preparation and coordination of working conditions of the IO of the UN-CS. One of the main tasks is to present proposals for the annual salary adjustment of staff to the General Assembly (see, for example, ILOAT Judgment 2420). In accordance with Art. 10(b) of its statute, the ICSC makes recommendations for the salary scales for staff in the Professional and higher categories to the UNGA and in accordance with Art. 12(1) of its statute recommendations for the salary scales for staff in the general service to the Administrative Committee on Co-ordination and for decision by the UN-SG (Annex I(6) UN-SR). Subsequently, these tables are taken over by the other IO connected to the UN-CS.

The salary method used by the ICSC is still largely based on principles from the time of the League of Nations. For professional and higher categories, the Noblemaire Principle applies, named after the chairman of a committee of experts of the League of Nations in 1921. For the general service category, the Fleming Principle applies whose name derives from the chairman of a committee of experts of the UN 1949.

The salary adjustment system of the UN-CS has meanwhile become very complex and can only be presented in outline here. A comprehensive and up-to-date description is available on the website of the ICSC under the heading "Compendium".

– Salary adjustment for the Professional and higher categories

The Noblemaire Principle (see in more detail above) is based on the recruitment principles in the UN-CS, according to which the officials are recruited on as wide geographical basis as possible (proportional representation of nationalities) and the paramount consideration is the necessity of securing the highest standards of efficiency, competence and integrity (Art. 101(3) UN Charter and Reg. 1(1)(d) UN-SR).

These recruitment principles require a salary structure that is attractive even for staff from the member states with the highest salary level in the national civil service.

The ICSC reviews regularly which national public service is used for reference purposes. So far, the federal civil service of the USA has been taken as the benchmark ("comparator civil service") for the application of the Noblemaire Principle, although it was repeatedly considered switching to the German, Swiss or Japanese civil services was considered on several occasions (ICSC Compendium, Section 2(1)(20)).

Periodic equivalent studies are made between each of the grades (P-1 to D-2) of the UN (New York) and the respective national grades in Washington D.C.. The net remuneration (base floor salary plus post adjustment) at New York is compared to the net remuneration at Washington D.C.. The comparison is expressed as an average ratio called "the margin". "The margin" in favour of UN staff remuneration is considered necessary in order to compensate for the different costs of living in the UN headquarters in New York and specific factors of the expatriate status of UN officials (it effectively represents an "integrated expatriation allowance", for more details see the ICSC Compendium, Section 2(1)(40)). "The margin" is 15% of the basic salary on average.

In addition to the base floor salary, a post adjustment is paid. It ensures that the staff dispose of a purchasing power of their salaries on the basis of New York at all locations. While New York is the reference city there is also a post adjustment element in the net remuneration in New York to compensate for cost of living increases (see the booklet "Common System of Salaries, Allowances and Benefits" and "The Post Adjustment System" on the ICSC internet portal). The post adjustment is updated continuously.

– Salary adjustment for the general service category

Starting from the basic premise that a majority of staff in the general service category will be locally recruited and will remain on that post throughout the professional career, there is no uniform salary table for all IO of the UN-CS (see their salary scales for staff in the general service and related categories at headquarters duty stations in Geneva, London, Madrid, Montreal, New York, Paris, Rome and Vienna on the ICSC internet portal).

According to the Fleming Principle (see above) the working conditions (not only the salaries as in the Noblemaire Principle) must be among the best at each duty station. For the adjustment of salaries, the working conditions at the duty station are either taken from reliable publicly available data or are supplemented by the IO's own investigations (see ICSC Compendium, Section 2(2)(10)). However, it is obvious that the salary adjustment method for the determination of the local best working conditions opens up a wide discretion, which often leads to litigation. This concerns questions such as which companies' employment conditions will be used for comparison or how the health care, the allowances and benefits are rated (see the case law).

**Case law of the ILOAT regarding the Noblemaire and Fleming Principles**

(see under general legal principle)

**The case law of the ILOAT and the CJEU on the salary adjustment systems in IO having regard to the principle of stability, foreseeability and a clear understanding of the results**

ILOAT Judgments

The jurisprudence of the ILOAT on salary adjustment procedures extends, beyond the IO of the UN-CS to numerous IO outside the three international civil service law systems, e.g. the EPO, EMBL, CERN and ESO. This jurisprudence is therefore of a considerable general importance for salary adjustment procedures of IO.

According to the tribunal's case law, all IO must adapt an objective methodology for adjusting salaries and pensions (Judgments 1821, 986). Otherwise, the

IO are at risk of violating the principle of acquired rights or the Noblemaire or Fleming Principle due to loss of purchasing power of salaries and pensions or through inflation. For the selection of an adjustment system, IO have, however, a very wide discretion (Judgments 1682, 1498, 1265, 1000).

Neither a periodic adjustment nor an indexing is required (Judgment 2533 para. 22). Each IO or system of the IO can develop its own methodology or resort to the adjustment procedure or the result of such a procedure in other IO, or to other external data (Judgment 1912, external data as a guideline). In accordance with the general principle of the international civil service law "*patere legem quam ipse fecisti*" (see above), an IO is bound by the chosen method (Judgment 1265) as long as it is valid. Afterwards the IO is again free to choose another methodology, system or standard of reference for determining salary adjustments (Judgment 2632) within the limits of the general principles governing the international civil service law (Judgment 1912).

(For more detail on the case law see above under the respective general legal principle).

CJEU Judgments/Orders

The jurisdiction of the CJEU on salary adjustment methodology is on a relatively small scale. The reason may be that the EU salary adjustment procedure has proven to be most effective and therefore rarely exposed to the scrutiny of the CJEU. (But see new Judgments C-40/10, C-63/12, C-66/12, referred to above under the respective general legal principle.)

In Judgment T-98/92 and T-99/92 the court found that the parallelism between the trend in the purchasing power of salaries of national officials and the EU officials included a possible loss. Such a procedure does not violate the principles of equality, welfare and good governance. The annual salary adjustment procedure does not require detailed technical aspects. In determining the salary adjustment, the bodies involved have a reasonable assessment period, depending on the circumstances in each individual case and the difficulty of the decision (Judgment T-16/89). The obligation to pay a salary adjustment arises only after the Council has adopted the amount of the adjustment. If the Council acts within a reasonable time, there is no right to default or compensatory interests (Judgments 174/83, T-16/89, C-136/92 P).

### *4. The social security*

#### a) General

The SR of IO cover a wide area of law that as a rule comprises the IO's own social security system, for its active and retired staff. An IO's own organisational power and its autonomy in personnel matters granted for the purpose of independence from the law of the contracting states and its role as a substitute state, does require exemption from the national social security system. The need for independence from national impact does, however, not rule out the possibility that an IO takes the sovereign decision not to offer a social security system of its own but makes reference to the municipal system of its host country (see, for example, the CoE medical and insurance scheme, CoE Rule No. 1331). For locally recruited staff serving in a third country this applies most frequently (see, for example, Art. 121 EU-CEOS; EPO auxiliary staff see EPO Codex). At the EPO, contract staff may opt for a national security scheme, see Art. 10(3) conditions of employment for contract staff).

Contracting states, in particular the host countries, have a significant interest in not having to bear the consequences of a missing or inadequate social protection for officials of IO. The PPI's of IO in practice exempt the staff members from compulsory contributions to the national social security schemes if they adhere to a social security scheme offered by the organisation (see, for example, Art. 14 EU-PPI: The "scheme of social security benefits" shall be laid down by European Parliament and the Council, CoE Res x(69)29 of 26 September 1969, §§ 175–182 stipulates this obligation in general terms for IO; Art. 18 EPO-PPI: " In the event of the Organisation establishing its own social security scheme, the Organisation and the employees … shall be exempt from compulsory contributions to national social security schemes …"). Occasionally, the exemption is only granted if a review of the organisation's social security scheme shows the equivalency to the national security scheme of the host state (Art. 18 ESO-PPI: "exempt … in the event that it establishes its own social security system providing adequate benefits …"); Art. 22 EMBL-PPI: "… with, in the opinion of the Federal Republic of Germany after consultation with the Laboratory, adequate social benefits.")

At the UN, the UN-CPI does not explicitly provide for an exemption of staff members from compulsory contributions to national social security systems. The UN did, however, successfully refer to Art. 5 Section 18(b) UN-CPI exempting the salaries and emoluments of staff members from national taxation in order to achieve exemption from compulsory contributions to national social security schemes (see Bandyopadhyay/Iwata, commentary, p. 342 § 81).

The social security system of IO covers a wide range of social protection, essentially insurances against health care expenses, incapacity, accidents, total and partial invalidity, maternity, birth and death. In addition, some IO also provide for long-term care insurance, protect their officials in the case of unemployment and grant loans and advances.

In the broad sense, the social security system also comprises the pensions (retirement pensions) as well as invalidity pensions and allowances (see below under point 4c)).

Social benefits which supplement the basic salaries and pension, such as family allowances etc., are dealt with in connection with the emoluments they complement (see above).

### b) The social security system in case of illness, maternity, birth, long-term care, unemployment and in case of hardship

#### *aa) Health care*

Today, the health insurance is part of the minimum standard of social security in IO (EU: Art. 72 et seq. EU-SR; UN: Reg. 6(2) UN-SR; CoE: Art. 43(1) CoE-SR; EPO: Art. 83 EPO-SR). The legal structure of the health insurance schemes varies even in the UN-CS and in the CO system since it does not fall under the unified employment standards for these systems. The health insurance schemes range from the organisation's own insurance scheme (EU, EPO: with effect from 1 January 2017, see EPO doc. CA/D 3/16 available on the EPO website) to the conclusion of insurance contracts with national insurance companies (CO, EPO until 31 December 2016) and even to the possibility for the staff to enrol in private health insurance schemes which are only subsidised by the organisation (UN). Apart from the UN, the health insurance of officials, spouses, children and other dependants is compulsory. Also in most organisations of the UN-CS staff are, however, "strongly urged" to enrol in a group health insurance scheme offered by the respective UN organisation (see, for example, UN doc. ST/IC 2016/13 §30). Nevertheless, the issue of health insurance is at present not considered as a "common system" matter of the UN-CS and therefore not a matter reviewed by the ICSC, which, however, is strongly recommended by the UN Joint Inspection Unit (see UN doc. JIU/REP/2007/2). The UN health insurance plans were established by the UN-SG on the basis of Reg. 6(2) UN-SR. UN staff members are free to enrol in one of the USA-based group insurance plans offered by the UN (Aetna, Empire Blue Cross, HIP health plan of New York) or in the worldwide plan offered for staff based outside the USA. For details see the UN doc. ST/IC 2017/10 Annex I (comparison chart).

Also the after-service health insurance for retired UN staff (ASHI) is optional (see the "Administrative Instructions" in UN doc. ST/AI/2007/3 and see below).

The UNJSPF has an emergency fund, which grants assistance to retired staff in cases of hardship in individual situations (for example, medical expenses, funeral expenses; for details see the UNJSPF internet portal under "Publications and Documents").

(1) Claims

If there is a mandatory health insurance scheme established by an IO and the organisations has concluded an insurance contract with a private insurer (like the EU), the organisation is ultimately liable if the insurance company refuses to reimburse medical expenses (like the EPO until 31 December 2016, see doc. CA/D 3/16 published on the EPO website). In such a case the official is advised to call for assistance from his organisation. The organisation may either enforce the claim (usually in an arbitration procedure) or may refuse the reimbursement. In the latter case the staff member may file an appeal against his employer. In the case of an optional health insurance scheme (see the UN health benefit plans above), the final decision in the reimbursement of medical costs rests with the insurance carrier and not with the UN (for more in detail see the United Nations Health and Life Insurance Section under: "How can I file a claim ?").

In addition to compulsory health insurance, the staff member may of course also conclude a private health insurance contract. In this case, he has to declare the amount of the reimbursement paid under this private cover (for example, Art. 72(4) EU-SR). As far as the working spouse of an official is covered by his own health insurance, he is generally urged to give priority to that.

(2)Premiums and contributions

In most IO, one third of the premium is charged to the official, for example, at the EU (in 2016) 1.7% (see on the EU website under Joint Sickness Insurance Scheme, JSIS), whereby limits sometimes apply (Art. 72(1) EU-SR: 2%). At the UN all plans are self-funded. The yearly premium is paid by the staff member and there is no fixed rate for the contribution by the employer, the organisation only "subsidises the remainder of the costs". For the USA-based plans, a "two thirds to one third" cost-sharing applies. For the worldwide plan a 50/50 cost-sharing applies. In various IO, officials do not contribute to the insurance cover or additional medical benefits in the event of occupational accidents at work or industrial diseases (see, for example, Appendix XII Art. 15 CoE-SR, see below).

For reasons of solidarity, often only one flat contribution rate is levied regardless of the marital status and number of children. In contrast, the health insurance plans for the UN staff have different contribution rates (effective 1 July 2015) for single officials (e.g. Aetna: 5.05%, Empire Blue Cross: 3.84%), staff with one child or spouse (e.g. Aetna: 8.83%, Empire Blue Cross: 6.80%) and staff with two or more family members (e.g. Aetna: 9.86%, Empire Blue Cross: 8.67%. For more details see UN doc. ST/IC/2015/10 Annex I.

At the CoE, the staff contributes one third of the insurance cover (Appendix XII Art. 15 CoE-SR). In 2016 the contributions were about 3% of the gross salary (see CoE doc. ADMIN/RH(2014)15E).

At the EPO, one third of the contributions is charged to the employee (Art. 83(1)(b) EPO-SR). The amount of the contributions is evaluated by actuaries (Art. 83(1)(d) EPO-SR) and is published in internal circulars which are not accessible via the EPO Codex. Any adjustment is, however, limited to 10% per year of the contribution rate in force (Art. 83(1)(e) EPO-SR).

The health insurance schemes of most IO also extend to retired staff, spouses and dependents. The insurance contribution calculated on the basis of the retirement pension corresponds to the rate for active staff. At the UN, the after-service health insurance is also voluntary (see below).

In some cases, the health insurance may lead to undesired results. For example, a working spouse with high income, who is therefore exempt from the mandatory national health scheme enjoys contribution-free coverage and may abstain from concluding a voluntary health insurance since he is insured under the family health insurance of the IO. These results can be avoided by levying of a higher premium like in the UN sickness schemes or an additional contribution in these cases (see the implementing rules to Art. 83 and 84 EPO-SR in the EPO Codex). Another questionable result is the level of the contribution rate for the sickness cover if the calculatory base for the premiums is the minimum retired pension, which senior staff may already receive after five years (10% of basic salary) and which can be drawn at the retirement age (for example, EU: 66 years of age), or even as an advanced (reduced) pension at an earlier age (for example, EU: 58 years of age).

(3) Benefits

Reimbursement in the event of illness will normally cover a large percentage of the medical costs (for example, at the EU: for pharmacy drug prescription: 80%, for hospital: 100%, see the Joint Sickness Insurance Scheme of the EU (JSIS) on the EU website and Art. 72 EPO-SR). For some benefits, maximum amounts per year are set (for example, for dental care, spectacle frames etc). For the medical benefits paid under the different UN health plans see the comparison chart in UN doc. ST/IC/2015/10 Annex II. For more in detail on the reimbursements granted at the EPO, see doc. CA/D 3/16 available on the EPO website. In some organisations, if the retained amount exceeds a certain percentage of the salary or the retirement pension, a special refund will be awarded (see, for example, Art. 22 EPO sickness insurance contract, cited in ILOAT Judgment 2843). In the event of occupational diseases and work accidents often 100% of medical expenses are often reimbursed (e.g. Art. 73(3) EU-SR, Appendix XII, Art. 14(4) CoE-SR, see also below).

The health insurance schemes in IO guarantee free choice of doctors and insurance cover worldwide.

In the case of a third party being responsible for the sickness or injury of the official, there is subrogation in favour of the organisation (see, for example, Art. 85a EU-SR and Art. 28 EPO-SR).

(4) Funding of the health insurance

The costs of the after-service health insurance under a pay-as-you-go system are increasingly projected by IO to accrue considerably, fuelled by demographic developments and increases in the rate of medical utilisation, and costs of medical treatment. Taking into account the relatively low calculatory basis of the retirement pensions, the IO are faced with increased budgetary requirements.

In his report (UN doc. A/70/590 of 4 December 2015) the UN-SG stated that there is a funding gap of the after-health insurance system of 13.5 billion USD. The current pure pay-as-you-go system of UN organisations is therefore unsustainable and there is a need for the adoption of a funding plan in respect of accrued liabilities.

The EPO established a funded system of its health insurance in 2010 as part of its Reserve Funds for Pensions and Social Security (see the EPO Codex).

*bb) Paid sick leave*

In the event of illness, staff members are entitled to sick leave with pay. If the employee is absent from service for more than a certain number of days for sickness reasons (for example, Art. 59(1) EU-SR: more than three days), he has to produce a medical certificate which has to be sent to his appointing authority within a deadline (for example, Art. 59(1) EU-SR: on the fifth day of absence at the latest). To prevent abuse, there is a maximum number of days for short-term sick leave without medical certificate within a certain time period (EU: Art. 59(2) EU-SR: twelve days within twelve months; UN: Rule 6(2)(c) UN-SR: seven days in an annual cycle).

After more than a certain period of sick leave in a certain time period, the organisation may involve an invalidity committee (EU: Art. 59(4) EU-SR: After more than twelve months' sick leave in any period of three years; UN: Rule 6(2)(b) UN-SR: different periods of months on full or half pay depending on the nature of the appointment and the duration of service). The medical panel (invalidity committee) gives proposals for further action (e.g. invalidity, part-time work, extension of sick leave).

The staff member is obliged to give his consent to a medical examination at any time during sick leave at the request of the appointing authority (Art. 59(1) EU-SR; Rule 6(2)(g) UN-SR).

Failure to observe the rules regarding the submission of medical certificates or in the event that the medical examination cannot take place for reasons attributable to the staff member, his absence is considered as unauthorised absence. As a result, the annual leave or salary can be reduced and disciplinary measures may be initiated (Art. 59(3) EU-SR; Rule 6(2)(d) UN-SR).

The CoE set up Rule No. 1331 of 24 March 2011 on the provisions applicable in the event of absence for reasons of health, maternity, paternity or adoption. The provisions provide for different periods of paid sick leave for permanent and temporary staff and for sick leave resulting from a work place accident or an industrial disease.

With effect from 1 April 2015, the EPO repealed its invalidity system and set up an incapacity system (Art. 62b EPO-SR). The new system forms part of the health insurance system of the EPO. It comprises four phases. In the case of sickness an official is placed on sick-leave with full pay up to a maximum of 125 working days, either in one unbroken period or in several periods within a rolling period of 18 consecutive months. If, at the expiry of that period, the staff member is still unable to perform his duties, he is placed on extended sick leave for a total of 250 days within a rolling period of 36 consecutive months. During the extended sick leave his basic salary is subject to a 10% reduction (Art. 62a EPO-SR). If, after the applicable maximum period of sick leave, a medical opinion confirms that he is partially or totally unable to perform his duties, the official receives 70% of his basic salary and of the allowances for the time he is discharged from his duties. The salary may, however, not be lower than 120% of the basic salary at grade G1 step 4. There are special provisions for, for example, the amount of contributions to be made to the social security system. If the official has been totally discharged from his duties for reason of incapacity (Art. 62b EPO-SR) for ten years and has reached the age of 55 years, the official is retired and receives a retirement pension for health reasons (Art. 13 EPO-PS). The amount of this pension is calculated in conformity with Art. 14 EPO-PS.

*cc) Long-term care insurance*

The long-term care (LTC) insurance represents a relatively young branch of the social security scheme of IO, therefore only sporadically provided for in the service regulations of IO. The WTO, CERN, ESO and the EPO (for the EPO see also ILOAT Judgments 2976, 2448, 2341) have shown leadership in this respect. In some IO without a proper LTC insurance there are at least provisions providing a subsidy (capital sum corresponding to a number of years' salary) if an invalid requires another person's assistance to perform the normal actions of everyday life (for example, Appendix XII Art. 12 CoE-SR). The LTC insurance for employees, spouses, children and other dependents aims at providing a fixed amount of financial support to defray some of the expenses occurred if the insured person is in need of assistance over an extended period of time due to an impairment of the ability to function independently in daily life. The LTC insurance does not cover the medical costs for illness, pregnancy or accident.

In line with national regulations (in particular the German and French LTC systems) the benefits of the LTC insurance normally cover three levels of care: low, moderate and high dependency care. The benefits lie in the range of about 40 to 90 EUR (2016) per day apart from special hardship cases (see Art. V EPO-LTC insurance in the EPO Codex). The funding of the compulsory LTC insurance for staff is generally split (1/3 staff, 2/3 organisation, see Art. II(4) and (6) EPO-LTC insurance; at the ESO 50/50 up to a maximum contribution from ESO of 0.25% of grade 7 step 13 basic salary). The LTC insurance may cover family members and other dependents on a compulsory or voluntary basis (see Art. I EPO-LTC insurance).

The management of the insurance is frequently transferred to a professional insurance broker to assure a more economic and experienced administration (see, for example, Art. III EPO-LTC insurance). The long-term budgeting of the insurance is sometimes dealt with by means of an internal fund of the organisation (see the EPO Reserve Funds for pensions and social security). During the initial phase a capital stock builds up since the amount of contributions exceeds the benefits paid by far.

Problems may arise in the area of the taxation of the benefits of the LTC insurance. Mostly those member states which do not have a national LTC insurance tend to view the benefits as income subject to national taxation, which contradicts the essence and purpose of the insurance (but see CJEU Judgment C-160/96: Even if long-term care benefits have their own characteristics they must be regarded as sickness benefits, see also under PPI above). Other states exempt the benefits from national taxation only for active staff, which appears to be a disastrously ill-conceived measure. Here IO have a duty of social care to provide for a uniform system of taxation, if needs be by compensation.

*dd) Protection against unemployment*

Some IO provide their contract staff with some kind of financial assistance even if their regular service has been terminated (for early termination benefits see above). The benefits paid under this heading should not be confused with the repayment ("severance grant") of accrued contributions to the pension scheme, if a pension is not due (see, for example, ILOAT Judgment 2613 (EPO)). This kind of assistance is of increasing importance, since IO are employing more and more staff on fixed-term contracts. These staff members are particularly vulnerable since they may not qualify for a national unemployment scheme after leaving the IO. For this reason, some member states of IO offer a special unemployment insurance for international staff after resignation (see, for example, in Germany on the internet portal of the Federal Foreign Office). Some IO offer access to the national unemployment insurance on a cost-sharing basis (for example staff of the IAEA in Austria may adhere to the Austrian unemployment insurance scheme). Even if it seems that up to now no international tribunal has recognised a general legal principle for the duty of the organisation to assists staff on limited contracts in the event of unemployment (see in this respect the ICSC Report for 2009, doc. A/64/30, §§ 42 to 60) it may be that member states will in future grant exemption of IO from mandatory national security schemes under the PPI's only if the IO includes unemployment cover in its own internal social security scheme.

At the EU, a temporary member of staff who is unemployed after leaving the service and does not receive a pension is entitled to a monthly unemployment allowance (Art. 28a EU-CEOS), provided, however, that he did not resign or was dismissed for disciplinary reasons, completed a minimum of six months in service and took up residence in one of the member states of the EU. The unemployment allowance is an insurance benefit and is granted as a declining amount of 60% to 30% of basic salary for a maximum of 36 months. Temporary staff contribute one third to the financing of the insurance. Unemployment benefits from a national unemployment insurance are deducted. An entitlement to the unemployment allowance only exists as long as the former staff member meets the national requirements for receiving national unemployment benefits and an according certificate is submitted to the competent EU institution monthly. Where appropriate, recipients of the allowance continue to be insured against sickness under the EU scheme (Art. 28a EU-CEOS) without having to make any contributions.

The EU's high-level public office holders are in receipt of a transitional allowance when they cease to hold office. For a duration of up to two years they receive between 40% and 65% of their basic salary, depending on the period of service (Art. 10 Council Reg. (EU) 2016/300 determining the emoluments of EU high-level public office holders).

At the UN, the topic of "separation payments" after service is under consideration in parallel with the "termination indemnity" (which has been in the system for many years). The ICSC has investigated the possibility of harmonising the "end of service" payments within the organisation of the UN-CS (ICSC report for 2009, doc. A/64/30 §§ 42 to 60), which can be considered "comparable in nature to an unemployment benefit ..." and has forwarded a proposal to the UNGA. A decision on the introduction of an "end of service" payment for fixed-term staff if their contract expires after ten or more years of service was deferred by the

UNGA at its 64th session on 22 December 2009 (UN doc. A/RES/64/231) and finally reverted to the ICSC (UN doc. 65/248). The ICSC did not consider it appropriate to set severance payments at the same level as the termination indemnity and decided in 2016 (UN doc. A/71/30) to submit to the UNGA its earlier recommendation that "end of service" pay be introduced for fixed-term staff leaving the organisation after ten years or more of service.

At the EPO, contract staff members receive a termination indemnity of one month's salary multiplied by the number of years in service (Art. 15b EPO conditions of employment for contract staff (see EPO Codex).

There are some decisions of the ILOAT concerning the unemployment schemes of Red Cross and Red Crescent (Judgment 2587), ESO (Judgment 2091), Interpol (Judgment 2087), CERN (Judgments 2380 und 1538) and of EMBL (Judgment 1395).

*ee) Paid leave in the event of maternity and adoption, unpaid parental or family leave, birth grant, allowances for parental and family leave, paid special leave*

– Maternity, adoption, birth

The service regulations of IO contain provisions ensuring the payment of full salary during maternity leave, usually in the range of 16 to 20 weeks (e.g. Art. 58 EU-SR, Rule 6.3 UN-SR). In some organisations there are similar rules in the case of the adoption of a child (e.g. Annex V Art. 6 EU-SR: paid special leave of 20 weeks). In addition, on the birth or adoption there is generally an entitlement to a capital sum (birth grant, adoption grant, for example Art. 74 EU-SR; Appendix XII Art. 22 CoE-SR).

– Parental leave (UN: paternity leave)

Employees are generally entitled to unpaid parental leave for a certain period after the birth of a child (see, for example, Art. 42a EU-SR: six months for each child to be taken during the first twelve years after the birth). During parental leave the contributions to the social security scheme are borne fully by the institution (Rule 6(3) UN-SR: 16 weeks), the promotion rules and the advancement in seniority often continue to apply. As a rule, a monthly allowance is paid (see, for example, Art. 42a EU-SR: EUR 911 per month).

– Family leave

Employees are generally entitled to unpaid leave for family reasons in the event of the serious illness or disability of the spouse or dependents. The duration is limited (see, for example, Art. 42b EU-SR: nine months over the entire career) and a monthly allowance equivalent to the parental allowance is paid.

– Paid special leave

Most IO grant special paid leave for several days in the following or similar cases: severe illness or death of a close relative or the spouse, marriage of the official or a child, birth of a child, training, examination, voting in national elections, court appearances (see, for example, Annex V Art. 6 EU-SR; Rule 5(3) UN-SR; Art. 45(4) and Appendix VII CoE-SR).

*ff) Hardship*

Occasionally, the SR of IO contain rules granting allowances or loans to staff in particularly difficult circumstances such as prolonged or serious illness or family reasons or difficulties in life or work at new duty stations (see, for example, Art. 76 and 76a EU-SR; Rule 3(14) UN-SR).

*gg) Special issues*

(1) Short-term employment, local staff

All permanent employees of IO (EU, EPO) and the vast majority of staff in a contractual relationship (CO and IO adhering to the mixed system) are compulsorily insured by the social scheme of most IO (for the UN see above). This social insurance cover is generally a precondition for the exemption of staff from compulsory contributions to national social security schemes under the PPI's of IO (see above under social security, general).

For other forms of employment like temporary workers, local staff and conference interpreters, special rules apply. This group of staff either continue their national social security cover throughout their international activities or else the organisation provides for special social security insurance cover. In either case the IO takes over the employer's share of the contribution (see, for example, Art. 121 EU-CEOS). In some organisations, these staff have a choice between the access to the scheme offered by the organisation or the continued adherence to the national scheme (see, for example, Art. 10(2) EPO conditions of employment of contract staff).

For conference interpreters who are engaged on an auxiliary basis for conferences special rules generally apply. At the EU, there is an "Agreement on working conditions and the pecuniary regime for auxiliary conference interpreters (ACIs) recruited by the institutions of the EU of 13 October 2004, the "Agreement"). Based on Art. 16 of the Agreement, the interpreters are covered against the risks of sickness and accident by an insurance concluded by the Commission. The respective institutions pay a contribution towards the cost of the insurance for each day that an interpreter is engaged by them. Other IO require their conference interpreters to demonstrate that they are covered by a social security system.

(2) Former staff

The PPI's and seat agreements of IO consistently extend the privilege of exemption of staff from mandatory contributions to the national social insurance also to former staff, spouses and dependants. In contrast to the national income taxation to which pensioners of IO are generally subject (see above), there is obliviously no interest by the member countries in a shift of the increased illness risk for former staff to the national social security schemes. Consequently, the social security schemes of IO usually continue to provide health insurance for former staff members. Mostly there is a mandatory membership (see, for example, Art. 72(2) EU-SR; Appendix XII Art. 16(1) CoE-SR), sometimes there is optional membership ("Administrative Instruction" in UN doc. ST/AI/2007/3 Art. 1(2); Appendix XII Art. 16(2) CoE-SR).

There is no general legal principle in the labour law of IO which grants a right to an after-service health insurance without contributions (ILOAT Judgment 1226: It was permissible to do away in 1989 with the free health insurance cover for pensioners who were not contributing to their health insurance since 1972. Because of numerous transitional measures lightening the impact of the change (grace period, maximum limit for contributions) there was no violation of an acquired right, rather the effect was to put all FAO pensioners on a par (ILOAT Judgment 1241: Assessment of premiums not on actual pensions but on notional pension figures corresponding to 30-years of contributory service is fully in line with the notion of mutual aid that underlies social security schemes).

### c) Retirement pensions, invalidity (pensions, allowances) and death benefits

Retirement pensions, invalidity and death benefits are consistently dealt with in the service regulations of IO as a common class of social security benefits. This structure is followed by this book.

*aa) Retirement benefits*

The normal retirements benefits are the retirement pensions triggered by reaching a certain age and seniority, the survivor's pension, and the orphan's pension triggered by the death of the pensioner or the person entitled to a survivor's pension (see, for example, Art. 77 et seq. EU-SR).

*bb) The general structure of pension systems*

The administration of the pension scheme of an IO is either in the hands of the executive body (pension administration) or is outsourced to a specialised external entity like ISRP/SIRP which carries out pension management services for about 40 IIO among them the CO and the EPO. Some IO have delegated the pension administration to special entities which are above all entrusted with managing pension funds (e.g. UNJSPF, CERN/ESO Pension Fund, Staff Retirement Plan and Trust of the World Bank Group).

*cc) General prospects for pension entitlements*

The entitlements under the pension scheme of IO in principle concern all staff members who are employed by the organisation and having completed a minimum period (as a rule five to ten years) of service (see below under conditions of entitlement). There are, however, certain limitations.

At the EU, members of contract staff have a choice between the pension scheme of the EU and remaining in their national scheme (Art. 112 EU-CEOS). Only full-time members of staff holding an appointment for a certain minimum period are participants in the UNJSPF (Art. 21(a) UNJSPF-Regulations). The CoE explicitly excludes temporary staff, auxiliary staff and personnel hired under local labour legislation from the application of its pension scheme (Appendix V Art. 1(3) CoE-SR). At the EPO, there are also provisions for non-permanent employees, excluding them from pension entitlements or offering a choice between the EPO's and their national pension scheme (Art. 10(3) EPO conditions of employment for contract staff).

*dd) Special issues concerning retirement benefits*

(1) The rate of contributions

For all pension schemes of IO, the long-term security of pension benefits is the most crucial issue. Generally, the following measures can be taken in order to guarantee the security of pension benefits: primarily the rate of contribution of staff members and of the organisation can be increased (see below under (1)); another method is the replacement of the defined benefit pension system (DBPS) by the defined contribution pension system (DCPS) (see below under (2)) , it is also possible to postpone the age of entitlement to a pension (see below under commencement entitlement), or to change the salary taken as a calculatory basis for the pension entitlement (see below); finally pension (reserve) funds can be set up in order to balance the financial burden of contributions for the present and the future staff members (see below under pension funds).

With their appointment, employees of IO are subject to compulsory membership to the organisation's own pension scheme and are exempt from membership to a national pension scheme (see above under immunities). As a rule, employees contribute of one third of the cost of funding the pension scheme, based on a certain percentage of the basic salary irrespective of the age and the marital status of the official (see, for example, Art. 83(2) EU-SR; Art. 25 UNJSPF-Regulations; Art. 41(3) EPO-PS; but see CoE-TPS Appendix Vter Art. 41 CoE-SR: the rate of staff contributions shall be in the long term 40% of the benefits provided). The staff contributions are currently between 8% and 11% on the basic salary (at the UN: of pensionable remuneration, in particular; EU (2012): 10.6%; UN (2010): 7.9%; CoE (2016 CoE-TPS): 9.4%; EPO (2015): 9.7%).

(2) The level of benefits

In general, IO guarantee the security and set out the level of pension benefits in advance so that the active staff member knows what level of income will be when he retires. The amount of the retirement pension is set in the pension regulations and depends mostly on the length of service and the grade and step which the staff member has reached at a certain period of time (usually one year) before his retirement. This pension scheme is known as a "defined benefit pension scheme" (DBPS). This system is co-funded by fixed contribution rates, which are periodically reviewed by actuaries. The risk that the defined retirement benefits can be delivered is on the IO.

Similar to some national pension schemes some IO have tried in recent years to shift the risk of secure benefits defined in advance, at least in part, to its staff members. This scheme is generally called a "defined contribution pension scheme" (DCPS). Since also in the DBPS the contributions are "defined", it would have been better to call it a non-defined benefit pension scheme). Most important examples for IO which partly or fully apply the DCPS are the World Bank Group, NATO and the new pension scheme of the EPO.

Irrespective of the fact that the IO which apply the DCPS stipulate that the staff member bears the risk of loss of the invested capital, there inevitably arises the responsibility of an IO for the management of the pension scheme (pension plan). An IO may not simply be absolved of any risks by transferring the administration of the pension scheme or the pension savings plan to an outside organisation. Its responsibility as an employer and substitute state inevitably remains for the *culpa in contrahendo* and *custodiendo* in respect of the management of the pension schemes savings plan. It may also be open to question whether such pension systems are in accordance with the Noblemaire and Fleming principles, since in the majority of member countries of IO (with the exception of the USA and the UK) the DBPS prevails.

(3) The DCPS more in detail

- The Staff Retirement Plan of the World Bank Group as of 1 January 2009

  The benefits consist of three components:

  a) defined benefit component. The benefit is fully funded by the bank and depends on the length of service (1% per year) and the highest three years average net salary; the maximum pension amount is 35% of this salary.

  b) a cash balance component funded by the bank (10% of net salary) and staff (5% of net salary). The benefits depend on the selection of investment options. 3% is the default option, guaranteed by the bank.

  c) a voluntary savings component exclusively funded by the staff member and comprising up to 15% of the net salary. There are different investment options. The staff member bears the risk of loss of capital.

- NATO DCPS for staff appointed on or after 1 July 2005

The new NATO pension scheme is a pure DCPS. NATO contributes 12% and the staff member 8% of his basic salary into an account administered by Previnet (Italy), the pension scheme administrator. The staff member may make additional contributions of up to 5% of his basic salary. The staff member can choose between several investment options (cash, equities, bonds). NATO cannot be held responsible for any losses incurred by movements in the investment markets (Annex VI Art. 10.3 NATO Pension Scheme). If the retirement pension is due, it is purchased by NATO from Previnet at commercial rates and paid to the retired staff member. The pensioner may request a tax-free lump-sum payment of the pension account holdings of up to 25%.

- The EPO introduced a new pension scheme for staff appointed after 1 January 2009 (see EPO Codex). The scheme consists of two components:

  a) a DBPS which guarantees a uniform basic retirement pension. 2% per reckonable year up to 70% of the salary paid at the last grade and step, however capped at twice the salary paid for grade G1 step 4 uniformly for all staff members. In contrast to the pension systems of the other civil service systems and the former EPO-PS there is no tax relief. Only the payment of the salary plan component is granted on termination of service (Art. 65(3) EPO-SR) and, therefore, covered by the tax exemption of salaries (Art. 16(1) EPO-PPI).

  b) a salary savings plan with several components which is outsourced (similar to NATO's DCPS) and EPO is not responsible for investment losses.

Both components are co-financed (EPO, staff member: 9.7% of basic salary (2016)).

*ee) Taxation of retirement benefits*

(see above under personal immunity of officials)

*ff) Attachment and subrogation of retirement benefits*

The attachment of retirement benefits is, like the attachment of salaries, in principle, excluded by the PPI's or seat agreements of IO since it is in conflict with the immunities of the IO. An IO may of course waive the immunity in a particular case (see, for example, Art. 3(1)(a) EPO-EPC). Most organisations have agreed with their seat countries that its immunity is deemed to be waived in respect of a court order relating to salaries or pensions owed by the organisation unless the organisation informs the competent national authorities that is does not waive its immunity (see, for example, Art. 3 DE/EPO Agreement and Art. 3 NL/EPO Agreement; see also above under personal immunity of staff members).

The question of assignability of pension benefits (as to salaries see above under personal immunity of staff members) is generally not regulated by IO. An exception is contained in Art. 45 UNJSPF-Regulations ("Non-assignability of rights").

*gg) Individual retirement benefits*

(1) Conditions of entitlement

After a certain number of actually completed eligible years of service, the staff member acquires entitlement to pension benefits. As a rule, five to ten years of service must be completed (Art. 77 EU-SR: ten years; Art. 28 UNJSPF-Regulations: five years; Appendix V and Appendix Vbis, CoE-NTS and Appendix Vter CoE-TPS Art. 7 CoE-SR: ten years; EPO: Art. 7 EPO-PS: ten years). If the minimum number of eligible years of service has not been reached the staff member leaving the service is entitled to a severance allowance (leaving allowance, severance grant, withdrawal settlement, see Annex VIII Art. 12 EU-SR; Art. 31 UNJSPF-Regulations; Appendix V Art. 11 CoE-SR; Art. 11 EPO-PS). An employee who leaves the service of an IO may, under certain conditions, also be entitled to an outward transfer of the actuarial equivalent of the retirement pension rights accrued to the new employer's pension scheme (see below under inward and outward transfer of pension rights).

(2) Commencement of entitlement

Demographic changes in the member states of IO and in particular the increase in the life expectancy requires that the mandatory retirement age and the age for pension entitlement of employees are increased in order to ensure the balance of social security systems.

IO are well aware of this trend and are adapting their pension schemes accordingly (see, for example, the report of the ICSC 2015 in UN doc. A 70/30 pp. 26–27 and UN doc. 64/30 pp. 12–14; EU Regulation No. 1023/2013 amending the EU-SR, preamble p. 14–16). In order to respect the acquired rights of their staff already in service extensive transitional provisions have been adopted (see, for example, Annex XIII EU-SR).

At the EU, the pensionable age was changed as from 1 May 2014 from 63 to 66 years (Art. 77 EU-SR). It will be re-assessed every five years on the basis of a report by the Commission. The mandatory retirement age has been raised from 65 to 66 years of age, but an employee may carry on working until the age of 67 or exceptionally until the age of 70 (Art. 52 EU-SR). An official leaving the service before the pensionable age may request a deferred pension until he reaches the pensionable age or he may request a reduced retirement pension after reaching 58 years of age (Annex VIII Art. 9 EU-SR).

At the UN, the mandatory retirement age is 65 years for staff members commencing participation in the UNJSPF on or after 1 January 2014 (Art. 1(n) UNJSPF – Regulations). A retirement benefit is paid to a participant whose age is the normal retirement age or more (Art. 28 UNJSPF-Regulations). Reduced early retirement benefits are payable to participants who are at least 58 years (participation in the fund on or after 1 January 2014).

At the CoE, a staff member becomes eligible for a retirement pension at the age of 65 (Art. 8(1) CoE-TPS). From the age of 55 years a staff member is entitled to a reduced early pension (Art. 8(4) CoE-TPS). A staff member must retire at the age of 65; he may, however, be retained in service up to the age of 67 (Art. 24 and 24bis CoE-SR).

At the EPO, there is still (2016) a difference (in line with the EU-SR up to 1 May 2014) between the age of entitlement to a pension (60 years of age, see Art. 8 EPO-PS) and the age of mandatory retirement (65 years, see Art. 54(1)(a) EPO-SR), which may exceptionally be extended to 68 years of age (see Art 54(1)(b) EPO-SR). If an official retires before the age of 60, the payment of his pension is deferred until he reaches the pensionable age (Art. 8(3) EPO-PS). He may, however, request a reduced early payment of his pension from the age of 50 (Art. 8(4) EPO-PS). It is likely that the EPO will adapt these provisions to the general trend in the near future.

Pension entitlements exist for the lifetime of the beneficiary (see, for example, Art. 27 UNJSPF-Regulations). The right to pension benefits may be forfeited (see, for example, Art. 46 UNJSPF-Regulations).

At the EU, the pension of a retired official may be withheld in part for a given period based on a disciplinary decision (see, for example, Annex IX Art. 9 EU-SR).

(3) Yearly accrual rate of pension benefits

The amount of the retirement pension basically depends on the number of reckonable years of service. The rate of acquired entitlements per year differs between the IO (Art. 77 EU-SR: 1.8% (but see the transitional provisions in Annex XII EU-SR); Art. 28 UNJSPF-Regulations: 1.5% to 2% depending on the participation period; CoE-SR: Appendix V and NPS, Appendix V bis Art. 10 CoE-SR: 2% and CoE-TPS Appendix V ter Art. 10: 1.75%; EPO: Art. 10(1) EPO-PS and Art. 10(1) new EPO-PS: 2%).

(4) Maximum and minimum rate of pensions

The maximum rate of pension benefits at IO is as a rule fixed at 70% of a certain basic salary (UN: pensionable remuneration) taken as the calculatory basis (Art. 77 EU-SR; Art. 28(b) UNJSPF-Regulations; Appendix V Art. 10 CoE-SR; Art. 10(2) EPO-PS).

The minimum pension corresponding to the salary amount of a lower pay grade is guaranteed (Art. 77 EU-SR: 4% of the minimum subsistence figure per year of service, for example, pay grade AST 1 step 1, see Annex VIII Art. 6 EU-SR; Art. 28(f) UNJSPF-Regulations: a certain minimum amount without reference to remuneration; Appendix V Art. 10(3) CoE-SR: 4% of the salary for grade C1, step 1, per year of service; EPO: Art. 10(3) EPO-PS: 4% of the salary for grade G1 step 4 per year of service).

(5) The salary taken as calculatory basis for the pension benefits

As a rule, the final basic salary carried by the last grade in which the official was classified for at least one year is taken for the calculation of the retirement pension (Art. 77(2) EU-SR; Appendix V Art. 10(1) CoE-SR; Art. 10(1) EPO-PS). The UNJSPF provides, however, for a "final average remuneration" (Art. 1(h) UNJSPF-Regulations) which is calculated on the basis of the highest pensionable remuneration within a certain period of service.

(6) Pension benefits for surviving spouses and dependants

If the recipient of the retirement pension dies, the spouse, the children and other dependants are entitled to a survivor's, orphan's or dependent's pension.

The survivor's pension is normally 60% of the retirement pension (see, for example, Annex VIII Art. 17 EU-SR). It is, however, reduced if there is a large difference in age between the spouses ("late marriage clause"). In the case of remarriage special rules apply (see, for example, the entitlement to the survivor's pension ceases and a capital sum is paid, Annex VIII Art. 26 EU-SR: equal to twice the amount of the survivor's pension). There are extensive rules concerning the calculation of the orphan's and dependant's pension (see, for example, Annex VIII Art. 21 and 22 EU-SR; Appendix V Art. 25 et seq. CoE-SR).

(7) Inward and outward transfer of pension rights

In most IO, pension rights of staff can be increased by transferring acquired pension rights from previous employment (Annex VIII Art. 11(2) EU-SR: previous employers under the EU legislation are obliged to allow a transfer, see CJEU Judgment 137/80; Art. 13 UNJSPF-Regulations; Appendix V Art. 12(1) CoE-SR; Art. 12(1) EPO-PS).

An employee who leaves the service of an IO and enters the service of another employer may transfer the actuarial equivalent of his retirement pension rights to the new pension scheme (Annex VIII Art. 11(1) EU-SR; Art. 13 UNJSPF-Regulations; Appendix V Art. 12(2) CoE-SR; Art. 12(2) EPO-PS).

Most IO have concluded agreements with member countries, national social insurance companies, private social insurance schemes and other IO in order to allow or facilitate the inward and outward transfer of pension rights (see, for example, the agreement of the EPO with Germany on the transfer of pension rights of 1995, see ILOAT Judgments 2413, 2101). There may even be an obligation under public internal law for the member states of IO to ensure the transfer of pension rights of staff members acquired under the national social security scheme (see Gruber, p. 151 et seq.; but see the ILOAT Judgment 2527 (Italy).

(8) Taxation of pensions

(see above under Privileges and Immunities)

(9) Allowances

Besides the pension benefits, pensioners are generally entitled to the family allowances (at the UN: dependency allowances) specified in the SR applicable to active staff (Art. 81 EU-SR; Art. 36 UNJSPF-Regulations; Appendix V Art. 28 CoE-SR; Art. 28 EPO-PS).

(10) Annual adjustment of pensions

At the EU, the pensions are adjusted annually with effect from 1 July in parallel with the adjustment of salaries (Art. 82(2) EU-SR).

At the UN, the pension adjustment system is described in Annex III of the UNJSPF-Regulations. The rather complex adjustment system provides for a periodic review of the pensions in order to adjust them to the development of the

United States' consumer price index (CPI) and to preserve the purchasing power of the pensions in the local currency of the pensioner's country of residence. The pensioner has a choice between a so-called "dollar track system" and the "local track system". In the event the pensioner opts for the "local track system" the adjustment follows the movement of the CPI of the country of residence outside the USA ("local track") and is compared to the "dollar track". The pensioner is generally entitled to the higher of the two. However, there is a certain maximum amount (a maximum "cap amount" of the local track amount at a defined date) and a certain minimum amount (80% of the adjusted "dollar-track amount"). It is therefore possible that the dollar track amount is sometimes more beneficial than the two-track amount (for details see the Annex III of the UNJSPF-Regulations and a booklet also available via the UNJSPF internet portal).

The pension system (including the pension adjustment system) of the CO underwent a significant change in the year 2001. The old adjustment procedure (see Appendix V Art. 36 CoE-SR) provided for an adjustment of pensions in relation to the cost of living (consumer price index). For an adjustment in the relation to the standard of living a special decision by the Council is required. Under the new pension scheme rules (Appendix V bis and V ter, NPS and TPS Art. 36 CoE-SR), the adjustment of pensions provides only for an adjustment in relation to the revaluation coefficient based on the consumer price index for the country of the scale used to calculate each pension. Only "where appropriate" may the Secretary Generals of the CO may propose measures to reduce the difference between increases in salary and increases in pensions.

At CERN/ESO, the pensions are adjusted in accordance with Art. II.1(14) of the Rules of the Pension Fund. The annual adjustment differs pursuant to the date on which the staff member became a beneficiary of a pension (before 31 December 2011, between 1 January 2012 and 31 July 2019, or afterwards). The adjustment of pensions depends on a rather complex calculation of the development of the consumer price index of Geneva and the individually calculated loss of purchasing power and the funding ratio of the fund. For details see Annex C to the Rules of the Pension Fund.

The EPO procedure for the adjustment of pensions is even stipulated in the primary law of the organisation (Art. 33(2)(c) EPO-EPC). It guarantees that the increases in pensions have to correspond to the increases in salaries.

Negative adjustments of pensions of IO are avoided (even without an explicit nominal guarantee in the PS) by deferring the reduction and setting it off against the positive adjustment at a later date, in parallel to the adjustment of salaries.

**Jurisprudence**

ILOAT Judgments

2633: The right to a pension is inviolable, a pension contribution is, however, by its very nature subject to variations (rise in contribution warranted for sound actuarial reasons). Pensioners residing in different countries are not in the same position, they cannot claim to be discriminated (2632, 1392); 2089: A change in the adjustment procedure for pensions (only adjustments for cost of living but not for standard of living) is within the authority of the legislator but subject to the respect of acquired rights; 1456: Enhancement of pension benefits for EPO staff who joined the EPO under the sponsorship by German national administration where a transfer of pension entitlements was not allowed.

### *hh) Permanent invalidity and death benefits*

#### (1) General benefits

Active staff members of IO are protected against total permanent invalidity which must be medically identified (medical board, medical committee). There is often also some form of death insurance and in some IO there is protection against partial permanent invalidity. There is no coherent form for invalidity benefits across the various service regulations (EU: "invalidity allowance", before 1 May 2004: "invalidity pension"; UN: "disability benefits"; CoE: "invalidity pension"; EPO: "invalidity allowance", before 1 January 2008: "invalidity pension"). The EPO's invalidity system was replaced completely (including the abolition of the payment of capital sums, which had been similar to the CO, see the CoE below) with effect from 1 April 2015 (see under sickness insurance).

The status of an official in permanent total invalidity is mostly assimilated to a retired staff member; he is therefore mostly exempt from paying contributions to the pension scheme. At the EU, an invalid official is automatically "retired" in conformity with Art. 53 EU-SR. Art. 78(4) EU-SR nevertheless stipulates that the invalidity allowance is subject to contributions to the pension scheme.

The amount of the invalidity benefits often corresponds to the pension that the staff member would have received if he had remained in employment until reaching the retirement age (UN: Art. 33(c) UNJSPF-Regulations; CoE: Appendix V Art. 14(1) CoE-SR). At the EU, the invalidity allowance is equal to 70% of the official's last basic salary (Art. 78(3) EU-SR).

In some IO there is, in addition to the general invalidity benefits, an additional insurance cover providing for the payment of a certain lump sum of a number of years' basic salary if the invalidity results from an occupational disease or an accident at work (see below).

At the CoE, there is entitlement to disability benefits (after the age of 56, progressively decreasing) in the form of a capital sum, which depends on the degree of invalidity under the French social security scheme classification, and corresponds to two to four years' salary for total permanent disability or reduced capital sum for partial permanent disability (Appendix XII Art. 12 CoE-SR). In the case of death, a capital sum of two to four years' salary is paid to the persons entitled (Appendix XII Art. 13 CoE-SR).

The funding of the additional cover is normally shared between the official and the organisation (1/3: 2/3). At the EU, the officials contribute up to 0.1% of the basic salary to the cost of insuring against non-occupational risks (Art. 73(1) EU-SR). In the event of total permanent invalidity, the official receives a payment of eight times his annual basic salary (Art. 73(2)(b) EU-SR and in case of partial permanent invalidity a proportion of this sum (Art. 73(2)(c) EU-SR. In the event of death, the persons cited in the provision will receive five times the annual basic salary of the deceased staff member (Art. 73(2)(a) EU-SR).

At the EPO, in the case of the death of an official, 2.75 times the annual salary is granted to the person entitled (Art. 84(1)(b) EPO-SR).

(2) Occupational disease and accident at work

In the event of total or partial permanent invalidity or death in course or in connection with the performance of official duties (including missions, journeys to and from the working place and in the event of a public-spirited act) particular provisions exist in many IO.

According to case law (see in particular CJEU Judgments T-262/06 P; Judgment F-52/05; C-257/98 P; 169/83 and 136/84 and ILOAT Judgment 2804), in the event of occupational accidents and diseases there is an entitlement to full compensation on the basis of a fault rendering the organisation liable beyond the basis of a no-fault regime if the benefits under the service regulations are not sufficient. The additional compensation may be due on the basis of the general principle of law that an IO is under a duty to safeguard the health and safety of its staff by putting adequate measures in place (see above under general principles).

The civil service system of the EU provides for the insurance of officials against the risk of accidents or occupational diseases, adopted on the basis of Art. 73(1) EU-SR ("Common Rules" of 13 December 2005; doc. OJ L 8 of 12 January 2005, p. 1). This extensive scheme contains definitions of occupational diseases and accidents. The list of occupational diseases is annexed to the Recommendation of the Commission of 19 September 2003 (doc. OJ L 238 of 25 September 2003, p. 28).

In addition, according to Art. 3(2) of the "Common Rules" any disease or aggravation of a pre-existing disease is considered as an occupational disease, if it is sufficiently established that it arose of in the course or in connection with the performance of duties. Similarly, under Art. 2, all accidents (not just occupational) are covered (exclusion of benefits are set out in Art. 7). According to Art. 73(2) (a) and (b) EU-SR the EU pays a death a lump sum of five times the annual basic salary to the persons cited in this provision and in the event of total permanent invalidity of the official the EU pays (in addition to the invalidity allowance) a lump sum of eight times the annual basic salary. In the event of partial permanent invalidity resulting from an accident or occupational disease, a partial amount of the lump sum payment for total permanent invalidity (Art. 73(2)(c) EU-SR) is granted. The extensive Annex A to the "Common Rules" contains a disability rating scale which serves as a calculatory basis for determining the lump sum provided for in Art. 73(2)(c) EU-SR. According to Art. 13 and 14 of the "Common Rules", an additional allowance is granted for physical disfigurement, sexual impairment or medically plausible exceptional pain. Art. 12 of the "Common Rules" provides for an annuity payment instead of a lump sum grant. In the event of an accident or an occupational disease all appropriate medical expenses that are not covered by the normal rules under Art. 2 EU-SR are reimbursed (Art. 73(3) EU-SR and Art. 9 of the "Common Rules").

The contributions to the pension scheme are exclusively paid by the EU institution (Art. 78(5) EU-SR) if the invalidity arises from an occupational disease or accident in course of or in connection with the performance of an official duty or in the event of a public-spirited act.

The UN enacted in "Appendix D" to the UN-SR rules on compensation in the event of death, injury or illness attributable to the performance of official duties on behalf of the UN (UN Doc ST/SGB/Staff Rules Appendix D). The compensation awarded under these rules supplements benefits awarded under the Regulations of the UNJSPF (Art. 4 "Appendix D").

In the case of the injury or the illness of staff or former staff which is attributable to the performance of official duties and which results in total invalidity the staff member receives a compensatory allowance equivalent to two-thirds of his final pensionable remuneration plus one-third of such annual rate in respect of each unmarried child under certain restrictions (Art. 11(1)(c) "Appendix D").

In the case of partial invalidity, if the staff member is reassigned to a post at a lower grade, there is an entitlement to compensation (Art. 11(2)(c) "Appendix D").

In the case of death, the UN pays an annual compensation to the deceased staff member's spouse or dependant(s), calculated as part of the annual pensionable remuneration of the staff member and additional compensation (Art. 10 "Appendix D").

Regardless of any other compensation, in the event of permanent disfigurement or permanent loss of functions to the limbs or senses, certain capital payments are due (Art. 11(3)(c) "Appendix D").

The CoE has adopted in Appendix XII Art. 14 CoE-SR special rules for occupational accidents including industrial diseases (also covering accidents occurring on normal journeys to and from work, see also CoE Rule No. 1331 of 24 March 2011 on the provisions applicable in the event of absence for reasons of health, maternity, paternity). In such cases, 100% of the medical costs are covered, applying the French social security scheme. The funding of these medical expenses is solely at the charge of the CoE (Appendix XII Art. 15 CoE-SR). The entitlement to full salary is extended until health is restored or the official is declared disabled (Appendix XII Art. 14(4)(b) CoE-SR). The amount of the invalidity pension in these cases is (independent of the length of service) set at 70% of the salary (Appendix V Art. 14(2) CoE-SR).

Most IO outside the three international civil service law systems dispose of similar provisions in the event of accidents or occupational diseases. However, in the event of partial permanent invalidity the protection of staff members leaves much to be desired.

When the invalidity system of the EPO was repealed on 1 March 2015 (see EPO doc. CA/D 2/15 on the EPO website), the special provisions on occupational disease and accidents at work granting a lump sum payment of 2.75% times the annual basic salary (see ILOAT Judgment 2804) and a higher invalidity pension (see EPO doc. CA/D 2/15 Art. 74) were deleted.

In accordance with the case law of international administrative tribunals, the liability of IO in the case of occupational disease and accidents at work is, however, extended beyond the no-fault regime if the complainant can prove negligence or an intentional breach of a duty (see ILOAT Judgments 2843: Slipping on liquid in the car park of the organisation; 2804: Repetitive strain injury and eye problems related to computer use; 2533: The organisation admits work-related injuries. It is common for a mature legal system to provide compensation on a no-fault basis to employees who suffer workplace injuries, the law of the international civil service can do no less. The present dispute is about quantum, not liability; 435: No liability beyond the requirements of the SR because the complainant was not exposed to a degree of danger incompatible with the normal performance of his duties).

(3) Taxation of invalidity benefits

(see also above under personal immunity of officials)

EU: The invalidity allowance is subject to the internal tax of the EU and exempt from national taxes (Art. 12(2) EU-PPI).

UN: The disability benefits are fully taxable under national law like a retirement pension (see item F of the Guide to taxation on the internet portal of the UNJSPF).

CoE: The invalidity pension (Appendix V Art. 13 CoE-SR) is subject to national taxation. The pensioner receives a tax adjustment of 50% of the amount by which his pension would theoretically need to be increased, were the balance remaining after deduction of the amount of national income tax on the total to correspond to the amount of the pension (Appendix V Art. 42 CoE-SR).

EPO: With effect from 1 April 2015 the EPO repealed its invalidity system (see under sickness insurance).

### *5. The pension schemes of international organisations*

#### a) Introduction

The organisational power of IO includes the management of the pension scheme. In principle, the human resources department applies the provisions of the pension scheme. However, in a number of IO, the management of the scheme is transferred to the pension fund, which is a specialised body within the legal umbrella of the organisation competent for the full or partial funding of the pension benefits.

The pension funds or pension reserve funds are in some cases established by IO even without an explicit legal basis in the primary law. According to international jurisprudence (Meroni Judgments of the CJEU 9/56 and 10/56), the creation of such bodies is permitted in such a case if the balance of powers characteristic of the institutional structure of the organisation is respected (see, for example, this precaution was observed by the EPO when its Pension Reserve Fund (EPO-PRF) was established in 1992, nearly a decade prior to the decision on an explicit legal basis in the primary law of the EPO (Art. 38(b) EPO-EPC) in 2000.

#### b) Legal structures of the pension schemes

The administration and the funding of the pension schemes takes place in one of two ways following basic categories: the pension (reserve) fund system or the budget system. Nowadays, the pension (reserve) system is the rule.

In the budget system, the administration and financing of the pension system lies in the hands of the administration of the organisation. No pension fund is involved. The pensions are paid out of the budget and are financed on a pay-as-you-go basis by contributions from the staff and the organisation. The EU applies this system to its officials. This system is exposed, in the long run, to the risk of overloading the budget and of a later generation of staff having to pay greatly increased contributions as a consequence of demographic developments in the age structure of staff and the higher life expectancy of retired staff. This type of pension scheme can also create significant problems upon the possible dissolution of the organisation. In this case, the question of the liability of the member countries (piercing the corporate veil of the contracting states arises (see below)).

The IO with pension funds have transferred the funding of the pension system to a special body (organ, subsidiary body) of the organisation. This entity may also become responsible for the administration of the pension regulations. The most prominent examples of this kind of pension scheme are the CERN/ESO-PF, the UNJSPF, the World Bank – Staff Retirement Plan and Trust, and the ECB – Pension Scheme. These funds aim to cover all future pension entitlements. Even in the event of the cessation of the regular contributions (as in the case of the dissolution of the IO) the pension fund should be able to ensure that all pension obligations can be met right up to the death of the last beneficiary. In this case, therefore, the question of piercing the corporate veil of the contracting states is of lesser importance than in an IO with a pay-as-you-go budget pension system.

Some IO do without a fully funded pension scheme. This so-called mixed pension system consists of a budget system with a partly funded pension component. These funds are usually referred to as pension reserve funds. The predominant aim of these pension reserve funds is to lessen the risk of an excessive increase in the percentage of contributions and thereby balance the burden of funding for future generations of staff. These funds are therefore often described as "buffer funds". It has, however, to be pointed out that the difference between a pension fund and a pension reserve fund is blurred. Some organisations falling under this category strive for a full coverage of pension liabilities in order to avoid a later piercing of the corporate veil of the contracting states. Examples for this category are the EPO-RFPSS and most organisations of the international civil service system of the CO.

### c) Actuarial balance of pension schemes

For all pension schemes, a periodic review of the intended actuarial balance of the scheme is required in order to adjust the amount of contributions needed (EU: Annex XII Art. 3 EU-SR: every five years; UN: Art. 12(a) UNJSPF-Regulations: at least once every three years; CoE: Appendix V CoE-SR Art. 41: every five years; EPO: Art. 41(3) and Art. 50(2) EPO-PS: no fixed deadline). In simplified terms, there is an examination as to whether the contributions of staff and of the organisation are sufficient to cover the guaranteed benefits. In addition to an adjustment of the contributions, the actuarial balance of the scheme can be assured by various other adjustment mechanisms. (For more detail, see above under: the age of entitlement to the pension, the change from a DBPS to a DCPS, the percentage of the annually accrued pension rights and the salary taken as calculatory basis for the pension entitlement). In the case of a fully or partly funded pension scheme, the most important parameters for the actuarial review are the evolution in the overall life expectancy of pensioners, the change in the demographic structure of active staff, the annual pension adjustment provisions and the economic return of the fund. Whereas the underlying aim of the actuarial review in a fully funded pension system is the cover of the pension benefits for the life-time of the beneficiaries, the aim of a partly funded system is the fair distribution of the burden among the present and future staff members and to keep the budgetary burden at an acceptable level.

### d) Legal protection of beneficiaries

The legal protection of beneficiaries under the pension scheme generally follows the legal protection offered to active employees (see Ullrich, Pension Schemes).

At CERN/ESO-PF the decisions are taken by the chief executive officer of the PF on behalf of CERN/ESO. Appeals are directed to the Chairman of the Governing Board of the PF (Art. III 1.04 CERN/ESO-PF Statute and Art. 2 Regulations for Appeals). Appeals against the decision of the Governing Board may be brought before the ILOAT (Art. 13 Regulation for Appeals; see, for example, ILOAT Judgment 2410).

For the pension reserve funds of the EPO it is the general administration of the organisation that is competent for all staff related decisions and the same system of legal protection is available as for active staff.

At the UNJSPF, the beneficiaries of the 23 member organisations (2016) have recourse to the UN Appeals Tribunal (Art. 48 UNJSPF-Regulations and Annex I, Section K, Review and Appeal). This is also valid for former staff members of one of the European-based organisations adhering to the UNJSPF, which have otherwise recognised the jurisdiction of ILOAT in labour law disputes (see, for example, ILOAT Judgment 2872).

The legal protection of beneficiaries of the World Bank in the execution of the Pension Plan is provided by the WBAT (Art. II WBAT-Statute).

Appeals by beneficiaries of the ECB-PS have to be directed to the CJEU (Art. 35 ECB-PS and Part 8 Art. 42 ECB-Conditions of Employment and Art. 8(2) ECB-SR).

### e) Financing guarantee of the pension scheme

The guarantee of the security and the level of pension benefits applies to all IO that have a defined benefit pension scheme (DBPS, see above).

*aa) During the existence of the international organisation*

The pension entitlements of staff, former staff and their successors are in principle recognised as acquired rights. It is, however, doubtful that the ILOAT in judgment 429 did not confirm the principle of an acquired right with respect to Agency's contribution to the pension scheme: "the rate of contribution by the Agency was a matter of lesser importance to them". Any reduction in pension entitlements is subject to legal scrutiny by the respective international tribunal, based on its case law on the legal principle of acquired rights (see above). A violation of an acquired right to pension entitlements may lay, for example, in the reduction of the annual accrued benefit entitlements. The respect of the vested rights of staff and former staff to the accrued pension benefit entitlements and pension claims rests in principle on the IO, but ultimately the contracting states must supply the cash necessary to ensure the entitlements.

An explicit guarantee of the contracting states for the benefits under the pension scheme is contained in the secondary law of the CO and the EPO (Art. 40(2) of the respective SR: "The member states of the Organisation jointly guarantee the payment of the benefits"). In 1977, Eurocontrol also adapted a direct liability of the contracting states for the payment of pensions (Art. 83(1) SR). The beneficiaries of the guarantee of the contracting states are ultimately the staff and former staff of the organisation. This specific guarantee has to be distinguished from the general guarantee of the contracting states of an IO in the primary law for the financing of the general budget of the organisation (see, for example, Art. 37 EPO-EPC). The specific guarantee clause for the pensions benefits entitlements of staff provides an additional direct guarantee for them.

*bb) After dissolution of the international organisation*

(1) Pensions

In the event of the dissolution (as well as integration, merger, transfer etc) of the IO, the appropriate plenary organs normally make arrangements for ensuring the accrued pension benefits and pension claims of staff and former staff until the cessation of entitlement of the last beneficiary (see, for example, Art. 40(3) PS of the CO and the EPO). In the case of transfer or integration there is generally a universal succession of rights (see, for example, the transfer of the IIB into the EPO in 1978, Section I(b) of the Protocol on the Centralisation of the European Patent System and on its introduction, see doc. OJ/EPO 2001, Special edition No. 4, p. 55; similarly, the integration of INPADOC into the EPO in 1990, doc. AT/BGBl. Nr. 671 of 6 November 1990, p. 4059 et seq.). The existing acquired rights of staff with respect to accrued pension entitlement and pension claims are not eliminated by the dissolution, nor by a transfer or integration of the IO (see, for example, ILOAT Judgments 365, 368, 369, 372 concerning the integration of the IIB into the EPO). With the dissolution of an IO, however, the competent international administrative tribunal loses its jurisdiction and the staff's complaints are no longer admissible. In so far as the legal system of the dissolved IO contained specific liability guarantees of the contracting states for pension entitlements, the staff and former staff members are legitimised to prosecute their claims before national courts. In denial of legal protection or legal review by national courts, the staff could ultimately enforce their right against the contracting states that have ratified the EConHR before the ECHR, since the accrued pension benefits are part of the fundamental social rights protected by the EConHR.

For IO without an explicit direct liability of the contracting states, the issue of liability is more difficult to answer. For example, the CERN/ESO Pension Fund Rules (Art. I 3.03) provide a guarantee of the organisations CERN and ESO for the continuation of the pension claims and accrued pension entitlements in the case of a merger or reconstitution of the organisation, until the extinction of the right of the last beneficiary. In the event of the dissolution of CERN, its Council will set up a foundation under Swiss law to succeed the fund without prejudice to other systems providing equivalent guarantees. In the event of the dissolution of ESO, its Council will take the necessary steps to guarantee the rights acquired by the members of the personnel of ESO who are members of the fund. There is no guarantee of the member states for pension entitlements.

The Regulations of the UNJSPF (Art. 26(a)) also merely contain a duty of each member organisation of the fund to make good the deficiencies of the fund, without a guarantee of the member states of the respective organisation. In literature the direct liability of the contracting state is advocated (see, for example, Conforti/Domenicé/Ress). There are, however, also critical voices on the question of liability of member states (see, for example, Wenckstern, Haftung, p. 113). In the absence of a judicial decision the question remains doubtful (the decision of British courts in the case of insolvency of the International Tin Council only concerned outside parties and non-organisational beneficiaries with an appropriate guarantee of the contracting states, see Conforti/Domenicé/Ress; see also Morgenstern, p. 588).

(2) Health and long-term care insurance

In the event of the dissolution of an IO it is also necessary to address the issue of direct liability of the contracting states regarding social benefits, in particular the future reimbursement of medical expenses and claims arising from long-term care and disability.

It appears that these benefits are, as a rule, not ensured by explicit guarantees of the contracting states. Even if in some IO reserve funds for social security exist, these funds only serve to avoid excessive contribution rates (buffer funds). They are not fully-fledged capital funds which could avoid the problem of the bringing of a suit against a contracting state in the case of the dissolution of the IO.

CERN/ESO has set up a fund for capitalisation of the long-term care and a fund for the health insurance scheme (see the CERN Health Insurance Scheme of 1 June 2014 Art. IX 2.01). Until now, no similar guarantee of the Council on the dissolution of CERN exists for the health insurance (see Bulletin 45 of the gap-epa association on the internet). Explicit guarantees of the contracting states for the social benefits do, as with the pensions entitlements, not exist at CERN.

In recent times, ever more IO are investigating the possibilities of setting up a funding system for the social security systems of the organisation which would avoid excessive contribution rates in the long run and could provide security for staff, at least temporarily in the case of the dissolution of the IO. The EPO created a reserve fund for the long-term care insurance (2001) and the sickness insurance (2010), the UNGA requested in 2014 (doc. A/RES/68/244) that the UN-SG set-up a working group for managing after-service health insurance liabilities. A package of actions was presented in a report by the UN-SG (doc. A/70/590) with the option of a further study after 2016.

#### f) Legal status of the pension (reserve) funds

All pensions and pension reserve funds of the IO are inter-organisational bodies (organs, auxiliary or annex bodies). They are an integral part of the respective organisation. Funds of IO do not exist as independent entities in international public law. The legal basis for the establishment of a fund may be reflected in the primary law of the IO (EPO-RFPSS: Art. 38(b) EPO-EPC) or in the secondary law (UNJSPF: Decision by the UNGA based on Art. 7(2) and Art. 22 UN Charter; CoE Reserve Fund: Resolution Res(2006)1 by the Committee of Ministers; ECB Pension Fund: Annex III, Section IV to VI of the PS). Ultimately, even without an explicit authorisation, the right to establish a pension (reserve) fund results from the right to self-organisation and autonomy in personnel matters of each IO (Seidl-Hohenveldern/Loibl, para. 0921 et seq., 1522 et seq.; Ullrich, Versorgungssysteme, p. 226 et seq.).

The operations of the fund are necessary for the fulfilment the duties of an IO, because it serves both to secure the budgetary commitment of member states for the payment of retirement benefits and for the long-term financial stability of the contributions. The performance of a fund is therefore to be qualified as an official activity as defined by the protocols on privileges and immunities and seat agreements of the IO. The funds are therefore participating from the tax privileges of the IO and enjoy immunities from national jurisdiction and enforcement. This legal status which is not easy to enforce in all contracting states would be lost if a fund were to lose its intra-organisational status. Hereby, the legal status of the fund in municipal law is immaterial (Seidl-Hohenveldern/Loibl, para. 0328). Pension funds can act (even without an explicit legal basis in national law) as independent legal entities. Their actions are to be attributed to the IO they belong to under international public law.

The legal status of the pension (reserve) funds in relation to the staff, the former staff members and their legal successors does, of course, not depend on their status under national law but on the internal allocation of competences. For example, decisions of the Standing Committee of the UNJSPF can be directly appealed before the UNAT (Art. 2(9) Statute of UNAT and Art. 48 UNJSPF-Reg.), whereas the decisions of the chief executive officer of the CERN/ESO Pension Fund can be only appealed before the ILOAT after a final decision of the governing board of the fund has been taken (Art. III 1.04 Statute of the Fund and Chapter II Reg. for appeals). The administration of the EPO-RFPSS can take no decision at all with legal effects on the staff members, since the administration of the pension scheme has not been transferred to the fund.

It is common to all funds and reserve funds that they are treated as a special class of asset (see, for example, Art. 38(b) EPO-EPC) of the respective organisation. The ownership of IO of the fund's assets takes the form of trust property.

For the internal accounting, the structural separation of the fund from other assets of the IO allows for full coverage of the pension obligations in accordance with the international public sector accounting standards (IPSAS), which is the accounting standard generally applied by IO. The relevant standard is E 31, "Intangible assets".

### *6. Brief overview of major pension and pension reserve funds of international organisations*

Major pension (reserve) funds and pension plans of IO include: the common pension fund for staff of the UN (United Nations Joint Staff Pension fund, UNJSPF), the CERN/ESO Pension Fund, the EPO Reserve Funds for Pensions and Social Security (EPO-RFPSS), the Scheme Assets of the European Central Bank and the Pension Reserve Funds of the CO. The EU has not yet established a pension fund (for pension funds of IO in more detail, see Ullrich, Pension Schemes).

#### a) The United Nations Joint Staff Pension Fund (UNJSPF)

The UNJSPF was established by decision of the UNGA in 1949 as a subsidiary body of the UNGA within the meaning of Art. 7(2) and 22 UN Charter. It is a capital fund responsible for the administration of the fund's assets and the administration of the pension scheme regulations for the staff of the UN and the member organisations. In legal literature, the UNJSPF is often called "one of the most complex pension payroll and entitlement systems in the world" (UNJSPF, Analysis of workflow statistics – As of 1 January 2017, see also Szasz, The complexification of the United Nations System, in: Max-Planck UNYB 3 (1999), pp. 45 et seq.; Busch, p. 191). The fund is administered by the UN joint staff pension board ("the Board", Art. 5 Reg.). Twelve members are appointed by the UN staff pension committee (four of whom are members or alternate members elected by the UNGA, four are appointed by the UN-SG and four are elected by participants in service in the UN), twenty-one members are appointed by the staff pension committee of the other member organisations (seven of whom are from members or alternate members chosen by the respective General Assembly, seven are appointed by the respective chief administrative officer from the member organisations and seven are elected from participants in service). (As to the composition see Appendix I.) The board is assisted by staff pension committees for the UN and each member organisation (Art. 6 Reg.). The board meets not less frequently than once in every two years (Annex III, Section A.1), between the meetings, the standing committee acts on its behalf (Annex III, Section B4). The administrator of the fund (the chief executive officer, Art. 7 Reg.) is appointed by the UN-SG (Art. 7(a) Reg.) on the recommendation of the Board. The chief executive officer is also responsible for the payment of all benefits under the UNJSPF.

The fund assets (as of 21 July 2016: more than USD 54 billion) are managed in trust as a special class of assets of the UN (Art. 18 Reg.). The investment of the assets of the fund are decided upon by the UN-SG after consultation with an investments committee, and observations and suggestions made by the Board (Art. 19(a) Reg.).

Besides the UN and its agencies, the fund has (as of 31 December 2016) 22 member organisations (Art. 3 Reg.). On 31 December 2015, the fund had more than 126,000 active participants and more than 71,400 beneficiaries.

The fund has no own international legal personality and does not enjoy the explicit legal capacity accorded to legal persons under municipal law. The fund, however, acts in the national legal relations in much the same way as a legal person (see Ullrich, Pension Schemes, p. 612; on the relationship between international and national legal capacity see Seidl-Hohenveldern/Loibl, para. 0327 et seq. and 0921 et seq.; see also Section 18 of the Headquarters Agreement No. 8679 between the UN and the Republic of Austria of 13 April 1967). Decisions of the Board taken in the name of the UNJSPF may be challenged by the participants and beneficiaries of the UNJSPF before the UNAT (Art. 48 UNJSPF Reg. and Art. 2(a) UNAT-Statute).

### b) The CERN/ESO Pension Fund

The CERN Pension Fund is a capital fund (see pensionfund.cern.ch on the internet). It was established by the Council of CERN as a subsidiary body in 1955. Based on cooperation agreements (1 July 1968 and 1 July 1983), it also covers assets of the ESO. The pension fund is also responsible for the administration of the pension scheme regulations integrated into the rules and regulations of the pension fund (updated version of 15 September 2016). The fund enjoys operational autonomy within CERN. The Director General has no responsibility with respect to the management of the fund (Art. I.2.02 Rules).

The main bodies are the Governing Board and the Fund's Chief Executive Officer (Art. I.2.04 f Rules). The afore-mentioned bodies are assisted by the Investment Committee and the Actuarial and Technical Committee. The fund is a special class of assets which institutes an integral part of CERN/ESO assets (Art. I.2.01 Rules). CERN/ESO may not reclaim, borrow, pledge or mortgage the assets of the fund (Art. I.2.03 Rules). The assets of the fund amounted to over CHF 4 billion on 31 December 2015.

The fund has no legal personality under international law, nor is it explicitly accorded legal capacity under national law. In practice, however, the fund acts legally on behalf of CERN.

### c) The EPO Reserve Funds for Pensions and Social Security (EPO-RFPSS)

The EPO-RFPSS was initially set up as a budgetary reserve of the EPO in 1983 and established as a subsidiary body of the EPO on 1 January 1992 and extended by a reserve fund for the long-term care insurance of staff in 2001 (Ullrich, Versorgungssysteme, Pension Schemes; see the regulations for the Reserve Funds for Security and Social Security of the EPO on the EPO website). In 2009, a reserve fund for sickness insurance liabilities and for lump sum payments as a partial compensation for national tax levied on pensions was set up.

In conformity with Art. 38(b) EPO-EPC, the resources of the EPO-RFPSS are to be treated as a special class of assets of the EPO. On 31 December 2015, the assets were approximately EUR 6.6 billion (EPO doc. CA/60/16 available on the EPO website). The capitalised stock of the EPO-RFPSS serves to slow down an excessive increase of contributions ("buffer funds") and thus guarantees some sort of inter-generational equity. The reserve funds are fed by surpluses from the budget of the EPO, left over after deduction of the ongoing payments to staff from the contributions of staff and the EPO. There is a trend towards a fully capitalised fund.

The administration of the pension and social security schemes rests with the management of the human resource department of the European Patent Office. This also goes for the regular assessment of the actuarial balance of the reserve funds. The funds therefore have neither participants nor beneficiaries.

The funds are administered by a Fund Administrator who fulfils his responsibilities under the control of the Supervisory Board. The Board is composed of six members, two members are appointed by the EPO Council, two members by the European Patent Office and two members by the staff representation. (This is one of the exceptional cases where staff is granted some sort of co-determination). Pensioners may be represented by an observer. Since the Administrator of the funds has no authority towards the employees and former employees, he can take no appealable decision (Ullrich, Pension Schemes).

#### d) The Scheme Assets of the European Central Bank

Until 30 June 2009 all contributions, monies, property and other assets of the retirement plan of the employees of the ECB were kept in trust by the ECB as a "pension fund" (Annex III of the Conditions of Employment). On 1 July 2009, a new ECB Pension Scheme (PS) entered into force (Annex IIIa of the Conditions of Employment). Whereas the term "fund" has been replaced by "Scheme Assets", the legal structure has remained untouched (see Section IV of Annex IIIa on the website of the ECB). The "Scheme Assets" are kept by the ECB as its property in trust separate from all of its other assets. This separate class of asset may be used solely to provide benefits under the pension scheme and to pay the expenses of the scheme as decided by the Governing Council (Art. 15(d) PS). The "Scheme" is administered by an administrator (Art. 19 PS). The Scheme assets are invested – in accordance with the policies and strategies determined by the Executive Board Art. 17(a) PS) – by the investment manager under the supervision of an investment committee (Art. 16 PS). An Oversight Committee monitors the overall running of the Scheme as the representative of the beneficiaries' interests (Art. 26(a) PS).

#### e) The Pension Reserve Funds of the co-ordinated organisations

Until the 1990's, the CO saw no need for pension reserves in the form of pension funds or pension reserve funds. The pension benefits of the relatively small number of pensioners could be funded from the current pension contributions of active staff and the organisation. In the subsequent years, the governing bodies of the CO gradually decided to establish pension reserve funds in order to avert the threat of a budget overload of the households through retirement benefits. ESA established its Pension Reserve Fund (not published) in 1995, the CoE in 2003 (Resolution (2006)1, the OECD in 2000, ECMWF in 2003 (not published), WEU:

because of termination of operational activities, liquidation of the establishment of a fund (see doc. A/1934 of 20 June 2006 on the WEU internet portal); NATO in 2005 (partly published on the internet), managed by Previnet (Italy).

Also the Pension Reserve Funds of the CO represent a special class of asset (trust funds) at the respective CO. They serve to secure the pension obligations (guarantees) of the member states (see, for example, Annex Va, Art. 40(2) CoE-SR). The funds are managed either by the CO themselves or by external experts, like ISRP (OECD and CoE funds). In view of the population of each CO the assets of the funds are still relatively small.

### *7. Other rights*

#### a) Leave entitlements

##### *aa) Survey*

In addition to the leave entitlements under the social security system (sickness, maternity, parental and adoption leave, family leave and special leave for family reasons which for systematic reasons are treated there, see above), international employees are entitled to annual leave, leave for personal reasons, and home leave, and benefit from public holidays at their working place. The content and scope of these entitlements vary significantly among the service law systems. An official on leave for any reason whatsoever remains bound by all his professional obligations except for the performance of duties (ILOAT Judgment 1363 para. 25).

##### *bb) Annual leave*

Most IO grant annual leave of 30 working days (Art. 57 EU-SR: for EU institutions between 24 and 30 working days per year; Rule 5(1)(c) UN-SR: two and a half days per month for staff members holding a fixed-term or continuing appointment; Art. 45(1) CoE-SR; 2.5 working days per month; Art. 59 EPO-SR: thirty working days per calendar year). Age and seniority in service are as a rule of no concern for the length of annual leave (see, however, Art. 59(1)(b) EPO-SR: officials aged at least 65 years and who have reached the maximum rate of retirement pension benefit from twelve days' additional leave). Annual leave is holiday. It serves individual life planning and physical and psychological regeneration. It ultimately derives from the general duty of care.

In contrast to most IO, the UN staff leave entitlement only arises after completion of the relevant service period. Only in exceptional circumstances may annual leave of up to ten working days be granted (Rule 5(1)(f) UN-SR). Annual leave may generally be taken in units of days and half-days (Rule 5(1)(e) UN-SR). In the EU, however, the annual leave must comprise at least one period of two consecutive weeks (Annex V, Art. 2 EU-SR). If a proven illness occurs during annual leave, the leave is extended by the duration of the incapacity (see, for example, Annex V, Art. 3 EU-SR).

The transfer of unused annual leave to the following year is limited (see, for example, Annex V, Art. 4 EU-SR: twelve days). The limits of carry-over annual leave not only serve the concern of the organisation for the staff's health, but they should prevent an excessive accumulation of holiday entitlement prior to retirement, which would lead to substantial compensation payments exempt from national taxation, since pensions paid by IO are mostly subject to national taxation (see above). If a staff member at the time of leaving the service has drawn annual leave in excess of his entitlement, a deduction from the payments due takes place (Annex V, Art. 4(3) EU-SR).

*cc) Leave on personal grounds*

IO generally grant their employees unpaid leave on personal grounds (Art. 40 EU-SR; Reg. 5(3) UN-SR: leave on personal grounds is granted under the provision for "special leave", which also comprises "family leave" and leave granted in special cases, like death of family members or in the case of serious family emergency; Appendix VII Art. 3(1) CoE-SR; Art. 45 EPO-SR).

Leave for personal reasons may be granted e.g. for study or research, for other forms of personal development or the exercise of a temporary professional activity, which must, however, be compatible with the obligations stipulated in the SR (see ILOAT Judgment 1363: Running of a consultancy firm incompatible with his activity as a patent examiner of the EPO).

Leave on personal grounds is generally for a limited period (Art. 40(2) EU-SR): one year with possible yearly extensions up to fifteen years over the entire career of an official; Appendix VII Art. 4(1) CoE-SR: Minimum period one year, maximum period together with family leave six years, but restricted to three years in respect of most reasons for entitlement). During leave, staff members are not qualified for promotion and step increments (Art. 40(3) EU-SR; Reg. 5(3)(e) UN-SR; Appendix VII Art. 6(2) CoE-SR).

At the end of their leave, staff members are entitled to be reinstated in their post (Appendix VII Art. 8(1) CoE-SR) or in the first post of equal grade which falls vacant (Art. 40(4)(d) EU-SR). If the staff member declines the post offered, he is deemed to have resigned (Appendix VII Art. 9 CoE-SR). At the EU, he may be required to resign if he declines the post offered a second time and after the Joint Committee has been consulted (Art. 40(4)(d) EU-SR).

*dd) Home leave*

Staff members of IO are recruited on the broadest geographical basis from among nationals of the member states ("international recruitment", see, for example, Rule 4(5) UN-SR). It is in the interest of an IO to main the international character of its staff and the international administrative tribunals have justified a general principle of law on this ground (see above). In addition to the expatriation allowance, all IO grant some sort of special benefits for this staff in order to foster the regular return to their home country. The facilities granted may be extra days off (Art. 45(2) CoE-SR and Art. 60(1) EPO-SR: additional home leave of eight working days every two years) or supplementary leave of at least 2.5 days per year for travelling time (Annex V, Art. 7 EU-SR) and travel expenses to the place of origin or a lump-sum payment (Annex VII, Art. 8 EU-SR; Art. 42(1)(c) CoE-SR; Art. 77(3) EPO-SR). According to UN-SR (Rule 5(2)(a)) a staff member may spend a reasonable period of his annual leave in the home country. He may claim travel time and travel expenses once in every twenty-four months of service (Rule 5(2)(i) UN-SR).

The entitlement to home leave is generally linked to the place of origin, that is the place where the staff member has been recruited or where he has the centre of his interests (Annex VII, Art. 7(4) EU-SR). Other IO take account of the place to which the staff member has the closest ties (e.g. the place of his family, the place where he grew up or where he owns property). Under Rule 5(2)(d) UN-SR in determining the country for which home leave is granted, the recognised nationality of the staff member is, in principle, decisive subject to special conditions and exceptions. A subsequent change of the place or origin is in principle possible. The administrative tribunals have had many opportunities to comment on the definition and the change of the place of origin (see below).

*ee) Public holidays*

Although national holidays are without legal significance for the autonomous internal regulatory system of IO, organisations generally accept the public holidays effective at the duty station, in addition to the work-free weekends, out of respect for religious sentiments, national traditions and for purely practical reasons (family, public transport). IO with headquarters, sub-offices or branches in more than one member state frequently compensate any higher number of holidays at a duty station by granting the corresponding number of additional days off at other duty stations. In addition, the head of administration is generally empowered to restrict the activities in special cases (e.g. traditional events at the duty station) or to decide on seasonal closure of the headquarters during the Christmas period.

In the case of illness on a public holiday, there is, as with illness at the weekend, and in contrast to illness during annual leave, no entitlement to additional leave.

**Jurisprudence**

Annual leave

ILOAT Judgments

2069: The SR do not justify a deduction from annual leave for assisting a colleague in an internal complaint procedure; 1985: Annual leave may only be claimed for actually worked periods or periods treated alike; 959: Prohibition of concurrent employment at another IO also applies during the holiday period; 769: No entitlement to leave for illness on a public holiday; 36: An application for annual leave can be rejected for official reasons (discretion).

CJEU Judgments/Orders

F-41/14: It is unacceptable to feign illness and thereby falsely claim an additional day of annual leave; C-579/12: It is constant case law that annual leave cannot be reduced if the official is not able to fulfil his obligation to work due to illness. Annex V Art. 4 EU-SR (no carry-over of annual leave in excess of twelve days) does not deal with the question of the carry-over of annual leave which cannot be taken because of long term sick leave. A carry-over period of fifteen months in such a case would not be contrary to the purpose of the right to annual leave; T-368/04: Compensation for annual leave not taken (T-80/04); C-348/90 P: Compensation for leave not taken.

**Jurisprudence**

Special leave

ILOAT Judgments

2619: Grant of special leave as a discretionary decision; the interests of the organisation take precedence over the interests of the complainant; 2593: During a period of unpaid special leave there is no entitlement to sick leave; 2379: Special leave for vocational training; 2053: Service regulations do not allow for professional experience acquired during unpaid leave for personal reasons to be counted for promotability; 1855: Grant of special leave denied due to service requirements; 1706: If early termination of contract has been agreed and special leave is granted during this period, the complainant still remains a staff member and rules on preferential treatment for staff in service apply; 1363: Staff members on leave for any reason remain bound by all professional obligations except performance of service; 991: Granting of a bonus can be restricted on objective reasons and therefore be refused to staff on unpaid leave.

CJEU Judgments/Orders

C-284/98 P: Reinstatement after leave on personal grounds depends, according to Art. 40(4) (d) EU-SR, only on the existence of a post for which the employee has the required qualifications, no further conditions are allowed; C-315/97 P: Special leave for elections and travelling time; T-48/90: After leave on personal grounds the organisation has systematically to verify each vacant post as to whether it fits for the official; 267/85: Review of required qualifications for reinstatement in a new post after leave on personal grounds; 785/79: No suitable post offered after leave on personal grounds; 108/79: Successive refusal to take a post offered after leave on personal grounds justifies compulsory resignation; 58/75: Failure to reinstate an official after leave on personal grounds; compensation.

**Jurisprudence**

Home leave

ILOAT Judgments

2639 (2637): Nationality of duty station acquired before obtaining a contract, no entitlement to home leave; 2389: Object of home leave is not primarily to make a monetary concession to staff members but is granted in the interest of the IO; the home country is not necessarily that of the staff member's nationality but the country to which he has the closest personal and material connection; 1985: Home leave is not due since the complainant was required to work and was residing in his home country; 1472: The home is usually the country of birth, but this is not an absolute and invariable rule; 1364 (1324, 1189): Equal treatment, dual nationality and home country; 1217: Revision of home station is discretionary, it must be applied for in time, it does not serve to prepare for retirement; 976: Reimbursement of charges for shipment of baggage when taking home leave; 945: Calculation of a home leave which is granted every second year; 937: Dismissal as a result of giving false information about home leave and travel expenses; 905: No right to home leave one month before termination of appointment; 525: the term "home" should not be interpreted too narrowly, it is usually, but not always, determined by birth, nationality or former residence; 441: Entitlement to travel expenses to the home station as an acquired right; 371: The travel expenses to the home station are basically an acquired right but not their amount and the conditions of payment; 271: Refund of only a portion of travel expenses to the home station without setting a specific percentage is not permitted; 270: No refund for travel expenses for family members who already live at the place of home.

CJEU Judgments/Orders

F-39/06: The reimbursement of annual travelling expenses to the place of origin of the official does not depend on the publication of a consolidated version of the EU-SR; F-43/05: The reimbursement of the travelling expenses to the place of origin of the official is based on a discretionary decision of the legislative organ of the EU. There is no general principle of the EU legal system or of international public law from which an obligation may be derived for the legislator to grant such a reimbursement; T-354/03: Reimbursement of annual travelling expenses for the child of divorced officials; T-28/98: The place of origin and the place of recruitment are not necessarily identical; T-134/96: No legitimate expectation in maintaining a certain travelling time to the place of origin for subsequent years; T-44/89: The place of origin as the centre of vital interests depends on a stable relationship, which a staff member maintains because *inter alia* of his main family ties, heritable interests or essential civic interest, both active and passive; 144/84: When determining the centre of vital interests for establishing the place of origin, the place where a couple had established residence before entering the service, cannot be disregarded, account may be also taken of permanent heritable interests.

**Jurisprudence**

Public holidays

ILOAT Judgments

2250: If the last day of the 90-day period after receipt of the final decision is a public holiday, the deadline will be extended for filing the complaint to the following working day (517, 306); 1194: Discretion in granting additional leave for German staff on the day of reunification of Germany (3 October 1990), no unequal treatment, no infringement of the agreement on granting an equal number of public holidays at all duty stations; 769: No entitlement to compensatory leave or pay for sickness leave during a public holiday; 699: Number of public holidays in excess of the maximum number of holidays laid down in the service regulations. Additional working days lost to be made up by extending working hours, maximum of working hours per week to be respected however.

CJEU Judgment

T-23/01: Reduction of public holidays at a duty station in a third country in order to compensate days of annual leave is unlawful.

### b) The right to assistance and vocational training

Most service regulations contain provisions in varying degrees of detail on the right of staff to assistance and vocational training by the organisation.

#### *aa) Assistance*

The duty of assistance is stipulated in most SR of IO. In the case of lacunae reference has to be made to the general legal principle of the duty of care an IO owes its staff (see above). The duty of assistance is not identical with the duty to provide solicitude (duty of care) which, as a rule, is not stipulated in the SR of IO but has to be derived by the tribunals from the general legal principle of the duty of care (see above). (CJEU T-67/99: Solicitude is not obliging an organisation to act beyond the clear wording of the duty of assistance in the service regulations). The duty of assistance safeguards staff against attacks by individuals and entities outside the organisation, and by own staff members (see, however, the difference in the jurisprudence of the ILOAT and the CJEU above, under the general principle of the duty of care) in the form of threats, insulting, defamatory acts or utterances, or attacks to persons or property of the employee or his family (Art. 24 EU-SR; implicitly in Reg. 1(2)(c) UN-SR; Art. 40 CoE-SR; Art. 28 EPO-SR).

The duty to assist also extends to retired staff. There is, of course, no duty of assistance against the actions and decisions of the organisation itself. The duty of assistance requires a rapid and diligent intervention by the organisation. The extent of the duty of assistance depends on the circumstances of the individual case. The organisation may have to enact disciplinary proceedings if the perpetrator of a criminal act is another official. If the staff member suffers an injury in the exercise of his official duties and he cannot obtain full redress, the organisation must compensate it, if he has not wilfully or by grave negligence caused the damage (Art. 24 EU-SR). To the extent to which he receives compensation he has to assign any claim against the third party.

**Jurisprudence**

Assistance (care)

ILOAT Judgments and CJEU Judgments/Orders

(See the case law under the general legal principle of care and assistance).

*bb) Vocational training*

Most IO promote vocational training for their staff (Art. 24a EU-SR; Rule 1.3(b) UN-SR; Art. 53 CoE-SR; Art. 29 EPO-SR). The training must meet the interests of the staff member and be compatible with the smooth functioning of the service. In some IO there are plans for training set up in collaboration with staff representatives (Art. 53 CoE-SR). The training must be taken into account for the purposes of promotion (Art. 24a EU-SR).

### c) Protection of dignity and professional reputation

The protection of dignity and professional reputation is recognised by the case law of all international administrative tribunals as a general principle of law in the international civil service (see above). In addition, some aspects of this protection are laid down in the service regulations.

The organisations have a duty to supervise the conduct of staff in this respect and to implement all necessary measures to protect staff against all sorts of victimisation and attacks. An organisation is required to make good any damage suffered by a staff member caused by negligence on its part in connection with the performance of his duties.

Most IO have adapted specific procedures for the resolution of harassment-related grievances (confidential counsellor or ombudsman), with the aim of dealing with these issues in a confidential, competent and prompt way. These procedures may, however, not preclude the right to standard legal protection by appeals boards and tribunals.

Art. 12a EU-SR requires of staff that they refrain from any form of psychological or sexual harassment, it also contains definitions of both types of harassment. Similarly, Rule 1(2)(f) UN-SR prohibits any form of discrimination or harassment, explicitly including sexual or gender harassment as well as a psychological or verbal abuse at the workplace or in connection with work.

The CoE adopted its charter on professional ethics on 15 July 2005. This charter requires CoE staff members to base their work-related conduct and their life outside the working environment on certain ethical values. Such work-related values are respect for dignity, diversity, integrity, discretion, privacy, confidentiality and accountability (Art. I.1 and Art. II.3 to 10). The charter comprises rules to be observed outside the working environment (Art. III.11 to 15) and provisions on legal consequences in the case of failure to observe these standards (Art. IV.16 to 17).

With effect from 1 January 2013 the EPO set up rules on the protection of dignity of its officials (Circular 135 on a policy on the prevention of harassment and the resolution of conflicts at the EPO, see EPO Codex). The aim of this policy is to protect the dignity of all persons working at or for the EPO (Office) (Part I of the Circular). All forms of harassment are regarded as unacceptable (Art. 3). Conflicts with colleagues should be resolved amicably (Art. 6) if necessary with the assistance of a confidential counsellor (Art. 7). A formal allegation of harassment may be filed (Art. 10) and an investigation may be conducted by an investigation unit within the Principal Directorate Internal Audit and Oversight (Art. 11 et seq.). At the conclusion of the investigations a report is submitted to the President of the EPO (Office) who may initiate disciplinary proceedings (Art. 16).

#### d) Occupational safety and health (OSH)

The right to safety and health at work is part of the service regulations of IO and is recognised by the international administrative tribunals as a general principle of labour law (see above). Despite the autonomous regulatory powers of an IO, the international civil service law provisions on occupational health, safety and ergonomics and the corresponding municipal regulations cannot be seen in isolation. There is a common interest among the IO and the national authorities to observe certain basic standards at the headquarters of an IO in a member state. In many cases there is even an express duty of the organisation, established in the PPI or seat agreement to cooperate in this field (see above). Based on the general labour law principle of safety and health care at the workplace IO have adopted numerous regulations and entered into agreements with national authorities to comply with their obligations in this area.

The SR of IO provide for mandatory medical examinations of staff (see, for example, Art. 33 and Art. 59(6) EU-SR, officials must undergo a medical check-up before appointment and every year after appointment). Compulsory testing for HIV/AIDS is consistently not required (see, for example, UN doc. ST/SGB/2003/18: "Policy on HIV/AIDS in the workplace"). At the UN, there is compulsory testing within some services at the headquarters for illegal drugs (UN doc. ST/AI/2003/2: "Testing in the Security and Safety Service at Headquarters for use of illegal drugs and controlled substances").

Most IO have an occupational health service competent for protecting health at the workplace (staff counselling, psychological support, ergonomic issues, assistance in returning to work after a long illness, physiotherapy). Some IO dispose of special regulations in this field, e.g. guidelines for working with display screen equipment. In compliance with the safety and environmental standards of the member states and international regulations, most IO set up safety offices or special occupational safety committees which monitor the compliance with safety standards for technical equipment (air-conditioning, lifts, escalators etc). The maintenance work itself is usually carried out by national professional firms under the supervision of the organisation.

What are probably the most recent and comprehensive rulings on occupational health, safety and ergonomics were set up by the EPO (see Art. 26b, 26c and 38a EPO-SR accessible on the EPO website (EPO Codex)).

At the EU, Art. 1e(2) EU-SR stipulates that the officials shall be accorded working conditions complying with appropriate health and safety standards at least equivalent to the minimum requirements applicable under measures adopted in these areas to the treaties. With its decision C(2006)1623 of 26 April 2006, the Commission established a harmonised policy for health and safety at work for all Commission staff.

At the UN, doc. JIU/REP/2011/1 delivers a comprehensive review on the manner in which the UN occupational health system is pursued, managed, supported and monitored.

At the CoE, the SG takes appropriate measures to ensure the safety and hygiene of the work premises.

#### e) Privileges and immunities

The privileges and immunities enjoyed by staff of the IO have been dealt with above under the privileges and immunities of IO and of international civil servants.

#### f) Right to compensation for damages

As a rule, the service regulations of IO contain no explicit legal basis for staff members to claim damages from their organisation. All international administrative tribunals have, however, developed a general principle of labour law which grants officials the right to claim damages from their organisation in cases of illegal acts and decisions with regard to their employer – employee relationship (see above under general legal principles).

### g) Legal protection

The service regulations of all IO contain detailed rules on the legal protection of their employees by international administrative tribunals and appeals committees. IO cannot deny legal protection by pleading immunity from national jurisdiction. This is also valid in relation to their own staff. If IO failed to grant legal protection through international tribunals, they would have to provide legal protection through arbitration or even through national courts. However, as far as the statutes of an international administrative tribunal meet minimum international standards of procedural justice, the concrete bounds of legal protection are set by the jurisdiction of the respective tribunal (see the recommendation in the case of lack of jurisdiction by the ILOAT in Judgment 2657: no legal protection for job applicants). (For more details see the comments on the legal protection in the service regulations below and the legal protection as a general principle of law, dealt with above under general legal principles.)

### h) The right to inspect the personal file

All IO keep personal files in which important documents concerning the employer -employee relationship are registered, e.g. application forms, appraisal reports, promotion documents, marital status, disciplinary measures, etc.. Nowadays, personal files are mostly kept in electronic form.

Broadly consistent rules exist in all IO for the management of personal files. In principle, the management of multiple personal files for the same official is forbidden (Art. 26 EU-SR: "... only one personal file for each official"; Art. 46(1) CoE-SR; Art. 32(5) EPO-SR). However, a separate medical file is allowed (Art. 26a EU-SR; Art. 46(2) CoE-SR). The documents recorded in the personal file may only be used or cited by the administration if they were communicated beforehand to the official (Art. 26 EU-SR; Art. 46(3) CoE-SR). The personal file may not contain any references to political, trade union, philosophical or religious activities and views or to the official's race, ethnic origin or sexual orientation (Art. 26 EU-SR; Art. 46(4) CoE-SR; Art. 32(4) EPO-SR). The personal file is kept confidential. It may be consulted by the official or his representative at any time via intranet or in the appropriate administration office (Art. 26 EU-SR; Art. 46(6) CoE-SR; Art. 32(7) EPO-SR). Also copying is permitted (Art. 26 EU-SR). Some committees of the organisation (e.g. promotion committee) need, as part of their mandate, access to personal files. To this end, some organisations have formal access arrangements (Art. 46 CoE-SR).

The regulations for personal files at the UN differ in some aspects from this common standard. Due to the administrative directive (still in force) dated 24 February 1955 (doc. ST/AI/108) there is an "Official Status File", which records the development of the career, as well as a "Financial File" with a list of payments made to the staff member, and a "Travel File" containing a record of missions. In 1982, the "Confidential Files" (doc. ST/AI/292: "Filing of adverse material in personal records") were forbidden. Since then, every official has the right to be heard before an adverse document will be included is added to the personal file. The staff member has, apart from exceptional cases (e.g. if he wants to file a complaint), the opportunity to inspect his personal file once a year only.

A violation of the correct management of the personal file may result in a claim of immaterial damages (see, for example, CJEU Judgment T-73/89).

#### i) Data protection

Most IO have internal regulations on the protection of staff with regard to the automated processing of personal data. Despite certain differences in the scope of protection (e.g. automated, partially automated or manually processed data) and in technical and formal details (mostly laid down in hierarchically lower-ranking guidelines), the following core principles of data protection are guaranteed (the relevant articles of the EU Regulation on the protection of personal data by Community institutions (EC) doc. No. 45/2001 of 18 December 2000 are quoted in parentheses as an example):

- The legitimate purpose of the data processing (Art. 4 to 6);
- The duty to supply the data subject with information about the processing of his data and the right of access to his personal data (Art. 11 to 13);
- Data quality (Art. 4);
- Prior checking of the processing of specific data (Art. 27);
- The security of data processing (Art. 22);
- The duty to rectify, block or erase data (Art. 14 to 16);
- The internal and external transfer of personal data (Art. 7 and 8);
- The appointment and tasks of data protection officer (Art. 24 and 25);
- Legal protection (Art. 33).

In case the internal guidelines on data protection showing lacunae or are in need of interpretation, the international administrative tribunals will have recourse to the general law principle of privacy (see above).

*EU*

The EU Regulation (EC) doc. No. 45/2001 of 18 December 2000 (doc. OJ 2001 L8, p. 1–22) on the protection of individuals with regard to the processing of personal data by Community institutions and bodies and on the free movement of such data

This regulation protects all persons whose personal data are processed by the EU institutions and bodies in any context, including its employees (preambule para. 7). It applies to the wholly or partly automated processing and the non-automated processing of personal data which form part of a filing system or are intended to form part of such a system. EU employees may lodge a complaint with the European data protection supervisor regarding an alleged violation of the regulations on data protection (Art. 33). This right to complain is in addition to the right to file a legal appeal under Art. 90 et seq. EU-SR. Even no violation of own rights on data protection of the staff member is required ("whistle blower", "popular action").

*UN*

Guidelines for the Regulation of Computerized Personal Data Files (Resolution 45/95 of the UN General Assembly of 14 December 1990, doc. A/RES/45/95)

The Guidelines contain minimum guarantees for computerised personal data. The Guidelines should apply to personal files kept by IO (point B. of the Resolution).

Even without a formal implementation in the internal law of the UN by the UN-SG, it is constant case law (see, for example, ILOAT Judgment 848; UNAT Judgments 378, 273) that IO are internally bound by the legal principles which they want their member states and other organisations to respect (see above under general legal principles of privacy). It would nevertheless be desirable that the UN adapt specific rules for the internal data protection of employees as a means to guarantee the fundamental human rights of staff. (For more details see the UNHCR doc. on Policy on the Protection of Personal Data of Persons of Concern to UNHCR on the UNHCR website).

*CoE*

The Secretary General's Regulations instituting a system of data protection for personal data files at the Council of Europe of 17 April 1989

The Regulation is based on the Convention for the Protection of Individuals with regard to Automatic Processing of Personal Data of 28 January 1981 (Convention No. 108). It is applicable to all personal data of staff members and of non-staff members which are collected, stored and used by the CoE automatically or manually (Art. 1 of the Regulation and Art. 3(1) and 3(2)(c) of the Convention).

The Regulation takes up all core principles of the Convention. In addition, the data protection officer also acts within the scope of staff complaints that concern data protection issues (Art. 6(a) Appendix of the Regulation).

*EPO*

On 1 April 2014 new EPO guidelines for the protection of personal data (accessible on the EPO Codex) entered into force replacing the former guidelines of 1 July 1992.

The guidelines take account of all core data principles (see above).

Art. 3 lays down that the guidelines apply to the processing of personal data wholly or partly by automatic means;

Art. 4 states the principles relating to data quality;

Art. 7 to 8 deal with the transmission of personal data to recipients within or outside the EPO;

Art. 9 to 12: contain special provisions relating to the processing of data;

Art. 13 to 15 deal with information to be supplied to data subjects and rights of the data subjects;

Art. 16 to 17 contain principles of confidentiality and security of processing;

Art. 18 to 25 contain institutional provisions on the data protection officer, the controller and complaints by the data protection officer and requests from data subjects to the data protection officer.

The guidelines need to be supplemented by a reference to Art. 8 of the AT/EPO agreement. In conformity with this provision, the EPO shall ensure that persons whose data are processed electronically are able to enforce their rights vis-à-vis the EPO in matters of data protection at least to the extent provided for in the Convention for the Protection of Individuals with regard to Automatic Processing of Personal Data (Convention of the Council of Europe No. 108 of 28 January 1981).

### j) Other benefits

In many cases, officials or departments are entitled to certain lump sum payments for social gatherings of staff, special anniversaries in service, and the costs of a party on retirement of as staff member etc. IO regularly support internal committees of a social character of staff (social services, Amicale) by granting financial subsidies and access to the facilities (room, equipment, secretary etc) of the organisation. Staff restaurants are regularly subsidised. The use of means of telecommunications of the organisation for private purposes is usually tolerated (local telephone call, e-mail, internet access) within certain bounds.

### *8. Collective rights of staff*

#### a) Survey

The collective rights of international officials to participate in issues relating to working conditions and staff welfare are limited to consultation. Compared with the right to negotiation or co-determination, this is the weakest form of participation. Nevertheless, is has an important protective function for the international staff. International administrative tribunals, above all the ILOAT, have underlined the practical importance of this collective right in a large number of cases. (For more detail, see above under the freedom of association, assembly and in trade union matters.)

Staff committees derive their general mandate through staff elections. During the period of office, the opinion of the staff is ascertained by general staff assemblies and referenda. The staff representation acts on behalf of the total staff. Its functions and powers are exhaustively vested in the service regulations of the respective organisation.

In addition to the staff committees, all IO have one or even several international trade unions (staff union, union syndicale). Occasionally, there are also professional associations or occupational unions which are established by certain categories of staff members (e.g. interpreters, translators) to promote professionalism and represent their specific interests within an IO. These are interest groups outside the formal institutional structure of staff participation set-up, under the service regulations. These groups primarily represent the interests of their members in issues relating to working conditions and staff welfare. Their functions and powers are based on general principles of freedom of association (see more in detail above). A specific system applies to the UN family of IO (see below).

All activities of staff unions are attributable to their representatives who in their capacity as staff members are in principle subject to the service regulations of the organisation. Actions of representatives of the staff unions are within the ambit of the official activities of the organisation and therefore enjoy immunity from national jurisdiction.

Legal disputes with their organisation are subject to the jurisdiction of the respective international administrative tribunal.

On 20 January 2017 the Supreme Court of the Netherlands (ref. 15/02186) issued an important ruling on the immunity of the EPO from the jurisdiction of Netherlands' Courts in an action brought by the trade union of the EPO (SUEPO) against a possible curtailment of the right to strike and a possible restriction of the activities of the trade union. The court stated that granting the EPO immunity from national jurisdiction is essential for the proper functioning of the EPO. The individual right of access to a court under Art. 6 EConHR is not absolute (see the decision of the ECHR of 18 February 1999, Waite and Kennedy v. Germany Appl. No. 26083/94) but subject to limitations as long as the essence of the right is not impaired. Although there is no collective right of SUEPO to direct access to the ILOAT, the individual staff members of the EPO and the staff representative may invoke the collective right and interests of all employees. There are therefore, reasonable means to protect the rights guaranteed under Art. 6 and the freedom of collective action under Art. 11 EConHR. The court declared that the courts of the Netherlands had no jurisdiction to hear the claims of SUEPO against the EPO.

The Munich Higher Labour Court (MHLC) dismissed two appeals lodged by the trade union of the EPO (SUEPO) against two judgments of the Munich Labour Court rendered against the EPO (Germany) in disputes concerning *inter alia* the introduction of new rules on strikes and the recognition of the SUEPO as a trade union (Judgments of 30 June 2016, ref. 2 Sa 168/15 and 2 Sa 167/15).

The MHLC held that the EPO enjoys immunity from German jurisdiction which is proportionate and reasonable within the meaning of the case law of the ECHR. The right of SUEPO to have access to a court under Art. 6 EConHR is protected by the access to the ILOAT. SUEPO has not attempted to obtain a fair hearing through an appeal to the ILOAT. It cannot be presumed from the outset that the ILOAT will consider the SUEPO to have no standing. Only through a complaint to the ILOAT can it be ascertained whether any loophole excluding the SUEPO from that system can be closed and whether the restriction on access to the German courts resulting from the immunity of the EPO is disappropriate within the meaning of the case law of the ECHR. It is for the ILOAT to decide under Art. II.7 of its Statute whether it has competence. Even if there is no provision on the standing of SUEPO it cannot be presumed that no protection is available. The court explicitly referred to the decision of the ECHR in the case Klausecker v. Germany (Appl. No. 415/07) where the ILOAT in its Judgment 2657 considered it highly desirable that the EPO should seek a solution affording the complainant access to court either by waiving its immunity or by submitting the dispute to arbitration (see above).

In most IO there is considerable overlap in terms of the individual people who are the representatives of the trade union and of the staff association. A lack in their respective powers is therefore not an issue since it is easily corrected by a simple "changing of caps" between the representatives of the trade unions and the staff committee.

– The hybrid system of the IO of the UN family

A somewhat different structure is to be found in the UN and some organisations of the UN family. In these organisations staff interests are collectively represented by a staff union which can be qualified as a *mixtum compositum* of a trade union and a staff committee. The so-called "staff representative bodies" include staff associations, unions and other corresponding staff representative bodies (Rule 8(1)(a) UN-SR). The representative bodies for staff participation (all issues relating to the conditions of work, staff welfare, conditions of life and other human policies) are the executive committees of the unions (Rule 8(1)(f)(g) UN-SR).

The hybrid collection of bodies represents the collective staff interests in the "joint" staff-management machinery (Reg. 8(2) and Rules 8(1) and 8(2) UN-SR). (For more detail see above under the freedom of association and below under trade unions.)

– The framework agreements

In the service law systems of the EU and of some organisations of the UN-CS (for example the ILO), there are special framework agreements between the organisations and the staff union(s). They provide *inter alia* a more intensified staff participation (dialogue, negotiation or conciliation procedures) in comparison to the "normal" consultation process safeguarded by the staff committees. (For more details see below.)

The following sections describe the structures and elements of the collective participation of staff committees and trade unions in issues relating to working conditions and staff welfare, as well as the main features of a framework agreement between trade union(s) and an IO. (For more detail see also above under the freedom of association, assembly and trade union matters.)

### b) The staff committees

#### *aa) General remarks*

The service regulations of IO do not, as a rule, explicitly regulate a general right of staff to collective participation in staff matters. The case law of the international administrative tribunals has, however, developed a general participation right for staff members in the international civil service (see above under participation rights).

The SR regularly contain basic principles for the composition, structure and activities of the staff committee of an IO. These provisions relate to the election process (e.g. secret ballot), the term of office of the representatives, the setting-up of local sections of the staff committee in the different places of employment, the representation of all categories of staff in the committee, etc. (Annex II Art. 1 EU-SR; Rule 8(1) UN-SR; Appendix I Art. 3 CoE-SR; Art. 35(5)(c) EPO-SR, see doc. CA/4/14 Annex 2 of the Regulations for the staff committee elections available on the EPO website). Within this framework, the staff committee autonomously manages its affairs on the basis of the general principle of freedom of association and the regulatory order of the organisation. This applies particularly to the details of the electoral process (for an exception, see the EPO rulings), the internal structure, the internal rules of procedure, the internal assignment of activities and the like. Since, unlike the international trade unions, staff committees are internal bodies, which assume specific functions under the service regulations, there is a general obligation of the organisation to monitor the compliance of the election and the legal framework of the staff committee in the service regulations (CJEU Judgments T-368/94, 54–75; the somewhat deviating position of the ILOAT in Judgments 2636, 274, 78 is doubtful). The details of the election process for the staff committee and the regulatory order of the committee is, as a rule, decided by general assembly of staff. All staff members are entitled to vote or to be elected (sometimes a minimum length of service is required in order to vote or to be elected; see, for example, Appendix I, Art. 3(2) CoE-SR; the status of temporary staff may also be an issue). In contrast to membership in an international trade union, there are no financial contributions to staff committees by the officials (but see the hybrid representation system of the UN below).

The term of office of a staff representative is usually between one and three years (see, for example, Annex II Art. 1 EU-SR; Appendix I, Art. 31 CoE-SR: two years).

*bb) Facilities provided to staff committees*

(See above under participation rights)

*cc) Formal participation in staff matters*

The process of consultation with the staff committee is governed by specific provisions, which contain a list of subjects requiring consultation, as well as rules on consultation procedures and on the composition of consultation bodies.

The participation of staff representatives in the joint committees is generally based on an equal number of members appointed by the staff committee and by the administration. The chairman is appointed by the administration or in yearly alternation with the staff committee.

The number, denominations and competences of the joint committees referred to below vary from organisation to organisation. It is the task of all joint committees to present reasoned opinions or suggestions to the head of the appointing authority. Although their statements are not of a binding nature, the organisation must seriously consider them before taking a final decision.

– *The joint committees for service regulation matters and general staff matters (working conditions, general living conditions)*

EU: Art. 10 EU-SR: the Staff Regulations Committee is consulted on all proposals to revise the SR, it may put forward suggestions for reviewing the SR. The Staff Committee shall bring to the notice of the institution suggestions concerning the service and proposals concerning staff's working conditions or general living conditions (Art. 9(3) EU-SR).

UN: staff representative bodies are entitled to effective participation through their elected executive committee in identifying, examining and resolving issues relating to staff welfare, conditions of work, general conditions of life and other human resources policies. They are entitled to make proposals to the UNSG on behalf of the staff (Rule 8(1)(f) UN-SR). General administrative instructions or directives on questions within the scope of Rule 8(1)(f) UN-SR must be transmitted in advance (except in emergency situations) to the executive committee for consideration and comment before being placed in effect (Rule 8(1)(h) UN-SR).

CoE: Appendix I Art. 6. The staff committee is consulted on all alterations or amendments to the SR or other regulations concerning the staff. The staff committee is obliged to bring to the notice of the SG any difficulty concerning the interpretation or application of the SR or the implementing provisions or any measures of a general nature concerning the staff (Art. 5).

EPO: In 2014 the general advisory committee was replaced by a general consultative committee (see doc. CA/4/14 available on the EPO website). The general consultative committee is consulted on proposals to amend the SR, PS and implementing rules and any proposal which concerns the conditions of employment of the whole or part of the staff. It is also consulted on questions of the EPO Office (for a considerable case law see above under participation rights). The streamlined consultation process (doc. CA/4/14 p. 6) provides that the members of the committee shall primarily express their opinion by voting, whereas in the former general advisory committee the emphasis was on finding a compromise solution (see above under participation rights).

– *Committees for recruitment and promotion*

EU: Selection board, Annex III EU-SR; UN: Senior review group and central review bodies, Rule 4(15) UN-SR; CoE: Appointment board advising on recruitment, transfer and promotion matters, Appendix II CoE-SR; EPO: Selection boards, Art. 2 and Annex II EPO-SR. The provisions on promotion boards had been deleted on 1 January 2015.

– *Committees for disciplinary matters*

EU: Disciplinary board, Art. 9(1) EU-SR and Annex IX EU-SR; UN: together with the two-tier formal system of administrating of justice (UNDT, UNAT) the joint disciplinary committees have been abolished, a staff member may file a complaint against a disciplinary measure before the UNDT direct, see Rule 10(3) UN-SR; CoE: Disciplinary Boards, Appendix X CoE-SR; EPO: Disciplinary committees, Art. 97 et seq. EPO-SR.

– *Committees for internal complaints*

EU: No internal appeals body; UN: The provisions relating to the joint appeals board have been repealed and replaced by the new two-tier system of administrating of justice (UNDT, UNAT), see Rule 11(1) UN-SR, see ILO doc. GB304/PFA/16/2); CoE: advisory committee on disputes, Art. 59 CoE-SR; EPO: appeal committee, Art. 111 EPO-SR.

Additional joint committees may be set up *ad hoc*, for example, in particularly sensitive areas (e.g. performance appraisal systems, ombudsman procedures in harassment matters, invalidity committee, reports committee).

Staff committees may also be involved in the appointment of the data protection officer and be represented in committees dealing with issues of working conditions and other human resources policies (e.g. nurseries, restaurants, newsstands, leisure clubs, ergonomics, health protection, security and monitoring of technical equipment).

*dd) Informal participation in staff matters*

In addition to the formal participation of the staff committees explicitly described in the service regulations, there is a wide field for these collective bodies to contribute to the smooth functioning of the service by providing a channel for the expression of interests. In addition to the informal contacts with the head and the senior management of the organisation other forms of dialogue exist institutionalised to varying degrees. An exchange of views at a very early stage of the decision-making process in staff matters is to the advantage of both sides. Because of the abundance of power of the head of an IO (sole decision-making competence in relation to the officials) the success of a confident cooperation depends to a large extent on his personality and human skills.

The staff committee members also maintain contact ("lobbying") with the national delegations of the legislative body (Council, General Assembly, Committee of Ministers). Staff representatives are generally admitted as observers to the plenary meetings and committee meetings of these bodies. The staff committee may also present their own documents to these bodies (see, for example, Appendix I Art. 7 CoE-SR) and may take the floor in matters of their concern.

Staff committees can only fulfil their duties if they maintain permanent contact with the staff members they represent. For this reason, the staff committee convenes general meetings of staff, sets up working groups on specific issues, informs staff regularly on the outcomes of meetings of joint committees, discloses in a timely fashion matters affecting the interest of staff and assists staff members in defending their professional interests. In most of these areas there is nevertheless a grey area of inter-change with the respective trade union(s) which have more financial resources at their disposal and can act in a more dynamic and powerful manner.

The duties undertaken by the staff representatives and the officials appointed by them to the joint bodies are deemed to be part of their service they render to the organisation. By performing such duties they should not suffer any prejudice (Annex II Art. 1(6) EU-SR; Art. 10 CoE-SR; Art. 34(2) EPO-SR).

##### *ee) Co-determination*

In some IO, beyond the staff's participation in the form of consultation there is a kind of "entrepreneurial" participation. This participation is prevalent in the management of pension funds of IO. As a rule, the staff committees appoint their members to the supervisory boards. Retired staff members may also be appointed as observers (e.g. Art. 5 UNJSPF Statute; Art. I 2.05 Statute of CERN/ESO Pension Fund; Art. 5 EPO Reserve Funds for Pensions and Social Security; see Ullrich, Pension Schemes). (For more details, see above under participation rights.)

##### *ff) The right of staff committees to file complaints*

(See below under *locus standi* of staff committees)

#### c) Trade unions and professional associations

The trade unions and professional associations of the staff of IO are formed on the basis of the freedom of association, in general explicitly laid down in the service regulations of IO (Art. 24b EU-SR; Rule 8(1)(g) UN-SR; Art. 47 CoE-SR; Art. 30 EPO-SR), alternatively it can be derived from the respective general principle of law (see above under freedom of association, assembly and trade union matters).

In addition to the trade unions, there are also occupational unions and professional associations which represent the collective interest of particular groups of staff but they play a generally minor role (noteworthy are the professional associations of translators and interpreters, see on the internet: inboxtranslation.com). The dominance of these trade unions avoids divisions among the staff and strengthens the assertiveness in representing their interests. The following presentation is therefore limited to the trade unions in IO.

The trade unions of IO are largely outside the internal legal order provided by the organisation. The representatives of the unions are nevertheless subject, as "normal" staff members, to the staff regulations of the organisation but enjoying a somewhat wider discretion in the manner they use their freedom of opinion and speech (see above). The trade unions are permitted by their fundamental right to freedom of association to influence the organisation for the collective perception of staff's interests. Staff associations are required to have some agreement as to the persons by or through whom the association acts, the means by which those persons are selected or elected, the matters in respect of which they have authority to act and the powers that they have in relation to those matters (ILOAT Judgment 2672). In contrast trade union's own financial resources (membership fees) and the instrument of a collective labour dispute enable them to exert a far higher pressure on the organisation than the staff association which is largely limited to its participation in some consultation procedure. Many IO, therefore, try to conclude agreements with the union of their staff on certain forms of staff participation, as well as on conflict prevention and resolution. In some cases, these attempts fail because of the interest of the organisation in regulating the activities of the trade unions as much as possible and the fear of the unions of losing their "teeth" leaving the field to newly formed "free" trade unions (see below under framework agreement).

The number of trade unions in IO varies considerably. Whereas in some IO only one or a few unions have been established (EPO: SUEPO, see www.suepo.eu; CoE: Council of Europe Trade Union (SACE), see the reform of the contractual policy with SACE, www.unionsyndicale.eu) or where a hybrid representation system of trade union and staff association exists (UN, see below), there are other IO in which various unions represent the collective interests of the staff. This is the case in the bodies of the EU in which there are more than a dozen unions. The most important are:

- The Trade Union of the European Public Service or Union Syndicale (USB) (see www.unionsyndicale.EU) and the USF (Union des Syndicats) with 22 affiliated unions, including trade unions of the EU institutions, in particular: US-Brussels, US-Luxembourg; US-Karlsruhe; US-Petten and US-Ispra), unions of employees of Eurocontrol, the Council of Europe (SACE), the unions of the European Schools, the European University Institute and the EPO (SUEPO), and SACE of the CoE.
- The European Public Service Union (Conf-SFE, see www.conf-sfe.org)

The large number of trade unions in the EU institutions speaks for the great interest of the staff in diversity of opinion in the collective defence of their interests, but it complicates contacts with the administration, particularly in consultation procedures (see the framework agreement, below) and implies the risk of fragmentation of power and "cannibalism".

Most trade unions and union federations of IO belong to umbrella organisations. Of particular relevance here are the European Trade Union Confederation (ETUC), Public Service International (PSI) and the European Federation of Public Service Unions (EPSU) (see www.etuc.org; www.world-psi.org; www.epsu.org).

*aa) Statutes of international trade unions*

The statutes of the international trade unions are generally available on the internet (see, for example, "www.unionsyndicale.eu" under Rules). They consistently adhere to a similar pattern addressing the following matters:

Scope, title of the union, purpose of the union, the principles of independence and solidarity, members' rights and obligations, resources, the union bodies, the general meeting, the executive committee, the delegations, the audit board, the dispute board, electoral procedure, decision to strike, civil liability, disbandment of the union and use of its assets.

The unions emphasise their complete independence from all international and national institutions and in particular from the IO itself, to which their members belong. Although they primarily defend the collective interests of their members, the interests of the general staff are also taken into account. Their supreme body is the general assembly (general meeting) setting out the broad outlines of the trade union's politics. The legislative body is the council. The executive committee (staff committee) implements the decisions of the general assembly and is responsible for the affairs of the current administration. Industrial actions, as a rule, require the prior decision of the general assembly (as far as framework agreements exist with the administration – see below – they prevail). Trade unions often have significant resources at their disposal (membership fees), which they use, next to hire lawyers and commission external expertise, and also to support staff in need during industrial action. Compliance with the financial rules of the union is safeguarded by an audit committee. In the case of internal dispute, an arbitration committee decides.

Rules on the legal status of international trade unions under national law are frequently missing. The civil liability of the union and its members is limited to the assets of the union, with respect to the applicable municipal law. The question of legal disputes with the organisation and the staff members is dealt with separately (see above under freedom of association and below under *locus standi*).

The United Nations staff union (the "union") and the more than 50 other staff unions of the UN assure a somewhat hybrid position. Their statutes combine elements of a trade union with those of a staff committee. (See also above under freedom of association, assembly and in trade union matters).

After several years of disarray, the union approved a new statute (Part I) and regulations (Part II) on 14 December 2007, and withdrew from the Coordinating Committee of International Staff Unions and Associations of the United Nations System (CCISUA). The union created the United Nations International Civil Servants Federation (UNISER, www.myuniserv.org) in collaboration with the UNDP/UNFPA/UNOPS Staff Council.

The Secretary General of the UN endorsed the electoral provisions contained in the UNSU-statute (see Reg. 8(1)(b) UN-SR) in 2008. Apart from the internal difficulties in the UNSU, which seriously endangered their reputation (see doc. Inf/42/34 of 14 October 2008, Report of the Staff Union Leadership 42nd Session of the Staff Council 2006–2008) the promulgation of the new provisional staff rules of 21 October 2009, in which comments, observations and queries by the union seemed to have been ignored with no feedback provided as to the reasons (see working paper No. 43/12 of 17 November 2009), throws light on the functioning of the joint staff-management machinery. In 2013 the UN-SG derecognised the UN staff union's rights to negotiate. In the meantime, the former website of UNSU (u-seek.org) has been removed from the internet. That is why in the following section reference is made to the statute and rules of the Vienna staff union, which gives a mirror image of the UNSU statute and rules.

Besides the union which represents the staff of the UN Secretariat in New York (Art. 31 UNSU statute) there are more than 50 staff unions of the UN organisations, see e.g. "staffunion.unov.org" (Vienna staff union (UNOV)), the United Nations field staff union (UNFSU, www.unfsu.org) with headquarters in Italy.

The purposes of the unions are to represent, promote and safeguard the rights, interests and welfare of all members of staff of the UN at the different places of employment (Art. 2 UNOV statute). Unlike in the unions of other IO, all staff members assigned to the UN at Vienna are automatically members of the union. This is due to the hybrid function of the union as a combined staff association and trade union (Art. 4 UNOV statute).

The organs of the union are the executive body ("Staff Committee", Art. 24 UNOV statute and rules 12 et seq. UNOV rules of Staff council), the legislative body ("Council", Art. 20 et seq. UNOV statute and rule 1 et seq. UNOV Rules of Council) and the "General Meeting" (Art. 7 UNOV statute and rule 1 et seq. rules of the general meetings). The highest decision-making mechanism for establishing the policy of the union is a referendum (Art. 6 et seq. UNOV statute). One standing committee is the auditing committee (Art. 32 UNOV statute). The payment of membership contributions is voluntary. Staff members are, however, invited to pay their membership contributions (dues) amounting to 1.5 thousand of net salary plus allowances (Art. 30 UNOV statute). Paying members are getting a membership card entitling them to legal assistance in work-related issues and two free legal consultations per year in non-work-related issues. They also get special discounts in various shops and restaurants (for more details see the staff union www.unov.org website under "your union").

The union is represented in the "joint staff-management machinery" (Rule 8(2) UN-SR) which consists of "joint advisory committees" and a "joint staff-management body" (Rule 8(2)(a) (i) and (ii) UN-SR). It is therefore involved in numerous joint committees, like appointment and promotion panels.

The joint appeals boards of the UN were abolished as of 1 July 2009 with the introduction of the new formal system of justice establishing a two-tier legal protection system by the United Nations Dispute and Appeals Tribunal (UNDT, UNAT). As of 1 July 2009, the UN-SG also has the authority to impose disciplinary measures without the recommendation of a joint body.

Such measures can be appealed by the staff member directly before the UNDT without first requesting an internal evaluation. The joint disciplinary committees were therefore also abolished on 1 July 2009 (see doc. ST/SGB/2009/11 of the UN).

*bb) The right to strike*

(See above under the freedom of association, assembly and in trade union matters).

*cc) Framework agreements of international organisations with staff unions*

The most important examples of framework agreements are the agreements of the International Labour Office and the Commission of the EU. The recognition and procedural agreement between the International Labour Office and the ILO Staff Union is dated 27 March 2000 (Amendment 6 November 2003, see www.ilostaffunion.org at the internet; see also the Complementary Paper of the Report of UNJIU/REP/2012/10) and contains provisions on the recognition of the trade union, the granting of subsidies by the International Labour Office, regulations on a negotiating process and conflict resolution. Based on this agreement there is a collective agreement on conflict prevention and resolution dated 24 February 2004 (see ilostaffunion.org at the internet). At the EPO, the framework agreement on the recognition of the union and the procedure for the dealings between the EPO and the union did not go beyond the drafting stage in the year 2000.

Of great importance is the Agreement on Relations between the European Commission and the Trade Unions and Staff Associations of 18 December 2008. This agreement is based on the previous agreements dated 20 September 1974 terminated by the commission in 2001, and on the revised agreements in 2003 and 2006. The agreement of 2008 is not officially published (for an unofficial English version see sidtu.org/SID-UNION-FILES/SID/Accord-cadre 2008 or generation 2004 Bylaws of January 2015 Annex IV). This framework agreement was signed by representatives of twelve trade unions and staff associations of the EU area, comprises 47 articles concerning in particular the recognition of trade unions, the dialogue (in French "concertation") procedure, the facilities available to the unions and procedures in case of labour disputes. The legal basis for the agreement is Art. 10(c) EU-SR.

*Important details of the agreement*

Art. 2 (Trade union freedom)

Enshrines the trade union freedom and confirms the right of staff and pensioners to be able to belong to unions.

Art. 3 (Role of unions)

The Commission recognizes the role and responsibility of unions and the most transparent and effective integration into the activities of the institutions of the unions.

Art. 4 (Appearance)

Belonging to a trade union and participating in its activities shall neither adversely affect a staff member's professional situation nor his professional career.

Art. 7 (Conditions for recognition)

The official recognition of a union by the Commission requires that it is pursuing an objective to defend the interest of the staff, irrespective of any distinction whatever. It must confirm to be regularly constituted.

Art. 9, 10, 11 (Representativeness of unions)

The regulations contain details on the requirements (minimum number of personnel of the European Commission: 6% and a minimum of 400 members, evidence rules, withdrawal procedures), for a recognition as a "representative trade union".

Art. 12 (Dialogue)

The undersigned trade unions may, according to the following articles, conclude agreements in terms of a dialogue.

Art. 13 (Dialogue schedule)

At the beginning of every year a schedule comprising the most important items for a social dialogue is set up by the Commission. This list may be amended. The trade unions may communicate to the Commission additional items for the list.

Art. 14 (Areas of dialogue)

The social dialogue comprises political dialogue and dialogue on working conditions (staff regulations). The responsibilities of the staff association under the SR remain unaffected.

Art. 15–20 (Dialogue levels, bodies and processes)

The dialogue process takes place at the administrative level (director), technical level (Director General) and political level (commissioner responsible for personnel and administration). There are in part different codes of procedures for the dialogue levels. Following a dialogue there will be either an agreement or a document setting out the points of disagreement. Technical dialogue may be followed by the political dialogue. In the case of disagreement political consultation may be followed by a dialogue procedure.

Art. 22–32 (Conditions for trade union activities)

Recognised unions can hold their meetings on the premises of the Commission, use the facilities of the Commission for translation, reproduction and communication for payment against invoices and, upon request, set up a homepage on the intranet "IntraComm".
Resources are made available for representative unions, based on an agreement and on a yearly protocol on allocation.
For concrete and specific trade union activities, special leave may be granted in line with the conditions adopted by the Commission. Special leave may be granted for participation in trade union activities and training.

Art.33 (Official business)

Duties carried out on behalf of and authorised by representatives of trade unions in the context of dialogue activities are considered official business.

Art. 35 (Work stoppage after dialogue)

In case of a labour dispute a decision on work stoppage shall be taken only if all means of a social dialogue have failed, save in exceptional circumstances.

Art. 36–38 (Notice)

The intention to stop work must be announced to the commissioner five working days prior to the expected commencement, with reasons and specifying the procedures of the strike. For successive strikes, their timetable (if necessary, updated at least 24 hours in advance) must be disclosed. In exceptional circumstances, the commencement of the strike can be announced without precise dating and is valid for 15 days. However, the starting date of the strike must be announced no later than three working days in advance.

Art. 39 (Negotiations)

The notice period must be used for negotiations.

Art. 40, 41 (Service obligations)

A list of personnel obliged to work is established in a dialogue process after the strike notice and published. Personnel obliged to work include staff responsible for the safety of persons and property, and those having been agreed through dialogue.

Art. 42, 43 (Freedom to strike)

Staff who stop their participation in a strike or choose not to strike must be able to do so without let or hindrance.

Art. 45 (Return to work)

The arrangements for returning to work are subject to concertation.

Art. 47 (Termination)

Three years after 18 December 2008 either party could terminate the agreement with one month's notice. In 2015, the agreement had still not been terminated.

## II. Duties and breach of duties

### *1. Survey*

The duties of the personnel of IO derive from the conditions of employment and following legal doctrine, are usually divided into public service obligations and rules of conduct (Rogalla, p. 132 et seq., ILOAT Judgment 282: distinction between quality of work and a general attitude at variance with the duties of an official). These duties are frequently complementary and interrelated. Thus, for example, the refusal to comply the official duties (insubordination) constitute a breach of both performance and behavioural requirements (ILOAT Judgment 1381: bad performance and misconduct).

The public service obligations and rules of conduct are differently construed in the service law provisions of the IO, both in terms of the density of regulations and the systematic representation. Particularly extensive regulations on these duties are included in the SR of the UN (Rules 1(1) to 1(9)). In some IO such as the UN and the CoE, the staff member also has to affirm observance of the duties by taking an oath or signing a declaration (Reg. 1(1)(b) UN-SR; Art. 25 CoE-SR).

An extensive case law from the tribunals regarding the official duties and conduct obligations helps to clarify and systematise them. Of particular importance is the recognition of common rules of conduct that require the observation of general principles and human rights, laid down in the service law provisions themselves (see Reg. 1(2)(a) UN-SR: "Staff members shall uphold and respect the principles set out in the Charter, including faith in fundamental human rights, in the dignity and worth of the human person and in the equal rights of men and women."). Similar rules exist in the EU (Art. 12a EU-SR) and at the EPO (Art. 16 EPO-SR and Circular 341 accessible don EPO Codex on the EPO website).

Monitoring of the compliance with conduct obligations is not at the sole discretion of an IO. According to the general principle of law, an IO, in its treatment of officials, must care for their dignity and reputation (ILOAT Judgment 367). If an IO fails to take action against an employee in order to prevent, stop and prosecute victimisation or sexual harassment it risks having to pay damages for moral injury (see, for example, ILOAT Judgment 1376 and above under the protection of human rights).

### 2. *Public service obligations*

#### a) The duty to provide service

The main duty of staff is to provide the agreed service (ILOAT Judgment 1550: "... the primary obligation of an international civil servant is to devote his energies and capacity fully to the work of the organization he serves ..."). Staff members are required to uphold the highest standards of ability, efficiency, competence and integrity in the discharge of their functions (see, for example, Art. 27 EU-SR; Reg. 1(3)(a) UN-SR; Art. 12(1) CoE-SR; Art. 5 EPO-SR).

The content and scope of the duties arise from the individual employment contract and/or the act of appointment referring to the applicable service regulations and complementary provisions. Whereas the SR generally refer to abstract descriptions of activity levels (job description), the concrete duties and responsibilities assigned are contained in the job specifications. Job specifications present virtual snapshots of the current activities of a staff member and they can be adjusted at any time to the service and organisational needs. The staff member has an enforceable claim that his duties comply with the level of importance and the scope attributed to his budget post (ILOAT Judgment 2819; CJEU Judgment T-76/03). In addition to the summarily assigned official duties, the international civil servant has a duty to comply with individual orders.

**Jurisprudence**

ILOAT Judgments

1175: The organisation is free to set quotas for the output of patent examiners; 324: Duty of staff strictly to respect the limits of his duties.

CJEU Judgment

T-76/03: Principle of equivalence of grade and post.

*aa) The duty to execute orders (duty to obey, subordination)*

International employees basically have (at least after a written confirmation of an order) the duty to obey the official instructions from their superiors and other authorising officers. This commitment is, as a rule, explicitly stated in the terms of service (see, for example, Reg. 1(2)(c) UN-SR: "Staff members are subject to the authority of the Secretary-General and to assignment by him ..."; ICSC-Standards of Conduct, point 18: "International civil servants must follow the instructions they receive in connection with their official functions ..."). The authority to issue directives always ultimately derives from the power of authority of the organisation. The content and scope of these powers to instruct employees are generally transferred by way of delegation on a case-by-case basis. According to a practice frequently followed, the person who has the delegated powers "notifies" the staff member of the decision taken by the Director-General (President).

A staff member is obliged to perform the duties assigned to him under his own responsibility (see, for example, Art. 21(2) EU-SR; Art. 30(1) CoE-SR; Art. 24(1) EPO-SR). If he considers an official order to be irregular or to have undesirable consequences of a serious nature, he has the right to convey his opinion to the person giving the order.

Upon (written) confirmation of the order, he must carry it out unless its execution may be contrary to criminal law (Art. 21a(2) EU-SR: As far as the orders are not "manifestly illegal or constitute a breach of the relevant safety standards"; Art. 30(2) CoE-SR: "... unless its execution would constitute an act contrary to criminal law or to the safety regulations applicable to the Council"; Art. 24(1) EPO-SR; ICSC-Standards of Conduct, point 19: "They should not follow verbal or written instructions that are manifestly inconsistent with their official functions or that threaten their safety or that of others").

**Jurisprudence**

ILOAT Judgments

2601: Staff member and superior resort to physical assault (1725): 2468: Refusal of a staff member to recognise the authority of his superior; 1550: Failing to obey an explicit and unambiguous order from the superior; 1030: Refusal to perform duties, refusal to obey instructions; 805: Order to staff to perform their duties; 318: Insubordination (247); 63: Failure to comply with an order.

*bb) Hours of work, unauthorised absence*

According to most SR, the employee of an IO is in principle at all times at the disposal of the organisation for the performance of official duties (see, for example, Art. 55(1) EU-SR; Reg. 1(3)(b) UN-SR). An official may be required to work overtime in cases of urgency or exceptional pressure of work. The SR usually contain rules on the maximum weekly working time (see, for example, Art. 55(2) EU-SR: normal working hours range from 40 to 42 hours per week; for part-time work see, for example, Annex IVa EU-SR), provisions for leave entitlement under the social security system (see above) and entitlement for annual leave, leave on personal grounds and home leave (see above). Often there are special rules for granting additional (special) leave. For obvious reasons, IO usually follow the official holidays at the duty station (see above).

Except in the event of incapacity to work due to sickness or accident, a staff member is considered to be absent without authorisation and without prior permission from his superior. In such a case, the periods of absence are deducted from his annual leave or he forfeits his remuneration for this period. In addition, disciplinary measures may be imposed (see, for example, Art. 60 EU-SR; ILOAT Judgment 481: Calculation of reduction in salary for an unauthorised leave of two hours service).

*cc) Place of work*

In principle the staff member provides his services at the place where he is employed. However, it is within the international character of his activity that he cannot refuse that an appropriate discretionary decision be taken as to transfer him to another duty station. A refusal may lead to his dismissal (see, for example, Art. 53(1)(b) EPO-SR).

**Jurisprudence**

ILOAT Judgment

1250: Refusal to a transfer.

*dd) Overtime, shift work, on-call duty*

Staff members may be required, in specific cases, to work overtime, to perform shift work or to be on-call. In the higher grades, there is generally no entitlement to compensation for overtime (see, for example, Art. 56(2) EU-SR). Many SR contain detailed provisions on compensatory allowances for shift work and on standby duty (see, for example, Art. 56a, 56b EU-SR).

b) Additional duties, which directly ensure the duty to provide service

*aa) Duty of residence*

Many IO oblige their employees in the SR to reside at no greater distance from their working place as is compatible with the proper exercise of their duties (see, for example, Art. 20 EU-SR). In practice, these rules are handled fairly generously. Daily travel time of up to four hours in total is frequently tolerated.

### *bb) Duty to notify violations of privileges and immunities*

The immunity from national jurisdiction granted to staff in the exercise of their functions, and the exemption from certain national legal obligations, particularly in the area of registration, tax and employment law are granted exclusively in the interests of the unimpeded functioning of the organisation (see above under privileges and immunities). For this reason, the employees are obliged to report any violation of their immunities and privileges to the organisation immediately (Art. 23(2) EU-SR; Reg. 1(1)(f) UN-SR; Art. 39(3) CoE-SR; Art. 27 EPO-SR).

### *cc) Duty to transfer industrial property rights*

Most SR stipulate that all rights in any work done by a staff member in the exercise of his official duties (in particular inventions and copyright) shall be transferred or shall belong to the organisation (see, for example, Art. 18 EU-SR).

### *dd) Recovery of undue payment*

Any sum overpaid has to be refunded if there was no legal ground for the payment and the recipient was aware that there was no due reason for the payment, or if overpayment was patently such that he could not have been unaware of it. This obligation can already be derived from the general legal principle of unjust enrichment, which is also effective in the service law of IO. For reasons of legal clarity and certainty, it is, however, preferable that the repayment obligation is explicitly defined in the SR. The recovery of overpayment may be waived on social grounds (Art. 85 EU-SR; UN Administrative Instruction doc. ST/AI/2009/1; Art. 38 CoE-SR; Art. 88 EPO-SR).

**Jurisprudence**

ILOAT Judgments

2899: To require repayment must be fair and just; relevant circumstances are, for example, good or bad faith, the sort of mistake made, the respective responsibilities and the inconvenience of repayment for the staff member (1849, 53); 2847: Claims for recovery of undue payment must be brought – even in the absence of any provision to this effect – within a reasonable time (2565, 53); 2565: Without an explicit provision, two years (2230: three years) are not sufficient to extinguish the right to recover undue payment by prescription; 2257: The organisation is obliged to issue clear and comprehensible communications and it did not notice the error for more than four years, reimbursement ordered; 1195: Extinctive prescription for recovery of undue payment is much longer than two years; 81: The deceased husband of the complainant could not claim reimbursement of the contributions to the superannuation fund. The complainant is not entitled to claim a right which the official was not entitled to invoke.

CJEU Judgments/Orders

C-420/04 P: The appellant could not have been unaware of overpayment when exercising ordinary care corresponding to his experience and grade; T-195/03: A staff member is obliged to inform the administration if he has doubts as to the justification of the payment (T-14/03, T-122/95); T-180/02 and T-113/03: Obligation to make an effort to reflect and check an entitlement to a payment; T-312/02: Failure to deliver required information; no release from the obligation to return overpayment.

#### *ee) Duty to undergo a medical examination*

In the interests of the physical ability to perform his duties and the health of other staff in general, an employee can be obliged to pass a medical check (see, for example, Art. 59(3) EU-SR).

### c) Other obligations

In addition to providing the agreed service as a core requirement, the SR and supplementing directives are the source of a variety of additional duties relating to the entire scope of the status of a staff member. These indirect (collateral) obligations refer to the areas of information and cooperation. Examples are information regarding the residence of the staff member, his marital status, the information needed to grant allowances and subsidies, the notification of sick leave, the settlement of overtime, shift work, on-call duty and the necessary information for the reimbursement of mission expenses. A number of these commitments, such as the payment of the contributions to the social security scheme, and to the pension scheme and the levy of internal taxes are met by the organisation itself in the name of the staff member.

**Jurisprudence**

ILOAT Judgment

459: Obligation to disclose the date of birth.

## *3. Duty of conduct*

Besides carrying out the allotted tasks, a staff member has a duty to show such dignity of behaviour as not to harm the good name that the organisation must enjoy if it is to carry out its functions properly (ILOAT Judgment 1584). The international staff is required to respect certain values, principles and standards essential to achieving the tasks of the IO (see the ICSC-Standards of Conduct, point 52 and Reg. 1(1) UN-SR: "... securing staff of the highest standards of efficiency, competence and integrity."). The standards of conduct are based on common principles of the national public administrations. These duties of conduct are supplemented and modified due to the special requirements for the international public service "special calling", see ICSC-Standards of Conduct, point 2). Without these specific duties of conduct, the accomplishment of the tasks of an IO would be endangered. These duties include in particular the loyalty to the international mission and goals of the IO, ensuring the independence of the organisation and equal treatment of member states, the respect for their delegates and the diversities of the government systems, traditions and cultures of the member states.

The general duties of conduct of an international employee evade an exhaustive enumeration (see the attempt of an enumeration of the "guiding principles" of conduct in ICSC-Standards of Conduct, points 3 – 14). From the ICSC-Standards of Conduct and the case law of the administrative tribunals of the IO, essential duties of conduct of an international civil servant can be derived, but a clear differentiation between the terms remains difficult.

Loyalty and integrity are closely linked and represent the main duties of conduct (Art. 25 CoE-SR: "Loyalty and integrity"; ICSC-Standards of Conduct, point 34).

The duty of loyalty (allegiance) (ICSC-Standards of Conduct, point 7) to the organisation is the focal point of all duties of conduct. Loyalty and devotion to the tasks and objectives of the IO are defining to the entire employment relationship and serve as a point of reference for the more specific duties of conduct.

The duty of integrity (ICSC-Standards of Conduct, point 5) includes a variety of behavioural issues that relate to the dignity, personality and moral maturity of the staff member. These specific duties include the duty of independence from any instruction outside the organisation, impartiality, incorruptibility, secrecy, the general duty to respect the law, the duty to respect the dignity and integrity of colleagues (prohibition of victimisation and harassment) and the duty of reporting serious abuses. Nowadays, most of these duties of conduct are dealt with in the service regulations of IO. All these duties of conduct apply generally and objectively. It is therefore immaterial whether the staff member took advantage from their violation or whether the organisation suffered a damage (CJEU Judgment T-24/98 and T-241/99).

#### a) The duty of loyalty and allegiance

The duty of international staff to professional loyalty and allegiance towards their organisation is in most cases laid down in the SR (Art. 11(1) EU-SR: "An official shall carry out his duties and conduct himself solely with the interest of the Union in mind"; see also Art. 12 and 21 EU-SR; Reg. 1(2)(e) UN-SR: "Loyalty to the aims principles and purposes of the United Nations …"; ICSC-Standards of Conduct, point 7: "International loyalty …"). Often this duty is paraphrased by the wording that staff members should solely be guided by the interests of their organisation in the exercise of their duties (Reg. 1(2)(e) UN-SR: "By accepting appointment, staff members pledge themselves to discharge their functions and regulate their conduct with the interests of the Organization only in view"; Art. 25(1) CoE-SR (declaration): "… in my official conduct I will have regard exclusively to the interests of the Council of Europe"; Art. 14(1) EPO-SR: "… and conduct himself solely with the interests of the European Patent Organisation"). This exclusive focus on the official obligations and the interests of the organisation forms the basis for the confidence of the organisation in the absolute reliability of the employee. The duty of loyalty finds its counterpart in the duty of care and assistance which an IO owes to its staff (for the "dual loyalty" of delegated staff, see Rogalla, p. 134 et seq.).

The private life of international staff "is their own concern and organisations should not intrude upon it" (ICSC-Standards of Conduct, point 42). On the other hand, staff have to align their private behaviour in a way that the interests of the organisation, in particular its prestige and reputation, are not damaged. This is also valid for the conduct of the members of the household of an employee.

The duty of loyalty does not, however, require the official to be unswervingly loyal. Rather, it is to be weighed against the legitimate self-interest of the staff member in each case. This is particularly true in the field of freedom of expression, in the exercise of the right to strike and the freedom of association and assembly. Of particular importance is also the right to remonstrate in the case of an instruction (see above).

**Jurisprudence**

ILOAT Judgments

3295: Dismissal was proportionate to the breach of loyalty; 3099: The dismissal of the complainant was neither based on a lack of loyalty nor of integrity but a smaller misconduct; 2569: False declaration of nationality as a lapse in loyalty; 2231: Offence of the theft of a cosmetic lotion as an egregious lapse in loyalty; 2133: Loyalty between employer and employee obliges the organisation to execute judgment in good faith; 2038: Fraud is a serious offence and lapse in loyalty.

CJEU Judgments/Orders

T-11/03: Commitment to loyalty of staff members; T-89/01: Staff members must be guided solely by the interests of the organisation; C-274/99 P: "Connolly case", violation of the duty of loyalty by publication of a book ("The Rotten Heart of Europe – The Dirty War for Europe´s Money") that violates the reputation of the EU; C-156/96 P: Public statements a serious insult, reflecting on the dignity of the office; T-273/94: Duty of loyalty to cooperate in an internal investigation; T-146/94: The duty of loyalty of the staff member is also valid in an election campaign for the staff association; T-146/89: By virtue of the duty of loyalty an official must refrain from conduct detrimental to the dignity and respect due to the institution and its authorities.

### b) The duty of integrity

The duty of integrity of staff is rarely explicitly cited in the SR of IO (but see Reg. 1(2)(b) UN-SR: "Staff members shall uphold the highest standards of … integrity. The concept of integrity includes, but is not limited to, probity, impartiality, fairness, honesty and truthfulness in all matters affecting their work and status"; ICSC-Standards of Conduct, point 5: "The concept of integrity … embraces all aspects of an international civil servant's behaviour, including such qualities as honesty, truthfulness, impartiality and incorruptibility"). Integrity is a sort of collective term for a variety of individual, particularly ethical and socially influenced behaviours, which the IO expects from their staff in order to optimise the performance of their official duties and this ultimately ensures the unimpeded functioning of the organisation. In the SR, however, no systematic and exhaustive behavioural catalogues can be found, rather only sporadic integrity requirements (see, for example, Art. 11a EU-SR: Independence in the exercise of an office; Art. 12 EU-SR: Reputation of the Office; Art. 16 EU-R: Honourable behaviour and restraint; Rule 1(2)(f-j) UN-SR: Specific fields of prohibited conduct; ICSC-Standards of Conduct, point 9: "Impartiality implies tolerance and restraint …").

In summary, the following most frequently referred aspects of integrity requirements for international civil servants are reflected in the case law of the administrative tribunals:

- Keeping with the reputation and standing of the organisation;
- Independence and impartiality;
- Honourable and trustworthy behaviour;
- Restraint, moderation;
- Discretion, secrecy;
- Truthfulness;
- Fairness;
- Respect the dignity of colleagues and superiors;
- Respect the law and ethical standards;
- Report on illegal activity.

For lack of sharp differentiation of each aspect, frequently overlapping occurs. The most frequent aspects of integrity and case law are dealt with below under aa) to ee) and the special issue of the duty of conduct and the freedom of expression under ff) below.

**Jurisprudence**

ILOAT Judgments

2569: False declaration of nationality, violation of loyalty and integrity; 1764: Common decency, good faith and honest dealing lie at the root of relations between employer and employee; 1732: Staff member may not degrade the reputation of the organisation; 1584: Violation of the reputation or the organisation by prison sentences for offences against national law; 1532: Intemperate language of submissions the complainant has failed in duty to respect towards the organisation; 1480: Endangering the reputation of the organisation by private financial irregularities; 1381: Serious misconduct and insubordination, ignoring normal channels of communication; 1363: Activity in the area of the organisation's own work (grant of European patents) while on leave for personal reasons, infringes integrity; 1277: Leaving work because of dissatisfaction with superior is intolerable and alien to due process, if tolerated would wreak havoc in any administration; 1128: Misbehaviour towards national authorities as a prejudice to the UN image; 349: Disrespect to superior; 274: The behaviour in private life and activities within the staff council of the organisation are *prima facie* outside the official duty. There are, however, exceptional cases. As a general rule there could be no true freedom of association if the disapproval of the Director General, whether justified or not, of what was said could lead to disciplinary measures; 96: Constant abuse of the right of appeal has affronted the dignity of the IO and of the administrative tribunal.

CJEU Judgment

T-137/03: Duty of integrity and independence and duty of information about possible conflicts of interest.

### *aa) The duty of independence, impartiality and incorruptibility*

Independence, impartiality and incorruptibility of the staff has a high priority at IO (ICSC-Standards of Conduct, point 8: "It cannot be too strongly stressed that international civil servants are not, in any sense, representatives of Governments or other entities nor are they proponents of their policies"). This standard of value is secured by a number of specific duties of conduct. The mere appearance of a possible infringement of independence, impartiality and incorruptibility is to be avoided in order to ensure the trust of the member states in the proper performance of the tasks of the IO (see, for example, 1(2)(f) UN-SR: Staff shall avoid any action that may adversely reflect "on their status or on the integrity, independence and impartiality that are required by that status"). For this reason, international civil servants are, among other things, forbidden to accept instructions from any authority external to the organisation, especially from governments or authorities of the member states, but also from other sources, like other IO (Art. 11(1) EU-SR; Reg. 1(2)(d) UN-SR; Art. 25(1) CoE-SR; Art. 14(1) EPO-

SR; ICSC-Standards of Conduct, point 8). Likewise, it is generally prohibited, without the consent of the IO, to accept any honour, decoration, favour, gift or remuneration from any source outside the IO (Art. 11(2) EU-SR; Reg. 1(2)(j) and (l) UN-SR, but see the exception in Reg. 1(2)(k) for minor gifts of nominal value and occasional invitations to meals and diplomatic receptions etc.; Art. 25 CoE-SR; Art. 14(2) EPO-SR; ICSC-Standards of Conduct, point 17). The protection of independence and impartiality of civil servants is also the reason behind the rules concerning the duty of reporting or the granting of special leave or transfer to inactive status of an official elected or appointed to public office or the approval of a secondary activity (Art. 15 EU-SR; Reg. 1(2)(o) UN-SR; Art. 34, 35 CoE-SR; Art. 16, 18 EPO-SR). Sometimes this applies even to the official's spouses (Art. 13 EU-SR; Art. 32 CoE-SR; Art. 16(2)(3) EPO-SR). Higher-ranking staff may be required to file financial disclosure statements on appointment and at intervals thereafter (Reg. 1(2)(n) UN-SR). In order to avoid any conflict of interest, international staff may not be active in any matter in which directly or indirectly, he has a personal interest such as to impair his independence (Art. 118a) EU-SR; Art. 36 CoE-SR; Art. 17 EPO-SR).

**Jurisprudence**

ILOAT Judgments

1550: Improper auxiliary activities (misuse of a diplomatic pouch for currency exchange activities); 1363: Activity in the area of the organisation's own work (grant of European patents) while on leave for personal grounds; 1061: To work as city councillor and to give statements to the press and radio relating to the activities of the organisation are acts of serious misconduct.

CJEU Judgments/Orders

T-89/01: Declaration of spouse's employment, personal interest such as to impair independence; T-197/00: Activities falling within the realm of corruption; T-75/00: Engagement in outside activities without prior authorisation.

### *bb) The duty of maintaining discretion and secrecy*

International civil servants are obliged to exercise utmost discretion with regard to all matters of official business unless the information has already been made public or is accessible to the public (Art. 17 EU-SR; ICSC-Standards of Conduct, point 39). The obligation exists even after leaving the service, but not in all IO is there a possibility to impose disciplinary sanctions on pensioners (see above). The obligation to secrecy concerns in particular the involvement of the press, the transmission of information to national authorities, especially to delegates of the Council, as well as the publication of newspaper articles, brochures, books, etc. on the activities of the IO. The staff member needs prior authorisation for the disclosure of information (Reg. 1(2)(i) UN-SR). At the EU, there is merely a duty to provide information on an intended publication. The publication can only be prohibited if the appointing authority can demonstrate that the matter is liable seriously to prejudice the legitimate interests of the EU (Art. 17a(2) EU-SR; regarding the balance between the fundamental right of employees to freedom of expression and the duty to maintain secrecy, see also below). Occasionally, there are special provisions regarding the disclosure of work-related information in national court proceedings (waiver of immunity). This immunity does not apply if evidence is required before the competent international administrative tribunal (see, for example, Art. 19 EU-SR).

**Jurisprudence**

ILOAT Judgments

2879: A newspaper article reported that the official of an IO had raped other officials. The evidence fell short of establishing a reasonable doubt that the complainant was responsible for the article (2786); 2861: An international civil servant is under an obligation of discretion; 2705: Obligation of secrecy (promotion and selection boards); 1608: Discretion also exists in relation to the supervisory bodies of an IO; 1475: Duty of secrecy towards government authorities of a member state; 1115: Disclosure of internal reports to outsiders; 635: The burden of proof for the alleged breach of the duty of discretion lies with the organisation, the duty of discretion varies in scope according to the grade of the official and the circumstances; 65: Violation of discretion by disclosing details of an internal conversation to press; 63: Violation of discretion by public accusation of a colleague; 42: Disclosure of internal information to outsiders (hostile attitude of a staff member towards the King of Jordan).

CJEU Judgments/Orders

T-74/01: The duty to get permission before disclosing internal information on legal proceedings is also valid for the delivery of documents; C-274/99 P: "Connolly case", publication of the book ("The Rotten Heart of Europe – The Dirty War for Europe's Money") violates the reputation of the EU; C-54/90: Testimony before a national court not liable to affect the relationship which the Commission's services must have with national administrations.

### *cc) The duty to report possible illegal activity*

Some SR explicitly oblige staff members to inform the organisation of possible illegal activities they become aware of in the course of or in connection with the performance of their duties (see, for example, Art. 22a and 22b EU-SR). This duty is based on the experience that staff of IO is also not immune from illegal activities. For this reason, the EU has even set up a European Anti-Fraud Office (OLAF). The "whistle-blowers" may not suffer any prejudicial effect when acting reasonably and honestly, otherwise they would risk disciplinary actions. In the financial departments of IO, there is an enhanced obligation upon authorising officers to give notice to the respective authorities if illegal activity, fraud or corruption occurs (see, for example, Art. 72(2) EU-Financial Regulations).

### *dd) The duty to respect the law and ethical standards*

International civil servants have the duty to respect the fundamental principles and human rights, the common principles of municipal laws of member states and the ethical rules and traditions of the country in which they serve (Reg. 1.2(a) UN-SR: "Staff members shall uphold and respect the principles set out in the Charter including faith in fundamental human rights ..."; ICSC-Standards of Conduct, point 44: "... acts that are generally recognized as offences by national criminal laws will normally also be violations of the standards of conduct for the international civil service" and point 2: "... respect for fundamental rights ..."). In practice, the respect for the dignity of colleagues, in particular the prohibition of harassment is of particular importance. Violations of national criminal law will as a rule result in most serious disciplinary actions. If a staff member commits a criminal act in connection with the performance of his duties, the organisation will waive its immunity and apply for the initiation of criminal proceedings.

**Jurisprudence**

ILOAT Judgments

2602: False declarations and falsified documents infringe the standard of integrity: 2569: False declaration of nationality; 2231: An intent to defraud the organisation (theft of a cosmetic lotion) is in contradiction to the highest standards of integrity expected; 2009: Submitting false statements and a falsified document of the organisation to a national court; 1977: Fraud against the organisation through falsification of documents; 1925: Theft; 1828: Fraud in mission costs infringes integrity; 1764: Fraud by falsifying tickets of a mission; 1661: Illicit games, selling cars of the organisation, import of duty free petrol breaches not only the law but gives the impression of arbitrariness, favouritism and graft; 1599: Intentional injury (slapping a colleague in the face); 1584: Non-observance of national laws and public order; 1501: Duty to respect the ethical standards of the host country; 1441: Violation of ethical standards; 1261: Incorrect information on paid overtime; 1128: Violation of the moral laws of the country in private life can harm the reputation of the IO; 937: Violation of the financial integrity by presenting false information as to the home leave; 237: Use of official car for private purposes, smelling of alcohol.

CJEU Judgments

T-307/01: Criminal and disciplinary proceedings; T-197/00: Corruption; T-74/96: Concurrent disciplinary and criminal proceedings.

### *ee) The duty to respect the dignity of colleagues (psychological and sexual victimisation)*

(See also under general legal principles)

The fundamental human rights are derived from the respect for human dignity as a kind of "legal cosmic egg" ("juristisches Weltenei", cited by Isensee, Menschenwürde in: AöR, 2006, 173ff). This is also true for the employment relationship in IO, which are basically governed by the labour law principles of the international public service. IO are committed to observe human dignity in all their decisions and actions regarding staff. Similarly, the IO also has a position as a guarantor for staff in relation to each other (CJEU Judgment T-333/99: Sexual and psychological harassment through abuse of internet services). If the organisation violates this duty to care and protect, the staff member whose dignity has been violated may claim damages from the organisation (ILOAT Judgment 1376: Duty of an IO to protect its staff by taking proper action against sexual harassment). He may not claim damages under the SR from the harasser, but he may initiate criminal proceedings before national courts.

Following a tendency in member states, IO in recent years have increasingly included not only the general duty of staff to respect the dignity of their colleagues in the service regulations or supplementary provisions, but the explicit duty of staff to refrain from discrimination and psychological and sexual harassment at workplace (see, for example, Art. 12a EU-SR; Rule 1(2)(e) and (f) UN-SR; EPO Circular 341). In the event of possible violations of rights in this sensitive area, specific procedures have been set up in order to tackle flagrant violation of human dignity at work in a rapid and effective manner (see, for example, the sexual harassment procedures in ILO Circular No. 543 (Rev. 1) and EPO Circular 341).

**Jurisprudence**

(see above under the protection of human dignity at work).

### *ff) Excursus: The duty of conduct and the freedom of expression*

The duty of conduct of staff members are closely related to the freedom of expression (see, for example, Art. 10 EConHR). As any freedom, the freedom of expression (freedom of speech) has its bounds; it has to be balanced against the responsibility of staff to loyalty and integrity, moderation and the duty of secrecy (Art. 17a(1) EU-SR: "An official has the right to freedom of expression with due respect to the principles of loyalty and impartiality"). The duty of allegiance of staff to the EU cannot be interpreted in such a way as to conflict with the freedom of expression, a fundamental right which the court must ensure (CJEU Judgment C-100/88: civil servant as a journalist). It only has the effect of being "inhibiting and delaying" on the use of freedom of expression (see the German Constitutional Court, decision of 26 September 2001, 2 BvR 496/00 available on the internet).

According to the case law of the CJEU, due to the special importance of the freedom of expression to democratic society, the requirement of prior consent of the IO to a publication of the staff on the activities of the organisation must be narrowly interpreted. Permission may only be refused if the disclosure is capable of causing serious damage to the interest of the organisation, in particular to its reputation (CJEU Judgment C-340/00 P; C-274/99 P "Connolly Case", publication of the book "The Rotten Heart of Europe – The Dirty War for Europe's Money").

The obligation to protect the reputation of the IO applies to civil servants in all circumstances. However, the freedom of expression at a general staff meeting is only limited in the case of a serious insult or serious defamation.

In the case of labour disputes with the organisation, the oral and written statements of the appellant in legal proceedings are privileged. This "in-court privilege" (privilege of judicial proceedings) exists for the benefit of proper proceedings (ILOAT Judgments 2751, 1391). Statements are even privileged if there is no clear justification supported by the evidence, if they are offensive, ill-chosen, damaging, unseemly, or in breach of good taste; only under exceptional circumstances ("wild and unnecessarily wounding allegations") disciplinary actions be justified (ILOAT Judgment 2751).

**Jurisprudence**

ILOAT Judgments

3156: Prior authorisation of messages circulated by the staff representation is unlawful only if the refusal to give that authorisation is unjustified; 3106: Legitimate defence to a claim on defamation; 2751; Statements in legal proceedings are privileged (1391); 2656: Serious allegations of misconduct against other staff members, reckless indifference to the truth and callous disregard for the feelings of others. Disciplinary action was proportionate; 2626: Immoderate nature of a corrigendum justifies refusal to publish it in the in-house magazine; 2228: Restriction of staff committee's access to internal message system; 2227: Bounds of the freedom to speech. No right of staff committee to distribute an "Appeal for donation"; 2114: A letter by an employee to his national parliament on internal matters is not covered by the right to freedom of expression; 1061: Radio interview, article in newspaper, breach of SR, dismissal justified; 911: Staff association enjoys special rights including broad freedom of speech, but must respect the boundaries (gross abuse); 87: Staff representations have a great discretion in their freedom of expression and criticism; 65: Damage to the reputation of the organisation by passing on internal matters to press; 54: Freedom of expression of a staff representative, respect of boundaries (secrecy in respect of joint bodies, confidential information communicated by virtue of trade union position).

CJEU Judgments/Orders

T-76/03: Adequate balance between freedom of expression and legitimate interests of the organisation; C-274/99 P: "Connolly Case", see above; T-82/99: The publication of the opinion of a staff member is covered by Art. 17a EU-SR, even if it dissents from the official opinion of the organisation, it is covered by the freedom of speech, if the organisation cannot prove that its interests are endangered (confirmed by Judgment C-340/00 P); T-259/97: Freedom of expression at a staff meeting is only limited by serous insult or serious libel; C-150/98 P: Observance of freedom of expression is particularly important for making comments on staff reports, limited by seriously insulting language; C-156/96: Serious insults by an official detrimental to the dignity of his office; T-74/96: Press contacts of staff; C-100/88: Duty of allegiance cannot be interpreted as to conflict with the freedom of expression.

### *4. Legal consequences for breaches of duties*

#### a) General

The breach of official duties of an international employee may (discretion!) lead to disciplinary proceedings or recourse claims against the staff member. If a staff member violates national law, he enjoys, even after termination of service, immunity from national jurisdiction in respect of all acts performed by him in his official capacity. The appointing authority may, however, waive his immunity where it considers that such immunity prevents the normal course of justice and that it is possible to dispense with such immunity without prejudicing the interests of the organisation.

In the case of a crime which is not performed in an official capacity there is no impediment to the enforcement of national criminal law. Where appropriate, the organisation is obliged to cooperate with the competent national authorities. The authorities may even get permission from the head of the organisation to enter the premises of the organisation for the purpose of criminal investigations.

#### b) Disciplinary and administrative consequences

Criminal proceedings under domestic law and disciplinary proceedings under the employment law of an IO are separate from one another and pursue different aims (CJEU Judgment T-198/02 para. 57–58, 98). Whereas criminal proceedings concern compliance with the proper workings of society as a whole, the disciplinary sanctions relate to the proper functioning of the IO. The same conduct must, therefore, be differently appraised and the same fact may incur a disciplinary measure but not a criminal conviction (CJEU Judgment T-144/96 para. 38; ILOAT Judgment 1984, para. 5: "when disciplinary sanctions are applied it is immaterial whether or not an act is criminal"). The principle *ne bis in idem* does not apply between criminal sanctions and disciplinary measures. It is, however, also applicable within the disciplinary law itself (see, for example, Art. 54(3) CoE-SR: a single offence shall not give rise to more than one disciplinary measure).

This does, however, not exclude that a national criminal conviction is of relevance for the disciplinary proceedings. Some SR of IO, therefore, provide that a final decision in disciplinary proceedings shall only be taken after a final judgment has been handed down by the national court hearing the case (see, for example, Annex IX Art. 25 EU-SR: Parallel criminal prosecution; Art. 102(2) EPO-SR: the disciplinary committee may decide not to deliver its opinion until after the court has given its decision). A disciplinary decision is, however, not flawed if the criminal court proceedings come after the completion of the disciplinary procedure and after the appointing authority has taken its final decision (ILOAT Judgment 3297).

As in the case of national disciplinary law, for the law of the international civil service the principle of *nulla poena sine lege* also does not require in advance an exhaustive list of all possible types of misconduct that might occur in the accomplishment of the official duties of an international employee. The disciplinary measures provided for in the SR of an IO neither specify a fixed relationship between the disciplinary measure and the kind of breach of duties by the employee, nor do they determine the extent to which the existence of aggravating or extenuating circumstances may affect the choice of a disciplinary measure. It is for the appointing authority to choose the appropriate penalty and to evaluate the aggravating or mitigating circumstances (discretion/value judgment). In their judicial review of the adequacy and proportionality of disciplinary sanctions, the role of the judicature is restricted to verifying whether the weight attached by the appointing authority to the choice of the penalty and the circumstances is proportionate. The judicature cannot substitute its own assessment for that of the appointing authority (CJEU Judgments T-11/03, T-198/02, T-12/94). The principle *nulla poena sine lege* is satisfied if the charges levelled against an official are stated in the SR in general terms (ILOAT Judgment 1764, para. 7; Opinion No. 3 of the Consultative Council of European Judges of 19 November 2002, CCJE doc. CCJE(2002)).

The *nulla poene sine lege* principle is, therefore, only applied with certain restrictions emerging from the disciplinary law (decision of the German Constitutional Court, 26,186(204) of 11 June 1969, 2 BvR 518/66). An IO is, however, obliged to deliver proof that an alleged misconduct is fundamentally contrary to the official duties of the international employee.

The conduct of an employee in his private life is *prima facie* outside his official duties. If, however, the conduct of his private life brings the organisation in disrepute, it may be incompatible with the rules governing the international employment relationship (ILOAT Judgments 3106, 1584, 274, 79).

*aa) Disciplinary measures*

Disciplinary measures serve the purpose of ensuring the proper functioning and the reputation of an IO (Rogalla, p. 142). Those measures have corrective and preventive effects. They call the official to order so as to ensure that he in future accomplishes his duties that is unless the seriousness of the breach of his duties requires the removal from service.

In general, the SR of IO provide for the following disciplinary measures (see, for example, Annex IX Art. 9 EU-SR):

- Written warning;
- Reprimand (Rule 10.2(b) UN-SR: no disciplinary measure, but an administrative measure);
- Demotion (loss of grades or steps, down-grading to a lower function group);
- Deferment of eligibility for salary increment for a specified period;
- Barring for a specified time from eligibility for consideration for promotion;
- Separation from service (dismissal) and, where appropriate reduction *pro tempere* of a pension or withholding for a fixed period of an amount from an invalidity allowance, but not less than the minimum subsistence and the measure shall not extend to the official's dependants.

The SR of the UN, the CoE (Rule 10.2; Art. 45 CoE-SR) and other IO do not provide for a reduction of pension rights or for disciplinary actions against retired staff members. At the UN, former staff members' only legal relationship is with the UNJSPF).

In the case of a presumed serious misconduct, most SR of IO provide for the suspension of the perpetrator of the misconduct from service. The suspension is an interim precautionary measure not normally considered a disciplinary measure (but see Rule 10(2) (iv) UN-SR: Suspension without pay for a specified period is considered a disciplinary measure). The suspension is a discretionary decision which must be in accordance with the principle of proportionality (ILOAT Judgments 3035, 2365, 1927).

The decision to suspend an official is taken after a hearing save in exceptional circumstances (Annex IX Art. 23 EU-SR). The situation of suspension must be settled within a certain period (Annex IX Art. 24(2) EU-SR: within six months; Art. 57 CoE-SR: within four months; Art. 104(3) EPO-SR: within six months for officials appointed by the President of the EPO (Office) and 24 months for officials appointed by the EPO Council, extension possible in exceptional cases. In the case of parallel criminal proceedings, a further suspension is possible, Art. 105 EPO-SR).

*bb) Disciplinary proceedings*

– Disciplinary measures without formal proceedings

A minor breach of official duties may trigger the administrative action of an oral or written warning issued by the administration without formal disciplinary proceedings (Annex IX Art. 11 EU-SR; Rule 10(2)(b) UN-SR: considered as not being a disciplinary measure at all; Art. 54(2) CoE-SR; Art. 94(1) EPO-SR, see ILOAT Judgment 2114).

– Formal disciplinary proceedings

A decision to initiate formal disciplinary proceedings is at the discretion of the IO after hearing the employee concerned. If the appointing authority becomes aware that an employee has failed to comply with his official duties, it may initiate disciplinary proceedings. This decision is at the discretion of the head of the organisation after hearing the employee concerned (see, for example, Art. 56(1) CoE-SR). The decision may be reviewed by the competent tribunal subject to the constant case law concerning the bounds of discretionary powers. In some IO, staff members are expressly encouraged by internal rules to report the possible misconduct of a staff member. As a rule, even anonymous allegations may trigger investigations (ILOAT Judgment 3295). Art. 22a and 22b EU-SR contain detailed rulings on whistleblowing of officials; EPO Circular 342 encourages officials to report possible misconduct.

As a rule, the decision to initiate disciplinary proceedings is based on a report established by an investigative unit of the organisation verifying the occurrence of misconduct (see, for example, Annex IX Art. 2 EU-SR; Rule 10(1) UN-SR; but see CJEU Judgment F-106/11: the ECB-SR do not provide that the initiation of disciplinary proceedings must be preceded by an administrative investigation. Already at the investigation stage the safeguards of due process have to be observed (ILOAT Judgments 3200, 2771, 2552, 2475). At the EU, investigative proceedings may also be initiated by the European Anti-Fraud-Office (OLAF), if any person or entity reports information liable to raise serious suspicion of fraud, corruption or any other illegal activity that may affect the financial interest of the EU (see the website of OLAF and EU Reg. No. 883/2013 concerning investigations conducted by OLAF).

Internal investigative reports cannot be the sole basis for disciplinary measures against a staff member, but they serve as a basis for deciding on the necessity to initiate disciplinary proceedings, (ILOAT Judgment 2773, para. 9). In the disciplinary proceedings the organisation is not obliged to repeat all the investigations but must ensure that the employee is given the opportunity to reply to any findings.

Some IO provide in their SR for special investigation rulings applicable to harassment cases. It is constant case law of the ILOAT that an allegation of harassment must be investigated "promptly and thoroughly" (Judgments 3071, 2642) and that the investigating body must function properly (Judgment 3069). Allegations of harassment must be supported by specific facts which have to be proven by the employee alleging harassment (for more details see above and harassment and ILOAT Judgments 2521, 2406, 2370, 2100, 2067).

The disciplinary proceedings are as a rule submitted by the appointing authority to an independent disciplinary body (board, council, committee) composed of members appointed by the administration and the staff representation (Annex IX Art. 5 et seq. EU-SR; Art. 55 CoE-SR; Art. 97 EPO-SR). At the UN, the joint disciplinary committees were abolished by the reform of the administration of justice in the UN, effective from 1 January 2009. A disciplinary measure may, therefore, be imposed by the appointing authority directly after an investigation process. The employee concerned may directly file an appeal against that decision to the UNDT (Rule 10(3) UN-SR).

The chairman and the members of the disciplinary body are completely independent in the performance of their duties and the proceedings are secret (Annex IX Art. 8 EU-SR; Art. 55(9) CoE-SR). The proceedings are subject to the general procedural principles recognised by the international administrative tribunals even if they are not explicitly referred to by the SR; among those are the principles of *in dubio pro reo* (ILOAT Judgment 2351), *ne bis in idem* (ILOAT Judgments 3126, 934: "double jeopardy"), *audi alteram partem* (ILOAT Judgment 1639), adversarial proceedings (ILOAT Judgments 3295, 2771, 2254) and due process. The principle of due process requires that an employee be given the opportunity to test the evidence relied upon (ILOAT Judgments 3295, para. 11; 2786, para. 13 and 2496; see also Amerasinghe, The law, p. 190). It is constant case law that an employee has the right to be heard in disciplinary proceedings and to participate in the examination of the evidence, even in the absence of an explicit text, and he is entitled to confront his accusers (ILOAT Judgment 2475 para. 20, 203).

The person concerned must be granted a reasonable period to defend his case (ILOAT Judgment 2288, para. 5). The principle of *patere legem* is especially relevant in disciplinary proceedings (ILOAT Judgment 3123 para. 11).

Disciplinary proceedings are, however, not subject to the safeguards of Art. 6 ECHR since they are not "penal proceedings" (CJEU Judgment T-26/89 para. 94) and the proceedings are of an administrative nature and the disciplinary body is not a tribunal (CJEU Judgment F-40/05).

The application of disciplinary measures is subject to the condition that the misconduct was committed intentionally or through negligence (CJEU Judgment 12/68 para. 7; Art. 86(1) EU-SR). A disciplinary measure may only be imposed if the culpability of the employee is established. A mere psychological disorder, however, even if a serious one causing a diminution in responsibility cannot be regarded as excluding a disciplinary measure (CJEU Judgment 12/68 para. 9).

The disciplinary body delivers to the appointing authority a reasoned opinion on the results of the proceedings. If misconduct has been established, the disciplinary body delivers a proposal for an appropriate disciplinary measure (Annex IX, Art. 18 EU-SR; Annex X, Art. 8 CoE-SR). The decision taken by the appointing authority based on the opinion of the disciplinary body is a discretionary decision (ILOAT Judgments 2944, 2773, 2114, 1984, 207; CJEU Judgments F-40/05, T-198/02). The general rules for judicial review of discretionary decisions apply. If the appointing authority deviates in its decision from a recommendation of the disciplinary body to the disadvantage of the official, it must deliver proper reasons (ILOAT Judgment 2261; see also Judgment 2391; CJEU Judgments T-24/98 and T-241/99 para. 82, 228/83 para. 32).

The judicial review is mostly concerned with the issue of whether there is proportionality between the disciplinary measure and the seriousness of the misconduct.

The lack of proportionality is to be treated as an error of law (ILOAT Judgment 2656). In determining the proportionality both objective and subjective features are to be taken into account by the tribunal and in the case of dismissal the "closest scrutiny" is necessary. The more serious the allegation, the greater is the need for care (ILOAT Judgments 2656, 937). Annex IX Art. 10 EU-SR explicitly stipulates that the severity of the disciplinary measure imposed shall be commensurate with the seriousness of the misconduct. It further contains a list of circumstances which must be taken into account in order to establish this proportionality. The organisation shall, therefore, in particular take account of:

a) The nature of the misconduct and the circumstances in which it occurred;
b) The extent to which the misconduct adversely affects the integrity, reputation or interests of the institutions;
c) The extent to which the misconduct involves intentional actions or negligence;
d) The motives for the official's misconduct;
e) The official's grade and seniority;
f) The degree of the official's personal responsibility;
g) The level of the official's duties and responsibilities;
h) Whether the misconduct involves repeated actions or behaviour.
i) The conduct of the official throughout the course of his career.

It is, however, trite law that the competence of the judicial review body is restricted to verifying whether the organisation has transgressed the bound of its discretion (see the standard clause of the ILOAT for the review of discretionary decisions above under reasonable discretion).

**Jurisprudence**

ILOAT Judgments

3682: Right to due process respected even though the complainant was not permitted to attend the witness interview; 3649: Review of the evidence by the tribunal; 3640: An internal investigative report may serve as a basis for initiating disciplinary proceedings; 3312: Disciplinary sanctions cancelled for lack of sufficient reasons; 3297: Official notification of criminal proceedings after the organisation has taken a final disciplinary decision. The final decision is not flawed; 3295: The employee misused PAHO's resources and immunity in a fashion that was deliberate and careless. The dismissal was proportionate and the principle of due process (communication of charges and evidence, adversarial proceedings, possibility to state own version of facts, to refuse evidence and cross-question experts and witnesses) was respected (2786, 2496, 1661); 3289: If possible, an organisation should take action promptly when possible misconduct comes to its attention. In the present case there was no time limit set in the SR and the organisation submitted reasonable grounds for the delay; 3200: Due process in disciplinary proceedings normally requires that the employee knows the name of the accuser; 2123: The principle of *patere legem* is especially relevant in disciplinary matters; 2899: The right to be heard must be respected in an especially rigorous manner in disciplinary proceedings; 2861: Disciplinary proceedings are irrelevant for the non-renewal of a fixed-term contract (1405). The delegation of good faith requires, however, that the organisation at least gives the official the opportunity to be heard and to answer the accusation levelled against him; 2786: Requirement of due process in disciplinary proceedings; 2771: Due process principle (2475, 2468, 1384, 999). The investigative body is not a judicial body; 2616: It was an error of law to impose a disciplinary sanction without taking into account the highly relevant evidence as to the health of the complainant; 2496: Disciplinary proceedings are flawed if the impugned decision penalised acts other than those with which the employee was chiefly charged; 2494: The right to strike must not lead to a sudden stoppage of activity in an operational environment relating to the safety of air navigation (Eurocontrol). The sudden abandonment of the workplace could justify a penalty; 2396: The presumption of innocence must be maintained in the disciplinary proceedings and the dignity and reputation of the staff member must not be impaired; 2391: Obligation to state the reasons for disregarding the recommendation as to disciplinary sanctions; 2365: Suspension is an interim discretionary measure (3035, 1927); 2351: Likelihood, if it is not incontrovertibly ascertained, cannot make up for the lack of conclusive evidence; 2288: Breach of due process since the complainant only had a few hours to defend his case; 2261: If the administration refuses to follow the recommendation of a committee that the various charges do not hold water, reasons must be given for each of the charges; 2254: Need for the opportunity to put forward a proper defence and to take part in adversarial proceedings; 2232: Even in the case of the head of an IO there is no unfettered discretion to terminate the appointment. A procedure must be followed enabling the incumbent to defend his case effectively before an independent and impartial body; 2229: Transfer decisions may be disciplinary, non-disciplinary or even mixed in nature; 2190: The tribunal has no jurisdiction to issue injunctions against IO to undertake disciplinary investigations against another staff member; 1984: It is immaterial for the application of disciplinary sanctions whether or not under national criminal law mitigating circumstances would apply; 1972: Even if a transfer cannot be regarded as a disciplinary sanction, the organisation must heed the dignity and good name of the staff member; 1925: Theft of goods of the organisation warrants summary dismissal; 1906: No obligation of an IO to launch disciplinary proceedings against a staff member. Possible disciplinary infractions may, however, be considered when the organisation is deciding whether or not to offer a new contract; 1899: A decision regarding disciplinary measures relating to one staff member will not adversely affect other staff; 1878: Example of a disproportionate disciplinary measure; 1828: Dismissal for fraud not disproportionate; 1599: Striking someone in the face at work justifies a written reprimand; 1391 (leading judgment): No punishment for offensive remarks which are not justified by evidence, freedom of speech, statements in judicial proceedings are privileged; 1363: Secondary employment under cover of main professional activity (patent consultancy and patent examiner) justifies dismissal; 1346: Dismissal for wilful and repeated insubordination; 969: Summary dismissal for documents calculated to intimidate by threats to the life of senior official.

CJEU Judgments/Orders

F-54/11: Suspension of disciplinary proceedings pending the conclusion of national criminal proceedings, interpretation of Annex IX Art. 25 EU-SR; F-106/11: Restricted competence of the tribunal to verify the proportionality of a disciplinary sanction, the tribunal may not assume the discretionary competence of the appointing authority (F-40/05; T-333/99, T-549/93); T-11/03: In disciplinary matters the examination of the judicature is limited, it cannot substitute its own assessment for that of the appointing authority (T-277/01, T-203/98, T-141/97); T-198/02: Criminal and disciplinary measures pursue different aims. A disciplinary measure is not disproportionate or manifestly incorrect if a sanction is imposed even if the official is not found guilty of any criminal offence (T-144/96); T-120/01 and T-300/01: The suspension of an official is an act adversely affecting him, unless special circumstances are duly established, a suspension may be adopted only after a hearing of the official concerned; C-73/99 P: The publication of the book "The Rotten Heart of Europe" without the prior permission of the appointing authority is constitutes serious misconduct, justifying the suspension of the official under Art. 88 EU-SR; C-252/97: The choice of the disciplinary measure may be reviewed only in the event of a manifest error or misuse of power; C-188/96 P: The statement of reasons for a disciplinary decision must provide a sufficiently precise indication of the reasons to enable review by the judicature (C-166/95 P); T-8/92: The complainant is not adversely affected by a disciplinary decision to close the proceedings without congratulating him as had been recommended by the disciplinary committee; C-326/91 P: No limitation period for the invitation of disciplinary proceedings; they must, however, be conducted within a reasonable period. Obligations to consider the responsibility objectively without reference to any lawfulness or unlawfulness of the decision taken with respect to the other official (T-26/89); T-26/89: Art. 6 EConHR does not apply to disciplinary matters since such proceedings are no "penal proceedings"; 175/86 and 209/86: Factors appertaining to the private life of an official may be regarded as aggravating the incompatibility of his integrity and honesty which each official is required to show vis-à-vis the administration; 255 and 256/83: If there are no rules for determining the new step after a downgrading for disciplinary reasons, that determination is at the discretion of the appointing authority.

### c) Hidden disciplinary measures

An administrative measure which seems to be adopted in the interest of the organisation may in reality be a disciplinary measure imposed as a penalty. A staff member may, therefore, be deprived of the opportunity to have his issue decided in accordance with the applicable disciplinary procedures and thus of the safeguard of his right to due process. In the event of a suspicion of a hidden disciplinary sanction, the judicial review must extend to the particular circumstances of the case (ILOAT Judgment 2659). In practice, the most typical cases are the termination of a contract and the forced transfer to a post with equal pay but with significantly lower competences.

In a number of cases, the ILOAT did not appraise the treatment of an official under the legal aspect of a hidden disciplinary measure but qualified the action as an attack on the complainant's dignity and good name. For example, in Judgment 2819 the ILOAT held that the duties of the complainant in the post to which he had been transferred differed to such an extent from his previous duties as a principal director of the EPO that the organisation did not respect the dignity of the staff member.

**Jurisprudence**

ILOAT Judgments

3162: Termination of a contract based on an allegation of dishonesty must be dealt with in accordance with the applicable disciplinary procedures; 2944: The decision not to promote the complainant did not constitute a hidden disciplinary measure. The administration has discretion to determine the severity of a disciplinary measure provided that it is not manifestly out of proportion to the offence; 2907: The existence of a disguised disciplinary measure cannot be inferred by mere conjecture, it has to be proven; 2861: Since disciplinary proceedings are irrelevant to the non-renewal of a fixed-term contract, a complainant may not properly allege hidden disciplinary action. Good faith, however, requires that he had the opportunity to answer the matters levelled against him (1906, 1405, but see 136); 2854: The termination of the contract was a disguised disciplinary measure; 2819 (see above); 2659 (leading judgment): A hidden sanction is a measure which appears to be adopted in the interests of the organisation but which in reality is imposed as a penalty; 2540: Retaliation for having filed an internal appeal is an abuse of power; 2229: A transfer may be motivated by the need to eliminate tensions among the staff. A transfer of a non-disciplinary nature is subject to the general principles governing the status of the official (respect for dignity) and the work must be of the same level as his previous duties, matching his qualifications; 1972: Assignment to new duties based on the complainants conduct and the tension among staff; 1929: The transfer partly constituted a disciplinary sanction; 1590: The change in duties of an employee is not a hidden disciplinary sanction if it was merely based on poor performance; 1501: Transfer because of infringement of ethical rules of the host country is not a hidden disciplinary sanction.

CJEU Judgments/Orders

T-50/92: The reassignment was not a covert disciplinary sanction; T-69/92: No covert penalty, the plea alleging the progressive reduction of duties was not supported by the documents.

### d) Non-disciplinary actions and recourse claims

*Non-disciplinary actions*

The rule against double jeopardy does not prevent disciplinary and non-disciplinary consequences being attached to the same acts or events (ILOAT Judgment 3126).

– Suspension

The suspension of an employee is an interim precautionary measure in the case of alleged serious misconduct and generally lasts as long as the disciplinary procedure (ILOAT Judgment 2365). The suspension has to be proportional to the alleged misconduct and may be legally reviewed in the same way as other discretionary decisions (ILOAT Judgment 3035). The suspension by its nature is generally not considered a disciplinary sanction but it is nevertheless a decision which causes injury to the person concerned (ILOAT Judgment 1927 para. 6; but see Judgment 136 and Rule 10(2)(a)(iv) UN-SR: a suspension without pay is a disciplinary measure): The suspension is ordered by the appointing authority with (CoE) or without (EU, UN, EPO) prior consultation of the chairman of the disciplinary committee (Annex IX Art. 23 EU-SR; Rule 10(4)(a) UN-SR (placed on administrative leave; Art. 57 CoE-SR; Art. 104(1) EPO-SR).

The situation of a suspended official must be definitely settled within a certain period of time (EU Annex IX Art. 24(1): six months; UN Rule 10(4)(b): the administrative leave shall as far as practical not exceed three months; CoE Art. 57 SR: four months; EPO: Art. 104(3) SR: six months or 24 months if the appointing authority is the Council, with the possibility of extension in exceptional cases). If the employee is subject to criminal proceedings for the conduct giving rise to his suspension, a final decision is only taken after a verdict of the court hearing the case has been delivered (Annex IX Art. 25 EU-SR; Art. 105 EPO-SR).

- Non-fulfilment of official duties (underperformance, professional incompetence)

A staff member participating in a lawful strike action is not exposed to disciplinary sanctions, but he is not entitled to payment for the period of strike. This is a corollary to the principle that remuneration is due only for service rendered (see ILOAT Judgment 3369 and the case law cited; CJEU Judgments 44, 46 and 49–74).

In the case of insufficient performance (underperformance, incompetence), advancement to a higher grade and promotion may be delayed (Art. 43 et seq. EU-SR; Rule 3(3)(a) UN-SR) or there may be a relegation in step, demotion or dismissal (Art. 51 EU-SR; Rule 9.6(h) UN-SR; Art. 22 bis (3) CoE-SR; Art. 22 EPO-SR).

- Non-renewal of a fixed-term contract

In the case of the non-renewal of an employment contract after expiry (for example for reasons of misconduct or unsatisfactory performance), disciplinary proceedings do not apply (ILOAT Judgment 1906 para. 8: "When an official by his own actions renders himself unacceptable for reappointment there is no longer any obligation on the part of the organisation to consider him for such reappointment", see also Judgments 1441, 1405, 1381, 1271, 1262, 1052).

- Unjust enrichment

The recovery of money owed to the IO (undue payment) is not considered as such a disciplinary measure (see the explicit statement in Rule 10(2)(b)(ii) UN-SR). It is, however, without prejudice to the opening of disciplinary proceedings if the organisation has deliberately been misled.

- Written or oral reprimand

In the UN-SR (Rule 10.2(b)(i) a written or oral reprimand is not considered to be a disciplinary measure but an administrative one (see, however, Annex IX Art. 9(1)(b) EU-SR).

- Recourse claims (reparation)

In the case of damage caused by an employee in the course of or in connection with his duties there is a direct and exclusive liability of the organisation. The personal liability of an international employee towards his organisation for any damage caused in the course or in connection with the performance of his duties is governed by the SR (see, for example, Art. 340(4) TFEU in conjunction with Art. 22 EU-SR; Art. 9(3) EPO-EPC in conjunction with Art. 25 EPO-SR, see Kunz-Hallstein/Ullrich, Art. 9 § 30).

Three conditions must be met:

- Breach of a legal obligation
- Financial damage must be caused
- Liability of a serious personal misconduct, this covers deliberate misconduct or misconduct arising from gross negligence, and excludes ordinary negligence.

The provisions are applied very rarely.

The reparation of the damage extends to damages directly inflicted on the organisation (for example, theft of office supplies) or third party damages (for example, breach of a contract or a tendering procedure).

The employee may be required to make good the damage in whole or in part. Some SR require that a reasoned opinion is given in accordance with the procedure laid down in regard to disciplinary measures (see, for example, Art. 22(2) EU-SR; Art. 25(2) EPO-SR).

For damage caused by an employee towards the organisation or a third party outside his official duties, he is liable under the rules of the applicable domestic law.

In contrast to the liability of the organisation for compensation of damages inflicted on its employees, the liability of staff members towards its organisation is of no great importance in practical terms. Moreover, IO have insurance arrangements in high-risk areas such as for authorising officers, accounting officers, pension administrators, etc.

*Part 3*

# The system of legal protection for the international civil service – The international administrative tribunals

*Chapter 1*

## General

### A. The obligation to grant legal protection

In their capacity as subjects of international public law, IO are endowed by member states with the necessary power of organisational autonomy to set up an adequate internal legal system to achieve their tasks. The legal protection of this autonomy requires that IO enjoy immunity from national jurisdiction and execution within the scope of their official activities. The immunity is, however, not a privilege, it does not free the organisation from any obligation. The laws remain applicable, it is only the adjudication in the courts which is prevented (Schermers/Blokker § 1612 and above under immunity). IO are, therefore, not absolved from the obligation to grant legal protection in the form of judicial or arbitral remedy which undoubtedly constitutes an integral part of human rights obligations and which is also considered by international administrative tribunals as a general legal principle applicable to the international civil service. Since national courts of member states would be subject to suspicion of not independently granting legal protection, IO do not, as a rule, waive immunity in disputes with third parties but instead offer the settlement of disputes by arbitration. As far as labour law disputes with staff members are concerned IO take account of the fact that service-related disputes occur relatively frequently and waive their immunity by accepting the jurisdiction of an international administrative tribunal. (Only for peripheral areas of employment (preferably manual labour) where an infringement of IO's autonomy in its core functions is not to be expected, may national jurisdiction be declared applicable). (ILOAT Judgment 1451: The tribunal has been "at pains to except any case in which there is express renvoi to municipal law and jurisdiction is an organisation's rules in the terms of appointment"; see the case law cited therein and Art. 122 EU-CEOS: the dispute between the institution and a member of the local staff serving in a third country is submitted to arbitration, and point 5 of the Conditions of employment for auxiliary staff of the EPO).

In so far as the jurisdiction of an international administrative tribunal applies in conformity with the internal rules of an IO (see, for example, Art. 270 TFEU; Reg. 11(1) UN-SR; Art. 60 CoE-SR; Art. 13 EPO-EPC) and with the statute of the respective international administrative tribunal an IO is bound to respect this jurisdiction and may in general not waive its immunity or offer arbitration (see, however, ILOAT Judgment 2657, where the tribunal declared an appeal as being outside its jurisdiction and recommended access to a municipal court either by waiving immunity or by submitting the dispute to arbitration). A tribunal may, however, at any time propose an amicable settlement (Art. 8(5) statute of ESMAT or even propose sending a case to mediation (Art. 10 statute of the UNDT).

## B. The legal basis for establishing an international administrative tribunal

As far as the founding convention of an IO does not expressly provide for authorisation to establish an international administrative tribunal for disputes between the organisation and its employees (see, for example, Art. 270 TFEU and Art. 13 EPO-EPC), the setting up of a tribunal can be based on the principles of "implied powers", "inherent powers" or "effet utile" (Priess, p. 89 et seq. and above) or on the organisational power of the organisation for the establishment of subsidiary and auxiliary bodies (see, for example, the establishment of the Pension Reserve Fund of the EPO in 1993, i.e. prior to the insertion of Art. 38(b) in the EPO-EPC in 2000 and the later establishment of other social security funds without an explicit legal basis in the EPC, see Ullrich, Pension Schemes, p. 5; see also the Advisory Opinion of the ICJ of 13.7.1954, ICJ Reports 1954, p. 57 on the establishment of the UNAT and Schermers/Blokker, § 233; see also the Recommendation 856(1979) of the Parliamentary Assembly of the CoE, points 4 and 9 as to the right of staff members of the CoE to file appeals against their appointing authority: "it would be unacceptable if the Council of Europe did not apply to its own staff the principles laid down in its Convention on Human Rights and the Social Charter"; "it should be possible for individual staff members, the Staff Committee and the Trade Union(s) to make appeals").

## C. The limited jurisdiction of the international administrative tribunals

### I. The principle of limited subject matters

International administrative tribunals are either established by the constituent instruments of an IO (Art. 256 TFEU) or subject to the jurisdiction of a pre-existing tribunal (Art. 13 EPO-EPC), or else set up later on by an internal decision of the plenary organ of the organisation (statute by the ILOAT adopted by the International Labour Conference on 9 October 1946). Provisions in the statute of an international administrative tribunal determine the limits of its jurisdiction. In addition to labour disputes some international administrative tribunals are competent to hear other disputes. This applies, for example, to the ILOAT (Art. II(4): disputes arising out of contracts to which the ILO is a party and which provide for the competence of the tribunal on any case of dispute with regard to their execution) and to the CJEU (Art. 256 TFEU) and to the complaints board of the European Schools (Art. 27 Convention defining the statute of the ES) which is competent to hear appeals from staff members (Art. 80 Reg. for members of the seconded staff of the ES) and from legal representatives of a pupil in an ES (Art. 66 General Rules of the ES).

The jurisdiction of an international administrative tribunal is restricted *ratione personae* to the officials of the organisation that has recognised its jurisdiction (see, for example, Art. II(5) of the statute of ILOAT in conjunction with the annex to the statute).

The right to submit a complaint is also limited *ratione personae* to claims relating to rights occurring as a result of the employment relationship with the organisation (ILOAT Judgments 2376, 1845). An official only has *locus standi* before a tribunal if there is evidence that he is connected by an employment contract or has permanent employee status (ILOAT Judgments 2649, 2157). Third persons have *locus standi* if, on the death of the official the official's rights have passed on to them or if they are entitled to some rights under the SR (see, for example, Art. II(6) statute of ILOAT).

In Judgment 621 (307) the ILOAT ruled that a binding employment contract already exists if the essential terms have been settled and only formalities remain to be done.

In Judgment 2657 the ILOAT held that the claim of an applicant for a post was irreceivable *ratione personae* since he had no contract relationship with the organisation (here: the EPO). It recommended, however, that the vacuum of legal protection be filled by offering arbitration or a waiver of immunity before national courts (see, however, CJEU Order C-126/90: successful candidates in an open competition have *locus standi*, see more in detail below).

The statutes of the international administrative tribunals determine the limits of their competence *ratione materiae*. For example, Art. II(1) of the statute of ILOAT limits the competence of the tribunal "to hear complaints alleging non-observance, in substance or in form, of the terms of appointment of officials" and of such "provisions of the Staff Regulations as are applicable to the case" (Art. II(2) of the statute of ILOAT extends the competence to hearing complaints concerning the compensation provided for in the event of invalidity, injury or disease incurred in the course of the employment and to fixing finally the amount of compensation; see also Art. 2 of the statute of the UNDT which contains a very detailed list of competences; by contrast Art. 50a of the statute of the CJEU in conjunction with Art. 270 TFEU describes the competence of the GC in staff matters in very general terms).

The ILOAT held in several judgments its incompetence to adjudicate *ratione materiae*. Judgment 3343 (whether the procurement of goods violated the internal tendering rules), 2649 (salary scales of agency staff supplying temporary work), 2306 (a claim concerning the creation of the office of an ombudsman), 1543 (a claim to waive the immunity of the President of the EPO (Office), 1020 (the transfer of the headquarters of an organisation), 933 (to waive the immunity of EPO officers). In its Judgment C-430/97 (preliminary ruling), the CJEU held that the EU-SR are intended to regulate the legal relationship between the EU institutions and their officials. The right of the spouses in divorce proceedings are governed by the rules of private law and family law applying in the member states. The CJEU would have no competence *ratione materiae* to decide on the appointment of pension rights in divorce proceedings.

The competence *ratione temporis* of an international administrative tribunal primarily refers to the receivability of a complaint. A tribunal loses jurisdiction if the time limit set in its statute for filing a complaint has expired. This is in the interest of the legal stability (see, for example, ILOAT Judgments 3147, 2722, 1393).

An abstract control of norms is, as a rule, not known by the judicature of the international administrative tribunals. An appellant may, however, incidentally challenge the general legal ruling which forms the basis of law for the individual decision impugned (see, for example, ILOAT Judgments 3146, 1786, 1329 and more in detail below).

### II. The principle of limited remedial powers

International administrative tribunals are not empowered to award whatever legal remedies they find appropriate to adjudicate. They may only make use of such remedies as are provided explicitly or by implication in their statute (see, for example, ILOAT Judgment 933 para. 6, 1419, 69; see more in detail above under the right to material and moral damages). The remedial powers of international administrative tribunals are, therefore, confined to ordering the rescission of the decision impugned or the performance of the obligation relied upon. If this is not possible or advisable, the tribunal awards the complainant compensation for the injury caused to him (see CJEU Art. 266; 270 TFEU; Art. 91 EU-SR; ILOAT statute Art. VIII; UNDT statute Art. 10(5); UNAT statute Art. 9(1)). The tribunals have no jurisdiction to order injunctions against the organisation (CJEU Judgment F-29/11 para. 93). (For more in detail see above under the right to material and moral damages.)

A tribunal may not entertain a claim for action against the management of an IO (ILOAT Judgment 654 para. 4; 655 para. 6), or order renegotiation of existing obligations or the creation of new obligations (ILOAT Judgment 2952), order the imposition of disciplinary measures on a staff member (ILOAT Judgment 2811) or an apology (ILOAT Judgments 3339, 3149), or order a management audit or the placing of the complainant in a particular post (ILOAT Judgments 1213, 968). Nor may a tribunal issue a warning against another staff member (ILOAT Judgment 1049). A tribunal may also not waive the immunity of another official (ILOAT Judgments 1543, 933, this is also *ratione materiae* outside its jurisdiction). It is also not for a tribunal to make statements of law (CJEU Order F-87/07) or to issue directions to the appointing authority (CJEU Judgments F-9/08; T-56/92; 62–65: The court cannot encroach upon the prerogatives of the appointing authority by addressing to it instructions in relation to the choice in recruiting officials). The tribunal cannot order a pre-recruitment medical examination (CJEU Judgment F-46/09) or a competition test in written French (CJEU Judgment F-29/11).

The statutes of some international administrative tribunals provide for additional limitations of remedial powers. For example, Art. 10(7) statute of the UNDT and Art. 9(3) statute of the UNAT forbids the award of exemplary or punitive damages by the tribunal and Art. 10(5)(b) statute of the UNDT (Art. 9(1)(b) statute of the UNAT) stipulates that the tribunal shall normally not order a compensation exceeding the two years' net base salary for an applicant. Art. XIV(2) of the statute of the IMFAT provides that the tribunal shall fix an amount of compensation in lieu of a measure which the organisation may not implement in the interests of the IMF (for example, the reinstatement of a staff member). The monetary award shall normally not exceed 300% of the last annual salary of the applicant. A similar ruling is provided in Art. IX(2) of the statute of OASAT with the proviso that the indemnity shall normally not exceed two years' salary for the applicant.

### III. The principle of limited standards of judicial review

The legal yardstick applied by international administrative tribunals for assessing the legality of the administrative decisions of IO in staff matters is in general restricted to international law. There are three sources of law applied: the SR, the letters of appointment of the respective IO, and the general legal principles applicable to the international civil service in general (Schermers/Blokker § 539).

The statutes of the tribunals mostly do not provide for all of the above standards for their judicial review (see, however, the SR referred to below). For instance:

- Art. II(1)(5) statute of the ILOAT only refers to the non-observance of the terms of appointment of officials and the applicable SR;
- Art. 60 CoEAT: The tribunal shall decide as to the law;
- Art. 2(1)(a) statute of the UNDT (Art. 2(9) statute of the UNAT) refers to the terms of appointment, the contract of employment or the regulations of the UNJSPF (Art. 7(2) statute of the UNAT);
- Art. 270 TFEU refers to the EU-SR and the EU-CEOS;
- In conjunction with Art. 6 TEU, which recognises the rights, freedoms and principles set out in the CFREU (Art. 6(1)) and provides (Art. 6(2)) that the Union shall accede to the EConHR. Art. 6(3) provides that the fundamental rights, as guaranteed by EConHR and as they result from the constitutional traditions common to the member states, shall constitute general principles of the Union's law;
- See however: Art. III IMFAT which refers to the internal law of the fund, including generally recognised principles of the international civil service law concerning the judicial review of administrative acts.

Since the SR, the letters of appointment and the supplementary internal rulings, decisions and assurances do not comprise a complete legal system, all international administrative tribunals have to resort to the application of general legal principles as a standard of their judicial review (ILOAT Judgment 11: "Considering that the administrative tribunal, by virtue of the very purpose for which it was created, should be considered as governed by general legal principles (instance de droit commun) with the necessary powers to guarantee the security of employment of all officials attached to the International Labour Organization"; ILOAT Judgment 2292 para. 11: "human rights … in compliance with the tribunal's case law, apply to relations with staff"; CJEU C-274/99 P: "freedom of expression constitutes a fundamental right, which Community officials also enjoy"; C-150/98 P: "… it is settled case law of the court of Justice that fundamental rights form an integral part of the general principle of law whose observance the court ensures …").

As a rule, the SR of IO only contain a small number of references for the application of general legal principles. For example:

EU-SR: Art. 12a (Prohibition of harassment); Art. 17a (Freedom of expression); Art. 24b (Right of association).

UN-SR: Reg. 1(1)(c) (Respect of the rights in the Charter); Reg. 1(2)(f) Inviolability of personal views and convictions); Reg. 8(1) (Staff relations).

CoE-SR: Art. 3 (Non-discrimination); Art. 47 (Freedom of association); Art. 47a (Right to strike).

EPO-SR: Art. 30 (Freedom of association); Art. 30a (Right to strike, see doc. CA/D 5/13 on the EPO website. In 1994 the Administrative Council of the EPO has adopted the following declaration: "The Administrative Council and the President of the Office note that when reviewing the law applied to EPO staff the ILO Tribunal considers not only the legal provisions in force in the European Patent Organisation but also general legal principles, including human rights. The Administrative Council also noted with approval the President's declaration that the Office adheres to the said legal provisions and principles.").

## IV. Details of the case law of the CJEU, ILOAT, UNDT/UNAT and the CoEAT on the application of general legal principles as standards for their judicial review

– CJEU

At the EU, the provisions of the CFREU are addressed to all institutions, bodies, offices and agencies of the Union (Art. 51(1) CFREU in conjunction with Art. 6 TEU). The CFREU explicitly forms, therefore, an integral part of the standards for its judicial review.

The CJEU refers in consistent case law to the general legal principles enshrined in the CFREU (see, for example, CJEU Judgments C-579/12 RX; F-122/12, F-84/12, F-38/12, F-46/11, F-41/10).

– ILOAT, UNDT, UNAT

The keyword "general principle" is constantly referred to in the case law of the ILOAT (in 2016: 246 extracts in the Triblex case law database), see, for example, Judgment 3046 para. 8: "The Tribunal accepts that various international norms and other general legal principles form part of an official's terms of appointment"; 2292 para. 11: The EPO is not formally bound by the EConHR, nevertheless the general legal principles enshrined in the Convention apply.

The same holds good for the UNDT and the UNAT, see, for example, Judgment UNDT 2010/030 para. 15; Judgment No. 2014-UNAT-409. Moreover, reference has to be made to the Advisory Opinion of the ICJ of 13 July 1954 (Reports 1954, p. 57): The aim of the UDHR to promote freedom and justice for individuals also applies to the UN's own staff (see more detail, above): "It would … hardly be consistent with the expressed aim of the Charter to provide freedom and justice for individuals and with the constant preoccupation of the UN Organisation to promote this aim that it should afford no judicial or arbitral remedy to its own staff for the settlement of any disputes which may arise between it and them".

– CoEAT

Art. 4 statute of the CoEAT in conjunction with Art. 60 CoE-SR does not explicitly specify the standards of judicial review of the tribunal. The tribunal does not, however, only apply the SR and the letters of appointment of staff members but also the general legal principles recognised in international case law (see, for example, Appeal No. 181/1994 para. 24: The tribunal must satisfy itself "that the decision complained of complied with the Organisation's regulations and with general legal principles, to which the legal system of international organisations are subject").

Questions regarding delimitation

International administrative tribunals are in no way bound by the rulings of other international administrative tribunals (ILOAT Judgment 3138 para. 7: "... it is in no way bound by the case law of the international courts ..."; 860 para. 24: "...will rule by its own lights on any case before it"). The rulings of other tribunals may, however, carry "persuasive authority" under certain conditions (ILOAT Judgment 1296).

As a rule, a tribunal will not review criteria laid down in any national law (ILOAT Judgments 1020, 899, 780, 435, 322), unless there is express renvoi thereto in the SR of contract of employment (ILOAT Judgments 1450, 1369, 1311) or if there are common general legal principles to be found in the labour law of member states (ILOAT Judgment 2533: mature legal systems provide for compensation on a "no fault" basis). Municipal law may also be applied if the SR of IO have, for lack of competence of the IO, to derive certain legal terms from it, e.g. marital and non-marital relationship (Annex VII Art. 1(2)(c)(ii) EU-SR), divorce (Annex VII Art. 1(2)(b) EU-SR), adoption (Annex VII Art. 2(2) EU-SR), nationality (Annex VII Art. 4(3) EU-SR). There is abundant case law on the treatment of same-sex partnerships in the SR of IO (see above under Excursus: same sex partnership).

The constant case law of the international administrative tribunals allows the complainant to challenge the lawfulness of a regulation forming the legal basis of the individual decision under review as an incidental issue, notwithstanding the expiry of the time limit set for the complaint (see, for example, ILOAT Judgment 3146 para. 10; see also Art. 277 TFEU and, below, under incidental challenge of an act of general application).

The judicial review of the decision is assessed on the basis of the facts and the law as they stood at the time when it was taken (*tempus regit actum*), otherwise the general principle against retroactivity would be violated (ILOAT Judgment 2459 para. 9; 986 para. 21; CJEU Judgments T-115/94, CJ 15/76 and 16/76).

## D. The international administrative tribunals as genuine judicial organs

The employment relationship between an IO and its staff is characterised by the autonomy of the IO in organisational and personnel matters. IO function with regard to their staff as a substitute state (see above). They also enjoy functional immunity from national jurisdiction in disputes with their employees. Since the immunity of IO does not, however, exempt them from the rule of law (see above), IO have to provide other means for protecting the fundamental rights of a staff member to a fair trial by a genuine judicial body.

Internal grievance and appeal procedures as well as mediation and conciliation procedures cannot fully replace judicial proceedings.

The occasional setting up of arbitration boards, which is current practice in disputes with third parties (contractors, tenderers), would not seem to be advisable. The frequency of staff disputes and the fragmentary nature of the institutional law requires a judicial system which guarantees legal certainty, stability and at least some foreseeability.

In labour law disputes with their staff, IO may adopt procedures adapted to the special features of an IO and different from the remedies available under municipal law if the alternative means of legal process available do not impair the essence of the right to a court and are not disproportionate for the purpose of a fair trial (see, for example, Judgment ECHR, Waite and Kennedy v. Germany, Application no. 26083/94, para. 65, 66, 72, 73).

The legal sources to be applied as standards of judicial review for verifying the judicial role of an international administrative tribunal are enshrined in international conventions (see, for example, Art. 10 UDHR, Art. 6 EConHR) and in the constitutions of most member states of IO.

The ECHR (see Judgment White and Kennedy v. Germany, Application no. 26083/94; Beer and Regan v. Germany, Application no. 28934/95) and various national high courts (see, for example, the landmark decision of the German Constitutional Court "Eurocontrol II" of 10 November 1981, for an English translation see the website of the University of Texas at Austin, Institute for Transnational Law, Foreign Law Translations; the Judgment of the Supreme Court of the Netherlands, Anonymous v. EPO of 23 October 2009, Nederlandse Jurisprudentie 2009, 527 et seq. and the decision of the Belgian Cour de Cassation, WEU v. Siedler of 21 December 2009, Belgian database: jure.juridat.just.fgov.be, ref. no. S. 04.0129 F) referred to Art. 6(1) EConHR in order to evaluate whether the international judiciary adopted by an IO corresponds to the purpose and essence of the "right to a fair trial". In contrast to the ECHR and other supreme courts the findings in the Eurocontrol II decision of the German Constitutional Court is characterised by a rather detailed analysis of the role of an international administrative tribunal (in this case the ILOAT) as a genuine judicial body.

The court thereby held that the statute and the rules of court of the ILOAT meet an "international minimum standard of elementary procedural justice ... such as arises from developed systems of rule of law and from the procedural law of international courts ...". It can further be deduced from constant case law that the court took account of Art. 6(1) EConHR (see Ullrich, ZaöRV, p. 166 et seq.).

Going into more detail, the analysis of the German Constitutional Court is based on the following elements of procedural law applied by the ILOAT.

The court held:

- the ILOAT was set up by an act in international law (decision of the International Labour Conference on 9 October 1946);
- the tribunal decides on the basis of legally established powers and in accordance with a legally ordered procedure (statute and rules of procedure);
- the judges are bound to independence and impartiality (these qualifications may implicitly be deduced from the statute (Art. III of ILOAT's statute);
- the access to the ILOAT is not made unreasonably difficult (Art. VII of ILOAT's statute);
- the ILOAT guarantees a legal hearing and a minimum degree of procedural equality (Art. IV and V of the statute and the rules of court). In consistent case law the ILOAT, however, has held that with respect to the right of the complainant to put his case freely "either in writing or orally, the appeal body is not obliged to offer him both possibilities" (ILOAT Judgments 3447 para. 8, 3023 para. 11, 2893 para. 5; see also Judgment 3059 para. 9: "... no issue that would justify the tribunal departing from its consistent practice not to grant an oral hearing in cases which turn essentially on questions of law". In contrast the UNDT and the CJEU (CST) hold oral hearings as a matter of routine (see below under proceedings before the tribunals).

It has, however to be noted that neither the UN-SR nor the EU-SR provide for an internal appeals procedure which guarantees a fair hearing before an independent body in which staff representatives and the administration are represented. That is why the oral hearing takes place for the first time before the Court of First Instance. By contrast, the appeals before the ILOAT are as a rule preceded by an oral hearing before the internal appeals board (ILOAT Judgment 3282 para. 3: "The tribunal encourages organisations to provide efficient internal appeal mechanisms which can provide a broad range of remedies which may not otherwise be available before the tribunal"; see in more detail below).

- the ILOAT guarantees a minimum degree of procedural equality of those involved (see ILOAT's rules of procedure);
- the ILOAT exercises its jurisdiction (see the "Triblex" database of the ILOAT).

It can generally be assumed that the international administrative tribunals meet the minimum standards of elementary procedural justice. This holds especially true for the UNDT/UNAT and the CJEU. The ILOAT's judicial system which has up to now not adapted its approach to the UN judicial system, may be rated as still being at the very minimum standard of what may be requested from a mature system of international judiciary. In particular, it should be noted that the right to an oral hearing is systematically denied. The relatively short term of office of the judges (three years) may rise doubts regarding their independence. In contrast to the twin tribunals UNDT/UNAT there is still no two-tier-system of legal protection. Applicants for a post in an IO are generally barred from access to a tribunal (ILOAT Judgments 2657, 1964, but see CJEU Judgments 81 to 88/74 and consistent case law granting applicants for a post a right to appeal). The tribunal has no authority to issue an interim injunction against the defendant (ILOAT Judgment 2623 para. 3).

## E. The legal status of the international administrative tribunals and their judges

International administrative tribunals are judicial bodies which adjudicate on labour law disputes between an IO and its staff members. They pronounce final judgments on the basis of the institutional law of the respective IO. International administrative tribunals have to be differentiated from other international courts and tribunals like the ICJ, the International Tribunal for the Law of the Sea (ITLOS), the International Criminal Courts of the UN (see the UN website) and regional international courts applying and interpreting the law of a union of member states, like the CJEU and the EFTA Court as well as international courts like the ECHR ruling on the alleged violations of human rights.

The CJEU and the EFTA Court also exercise jurisdiction as international administrative tribunals in civil service disputes. The ILOAT is, in addition to labour law disputes, also competent to hear disputes arising out of contracts to which the ILO is a party, and which provide for the competence of the Tribunal in any case of dispute with regard to their execution (ILOAT statute Art. II(4)).

International administrative tribunals are as a rule not endowed with their own international legal personality or legal capacity in the member states. They thus depend on the legal status of the funding IO (see, for example, the CJEU, the UNDT/UNAT and the ILOAT).

In its Advisory Opinion of 13 July 1954, ICJ Reports 1954, p. 53, the ICJ held in regard to the status of the UNAT that the tribunal was not established as an advisory organ but "as an independent and truly judicial body pronouncing final judgments without appeal within the limited field of its functions".

Since international administrative tribunals exercise core functions of the IO they "benefit from the immunity of the IO which established them (A. Reinisch, The Immunity, pp. 285–306).

The judges of international administrative tribunals are "usually chosen from a pool of people that have advanced enough in their career in life" and they "would like to leave the legacy of good name" (A. Gordillo). The candidates applying for the post of a judge have to undergo a selection procedure. They are appointed by a special committee of the organisation on the basis of a contract for a limited term of three to seven years (CJEU: six years, ILOAT: three years, UNDT: seven years).

As a rule, they enjoy the same privileges and immunities as the staff members of the funding organisation (Art. 3(4) statute of the CJEU; UN doc. A/63/314 para. 83 and UN doc. A/RES/63/253 para. 30; Art. VIII statute of IMFAT). The short term of office of the ILOAT judges give rise to doubts regarding their independence.

The judges enjoy full independence (Art. 19(2) TEU; Art. 253 TFEU; Art. 4(8) statute of the UNDT; a similar provision is missing in the statute of the ILOAT, the independence of the judges may, however, be deduced form Art. III of the statute of the ILOAT (Priess, p. 182)). The judges must perform their duties impartially and conscientiously (Art. 2 statute of the CJEU and Art. 4(3)(a) UNDT statute and Art. 3(3)(a) UNAT statute). At the ILOAT, the necessary guarantee for impartiality may be deduced from Art. 8(1), 9(1) and 16 of the rules of procedure of the ILOAT. In the event of misconduct or incapacity a judge may be removed under very restricted conditions and after a formal procedure.

## F. The number of international administrative tribunals

Just as for IO there are no reliable statistics on the number of international administrative tribunals which adjudicate upon staff disputes. A good overview may be obtained from the website of the CoEAT ("other courts"). There are about two dozen of the most important international administrative tribunals and comparable judicial bodies: UNDT, UNAT, ILOAT, IMFAT, WBAT, the five AT of OECD, NATO, CoE, ECMWF, EUMETSAT and the Appeals Board of ESA (the six CO), the Complaints Board of the European School, the CJEU (CJ and GC), the EBRDAT (European Bank for Reconstruction and Development AT), UNIDROIT (International Institute for the Unification of Private Law AT), ATBIS (Bank for International Settlements AT), CSAT (Commonwealth Secretariat Arbitral Tribunal), TRIBAD (AT of the Organisation of American States), IDBAT (Inter-American Development Bank AT), ADBAT (Asian Development Bank AT), AfDAT (African Development Bank AT), ESMAT (European Stability Mechanism AT).

## G. The success rate of complaints

The average success rate of complaints (in full and in part) before the international administrative tribunals over an extended period can be estimated at between 25% and 35%. In conformity with the statistics of judicial activity of the CJEU published in the annual report of the CJEU (accessible on the "curia" website of the CJEU), the success rate over a period of eight years was about 25%. The rate before the ILOAT over a period of about 15 years was between 25% and 30% (see UN special No. 614 of January 2003, and No. 629 of May 2004, published on the internet on www.unspecial.org). The rate before the UNDT/UNAT over a period of eight years was over 30% (see the statistics set up by the Activity Report of OAJ published on the website of the OAJ under "Statistics").

## H. Legal assistance for staff in employment disputes

The right of staff to an assistance in informal and formal staff management disputes is generally acknowledged by IO. Most IO leave it, however, to the individual staff member to get legal support from an attorney or from the staff union or staff representation. Some IO, however, consider it their own duty to provide independent support in this field.

A good example is provided by the establishment of the Office of Staff Legal Assistance (OSLA) within the UN Secretariat which became operational as of 1 July 2009 (see the website of OSLA; UN doc. A/RES/63/253 para. 13, A/RES/62/228 and A/65/373). OSLA is the successor of the UN Panel of Counsel (POC) established in 1956 and restructured in 1984 (see UN doc. ST/ADM/SER.A/360 and A/61/205). OSLA is staffed by legal officers who must abide by a code of conduct. It is an independent unit providing legal advice and assistance free of charge in all staff-management disputes, informal and formal. A staff member may seek the assistance by a member of OSLA at any stage during the resolution of a workplace issue. OSLA may, however, refuse to give legal assistance if an application has little chance of success (see Judgment UNDT/2010/025 para. 37). A growing problem is the funding of OSLA. To this end, OSLA has set up a trust fund to collect donations (see UN doc. A/66/275 para. 86 and the UN website of OSLA).

## I. Conflict of jurisdiction

International administrative tribunals generally assume sole jurisdiction in disputes between an IO and its staff members based on their immunity from national jurisdiction. There may, however, exceptionally be cases where the employment law of an IO has close connections "with both municipal and international law to warrant recognition of both jurisdictions, each for different issues" (ILOAT Judgment 1451 para. 27).

In the case underlying Judgment 1451 of the ILOAT the IO has vested jurisdiction in regard of the pension scheme both in national courts and the ILOAT. The tribunal held that based on the latent conflict of jurisdiction a staff member may file suit before the ILOAT or the national court, as he deems competent. It is then up to the respective tribunal to determine "whether the material issues of the particular case make it the most suitable jurisdiction" (ILOAT Judgment 1451 para. 27).

In any case, a "... conflict of jurisdiction must invariably be so resolved as to allow no judicial void where conflicting jurisdictions decline competence" (ILOAT Judgment 1451 para. 28). The ILOAT assumed jurisdiction, quashed the decision and restored its sole competence in this matter based on the requirement of rational division of jurisdiction in the international context of the Pension Scheme (funding, coverage under the terms of the contracts of service and execution by the IO as the guarantor of its obligations).

In Judgment 1773 the ILOAT held that if a contract of employment does not vest competence in the tribunal but expressly provides for arbitration over any dispute, and the organisation refuses arbitration the tribunal assumes competence in order to warrant legal protection.

If a staff member files suit against the employing organisation before a national court, he is not barred to bring an action before the ILOAT on the same matter. It is for the municipal labour court to rule on its own competence (ILOAT Judgment 1258).

In the case underlying ILOAT Judgment 1450 there was a conflict of jurisdiction between the ILOAT and municipal courts. The EPO engaged auxiliary staff primarily on the basis of regulations subject to national law, whereas grading, leave and the limited duration of the contracts were governed by internal law. In the case of a dispute, the applicable law is decisive for the issue of jurisdiction. In a dispute about the limited duration of a contract, the German courts resolved the dispute by declining jurisdiction whereas the ILOAT assumed jurisdiction and ruled on the merits of the case.

## J. Alternative dispute resolution (ADR) mechanisms (arbitration, mediation, ombudsman services)

### I. Overview

The formal litigation in workplace disputes by judicial proceedings before an internal appeals (grievance) body and finally by an international administrative tribunal is cumbersome. The staff member is not usually familiar with the legal procedures, time limits and other formalities. He often has to seek assistance from the staff union, staff legal assistance bodies (see OSLA at the UN see below) or legal counsel.

The formal procedures are costly, both for the organisation and for the complainant. The costs for the internal and the court proceedings may be estimated roughly at EUR 20,000 to 30,000 (comprising the internal costs for the various briefs, the salaries of the members of the internal boards of appeal and the financing of the tribunal).

The formal procedures are sometimes extremely long. The average time for processing an appeal through the internal board of appeal and the old United Nations Administrative Tribunal was about five years (see para. 6 of the Report of the Commission of Experts on Reforming Internal Justice at the UN of 12 June 2006). After a reform the processing time before the UNDT was reduced to approximately twelve to 24 months (see UN doc. A/65/373 of 16 September 2012). At the WBAT the processing time dropped from twelve to nine months in 2014. At the ILOAT, it presently takes extremely long for officials of some IO with a high number of appeals (see, for example, the Judgment of the District Court of The Hague of 16 July 2013 which held that a processing time of probably 15 years before the ILOAT was in conflict with the principle of a fair trial. The court, therefore, assumed his jurisdiction in case Verveer v. EPO (Case no.: 1223887/12–31860) which was, however, annulled by a Judgment of the Hague Regional Court of Appeal of 30 September 2014 (Case no.: 200.136.028/01).

The formal procedures are adversarial. This may lead to an escalation of the conflict and result in a detrimental impact on the future working relation between colleagues and superiors.

It is, therefore, in the common interest of both parties of an employment relationship to deal with tensions and conflicts in a smoother way. To this end, additional channels of conflict resolution had been established in many IO. These procedures are easily accessible, cost effective, expeditious and offer less confrontational ways of dispute resolution. These soft dispute resolution mechanisms are generally referred to as "informal", "consensual" or "alternative" dispute resolutions.

A soft dispute resolution is "non-legalistic" in character and aims at enabling an amicable settlement of management-staff disputes at an early stage.

The ADR mechanisms are manifold. Sometimes the most appropriate mode of dispute settlement is achieved by indicating to the other party the willingness to negotiate or by offering a compromise solution.

The formal channels of ADR frequently available to the international civil service are:

- arbitration (binding or non-binding), a decision is rendered.
- mediation, no decision rendered but assistance in dispute settlement.
- ombudsman services, impartial assistance in employment issues.

In preparation for a conference on Best Practices in Resolving Employment Disputes in IO, hosted by the ILO in September 2014, a survey was launched among IO with the aim of collecting background information on conflict resolution mechanisms. According to the reply of 36 IO, organisations with no ADR mechanism receive twice as many formal appeals per staff member and per year on average than organisations with mediation or ombudsman services and six times more appeals than IO with both mediation and ombudsman services.

## II. Internal ADR mechanisms

- EU

An EU official who prefers not to file an appeal with the CJEU (Art. 20, 91 EU-SR) may apply to the European ombudsman after having exhausted the internal means of redress (Art. 2(4)(8) Decision of the European Parliament on the regulations and general conditions governing the performance of the ombudsman's duties of 9 March 1994, "the Decision"). The ombudsman may not intervene if the official has filed an appeal with the CJEU (Art. 1(3) of the Decision). Special rules apply to whistleblowing by officials (Art. 22a, 22b EU-SR).

On 26 April 2006 the Commission of the EC took a decision on its policy for protecting the dignity of the person, and preventing psychological and sexual harassment (doc. C(2006) 1624/3). This decision can be considered as an implementing ruling to Art. 1d, 12 and 12a EU-SR and Art. 11 EU-CEOS. The ruling opened informal procedures common to the two forms of harassment through the network of confidential counsellors and the commission mediator. The procedures may lead to an amicable solution. No formal recording of the facts takes place and no penalties are applied. There are no fixed deadlines to start informal proceedings. The victim should, however, start to act within a reasonable period (CJEU Judgment F-95/09 para. 35, 36).

- The confidential counsellor procedure (Point 6.2.1 of the Decision)

The official who feels he is a victim of harassment may contact a confidential counsellor of his choice from the list published on the website of the administration. The confidential counsellor may, with the prior agreement of the victim, take any action he deems appropriate and may place the victim in contact with all persons and bodies of the organisation, he deems appropriate. If, after a period of two months, no solution can be found, the counsellor may propose to the victim to contact the commission mediator in order to reach an amicable solution, or to lodge a formal complaint.

– The commission mediator service procedure (Point 6.2.2 of the Decision)

The official who feels a victim of harassment may either at first instance or after the unsuccessful confidential counsellor's procedure contact the commission mediator. The mediator strives to resolve the dispute by mutual agreement or a compromise solution without having to respect any deadline.

At any time during the informal procedures emergency measures may be proposed by the confidential counsellor, by the mediator or by one of the parties concerned (Point 6.2.3 of the Decision).

At any time, the victim may initiate a formal procedure on the basis of a request for assistance provided for in Art. 24 EU-SR. If the request is rejected, the official concerned may start the pre-litigation procedure by submitting a complaint to the appointing authority (Art. 90(2) EU-SR).

– UN

The Redesign Panel of the UN system of administration of justice quotes seven different ways of ADR at the UN (UN doc. A/64/640 para. 81–82 and A/61/205 para. 22; see also R. Gulati). The new system of administration of justice in the UN may serve as a model for ADR.

The new informal system of ADR (Rule 11(1) UN-SR) is centred on the office of staff legal assistance (OSLA), the office of the ombudsman and the mediation services (see the website UN Ombudsman & Mediation Services).

The ombudsman provides "confidential off-the-record and impartial assistance for the informal resolution of concerns that are related to employment with the United Nations" (see the website quoted above and "A guide to resolving disputes", Administration of Justice in the UN, 2009, p. 2–3).

The OSLA may, after assessment of the case involving an administrative decision, propose to the official concerned that an informal dispute resolution should be explored with the assistance of the ombudsman. The ombudsman may propose mediation. The official may also ask for direct mediation at the mediation division. Mediation may also be sought by the SG (Rule 11(1)(b) UN-SR). The mediation may result in a binding memorandum of understanding which is legally enforceable (Rule 11(1)(d) UN-SR). More details are available on the website of the UN Ombudsman & Mediation Services. The informal dispute resolution process by the ombudsman or by mediation may result in the extension of the deadlines applicable for a management evaluation and for filing a legal action with the UNDT (Rule 11(1)(c) UN-SR).

Similar ADR mechanisms are offered by other IO of the UN family and by the IMF. The WB Group's website provides an excellent overview of the staff's choices for assistance in workplace conflicts. Staff members may address their issues to a "respectful workplace advisor" who will assist and guide the colleague at a very early stage of all possible tension and conflicts without intervening, investigating, mediating or participating in resolving issues. A staff member may also seek the support by the "ombudsman services" for the resolution of workplace issues. The consultation is strictly confidential, independent and impartial. Finally, an informal conflict resolution is offered by the "mediation services". The mediation process is very user-friendly and may even be initiated by a phone call. If an issue is settled by mediation, a memorandum of understanding binding both parties is signed.

At the ILO, there is a collective agreement on the prevention and resolution of harassment-related grievances between the ILO and the ILO staff union signed on 26 February 2004. The agreement covers both psychological and sexual harassment and an informal (Art. 2) and formal (Art. 3) conflict resolution. In conformity with Art. 6(2) a request for resolving harassment grievances must be submitted within six months of the incident giving rise to a harassment-related grievance. The ombudsman, however, has the power to decide if the harassment-related grievance should be heard notwithstanding a delay.

– EPO

The existing ADR in cases of harassment (see ILOAT Judgment 3337) was revised and updated in 2014 (see doc. CA/39/14, p. 6 accessible on the EPO website; the new Circular No. 341 on the prevention of harassment and amicable conflict resolution is accessible on the EPO website (EPO Codex)). At least two confidential counsellors are appointed per place of employment to encourage amicable settlement and to restore and maintain the professional relationship between staff members. In 2013, 63 cases were subject to informal conflict resolution.

In the case of disagreement on an appraisal report the parties concerned must endeavour to settle their dispute through conciliation (Art. 110a(1) EPO-SR; see doc. CA/D 10/14, accessible on the EPO website). The President of the EPO (Office) established guidelines on the prevention of harassment and the resolution of conflict at the EPO in Circular No. 341.

**Jurisprudence**

ILOAT Judgments

3180: If the organisation is of the opinion that the amount at stake is derisory it ought to have tried to reach an amicable solution; 3067: The very purpose of conciliation procedure is to endeavour to resolve a dispute amicably; 2584: The duty of good faith requires that the time needed for ongoing settlement discussions is not taken into account for the calculation of deadlines for further actions (but see 2878, 2841); 1938: If the parties freely accepted recourse to arbitration to settle disputes they are perforce excluding them from the tribunal's jurisdiction; 1934: A staff member is bound by the terms and conditions of a settlement which he freely accepted; 1924: If an offer of amicable solution is accepted, the other party cannot withdraw from it; 1699: A staff member may file an appeal in order to have a stronger negotiating position; 28: The complainant has acquiesced in the actual payments and under general principles of law he has relinquished the remainder of his claims.

CJEU Judgments/Orders

F-3/14: Amicable settlement requested by the parties; removal from the register; F-130/12: Amicable settlement between the parties after invention of the European ombudsman; F-47/12: Agreement between the parties at the initiative of the tribunal; removal from the register.

## UNDT Judgments

2014/031: Withdrawal of a case after reaching an amicable solution which "saved significant resources of the tribunal and both parties"; 2013/148: The case is amenable to amicable solution.

*Chapter 2*

# International administrative tribunals and their legal proceedings

## A. International administrative tribunals

### I. Unity within diversity

International administrative tribunals apply the international civil service law of the respective IO and the general legal principles applicable to the international civil service (see above). They are in no way bound by the case law of other international courts (see, for example, ILOAT Judgment 3138 para. 7). The same holds true for the application and interpretation of their statutes and rules of procedure. Each tribunal is bound only by its own statutory provisions (see, for example, ILOAT Judgment 176 para. 33, see also Art. II(7) ILOAT statute).

Notwithstanding this apparent isolation of the statutory provisions of the tribunals there is a widespread unity in this matter. Apart from some differences in particular topics there is a high degree of similarity between the structures and elements of their judicial proceedings. In view of such circumstances the presentation of the judiciary system of the international administrative tribunals (see below under C to J) can be limited to only one judicial body as *pars pro toto.* The judiciary of the ILOAT seems to be the most appropriate means to achieve this objective. It is the successor of the League of Nations Administrative Tribunal and as such probably the oldest international administrative tribunal, its jurisdiction extends to 62 IO and its case law comprises over 3,800 judgments.

### II. ADR and court proceedings

International administrative tribunals are general fostering an amicable settlement by mediation or by arbitration during court proceedings. Some statutes or rules of procedure of international administrative tribunals even explicitly provide for the fostering of an amicable settlement or arbitration.

#### *1. The UNDT*

Art. 10(3) UNDT statute and Art. 15(2) UNDT rules of procedure stipulate that at any time during the deliberations the tribunal may, with the consent of the parties, refer the case to mediation and suspend proceedings. Also, the parties may at any time during the proceedings refer the case to mediation (Art. 15(3 to 7) UNDT rules of procedure. If parties have sought mediation within the deadline for filing an application and the mediation has been unsuccessful, a new deadline for filing an appeal begins to run from the day after the mediation broke down (Art. 8(1)(d)(iv) UNDT statute). An application is not admissible if the dispute arising from the contested administrative decision has been resolved by mediation. However, the official may file an application to enforce the implementation of the agreement reached by arbitration (Art. 8(2) UNDT statute). In 2015, 23% of the mediation cases were referred by the UNDT (see the Report of the UN-SG on the activities of the office of the UN Ombudsman & Mediation Services, doc. A/71/157 p. 11).

#### 2. *The CJEU*

The GC may at any stage examine the possibility of an amicable settlement of the dispute or even instruct the reporting judge to seek such a settlement (Art. 125a GC rules of procedure). If a negotiated settlement of a dispute is achieved, the agreement is recorded in a document and the case is removed from the register (Art. 125b GC rules of procedure).

#### 3. *The ILOAT*

Although the Statute and the rules of procedure of the ILOAT do not explicitly provide for an alternative workplace dispute resolution the tribunal held in constant case law that sound judicial policy requires that international administrative tribunals encourage the parties to settle their dispute amicably at any time during legal proceedings (see, for example, Judgments 2584 para. 13, 2220 para. 6, 1924 para. 10). Both parties are bound by a settlement agreement (Judgments 1938, 1934, 1924, 1699). In order to try to reduce the enormous backlog of pending appeals the ILOAT has in some cases even invited the litigants in writing to explore the possibility of an amicable settlement to the dispute.

## B. The most important international administrative tribunals

### I. Tribunals extending their jurisdiction to several international organisations

#### 1. *The ILOAT*

The ILOAT was established in 1946 as the successor to the Administrative Tribunal of the League of Nations (for more details see the website of the ILOAT). After amending its statute in 1949, other IO besides the ILO, could submit their labour law disputes to the jurisdiction of the ILOAT (Art. II(5) statute of the ILOAT).

The jurisdiction of the ILOAT extends to the ILO, other UN organisations and other IO outside the civil service systems of the UN, the EU and the CO (see the website of the ILOAT). Subject to its jurisdiction are more than 58,000 serving or former employees of 62 IO (see the presentation of the ILOAT on its website). The tribunal has so far (2016) delivered over 3,800 decisions in 123 sessions.

As a rule, there are two sessions a year where the tribunal deals with about 100 cases. The ILOAT has an increasing backlog (in 2013 about 425 pending cases, thereof 150 concerning the EPO, see the Judgment of the District Court of The Hague of 16 July 2013 (case no. 1223887/12 – 31860 – case "Verveer") in which the Court referred to a statement of the registrar of the ILOAT that the tribunal decides approx. 100 cases a year, thereof four to five against the EPO, the procedural waiting time for officials of the EPO would be about 15 years should the situation not change. The court therefore held that the complainant was deprived of a fair process within a reasonable period (Art. 6 EConHR) and that the immunity of the EPO was overruled and the court was competent to hear this case. The judgment was, however, annulled by the Hague Regional Court of Appeal by a judgment of 30 September 2014 (case no 200.136.028(01)) on the grounds that the ILOAT will do its utmost to prevent unacceptable delays and it cannot be presumed automatically that the essence of the right of access to a court is impaired.

In 2014, the ILOAT held an additional session in order to reduce the number of pending cases. It delivered 146 decisions in 2014 thereof 39 decisions concerning the EPO.

The judicial proceedings (the statute and the rules of the tribunal are posted on the website) are, in contrast to most other international administrative tribunals, almost without exception only in writing (see above), they comprise the complaint, the opinion of the organisation, a rejoinder and a surrejoinder. The tribunal's expenses (general costs of the secretariat and the costs for each procedure) are borne by the defendant organisation. In contrast to other international administrative tribunals (see, for example, the CJEU), the statutory rules of the ILOAT do not provide that the tribunal may examine the possibility of an amicable settlement to the dispute. The tribunal even held in its Judgment 3067 para. 24 that the task of the tribunal "is plainly not to explore possible settlements before the Tribunal". In the meantime, however, the tribunal in some cases even invites the parties to the complaint to state whether they have considered an amicable settlement. This measure appears to serve the reduction of the backlog of pending appeals.

The jurisdiction of the ILOAT extends to disputes arising out of contracts with the ILO which provide for the competence of the ILOAT (Art. II.4 of the ILOAT statute).

The website of the ILOAT offers various useful links allowing access to the "Triblex" database, the composition of the tribunal, the statute, the rules of procedure and the complaint form.

### *2. The UNDT and the UNAT*

The internal system of administration of justice of the UN was redesigned in 2007 and became operational on 1 July 2009 (UN doc. A/RES/63/253 of 17 March 2009, for details and a bibliographic review see Otis/Reiter and R. Gulati; see also the UN Guide to resolving disputes, 2009 on the UN website). Its organisational structure encompasses the office of staff legal assistance (OSLA), the UN Dispute Tribunal (UNDT) and the UN Appeals Tribunal (UNAT). The new two-tier system replaced the old UN Administrative Tribunal and various internal advisory bodies like the joint appeal board and the joint disciplinary committees.

The tribunal's jurisdiction extends to staff disputes between the staff of the UN Secretariat and more than three dozen other entities (for further details see the website of the UNDT). The UNDT is responsible for complaints of more than 60,000 staff members and former staff members and their legal successors (see the Report of the ICSC for the year 2012, UN doc. A/67/30 p. 92 indicating the number of staff of the largest UN bodies falling under the jurisdiction of the UNDT).

Appeals before the UNAT may be filed against judgments rendered by the UNDT and *inter alia* against decisions of the standing committee of the UNJSPF (for more details see the website of the UNJSPF). The UNJSPF has (2015) almost 200,000 active participants and beneficiaries (also comprising the staff members and pensioners of UN organisations who are under the jurisdiction of the ILOAT, see Art. 48 Reg. of the UNJSPF). The UNAT may, therefore, be considered the international administrative tribunal with the highest number of staff members under its jurisdiction worldwide. Between its inception in 2009 and 2014, the UNDT delivered more than 1,000 and the UNAT almost 500 judgments. The average time required to adjudicate a case by the UNDT was reduced to about six months (UN doc. A/65/373 para. 22).

The procedures before the UNDT and the UNAT always include a written part and an oral hearing may be ordered by the judge. The written procedure normally comprises the application by the staff member and the reply by the defendant organisation.

In contrast to the ILOAT and the AT of the CO, the UNDT operates on a full-time basis three full-time judges and two half-time judges), whereas the UNAT holds two sessions a year. The expenses of the UNDT and the UNAT are borne by the UN and shared with the other IO which by special arrangement have accepted the jurisdictions of the UN tribunals for their disputes with staff members.

An informal resolution of disputes is expressly favoured in the resolution UN doc. A/RES/63/253 of the UNGA. It emphasises that all possible use should be made of it to avoid formal litigation. The informal resolution of disputes is also explored through OSLA (for details see above). In contrast to the ILOAT, the statutory provisions of the UN tribunals explicitly provide for a referral of the case to mediation at any time during the proceedings on a proposal by the judge. The parties may also seek mediation at their own initiative.

The website of the UN office of administration of justice (OAJ) contains information about the statutes, rules of procedure, judgments and orders of the UNDT and UNAT and *inter alia* about the staff legal assistance (OSLA). In addition, the OAJ's annual report outlines the activities of the OAJ, OSLA and the judicial statistics of UNDT/UNAT.

### *3. The CJEU (CJ, GC, CST)*

Unlike most other international administrative tribunals, whose competence extends only to staff disputes, the jurisdiction of the CJEU primarily concerns non-staff disputes.

About 10% of the decisions of CJEU are staff cases (see the Reports on Judicial Activity of the CJEU on the Curia website).

With the establishment of the Court of First Instance of the EC in 1988 (Council Decision No. 88/591 of 24 October 1988) the jurisdiction in staff disputes was transferred to this new court (which was renamed as the "General Court" (GC) under the Treat of Lisbon in 2009).

The number of completed staff cases at the Court of First Instance increased from 101 cases in the year 2000 to 236 cases in the year 2005 (see the statistics of the judicial activity of the court). By Council decision No. 2004/752 of 2 November 2004 the CST was established to exercise first instance jurisdiction in disputes between the EU and its servants (Art. 270 TFEU).

The duration of a full procedure for a new case brought before the CST was about 13 months in 2015 (annual report of the CJEU, 2015, p. 206). Between 2011 and 2016 the CST completed between 166 and 152 cases per year.

In view of the increase in litigation and the length of proceedings before the GC, the EU decided in September 2016 to transfer first instance jurisdiction in civil service cases to the GC. The CST was dissolved and the posts of judges of the CST were transferred to the GC.

The website "Curia" of the CJEU provides comprehensive information on the institutions in general, the procedures, statistics of judicial activity, access to the case law and a digest of the case law. Additional information can be found on the website EUR-Lex of the EU.

### *4. The Administrative Tribunal of the World Bank Group (WBAT)*

The WBAT was established in 1980. Its jurisdiction extends to staff disputes of the IBRD, IDA, IFC, MIGA and the ICSID, with about 10,000 active employees (see the website of the World Bank). The WBAT has so far (2016) issued almost 600 judgments. The website of the tribunal provides ample information on its statute, the rules of procedure and the judgments. The period between the filing of an application and a Judgment is, on the average, about eight months.

### *5. The Administrative Tribunal of the Council of Europe (CoEAT)*

In its Resolution 2014(4) of 11 June 2014, the Committee of Ministers of the CoE amended Art. 15 of the statute of the CoEAT (Appendix XI to the CoE-SR) by extending the jurisdiction of the tribunal to disputes between other IO and its staff. At present, the CoE Development Bank and the Central Commission for the Navigation of the Rhine have recognised the jurisdiction of the CoEAT. The tribunal had issued about 600 appeals up to 2016. The tribunal's website provides comprehensive information and offers a link to the internet sites of other international administrative tribunals.

### *6. The Administrative Tribunal of the Organization of American States (TRIBAD)*

The TRIBAD's jurisdiction extends to about 1,000 active staff members of the OAS and the Inter-American Institute for Cooperation on Agriculture. The tribunal has issued 165 judgments (status as of 2016).

## II. The tribunals competent for individual organisations

The following list of tribunals is not exhaustive. There are even tribunals which due to the very small number of staff did not exercise their jurisdiction (see, for example, the Tribunal of the International Institute for the Unification of Private Law, UNIDROIT, see Art. 7bis of the Statute of UNIDROIT and the annual report 2014).

### *1. The tribunals of the co-ordinated organisations*

The six CO (CoE, NATO, ESA, OECD, ECMWF, EUMETSAT) have established their own administrative tribunal (at ESA the term Appeals Board is still used, see Reg. 33 ESA-SR). The CoEAT has already been addressed above.

The number of decisions of these tribunals is relatively small (OECD AT 75 judgments between 1992 and 2017, ESA Appeals Board 100 judgments between

1976 and 2016). More details about these tribunals (statutes, rules of procedure, judgments) may be found on the websites of the CO.

Despite the coordination of the pension schemes and to some extent of the SR there is the risk of diverging decisions of the tribunals of the CO. In spite of great efforts, the CO have not yet succeeded in establishing one single tribunal for all CO.

### *2. The Administrative Tribunal of the International Monetary Fund (IMFAT)*

The IMFAT delivered more than 50 judgments between 1994 and 2016. The website of the tribunal provides a comprehensive information on the tribunal, including its statute, rules of procedure, judgments and orders. It also provides a comprehensive commentary on the statute of the tribunal (Author, Mrs. C. Goldman, Registrar of the Tribunal).

### *3. The African Development Bank Administrative Tribunal*

The Tribunal delivered about 100 judgments between 1998 and 2015. More information is provided on the tribunal's website (statute, rules of procedure, judgments).

### *4. The Asian Development Bank Administrative Tribunal*

The tribunal delivered more than 100 judgments between 1992 and 2016. More information is provided on the tribunal's website (statute, rules of procedure, judgments).

### *5. The Inter-American Development Bank Administrative Tribunal*

The Tribunal delivered about 100 judgments between 1983 and 2016. More information is provided on the tribunal's website (statute, rules of procedure, judgments).

### *6. The Administrative Tribunal of the European Stability Mechanism (ESMAT)*

The statute of the tribunal was adopted at the end of 2013. The judges were appointed in 2014. The tribunal's website provides information on the statute of the tribunal. Due to the small number of staff members no judgments have yet been rendered.

### *7. The Complaints Board of the European Schools*

Complaints may be filed *inter alia* by seconded teachers and by students having reached the age of majority or by their legal representatives. About 20% of the decisions are related to staff disputes.

## C. The right to bring an action (*locus standi*)

### I. Staff members and legal successors

All persons who have the status of an official or who are contractual employees of the respective IO, or persons claiming that status (CJEU Judgment 286/83), have a right to bring an action before the tribunal whose jurisdiction has been recognised by the organisation. The same right is accorded to former staff members, retired staff members, and parties deriving rights from a deceased staff member (see, for example, Art. II.6 statute of the ILOAT). Nevertheless, in special cases the SR may provide for the jurisdiction of national courts (see, for example, auxiliary staff of the EPO, Judgment 1450) or for the competence of an arbitration board for local staff (see, for example, Art. 122 EU-CEOS).

### II. External candidates for a vacant post

The right of candidates for a vacant post has not been harmonised in the case law of the international administrative tribunals. The case law of the CJEU (Order C-126/90 P; Judgment 81 to 88–74; Judgment 44/71) and Art. 1(c) of the statute of the OECD AT and Art. 59(8d), 60 CoE-SR in conjunction with Art. 5(1) of the statute of the CoEAT grant *locus standi* to candidates who are applying for a post and are contesting a negative decision.

In contrast other tribunals, the ILOAT, UNDT/UNAT and IMFAT for lack of jurisdiction do not entertain the complaints from outside candidates whose application for a post was unsuccessful. The ILOAT, thereby, refers to Art, II(6) of its statute, which restricts the right to appeal to present and former officials and to the legal successors of a deceased official (see Judgment 661; see also Judgments 3382, 3112, 1554, 803, 307, 67). Only in a case where, even in the absence of a signed contract, the parties made commitments which are "equivalent to a contract" can the Tribunal decide to retain jurisdiction (Judgment 2657 para. 5, 339, 621 para. 1: "A contract is concluded only if both parties have shown contractual intent, all the essential terms are worked out and agreed on, and all that may remain is a formality").

In Judgment 2657 ("case Klausecker") the tribunal has expressly recognised a "legal vacuum" in a case where the complainant was not appointed as an employee since he did not meet "the physical requirements of the post". The tribunal, having no authority to order the EPO to waive its immunity considered it "highly desirable" that the organisation waive its immunity or submit the dispute to arbitration (see also above and Judgment of the German Constitutional Court of 22 June 2006, ref. 2 BvR 2093/05 and ECHR Appl. No. 415/07).

Also, the UNDT/UNAT and the IMFAT are interpreting their statutes restrictively so as to not allow unsuccessful external candidates to a post to bring a claim. The UNDT/UNAT, however, extends its jurisdiction to external candidates who have unconditionally accepted an employment offer even before the issuance of a formal letter of appointment under the condition that the person is legitimately entitled to similar rights to those of a staff member (UNAT Judgment 2011-UNAT-120). For the IMFAT see the commentary to Art. II(2)(c) of its statute on the website of IMFAT.

The concept of these tribunals of refusing external candidates for a post access to their jurisdiction based on a mere reference to the wording of their statutes may be considered as being too formalistic (see on the other hand the CJEU (CJ, GC, CST) which interprets the wording of Art. 81 EU-SR in conjunction with Art. 270 TFEU extensively: "The CJEU shall have jurisdiction in any dispute between the Union and any person to whom these Staff Regulations apply ..."). There are numerous examples where international tribunals have recourse to a broad interpretation of their statutes (see, for example, the reference to general principles of law applicable to the international civil service, see, for example, the "inherent power to impose costs on a complainant", ILOAT Judgment 1962 para. 4; see also ILOAT Judgment 3003 para. 28: The possibility of submitting applications for review, interpretation or execution is not expressly provided for in its statute, nevertheless it is current practice, but see now Art. VI(1) ILOAT-Statute amended in June 2016). The construction of a *pactum de contrahendo* would, therefore, be the most effective means avoiding a "legal vacuum".

## III. *De facto* employment relationships

There are cases where an external consultant is working under a service contract for an IO and performing duties similar to those of an official on a regular basis and under the supervision of the organisation. Those persons may, therefore, be considered as *de facto* employees of the organisation. In its Judgment 3051 the ILOAT denied a *de facto* employment relationship of the complainant with the EPO since he had no direct contractual relationship with the EPO. He was paid by a firm and was also working during the material time as a consultant for several other agencies.

## IV. Experts, independent contractors and agency staff

Persons who have contractual relations with an IO without being a member of its staff, like external experts, consultants or legal counsels or who provide services or work according to a contract concluded between their employer and the IO do not have *locus standi* before an international administrative tribunal. In these cases, legal protection is provided by municipal courts or through arbitration (see, for example, ILOAT Judgments 2888, 2688, 2017, 117, 77, 75).

## V. *Locus standi* of staff committees and trade unions

In conformity with their statutes and the SR, most international administrative tribunals apply a system of individual complaints, i.e. staff associations (staff committees, staff unions) have no right to file a suit (see, for example, CJEU Order T-78/91; Judgment C-193 and C-194/87, C-18/74, 15–63; ILOAT 2791; UNDT Art. 2(1) statute: "an application filed by an individual").

Despite the recommendations in the report of the Redesign Panel on the UN system of administration of justice in 2006 (Report doc. A/61/205) para. 82) that staff associations should have an independent right to bring action to enforce the SR, class actions by staff associations are not admissible before the UNDT/UNAT. As for the ILOAT, see ILO doc. GB 310/PFA/14/2 of 13 January 2011, which declares it desirable to maintain to status quo until the UNGA comes to other conclusions.

In consistent case law the ILOAT, however, held that, to "preserve common rights and interests of staff" individual members of a staff committee must have the power to bring an action as representatives of that body (ILOAT Judgments 2791 para. 2 and constant case law: 2649, 2562, 2036, 1897, 1315, 1269, 1147). This also holds good for trade unions of IO (see ILOAT Judgments 3106, 2228, 1547, 274). A member of the union may file a complaint to defend the collective rights of the unions which are exercised *prima facie* from outside the organisation. A staff representative can, however, not challenge a general decision which will require individual implementing decisions (ILOAT Judgment 3515 para. 3 and below under the direct challenge of a general decision).

There are, however, some international administrative tribunals which, in conformity with the SR and their statute, have jurisdiction over applications filed by the staff committee (CoEAT, see Art. 59(8)(c) CoE-SR) and even by trade unions and professional associations (OECD AT) in respect of acts affecting them or prejudicing any rights accorded to them by the SR and instructions (see Art. 1(b) statute of the OECD AT).

### VI. Limited right of the organisation itself to bring an action

According to the statutes of the international administrative tribunals the IO have a limited right to bring an action against a staff member in a case of dispute. IO protect their interests primarily by enforcing their decision against the staff member.

As a rule, AT do, however, permit applications for a review, interpretation or execution of a judgment (see, for example, ILOAT Judgment 570: review; 3154, 2483: interpretation; 3003: suspension of execution; see Art. VI(1) of the Statute of the ILOAT).

In the new two-tier system of administration of justice of the UN (UNDT/UNAT) and in the two-tier legislative process of the CJEU (CJ, GC) the organisation also has a right to appeal. Based on Art. 263(2) TFEU *inter alia,* the European Commission is even empowered to file a complaint before the CJEU in regard of the EU-SR adopted by the Council.

In 2010, the Commission brought an action against the Council for annulment of Regulation No. 1296/2009, adjusting the remuneration and pensions of EU officials as from 1 July 2009 on the basis of the exception clause (Art. 65 EU-SR in conjunction with Art. 3 of Annex XI to the EU-SR). In Judgment C-40/10 the CJEU annulled the new salary amounts fixed by the European Council on the basis that the exception clause (serious and sudden deterioration in the economic situation within the EU) adjustment differed from that proposed by the Commission.

## D. Persons taking part in the proceedings

### I. Representation by another staff member or by a legal counsel

In general, an official may represent himself in court in disputes with his organisation. At the ILOAT, an official may also appoint a colleague or an agent who is a serving or former official of another IO which has recognised the tribunal's jurisdiction or of the UN, or a member of a bar in a member state of one of those organisations, or, with leave from the President of the tribunal, someone who is qualified to deal with issues relating to the international civil service (ILOAT Art. 5(1) rules of procedure). The costs involved in legal representation and assistance by legal counsel are normally at the expense of the official. For reasons of economy, an IO may submit a declaration that all staff members in the same factual and legal positions as the complainant will be treated as interveners by the organisation for the purpose of executing the tribunal's decision, even without filing a formal application to intervene (ILOAT Judgment 726 para. 4).

At the UNDT, a party may be represented by another (also a former) staff member or a legal counsel from the OSLA (for free) or by a legal counsel authorised to practise law in a national jurisdiction (Art. 12 rules of procedure) at the expense of the complainant.

At the CJEU, officials must be represented by a lawyer authorised to practise before a court in a member state (Art. 19(3) and Art. 53(1) statute of the CJEU). An official may, however, apply for legal aid if he is wholly or partly unable to meet these costs (Art. 146 rules of procedure of the GC, see also the legal aid application form available at the "Curia" internet platform).

At the CoEAT, the appellant may be represented and assisted by one or several advisers of his choice (Rule 12 rules of procedure).

### II. Intervention

The intervention of officials in the complaint of another official is available as a means of judicial economy on the grounds that the ruling of the tribunal may affect them (Art. 13(1) rules of the ILOAT; Art. 40(2) and Art. 53(1) statute of the CJEU: if they "can establish an interest in the result of a case"; Art. 22 UNDT rules of procedure). The intervener must be in the same situation in fact and in law (ILOAT Judgments 2985, 2636, 2237, 1462, 496). The intervention is limited to the same claims (ILOAT Judgment 2311, 2239) and to seeking the same redress on the strength of these claims (ILOAT Judgments 1792, 1442). An application to intervene is receivable without the need to exhaust internal legal remedies but must arrive at the tribunal no later than sixty days before the opening of the session for which the complaint is listed (Art. 13(4) rules of the ILOAT).

In conformity with Art. 13(2) rules of procedure of the ILOAT also an IO which has recognised the jurisdiction of the ILOAT may intervene in a complaint on the grounds that the ruling may affect it.

Some international administrative tribunals grant a right to staff committees to intervene in the case of a staff member (Art. 5(c) statute of the OECD AT; Art. 10(1) statute of the CoEAT in conjunction with Rule 38 rules of procedure. No right to intervention is provided by the ILOAT, the UNDT or the CJEU (see CJEU order F-127/10).

### III. Friend-of-the-court briefs (*amicus curiae* briefs)

Since the possibility of a staff association (staff committee, staff union) to file a complaint is not provided for in the statutes of most international administrative tribunals, they consider it all the more beneficial to gather observations from staff associations representing staff interests by accepting friend-of-the-court briefs (*amicus curiae* briefs) (see ILOAT, Judgment 2420 para. 7).

Whereas the right to submit an *amicus curiae* brief is explicitly provided for in Art. 2(3) of the statute of the UNDT and Art. 24 of the UNDT rules of procedure, the ILOAT admits *amicus curiae* briefs are based on a broad interpretation of its powers conferred on it by its statute (ILOAT Judgments 2672, 2423, 2422, 2420).

## E. The admissibility of a complaint

### I. Overview, general questions and preconditions for admissibility

The jurisdiction of the international administrative tribunals is not determined by the SR of the IO, but by the terms of their own statutes and the submission to them by the defendant organisation (ILOAT Judgment 2312 para. 3). With the declaration of competence the organisation accepts the provisions of the statute and the rules of the tribunal and "any provisions in its own rulebook on the receivability of complaints filed with the tribunal are of no effect, whether they comply with the tribunal's rules or not" (ILOAT Judgment 532 para. 1).

#### *1. The formal conditions of an application*

Before a case can be examined by a tribunal, the formal conditions of a complaint and the substantive requirements of its admissibility as set out in its statute and rules of procedure must be satisfied. General principle dictates that an official cannot simultaneously submit the same matter for decision in more than one proceedings (ILOAT Judgment 3291 para. 6; 3146 para.11; 2742 para. 16).

If the complaint does not meet the essential formal requirements stipulated in the rules of the tribunal the complaint is formally inadmissible. If the deficiencies are of subordinate significance the registrar sets a time limit for the complainant to correct them (see, for example, Art. 6(2) ILOAT rules of the tribunal; Art. 78(6) CJEU GC rules of procedure).

**Case law of the ILOAT regarding formal requirements:**

Judgment 3225: A complaint form filed without the brief and supporting evidence may be corrected; 3116: The essential requirements of form, for example, the relief claimed, must be met otherwise the complaint cannot be registered as filed; 2439: The possibility of correcting a complaint is given as a means of protecting complainants against strict implications of a procedure with which they are not necessarily familiar; 1500: Not all formal requirements must be met by the date of filing, it is sufficient to be able to identify the impugned decision and the relief claimed; 1102: The complainant *inter alia* failed to explain what he wanted or to file any legal plea in support; 995: The internal appeal filed by the counsel of the complainant was not valid since under the special rules of the UNESCO he was not allowed to represent the complainant (the internal appeals board was not conceived as a quasi legal body but as a non-judicial encounter between the disputing parties).

On the website of the tribunals there is usually a complaint form (Aide-Mémoire-Application) for filing an application (see, for example, ILOAT, CJEU (GC), UNDT/UNAT). Some tribunals even provide templates for submitting notions and authorisations (see, for example, the website of the UNDT where twelve forms are available) in order to facilitate the compliance of the complainant and the registrar with the formal requirements of judicial proceedings.

Methods of filing a complaint

The ILOAT still (2017) requires that the complaint form available on the website is printed out, signed by hand (also the copies required) and sent by mail to the tribunal's registry.

The CJEU (GC) provides for lodging of an application by a legal practitioner in electronic form, provided he has an account giving access to the "e-curia" system for filing in electronic form (see the Union website) or in print formats.

The UNDT/UNAT requires that all complaints are submitted electronically through its "e-filing portal". If the complainant has no access to the e-filing portal the filing may be made by e-mail or in hard copy by mail or hand-delivery (see the website of the "office of administration of justice UN internal justice system").

The complaint and all appendices must be submitted in one of the official languages of the tribunal. The translations must not necessarily be made by a professional translator (see, for example, point B.10 Advice to litigants: proceedings before the ILOAT). If the official languages of the IO are not identical with those of the tribunal, the organisation will for reasons of equality provide for a translation free of charge (see, for example, for the EPO which provides translation from German into the official languages of the ILOAT, Kunz-Hallstein/Ullrich Art. 13 para. 52).

Most tribunals publish extensive information for applicants and legal counsels on their websites.

There is no general principle of law of the international civil service requiring a decision of the administration to include advice on the means of redress available (ILOAT Judgment 1734 para. 3(f); CJEU Orders F-84/11 para. 35; C-163/07 P para. 31).

### 2. *Examination of admissibility proprio motu*

The tribunals rule *proprio motu* on the admissibility of an application based on their statutes, rules of procedure and the applicable general legal principles. They are by no means bound by opinions expressed by the internal appeals board. This extends, for example, to the question of whether a preceding internal appeal was time-barred (ILOAT Judgment 677 para. 5).

If a complaint is clearly unfounded, the tribunal (court) need not address the question of receivability (ILOAT Judgments 2459 para. 7(e), 2049 para. 4; CJEU Judgment F-112/11 para. 19).

### 3. *Strict application of the rules regarding admissibility*

The rules governing receivability must be strictly complied with, they are a matter of public policy and are not subject to the discretion of the parties or the Court (CJEU Judgment T-14/03 para. 1). They must, however, "not be construed too pedantically or set traps for staff members who are defending their rights" (ILOAT Judgment 2882 para. 6). If strict compliance would cause a flagrant miscarriage of justice, good faith must prevail (ILOAT Judgment 1734 para. 3). (See also ILOAT Judgments 1502, 1376, 1317; CJEU Judgment 276/85: there can be no derogation unless there is a quite exceptional case of unforeseeable circumstances or *force majeure*).

If an organisation does not raise an issue the receivability of a complaint in the internal appeal proceedings, this precludes the argument being raised before the tribunal. This is in the interest of justice (ILOAT Judgments 3160 para. 10, 2255 para. 13, 522).

### 4. *Misdirection of an appeal*

If an appeal is filed in time but misdirected to a wrong internal body of an IO, this body is under a duty arising from good faith to forward the appeal to the competent body (see, for example, ILOAT Judgment 3027: Wrong choice between the registrar of the ICC and the secretary of the appeals board, ILOAT Judgment 1832: Wrong choice between the Council and the President of the secretariat of the EPO). In Judgment 2431, however, the ILOAT did not consider that the EPO Council to which the appeal by the controller was made, should have been forwarded to the President of the secretariat of the EPO which was the appointing authority of the complainant. In this judgment the ILOAT did not give relief for the consequences of turning to the wrong body presumably because the controller "knew it was the wrong one but addressed it for the purpose of pursuing some unactionable interest" (ILOAT Judgment 1832 para. 6).

### 5. *Summary dismissal*

Where it is clear that a court has no jurisdiction to hear an action or where the action is manifestly inadmissible or manifestly devoid of merit, it may be summarily dismissed, i.e. the court will issue a decision by reasoned order without taking further steps in the proceedings" (Art. 126 rules of procedure of the GC of the CJEU; Art. 7(2) ILOAT rules of procedure; Art. 9 UNDT rules of procedure). Case law: ILOAT Judgment 3393: The complaint was filed out of time and justifies a summary procedure; Judgment 3392: The application for review and interpretation is summarily dismissed; Judgment 3388: The internal means of redress not being exhausted the complaint is summarily dismissed; Judgment 2815: The principle of *res judicata* justifies a summarily dismissal.

### 6. *Types of admissible actions*

(See above under the competence of international administrative tribunals and under the principle of limited remedial powers).

### 7. *Filing fees (deposit)*

The access to the tribunals is generally not subject to the payment of filing fees or the ordering of a deposit for such purposes. The provisions of some former boards of appeal requiring the payment of security fees for filing an application (Priess, p. 217) have been repealed. But see now Art. 5(3) Implementing Rules for Art. 106 to 113 of the EPO-SR of 29 June 2017 (doc. CA/D 7/17): EUR 200 registration fee.

The basic costs incurred by the tribunal (secretariat, registrar) and the procedural expenditure per case (judges) are borne by the IO having established the tribunal. If a tribunal assumes jurisdiction for several IO, the basic costs of the tribunal are borne by the IO in proportion to the number of its staff members. The expenses occasioned by each case are borne by the organisation against which the complaint was filed (see, for example, the statute of the ILOAT Art. IX(2) in conjunction with the annex to the statute).

At the CJEU, the court may order a party, even if successful, to pay some or all of the costs, if this appears justified by the conduct of that party (Art. 135 CJEU (GC) rules of procedure).

Since the parties before the CJEU (GC) must be represented by a lawyer (Art. 19 in conjunction with Art. 53 statute of the CJEU), legal aid may be granted by order of the CJEU (GC) (Art. 146 to 150 CJEU (GC) rules of procedure). The parties to litigation have in principle to bear their own costs.

### 8. *Precise terms of the claims*

The claims of a complaint must be couched in terms precise enough to enable the tribunal to make an enforceable decision (ILOAT Judgments 654: The formulation of an obligation was too vague and general for their performance to be subject to judicial review, 649, 637).

### *9. Waiver to bring an action*

The guarantee of the access of international officials to justice before international administrative tribunals ensures respect of the right to effective judicial protection of their statutory rights and the general basic rights acknowledged in the case law of the international administrative tribunals. It is consistent case law, however, that an official is permitted in agreement with the administration to waive the jurisdiction of internal appeals boards and appeal direct the ILOAT (ILOAT Judgments 2232, 592). Also, the right to appeal may be waived (ILOAT Judgment 2368).

**Jurisprudence**

ILOAT Judgments

3127: An official should not in principle be denied the right to have a decision effectively reviewed; 2868: The waiver of a right to bring an action may not be presumed. A waiver is binding only if it is express or clearly implied on the facts (592, 580, 567, 431); 2715: A clause which makes the payment of compensation which was already awarded but had not been paid subject to an undertaking from the complainant that he would renounce of all means of appeal is unlawful and should definitely be censured; 2368: An express waiver of the right to appeal in an overall financial settlement; 2040: The official was bound by his agreement to waive appeal rights in respect of the disputed salary adjustments; 2049: The mutual agreement on a termination indemnity was not invalidated by mental deficiencies; 1938: The freely accepted arbitration clause excludes the tribunal's jurisdiction; 1934: Waiver of the right to appeal by accepting a separation package (893); 88: Jurisdiction confined to fixing the amount of compensation in an agreed settlement of dispute.

CJEU Judgment

T-404/06 P: No implicit waiver of the right to appeal. A waiver must be clear and unconditional.

### *10. Amicable settlement of a dispute*

See above under ADR mechanisms.

## II. The specific admissibility requirements of a complaint

### *1. Overview*

Apart from the preconditions for a complaint referred to above, a complaint is admissible if:

a) It is directed against a decision adversely affecting the complainant;

b) The complainant has exhausted the internal means of redress open to him under the SR of the IO;

c) The complaint has been filed within the time limits stipulated in the statute of the respective tribunal or in the SR of the IO.

### *2. Individual and general decisions*

#### a) The appeals system

*aa) The individual decision*

The appeals procedure before the international administrative tribunals is generally determined by an individual appeals system.

In consistent case law the ILOAT holds that its statute makes provisions for a system of individual appeals (see, for example, Judgments 2459 para. 7(a), 2379 para. 5, 1392 para. 24). In Judgment 1134 para. 4 the ILOAT ruled that Art. VII(2) of its statute is to be read together with Art. VII(1), which provides that "A complaint shall not be receivable unless the decision impugned is a final decision…", "… a complaint will be irreceivable if it challenges a general decision that must ordinarily be put into effect by individual decisions against which internal appeal will lie".

As for the CJEU, the individual appeals system is derived from Art. 90 EU-SR in conjunction with Art. 270 and Art. 263(4) TFEU. Art. 263(4) TFEU provides that a general decision (regulatory act) cannot be challenged if it entails implementing measures, i.e. individual decisions which form the subject of an individual appeal. Whereas a general decision (see in more detail below) entails legal effects for categories of "persons regarded generally and in the abstract" (CJEU Judgment 171/00 P para. 31), an individual decision is an act which decides a specific case and is capable of having direct binding legal effects on an official (ILOAT Judgments 3141 para. 21, 2573 para. 8, 2629 para. 6, 532 para. 3, 112 para. 7(c); CJEU Judgments F-125/11, F-19/08, C-154/99 P).

A decision does not require any particular formality and may be constituted by any communication capable of being understood to constitute a decision on a matter (even if it is not put in writing) (ILOAT Judgments 3141, 2629, 2573, 532).

A bank statement on monthly pension payments reflects a decision of the organisation to credit the pensioner's account and may be challenged (ILOAT Judgment 2410). The termination of the appointment of the Director General of an IO is a decision in the meaning of the statute of the ILOAT (Judgment 2232). An entity outside the organisation (e.g. an insurance representative) is not able to take a decision in the meaning of the statute of the ILOAT (Judgment 2290).

The admissibility of a complaint does not depend on proving actual and certain injury. It is sufficient to show that the decision under challenge may impair the rights and safeguards of the official (ILOAT Judgments 2856, 2630, 1330) (see in more detail below).

There is no formal requirement as to the admissibility of a complaint that the authorised decision-maker has to be the signatory to the final decision (ILOAT Judgments 3177 para. 11 and 12, 2994 para. 6 and 7, 2558 para 4(a)). There is, however, the requirement as to the merits, that evidence must be adduced that a person with authority actually made the decision or properly delegated it. The onus of proof is on the organisation (ILOAT Judgments 2324 para. 10 and 11, 2028 para. 8(3)). The head of an IO must not be the first person to take an action to terminate the appointment of a staff member. It suffices that the action be on his behalf and with his prior approval (ILOAT Judgment 1834 para. 3).

A complaint must be clearly identifiable (ILOAT Judgments 2410, 654, 649, 637).

The individual decision challenged is normally an explicit refusal of a request. If the administration did not reply to the request for a decision within a certain period of time, the official may file a complaint against an implied decision (see, for example, Art. VII(3) Statute of the ILOAT; Art. 90(1) EU-SR; ILOAT Judgments 2975, 2901, 2631, 2626, 2538). An implied decision occurs only when the complaint is entitled to treat the inactivity or some other failure as constituting a decision to reject the claims and elects to do so (ILOAT Judgment 3089).

The forwarding of the complaint to the internal advisory committee constitutes a rejection (ILOAT Judgments 2948, 2681). Also, the rejection of an application for a post implied in the appointment of someone else may be challenged (ILOAT Judgment 1223). An appeal is irreceivable if it puts forward a claim to compensation that is unconnected with a final decision (ILOAT Judgment 1270).

*bb) The general decision*

General decisions (regulatory acts) are abstract rules (SR enacted by the legislative body of an IO or general administrative decisions like circulars, adopted by the executive body of the organisation). A general decision normally only affects the interest and safeguards of staff members theoretically, as long as they are not applied by implementing individual decisions (ILOAT Judgments 3291 para. 4(b), 2953 para. 2, 2822 para. 6, 1852 para. 3; CJEU Order T-20/01 para. 35).

As a rule, general decisions (regulatory acts) cannot be challenged directly unless they are not necessarily to be followed by implementing individual decisions entailing direct and immediate legal consequences (see in more detail below). In admissible proceedings against an individual decision, a staff member may also plead incidentally the inapplicability of the general decision which constitutes the legal basis for the implementing individual act (see in more detail below, under incidental challenge of an act of general application).

**Jurisprudence**

ILOAT Judgments

3291: A general decision of the legislative organ cannot as such be challenged in a prejudicial matter to each complainant by an individual decision (2953); 3146: An employee may not challenge both the underlying regulation and the implementing individual decision; he may, however, when challenging the individual decision in the same appeal challenge the related underlying regulation; 2833: Regulations concerning the redefinition of functions and grades are rules of general application and cannot be attacked until they are applied by individual decisions; 2625: Pension regulations are regulatory texts which entered into force long ago and apply to all retired officials. Their lawfulness may be challenged only by appealing against a decision applying those provisions which actually cause present damage (2459); 2410: The lawfulness of a legislative decision on pension adjustment may be challenged in the context of a complaint against an individual decision concerning a retired staff member's pension; 2379: The circular is a regulatory text which affects the individual staff member only in theory, it can only be challenged in the context of an appeal against a decision applying these provisions (1786, 1451, 1393, 1134, 1000, 663); 1852: The agreement of the IO with a country on the harmonisation of local labour law is a rule of general application which can be challenged only if it is applied by an individual decision; 1520: A complaint against the new SR is irreceivable. A staff member may, however, plead the unlawfulness of any general measure that affords the basis for it in law (1329).

CJEU Judgments/Orders

T-261/09 P: A decision of OLAF to communicate information to national judicial authorities has no binding legal effects and is, therefore, not challengeable; F-137/07: An agreement between the EU institutions and the trade union is not an individual decision affecting an official; T-20/01: Complaints may only be directed against individual decisions, not against acts of general applications (abstract rules); T-192/99: A measure of general application cannot be the subject of a direct action (T-13/93, T-72/92, T-14/91).

### b) Preparatory, provisional and preliminary acts

Ordinarily, the process of decision-making involves a series of preparatory steps and findings. Such acts may be challenged only as part of a final individual decision which produces "binding legal effects" capable of affecting the official's interests by bringing a significant change in his legal situation (ILOAT Judgment 2366; CJEU Judgment F-107/11).

It is therefore consistent case law that reports, recommendation and opinions of the advisory boards (appeals committee, medical board, disciplinary committee, etc.) are generally (for exceptions see under pre-litigation procedures below) not to be considered as challengeable final decisions (ILOAT Judgments 1401, 1363, 1104; CJEU Order F-115/06).

However, in complex administrative operations, such as, for example, the EU recruitment and promotion procedures composed of a series of closely-linked but distinct decisions each entailing a binding and definitive legal effect and capable of affecting directly and immediately the interests of an official by bringing about a significant change in his legal position, it is possible to challenge an intermediate decision. For example, if an official does not wish to risk challenging a decision not to promote him, he may only separately challenge the underlying decision concerning the number of cumulative merit points kept for the subsequent promotion procedure (CJEU Judgments T-311/04 P para. 91 to 93; F-19/08, T-100/04).

Provisional decisions paving the way for a final decision are not open to review (ILOAT Judgment 1100: A decision concerning the provisional reckoning of pension entitlements may not be challenged; 762, 689: The preliminary rejection of an internal complaint and the forwarding to the appeal committee for opinion is not a final decision).

**Jurisprudence**

ILOAT Judgments

3198: A warning for low performance cannot be challenged; 2698: The measure of suspension for alleged serious misconduct is a provisional temporary measure which nevertheless imposes a constraint on the official. It may, therefore, be challenged. The necessary investigation must be conducted with due speed (2365, 1927); 2573: The notification that a contract of employment will expire according to its terms is a decision having legal effect; 2366: A decision which does not resolve an entire dispute but separate and distinct issues may be challenged; 1832: A proposal by the President of the EPO (Office) to the Council for appointments to a technical board of appeal is not a final decision which may be challenged; 1694: A staff member may not challenge just an element of a complex procedure; only the final outcome is subject to appeal (468, but see 2366 para. 16); 1044: A preparatory decision (involvement of a medical expert) is actionable if it contains a disciplinary warning (where the complainant refuses the medical examination) which in itself causes injury to the complainant; 801: The mere intention of imposing a reprimand is not an appealable decision.

CJEU Judgments/Orders

T-261/09 P: The provision of information by the EU Anti-Fraud-Office (OLAF) to national judicial authorities is not an act adversely affecting the official since it does not bring about a significant change in his legal position; T-311/04: A complaint solely against the total numbers of points in a promotion exercise is admissible. The adaption of the list of promoted officials constitutes a "cluster of acts" affecting specific individuals, it may be challenged; T-96/03: A decision to withdraw an investigator from the investigation team because of potential conflict of interest constitutes an interim measure which is not appealable.

### c) Cause of action – the adverse effect of a decision

An internal complaint may be submitted by a person to whom the SR apply only against an act adversely affecting him (Art. 90(2) EU-SR; Art. VII(2) statute of the ILOAT). The decision must be binding on the official and capable of affecting directly and immediately his interest by bringing about a distinct change in his legal position (CJEU Judgment F-19/08; ILOAT Judgments 3291 para. 4(b), 2953 para. 2, 2573 para. 10).

There may be a cause of action even if there is not actual and certain injury but an actual and reasonable presumption that a decision will affect the rights and interest of an official (ILOAT Judgments 2630, 1712). For example, even if a complainant is still far from the age of retirement, he has an obvious interest in ascertaining as soon as possible the conditions on which his pension rights are acquired (ILOAT Judgments 2633, 2583, 2204, 1330; but see below under the direct challenge of a regulatory act, Judgments 3428, 3427).

Preparatory and provisional measures are not in principle final decisions which may be challenged.

**Jurisprudence**

ILOAT Judgments

3698: The abolition of the audit committee does not relate to the administrative status of the complainant; 3671: The service order constitutes a regulatory measure which may ordinarily only be challenged indirectly. A staff committee member has, however, a direct cause of action if the staff committee was not consulted; 3546: No cause of action to order the organisation to reimburse sums in respect of another staff member; 3544: The complainant had a cause of action even if in the past the staff union had never thought it necessary to challenge a practice of the organisation; 3343: A complaint is irreceivable if it is directed against an alleged violation of financial provisions in regard of procurement operations for the supply of goods and services. The employment relationship of staff members is not adversely affected; 3342: A complaint filed by a member of the staff committee about the respective power vested in the head of administration or the Council to appoint a vice-president is inadmissible. Legitimate interests in a broad or organisational sense are not rights or interests of a character that are actionable in the tribunal; 3337: The claim to instruct the President to ensure that the future career of the complainant is not influenced negatively points to a future possibility and not to a current grievance and present injury; it does not provide a cause of action; 3280: Cause of action in losing an opportunity for promotion; 3206: No cause of action in seeking the repayment of emoluments to another official or questioning his pension rights; 3198: A written warning based on low performance added to the personal file is not a final decision. The official suffers no injury from having to wait for a later decision on his performance; 3053: The challenge of decisions is admissible only if they affect in some way the employment relationship with the organisation. Complaints against decisions relating, for example, to the grant of European patents by the EPO are irreceivable; 2993:

If an organisation conceals the cause of action the time for filing a complaint will run only from such time as the cause of action is discovered; 2919: Members of the staff committee have in the interests of efficiency and consistency in decision making and the timely resolution of disputes a cause of action in challenging decisions, which allegedly have a broad adverse impact on a large number of officials; 2856: There may be a reasonable presumption that a decision affects the complainants' rights if there is a live controversy on the plea of mootness of a claim; 2832: A retired official has no cause of action to be appointed to an advertised post; 2626: The refusal to publish a corrigendum to an article in the in-house magazine may cause injury; 2324: The mere fact that a final decision has been reversed or withdrawn does not deprive it of its character as a final decision, which may be challenged, for example, to receive compensation for moral damages (1927); 2092: The reasons given for taking a decision which affects the interests of the complainant are binding and the organisation cannot later seek to justify its action on other grounds; 2037: A staff member has a cause of action to challenge the appointment. The time limit for an appeal does not depend on formalities like the signing of the contract or the medical examination; 2027: Even a simple matter like a transfer may sometimes impair the rights of an official and may show a cause of action; 1549: Even if the quashing of someone else's appointment is moot, there may be a cause of action (e.g. award of damages for breach of due process); 1435: No cause of action since the complainant was not adversely affected by the promotion of another official; 1423: No cause of action since the complainant belongs to another category of staff and the salary revision cannot cause him injury; 1363: Even if the disciplinary procedures have begun, there is not act adversely affecting an employee until there is a final decision by the competent authority; 1272: A cause of action does not depend on whether he is a serious contender for the post; 1104: A warning, which qualifies as a disciplinary measure is actionable (see, however, Judgment 3198; A warning based on low performance); 523: If an act is only a step in a complex procedure, only the outcome is subject to appeal (468).

### CEJU Judgments/Orders

F-61/11: A provisional measure intended to pave the way for a final decision (procedure of several stages) is not open to legal review; T-12/10 P: A note informing an official of the mere intention take a decision if he does not take a certain action, does not yet directly and immediately affect his interests; T-234/02: Measures concerning only the internal organisation of the department do generally not adversely affect the position of an official.

## d) Confirmatory decisions

A decision that merely confirms or reproduces the original one and is not based on any further inquiry or on new grounds (identity in substance) does not trigger a new deadline for a legal challenge (ILOAT Judgments 2823, 1490, 1304, 759, 659, 586, 478; CJEU Order F-28/08, but see Judgment T-55/03). A decision may, however, be challenged if it is not merely confirmatory (ILOAT Judgments 507, 333).

A reply to a further request for reconsideration is not a new decision resetting the time limit for an appeal (ILOAT Judgment 1528). If an organisation states that it will reconsider a decision, an appeal is not admissible. If the organisation ultimately decides, however, to uphold its former decision, the rule that confirmatory decisions of an earlier decision does not generate a new time limit for an appeal, does not apply (ILOAT Judgment 2066). A decision is not considered merely confirmatory but as a new one if it alters the previous decision and is not identical in substance, or at least provides further justification and relates to different issues from the previous one, or is based on new grounds (ILOAT Judgment 2011). The fact that discussions take place after a final decision has been taken does not mean that a new final decision has been taken (ILOAT Judgment 2011). A decision made in different terms, but with the same meaning and purpose as a previous one, does not constitute a new decision (ILOAT Judgment 586).

#### e) Decisions with recurring effect

Every salary slip is an individual decision that may be challenged as may incidentally the rules and policy decisions which afford the basis for individual decisions on pay (ILOAT Judgments 2951, 1798, 978). Salary slips cannot, however, be challenged as new decisions if they merely confirm a decision which was taken at some earlier time and outside the time limits in which an appeal may be brought.

The lawfulness of the regulatory act which affords the basis for salary slip (determination of seniority and reckonable experience) is, however, in principle restricted to the latest general decision on pay scales and will "not lie *sine die* against earlier general decisions" (ILOAT Judgments 2823 para. 10, 1368 para. 8, 1329 para. 9) but must be challenged within the deadline for its original determination. In the plea of a breach of acquired rights, the tribunal may, however, take into account a gradual decline of the salaries in previous salary scales (ILOAT Judgment 1368 para. 8).

#### f) Consistency between the administrative complaint (pre-litigation procedure) and the legal action

In line with constant case law, a rule of correspondence between the facts and the heads of claims submitted in the proceedings before an international administrative tribunal and the facts and heads of claims in the administrative complaint and the pre-litigation procedure has to be observed (ILOAT Judgments 3223, 2649, 435; CJEU Judgments F-128/12, F-26/12, T-401/11 P). The rule is justified by the general legal principle of effective judicial protection (see, for example, Art. 47 CFEU: right to an effective remedy and to a fair trial), ensuring that the complainant is in a position to properly challenge the decision which adversely affects him, and by the principle of legal certainty, that the administration may be aware of the arguments levelled by the complainant. In addition, it permits the possibility of an amicable settlement at an early stage of the dispute (ILOAT Judgment 3222; CJEU Judgments F-26/12 para. 31, 32, F-45/07 para. 109, 110 with references).

The heads of claims may, however, be developed before the tribunal "by means of pleas and arguments which did not necessarily appear in the complaint, but are closely linked to it" (CJEU Judgments F-26/12 para. 33, T-58/91 para. 83; ILOAT Judgment 2360).

Ordinarily, the failure to lodge a prior complaint within the time limit and failure to exhaust the pre-litigation procedures renders the legal action inadmissible (Art. VII(1) statute of the ILOAT; CJEU Order F-91/11, Judgment F-50/09, Order 317/85).

**Jurisprudence**

ILOAT Judgments

3222: A claim about an entirely different subject matter cannot be introduced at a later stage in an internal appeal; 2649: The scope of an appeal before the tribunal may not exceed the limits of the internal appeal; 2457: Claims for damages made for the first time in the course of the internal proceedings, and only orally and in general terms, are receivable before the tribunal; 909: Claims put forward in a rejoinder are receivable only if they come within the ambit of the claims as stated in the complaint; 899: If a claim did not form part of an internal appeal, it may not be put forward for the first time in the complaint before the tribunal; 589: Claiming promotion in the appeal to a different grade than in the complaint is inadmissible; 565: A claim made in a rejoinder is receivable only if it comes within the scope of a claim made in the complaint before the tribunal. Claims to compensation are receivable if linked with a claim for breach of the SR or the contract of appointment; 435: A complainant may not claim before the tribunal a higher sum of compensation than in his internal appeal.

CJEU Judgments/Orders

50/08: The rule of correspondence is not only complied with where the judicial action alters the relief sought in the internal complaint or its cause of action, and the concept of "cause of action" must be given a broad interpretation (F-45/07).

### g) Class actions, representative complaints

The statutes of the international administrative tribunals do not in general provide for class actions (judicial collective redress mechanisms). Staff committees may, therefore, not as such bring an action in the name of the staff members. Only an individual staff committee member may file a complaint against the non-observance of the SR (ILOAT Judgments 2649, 1897, 1147). The UN rejected the proposition of allowing class actions (representative complaints) in the reform of the internal justice system on 1 July 2009 (UNDT Judgment UNDT/2011/136). There is also no right to bring a class action before the CJEU (CJEU Order

T-236/04 and T-241/04: "... no right to bring a class action before the Community Courts...").

### h) The incidental (indirect) challenge of an act of general application (regulatory act)

It is well-settled case law of the ILOAT and the CJEU that an official may in the context of an appeal against an individual decision plead the illegality of a measure of general nature (general decisions, regulatory act) that affords the basis for it in law (ILOAT Judgments 3146 para. 10, 2793 para. 13, 2625 para. 3, 2459 para 7(b), 2379 para. 5, 1852 para. 3, 1786 para. 5, 1510 para. 4, 1329 para. 7, 1000 para. 12 and the case law cited therein; CJEU Judgments F-128/12, T-173/04, C-171/00 P; 181/86 to 184/86). The lawfulness of the general decision may even be challenged on the grounds that it was based on another unlawful one (ILOAT Judgment 1265: An organisation assumes responsibility towards its staff for incorporating standards of the common system in its own rules which may contain unlawful elements).

In EU law, Art. 277 TFEU gives expression to the "general principle" that an official may challenge incidentally the legal basis of a contested measure (CJEU Judgment F-26/12 para. 45).

An act of general application (regulatory act) which applies to an objectively determined situation and entails legal effects for categories of staff members is not subject to any time limits (ILOAT Judgments 3146 para. 10, 2625 para. 3, 1786 para. 5: "... must impugn an individual decision applying a general one and, if need be, may for that purpose challenge the lawfulness of the general one without any risks of being told that such challenge is time-barred"). In EU law, this principle is explicitly stipulated in Art. 277 TFEU giving expression to a general principle that an official may challenge incidentally the legal basis of a contested measure, notwithstanding the deadline for individual appeals (Art. 263(6), Art. 270 TFEU, Art. 90 EU-SR; see CJEU Judgment F-26/12 para. 45). The form of the regulatory measure (legislative act, circular of the administration, rule of practice) and the competence of the internal body are irrelevant.

The incidental challenge of an act of general application has to be distinguished from the direct challenge of a general decision (see more in detail below). The incidental challenge does not constitute a separate type of legal remedy but only a plea admitted by the international administrative tribunal.

The general decision is not direct subject-matter of the complaint but is a legal issue which needs to be addressed in the context of reviewing the legality of the individual decision under challenge. If the incidental plea of illegality is well-founded, the general decision is declared inapplicable with *inter partes* effect. The judgment does not affect the legislative act itself with *erga omnes* effect

(ILOAT Judgment 667; CJEU Judgments F-128/12, F-26/12). That is why the illegality of the general decision is not stated in the operative part of the judgment but only in the grounds of the judgment. In practice, however, the regulatory act which has been declared by the tribunal null and void with *inter partes* effect is fairly quickly repealed or amended in order to avoid similar actions by other employees.

**Jurisprudence**

ILOAT Judgments

3494: A decision is unlawful if it is based on an invalid delegation of authority to issue a regulatory text; 2793: Change of the method of adjusting pensions, no general principles are violated; 2615: Incidental challenge of pension adjustments; 2410: Incidental challenge of pension rates; 2129: Incidental challenge of a circular; 1733: Incidental challenge of an administrative manual; 1682: The salary adjustment violated the *patere legem* principle; 1368: Incidental challenge of salary scales by bringing an action against salary slips (1329); 1200: Incidental challenge of an improper amendment to the SR; 1000: Incidental challenge of the salary scales violating the Fleming principle.

CJEU Judgments/Orders

F-105/05: Incidental challenge of the rules for maintaining the actuarial balance of the pension scheme; T-35/05 to 139/05: The inadmissibility of the complaint entails the inadmissibility of the incidental challenge to the regulatory act; C-171/00 P: Incidental challenge to rules of practice regarding the calculation of professional experience; C-274/99 P: Incidental challenge, Art. 12 of the EU-SR does not constitute a bar to the freedom of expression laid down in Art. 10 ECHR; C-181/86 to C-184/86: Incidental challenge to the rules of practice concerning the transfer between categories of officials (44, 46 and 49/74); 262/80: Incidental challenge to the regulations providing for the remuneration of officials (783 and 786/79).

### 3. *The direct challenge of a general decision (regulatory act)*

#### a) General

The appeals procedure laid down in the statutes of most international administrative tribunals or in other legally binding regulations is an individual appeals system. A direct challenge of a measure of general nature (general decision, regulatory act) is inadmissible if the regulatory act "entails implementing measures" in order to produce a legal effect or leaves any discretion as regards its application. In such a case, the legal interests of the official are only theoretically and not directly affected (Art. 263(4) TFEU; CJEU Order T-20/01 para. 35; Judgment T-192/99 para. 62 with further references). The jurisprudence of the ILOAT reaches the same conclusions by referring to Art. II of its statute which "makes provisions for a system of individual appeals" (Judgments 2459 para. 7(a), 2379 para. 5, 1392 para. 24).

Regulatory acts may ordinarily be challenged only indirectly in the context of an admissible appeal based on an individual decision. Members of a prerogative body like a consultation committee may, however, have a cause of action against regulatory acts (ILOAT Judgments 3671 para. 3, 3546, 2919). The case law is, however, not clear on this point. In Judgment 3515 the tribunal held that a staff member cannot challenge a general decision which requires individual decisions: "To the extent that Judgment 2915 (…) indicates otherwise, it is at odds with the general jurisprudence of the tribunal" (see also Judgment 3615).

**Jurisprudence**

ILOAT Judgments

3812: The general decision to eliminate the ceiling of 2.4% on employees' contribution to the sickness insurance requires further individual implementation. It can be challenged only through impugning an individual decision (3628); 3671: If a staff member alleges a failure to respect the prerogatives of a body of which he was a member (consultation before a service order is published) he has a cause of action even though the service order constitutes a regulatory act which may ordinarily be challenged only indirectly in the context of an appeal lodged against an individual decision based on it (see also Judgment 3546); 3615: A staff representative challenged the outsourcing practice of the organisation. The complaint was dismissed as being irreceivable since it had not been established that the practice in question amounted to a general decision. In any event, even if it were a general decision, it could not be challenged by the complainant as stated in Judgment 3515; 3515: The complaints of staff representatives against the general decision to pay a collective reward to officials in active service are irreceivable. The general decision requires implementation; 3428: The decision to introduce a new pension system is a general one. A complaint is receivable only if it is filed against an individual decision (3427); 2919: An informal general policy of hiring external contractors as a new category of staff (in addition to permanent officials) may have a broad adverse impact on permanent employees without the need for implementing decisions. The members of the staff committee have a cause of action to challenge such a general policy in the interests of efficiency and consistency in decision-making and timely resolution of disputes (1618, 1451); 2300: The direct challenge of staff instructions (general decision) on working hours; 2279: A circular introducing a clocking-in system may be challenged without the need to await an individual decision; 2244: The change of the internal appeals system immediately affects the rights of staff members without the need to await individual decisions; 1618: The adoption of rules for contract staff that have a general and indirect effect on the status of permanent staff without the need for implementing provisions; 1451: Rules conferring jurisdiction on pension disputes from the ILOAT to a municipal tribunal do not need to be implemented to have potentially a negative impact on staff members.

CJEU Judgments/Orders

F-100/13: The change of the EU-SR results in a reduction of an allowance for EU officials in some countries outside Europe. Entitlement to bring an action against this measure of a general nature which does not require any implementing measure or have any discretion; T-13/10: The guide for the evaluation procedure is an act of general application and cannot be subject of a direct action; T-120/01 and T-300/01: Articles of the SR constitute a measure of general application and cannot, therefore, be subject of a direct action; T-192/99: The abolition of the system of special conversion rates is a measure of general application and cannot be the subject of a direct action; T-72/92: Claims for compensation of material damages cannot be brought against a regulation of general application concerning the weighting of a monthly insurance premium transferred to a financial institution; T-14/91:The official may not directly seek annulment of a regulation introducing special measures to terminate the service of officials; 125/87: Direct challenge of a method concerning the classification and remuneration of officials; 146/85 to 431/85: Direct challenge of the electoral regime for the staff committee; 54/75: Direct challenge of a staff election procedure.

### b) The special case of the EPO

Unlike most IO, the EPO has two appointing authorities, the Council and the President of the EPO (Office). In Judgment 3515 para. 2 the ILOAT declared a complaint against a general decision of the Council as being irreceivable on the basis that a decision of a general application had not been individually and prejudicially applied to the complainant.

In recent Judgments 3786, 3796 and 3700 the ILOAT further developed its case law with references to the special internal structure of the EPO.

Complaints against individual decisions concerning officials appointed by the President of the EPO (Office) had to be lodged and dealt with by the President. The only individual administrative decisions taken by the Council concerning officials appointed by the Council relate to the appointment and disciplinary matters. Decisions on all other matters are taken by the President because these staff members are also subject to most of the provisions of the SR. In Judgments 3786, 3796 and 3700 the complainants were appointed by the President and therefore the requests for review also had to be lodged with and dealt with by the President and not with the Council. The Council discussed the requests for review as irreceivable, it did so on the basis that the requests concerned a general decision. However, this in effect concerns the merits of the request. The Council should have recognised that it was not the competent authority at all and should have referred the requests to the President. The flaw identified, stemming from the Council's lack of competence to review the requests, warranted setting aside the impugned decision and remitting the matter to the EPO in order for the President, as the competent authority, to take decisions on the requests for review.

### *4. The formal pre-litigation procedures*

#### a) Overview

According to the statutes of most international administrative tribunals and/or the SR of the IO, a legal action by an official is in general admissible only if he has previously submitted a complaint to the appointing authority and the complaint has been rejected by an express or an implied decision (Art. 91(2) EU-SR; CJEU Judgment F-122/12 para. 37, Rule 11(4)(a) UN-SR and Art. 8(1)(c) UNDT statute; UNDT Judgment 2014/135 para. 27; Art. VII(1) ILOAT statute; ILOAT Judgment 3388; Art. 59 CoE-SR; Appeal no. 538/2013). In this connection it is of interest to note that the European ombudsman has frequently held that an implicit rejection of the complaint constitutes maladministration; see, for example, the annual report of the European ombudsman 2006, p. 80.

There are, however, cases where a direct application to a tribunal is admissible without a pre-litigation procedure (see below under point c)).

The review procedure

Before taking a final decision on the complaint some IO conduct a pre-litigation procedure comprising an internal review of the decision under challenge. This review procedure is a unilateral "non-peer" review (i.e. without the involvement of an independent internal appeals body equally represented by members appointed by the administration and the staff committee) of the decision, in order to verify its legality and appropriateness. In conformity with most statutes of international administrative tribunals and/or SR of IO it is a mandatory first step before an action may be brought before a tribunal.

The non-peer administrative review procedure is sometimes considered as "largely unsatisfactory", primarily based on the insufficient independence of the appointing authority "to have a rethink" (EU Parliament, Directorate General for Internal Administration Procedures Policy, EU civil service law, 2011, p. 19). The same may be true if the reasoned opinion given by the advisory body is not seriously considered by the appointing authority before taking its final decision. If this occurs without giving valid reasons, the decision of an IO, subject to the jurisdiction of the ILOAT will be quashed (Judgments 2355, 2261, 2092).

In quite a number of IO the pre-litigation procedure includes the involvement of a peer advisory body (internal appeals board, advisory committee on disputes) composed of members appointed by the administration and the staff representation (for details see de Cooker, pre-litigation and H.P. Kunz-Hallstein, IOLR). The appointing authority takes its final decision in the full knowledge of the reasoned opinion of this consultative body but is not bound to follow it.

The importance of these internal advisory committees on conflicts has been stressed in particularly in the jurisprudence of the ILOAT (Judgments 3075 para. 7: "... in the remedying of disputes an appeal body's competence is broader than that of the tribunal"; 2355 para. 9: The organisation has to give reasons if the executive board has decided not to follow the recommendation of the appeals board. Furthermore, it may not rely on new and different reasons before the tribunal, which it failed to invoke in the impugned decision; 1317 para. 31: "An internal appeal procedure that works properly is an important safeguard of staff rights and social harmony in an international organisation and, as a prerequisite of judicial review, an indispensable means of preventing dispute from going outside the organisation").

In its Judgments 2671, 3694 and 3785, the ILOAT stressed the importance of a proper statutory composition of the peer review body with an equal number of members appointed by the administration and by the staff committee. If the staff committee fails to appoint their committee members and the administration appoints volunteers to replace them, the committee is improperly composed and cannot assume its quasi-judicial function. Its composition is fundamental and changing it changes the body itself. The volunteers did not have representative capacity and the committee cannot be considered to be balanced as provided for by the rules. The tribunal sent the case back to the organisation so that the committee composed in accordance with the applicable rules may examine the appeal. It should also be noted that in the light of Judgment 2671, a member of a committee that has already expressed a concluded view as to the merits of the appeal is bound to withdraw in order to bring an impartial and objective mind to the issues involved.

The involvement of an internal appeals body in the pre-litigation is of special importance if the subsequent court proceedings do not provide for a two-tier system of judicial protection such as the IO that have recognised the jurisdiction of the ILOAT or the tribunals of the CO. It is only the EU institutions and the IO of the UN family subject to the jurisdiction of the CJEU and the UNDT/UNAT respectively, that do not provide for an internal appeals body in their pre-litigation procedure.

In various IO, the peer review procedure by an internal appeals body is substituted by the involvement of another advisory body, such as the disciplinary committee, the medical committee (or independent medical advisors) or an appraisal committee. In such cases there is even no internal administrative review by the appointing authority at all.

If the organisation fails to take a final decision within a defined period (stipulated in the statute of the tribunal or the SR of the IO or developed by the case law of the IO), an action may be brought before the tribunal. (For more details see below under d) cc)).

An IO may also give permission to file an appeal direct with the tribunal if special rulings in the SR so provide (ILOAT Judgment 1000, see also 1660, 146) or in other special cases (ILOAT Judgment 2232: The DG of an organisation cannot file an internal appeal against the decision of the Council to terminate his appointment). (For more details see below under c)).

The mandatory pre-litigation procedures serve several purposes (see, for example, ILOAT Judgments 2811, para. 11, 1141, para. 17; see also: A guide to resolving disputes, published by the Administration of Justice in the UN, June 2009, p. 4). The main purpose is to compel the authority to reconsider its decision in the light of objections made by the complainant, in order to restore legal peace as soon as possible. This above all includes the informal (amicable) dispute solutions, CJEU Judgment T-53/92 para. 16; 142/85).

Pre-litigation is also aimed at reducing the number of cases that need to proceed to litigation and contributes to savings in costs. Finally, the pre-litigation supports the tribunals in the process of reaching a verdict. This is particularly true if the pre-litigation encompasses the involvement of an internal peer review body (ILOAT Judgments 2811 para. 11, 1141 para. 17).

### b) Non-peer administrative review

EU

An administrative complaint must be lodged within three months of the date of the notification of the challenged decision (Art. 270 TFEU in conjunction with Art. 90(2) EU-SR).

In view of the specific nature of psychological harassment and the requirement for legal certainty, the relevant time limits do not start to run before the last act of harassment. Claims for compensation in connection with psychological harassment may be filed within a reasonable period (up to five years) in analogy to Art. 46 of the Statute of the CJEU (non-contractual liability) (CJEU Judgment F-95/09 para. 49).

In a case of alleged harassment, the official who claims to be a victim of harassment by a colleague may not sue the harasser but has to submit a request for assistance by the appointing authority (see, for example, Art. 24 EU-SR).

The pre-contentious procedure is informal in character and without the assistance of an attorney (as is mandatory in the court proceedings before the CJEU). The late communication of an annex to the complaint may, therefore, not automatically be a breach of time limits (CJEU Judgment F-43/10, para. 51). In the pre-litigation procedure, the complaint must not be interpreted "restrictively" but considered "with an open mind" (CJEU Judgment T-49/03 para. 37–39). (For more details on the internal processing of complaints see de Cooker, pre-litigation). If the authority does not notify the person concerned of its reasoned decision within four months of the date on which the complaint was lodged, this constitutes an implied decision against which an appeal may be filed (Art. 90(2) EU-SR).

In consistent case law, the CJEU has held that where the appointing authority is not empowered to annul or amend a decision of an internal body, a direct action to the CJEU is admissible without the necessity to lodge a formal complaint. This applies to decisions of the competition selection boards (CJEU Judgment F-96/09 para. 53) and decisions on staff reports (CJEU Order F-91/11 para. 15, Judgments F-66/11 para. 37, T-386/00 para. 34, T-1/91 para. 23, 144/82 para. 16).

UN

On 1 July 2009, the new UN system of administration of justice became operational. Among other changes, the former system of pre-litigation involving joint appeal boards and joint disciplinary committees was replaced by a management evaluation procedure as a mandatory first step in the formal system of dispute resolution and a two-tier judicial system, comprising the UNDT and the UNAT.

Pursuant to Art. 8(1)(c) UNDT statute and rule 11(4)a UN-SR, the jurisdiction of the UNDT can only be invoked if a contested administrative decision has previously been submitted for management evaluation. This is normally a mandatory first step (UNDT Judgment 2014/135, UNAT Judgment 2013-UNAT-300).

A request for management evaluation must be lodged within 60 calendar days of the date of notification of the complaint (Rule 11(2)(c) UN-SR).

In the UN's pre-litigation system, a prior complaint is not required if the administrative decision was taken pursuant to advice obtained from technical bodies or decisions imposing a disciplinary or non-disciplinary measure following the completion of a disciplinary process (Rule 11(2)(b) UN-SR). With regard to the deadlines which have to be observed, see Rules 11(2)(d) and 11(4) UN-SR.

CoE

An administrative complaint must be lodged within thirty days of the date of notification of the challenged decision. In exceptional cases and for duly justified reasons, a complaint filed after this date may be declared admissible (Art. 59(3) CoE-SR). In the event of either the explicit or implicit rejection of the complaint, the complainant may appeal to the CoEAT. (For possible consultation of an advisory committee see below under c)).

EPO

A request for review of the administrative decision is compulsory prior to lodging an internal appeal. It must be submitted within three months of the notification of the challenged decision (Art. 109(1)(2) EPO-SR). A review procedure is not provided for in the case of decisions on the basis of medical opinions, after an arbitration procedure on medical questions (Art. 109(3)(a) EPO-SR in conjunction with Art. 89, 90 and 91 EPO-SR) or against appraisal reports (Art. 109(3)(b) EPO-SR). Disputes on appraisal reports are settled through a conciliation and, if the official is still dissatisfied, by an appraisals committee (Art. 110a EPO-SR).

After the review procedure an official who is dissatisfied with the decision may lodge an internal appeal within three months of the formal notification (see below under c).

In harassment cases, an official may submit a request for assistance by the organisation to protect his dignity. In conformity with consistent case law of the ILOAT (Judgments 3347 para. 8, 2100 para. 13) for the calculation of the time limits in harassment cases based on an accumulation of events, the last event is decisive for initiating harassment proceedings.

The EPO used to provide a formal dispute resolution mechanism in harassment cases by Circular No. 286 (see ILOAT Judgments 3337, 3212, 2984, 2795). In 2014, the EPO adopted some modifications of this internal framework (see doc. CA/39/14 p. 6 and Circular No. 341 Policy on the prevention of harassment and the resolution of conflicts at the EPO, published on the EPO website). After the filing of a formal allegation of harassment the internal investigation unit is charged with confidential and expeditious fact finding and reporting. On the basis of this report, the appointing authority takes its decision. If the victim is dissatisfied with the decision, he may submit a request for review within three months of the notification, prior to lodging an internal appeal (Art. 109(1) EPO-SR).

### c) Administrative review with the involvement of a peer advisory body

With the exception of those organisations of the UN family which are subject to the jurisdiction of the UNDT/UNAT and the organisations adhering to the EU system subject to the CJEU, the pre-litigation procedure of most IO includes the involvement of an internal appeals body. In this peer evaluation body, members appointed by the administration and by the staff representation are equally represented (for details see de Cooker, pre-litigation). The opinion of this body is not binding on the head of

administration. However, in conformity with the consistent case law of the ILOAT, which is the tribunal that has most frequently been engaged with this kind of pre-litigation procedure, the decision-maker may not deviate from the recommendation of this body without stating valid reasons (ILOAT Judgment 2355).

CoE

In conformity with Art. 59(5) CoE-SR, a complaint may be referred to the advisory committee on disputes on the initiative of the SG or at the request of the complainant.

EPO

If an official is dissatisfied with an administrative decision after exhaustion of the administrative review procedure, he may submit an internal appeal within three months of the date of notification (Art. 110(1) EPO-SR, see ILOAT Judgment 3464). If no decision has been taken within two months of the request for review, this is deemed to constitute an implied decision rejecting it and an internal appeal may be lodged (Art. 109(7) and Art. 110(1) EPO-SR).

The following decisions are, however, excluded from the internal appeal procedure and the official may bring an action direct before the ILOAT (Art. 110(2) EPO-SR).

- decisions taken on the basis of medical opinions or in accordance with an arbitration procedure on medical questions;
- decisions taken on request to carry on working after reaching the mandatory retirement age;
- decisions taken after consultation of the disciplinary committee;
- decisions on a request for home working;
- decisions on appraisal reports.

In these cases, the administrative decision is, therefore, to be considered as a final decision after exhaustion of such other means of resisting it as are open to the official under the applicable SR (Art. VII(1) ILOAT statute). As for the difference between internal appeals against decisions of the President of the EPO (Office) and those of the Administrative Council of the EPO, and the composition of the respective appeals committees, see Art. 111(1) EPO-SR and ILOAT Judgments 3796, 3786 and 3700 and more in detail above under point 3b). As to the importance of a proper statutory composition of the peer advisory body, see ILOAT Judgments 3785, 3694, 3671 and above under 4a).

If the appointing authority deviates in its final decision from the opinion of the appeals committee, it is under a duty to state valid reasons, and may in its pleading before the ILOAT not rely on new and different reasons which it failed to invoke in the impugned decision (ILOAT Judgments 2355, 2261, 2092).

### d) The interaction between internal appeal proceedings and court proceedings

*aa) The importance of internal appeals committees*

In view of the fact that staff complaints before the UNDT and the CJEU are not preceded by an internal complaint with the involvement of a peer review body (see above), the jurisdiction of the ILOAT with its abundant case law is best placed to illustrate the interaction between internal appeal proceedings and court proceedings.

It is only the express or implied rejection of a request for a decision that constitutes a decision adversely affecting the official and against which he may submit a complaint, and it is only after the express or implied rejection of that complaint that an official complaint may be brought before the tribunal (see also CJEU Judgment F-30/08 para. 83). In conformity with Art. VII(1) of its statute, a complaint submitted to the ILOAT is not receivable unless the decision impugned is a final decision and the complainant has exhausted all internal means of redress as are open to him under the respective SR of the IO which is subject to ILOAT's jurisdiction. The statute does, however, "not specifically require the organisation to provide specific internal remedies, it only requires that those actually existing be exhausted" (Judgment 2461 para. 3). Even the absence of any internal appeal mechanisms is in itself not a fatal flaw which violates a final decision (Judgment 3282 para. 3). The tribunal encourages organisations to provide efficient internal appeal mechanisms (Judgment 2616 para. 15). An efficient internal appeal mechanism would "not only make the tribunal's task easier but also substantially reduce its workload by bringing a satisfactory and less expensive resolution to many disputes ..." (Judgment 2312 para. 5; 1317 para. 31). To this end the ILOAT has enhanced the role of the appeals committees to quasi-judicial bodies "in order the ILOAT does not become, *de facto*, a trial court of staff grievances but continuing as a final appellate tribunal" (Judgment 3222 para. 10). In respect of fact finding, taking evidence and the ensuring of oral hearings, the appeals committees assume to a certain extent the functions of a judicial body of the first instance (Judgment 1317 para. 31; see also Judgments 3253 para. 15; 3184 para. 15). This is the logical consequence of the single-tier system of judicial review by the ILOAT, in contrast to the two-tier judicial review system of the CJEU (CJ, GC) after the dissolution of the CST on 1 September 2016 and to the two-tier judicial review system of the UN (UNDT/UNAT) established in 2009.

In order to increase the important functions of the internal appeal committees further, ILOAT case law requires that the administration of an IO must provide adequate, clear and cogent reasons if it departs from recommendations of the appeals committee (Judgments 3361 para. 14; 3266 para. 9; 3208 para. 11; 2833 para. 4; 2699 para. 24; 2643 para. 8). This duty to give reasons is not fulfilled by simply saying that the decision-maker does not agree with the recommendation of the appeal committee (Judgments 2278, 2092). How ample the reasons need to be turns on circumstances (Judgment 2391). It is not for the tribunal itself to find the justification for an unmotivated decision (Judgment 2261).

In order to fulfil its quasi "judicial" functions properly (ILOAT Judgment 852 para. 21), an IO bears the responsibility of "providing adequate staffing in keeping with its obligation to provide an efficient means of internal redress" (ILOAT Judgments 3168 para. 13; 2392 para. 6). A large backlog of pending internal appeals "may be a reason for the inordinate delay, but it is not an excuse" (ILOAT Judgments 2196 para. 9; 1968 para. 5). The requirement to exhaust the internal remedies cannot have an effect "paralysing" the exercise on the complainant's right to a fully functioning internal appeals board (ILOAT Judgments 2170 para. 9, 2104 para. 3).

The members of the appeals board should be impartial and objective in their fact finding and should enjoy the staff's confidence in internal appeal proceedings (ILOAT Judgments 3184 para. 15; 2671 para. 7, 11; 1317 para. 31; 179 para. 1). The internal appeal procedure must observe "the minimum standards of justice" (ILOAT Judgment 1317 para. 33), above all the principle of due process (ILOAT Judgments 2598 para. 7: the right to be heard; 2513 para. 11: the right of the parties to be present at the hearing of witnesses and to give full answers in defence). For the sake of transparency and due process a complainant must be informed about the substitution of a member of the appeals committee immediately so that he can exercise his right to contest the composition (ILOAT Judgment 3158 para. 4; see also Judgment 3354 para. 5).

#### *bb) Consequences of the admissibility of an action brought before the tribunal based on an implied decision*

If an IO fails to reply to the request of an employee to take a decision relating to him this is deemed after a certain lapse of time to constitute an implied decision (Art. VII(3) ILOAT Statute: sixty days; Art. 90(1) EU-SR: four months). The provision must, however, be read in conjunction with Art. VII(1) ILOAT statute (ILOAT Judgments 2631, 185) which established the obligation to exhaust the internal means of redress before filing a complaint with the tribunal. The official is then required to file an internal complaint. Otherwise an action brought before the tribunal will be inadmissible. If the organisation does not take an explicit decision on the internal complaint within the respective time limit of sixty days (Art. VII(3) ILOAT statute; four months Art. 90(1) EU-SR) this constitutes an implied final decision rejecting the complaint against which an appeal may be lodged.

If a complaint against an implied decision is declared receivable the complaint is assessed by the tribunal at the time it was filed and events subsequent hereto "while possibly of interest, can have no impact on the outcome" of the complaint (ILOAT Judgment 2196 para. 11). The later recommendation of an appeals committee and an express final decision of the administration become, therefore, "simple nullities" (ILOAT Judgments 2196 para. 11; 1968 para. 5; see also: CJEU Order F-53/13: The total absence of a statement of reasons before an action is brought cannot be remedied by explanations provided by the administration at a later stage). If the complainant has brought an action with the tribunal against an implied rejection of the internal appeal and the administration informed him afterwards that the complaint had been forwarded to the internal appeals committee for consideration, the complainant may elect not to proceed with the appeal before the tribunal, but proceed with the internal forum. (It is fundamental that the litigant cannot pursue the same claim before different adjucative bodies at the same time (ILOAT Judgment 2853)). The same holds good if the complaint has been declared receivable by the tribunal because of an undue delay of the internal appeal procedure (ILOAT Judgments 2039 para. 4; 1968 para. 4).

There is a special ruling with respect to the time limit in the case of an implied decision in Art. 91(3) EU-SR. Where a complaint is rejected by express decision after being rejected by implied decision (Art. 90(2) EU-SR: No reasoned decision within four months from the date on which the complaint was lodged), the period for lodging an appeal starts to run afresh.

### *cc) Internal appeal proceedings and legal actions brought before the ILOAT – interpretation of Art. VII of its statute*

Art. VII of its statute, stipulating the conditions under which an appeal is receivable, are construed by the case law of the ILOAT as follows:

- The purpose of Art. VII(3) (implied decision) is twofold. Firstly, it aims at enabling the complainant to defend his interests even if the organisation has failed to take an explicit decision, and secondly to serve the stability of the parties' legal relations. It is therefore mandatory that the official refers the matter to the tribunal within 150 days of his complaint being received by the organisation (Judgments 2901; 2600; 456).
- If there is any decision, i.e. a measure which has legal effects (a mere acknowledgement of the receipt will, therefore, not do), taken by the organisation on a complaint within 60 days of the notification of the complaint there is no implied decision within the meaning of Art. VII(3) (ILOAT Judgments 3060, 2948 and consistent case law).

If the organisation takes no decision at all on an appeal within the 60 days provided for in Art. VII(3), the complaint may bring an action before the tribunal within the 90 days time limit (Art. VII(2)). This holds good even if the organisation has taken an express decision to reject the appeal and forwarded it to the appeals committee before the appeal to the tribunal has been filed (ILOAT Judgments 2866; 2562). Earlier decisions of the tribunal requiring that the appeal must be submitted to the tribunal before the organisation has belatedly taken an express decision (ILOAT Judgment 533; see also Judgments 2681 para. 4; 786; 762) are deemed to be restricted to the very particular facts of these cases, i.e. the complainant explicitly asked the appointing authority to confirm the implied rejection of the appeal instead of going straight to the tribunal and the complainant "has only himself to blame" for having to challenge the new decision which has superseded the implied rejection he had initially challenged.

- Since the internal appeal proceedings are "judicial in character" (Judgment 852 para. 21) they are, in principle, not subject to time limits (see, however, Art. 90(2) EU-SR where a time limit of four months from the date on which the complaint was lodged is defined). If, however, the appeals committee does not deliver its opinion within a reasonable lapse of time (see below), an implied decision is presumed and the complainant may lodge an appeal with the tribunal (Art. VII(1) ILOAT statute).
- If the organisation does not take a decision within sixty days (Art. VII(3) ILOAT statute) after getting the opinion of the appeals board a decision rejecting the complaint is inferred from its failure to act and an appeal may be submitted to the tribunal within the time limit of ninety days (Art. VII(2) ILOAT statute; ILOAT Judgment 762 para. 3).
- Jurisprudence as to the "reasonable lapse of time" within which an appeal board is expected to render its opinion.

ILOAT Judgments

3302: The internal appeals procedure is deemed to be exhausted (Art. VII(1) ILOAT statute) "where the pursuit of the internal remedies is unreasonably delayed" (with reference to Judgment 2939 para. 9). The complainant must show, however, that for his part he has done everything to get the matter concluded (Judgment 2929 para. 9 and the cases cited therein) and is in no way "responsible for a failure to exhaust the internal means of redress" (Judgment 2811 para. 13). What constitutes a reasonable lapse of time varies "according to the particular circumstances of each case" (3302 para. 5; 1968 and the numerous judgments cited therein). A delay of four years is excessive by any standards, but the complainant greatly hampered the proceedings "by deliberately filing as many appeals as possible in an attempt to pressure the Administration into acceding to various requests". The complainant had, therefore, not exhausted the internal remedies available to him and no exception to the requirement set out in Art. VII(1) of the ILOAT statute was justified in this case; 3200: Although the case was complex and detailed (harassment case), the internal proceedings (approximately 16 months) were considered as being excessive due to delays by the decision-maker; 3188: The processing of the appeal was delayed by 14 months and in consideration of the special circumstances not conducted with due diligence; 2891: A delay of approximately 42 months is unacceptable for internal proceedings; 2768: The delay of about three years in processing the internal appeal is unacceptable by any standards – the appeal was "not handled with the diligence required by the circumstances and with the care " which IO owe to their staff (2705); 2626: The refusal to publish the corrigendum of an article in the in-house magazine constitutes a breach of the personal rights of the official concerned and his freedom of expression. In view of the special circumstance of the case the tribunal declared receivable a complaint brought already some four and a half months after filing an internal appeal. The internal dispute was such that it had to be resolved rapidly if resolution was to serve any purpose; 2522: The appeal procedure, which took more than 14 months, was not conducted with due diligence and care; 2392: A complainant does not implicitly accept delays in internal appeal proceedings if he does not directly bring action before the tribunal; 2197: Internal appeal proceedings must move forward with reasonable speed.

### e) Time limits for the internal appeal proceedings

Time limits for lodging internal complaints are a matter of public policy, legal certainty and stability in law and are, therefore, binding on the parties and the tribunal (ILOAT Judgment 1279; CJEU Judgment C-154/99 P). IO may not depart from the time limits stipulated in the statute of the competent international administrative tribunal (ILOAT Judgments 2863 para. 3: three months in the SR instead of 90 days in the Statute is unlawful; CJEU Judgment C-154/99 P). The rationale behind this rule is that the IO did not only recognize the jurisdiction of the tribunal as such, but also the applicability of its statute and the rules of procedure (ILOAT Judgment 532 para. 1: "… any provisions in its own rulebook on the receivability of complaints filed with the tribunal are of no effect, whether they comply with the tribunal's rules or not"; see also Judgments 2863, 2312, 1095, 852, 786, 762).

The time limits for filing an internal complaint are at the legislative discretion of the competent body of the IO. They are set up in the SR. Where the SR lay down a procedure for internal appeals, it must be strictly adhered to. There must also be compliance with the set time limits (ILOAT Judgments 1653, 1469, 1132). The rules on time limits are, however, not supposed to be traps for catching out an official (ILOAT Judgments 1720, 1376, 1247, 607), misleading him or concealing some paper or practice from him (ILOAT Judgments 2907, 2821, 752), or depriving him of the possibility of filing an appeal in breach of the principle of good faith (ILOAT Judgment 2996). If an appeal was filed in time but with the wrong internal body, it is receivable (ILOAT Judgments 1832 para. 6, 1734, 1720, 1393).

The SR may also contain provisions for waiving the time limits for filing an internal complaint in specific cases (ILOAT Judgments 3267, 1700, 1356, 1230) or set no time limits at all (ILOAT Judgment 1659). An IO may even exempt a complainant from filing an internal appeal in a specific case, for example, for reasons of delay or expense (ILOAT Judgments 458, 339; see also 408). In conformity with Art. 110(2) EPO-SR the following decisions are excluded from the internal appeals procedure: decisions taken on the basis of medical opinions, decisions on requests to carry on working beyond the age of 65 years, decision after consultation of the disciplinary committee, decision on a request to perform duties outside the Office's premises, appraisal reports. If an organisation has failed to provide internal means of redress or explicitly notifies its refusal to take any action at all, the official may appeal straight to the tribunal (ILOAT Judgments 2996, 2866, 2740, 2562, 1660). Based on the principle of good faith a time limit for filing an internal appeal will not start to run if an organisation invites the official to discuss the possibility of an amicable settlement, unless the organisation expressly states otherwise (ILOAT Judgments 2878, 2584, 1066, 509) or if the organisation hints that it will reconsider the case (ILOAT Judgment 2066). The time limit also does not start to run if the Office of the UN ombudsman is making efforts for an informal resolution (Rule 11(2)(c) UN-SR).

As part of its duty of care towards its staff an organisation must help an official in the exercise of his right to file an appeal. The international administrative tribunals are competent *proprio motu* to review whether the time limits for filing an internal complaint or an internal review have been respected. A tribunal will, therefore, not entertain an action if the internal appeal or the request for internal review was time-barred even if the organisation goes into the substance of such a complaint (ILOAT Judgments 2297, 775; CJEU Judgment T-54/90). This also holds good if an internal appeals body has held an internal appeal receivable which was filed out of time (ILOAT Judgments 3351, 2966, 2297, 775). If an internal appeals body erred in dismissing the appeal as irreceivable, the tribunal will remit the matter back to the board for consideration (ILOAT Judgment 3253).

An internal complaint is "lodged" within the meaning of Art. 90(2) EU-SR not when it is sent but when the institution receives it (CJEU Judgments F-27/06 and F-75/06, F-3/05; T-54/90); but see Art. 4(2) ILOAT rules of procedure for the dispatch of complaints).

It is settled case law that it is upon the sender to establish the date on which a communication was received. This is easily proved if the communication is made by registered mail or by hand delivery against receipt (ILOAT Judgment 3253 para. 7 with abundant case law; CJEU Order F-3/05; Judgment 195/80). If a sender cannot produce evidence for the date of receipt, the tribunal ordinarily accepts what is said by the addressee about the date of receipt (ILOAT Judgments 3253 para. 7; 2494 para. 4; CJEU Judgment 195/80 para. 11).

As to the methods for calculating the time limits, see below.

#### f) The failure to exhaust the internal appeal proceedings

If a complainant is responsible for a failure to exhaust the internal means of redress provided for in the SR, a complaint is inadmissible (ILOAT Judgment 3302 with references). A complainant is not allowed to evade the internal means of redress on his own initiative (ILOAT Judgments 3190, 2811). An official must state, for example, in clear wording his intention to lodge an appeal (ILOAT Judgments 1172). A notice to the legal adviser of an organisation who is not a member of the staff, is not a valid notice of appeal filed within the time limit (ILOAT Judgment 840). If a complainant has done all that could reasonably expected of him to have the internal appeal effectively examined, he cannot be held responsible for an unreasonable delay and thus the internal means of redress are deemed to be exhausted.

It is not necessary to exhaust internal means of redress before filing an application for the execution of a judgment of the ILOAT. This does not, however, exclude the possibility of first filing an internal appeal (ILOAT Judgments 1978, 1887 and the case law cited therein).

(As to the explicit exemptions from filing an internal appeal or a request for review provided for in the SR, see above).

### *5. The time limits for bringing an action*

The strict application of time limits for lodging an appeal are a matter of public policy and are not left to the discretion of the parties or the tribunal (ILOAT Judgment 1140 para. 14; CJEU Judgment T-54/90 para. 24). The time limits are intended to ensure legal certainty and the need to avoid discrimination or arbitrary treatment in the administration of justice (ILOAT Judgment 3002 with abundant case law cited; CJEU Judgments F-113/11, 152/85, 42/85, 33/72).

The conditions of receivability of actions brought before the ILOAT are governed exclusively by the provisions of its own statute (ILOAT Judgment 2863 para. 3: t is, therefore, unlawful to set a different time limit of three months in the SR instead of ninety days in Art. VII(2) ILOAT statute; see in this context also Judgment 2312 para. 3: An IO cannot unilaterally preclude the right to lodge an appeal; Judgment 786 para. 2: Art. VII(3) ILOAT statute is the only rule that matters in determining whether to entertain a complaint against an implied decision). But see the ruling in Art. 110(2) EPO-SR excluding quite a number of decisions from the internal appeals procedure.

Derogations from the strict application of time limits are permitted for the purpose of safeguarding general principles of law. This holds good if the official was prevented by *vis major* from learning of the impugned decision in good time, was unlawfully deprived of the possibility to exercise his right of appeal within the specified time limit, if the official has asked for review of the decision following the emergence of some new and unforeseeable facts of decisive importance since the decision was taken, or when the organisation relied on facts or evidence of decisive importance of which the official was not and could not have been aware before the decision was taken (ILOAT Judgment 3304). A complaint against an implied rejection is receivable notwithstanding the expiry of the time limit if the complainant has good reasons to infer from a dilatory reply that his case is still under consideration (ILOAT Judgment 2901). If an organisation invites a complainant to settlement discussions, or even participates in discussions of that kind, its duty of good faith requires that, unless it expressly states otherwise, it is bound to treat those discussions as extending the time limit for the taking of another step (ILOAT Judgment 2584). As part of its duty of care to its staff, an organisation must help an official in the exercise of his right to file an appeal. If, for example, an official asks the organisation for authorisation before filing an appeal with the tribunal and then filed the appeal out of time because he did not get a prompt reply, the appeal is nevertheless admissible (ILOAT Judgment 2345).

The time limit (period) for lodging an appeal is generally expressed in the SR or the statute of the tribunal in days or months.

In order to have a fair ruling it is not the moment when the decision was notified but the end of the day of notification of the impugned decision (*dies a quo*, starting day) that is taken into consideration for the calculation of the time limit for filing an appeal (*dies a quo non computatur in termino*).

The day following the *dies a quo* is the day on which the period starts to run but it is not the day which fixes the timing for that period (for more details see the detailed presentation by the advocate general in its opinion to the CJEU Judgment 152/85 para. 3). For example, if a decision is notified on 1 September and the time limit is defined as a period of 30 days, the period ends on 1 October and the official may exercise his right to appeal until midnight of this day (*dies ad quem computatur in termino*). Taken together the complainant has a full period of 30 days for the execution of his right to appeal (the complainant in the case CJEU 152/85 erred, therefore, in supposing that the timing of the period started to run on 2 September and terminated on 2 October. In applying such a method of calculation, the time limit would be extended to 31 days). If the time limit is calculated in months, it ends with the expiry of the day in the month in which the period ends and which bears the same number as the starting day (Art. 58(1)(9) GC rules of procedure; CJEU Judgment 38/84 para. 20).

For further examples, see CJEU Judgment 152/85 para. 8: notification of the impugned decision on 18 February, meant that the period of three months expired on 18 May at midnight, plus two days extension on account of distance; CJEU Order F-3/05: notification of the impugned decision on 3 December, means that the filing period expires on 3 March.

Recently, the ILOAT has been applying an identical method for calculating the time limit of ninety days laid down in Art. VII(2) ILOAT statute for filing a complaint (for example, ILOAT Judgment 3393: Notification of the impugned decision on 20 July, the filing period expired on 18 October; Judgment 3344: Notification of the impugned decision on 17 October, the filing period would expire on 18 January; Judgment 3116: Notification of the impugned decision on 11 February, the filing period expired on 12 May).

The date of lodging an appeal

In the case law of the CJEU an appeal is "filed" in accordance with Art. 91(3) EU-SR if the appeal in paper format is received at the registry (CJEU Order F-113/11 para. 25) and not when it is dispatched. An appeal may, however, also be lodged by means of electronic transmission (e-curia, see the Aide-Mémoire-Application lodged by means of E-Curia and E-Curia: Conditions of use of 11 October 2011). If an appeal is lodged by fax, the original must be lodged at the registry by mail within a period of ten days (Art. 73(3) GC rules of procedure). The appeal must be lodged in paper format without any corrections or amendments, even of a minor nature (CJEU Order F-113/11 para. 25 to 33). If the time limit for filing an appeal is extended on account of distance in accordance with Art. 58(2) GC rules of procedure, and ends on a Saturday, Sunday or an official holiday, it is extended until the end of the first subsequent working day.

In the proceedings before the ILOAT, the date of dispatch of the complaint is decisive for the filing of a complaint within the prescribed time limit (Art. VII ILOAT statute and Art. 4(2) rules of procedure). It is, therefore, "a sensible precaution" to send the application by registered mail with receipt by the post office (see the "Advice to litigants" on the ILOAT's website). If the complainant cannot deliver evidence, the date of delivery at the registry is decisive (ILOAT Judgment 3253 para. 7 with abundant case law). In the case of urgency, it is sufficient that the essential parts of the complaint form are filled out and dispatched within the time limit. The registrar may then ask the complainant to amend the complaint within a fixed time limit (ILOAT Judgment 3390: The brief was lacking necessary elements to identify it as a complaint). A complaint may in the case of urgency also be filed by sending the scanned complaint by e-mail (ILOAT Judgment 3390, 3116). If a time limit ends on a day which is not a working day of the organisation, the time limit for filing an internal appeal is extended until the next working day (ILOAT Judgment 2831).

### 6. *Restitutio in integrum (Re-establishment of rights)*

The doctrine of *restitutio in integrum* means that the *status quo ante* (the previous situation) on procedural or substantive rights of a complainant may be re-established in order to restore justice.

In substantive law, *restitutio in integrum* is intended to remedy the damage caused by restoring the position of the complainant to that which it would have been, had the damage not occurred. If that is not possible or desirable, a pecuniary compensation is awarded (ILOAT Judgments 1317, 145; old UN Administrative Tribunal Judgments 464, 465, 145).

In procedural law, *restitutio in integrum* is the re-establishment of procedural rights of the complainant who has failed to meet a time limit (see, for example, Art. 45(2) CJEU statute; Art. 8(3) UNDT statute and Art. 35 UNDT rules of procedure; Art. 122(1) EPO-EPC). Time limits are a matter of public policy, they are established to ensure legal clarity and avoid discrimination or arbitrary treatment in the administration of justice and may, therefore, as a matter of principle not be waived (ILOAT Judgment 2722 para. 3 and further judgments cited therein; CJEU Order F-113/11, Judgment F-95/09). Art. 45(2) CJEU statute stipulates that no right shall be prejudiced in consequence of the expiry of a time limit if the party concerned proves the existence of unforeseeable circumstances or of *force majeure*. Art. 8(3) UNDT statute and Art. 35 UNDT rules of procedure provide for the extension of time limits when the interests of justice so require. According to the case law of the ILOAT, the waiver of a time limit is permissible only if the complaint has been prevented by *vis major* from learning of the decision in good time or where the organisation has misled the complainant, concealed some paper from him, or deprived him of the possibility of exercising his right of appeal in breach of the principle of good faith (ILOAT Judgments 2722 para. 3, 1466).

## III. Interim measures

In the same manner as internal appeals, actions before the international administrative tribunals do not, in principle, invoke the suspension of the execution of the impugned decision (Art. VII(4) ILOAT statute; Art. 278, 279 TFEU; Art. 156 et seq. rules of procedure; Art. 91(4) EU-SR; Art. 60(4) CoE-SR; Art. VI(4) IMFAT statute; Rule 13(1) WBAT procedure; Art. 10(2) ESMAT statute).

Most international administrative tribunals are, however, empowered to order interim measures (interim relief). Such temporary relief "must not prejudice the points of law or of fact at issue or neutralise in advance the effects of the decision subsequently to be delivered in the main action" (CJEU Order F-61/11 R para. 55). The purpose of the interim measure is not to secure reparation of damages but to ensure that the judgment on the substance of the case takes full effect (CJEU Orders F-62/10 R para. 45, 47; F-52/08 R para. 34).

The power to order interim measures does not include the issuing of interlocutory orders. Taking into account the principle of limited remedial powers (see above), an obligation may be imposed on the organisation only as a result of a tribunal's judgments (ILOAT Judgments 1468, 61; CJEU Judgment F-104/10 para. 63). It is, therefore, for example, inadmissible to apply for injunctions to remove medical files from an internal register or to order a pre-recruitment medical examination (CJEU Judgments F-46/09 para. 63).

Taking into consideration the principle of limited remedial powers of the tribunals (see above) and the right of staff members to an effective judicial protection, tribunals have developed abundant case law to grant interim relief in order to avoid serious and irreparable damage to the applicants in urgent cases. There is, however, no one system of the grant of interim measures by the international administrative tribunals.

The power to adopt interim measures is in most cases explicitly ruled in the statutes or rules of procedure of the tribunals, or in the SR of the IO. Interim measures mainly relate to the suspension of the execution of the impugned decision.

- CJEU

Art. 278, 279 TFEU; Art. 156 et seq. GC rules of procedure; Art. 91(4) EU-SR.

An application for suspension is admissible if the applicant has challenged the decision in an action before the GC. An application for other interim measures referred to in Art. 279 is admissible only if it is made by a party to a case before the GC and relates to that case (Art. 156(2) GC rules of procedure). In its Order C-393/96 P (R) summary point 6 the CJEU held that: "the right of individuals to complete an effective judicial protection under community law … implies in particular that interim protection be available to them …".

- UNDT

Art. 10(2) UNDT statute; Art. 14(1) UNDT rules

The tribunal may order interim measures to provide temporary relief. The relief may include an order to suspend the implementation of the contested administrative decision, except in cases of appointment, promotion or termination.

- CoEAT

Art. 60(4) CoE-SR

If a stay of the execution of an administrative decision has been granted by the chair of the CoEAT for the complaint proceedings, the stay is maintained during the appeal proceedings unless the CoEAT decides otherwise.

- WBAT

  Rule 13 WBAT rules of procedure

  The Tribunal is empowered to suspend the execution of impugned decisions.

- ESMAT

  Art. 10(2) ESMAT statute

  The President of the tribunal is empowered to grant interim relief.

- IMFAT

  Art. VI(4) IMFAT statute does not empower the tribunal to grant interim relief. The official commentary to this Article does, however, state that this Article would not preclude the tribunal from ordering interim measures if warranted by the circumstances of a particular case.

- ILOAT

  The ILOAT statute does not explicitly empower the tribunal to order interim measures. The tribunal, therefore, declines to order the suspension of impugned decisions and does not address the issue of inherent powers (Judgment 1584 para. 6: According to Art VII(4) of its statute the tribunal is not empowered to suspend the impugned decision). In the light of the great number of pending appeals and the resulting extremely long duration of its proceedings the granting of interim measures based on its inherent powers would be in the interest of a complete and effective judicial protection.

It is common to all the international administrative tribunals that grant interim relief that they only suspend the execution of an impugned decision if certain conditions are met. Details on this subject matter are developed most comprehensively by the case law of the CJEU. The conditions for the adoption of an interim measure to suspend the execution laid down in Art. 156(2) GC rules of procedure were specified in the case law (including the case law of the former CST) as follows:

- The circumstances of fact and of law must justify *prima facie* (*fumus boni iuris*) such an order (CJEU Order F-120/06 R para. 41). In this regard it is sufficient that the judge has "serious doubts" as to the legality of the impugned decision (CJEU Order F-92/09 R para. 93), or that the application is not "at first sight manifestly devoid of all foundation". Thereby the examination of extremely delicate questions of fact and law is a matter for the ruling on the main proceedings (CJEU Order T-41/96 R para. 52). As to the question of a possible transformation of the normal test of *fumus boni iuris* into a test of *fumus non mali iuris* see CJEU Order T-184/01 R para. 58.

- The measure must be urgent in order to avoid a serious and irreparable damage to the applicant's interests and ensure that the judgment on the substance of the case takes full effect.

The occurrence of damage need not be demonstrated with absolute certainty, only a sufficient degree of probability is necessary (CJEU Orders F-19/08 R para. 25; F-64/07 R para. 31). Whether there is a serious and irreparable damage must be determined in the light of the particular circumstances of each case. Purely financial damages cannot, in principle, be regarded as irreparable, or even difficult to repair. The judge must, however, ensure that the appellant has enough money to meet all the essential expenditure to cater for his own basic needs until a financial decision is taken on the main action (CJEU Orders F-38/12 R; F-61/11 R; F-92/09 R; F-19/08 R; F-98/07 R; F-120/06 R).

- The order must be provisional and may not prejudice the decision on the substance of the case (CJEU Order F-61/11 R para. 55).

The conditions are cumulative (CJEU Judgment T-120/01 and T-300/01).

The judge hearing such an application must weigh up the interests involved (CJEU Order F-120/06 para. 42; C-445/00 R para. 73).

## IV. Interlocutory judgments/orders

International administrative tribunals may deliver interlocutory (interim) judgments. These judgments do not terminate judicial proceedings. They are intended to decide on preliminary questions of law or facts as an indispensable prerequisite for the final judgment. Tribunals have inherent power to render interlocutory judgments.

**Jurisprudence**

ILOAT Judgments

3209: Order to produce the files of the selection process; 3145: Order the appointment of a medical expert (2094); 2700: Order the filing of further submissions; 2603: Order the appointment of a chartered accountant in order to determine the a of the amount of the complainant's debt; 2192: Order to submit documents; 2136: Order the defendant organisation to submit arguments on the merits (the organisation had in its submissions confined itself to a challenge as to the receivability of the complaints); 1468: Order further submissions from the parties; 1417: Order further submissions from the ICSC and the complainants; 1373: Appointment of an expert by the President of the tribunal; 1188: Order the submission of an item that formed part of the internal appeal proceedings; 1177: Order the submission of a table showing the ratings of the complaint; 875: Order the appointment of an expert.

CJEU Judgments

F-98/07: Order to deliver figures as to the amount of monetary compensation; F-1/05: Order to deliver submissions on the amount of monetary compensation; T-10/02: Order to deliver figures as to the amount of monetary compensation; T-40/03: Order to deliver figures for an appropriate compensation or conclusions with figures as to the assessment of the loss sustained.

### V. Stay of proceedings

Like municipal courts the international administrative tribunals are authorised to suspend judicial proceedings either on an application of a party or on its own initiative. An order on the staying of proceedings is generally issued where the proper administration of justice so requires. In most cases the authorisation is explicitly laid down in the rules of procedure of the tribunals.

Art. 10(3) ILOAT rules of procedure states that the tribunal rules on an application by either party for a stay of proceedings or the adjournment of a listed case to a later session. (Judgment 3449: Stay of proceedings *sine die* on request of the complainant; Judgment 3431: Stay of proceedings requested by the organisation has been rejected; 1390: The tribunal will not stay the proceedings pending possible changes in the rules).

Art. 69 GC rules of procedure rules on the conditions and the procedure for staying proceedings. Proceedings may be stayed in the specific cases referred to in Art. 69(a) to (c) and in other cases where the administration of justice so requires.

Art. 19 UNDT rules of procedure stipulates that the tribunal may, at any time, either on an application of a party, or on its own initiative make an order appropriate for a fair and expeditious disposal of the case and to do justice to the parties. This rule implies the authorisation to rule on a stay of proceedings (UNDT Judgment UNDT/2009/020).

## F. Procedural matters

### I. The principles of procedural law applicable to the international administrative tribunals

#### *1. General*

In their search for justice the international administrative tribunals have to apply the substantive labour law of the IO in a legally ordered procedure. In the absence of a *corpus iuris* or a generally accepted international doctrine of court proceedings, the tribunals apply the rules of their own statutes, set up by decision of the respective legislative body of the IO. As with IO which are not bound by the SR of other IO, the international administrative tribunals are not bound by the statutory rules of other tribunals (see, for example, UNDT Judgment UNDT/2009/036 para. 25: "neither are they bound by the case law of other international administrative tribunals"; ILOAT Judgment 3138).

As courts of limited jurisdiction (see above), international administrative tribunals are bound by the mandatory provisions governing their competences (see, for example, ILOAT Judgment 67 para. 3) and in particular may not extend their jurisdiction to persons or subjects beyond the limits stipulated in their statute. This limited jurisdiction may also not be disregarded with reference to the general right of access to a court.

In general, the international administrative tribunals are, however, reluctant to decline their jurisdiction on the grounds that they are bound by mandatory provisions. (Sometimes a tribunal even tries to avoid "to express a critical opinion on provisions of its own statute"; see ILOAT Judgment 3003 para. 46). This objective is achieved by a wide interpretation of the procedural rules to which they are subject. This may be best exemplified by the following case law of the ILOAT.

In conformity with Art. XII (and the annex) of the statute of the ILOAT in the version applicable until 6 June 2016 (see ILO doc. GB 326/PFA/12/1), a judgment of the ILOAT could be challenged before the ICJ by the respective IO if it considered that the decision was vitiated by a fundamental procedural fault (including the principle of equality of parties in court proceedings as an essential part of the right to a fair trial). The advisory opinion of the ICJ was binding on the ILOAT, the IO and its staff (ILOAT Judgment 3450 para. 8; Art. XII(2) and the annex of its statute).

Since the recourse to the ICJ was confined to the IO there was fundamentally an "imbalance" in the equality of procedural right of the parties involved (ILOAT Judgment 3003 para. 40). In its Judgment 3003 ("IFAD case"), the ILOAT declared inadmissible the request of the IO for a stay of execution of its judgment until the ICJ had rendered its advisory opinion in order not to "amplify the consequence of this inequality" (para. 46). The ICJ underlined this concern in its advisory opinion of 1.12.2012 (see on the website of the ICJ). It was, however, of the opinion that this inequality was alleviated by the procedural measures it had taken (advisory opinion para. 45 to 48), for example, by allowing an exchange of briefs, granting equal time for these briefs and disallowing a unilateral hearing of the IO. This more or less reflects the reasoning given in the "Eurocontrol II" decision of the Federal Constitutional Court of Germany of 10 November 1981, BVerfGE 59, 63 (for an English version see the website of the University of Texas at Austin, School of Law, Institute for Transnational Law) in order to minimise the impact of inequality of the judicial procedure before the ILOAT. The very clear wording in ILOAT Judgment 3003 para. 40 had to be seen, however, as a request for action addressed to the lawmaker of the ILO. The governing body of the ILO repealed Art. XII of the statute of the ILOAT at its 105th Session (June 2016), see ILO doc. GB 326/PFA/12/1.

Another example of providing judicial protection by an extensive interpretation of rules of procedure is the case law of the ILOAT in regard of collective rights of staff. Despite the restriction of its competence to individual complaints, the ILOAT grants judicial protection for collective bodies of staff (staff representation). (Some statutes of international administrative tribunals or SR of IO even provide for a right of these bodies to bring an action before court, for example see above under *locus standi*). By opting for a broad interpretation of its mandatory procedural rules, the ILOAT held that the individual staff representatives must have *locus standi* in order "to preserve common rights and interests of staff" (Judgment 2791 with further references). "However, the rights that are comprehended within the notions of freedom of association and collective bargaining … are individual rights inhering in individual staff members" (ILOAT Judgment 2827 para. 4). In this context, reference has to be made to the judgment of the Hague Court of Appeal of 17 February 2015, case no. 200.141,812/01, trade union of the EPO (The Hague Office, VEOB) and the staff union of the EPO (SUEPO) v. EPO. The court ruled that VOEB/SUEPO had no access to the judicial process before the ILOAT. The protection of this fundamental right to association and assembly (for example, Art. 11 EConHR, consistent case law of the ILOAT and Art. 30 EPO-SR) was, therefore manifestly deficient. That was why Dutch courts were obliged to safeguard the collective right of VEOB/SUEPO to a fair trial (Art. 6 EConHR). On 20 January 2017, the Supreme Court of the Netherlands set aside the Judgment of the Hague Court of Appeal and declared the Netherlands courts to have no jurisdiction to hear the claims of the EPO trade union against the EPO (ref. 15/02186). Art. 6 and 11 EConHR are individual rights and not collective rights. The individual right of access to the courts under Art. 13 EPO-EPC is sufficiently guaranteed and there is no independent right of direct access to court for trade unions of an IO (see the opinion of the procurator general at the Supreme Court of the Netherlands, p. 13). Unions have no standing to bring claims to the ILOAT but EPO staff representatives may lodge an appeal for effectively protecting the right to collective action under Art. 11(1) EConHR.

In its Judgments 3447, 2893, 623 the ILOAT interpreted the right to a hearing as an essential element of the right to a fair trial. It ruled, however, that the right to a hearing required that the complainant was free to put his case either in writing or orally and there was no obligation to offer him both possibilities.

In the "Klausecker" Judgment 2657, the ILOAT, however, strictly adhered to its well-established case law that, according to its mandatory provisions, an external candidate for employment was outside the ambit of its jurisdiction (para. 6) (for exceptions, see Judgments 621 and 339, where the employment contract was not yet concluded but all the essential terms had been agreed). In this case the ILOAT did not even consider the possibility of a wide interpretation on the basis of *culpa in contrahendo*. It held that the complainant could not successfully invoke the case law of the CJEU, which is not binding on the ILOAT and would be in breach of its procedural rules.

In order to avoid a legal vacuum, the tribunal, however, considered it "highly desirable" that the EPO "should seek a solution affording the complainant access to a court, either by waiving its immunity or by submitting the dispute to arbitration" (para. 6). Thereupon the EPO offered arbitration, which was rejected by the complainant. His recourse to the ECHR was not granted (see more in detail above under the right to bring an action).

Apart from the mandatory provisions governing its competence, an international administrative tribunal is inherently empowered to interpret its statute "for taking such steps within its area of competence as it deems to be essential to ensure the proper administration of justice" (ILOAT Judgment 3003 para. 28). The ILOAT has, therefore, recognised the possibility of submitting requests for review, interpretation or execution of its judgments or a stay of execution or proceedings (see, for example, Judgment 3003 para. 28). With effect from 7 June 2016, the governing body of the ILO adopted a new version of Art. VI(1) of the statute of the ILOAT by adding the following sentence: "The tribunal shall nevertheless consider applications for interpretation, execution or review of a judgment".

On the other hand, the ILOAT has ruled in consistent case law that it has no authority under its Statute to issue interim injunctions against an IO (Judgment 2623 para. 2). In the absence of a mandatory ruling excluding this legal action, it is difficult to conceive this self-imposed restriction of its judicial power.

Despite their independence from the procedural court rules of other international administrative tribunals, the tribunals have developed a "notable degree of homogeneity" in court proceedings (Gaffney, p. 1181).

In the application of the procedural rules in its statute an international administrative tribunal is under an obligation to abide by the general international legal principles of procedural law, which form part of the general legal principles as enshrined in Art. 6 and 13 of the EConHR; Art. 47 CFREU; Art. 8 and 10 UDHR; Art. 38(1)(c) statute of the ICJ and applied by the constitutional courts of most states).

Some international administrative tribunals are even directly bound by these general legal principles of procedural law. The CJEU is directly committed to respecting the general legal principle established in the CFREU (Art. 6(1) TEU; Art. 51 CFREU) and the CoEAT is bound by those principles specified in the EConHR (see, for example, CoEAT Appeals No. 100/1984 of 20 December 1984 and No. 405/2008 of 19 December 2008).

It transpires from the case law of international administrative tribunals that, in contrast to the assessment of the substantive law of IO in its judicature, the international general legal principles of procedural court law only play a very subordinated role in the case law of international administrative tribunals. It can be assumed that only in a case of a blatant conflict of its rules with higher ranking law which cannot be solved by interpretation would an international administrative tribunal raise an issue before the legislative organ of the respective IO responsible for its statute.

Due to the aforementioned circumstances the most effective way to identify general legal principles governing the procedural law of international administrative tribunals is an indirect one, i.e. having recourse to the case law of the ECHR, the ICJ and national constitutional courts which adjudicate whether staff members of IO have available to them reasonable means to protect their rights effectively.

### 2. *General legal principles*

From the following case law of the ECHR, the ICJ, the Supreme Court of the Netherlands and the Federal Constitutional Court of Germany some general legal principles applicable to the procedural law of international administrative tribunals may be derived. It has to be underlined, however, that this list is far from being exhaustive. Other general legal principles like e.g. that of good faith or due process (see above under good faith and due process) are also applicable to the procedural law of the international administrative tribunals.

#### a) The essence of the right to a fair trial

In its Judgment Waite and Kennedy v. Germany, Appl. No. 26083/94 of 18 February 1999 and Beer and Regan v. Germany, Appl. No. 28934/95 of 11 May 2000, the ECHR only provided a very general evaluation of the right to access to a court under Art. 6(1) EConHR in regard of the ESA appeals board. It ruled that this right was not absolute but could be limited in the light of the immunity of an IO from national jurisdiction in order to perform its functions free from interference by national courts. The contracting states of the EConHR are, however, not absolved from their responsibility under the EConHR and have to ensure that staff members have reasonable means to protect effectively their right to a fair trial which are not disproportionate to the intended purpose and do not impair the essence of the right (para. 49). Unfortunately, the court did not disclose the details of its analysis (see in this conjunction the "Guide on Article 6 EConHR of 31 December 2013 p. 14, 15; available on the website of the ECHR).

#### b) Equality of the parties in the court proceedings

In its advisory opinion of 1 February 2012 on ILOAT Judgment 2867 (IFAD case) the ICJ expressed concern about the inequality of access to the ICJ based on Art. XII of the statute of the ILOAT (this provision was repealed with effect from 7 June 2016, for more detail, see above).

#### c) Fundamental errors in procedure – failure in justice

In its Advisory Opinion of 12 July 1973 on UNDT Judgment 158, the ICJ held (para. 30) that "certain elements of the right to a fair hearing are well recognised and provide criteria helpful in identifying fundamental errors in procedure which have occasioned a failure of justice" (see Art. 11 of the former version of the statute of the UNDT which was repealed by decision of the UNGA in 1995, doc. A/RES/50/54). As example of such elements of procedure the ICJ highlighted under para. 30 "for instance":

- the right to have the case heard and determined within a reasonable time,
- the right to comment upon the opponent's case (adversarial proceedings),
- the equality of proceedings,
- the right to a reasoned decision.

#### d) Publicity of an oral hearing

The ECHR ruled in its decision Klausecker v. Germany, Appl. No. 415/07 of 6 January 2015 in regard of the jurisdiction of the ILOAT that the lack of publicity of an oral hearing did not render the proceedings manifestly deficient for the purpose of the EConHR (for more details, see above under immunity of IO from national jurisdiction in staff matters and the decision of the ECHR in the case Gaspari v. Belgium, Appl. No. 10750/03 of 12 May 2009).

#### e) International minimum standard of elementary procedural justice

In its "Eurocontrol II" decision of 10 November 1981 (for more in detail, see above under immunity of IO from national jurisdiction in staff matters) the Federal Constitutional Court of Germany ruled in regard of the ILOAT that the minimum standard of international elementary justice comprises:

- a minimum degree of procedural equality of those involved,
- the grant of a legal hearing,
- there must be a legally ordered procedure exclusively in accordance with legal norms and legal principles,

- the access to court must not be unreasonably difficult,
- the court must exercise its jurisdiction.

#### f) Oral hearing, accessibility, length of proceedings

In its judgment Anonymous v. EPO of 23 October 2009, case No. 08/00118, the Supreme Court of the Netherlands ruled on the court proceedings of the ILOAT. It held that although the ILOAT was not bound by Art. 6(1) EConHR (see, for example, ILOAT Judgment 2662 para. 12) it afforded an "equivalent" legal protection to staff members. It was readily accessible and the dismissal of a request for an oral hearing was well-reasoned. It further ruled that the ILOAT's proceedings were not too lengthy and a complaint of "undue delay does not automatically mean that the procedure cannot be regarded as effective".

In connection with this reference has to be made to the judgment of the Hague Regional Court of Appeal of 30 September 2014, EPO v. Verveer, Case no. 200.136.028/01, quashing the judgment of the court of first instance (District Court of The Hague of 16 July 2013, case no. 1223887/12–31860) which was based on the submission of the appellant that the procedure before the ILOAT in EPO cases would probably last 10–15 years and, therefore, deprived him of fair trial. The Court of Appeal ruled that the Netherlands court must show restraint in concluding that the ILOAT did not meet the requirements of Art. 6 EConHR. It could be presumed that the ILOAT would do what was needed to prevent unreasonable delays. An impairment of the very essence of the right could not be automatically presumed. In the meantime, the ILOAT seems to have reacted.

Indeed, the ILOAT reduced the enormous backlog in EPO cases by rendering about 40 judgments in 2014 and 2016 respectively and 69 judgments in 2015, whereas in the preceding years 2012 and 2013 there were between ten and twenty judgments per year.

### II. The proceedings before the tribunals

In general, the proceedings before the international administrative tribunals comprise a written and an oral part.

The written part normally includes the reply (opinion) of the organisation to the complaint of the official. The CJEU (Art. 83(1) rules of procedure of the GC). The pleadings may be supplemented by a reply and a rejoinder unless the GC decides that a second exchange of pleadings is unnecessary.

The rules of procedure of the UNDT do not provide for a second exchange of pleadings; the parties may, however, request to file an application (see UNDT guidelines for filing an application).

The rules of procedure of the ILOAT (Art. 9) provide for an exchange of pleadings in four stages (complaint brief, reply, rejoinder and surrejoinder) in regular cases. The tribunal may in exceptional cases allow an application from the complainant for leave to file further submissions (see Advice to litigants B13 and B14).

The second part of the procedure normally includes an oral hearing.

The CJEU (GC) holds a hearing arranged either of the court's own motion or at the request of a party. Reasons must be stated (Art. 106 rules of procedure of the GC). There are special rules for appeals against decisions of the former CST (Art. 192 et seq. rules of procedure of the GC).

The new UN Administration of Justice system adopted in 2009 resulted in the abolition of the joint disciplinary committee and the joint appeals board and the establishment of a two-tier judicial system (UNDT, UNAT). The document-based proceedings before the old UNAT had therefore to be supplemented with an extended system of oral hearings in order to offset the loss of an oral hearing consistently held by the former internal bodies (Art. 16(1)(2) UNDT rules of procedure, see also UN doc. A/66/275 para. 128).

The oral hearing may take place either in the physical presence of a party or by video-link, telephone or other electronic means (Art. 16(4) UNDT rules of procedure). The costs associated with the travel and accommodation of the party, the counsel and witnesses are borne by the organisation (Art. 16(5) UNDT rules of procedure). The UNAT decides in the vast majority of cases on the basis of documentation.

From 2009 to 2015 the UNDT rendered 1196 judgments and 4825 orders in 1537 court sessions and in most cases provided an audio recording of the hearings (see UN doc. A/66/275).

From 2009 to 2015 the UNAT rendered 610 judgments and 247 orders and held 23 hearings, OAJ Report 2015).

The statute of the ILOAT provides for the possibility of an oral hearing (Art. V). The tribunal, however, declines in consistent case law to hold oral hearings. Whereas in the 1950s and 1960s, the tribunal held some oral hearings (see Judgments 26, 28, 29, 121, 122, 133, 137), the last hearing dates from 1989 (Judgment 986, in the meantime the number of judgments is approaching 4000). The rationale behind this restrictive practice may be seen in the statute and the rules of procedure which unlike to the UNDT, do not provide for the possibility to impose the costs for travel and accommodation of the parties, the counsel and witnesses on the organisation or to replace the physical presence of parties by using modern means of communication (see ILOAT Advice to Litigants, point D(3): "it is up to the parties to meet their own costs, such as travel and other expenses of counsel and witnesses, whatever award the tribunal may make in its judgment"). The tribunal is apparently reluctant to return to its former practice which was to include these costs in the general decision on costs in the judgment.

In this regard, the ILOAT attaches great importance to the findings of the internal appeal committee. Before the committee witnesses can be heard and questioned (Judgment 736 para. 4). The internal appeals procedure serves the purpose of providing a fair hearing process to resolve the dispute (Judgment 3222 para. 9). In its Judgment 3447 para. 8 the tribunal held that the right to a hearing required that the complainant should be free to put his case either in writing or orally and that the appeal body was not obliged to offer him both possibilities. (See, however, the report of the Amsterdam International Law Clinic of 3 August 2005 on the non-compliance of the ILOAT with the requirements of Art. 6 EConHR).

## III. Evidence and proof

### *1. General*

The international administrative tribunals follow a compromise between the adversarial and the inquisitorial systems (Benzing, p. 745). It is the official who decides to file a complaint and determines the scope of the dispute and the judiciary activity of the tribunal (*ne ultra petita*). Each party to the dispute has to adduce evidence in support of the facts and assertions they are pleading (burden persuasion, evidentiary burden *actori incumbit probatio*), whereas the tribunal is deemed to know the law (*iura novit curia*). The tribunals are not *ex officio* obliged to gather evidence. They may, however, of their own motion, use their power of investigation and order the parties to produce documents for evidentiary purposes (Art. 11(c) ILOAT rules: "measures of investigation"; Art. 92 CJEU (GC) rules of procedure: "measures of inquiry"; Art. 18(2) UNDT rules of procedure: The tribunal "may order the production of evidence for either party at any time"; see also ILOAT Judgments 3209, 3046, 1560, 436). The tribunals may shift the evidentiary burden to an organisation which refuses to disclose the reasons for a decision (UNAT Judgment 2012-UNAT-201; ILOAT Judgments 2654: The official was deprived proof by the organisation of allegations of harassment; 3234: Refusal to present evidence requested by the joint appeals board; 3415: Refusal of the organisation to present documents). ILOAT and UNDT do not apparently follow the Roman law principle that no one is under an obligation to produce documents against his own interests (*nemo tenetur edere contra se*) but tend to the common law system (Benzing, p. 746).

The law of evidence as applied by the international administrative tribunals is neither enshrined in international conventions nor do the statutes of the tribunals include a uniform and exhaustive set of evidentiary rules (Benzing, p. 740). Moreover, the rules of procedure of the international administrative tribunals "are fragmentary in relation to evidentiary questions" (Benzing, p. 740). This is all the more astonishing because the facts and assertions of the parties necessarily mostly diverge so the evidence adduced must be substantiated to the satisfaction of the judges who are not authorised to adopt a non-liquet decision. On the other hand, there is a remarkable degree of convergence of evidentiary law as developed by the case law of the international administrative tribunals.

## 2. *The burden of proof*

The burden of proof (*onus probandi*) comprises two different features. First, the burden of persuasion (evidentiary burden), i.e. the parties of the dispute have to adduce evidence in support of the facts and their assertions in order to persuade the judges. Second, only if both parties provide different but equally sound and conclusive arguments (a non-liquet situation), the objective burden of proof comes into play. It is intended to take into account the overarching principle that ensures the ending of a litigation in the public interest (*interest reipublicae ut sit finis litium*) and avoid a negation of justice (*negatio iuris*) (Castillo de la Torre/ Fournier; opinion of advocate general Kokott in CJEU Judgment C-8/08 and in Order C-105/04 P).

The burden of proof (evidence) in respect of facts and assertions is on the party that pleads it (*onus probandi incumbit actori*) (see, for example, Art. 85 CJEU (GC) rules of procedure; CJEU Judgment F-43/10 para. 222, F-98/09 para. 84; ILOAT Judgments 3347, 3222, 2116, 2074). The burden of proof implies a burden of persuasion which carries with it the risk of non-persuasion.

It is not the role of the international administrative tribunal to engage in fact-finding. The gathering and adducing of evidence is on the parties (ILOAT Judgment 2879 para. 14). The facts and assertions must be set out in the complaint itself. It is not for the tribunal to search for and identify the intended subject of a complaint in the annexes of the case (CJEU Judgment F-98/09 para. 84).

**Jurisprudence**

ILOAT Judgments

3443: The complainant bears the burden of proving that he was a victim of retaliation or unequal treatment; 3344: The burden of proof is on the sender of a communication. If that cannot be done the tribunal ordinarily accepts what is said by the addressee. It is, however, for the tribunal to evaluate the evidence provided by the parties (3253, 2678); 3215: The burden of proof for the failure to take reasonable steps to prevent a foreseeable risk of injury (negligence) is on the person seeking damage for negligence (2804); 3234: The refusal to present the evidence required by the joint appeals board is a violation of good faith and undermines the proper functioning of the internal appeals process; 3216: It is a fundamental principle of the adversarial process to give the complainant the opportunity to respond to new evidence; 3200: It is consistent with the fundamental right of due process to know the name of the accuser except in special circumstances; 2907: A hidden disciplinary measure cannot be inferred from conjecture, it must be proven; 2786: Due process requires that the complainant must be given the opportunity to test the evidence relied upon and the possibility to produce evidence to the contrary; 2706: An IO completely contradicts itself if, after reprimanding a superior for sexual harassment, it asserts that the complainant failed to discharge the burden of evidence with respect to her allegations of harassment; 2702: A party seeking to rely on an unwritten rule or established practice bears the onus of proof; 2700: Under normal circumstances a staff member must have access to all the evidence on which the organisation bases its decision against him (for special cases see 2229, 1756); 2475: Evidence of little probative value was delivered by the organisation and the principle of *in dubio pro reo* was violated; 1781: The best evidence available must be offered in proceedings before the tribunal; 1775 para. 7: The evidence provided must be of "sufficient quality and weight" to persuade the tribunal; 1756: Material information may not be withheld merely to strengthen the position of the administration or one of its officers in a dispute with an employee; 1637: No grounds for striking out a text that is material to the case or grounds of evidence and that in any event the tribunal may have ordered to disclose; 1384: The organisation was unable to prove satisfactorily the charge of theft of computer equipment; it simply reversed the burden of proof by expecting the complainant to show that his conduct was spotless; 1372: An item that forms part of the proceedings that led to the impugned decision may not be withheld from the scrutiny by the tribunal; 1157: An official who alleges material injury has to prove or offer at least cogent evidence of it.

### *3. Evidentiary presumption and shifting the burden of proof*

There is a presumption that administrative decisions of IO regarding officials have been regularly performed ("presumption of regularity", UNAT Judgment 2011-UNAT-122 para. 5). To this end it is sufficient that the IO is able even minimally to show that a decision was legal. It is thus for the official to rebut this presumption, to whom the burden of proof is shifted.

If an IO refuses to disclose the reasons for a contested decision the burden is shifted and the organisation has to establish that the decision is neither arbitrary nor tainted by improper motives (UNAT Judgment 2012-UNAT-201 para. 5). By failing to conduct an inquiry into the validity of an accusation of moral harassment the complainant was deprived of the opportunity to prove the allegations, and the burden of proof was shifted to the organisation (ILOAT Judgment 2654 para. 7).

It is unacceptable that an IO refuses to provide documents sought by the complaint that are patently relevant to his case and then to argue that the complainant has not furnished relevant evidence. In the absence of a clear and unequivocal denial by the organisation, an inference is drawn that the complainant had furnished evidence (shift of the burden of proof, ILOAT Judgment 3415 para. 9; 3272 para. 15; see however 3345 para. 9: a general "fishing" for documents is not permissible; Judgment 2510: The tribunal will not order the production of documents on a speculative basis).

In disciplinary matters staff members enjoy the presumption of innocence. In accordance with the principle of *in dubio pro reo* they have the benefit of the doubt (ILOAT Judgments 2913, 2849, 2351; CJEU Judgment T-48/05).

### *4. Standard of proof, evaluation of evidence*

The standard of proof "determines the requirements which must be satisfied for facts to be regarded as proven" (advocate general Kokott, opinion in CJEU Judgment C-8/08 para. 80 footn. 60). The other party has the right to comment on all evidence adduced or observations filed with a view to influencing the decision of the Court (see "The Guide on Art. 6 EConHR", para. 92 on the website of the ECHR). In order to reach proof, the evidence adduced by the parties must be evaluated by the tribunal (see, for example, ILOAT Judgment 2231 para. 5).

The tribunals do not require absolute proof (for example, ILOAT Judgments 3297 para. 8, 1384 para. 10) which anyway would rather difficult to achieve in social relations. It suffices that the evidence adduced from the coexistence of sufficiently strong, clear and concordant inferences or of similar unrebutted presumptions of fact is proven "beyond a reasonable doubt" (opinion of advocate general Sharpston in CJEU Judgment C-396/11 para. 78 and ECHR Judgment of 7 June 2007, Appl. No. 38411/02 para. 76; ILOAT Judgments 3297, 2879, 2849, 2786).

### *5. Means of evidence*

The rules of procedure of most international administrative tribunals provide for some rules on the adoption of means of evidence. These rules are not exhaustive (Benzing, p. 748). They primarily comprise documentary evidence, evidence by witnesses and experts, oral testimony, affidavits or an inspection of the place or thing in question (Art. 11 and 12 ILOAT rules; Art. 91 et seq.; CJEU (GC) rules of procedure; Art. 17, 18 UNDT rules of procedure).

In practice, the documentary evidence is by far the most frequently used item of evidence in the international judicial proceedings. As a rule, documentary evidence has already to be submitted in the annex to the complaint form and in the reply by the organisation. Further documentary evidence may be adduced if a secondary exchange of briefs (rejoinder and surrejoinder) is granted or at any time by the tribunal of its own motion.

Even if an international administrative tribunal regularly holds oral hearings (see, for example, the CJEU (GC) and the UNDT; see the judicial calendar on the "curia" website of the CJEU and the annual report of the CJEU and the activity report of the office of staff legal assistance (OSLA) of the UN internal justice system on the website of the office of administration of justice of the UN) the summoning of witnesses takes place very rarely (Sarvarian).

The ILOAT, which in consistent case law does not admit oral hearings (see above), also shifts the hearing of witnesses and experts to the internal appeal boards (see, for example, ILOAT Judgments 2771 para. 18, 1133 para. 7).

## IV. Change of claims

There is a rule of correspondence between the claims put forward in the administrative complaint and the claims in the subsequent action before the international administrative tribunals. This rule is justified *inter alia* by the purposes of the pre-litigation procedure, effective judicial protection and by the principle of legal certainty (see, for example, CJEU Judgments F-128/12, F-26/12, 133/88).

The case law of the ILOAT (Judgments 2457 para. 4, 2416 para. 11, 2360 para. 7) requires for claims of damages to be receivable that in the course of the internal appeal procedure damages are claimed as a minimum orally and in general terms. In contrast the case law developed by the CJEU consistently holds that an application for damages may be requested for the first time before the court since an administrative complaint which only requests the annulment of a decision may imply a request for compensation of damages (CJEU Judgments T-401/11 P para. 92, C-62/01 P para. 35).

**Jurisprudence**

ILOAT Judgments

3420: Precedent has it that a complaint may enlarge on the arguments presented before the internal appeals board, but may not submit new claims to the tribunal (2837 and further case law cited therein); 3222: If a claim (in the present appeal claim for moral damages of a very significant amount) is introduced at a later stage in the internal appeal about an entirely different subject and is therefore only briefly addressed it cannot be litigated before the tribunal for lack of exhaustion of the internal remedies; 2965: No new claims not contained in the initial complaint may be entered in the rejoinder; 2213: Financial claims in an application for review that are higher than those in the judgment are irreceivable; 1519: Pleas may be entered during the proceedings before the tribunal. The receivability depends on the making of prior claims not on pleas; 1443: The complainant may not put wider claims to the tribunal than in the internal appeal.

CJEU Judgments/Orders

T-401/11 P: There is a rule of correspondence between the administrative complaint and the action before the court. The beads of claim may be developed before the court by means of pleas and arguments which did not necessarily appear in the administrative complaint but are closely linked to it (C-62/01 P); C-150/03: The extent of the damage allegedly suffered need not to be particularised in the application to the court if the appellant has established the existence of special circumstances justifying the omission to calculate the damage; 224/87: A complaint may not submit to the court conclusions the subject-matter of which differs from that of those contained in the internal complaint or put submissions founded on a legal basis other than that relied on the complaint.

## V. *Ex tunc* assessment (*tempus regit actum*)

The lawfulness of a measure must be appraised as at the date of its adoption. In consequence thereof, all subsequent facts are irrelevant (ILOAT Judgments 3037, 2365).

**Jurisprudence**

ILOAT Judgments

3126: In disciplinary matters no new grounds going beyond the grounds specified in the notice of dismissal may be brought before an appeal board or the tribunal. Such a course would seriously infringe a staff member's right to be heard before a disciplinary measure is imposed; 2786: It is not open to an organisation to justify a decision by conducting further inquiries after the internal appeal proceedings have been conducted. The legal review of a decision is decided, para. 15: "in the light of facts as known at the time of the decision and the reasons given for that decision"; 2355: An organisation has a duty in its pleadings before the tribunal not to rely on new and different reasons which it failed to invoke in the impugned decision; 1390: The complaint must be reviewed in the light of the rules in force at the material time.

CJEU Judgments/Orders

C-485/08 P: The legality of a decision must be assessed at the basis of facts and the law as they stood at the time when the measure was adopted (C-443/07 P, C-449/98 P).

## VI. Withdrawal of complaint (discontinuance of proceedings)

The rules of procedure of the international administrative tribunals provide for a removal of the case from the register if the applicant informs the tribunal that he wishes to discontinue the proceedings (withdrawal of suit) in conformity with the general legal principle of party disposition (Note: The term "discontinuance" of proceedings is used in Art. 125 of the rules of procedure of the CJEU (GC) if the applicant wishes the case to be removed from the register. In ILOAT case law, the term "withdrawal" is used.

According to the case law of the ILOAT, the withdrawal of a suit is not permissible after the opening of the session at which the tribunal is to hear the case (Judgment 728).

The tribunals will generally not look into the reasons for an unqualified withdrawal of suit (ILOAT Judgments 1598, 951).

A complainant may withdraw a premature complaint and lodge a new one complying with the time limits in the statute of the tribunal (ILOAT Judgment 1611).

The withdrawal of a suit may not be presumed. A withdrawal may be cancelled at any time prior to its receipt by the competent body (ILOAT Judgment 567).

### VII. Joinder of cases

Cases concerning "the same subject-matter may be joined" (Art. 68 CJEU (GC) rules of procedure). This is in the interest of good administration of justice. In consistent case law, the ILOAT uses the wording that complaints should be joined if they raise "the same issues of fact or law and seek the same redress" (Judgments 3445, 1680, 1541). It is immaterial that the complainants advance more or less different pleas since "the content of the pleas lays no constraint on the tribunal's ruling" (ILOAT Judgment 762 para. 2).

### VIII. Prolongation of deadlines

The rules of procedure of the international administrative tribunals explicitly provide for the prolongation of deadlines either by the tribunal or its president.

Art. 14 ILOAT Rules: The tribunal or between sessions the president, may lengthen any time limit set in the rules. In practice the short deadline of 30 days for the dispatch of the reply, the rejoinder and the surrejoinder is regularly prolonged on request for a period of up to 90 days. Art. 60, 61, 81, 106, 179, 185, 207 CJEU (GC) rules of procedure: time limits may be extended.

## G. The judgment

### I. Content and other aspects

If an action is well founded in whole or in part, the tribunals render their judgments. A tribunal may order the rescinding of a decision and/or the performance of an obligation and/or the award of material and/or moral damages (see, for example, Art. VIII ILOAT statute; for more details on the kind of actions, see above under the principle of limited remedial power).

In contrast to most other international administrative tribunals Art. 10(5)(b) UNDT statute provides that the award of damages shall not normally exceed the equivalent of two years net basic salary of the applicant. The UNDT may also not award exemplary or punitive damages (Art. 10(7) UNDT statute).

If an action is manifestly (ILOAT: "clearly") inadmissible (irreceivable) or devoid of merit (unfounded), it may be summarily dismissed (see, for example,

Art. 7(2) ILOAT rules of procedure; Art. 208 CJEU (GC) rules of procedure) so that the resources of the system of administration of justice can be used more efficiently.

If a complaint is manifestly devoid of merit there is no need for a tribunal to address the issue of receivability, the complaint is dismissed by a summary judgment (ILOAT Judgment 3460).

If the defendant organisation does not respond to an application initiating proceedings in the proper form and within the time-limits, the complainant may apply to the tribunal for judgment by default (CJEU Judgment F-79/13).

If a case is examined by a panel of judges, the decision is taken by a majority vote (see, for example, Art. 5(3) UNDT rules of procedure, Art. VI(1) ILOAT statute).

The requirements in terms of the form and the content of a judgment provided for in the statutes and rules of the international administrative tribunals vary considerably. Whereas Art. VI of the statute of the ILOAT simply states that a judgment shall contain the reasons for the decision, Art. 117 CJEU (GC) rules of procedure provides for an exhaustive list of the necessary elements of a judgment. A judgment shall contain:

a) a statement that it is the judgment of the court;
b) an indication as to the formation of the court;
c) the date of delivery;
d) the names of the president and of the judges who took part in the deliberations with an indication as to the name of the judge-rapporteur;
e) the name of the advocate general, if designated;
f) the name of the registrar;
g) a description of the parties;
h) the names of their representatives;
i) the statement of the forms of order sought by the parties;
j) where applicable, the date of hearing;
k) a summary of the facts;
l) the grounds for the decision;
m) the operative part of the judgment, including the decisions of the costs.

In contrast to most other international administrative tribunals the ILOAT and the UNDT (Art. 5(3) rules of procedure) record any dissenting opinions (in 2017 the ILOAT Triblex database refers to 21 judgments with a dissenting opinion).

On a reasoned application by a party or on its own motion, the CJEU (GC) may omit the name of the applicant and other information if there are legitimate grounds for that anonymity (Art. 66 CJEU (GC) rules of procedure). In 2002 (ninety-third session) the ILOAT adopted a practice of not mentioning the names of individuals on the internet (Triblex database; see Judgment 2189).

Copies of the judgments are communicated in writing to the IO and to the complainant (Art. VI(2) statute of the ILOAT; Art. 118(2) CJEU (GC) rules of procedure). As a rule, the judgments of the international administrative tribunals are also published on the website of the tribunal (Art. 26(1) UNDT rules of procedure; Practice rules for the implementation of the rules of procedure of the CJEU (GC) item (K) and constant practice of the ILOAT).

The judgments of several international administrative tribunals are delivered in court (Art. 118 CJEU (GC) rules of procedure; the judgments of the ILOAT are read in open court based on longstanding practice).

Clerical and arithmetical errors in a judgment may be corrected by the tribunal either on the basis of explicit authorisation (see, for example, Art. 164 CJEU (GC) rules or by implied powers (see, for example, Art. 16 ILOAT rules).

### II. Application for the interpretation of judgments

Either party may apply for interpretation of a judgment (see, for example, ILOAT Judgments 3154, 2806, 2483), even if such an application was not explicitly provided for in the rules of procedure of the tribunal. (Now, as a result of an amendment to its statute in June 2016, Art. VI(1) statute of the ILOAT explicitly provides for the possibility to consider an application for interpretation). Art. 168 CJEU (GC) rules of procedure contains a detailed provision regarding the interpretation of judgments. The application may be made by any party or any institution establishing an interest therein. The application must be made within two years of the date of delivery of the judgment. Art. 30 UNDT rules of procedure provides a ruling on the interpretation of judgments. The application for interpretation must be sent to the other party who has 30 days to submit comments on the application, which will then be decided by the tribunal.

In its Judgment 1328 para. 10, the ILOAT held that a dispute referred to in Art. II ILOAT statute was not resolved until the judgment had been duly executed. The competence of the tribunal is, therefore, not exhausted when the judgment is rendered but the tribunal remains competent in all issues until the full execution of the judgment (see now the explicit ruling in Art. VI(1) statute of the ILOAT). The request is admissible only if the operative part of the judgment gives rise to uncertainty or ambiguity about its meaning or purport (Judgments 3392, 536, 240).

The application for interpretation may be filed with the tribunal direct without exhausting any internal remedies (ILOAT Judgment 2483). There is no time limit for an application (ILOAT Judgments 2483, 1064, 538: more than 40 months after delivery of judgment).

The application may only concern the grounds of the judgment if the decision refers to them explicitly (ILOAT Judgment 2483).

If the application for interpretation of an unfavourable judgment by the IO is not successful, the tribunal may also order a penalty and costs (ILOAT Judgment 2806).

Interveners have an independent right to apply for interpretation even if the party whose conclusion they support has not done so (CJEU Order 146 and 431/85).

## III. Supplementary decisions

### *1. Decisions as to costs*

A decision as to costs is given in the Judgment or Order which closes the proceedings (see, for example, Art. 133 CJEU (GC) rules of procedure).

As a rule, the proceedings before the international administrative tribunals are free of charge for the complainant (ILOAT, advice to litigants, point E; Art. 139 CJEU (GC) rules of procedure: except in respect of a manifest abuse of process; Art. 6(3) UNDT Statute).

The costs of the judicial proceedings are borne by the respective IO regardless of the outcome of the case.

A decision on the recoverable costs is apparent from the operative part of the judgment (see, for example, Art. 140 CJEU (GC) rules of procedure). Even if the statute of a tribunal does not explicitly rule on the imposition of costs a tribunal has an inherent power to do so (for example, ILOAT Judgments 3054, 1962).

According to the case law of the UNAT (Judgment 2013-UNAT-370 para. 23), however, it must be derived from Art. 10(6) UNDT rules that the UNDT has in general no power to award costs. Each party has, therefore, to bear its own costs. It is only if a party has manifestly abused the proceedings that the UNDT may award costs against that party.

Art. 134 to 140 CJEU (GC) rules of procedure contain very detailed rules as to the allocation of costs. The general rule is that the unsuccessful party bears its own costs and the costs incurred by the other party if they have been applied for in the successful party's pleadings (Art. 134(1) CJEU (GC) rules of procedure). For equity reasons or in the case of costs which are held to be unreasonable or vexatious a different distribution of costs may be ordered by the court (Art. 135 CJEU (GC) rules of procedure; see, for example, F-91/13).

The ILOAT holds in consistent case law that no express claim for recoverable costs by the successful complainant is required (Judgments 3084 para. 12 and the case law cited). Even in the case of an abuse of process, the ILOAT will, as a rule not award costs to the defendant organisation (Judgment 3301, para. 5).

The ILOAT asserted however in several judgments (see Judgments 3293, 3196, 3054, 3043) that it has an inherent power to impose a costs penalty upon a complainant: it will, however, avail itself of that possibility only in "exceptional circumstances" since it is essential that the tribunal should be open and accessible to international civil servants "without the dissuasive or chilling effect of possible adverse awards of that kind". On the other side, frivolous vexatious and repeated complaints absorb the tribunals' resources and are costly and time-wasting for the defendant. In its Judgment 2211, the ILOAT ordered for the first time the complainant to pay to the defendant a (nominal) award of costs (EUR 100).

As a corollary to the mandatory representation by a lawyer (Art. 19 of the statute of the CJEU), the complainants are entitled to aid (Art. 147 to 148 CJEU (GC) rules of procedure). The UN judicial system provides for the possibility to seek free legal advice from the OSLA.

The decision on the award of costs is a discretionary decision of the tribunal based on considerations of fairness and the precise information supplied (ILOAT Judgment 2278) or, in the absence of such information, on the basis of an equitable assessment (CJEU Judgment T-278/07 P-DEP para. 16).

**Jurisprudence**

ILOAT Judgments

2418: There is a nominal award of costs even if the counsel is a full-time member of the organisation; 1532: The tribunal disallowed the claim of costs in view of the intemperate language of the complainant in his submissions; 931: In the matter of costs the tribunal has absolute authority that no text can fetter. The award of costs depends on the circumstances of the case; 320 para. 19: Costs are payable only to the extent warranted by the circumstances of the case, "that is to say by its nature, importance, complexity and the actual contributions made by the complainant or his counsel to the proceedings".

### 2. *Default interest on damages*

On request, international administrative tribunals will grant default interest for late payment of sums due. The interest is a simple interest system which in contrast to the compound interest system does not itself accrue interest (ILOAT Judgment 3013 para. 1). The obligation to pay compound interest is an exception and must clearly arise from the operative part of a judgment (ILOAT Judgments 3013 para. 3 and the case law cited therein).

Most tribunals do not disclose the basis for the calculation of the default interest rate in their decisions; they simply fix the applicable rate.

The ILOAT awards a yearly interest rate for late payment ranging between 5% (Judgment 874) to 8% (Judgments 3180, 3013, 2782) or 10% (Judgments 1461, 1403, 1338, 706, 553).

The CJEU (GC) applies a rate of default interest which is calculated on the basis of the rates set by the ECB for principal refinancing operations plus two points, provided that it does not exceed the interest claimed (see, for example, Order F-14/08 DEP).

## H. *Res judicata, stare decisis*

### I. General

The judgments of most international administrative tribunals have the authority of *res judicata.* This legal principle comprises two aspects:

- Subsequent proceedings are barred if the issue has already been the subject of a final and binding decision between the parties (substantive *res judicata*) (see, for example, ILOAT Judgments 3106 para. 4, 2316 para. 11);
- There is no recourse to a higher court, i.e. no appeal is admissible (formal *res judicata)*;

### II. Substantive *res judicata*

The principle of substantive *res judicata* applies to the proceedings of all tribunals. If, however, there is no judgment on the merits, a new complaint is not barred by *res judicata.* A person cannot simultaneously submit the same matter for decision in more than one proceedings (*lis pendens*, ILOAT Judgment 3291).

The effect of *res judicata* on a judgment is restricted to the parties involved (*inter partes, ad personam*) and has no binding legal effect on anyone else (*erga omnes*; ILOAT Judgment 2463 para. 13). The *res judicata* principle applies to judicial rulings only and not to administrative decisions (ILOAT Judgment 3002; CJEU Judgment C-201/09 P and C-216/09 P).

The effect of substantive *res judicata* is regularly stated in the statutes and in consistent case law of the tribunals (Art. VI(1) ILOAT Statute: "Judgments shall be final"; CJEU Judgment C-352/09 P para. 3 and constant case law; Art. 11(3) UNDT statute: "The judgments of the Dispute Tribunal shall be binding upon the parties, but are subject to appeal").

– Rectification

Judgments may be rectified by the tribunal on its own motion or on application by a party in regard to typographical or arithmetical errors (see, for example, Art. 164 CJEU (GC) rules of procedure; Art. 31 UNDT rules of procedure).

### III. Right of appeal, review

The principle of formal *res judicata* has it that no appeals may be brought against the decision of most international administrative tribunals, e.g. those of the ILOAT (Art. VI(1) statute: "without appeal"), the tribunals and appeals board of the six CO, of WBAT, IMFAT, ESMAT and the TRIBAD.

Only the final judgments of the CJEU (GC) (Art. 56 et seq. CJEU statute) and of the UNDT (Art. 11(3) UNDT statute) are subject to appeal.

The single-tier system of legal protection does not violate the very essence of the right to a court as enshrined, for example, in Art. 6 EConHR (see the "Guide on Art. 6 EConHR, Right to a Fair Trial, 2013, point 79: "Article 6(1) does not compel the contracting states to set up courts of appeal or of cassation").

This legal position is shared, for example, by the case law of the ECHR, the ICJ and the German Federal Constitutional Court.

In its advisory opinion of 13 July1954 p. 53 to 55, the ICJ did not call into question the legality of the decision of the UNGA to confer on the UN Administrative Tribunal the power to pronounce final judgments without appeal similar to the corresponding power of the Administrative Tribunal of the League of Nations.

The ECHR held in its judgments Waite and Kennedy v. Germany of 18 February 1999, Appl. No. 26083/94, as well as in the case Beer and Regan v. Germany of 18 February 1999, Appl. No. 28934/95 and in the case A.L. v. Italy of 11 May 2000, Appl. No. 41387/98 that the respective single-tier system of legal protection for the staff of ESA and NATO by the internal appeal bodies (now international administrative tribunals) were in line with the requirements for a fair trial within the meaning of Art. 6 EConHR.

The German Federal Constitutional Court confirmed in its decision "Eurocontrol II" of 10.11.1981, BVerfGE 59, 63–95 (for an English version see The University of Text at Austin, Institute for Transnational Law, Germany, Constitutional Law, General Content) that the statute and rules of the ILOAT meet an international minimum standard of elementary procedural justice such as arises from developed systems of the rule of law and from the procedural law of international courts. As to the single-tier system, the court ruled that: "Comparable international tribunals similarly decided without a sequence of appeals".

In spite of the precept of a minimal legal protection of international employees by a single-tier judicial system, there is a widespread perception that the establishment of a second instance would be desirable in order to improve the level of protection and bring it in line with most national court systems. This is why the question of a two-tier legal protection was vigorously addressed in the context of the reform of the UN administration of justice and leading to the establishment of the UNDT and the UNAT in 2009. The Director General of UNESCO, the legal advisor of UNESCO as well as staff representatives of most UN organisations and human rights groups referred to this objective of the reform as one of its cornerstones (Reinisch/Knahr; see also the report of the joint inspection unit of the UN, doc. JIU/REP/2002/5, points 52 to 54).

– The ILOAT

In consistent case law, the ILOAT admits a review of its judgments in exceptional cases based on its competence under Art. II of its statute, despite the wording of Art. VI statute, that judgments shall be final and without appeal. In June 2016 this practice was formalised by introducing the following additional sentence to Art. VI(1) of the statute: "The Tribunal shall nevertheless consider applications for interpretation, execution or review of a judgment" (see ILO doc. GB.326/FA/12/1). This new wording is in line with the statute of the IMFAT (Art. XVI) and the WBAT (Art. XIII).

Judgments may be reviewed only "in exceptional circumstances and on strictly limited grounds" (Judgment 3371 para. 4). The only admissible grounds of review are "failure to take account of material facts, a material error involving no value judgment, an omission to rule on a claim, or the discovery of new facts on which the complainant was unable to rely in the original proceedings. However, the pleas must also be likely to have a bearing on the outcome of the case. Mistakes of law, failure to admit evidence, misinterpretation of the facts or the omission to rule on a plea afford no grounds for review (ILOAT Judgments 3371 para. 4; see also Judgments 3480, 3385, 3470, 3469, 3244, 3000 and case law cited).

If the execution of a judgment proves impossible owing to facts of which the tribunal was unaware when it adapted its judgment, the decision will be reviewed (ILOAT Judgment 2889 para. 7).

Optionally a defendant IO may challenge a decision of the ILOAT before the ICJ by way of an advisory opinion (Art. XII of the ILOAT Statute was repealed in June 2016) (for more details see ILO doc. GB.326/PFA/12/1). Given that the challenge open only to defendant organisations and not to officials, it has been heavily criticised by the ICJ as anachronistic and in conflict with the principle of equality of access to courts (ICJ Advisory Opinion of 1 February 2012, accessible on the website of the ICJ). The ILOAT has also expressed similar concerns (Judgment 3003 para. 43 et seq.). For similar reasons, the optional review of judgments was repealed in 2016.

The ILOAT requires that the application for review is filed within a reasonable time (ILOAT Judgments 1952, 2219: five months are not unreasonable; 788: nine years are wholly unreasonable).

In general, the prospects of success of an application for review are very limited. As far as can be seen of the 121 applications for review before the ILOAT only two were successful (Judgments 1255, 620).

– The CJEU

The EU Civil Service Tribunal (CST), exercising jurisdiction at first instance between the EU and its officials, was dissolved on 1 September 2016 (EU Reg. 2016/1192 of 6 July 2016). The CST had been established on 12 December 2005 and had delivered 1549 judgments. Its competences were transferred to the CJEU (GC) (Art. 50a CJEU statute). The appeal is limited to points of law, on the grounds of lack of competence of the GC, a breach of procedure which adversely affects the interests of the appellant as well as the infringement of Union Law by the GC (Art. 58 CJEU statute). The provisions of Art. 9 to 12 of annex I to Protocol No. 3 of the statute of the former CST are to continue to apply to the appeals against the CST of which the GC is seized as at 31 August 2016 or which are brought after that date (see the preamble in annex I to the CJEU statute).

– The UNAT

The UNAT is competent to hear and pass judgment on an appeal against a judgment rendered by the UNDT in which it is asserted that the UNDT exceeded the jurisdiction vested in it, erred in a question of law, committed an error in procedure or erred in

a question of fact, resulting in a manifestly unreasonable decision (Art. 2(1) UNAT statute). An appeal may also be filed by either party (Art. 2(2) UNAT statute). The UNAT is also competent to hear and pass judgment on an appeal against a decision of the standing committee acting on behalf of the UNJSPF (Art. 2(9) UNAT statute).

## IV. *Stare decisis*

The common law doctrine of *stare decisis*, i.e. the adherence of a court to its decisions in earlier cases as a binding precedent does not formally exist in the international judicial decision-making (Lecture of the President of the ICJ of 2 December 2013 on the Rule of Law and the Role of the ICJ in World Affairs, p. 7; see the website of the ICJ, under Statements by the President; see also Art. 59 ICJ Statute and judgment 656 point XIX of the old UN Administrative Tribunal).

Nevertheless, the ILOAT adopted the rule of *stare decisis* "as a matter of judicial practice or of comity". The ILOAT follows its own precedents "unless it is persuaded such precedents were wrong in law or in fact or that for any other compelling reason they should not be applied" (Judgments 3450 para. 8 and case law cited). The *stare decisis* rule serves the purpose of creating consistency and predictability in a legal system. It is also for an IO under its jurisdiction to follow and apply principles established by the case law of the tribunal in order to create "a stable, predictable and certain legal system concerning the rights and obligations of both staff and organisations" (ILOAT Judgment 3450 para. 8).

## I. Enforcement (execution)

### I. General

With the exception of the CJEU (see below), there is no straightforward mechanism available to enforce judgments rendered by international administrative tribunals. The means of municipal enforcement of a judgment in favour of an applicant would regularly be barred from execution by the IO's immunity.

IO are expected to comply with the judgments and orders rendered against them by the respective tribunal. Judgments in favour of the organisation are ordinarily enforced through offsetting against outstanding salary or pension claims of the official (see Annex VIII, Art. 46 EU-SR; Art. 85 EU-SR: for pension benefits; CJEU Judgment F-56/09 para. 59; T-214/00 para. 89: An express provision in the EU-SR is required.).

If an offsetting is not possible, the organisation must seek the enforcement under municipal law (by waiving the immunity of the employee) similar to the enforcement of the judgments of foreign courts. Ultimately the organisation would have to initiate proceedings before the competent national court.

If an organisation does not enforce a judgment within a reasonable period of time the appellant may, as a rule, file an application for execution with the respective tribunal. (for more details see Elias/Thomas).

### II. ILOAT Judgments

Until recently, the statute of the ILOAT did not expressly provide for the possibility of either party to submit an application for execution of a judgment. In its judgment 1328 para. 10 the ILOAT ruled, however, that a dispute is not resolved in the meaning of Art. II of its statute until it has been duly executed. The competence of the tribunal is, therefore, not exhausted when it renders its judgments but it remains competent until their full execution. In June 2016, Art. VI(1) of the ILOAT statute was amended explicitly to provide for an application for the execution of a judgment.

Judgments are final and without appeal and also have *res judicata* authority. They are immediately operative and must be executed as ruled (Judgment 3792).

An exception must be made to this principle when the execution proves to be impossible owing to facts of which the tribunal was unaware when it adopted its judgment (Judgments 3332 para. 4, 2889 para. 6 and 7).

Judgments must be executed within a reasonable period of time (Judgment 2684 para. 6). The enforcement of a judgment after 18 months is manifestly unreasonable (Judgment 3114). Internal debates and discussions do not warrant a delay in the execution of a judgment (Judgment 2327 para. 7). The exhaustion of all internal remedies is not necessary before filing an application for execution (Judgment 1514 para. 4). The official may, however, avail himself of the possibility of first lodging an internal appeal (Judgment 1978).

The tribunal may ensure the execution of a judgment by ordering, if appropriate, the payment of a penalty for default (Penalties for each month of delay in the execution of the judgment; Judgments 3394: CHF 5,000; 3152: EUR 25,000; 2806: EUR 10,000; EUR 20,000 for five years delay in executing a judgment).

In a series of judgments the tribunal referred the case back to the organisation in order that it executes in full the judgment under review (see, for example, Judgment 3635). In some cases, high damages were awarded in compensation for moral injury due to the unacceptable delay in executing the judgment (see, for example, Judgments 3792, 3637). In Judgment 3723 the tribunal held that an application for execution of a judgment is, by definition, premised on the contention that the judgment has not been properly executed. Determining whether or not that contention is correct does not relate to the question of receivability but invokes an examination of the merits of the application. In the case of the retroactive reinstatement of an official, there is an obligation to make a retroactive payment of pension benefits and contributions to the insurance system. Since unemployment benefits have to be reimbursed by the complainant to the national authorities, they cannot be deducted from the sum due to the complainant as a consequence of his reinstatement with retroactive effect.

## III. CJEU Judgments

A distinction must be made between the enforcement of judgments imposing preliminary obligations and judgments on an action for failure to act or annulling judgments.

A judgment against an EU institution concerning pecuniary and other matters is enforceable in accordance with Art. 270, 280, 299 TFEU. Art. 1 third sentence of the Protocol (No. 7) on Privileges and Immunities of the EU must be respected however. This kind of enforcement does not play any role in practice since the CJEU judgments are regularly enforced by EU institutions.

The EU institutions whose act has been declared void (annulling judgment, Art. 270, 266 TFEU in conjunction with Art. 91(1) EU-SR) or whose failure to act has been declared contrary to EU law (judgment on an action for failure to act) are "required to take the necessary measures" to comply with the judgment (Art. 90(1) EU-SR; CJEU Judgments F-117/13 para. 37; F-104/08 para. 35, 36; F-35/08 para. 73; F-9/08 para. 21). In these cases, the GC cannot substitute itself for the administrative authority. The court may only mention some possible measures by way of illustration which cannot be regarded as injunctions against the administration (CJEU Judgment C-412/92 P para. 30). It is for the EU institution in the exercise of the power of assessment conferred on it by Art. 266 TFEU to choose between various possible measures to eliminate the illegality committed with respect to the appellant (see, for example, CJEU Judgment T-84/91 para. 78). When the compliance with the judgment imposes special difficulties, a fair compensation may be paid (CJEU Judgment F-15/05 para. 132). A dialogue may even be established between the administration and the appellant with the aim of reaching an agreement on fair compensation (CJEU Judgments T-177/97 para. 23; T-81/96 para. 42).

If an institution allegedly failed to comply with a judgment and does not adopt the necessary measures the appellant may bring an action before the court (CJEU Judgment T-84/91: failure to comply with judgment; Order F-15/09: Application for an order to ensure compliance with judgment). In order to ensure an annulling judgment is implemented, the judicature may use its unlimited jurisdiction in proceedings concerning pecuniary matters and order the defendant to pay compensation for damages caused by the breach of its administrative duties (CJEU Judgments F-27/08 para. 142, 144; F-46/07 para. 214; F-6/07 para. 127).

An appeal against a decision of the GC may be brought before the CJ (Art. 56(1) CJEU statute). The appeal has no suspensory effect (Art. 60 CJEU statute, without prejudice to Art. 278 and 279 TFEU).

## IV. UNDT Judgments

Either party may apply to the UNDT for an order for execution of the judgment if the judgment requires execution within a certain period of time and such execution has not been carried out (Art. 32(2) UNDT rules of procedure; UNDT Judgment UNDT/2011/137 para. 21: Judgment on execution of judgment).

In the absence of an appeal, a judgment of the UNDT is executable following the expiry of the time provided for appeal (Art. 11(3) UNDT statute). The filing of an appeal has a suspensory effect (Art. 7(5) UNAT statute).

In contrast to the ILOAT, the UNDT may not award punitive damages to enforce its judgments (Art. 10(7) UNDT statute); it may, however, award compensation for excessive and inordinate delays in the implementation of a judgment (UNDT Judgment UNDT/2011/004: USD 25,000 compensation and if the sum is not paid within a certain period, an additional five per cent is added to the US prime rates until the date of payment).

## Bibliography

*Adorno, R.*: Human dignity and human rights as a common ground for a global bioethics, in The Journal of Medicine and Philosophy, Volume 34(3), 2009, pp. 223–240

*Ali, A.*: The International Civil Service: The Idea and the Reality, in de Cooker (ed.), pp. 3–20

*Alpa, G.*: General Principles of Law, in Annual Survey of International & Comparative Law, Volume 1 (1994), Issue 1, Art. 2, pp. 1–37

*Amerasinghe, C.F.*: The Law of International Civil Service: A Subject which needs Exploration and Analysis, in International Organizations Law Review, Volume 1, 2004, pp. 9–21 (cit. IOLR)

– Principles of the Institutional Law of International Organizations, Second revised edition 2005 (cit. Principles)

– Jurisdiction of specific international tribunals, 2009 (cit. Jurisdiction)

– The Law of the International Civil Service: As Applied by International Administrative Tribunals, Volume II, 1994

*Bandyopadhyay/Iwata*: VII Officials, Art. V Sections 17–21, pp. 313 et seq. in Reinisch/Bachmayer (ed.), The Conventions on the Privileges and Immunities of the United Nations and its Specialized Agencies (cit. Bandyopadhyay/Iwata, commentary)

*Beier/Haertel/Schricker/Strauss*: Munich Joint Law Book on the European Patent Convention (Münchner Gemeinschaftskommentar zum Europäischen Patentübereinkommen), since 1984

*Benzing, M.*: Das Beweisrecht vor internationalen Gerichten und Schiedsgerichten in zwischenstaatlichen Streitigkeiten (english summary), Beiträge zum ausländischen öffentlichen Recht und Völkerrecht, Volume 215 (2010), pp. 739–755

*Bouwhuis, S.*: The International Law Commission's Definition of International Organizations, IOLR 2012, pp. 451–465

*Busch, J.D.*: Dienstrecht der Vereinten Nationen – Das Common System, 1981

*Carillo Salcedo, J.A.C.*: Reflections on the Existence of a Hierarchy of Norms in International Law, in European Journal of International Law 8 (1997), pp. 583–595

*Castillo de la Torre/Fournier*: Evidence, Proof and Judicial Review in EU Competition Law, 2017

*Cheng, B.*: General Principles of Law as Applied by International Courts and Tribunals, 1953 (2006)

*Conforti/Dominicé/Ress:* Les obligations des états membres d'une organisation internationale à l'égard du system de pension du personnel, Revue générale de droit international public, 2003, pp. 801–834 *de Cooker, Ch.*: Pre-Litigation Procedures in International Organisations, in de Cooker, pp. 781–801 (cit. pre-litigation)

– (ed.): International Administration/Law and Management Practices in International Organisations, 2009 (cit. de Cooker)

*de Cooker/Süss*: Immunity of International Organisations from National Jurisdiction in Staff Matters, in de Cooker (ed.), pp. 541–572

*Dröge, C.*: Positive Verpflichtungen der Staaten in der Europäischen Menschenrechtskonvention, Max-Planck-Institut Beiträge zum ausländischen öffentlichen Recht und Völkerrecht, Volume 159 (2003), english summary, pp. 379–392

*Du Plessis, J.*: Comparative Law and the Study of Mixed Legal Systems, in The Oxford Handbook of Comparative Law, 2006

*Duxbury, A.*: The Participation of States in International Organisations, 2011

*Ehlers, D.*: General Principles, in European Fundamental Rights and Freedoms, in Ehlers, D. (ed.), 2007, Part II, pp. 25–66

*Elias/Thomas*: Enforcement Powers, in Ch. Giorgetti (ed.), The Rules, Practice and Jurisprudence of International Courts and Tribunals, 2012, pp. 177 et seq.

*Elliott, M.*: The Constitutional Foundations of Judicial Review, 2001

*EU Commentary*: Commentary of the Charter of the Fundamental Rights of the European Union, EU Network of Independent Experts on Fundamental Rights, 2006 (published on the internet) (cit. EU Commentary)

*Fürst/Weber*: Uniformity in Service Law and Judicial Remedies for Staff Members of the European Coordinated Organisations, in de Cooker (ed.), pp. 623–653

*Gaffney, J.P.*: Due Process in the World Trade Organization: The Need for Procedural Justice in the Dispute Settlement System, in American University International Law Review, Volume 14, Issue 4, 1999, pp. 1174 et seq.

*Gernigon/Odero/Guido*: ILO Principles concerning the right to strike, International Law Review, Volume 137 (1998)

*Gordillo, A.*: The Status of the Judge: Independence and Impartiality, in European Review of Public Law, No. 83 (2012)

*Gourgourinis, A.*: General/Particular International Law and Primary/Secondary Rules: Unitary Terminology of a Fragmented System, in The European Journal of International Law, Vol. 23, No. 4, 2011, pp. 993–1026

*Grabitz/Hilf* (ed.): The Law of the EU (TEU and TEC) commentary; (Das Recht der Europäischen Union (EUV und EGV), Kommentar, last additional delivery 2009

*Grabitz/Hilf/Nettesheim* (ed.): The Law of the EU (TEU and TFEU) commentary; (Das Recht der Europäischen Union (EUV und AEUV), Kommentar, 2012 et seq.

*Gruber/Benisch*: Privileges and Immunities of the European Central Bank, Legal Working Paper Series No. 4, June 2007

*Gruber, J.*: Das Schicksal von Versorgungsanwartschaften beim Wechsel zu internationalen Organisationen, in Die Rentenversicherung (The pension insurance, German Law Journal), 2010, pp. 151 et seq.

*Gulati, R.*: The Internal Dispute Resolution Regime of the United Nations, in Max Planck Yearbook of United Nations 2011, Volume 15, pp. 489–538 and pp. 593–536, The Informal Dispute Resolution System

*Hailbronner, K.*: Immunity of International Organisations from National Jurisdiction, with particular reference to Germany, in de Cooker (ed.), pp. 530–540

*Ipsen, R.*: Völkerrecht (international law), 6th ed. 2014

*Irion/Luchetta*: Online Personal Data Processing and EU Data Protection Reform, Report of the Centre for European Policy Studies (CEPS), April 2013

*Kanska, K.*: Towards Administrative Human Rights in the EU. Impact of the Charter of Fundamental Rights, in European Law Journal, Vol. 10, No. 3, 2004, pp. 296–326

*Karpenstein, U.*: Commentary to Art. 236 TEC, in Grabitz/Hilf (ed.)

*Kirchof, P.*: Grundrechtsinhalte und Grundrechtsvoraussetzungen, § 21 para. 16 et seq., in Handbuch der Grundrechte in Deutschland und Europa, Entwicklung und Grundlagen, Merten/Papier (ed.)

*Kokott, J.*: Grundrechtliche Schranken und Schrankenschranken, in Handbuch der Grundrechte in Deutschland und Europa, Entwicklung und Grundlagen, Merten/Papier (ed.), Volume I, 2004, pp.853–908

*Kunz-Hallstein, H.P.*: Die Gerichtsbefreiung internationaler Organisationen in der deutschen Praxis, in Festschrift für K. Hailbronner, Grenzüberschreitendes Recht – Crossing Frontiers, Jochum, Fritzemeyer, Kau (ed.) 2013, pp. 597–614 (cit. Crossing frontiers)

– Paralysing the Functioning of International Organisation's Internal Appeals Boards, in International Organizations Law Review 14 (2017), pp. 196–203

– Die Beteiligung Internationaler Organisationen am Rechts- und Wirtschaftsverkehr, in GRUR Int. 1987, pp. 819 et seq. (cit. GRUR Int.)

– Commentary to Art. 8 and EPO-PPI in Beier/Haertel/Schricker/Strauss, 1986 (cit. Art. 8 or EPO-PPI)

*Kunz-Hallstein/Ullrich*: Commentary to Art. 9 and 13 in Beier/Haertel/Schricker/Strauss, 1995 and 2004 (cit. Art. 9 or Art. 13)

*Labayle, H.*: Commentary to Art. 41 of the CFREU, in the EU Commentary

*Lammers, J.G.*: Immunity of International Organizations, The Work of the International Law Commission, in International Organizations Law Review, Volume 10, Issue 2, 2014, pp. 276–286

*Laubinger, H.P.*: Art. 41 CFREU (Right to good administration), in commemorative publication (Festschrift) for Hans-Peter Bull, Berlin, 2011, pp. 659–682

*Leawoods, H.*: Gustav Radbruch: An extraordinary Legal Philosopher, Washington University Journal of Law & Policy, 2000, p. 489

*Lindemann, H.H.*: Allgemeine Rechtsgrundsätze und europäischer öffentlicher Dienst, 1986

*Marschall, S.*: European parliaments in transnational organisations: Parliamentary Cooperation beyond the European Union, Paper prepared for the Conference „Fifty Years of Parliamentary Cooperation", 13 June 2007, Bundesrat, Berlin

*Martin, J.*: The International Civil Service: 90 years on a view from the Engine Room, in AAFI/AFICS Commemorative Report, December 2009, pp. 23–29

*Megzari, A.*: The Internal Justice of the United Nations: A critical History 1945–2015, 2015

*Miller, A.J.*: Privileges and Immunities of United Nations officials, in International Organizations Law Review, Volume 4, 2007, pp. 169–257

*Morgenstern, F.*: Social Security Problems in International Organisations, in de Cooker (ed.), pp. 573–608

*Nettesheim, M.:* Commentary to Art. 288 TFEU in Grabitz/Hilf/Nettesheim (ed.) (cit. Art. 288)

– Commentary to Art. 249 TEC in Grabitz/Hilf (ed.) (cit. Art. 249)

– Normenhierarchien im EU-Recht (hierarchy of norms in European Law), in EuR, 2006, pp. 737–772 (cit. EuR)

*Oppermann:* Europarecht (European Law), third ed. 2005

*Otis/Reiter*: The Reform of the United Nations Administration of Justice System: The United Nations Appeals Tribunal after one year, in The Law & Practice of International Courts and Tribunals, 2011, Volume 10, Issue 3, pp. 405–428

*Pauwelyn, J.*: Conflict of Norms in Public International Law, in Cambridge Studies in International and Comparative Law (No. 29), 2006

*Potacs, M.*: Effet utile als Auslegungsgrundsatz, in EuR, pp. 465–487

*Priess, H.J.*: Internationale Verwaltungsgerichte und Beschwerdeausschüsse, 1989

*Reinisch, A.*: The Immunity of International Organizations and the Jurisdiction of their Administrative Tribunals, in Chinese Journal of International Law, 2008, Vol. 7, No. 2, pp. 285–307 (cit. The Immunity)

– Transnational Judicial Conversations on the Personality, Privileges and Immunities of International Organizations – An Introduction in the Privileges and Immunities of International Organizations in Domestic Courts, Reinisch, A. (ed.), 2013, pp. 1–16 (cit. Privileges)

– Decision of the European Patent Organisation before National Courts, in Challenging Acts of International Organizations before National Courts, 2010, pp. 137–156 (cit. Challenging Acts)

*Reinisch/Knahr*: From the UN Administrative Tribunal to the UN Appeals Tribunal, in A. Bogdandy and R. Wolfrum (eds.), Max Planck Yearbook of United Nations Law, Volume 12 (2008), pp. 447–483

*Reinisch/Weber*: In the Shadow of Waite and Kennedy: The jurisidictional immunity of international organisations, the individual's right to access to the courts and administrative tribunals as alternative means of dispute settlement, International Organizations Law Review, 2004, pp. 59–110

*Rengeling/Szczekalla*: Grundrechte in der Europäischen Union: Charta der Grundrechte und allgemeine Rechtsgrundsätze, 2004 (cit. Rengeling)

*Rogalla, D.*: Das Dienstrecht der Europäischen Gemeinschaften, 1992

– Commentary to Art. 283 EGV (TEC), in Grabitz/Hilf (ed.) (cit. Art. 283)

*Ruzié, D.*: The Independence of International Civicl Servants from Governments, in Australian International Law Journal, 1998, pp. 168–170

*Sands/Klein*: Bouwett's Law of International Institutions, 6th ed., 2009

*Sarvarian, A.*: Common Ethical Standards for Counsel before the European Court of Justice and European Court of Human Rights, European Journal of International Law, Vol. 23, No. 4 (2012), pp. 1007 et seq., also available on the internet

*Schermers, G.*: Die Bedeutung der Menschenrechte für die internationalen Organisationen, Ansprache aus Anlass der Ehrenpromotion von Prof. Dr. jur. Dr. h.c. Henricus G. Schermers on 16 June 1994 (University of Osnabrück, Germany) (cit. Address)

*Schermers/Blokker*: International Institutional Law, 5th edition 2011 (cit. Schermers/Blokker)

*Schmitt, P.*: Western European Union v. Sielder and others, Belgian Court of Cassation, 21 December 2009, in Judicial Decisions on the Law of International Organizations, Ryngaert/Dekker/Wenzel/Wouters, pp. 424–431

*Schreuer/Ebner*: Art. 100, in Simma, B. (ed.)

*Seidl-Hohenveldern/Loibl*: Das Recht der Internationalen Organisationen, 7th ed., 2000

*Seidl-Hohenveldern/Stein*: Völkerrecht, 10th ed., 2000 (cit. Völkerrecht)

*Simma, B.*: The Charter of the United Nations: A commentary (ed.), second ed., 2002

*Singer/Geuß*: Commentary to the introduction of part 6, in Beier/Haertel/Schricker/Strauss, 1998, pp. 181–207

*Sobotta, C.*: Commentary to Art. 286 EGV, in Grabitz/Hilf (ed.)

*Stein, T.*: Demokratische Legitimierung auf supra-nationaler und internationaler Ebene, in ZaöRV (2004), pp. 563–570

*Teilhard de Chardin, P.*: The Phenomenon of Man, 1955

*Ullrich, G.*: Data Protection in International Organisations, in de Cooker (ed.), pp. 323–328 (cit. data protection)

– Pension Schemes for Staff at International Organisations – Institutional Structures of Pension Protection Funds, in de Cooker (ed.), pp. 609–620 (cit. Pension Schemes)

– Versorgungssysteme für Bedienstete der Internationalen Organisationen, in Zeitschrift für Beamtenrecht (ZBR), 1995, pp. 225 et seq. (cit. Versorgungssysteme)

– Die Immunität Internationaler Organisationen von der einzelstaatlichen Gerichtsbarkeit, in ZaöRV, Volume 71 (2011), pp. 157–167 (cit. ZaöRV)

– Procurement Law of International Organisations (Vergabe durch internationale Organisationen), in Grabitz/Hilf (ed.), Vol. IV, part B17 (cit. procurement)

*UN Special*: monthly magazine of the international civil servants working in the UN system in Geneva („www.unspecial.org“)

*Verdross/Simma*: Universelles Völkerrecht (universal international law), 3rd ed., 1984, reprint 2010

*Villiger, M.E.*: Commentary on the 1969 Vienna Convention on the Law of Treaties, 2009

*Vitzthum, W.G.*: Völkerrecht, 5th ed., 2010

*Voigt, Ch.*: The Role of General Principles in International Law and their Relationship to Treaty Law, 2008

*Weiss, T.G.*: The International Civil Service Revisited, in AAFI/AFICS Commemorative Report, 2009, pp. 15–22

*Wenckstern, M.*: Die Haftung der Mitgliedsstaaten für internationale Organisationen, in Zeitschrift für ausländisches und internationales Privatrecht, 1997, pp. 93 et seq. (cit. Haftung)

– Die Immunität internationaler Organisationen, in Handbuch des Internationalen Zivilverfahrenrechts, Band II/1

*Yearbook of International Organizations (YBIO)*: The YBIO is edited by the Union of International Associations. It contains comprehensive information on all non-profit international organisations. It includes profiles of all international intergovernmental organisations (IGO's) and all international non-governmental organisations (NGO's)

*Young, A.*: Deconstructing International Organizations Immunity, in Georgtown Journal of International Law, 2013, pp. 311–364

# Index

MIX
Papier aus verantwortungsvollen Quellen
Paper from responsible sources
FSC® C105338

Printed by Libri Plureos GmbH
in Hamburg, Germany